TOEIC® L&Rテスト 究極の模試600問+
模擬試験 ①
Test 1

JN112845

	1回目		2回目		3回目	
受験日	年 月	日	年 月	日	年 月	日
開始時間	時	分	時	分	時	分
Listening Section 終了時間	時	分	時	分	時	分
Reading Section 終了時間	時	分	時	分	時	分

◆Listening Section の音声は、ダウンロードしてご利用ください。詳しくは本冊のp.10に掲載されています。【Test 1】の音声を利用します。所要時間は**約46分**です。

テスト採点センター

◆解答には本冊巻末のマークシートを使用してください。マークシートA（勘ボックスあり）の使い方は本冊のp.12〜で説明しています。テスト採点センター（本冊p.11）もご利用いただけます。

◆解答一覧は本冊p.28〜にあります。

使用する音声ファイル一覧

Listening Section、Part 1 Directions	001_T1_P1_Dir.mp3
Part 1 No.1〜No.6	002_T1_P1_01.mp3〜008_T1_P1_06.mp3
Part 2 Directions	010_T1_P2_Dir.mp3
Part 2 No.7〜No.31	011_T1_P2_07.mp3〜035_T1_P2_31.mp3
Part 3 Directions	036_T1_P3_Dir.mp3
Part 3 No.32〜No.70	037_T1_P3_32-34.mp3〜051_T1_P3_68-70.mp3
Part 4 Directions	052_T1_P4_Dir.mp3
Part 4 No.71〜No.100	053_T1_P4_71-73.mp3〜063_T1_P4_98-100.mp3

矢印の方向に引くと、この冊子を取り外すことができます。

LISTENING TEST

In this section, your ability to understand spoken English will be shown. The Listening test consists of four parts and will take approximately 45 minutes. Directions will be given for each part. By following the directions you hear, select the best possible answer and mark your answers on your answer sheet. Please refrain from writing anything in your test book.

PART 1

Directions: In this part, you will see a picture in your test book and hear four statements. After hearing each statement, select the one statement you think is the best description for the picture. Then, mark the answer on your answer sheet. You will only hear the statements one time, and they will not be printed in your test book.

Statement (B), "They're sitting side by side," best describes the picture. Therefore, you should choose answer (B) and mark it on your answer sheet.

1.

2.

GO ON TO THE NEXT PAGE

3.

4.

5.

6.

GO ON TO THE NEXT PAGE ➡

PART 2

Directions: In this part, you will hear a question or statement. You will then hear three alternative responses to the question or statement. They will all be spoken in English. You will only hear them one time, and they will not be printed in your test book. Choose the best response to each question and mark the letter (A), (B), or (C) on your answer sheet.

7. Mark your answer on your answer sheet.

8. Mark your answer on your answer sheet.

9. Mark your answer on your answer sheet.

10. Mark your answer on your answer sheet.

11. Mark your answer on your answer sheet.

12. Mark your answer on your answer sheet.

13. Mark your answer on your answer sheet.

14. Mark your answer on your answer sheet.

15. Mark your answer on your answer sheet.

16. Mark your answer on your answer sheet.

17. Mark your answer on your answer sheet.

18. Mark your answer on your answer sheet.

19. Mark your answer on your answer sheet.

20. Mark your answer on your answer sheet.

21. Mark your answer on your answer sheet.

22. Mark your answer on your answer sheet.

23. Mark your answer on your answer sheet.

24. Mark your answer on your answer sheet.

25. Mark your answer on your answer sheet.

26. Mark your answer on your answer sheet.

27. Mark your answer on your answer sheet.

28. Mark your answer on your answer sheet.

29. Mark your answer on your answer sheet.

30. Mark your answer on your answer sheet.

31. Mark your answer on your answer sheet.

PART 3

Directions: In this part, you will hear conversations between two or more people. You will be asked to answer three questions about what the speakers say in each conversation. You will only hear the conversations one time, and they will not be printed in your test book. Choose the best response to each question and mark the letter (A), (B), (C), or (D) on your answer sheet.

32. What is the main topic of the conversation?

(A) A promotional booklet
(B) A company event
(C) A Web site revision
(D) A software program

33. What problem does the woman mention?

(A) The design is not attractive.
(B) Some information is out of date.
(C) Running costs are high.
(D) There have not been many visitors.

34. What does the man suggest doing?

(A) Choosing an employee for a task
(B) Using more colorful graphics
(C) Comparing prices online
(D) Holding meetings more frequently

35. What does the woman want the man to do?

(A) Choose a color scheme
(B) Interview a candidate
(C) Accept a delivery
(D) Write a report

36. What does the man ask the woman about?

(A) An arrival time
(B) The amount of a bill
(C) The cost of some materials
(D) A mailing address

37. What does the woman say she will do?

(A) Read some reviews
(B) See an accountant
(C) Hire a decorator
(D) Make a phone call

38. What is the topic of the conversation?

(A) Office equipment
(B) Employee training
(C) A meeting location
(D) Customer feedback

39. What does the woman ask about?

(A) The location of a hotel
(B) The name of a business
(C) The date of an event
(D) The availability of a client

40. What will the woman most likely do next?

(A) Pick up a client
(B) Announce some survey results
(C) Reserve a table
(D) Change her appointment

41. Who most likely is the man?

(A) A train station employee
(B) An event organizer
(C) A technician
(D) A driver

42. What does the woman mean when she says, "A phone call would have been nice"?

(A) She wishes the man had given her an update.
(B) She enjoys talking with the man.
(C) She forgot to bring her mobile phone with her.
(D) She wanted to take a job interview.

43. What will the woman probably do next?

(A) Announce a delay
(B) Test some equipment
(C) Buy a ticket
(D) Speak with a colleague

GO ON TO THE NEXT PAGE

44. What are the speakers discussing?

(A) Athletic events
(B) A moving company
(C) Employee records
(D) A summer sale

45. What is the man concerned about?

(A) The price of a service
(B) The office's opening hours
(C) Arrangements for a visit
(D) Damage to some merchandise

46. What does the woman say one of her friends recently did?

(A) Applied for a position
(B) Transferred to another branch
(C) Got a new qualification
(D) Put some goods in storage

47. Why did the woman contact the man's company?

(A) To request a replacement invoice
(B) To express thanks for a favor
(C) To announce the cancellation of a product
(D) To have some garbage removed

48. What does the man say he must do?

(A) Provide a refund
(B) Review some reports
(C) Charge an additional fee
(D) Take a vacation

49. What will the woman do this week?

(A) Replace some equipment
(B) Speak at a workshop
(C) Take employees on a trip
(D) Watch a movie

50. Where does the conversation most likely take place?

(A) At a hospital
(B) At a publishing house
(C) At a public library
(D) At a car dealership

51. What did the man hear about the Real Color 90?

(A) It has advanced software.
(B) It is reasonably priced.
(C) It was released recently.
(D) It is popular with colleges.

52. What does the man recommend the woman do?

(A) Ask for a demonstration
(B) Call a manager
(C) Go to a specific store
(D) Set up a meeting room

53. What is the purpose of the man's trip?

(A) To inspect a facility
(B) To negotiate with a supplier
(C) To meet with a client
(D) To visit a family member

54. Why does the woman say, "I know what that's like"?

(A) She has to meet with some new clients.
(B) She has had trouble finding accommodation.
(C) She does not want to visit Glen Ridge.
(D) She has made the necessary preparations.

55. What does the woman suggest the man do?

(A) Secure a seat
(B) Cancel a trip
(C) Check a map
(D) Request a change

56. Who most likely are the men?

(A) Fashion designers
(B) Automobile mechanics
(C) Factory managers
(D) Taxi drivers

57. What does Morris say about the business?

(A) It is too busy today.
(B) It will be relocated.
(C) It has multiple locations.
(D) It will be closed tomorrow.

58. What does Ms. Day say she will do?

(A) Use another business
(B) Come to work a little earlier
(C) Hire more staff
(D) Ask a coworker for a ride

59. Where most likely are the speakers?

(A) In a restaurant kitchen
(B) At a home improvement store
(C) At a food market
(D) At a souvenir shop

60. What does the man offer the woman?

(A) A discount
(B) A guided tour
(C) Gift wrapping
(D) Some samples

61. According to the man, what will happen next month?

(A) The business will be closed.
(B) An item will become available.
(C) A new location will open.
(D) Job applications will be accepted.

Location	Price
Rows 1 through 10	$120
Rows 11 through 21	$100
Rows 22 through 45	$90
Balcony	$60

62. What is the woman planning to see?

(A) An acrobatic performance
(B) A play
(C) A concert
(D) A ballet

63. Look at the graphic. How much will the woman be required to pay for each ticket?

(A) $120
(B) $100
(C) $90
(D) $60

64. What does the man advise the woman to do?

(A) Arrive early
(B) Eat beforehand
(C) Purchase a T-shirt
(D) Bring an umbrella

GO ON TO THE NEXT PAGE

7:00 P.M. ~ 8:00 P.M. Advertising Rates	
5 seconds	$3,000
10 seconds	$5,000
15 seconds	$7,000
20 seconds	$10,000

65. What kind of business do the speakers most likely work for?

(A) A shopping mall
(B) A construction company
(C) A clothing manufacturer
(D) An insurance firm

66. Look at the graphic. How long is the advertisement the speakers plan to broadcast?

(A) 5 seconds
(B) 10 seconds
(C) 15 seconds
(D) 20 seconds

67. What does the woman ask the man to do?

(A) Correct a mistake
(B) Lead a meeting
(C) Make a presentation
(D) Send out an e-mail

Formaster II	Grayson E56
	PM 10:12
Tanaka HTR	**XianBo T12**
	10:12 23.5°C 6/30 SUN

68. Where do the speakers most likely work?

(A) In a grocery store
(B) In a medical office
(C) In a health club
(D) In a cafeteria

69. Look at the graphic. Which clock does the woman recommend?

(A) Formaster II
(B) Grayson E56
(C) Tanaka HTR
(D) XianBo T12

70. When will the delivery most likely arrive?

(A) This morning
(B) This afternoon
(C) Tomorrow morning
(D) Tomorrow afternoon

PART 4

Directions: In this part, you will hear some talks given by a single person. You will be asked to answer three questions about what the speaker says in each talk. You will only hear the talks one time, and they will not be printed in your test book. Choose the best response to each question and mark the letter (A), (B), (C), or (D) on your answer sheet.

71. Where is the speaker calling from?

(A) A pharmacy
(B) A research center
(C) A fashion outlet
(D) A storage facility

72. What will the listener most likely do on Friday?

(A) See a doctor
(B) Administer a test
(C) Go on a business trip
(D) Participate in a seminar

73. What is the listener reminded to do?

(A) Submit a payment
(B) Cancel an appointment
(C) Bring some identification
(D) Read some instructions

74. Who is the talk intended for?

(A) Financial advisors
(B) Recent hires
(C) Company executives
(D) Retail shop owners

75. What problem does the speaker mention?

(A) A drop in customer numbers
(B) A lack of funding
(C) Unfavorable weather conditions
(D) Insufficient factory capacity

76. What does the speaker suggest?

(A) Expanding a factory
(B) Renting a parking space
(C) Holding an event
(D) Selling an asset

77. What is the occasion for the speech?

(A) A book signing
(B) A management workshop
(C) A trade show
(D) A retirement celebration

78. What has Ms. Dawe received recognition for?

(A) Writing a helpful book
(B) Reducing departmental spending
(C) Completing a successful career
(D) Founding a profitable business

79. What is Ms. Dawe planning to do in the future?

(A) Produce a television program
(B) Take a job at a university
(C) Relocate to a new city
(D) Lead a department

80. What is being advertised?

(A) A circus
(B) A workshop
(C) A sporting competition
(D) A theatrical production

81. How long will the event be held?

(A) For one day
(B) For two days
(C) For one week
(D) For two weeks

82. What does the speaker imply when he says, "You can't miss it"?

(A) Everyone is required to attend.
(B) A venue is very easy to find.
(C) A product is not popular with many people.
(D) Listeners will be given free tickets.

GO ON TO THE NEXT PAGE

83. What is the topic of the talk?

(A) A schedule update
(B) A company merger
(C) A marketing campaign
(D) A personnel change

84. What is Joe Baxter's area of expertise?

(A) Audio engineering
(B) Social network services
(C) Personnel administration
(D) Corporate financing

85. What does the speaker ask Joe Baxter to do?

(A) Register for a course
(B) Join a luncheon
(C) Explain a technology
(D) Address an audience

86. Where is the announcement being made?

(A) In a supermarket
(B) In a sporting goods store
(C) In a hardware store
(D) In an electronics shop

87. What does the speaker say about the business?

(A) It is open until late.
(B) It has won an award.
(C) It is holding a seasonal sale.
(D) It is employing new staff.

88. Why does the speaker say, "You really don't want to be last in line"?

(A) There is a limited number of the goods available.
(B) It will take a long time to serve customers.
(C) The store will close very soon.
(D) The line will extend outdoors.

89. What problem does the speaker report?

(A) A speaker will be unavailable.
(B) A venue is too small.
(C) A reservation may be wrong.
(D) A prototype is not ready.

90. What kind of event is the speaker planning?

(A) A product launch
(B) A company banquet
(C) A farewell party
(D) A weekend workshop

91. What does the speaker request?

(A) An agenda
(B) A telephone number
(C) An invitation
(D) A confirmation e-mail

92. Where does the speaker most likely work?

(A) At a movie theater
(B) At a warehouse
(C) At a garage
(D) At a dental clinic

93. What time will the facility open tomorrow?

(A) At 6:30 A.M.
(B) At 7:00 A.M.
(C) At 8:30 A.M.
(D) At 9:00 A.M.

94. What does the speaker mean when he says, "they're staying with it"?

(A) The company has chosen some accommodations.
(B) A plan seems to be successful.
(C) A client cannot change an appointment.
(D) Prices have been kept the same.

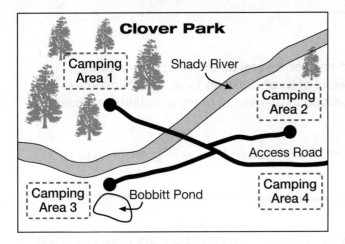

Clover Park

Camping Area 1

Shady River

Camping Area 2

Access Road

Camping Area 3

Bobbitt Pond

Camping Area 4

Departments	Section Leaders
Design	Nadia Becker
Marketing	Ahmed Lloyd
Administration	Daisy Chang
Customer Service	Simon Logan

95. What does the speaker say he has lost?

(A) The keys to his car
(B) Some camping equipment
(C) His mobile phone
(D) An address book

96. Look at the graphic. Which camping area did the speaker most likely visit?

(A) Camping Area 1
(B) Camping Area 2
(C) Camping Area 3
(D) Camping Area 4

97. According to the message, what might the speaker do?

(A) Contact a security guard
(B) Write a review
(C) Visit the ranger's center
(D) Purchase a map of the area

98. What is being distributed to staff members?

(A) Security passes
(B) Stationery items
(C) Work vests
(D) Annual bonuses

99. Look at the graphic. Where do the listeners most likely work?

(A) In design
(B) In marketing
(C) In administration
(D) In customer service

100. What does the speaker say about Ms. Chang?

(A) She will change departments.
(B) She is in a meeting.
(C) She has not arrived at work yet.
(D) She has a doctor's appointment.

This is the end of the Listening Test. Turn to Part 5 in your test book.

GO ON TO THE NEXT PAGE

READING TEST

In this section, you will read a variety of texts and answer several different types of reading comprehension questions. The Reading test consists of three parts and will take 75 minutes. Directions are given for each part. You are encouraged to answer as many questions as possible within the time allowed.

You must mark your answers on your answer sheet. Please refrain from writing anything in your test book.

PART 5

Directions: The following sentences are incomplete. Select the most appropriate word or phrase from the choices (A), (B), (C), and (D), and mark your answer on your answer sheet.

101. Employees should come to the ------- office to receive a windshield sticker for their vehicle.

(A) administration
(B) administrator
(C) administrate
(D) administer

102. The section meeting was ------- to finish at 5:00 P.M. but carried on for two hours longer.

(A) forced
(B) supposed
(C) refused
(D) postponed

103. Rules have been put in place which ------- the number of visitors to the national park each month.

(A) restrictively
(B) restrictive
(C) restriction
(D) restrict

104. Hotel guests are given a coconut juice drink immediately ------- arrival.

(A) over
(B) upon
(C) beyond
(D) across

105. The changes to the film's production schedule were ------- a result of unforeseeable weather conditions.

(A) large
(B) largeness
(C) largely
(D) larger

106. None of the plans can be carried out ------- additional funds are provided.

(A) only
(B) unless
(C) without
(D) again

107. Products ------- on the shelves to attract the attention of shoppers.

(A) are arranging
(B) have arranged
(C) arranged
(D) are arranged

108. Updating the car's design will increase costs ------- but the changes will result in long-term savings.

(A) accessibly
(B) initially
(C) maturely
(D) negatively

109. As no one else was qualified to operate the machinery, Rafael Barros took on the task -------.

(A) he
(B) his
(C) himself
(D) him

110. Glasgow Catering has always provided ------- levels of food quality for our in-flight meals.

(A) satisfactory
(B) protective
(C) periodical
(D) lengthy

111. Additional ticket sellers have been hired to ensure that lines for admission to the gallery are -------.

(A) tolerate
(B) toleration
(C) tolerable
(D) tolerably

112. Customers should ------- the instructions for Greyson teeth whitening gel.

(A) follow
(B) undertake
(C) establish
(D) convey

113. Attractions at Megaworld Theme Park have ------- inspections for safety issues.

(A) regularly
(B) regular
(C) regulate
(D) regulation

114. ------- the updates are installed, users should be able to start using the software.

(A) Whether
(B) Now that
(C) So
(D) As far as

115. Pear Tree devices are ------- more expensive than other manufacturers'.

(A) generalization
(B) generalize
(C) general
(D) generally

116. When ------- a delivery vehicle, aside from size, efficiency is usually an important factor.

(A) chose
(B) choose
(C) chosen
(D) choosing

117. Ms. Carter met a number of renowned architects ------- she was stationed in France.

(A) while
(B) seldom
(C) afterward
(D) so that

118. Greg Silva is the chief editor of the ------- acclaimed magazine *Indoor Outdoor*.

(A) mindfully
(B) personally
(C) critically
(D) virtually

119. ------- at this year's summer concert was higher than organizers had expected.

(A) Attend
(B) Attending
(C) Attendees
(D) Attendance

120. A range of ------- priced laptop computers has recently come onto the market.

(A) affordably
(B) constructively
(C) immensely
(D) completely

GO ON TO THE NEXT PAGE

121. *Lime Sky* is far ------- to receive an award than any other music video in the competition.

(A) most likely
(B) likely
(C) more likely
(D) likelihood

122. Details of the advertisement's production schedule will be ------- to the crew by the director.

(A) informed
(B) distributed
(C) suspended
(D) advised

123. Patients wishing to see Dr. Park must receive a ------- from their family physician before making an appointment.

(A) refer
(B) referred
(C) referring
(D) referral

124. Mr. Brown was offered an important position ------- his lack of experience.

(A) in
(B) around
(C) above
(D) despite

125. Companies must obtain written ------- before disposing of waste at public garbage processing sites.

(A) authorize
(B) authorized
(C) authorization
(D) authorizing

126. Applicants to the Dunham Auto Club must read all of the ------- explained in the members' agreement before signing.

(A) allocations
(B) circumstances
(C) qualifications
(D) regulations

127. *Business Plus* magazine is full of articles that modern business leaders should find both ------- and entertaining.

(A) beneficial
(B) actual
(C) objectionable
(D) portable

128. An up-to-date understanding of social networking technology is becoming ------- important for advertisers.

(A) responsibly
(B) increasingly
(C) adversely
(D) promptly

129. The president of Dixon Foods praises divisions ------- successfully reduce their use of paper.

(A) that
(B) if
(C) whom
(D) how

130. Harrison Concrete ------- as the leader in concrete production in Melbourne.

(A) is acknowledging
(B) acknowledges
(C) is acknowledged
(D) acknowledged

PART 6

Directions: Some of the following sentences are incomplete. Select the most appropriate word, phrase, or sentence from the choices (A), (B), (C), and (D), and mark your answer on your answer sheet.

Questions 131-134 refer to the following information.

Training

------- their previous experience in the finance industry, all consultants are required to take part
131.

in a two-week training course in New York. There, you ------- about the standards of conduct
132.

required of all Ogilvy and Horne employees. -------. Accommodation will be provided in a
133.

company-owned apartment for ------- coming from outside New York. Please call chief organizer,
134.

Cobie Patel, if you would like to make your own arrangements.

---

131. (A) In addition to
(B) With respect for
(C) Regardless of
(D) Along with

132. (A) learned
(B) learning
(C) were learning
(D) will learn

133. (A) This is only necessary for people who
have never worked in finance.
(B) The weeklong course is available for
only $250 per person.
(C) The course will be held in the first two
weeks of February.
(D) It is necessary for trainees to find
somewhere convenient to stay.

134. (A) applicants
(B) participants
(C) judges
(D) customers

GO ON TO THE NEXT PAGE

To: Laurence Keen <lkeen@bradleygroup.com>
From: Stephanie Dion <sdion@portlandprojects.com>
Date: June 23
Subject: July gathering

Thank you for agreeing to attend our two-day presentation for prospective investors in the Moreton Island Sterling Hotel and Resort project. ------- have arranged a variety of entertainment
135.
for you to enjoy after you have attended the project information sessions and toured the proposed building location. -------.
136.

You will be staying in luxury rooms at the Daydream Hotel on the Gold Coast. That, your meals, and your helicopter transportation between the ------- and our project offices will all be provided
137.
courtesy of Portland Projects. Please note that representatives of other ------- investors will also
138.
be visiting at the same time.

Sincerely,

Stephanie Dion
Investor Relations — Portland Projects

135. (A) We
(B) You
(C) They
(D) Ours

136. (A) Please remember to make your own arrangements in this regard.
(B) I hope it will help you understand how promising the area is for tourism.
(C) Unfortunately, we will not have time for any recreational activities.
(D) This opportunity is only available to frequent guests.

137. (A) site
(B) factory
(C) bank
(D) stadium

138. (A) confirmed
(B) reluctant
(C) defined
(D) potential

Questions 139-142 refer to the following excerpt from a report.

-------. In accordance with a company-wide push to reduce spending, every department was set
139.

a goal of ten percent, which ------- except one were able to achieve. The accounting department
140.

did manage to cut spending a little. However, their expenses were ------- so low that the goal may
141.

have been unrealistic. Their modest achievement was made by switching their paper supplier.

The new supplier, Ascot Paper offered to undercut the price of the previous supplier by five

percent. According to our calculations, the ------- will result in a saving of around €1,600 per year.
142.

139. (A) Expenditure is down this quarter.
(B) Running costs should increase as the
company grows.
(C) No objectives have been met since last
year.
(D) We are no longer using paper.

140. (A) each
(B) all
(C) neither
(D) other

141. (A) likewise
(B) quite
(C) indeed
(D) already

142. (A) change
(B) campaign
(C) program
(D) closure

GO ON TO THE NEXT PAGE

Questions 143-146 refer to the following notice.

Attention

On Friday, a company called Sensible Security Solutions ------- the security system at the main
143.

entrance. The work is scheduled to take place between 7:00 P.M. and 10:00 P.M. because that is

when we have the least -------. While the work is being carried out, you will not be able to use the
144.

automatic card reader. You will not be able to unlock the exterior doors using the electric buzzers

in the offices, either. -------. If you have a guest to whom you would like to grant entry, you should
145.

provide the building team with the name and the ------- arrival time in advance.
146.

---

143. (A) was upgrading
(B) have upgraded
(C) will be upgrading
(D) is upgraded

144. (A) confidence
(B) traffic
(C) evidence
(D) reference

145. (A) Unfortunately, no one will be allowed to
enter until the work is complete.
(B) However, it will be possible to allow
access remotely.
(C) Therefore, you should have all
employees leave before 7:00 P.M.
(D) Instead, we will have a security guard
standing at the front door.

146. (A) expecting
(B) expectation
(C) expected
(D) expectedly

PART 7

Directions: In this part, you will read a selection of texts, such as advertisements, e-mails, and instant messages. Each text or set of texts is followed by several questions. Select the most appropriate answer for each question and mark the letter (A), (B), (C), or (D) on your answer sheet.

Questions 147-148 refer to the following notice.

Attention Visitors

Walbran Park is a favorite place for families with young children to visit. Unfortunately, the popular playground has been fenced off so that maintenance workers can replace damaged and worn-out parts for safety reasons. The work will continue until the middle of March.

There are other parks in the area which have similar equipment, the closest of which is Vandelay Park on Butler Street in East Preston. The council encourages residents to make use of that facility until the work is complete.

If you would like any more information about the work or local city parks in general, please contact Nadine Salinger at gpm@haliburtoncitycouncil.com.

---

147. What is the purpose of the notice?

(A) To encourage people to make a donation
(B) To announce a change in admission rates
(C) To explain why a park is unavailable
(D) To ask for volunteers to help maintain a park

148. According to the notice, why might someone contact Ms. Salinger?

(A) To get a price estimate for playground equipment
(B) To learn more about public transportation
(C) To hire a landscaping business
(D) To discuss a construction project

GO ON TO THE NEXT PAGE

Drummond (September 6) — Blake Hawthorne, the president of Zeno Pharmaceuticals, announced today that he had finished negotiations for a takeover of Omicron Corporation. He stated that Zeno Pharmaceuticals would completely absorb the smaller company and that all their products would simply be rebranded.

Both companies have their headquarters and production facilities in Drummond so the change is not expected to have a very profound effect on staff members, who should be able to continue in their current positions albeit at a different address.

"I'll be retiring as soon as the deal is formalized" said Melissa Raver, the current CEO of Omicron Corporation. "I am very happy with the arrangement and expect the company to experience even greater prosperity as a result" she added.

149. What is the article mainly about?

(A) A new product
(B) A temporary closure
(C) A corporate merger
(D) An advertising strategy

150. What is indicated about Omicron Corporation?

(A) It has recently reported record profits.
(B) It has received an industry award.
(C) It is moving away from Drummond.
(D) It will have a change in leadership.

Questions 151-152 refer to the following text-message chain.

DEL WATKINS	8:50 A.M.

I just had a call from Ralph. He says that he can't come to the office tomorrow. The only problem is that we have to demonstrate the new equipment for the clients from Richmond.

ODETTE SOLOMAN	8:51 A.M.

I suppose you want me to fill in for him.

DEL WATKINS	8:53 A.M.

That's right. Are you available?

ODETTE SOLOMAN	8:53 A.M.

I'd made some plans, but I can change them if there's no other option.

DEL WATKINS	8:54 A.M.

I'll ask around some other people, then. If no one else is available, I'll give you another call.

ODETTE SOLOMAN	8:59 A.M.

Give me a call either way. I don't want to be wondering about this all day.

DEL WATKINS	9:02 A.M.

Good point. I'll let you know by 10 A.M.

ODETTE SOLOMAN	9:03 A.M.

Thanks, Del.

151. Who most likely is Ralph?

(A) A client
(B) A work colleague
(C) A supplier
(D) A safety inspector

152. At 8:59 A.M., why does Ms. Soloman write, "Give me a call either way"?

(A) She does not mind how Mr. Watkins calls her.
(B) She hopes that Mr. Watkins will not use another supplier.
(C) She is very eager to solve a problem.
(D) She wants to know whether or not she is needed.

GO ON TO THE NEXT PAGE

Help Save the Odeon Theater

On May 19, the Doraville Historical Society will host a screening of *Free Hearts* at the Odeon Theater on Cordon Street, Doraville. The Odeon Theater building is listed as a heritage asset of Doraville and has been protected from demolition by an order of the town council. The current owners have been unable to find a tenant and therefore, the building is not generating an income. As a result, little has been spent on its upkeep. The historical society hopes to generate interest in the old building and to find people willing to invest in a business there. Unless there is some investment and restoration work soon, the building may become unsalvageable. All money raised from admission fees for the event on May 19 will be used to carry out some emergency repairs on the roof and a couple of the exterior walls. Visit www.doravillehs.org/odeontheater for further details about the film screening and to purchase tickets for the May 19 event.

153. What is true about the Odeon Theater?

(A) It is scheduled for demolition.
(B) It has historical value.
(C) It has recently changed ownership.
(D) It is popular with local residents.

154. Why will the event most likely be held?

(A) To attract attention to an important building
(B) To provide a networking opportunity for business people
(C) To celebrate the foundation of a business
(D) To welcome new members to a community group

155. What is suggested about the tickets?

(A) They can be purchased at the theater.
(B) The price was determined by council employees.
(C) The revenue will be used to pay for repairs.
(D) They cannot be refunded within 24 hours of the event.

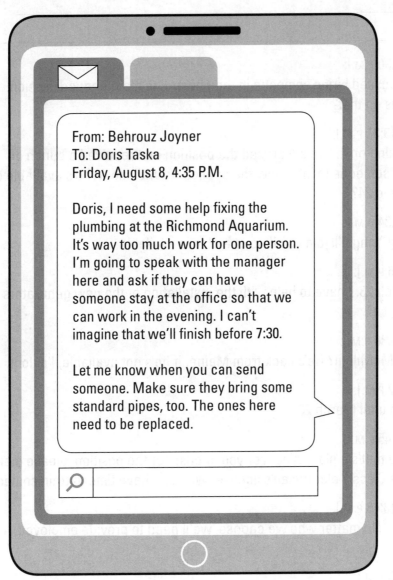

From: Behrouz Joyner
To: Doris Taska
Friday, August 8, 4:35 P.M.

Doris, I need some help fixing the plumbing at the Richmond Aquarium. It's way too much work for one person. I'm going to speak with the manager here and ask if they can have someone stay at the office so that we can work in the evening. I can't imagine that we'll finish before 7:30.

Let me know when you can send someone. Make sure they bring some standard pipes, too. The ones here need to be replaced.

156. Why did Mr. Joyner send the text message?

(A) To request assistance with a job
(B) To announce the date of an interview
(C) To comment on the price of some materials
(D) To apply for a position at an aquarium

157. What will Mr. Joyner do?

(A) Purchase some new equipment
(B) Deliver some supplies to a client
(C) Apply for a position at a manufacturing plant
(D) Make arrangements to work in the evening

GO ON TO THE NEXT PAGE ➡

Kevin Woods [3:30 P.M.]:
Hi guys. We discussed hiring someone in the power line maintenance division. What's the status on that?

Sung-Yong Lee [3:31 P.M.]:
I'm already working on it. I've advertised the position and received a bunch of résumés. I need someone to interview the applicants with me. Who's available on both March 23 and 24?

Kevin Woods [3:34 P.M.]:
Great work Sung-Yong. I'll join you if no one else is available.

Mel Chapel [3:36 P.M.]:
I'm busy on March 23. I have to help with the installation of the new generators in Hill Valley.

Denise Porter [3:38 P.M.]:
How about Rob McMillan? He's back from Maine. If he's not available, I'll do it.

Mel Chapel [3:42 P.M.]:
He's on vacation until March 26.

Kevin Woods [3:45 P.M.]:
Well, it looks like that's a plan. Whoever you choose for the position, please make sure they have a Class 1 electrician's license. We don't have time to train someone.

Sung-Yong Lee [3:46 P.M.]:
That reminds me. No matter who we choose, we'll need to provide employee orientation.

Mel Chapel [3:49 P.M.]:
I took care of that last time. It won't require any preparation for me to do it again.

Kevin Woods [3:52 P.M.]:
Thanks, Mel. Let's schedule that when we decide on the start date.

158. Where do the writers most likely work?

(A) At a fitness center
(B) At an electric company
(C) At a department store
(D) At a financial institution

159. Why does Mr. Woods praise Mr. Lee?

(A) He helped train some new employees.
(B) He has received a new qualification.
(C) He made a useful suggestion.
(D) He has made progress on a task.

160. Who will most likely assist Mr. Lee with the interview?

(A) Rob McMillan
(B) Denise Porter
(C) Mel Chapel
(D) Kevin Woods

161. At 3:49 P.M., why does Ms. Chapel write, "I took care of that last time"?

(A) She thinks it is another staff member's turn.
(B) She is ready to conduct an orientation.
(C) She has a lot of projects to complete.
(D) She would like to try something new.

GO ON TO THE NEXT PAGE

For more than 30 years, Cameron Associates has been helping our clients in the business world grow their companies and develop mutually beneficial relationships with people and organizations in both the public and private sectors.

Our vast network of connections enables us to put our clients together with both suppliers and clients whose needs and capabilities are a perfect match. Our clients also have complete access to the database of résumés on our job search Web site, ZipJobs.com, which is the most popular and highly rated in the country. Our team of consultants are also excellent motivational speakers and can be relied on to give your workforce the boost it needs when things are not going as well as they should. Please view the testimonials from our many satisfied customers on our Web site at www.cameronassociates.com.

We have just expanded our business, which means we now have the means to take on new clients. If you think your company could use the services of the United States' top consultancy firm, why not give us a call? One of our representatives will be happy to thoroughly explain our services and pricing structure so that you can make an informed decision. Call 405-555-8489 to arrange a free consultation.

Cameron Associates

162. What is the purpose of the information?
(A) To notify current clients of a change in pricing structure
(B) To describe a company's standards of customer service
(C) To advertise career opportunities
(D) To promote a company's services

163. What is NOT provided by Cameron Associates?
(A) Financial advice
(B) Professional introductions
(C) Recruitment services
(D) Employee motivational talks

164. What has Cameron Associates done recently?
(A) It has launched a new service.
(B) It has changed its address.
(C) It has won an award.
(D) It has grown.

Questions 165-167 refer to the following e-mail.

To: Fred Wilcox <fwilcox@essexprime.com>
From: Vanessa Zhi <vzhi@essexprime.com>
Subject: Dover
Date: 6 November

We have hired contractors to build a studio at the new office in Dover. They have encountered a problem that may cause us to delay the opening. — [1] — . It is going to be quite demanding in terms of both time and cost. Therefore, we need a company executive to go down there, authorize the work and oversee its completion. — [2] — .

I know you were supposed to spend some time there in December, but I would like you to go there immediately. It is important that everything go according to plan. We already have clients there and it would be a disaster if this were allowed to affect their businesses. — [3] — .

I will ask Silvia Durant to fill in for you here while you're gone. — [4] — . She has a good knowledge of the production schedule for the Pure Shine toothpaste commercial. I am sure she is qualified to complete that project.

Sincerely,

Vanessa Zhi

---

165. Why is Ms. Zhi sending the e-mail?

(A) To explain a change in plans
(B) To ask for an extension to a deadline
(C) To comment on the quality of some work
(D) To introduce a new member of staff

166. What will Ms. Durant most likely be asked to do?

(A) Attend a conference
(B) Produce a commercial
(C) Reduce department spending
(D) Meet with a prospective client

167. In which of the positions marked [1], [2], [3], and [4] does the following sentence best belong?

"There is a large fault in the building's foundation."

(A) [1]
(B) [2]
(C) [3]
(D) [4]

GO ON TO THE NEXT PAGE

https://www.comstockcitygardens.com

Comstock
25th Annual Arts and Crafts Festival
Comstock City Gardens
Saturday, May 17

9:00 A.M. – 6:00 P.M. *Arts and Crafts Demonstrations*
Local artists will be demonstrating their methods to audiences. Admission to seminars with hands-on learning opportunities can be purchased in advance from the festival Web site at www.comstockfest.org.

11:00 A.M. – 11:30 A.M. *Charity Auction*
Artworks donated by participating artists will be auctioned off in the main tent. The proceeds will be divided among a number of worthy causes. The auction will be conducted by Matt Hunt from the popular television show, Art Under the Hammer.

11:00 A.M. – 2:00 P.M. *Riverside Lunch*
A variety of local vendors will be offering meals, drinks, and snacks from stalls set up on the path along the Regent River. Food items will be priced fairly at between $1 and $12.

9:00 A.M. – 4:00 P.M. *Comstock Annual Art Exhibit and Competition*
The popular annual art competition will be held in the main tent. Anyone can submit paintings, sculptures or pottery to the event, which will be judged by a panel of local experts. View the Web site to learn more about the submission process.
www.comstockaac.com
Winners will be announced at the end of the lunch services.

There is limited parking in the area so visitors are encouraged to come by public transportation. Click here to view the area map.
For more information, visit the festival headquarters at Comstock City Hall on Dwyer Street.

168. According to the Web page, what can people buy online?

(A) Tickets to practical workshops
(B) Artworks by local artists
(C) Vouchers for meals
(D) Parking permits

169. At which event can visitors meet a celebrity?

(A) The Arts and Crafts Demonstrations
(B) The Charity Auction
(C) The Riverside Lunch
(D) The Comstock Annual Art Exhibit and Competition

170. When will the competition winners be announced?

(A) At 11:00 A.M.
(B) At 1:00 P.M.
(C) At 2:00 P.M.
(D) At 6:00 P.M.

171. What is suggested about Comstock City Gardens?

(A) It will be sold to a local business.
(B) It has some historical landmarks.
(C) The opening hours will be extended.
(D) There are few places to leave private vehicles.

GO ON TO THE NEXT PAGE

Supreme Furniture
267 North Fernanda Avenue
Aurora IL 60509

July 7

Madeline Asaba
356 Rinehart Road
Victoria BC V8P 4R7
Canada

Dear Ms. Asaba,

I am pleased to be able to inform you that your application for the position as the regional manager of our Portsmouth branch has been approved. — [1] — . As we discussed at your interview, the annual salary will start at $135,000 per year. This will increase in line with the Supreme Furniture pay scale, which you will find in the welcome package I mailed to you this morning. — [2] — . There are also some forms for you to fill out and turn in to us before you can start work. They should be fairly straightforward, but if there is anything you do not understand, please call Tony Burton in human resources.

We would like you to begin work as soon as possible. However, I understand that you will need some time to move from your current home in Victoria. — [3] — . Please let me know if there is anything I can do to make that transition go more smoothly. We have a company apartment near the office which you may use until your permanent accommodation is finalized. — [4] — . Please keep any receipts for the shipping of your belongings and your travel. Send them to the accounting department at head office by August 31. They will reimburse you with your first paycheck.

I look forward to having you on the team.

Sincerely,

Lynn Delany

Lynn Delany
President — Supreme Furniture

172. Why did Mr. Delany send the letter?

(A) To confirm the details of a contract
(B) To request an update on the progress of a project
(C) To thank a colleague for introducing a job applicant
(D) To announce the opening of a new branch office

173. According to the letter, why might Ms. Asaba contact Mr. Burton?

(A) To suggest ways to manage a project
(B) To find out more about a pricing policy
(C) To ask for an extension to a deadline
(D) To get assistance completing a form

174. What is implied about Supreme Furniture?

(A) It has relocated its head office to Victoria.
(B) Its employees are paid at the end of every month.
(C) It will cover the costs of Ms. Asaba's move.
(D) Its new recruits are required to attend a company retreat.

175. In which of the positions marked [1], [2], [3], and [4] does the following sentence best belong?

"That should arrive by tomorrow or Thursday at the latest."

(A) [1]
(B) [2]
(C) [3]
(D) [4]

GO ON TO THE NEXT PAGE

Beaudesert Regional Fair

The annual Beaudesert Regional Fair will be held this November 12 and 13 at the Beaudesert Showgrounds on Alice Street. There are prizes to be won for submissions to a number of exhibition categories. As this is a rural fair, many of the categories are agricultural in nature. The following list features the most popular exhibition categories. Only a limited number of entries will be accepted. If you would like to make a submission, you should apply by October 31 at the latest.

• Funniest Pumpkin Carving
• Juiciest Tomato
• Tastiest Yogurt
• Best Cheese
• Most Delicious Cherry Pie

An extensive list of exhibition categories is available on the Web page. Everyone submitting agricultural items must be registered with the State Board of Farmers. Furthermore, entrants in categories judged on flavor must submit a minimum of two samples.

All applications must be made in person at the administration office. Please note that the office at the showgrounds is only a temporary office and it will not be staffed until October 25. Until that date, we will be located on the third floor of the Beaudesert City Hall. You may contact chief organizer Harold Cake at hcake@beaudesertrfoc.org.

E-Mail Message	
To:	Harold Cake <hcake@beaudesertrfoc.org>
From:	Alexi Smirnoff <asmirnoff@novaduck.com>
Subject:	Beaudesert Regional Fair
Date:	November 3

Dear Mr. Cake,

I have already had my application accepted. I submitted it to the Giant Watermelon category, which I understand is new this year. Unfortunately, I misplaced the literature that the office staff handed to me so I am unclear about a couple of things. I did not deliver the watermelon with my application on October 27 as it is still on the vine. This is because I want to keep it fresh for as long as possible and because it is still growing. I understand that I must deliver it to a refrigerated warehouse at 19 James Street, but I would like to know the latest possible date on which I can do so.

Sincerely,

Alexi Smirnoff

176. What is indicated about the Beaudesert Regional Fair?

(A) It is sponsored by local businesses.
(B) It is staffed by volunteers.
(C) It is held once a year.
(D) It is growing in popularity.

177. What is most likely true about the Beaudesert region?

(A) It advertises the fair on television.
(B) It has a new administrative building.
(C) It attracts many tourists.
(D) It has a farming economy.

178. In which category are competitors expected to submit a single item?

(A) Funniest Pumpkin Carving
(B) Tastiest Yogurt
(C) Best Cheese
(D) Most Delicious Cherry Pie

179. What is NOT suggested about Ms. Smirnoff?

(A) She has viewed the Web page.
(B) She is registered with the State Board of Farmers.
(C) She has submitted items in more than one category.
(D) She obtained documents at the showgrounds.

180. Why did Ms. Smirnoff write to Mr. Cake?

(A) To ask for assistance planning an event
(B) To complain about a mistake
(C) To inquire about a date
(D) To announce a change to a plan

GO ON TO THE NEXT PAGE

Roman Rossi
Rossi Modeling Agency
Office 2, Level 19, Gibraltar Office Building
10 Well Street,
Wellington, 6011

16 January

Dear Mr. Rossi,

I would like to hire two of your models for a photography shoot on 27 January. I recently founded a company that imports various fashion items from manufacturers around the world and I am putting together a new catalog of our products that I will mail to customers. I was given your contact details by Michelle Leeds. She mentioned that she used your company exclusively in the past and that she found you and your employees extremely reliable.

We would require the models to come to a studio at 257 Barkley Street. The shoot should take about four hours from 2:00 P.M. to 6:00 P.M. However, I would appreciate it if the models could arrive one hour early. We require a male and a female model as we stock garments for both genders. I am sure you will be pleased to know that the photographer is Milo Milano. He was also introduced to us by Ms. Leeds. My e-mail address is on my business card, which you will find enclosed along with last year's catalog.

Sincerely,

Harriett Clutterbuck

Harriett Clutterbuck
CEO — Clutterbuck Fashion

To: Harriett Clutterbuck <hclutterbuck@clutterbuckfashion.com>
From: Roman Rossi <rrossi@rossima.com>
Date: 21 January
Subject: Request

Dear Ms. Clutterbuck,

Thank you for contacting me. I am happy to hear that Ms. Leeds is still in the industry. For many years she was my best client and the models all loved her designs. Ordinarily, we only accept appointments made at least a month in advance. However, I realize you are new to the business and I will do what I can to accommodate you. You can contact my secretary at 555-2423 to set up an appointment to look at the profiles of the people we represent.

By the way, our models will be happy with your choice of photographer. Mr. Milano's reputation in the industry is unmatched.

I look forward to meeting you when you come to our office.

Sincerely,

Roman Rossi

181. Why did Ms. Clutterbuck contact Mr. Rossi?

(A) She would like to work as a model.
(B) She is creating a brochure.
(C) She wants to interview him for an article.
(D) She is organizing a fashion show.

182. At what time should the models arrive on January 27?

(A) 1:00 P.M.
(B) 2:00 P.M.
(C) 5:00 P.M.
(D) 6:00 P.M.

183. Who gave Ms. Clutterbuck Mr. Rossi's contact details?

(A) An apparel importer
(B) A fashion model
(C) An advertising executive
(D) A clothing designer

184. Why does Mr. Rossi make an exception for Ms. Clutterbuck?

(A) She has limited experience in the fashion industry.
(B) She is paying for a premium service.
(C) Another client canceled unexpectedly.
(D) She requires only a little assistance.

185. What is suggested about Mr. Milano?

(A) He primarily works at 257 Barkley Street.
(B) He is an experienced fashion photographer.
(C) He helped create Clutterbuck Fashion's previous catalog.
(D) He charges extra for assignments outside Wellington.

GO ON TO THE NEXT PAGE

Dreamride Car Rental – Rental Agreement

Renter: *Jason Cox*	License Number: *16172334*
Address: *622 Lake Drive, Seattle*	Contact Number: *832-555-8348*
Rental Start: *9:00 A.M. March 16*	Rental End: *9:00 A.M. March 19*
Insurance: *$35 per day (Premium Protection)*	

Should the car be returned later than the time indicated on the form, the renter will be charged for an additional day of rental.

The renter is required to pay the cost of any damage repairs. When damage results from two vehicles coming into contact, renters with basic insurance will be required to pay the first $990 with the remainder being covered by the insurance company. If the damage is a result of contact with something other than a vehicle, the driver pays the initial $5,000 of repairs. For those with premium protection, the amounts are reduced to $300 and $1,000 respectively.

Please be sure to remove any personal items from the car before delivering it to the drop-off location indicated on the condition report, which can be found in the car's glove compartment.

I agree with all of the conditions explained in this agreement.

Signed: *Jason Cox*

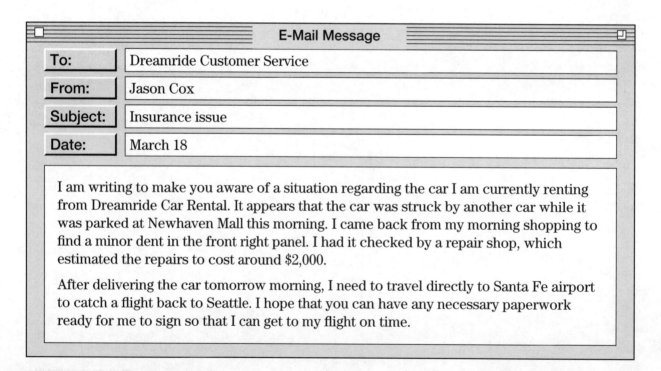

	E-Mail Message
To:	Dreamride Customer Service
From:	Jason Cox
Subject:	Insurance issue
Date:	March 18

I am writing to make you aware of a situation regarding the car I am currently renting from Dreamride Car Rental. It appears that the car was struck by another car while it was parked at Newhaven Mall this morning. I came back from my morning shopping to find a minor dent in the front right panel. I had it checked by a repair shop, which estimated the repairs to cost around $2,000.

After delivering the car tomorrow morning, I need to travel directly to Santa Fe airport to catch a flight back to Seattle. I hope that you can have any necessary paperwork ready for me to sign so that I can get to my flight on time.

Travel Report

Employee: Jason Cox

Expenses	Cost
Round trip ticket to New Mexico: March 16 **Depart** Seattle 9:20 A.M. **Arrive in** Santa Fe 4:55 P.M. March 20 **Depart** Santa Fe 7:40 A.M. **Arrive in** Seattle 1:27 P.M.	$789.00
Accommodation: March 16 to March 19 — Royal Palms Hotel March 19 to March 20 — Barato Airport Hotel	$570.00 $110.00
Other transportation: Rental Vehicle, March 16 to March 19 Taxi from Barato Airport Hotel to Santa Fe Airport, March 20	$720.00 $35.00

186. What information is mentioned in the agreement?

(A) The daily rental cost
(B) The penalty for late returns
(C) The return address for the vehicle
(D) The location of the driver's manual

187. How much was Mr. Cox most likely charged as a result of the damage?

(A) $300
(B) $990
(C) $1,000
(D) $5,000

188. What is Mr. Cox reminded to do before returning the vehicle?

(A) Refill the car's fuel tank
(B) Take out his personal belongings
(C) Fill out an online form
(D) Call the rental company office

189. In the e-mail, the word "ready" in paragraph 2, line 3, is closest in meaning to

(A) prepared
(B) willing
(C) approved
(D) examined

190. What is implied about Mr. Cox?

(A) He lives near a shopping mall.
(B) He left the rental car at Santa Fe airport.
(C) He was forced to change his travel plans.
(D) He has used Dreamride Car Rental before.

GO ON TO THE NEXT PAGE ➡

SANDER'S PRODUCTIONS
772 Rockatanski Road • Boise • ID 83644

March 23

Ms. Lawrence,

Thank you so much for putting me in touch with Todd Jensen. We were having difficulty finding someone with his qualifications and it felt like a miracle when you suddenly contacted us and explained his situation. He has been doing an excellent job on the Francis Inn television commercials. The project reminds me of the time we worked together on the Heathcliff Hotel advertising campaign.

If there is anything we can do to repay the favor, do not hesitate to let me know. I look forward to seeing you at this year's Producers' Conference in Boulder. I hear that Freda Watts is presenting. We attended her lectures at Kamloops University. It is great to see that she is finally getting the industry recognition she deserves.

Sincerely,

Reg Garibaldi

Reg Garibaldi

To: Reg Garibaldi <rgaribaldi@sandersproductions.com>
From: Carrie Lawrence <clawrence@eaglevl.com>
Subject: Instructional videos
Date: June 17

Dear Reg,

I have been communicating with Mr. Jensen of late and he informs me that you have secured a contract to shoot a series of instructional videos and need a second crew to cover the workload. While we have not received a formal invitation, I would like to offer our services as a subcontractor. I remember that our previous collaboration was regarded as a great success, and I hope that we can repeat that this time.

Best regards,

Carrie
Eagle Video Labs

ACVPA

Annual Corporate Video Production Awards Ceremony
Event Schedule (Confidential Information for Committee Members ONLY)
Chandler Plaza Hotel, December 2

7:00 P.M. – 7:10 P.M.	**Opening Speech** **By:** ACVPA President Sam Whitehall	
7:10 P.M. – 7:40 P.M.	**Dinner Service**	
7:40 P.M. – 7:50 P.M.	Award for Best Regional Advertisement **Recipient:** Voorhees Video	Presented by: Creed Norris
7:50 P.M. – 8:00 P.M.	Award for Best Public Service Announcement **Recipient:** Undecided	Presented by: Undecided
8:00 P.M. – 8:10 P.M.	Award for Best Instructional Video **Recipient:** Sanders Productions/Eagle Video Labs	Presented by: Luke Moore
8:10 P.M. – 8:20 P.M.	Award for Best Memorial Video **Recipient:** Undecided	Presented by: Undecided
8:20 P.M. – 8:40 P.M.	**Closing Speech** **By:** ACVPA Founder Cindy DuPont	

191. Why did Mr. Garibaldi write to Ms. Lawrence?

(A) To offer a suggestion for a title
(B) To express appreciation for an introduction
(C) To remind her of a condition in her contract
(D) To suggest she submit her work for evaluation

192. Who most likely is Ms. Watts?

(A) A conference organizer
(B) A software engineer
(C) A university lecturer
(D) A factory manager

193. What is indicated about the Heathcliff Hotel advertising campaign?

(A) It was considered a success.
(B) It will be completed in March.
(C) It has had its budget reduced.
(D) It is being managed by Mr. Jensen.

194. What will happen on December 2?

(A) Transportation will be provided for guests.
(B) Mr. Norris will receive an award.
(C) Chandler Plaza Hotel will host a ceremony.
(D) A committee member will greet the audience.

195. What is suggested about Mr. Garibaldi?

(A) He is a member of the awards committee.
(B) He will provide training to Mr. Jensen.
(C) He will give a presentation at ACVPA.
(D) He accepted Ms. Lawrence's business proposal.

GO ON TO THE NEXT PAGE

www.frontierwear.com/receipt9783903

FRONTIER WEAR ONLINE STORE

Customer name: Cliff Spence
Account number: 783834
Date: October 2

Quantity	Description	Price
1	Mountain Climbing Boots (GB839)	$125.00
2	Knitted Hat Blue (NH739)	$38.00
2	60L Backpack (ER331)	$178.00
1	Winter Socks Black (HB949)	$18.00
	Subtotal	$359.00
	Shipping	$12.00
	Amount Paid	**$371.00**

You will receive a hard copy of this receipt with your order. Frontier Wear will provide a full refund or exchange for any defective item for a period of 12 months from the date of purchase. Returns and exchanges can be made within 28 days of purchase if there is a discrepancy between the description and the actual article.

By spending over $100 at Frontier Wear you are automatically eligible to take part in our yearly hiking adventure. Click HERE for details.

To: Cliff Spence <cspence@youngpanda.com>
From: Holly Waters <hwaters@frontierwear.com>
Date: October 7
Subject: Your order
Attachment: 📎 careinstructions

Dear Mr. Spence,

I'm sorry to hear that the care instructions for the mountain climbing boots were not enclosed in the box. We source our footwear from overseas. Therefore, having instructions sent from the manufacturer would take a long time. Fortunately, I was able to find care instructions on the manufacturer's Web site. I have downloaded them and had them translated by a member of our staff. I can confirm that all of the items mentioned in the instructions are available from our online store. Please see the attachment to this e-mail. Should you require a paper copy, please let me know and I will have the store nearest to your home print one out.

Sincerely,

Holly Waters
Customer Service Officer — Frontier Wear

Manufacturer's Warranty

The Bradbury 60L Backpack (ER331) is the top of the line in backpacks for serious hikers. Whether you are climbing mountains, crossing deserts, or navigating glaciers, this sturdy backpack will keep your belongings safe and dry there and back. In fact, we are so sure about our product quality that we will guarantee it for five years. If you have any issues with the construction or materials used in this item, call our customer service hotline at 321-555-7838.

196. What is indicated about Mr. Spence?

(A) He is a frequent customer of Frontier Wear.
(B) He is eligible to take part in a store-run event.
(C) He has planned an international trip.
(D) He made the payment in installments.

197. Why most likely is Ms. Waters sending the e-mail?

(A) To accommodate a customer's request
(B) To apologize for a defective product
(C) To provide updates on a project
(D) To inform staff of a shipping error

198. What is NOT mentioned about Frontier Wear?

(A) It sells imported items.
(B) It operates stores in several locations.
(C) It has a translating team.
(D) It ships orders with a printed receipt.

199. In the warranty, the word "serious" in paragraph 1, line 2, is closest in meaning to

(A) affordable
(B) urgent
(C) passionate
(D) cautious

200. What is true about the Bradbury 60L Backpack?

(A) It comes with some accessories.
(B) The price is higher than many of its competitors'.
(C) It can be converted into different shapes.
(D) The manufacturer's warranty exceeds the seller's.

Stop! This is the end of the test. If you finish before time is called, you may go back to Parts 5, 6, and 7 and check your work.

TOEIC® L&Rテスト 究極の模試600問⁺
模擬試験 ②
Test 2

	1回目			2回目			3回目		
受験日	年	月	日	年	月	日	年	月	日
開始時間	時		分	時		分	時		分
Listening Section 終了時間	時		分	時		分	時		分
Reading Section 終了時間	時		分	時		分	時		分

◆Listening Section の音声は、ダウンロードしてご利用ください。詳しくは本冊のp.10に掲載されています。【Test 2】の音声を利用します。所要時間は**約46分**です。

◆解答には本冊巻末のマークシートを使用してください。マークシートA（勘ボックスあり）の使い方は本冊のp.12～で説明しています。テスト採点センター（本冊p.11）もご利用いただけます。

◆解答一覧は本冊p.144～にあります。

テスト採点センター

使用する音声ファイル一覧

Listening Section、Part 1 Directions	065_T2_P1_Dir.mp3
Part 1 No.1～No.6	066_T2_P1_01.mp3～072_T2_P1_06.mp3
Part 2 Directions	073_T2_P2_Dir.mp3
Part 2 No.7～No.31	074_T2_P2_07.mp3～099_T2_P2_31.mp3
Part 3 Directions	100_T2_P3_Dir.mp3
Part 3 No.32～No.70	101_T2_P3_32-34.mp3～115_T2_P3_68-70.mp3
Part 4 Directions	116_T2_P4_Dir.mp3
Part 4 No.71～No.100	117_T2_P4_71-73.mp3～127_T2_P4_98-100.mp3

矢印の方向に引くと、この冊子を取り外すことができます。

LISTENING TEST

In this section, your ability to understand spoken English will be shown. The Listening test consists of four parts and will take approximately 45 minutes. Directions will be given for each part. By following the directions you hear, select the best possible answer and mark your answers on your answer sheet. Please refrain from writing anything in your test book.

PART 1

Directions: In this part, you will see a picture in your test book and hear four statements. After hearing each statement, select the one statement you think is the best description for the picture. Then, mark the answer on your answer sheet. You will only hear the statements one time, and they will not be printed in your test book.

Statement (B), "They're sitting side by side," best describes the picture. Therefore, you should choose answer (B) and mark it on your answer sheet.

1.

2.

GO ON TO THE NEXT PAGE

3.

4.

5.

6.

GO ON TO THE NEXT PAGE ▶

PART 2

Directions: In this part, you will hear a question or statement. You will then hear three alternative responses to the question or statement. They will all be spoken in English. You will only hear them one time, and they will not be printed in your test book. Choose the best response to each question and mark the letter (A), (B), or (C) on your answer sheet.

7. Mark your answer on your answer sheet.

8. Mark your answer on your answer sheet.

9. Mark your answer on your answer sheet.

10. Mark your answer on your answer sheet.

11. Mark your answer on your answer sheet.

12. Mark your answer on your answer sheet.

13. Mark your answer on your answer sheet.

14. Mark your answer on your answer sheet.

15. Mark your answer on your answer sheet.

16. Mark your answer on your answer sheet.

17. Mark your answer on your answer sheet.

18. Mark your answer on your answer sheet.

19. Mark your answer on your answer sheet.

20. Mark your answer on your answer sheet.

21. Mark your answer on your answer sheet.

22. Mark your answer on your answer sheet.

23. Mark your answer on your answer sheet.

24. Mark your answer on your answer sheet.

25. Mark your answer on your answer sheet.

26. Mark your answer on your answer sheet.

27. Mark your answer on your answer sheet.

28. Mark your answer on your answer sheet.

29. Mark your answer on your answer sheet.

30. Mark your answer on your answer sheet.

31. Mark your answer on your answer sheet.

PART 3

Directions: In this part, you will hear conversations between two or more people. You will be asked to answer three questions about what the speakers say in each conversation. You will only hear the conversations one time, and they will not be printed in your test book. Choose the best response to each question and mark the letter (A), (B), (C), or (D) on your answer sheet.

32. What does the man want to discuss?

(A) Deadlines for sales reports
(B) The location of some furniture
(C) Plans for a business trip
(D) The cost of some upgrades

33. What does the woman say she will be doing in the afternoon?

(A) Attending a game
(B) Looking at a building site
(C) Meeting an auditor
(D) Dealing with some problems

34. Why will the woman call a client?

(A) To reschedule a meeting
(B) To give a progress report
(C) To introduce a coworker
(D) To request an extension to a deadline

35. What kind of business do the men work for?

(A) A cleaning service
(B) A solar power company
(C) A construction firm
(D) An Internet service provider

36. What do the men imply about the job?

(A) It will take a long time.
(B) It will be carried out on another day.
(C) It has been assigned to a different team.
(D) It was requested by a company executive.

37. What does the woman ask the men to do?

(A) Lock the door
(B) Return her keys
(C) Take out some garbage
(D) Send a text message

38. Who is Jules Martinez?

(A) A guest speaker
(B) A sales representative
(C) A council inspector
(D) A photographer

39. What problem does the woman mention?

(A) A portfolio has not been submitted.
(B) A kitchen has not been cleaned.
(C) Some information is inaccurate.
(D) Some equipment is out of order.

40. What is the man asked to do?

(A) Request some repairs
(B) Fill out a form
(C) Purchase a replacement
(D) Change an appointment

41. What are the speakers mainly discussing?

(A) A marketing strategy
(B) A news story
(C) An appliance
(D) A product description

42. What does the man mean when he says, "I only bought it a week ago"?

(A) He is not familiar with a procedure.
(B) He needs more time to test a product.
(C) He thinks he is eligible for a refund.
(D) He is certain a product works well.

43. What does the woman ask the man to do?

(A) Make a presentation
(B) Show her a product
(C) Send her some research data
(D) Delay a product launch

GO ON TO THE NEXT PAGE

44. Where most likely are the speakers?

(A) In an art gallery
(B) In a theater
(C) At the airport
(D) At a taxi stand

45. What does the woman ask about?

(A) An invitation
(B) A travel time
(C) Seating capacity
(D) Traffic conditions

46. What will the man most likely do next?

(A) Go to a train station
(B) Buy a bus pass
(C) Make a phone call
(D) Take out some identification

47. Who most likely is the woman?

(A) An author
(B) A lawyer
(C) An architect
(D) A financial advisor

48. What is the woman looking for?

(A) A computer
(B) A document
(C) An empty desk
(D) Her luggage

49. Why does the man suggest speaking with Ted?

(A) To discuss a strategy
(B) To learn about a product
(C) To ask for directions
(D) To get a password

50. Why is the man concerned?

(A) A client is dissatisfied.
(B) Bad weather was forecast.
(C) A supplier is closed.
(D) An order was incorrect.

51. What is the man planning to do later today?

(A) Take the afternoon off
(B) Evaluate employee performance
(C) Paint some walls
(D) Photograph a garden

52. What does the woman propose the man do?

(A) Borrow a van
(B) Wear protective clothing
(C) Check a telephone directory
(D) Use a staffing agency

53. Where do the speakers most likely work?

(A) At an assembly plant
(B) At a shipping facility
(C) At a legal office
(D) At a hotel

54. What problem does the man mention?

(A) Some guests will arrive late.
(B) Some products have been broken.
(C) A machine is too expensive.
(D) A deadline has passed.

55. What does the woman mean when she says, "They won't like that"?

(A) Product quality has dropped.
(B) Extra work will be assigned.
(C) A request is unacceptable.
(D) A warranty will expire.

56. What is the conversation mainly about?

(A) A photography club
(B) An office cleanup
(C) A fitness center
(D) Transportation routes

57. What does the woman say will happen tomorrow?

(A) Entries for a contest will be accepted.
(B) A truck will come to pick up garbage.
(C) Some cleaners will do some work.
(D) A discount will become available.

58. What does the man say he will bring?

(A) Some appropriate clothing
(B) Some cleaning products
(C) His employee card
(D) A copy of a certificate

59. What are the speakers discussing?

(A) A building opening
(B) A musical performance
(C) A client dinner
(D) A film premiere

60. What time will the event start?

(A) At 2:00 P.M.
(B) At 4:00 P.M.
(C) At 5:00 P.M.
(D) At 6:00 P.M.

61. What does the man say he will do?

(A) Invite a colleague
(B) Hire a catering company
(C) Send out a memo
(D) Have his suit cleaned

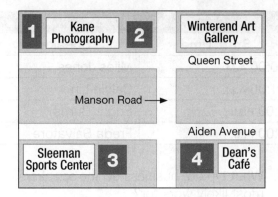

62. Why will the woman borrow the man's car?

(A) To go shopping
(B) To meet a client
(C) To make a delivery
(D) To return home

63. Look at the graphic. In which parking lot does the man say he left the car?

(A) Parking Lot 1
(B) Parking Lot 2
(C) Parking Lot 3
(D) Parking Lot 4

64. What does the man ask the woman to do?

(A) Have the car washed
(B) Pay the parking fee
(C) Bring back a receipt
(D) Refill the fuel tank

GO ON TO THE NEXT PAGE

Day 1	
Start Time	**Speaker**
10:00 A.M.	Miles Jones
11:30 A.M.	Calvin Lin
2:00 P.M.	Edgar Burns
4:00 P.M.	Freda Salvatore

Destination	Status	Departs
Paris	Delayed	To be advised
New York	On Time	4:30 P.M.
London	Delayed	6:30 P.M.
Tokyo	On Time	7:00 P.M.

65. What type of business do the speakers most likely work for?

(A) A utility company
(B) An advertising agency
(C) An accounting firm
(D) A printing company

66. Look at the graphic. Which presentation will the man attend?

(A) Miles Jones'
(B) Calvin Lin's
(C) Edgar Burns'
(D) Freda Salvatore's

67. What does the man say he will do on Friday?

(A) Stay in a hotel
(B) Take a train
(C) Introduce a speaker
(D) Attend a reception desk

68. What does the woman suggest doing?

(A) Calling a coworker
(B) Reserving a hotel room
(C) Renting a car
(D) Charging their phones

69. Look at the graphic. Where are the speakers most likely headed?

(A) To Paris
(B) To New York
(C) To London
(D) To Tokyo

70. What will the speakers most likely do next?

(A) Change their flight
(B) Have a meal
(C) Postpone a meeting
(D) Submit some forms

PART 4

Directions: In this part, you will hear some talks given by a single person. You will be asked to answer three questions about what the speaker says in each talk. You will only hear the talks one time, and they will not be printed in your test book. Choose the best response to each question and mark the letter (A), (B), (C), or (D) on your answer sheet.

71. What is about to take place?
    (A) A sales presentation
    (B) A college introduction
    (C) A book reading
    (D) A seminar

72. Who is scheduled to speak?
    (A) College professors
    (B) Career counselors
    (C) Artists
    (D) Journalists

73. What are the audience members encouraged to do?
    (A) Take notes
    (B) Complete evaluation forms
    (C) Open brochures
    (D) Ask questions

74. What has been ordered?
    (A) Tablecloths
    (B) A sofa
    (C) Flowerpots
    (D) Pamphlets

75. What problem does the speaker mention?
    (A) An item was damaged.
    (B) A delivery was late.
    (C) The color was wrong.
    (D) The address has changed.

76. What is the listener asked to do?
    (A) Send a replacement
    (B) Take another route
    (C) Pay for some repairs
    (D) Update an invoice

77. Who is the announcement intended for?
    (A) Residents
    (B) Tour participants
    (C) Hotel guests
    (D) Store clerks

78. What will happen next week?
    (A) An attraction will be closed.
    (B) Landscaping will be carried out.
    (C) A festival will commence.
    (D) A decision will be announced.

79. What does the speaker recommend listeners do?
    (A) Check their mail
    (B) Obtain tickets for an event
    (C) Attend a meeting
    (D) Keep windows closed

80. What is the purpose of the meeting?
    (A) To suggest buying some new equipment
    (B) To ask people to volunteer on a project
    (C) To update a reporting procedure
    (D) To introduce a new employee

81. What does the speaker mean when she says, "Ms. Gordon has a long history in television advertising"?
    (A) She thinks Ms. Gordon's knowledge is outdated.
    (B) She hopes Ms. Gordon has connections with many experts.
    (C) She has known Ms. Gordon for a long time.
    (D) She believes Ms. Gordon has valuable experience.

82. What did the focus group say about the commercial?
    (A) It was very interesting.
    (B) It was not inspiring.
    (C) It had too much music.
    (D) It had confusing dialogue.

GO ON TO THE NEXT PAGE

83. Who is George Wallace?

(A) A producer
(B) A writer
(C) A singer
(D) A videographer

84. What are listeners asked to do when they call?

(A) Suggest a title for a song
(B) Talk about an experience
(C) Name one of George Wallace's works
(D) Guess the location of a film set

85. What will the winner be given?

(A) A copy of a new book
(B) An invitation to a party
(C) An autographed album
(D) A ticket to a workshop

---

86. What is the purpose of the message?

(A) To make a complaint
(B) To announce a schedule
(C) To request a change
(D) To explain a delay

87. What does the speaker ask about?

(A) Ticket prices
(B) Workshop topics
(C) Parking allocation
(D) Accommodation options

88. What does the speaker imply when she says, "I hope this isn't a repeat of last year"?

(A) The same problem occurred in the past.
(B) The schedule looks similar to the previous year's.
(C) She did not receive an invitation to a prior event.
(D) Few people are showing interest in an event.

---

89. What kind of business is Rudolph's?

(A) An outdoor market
(B) A restaurant
(C) A grocery store
(D) A vocational school

90. According to the speaker, what has Rudolph's done recently?

(A) Started a new course
(B) Changed its opening hours
(C) Moved to a new location
(D) Hired more staff

91. What can listeners do on Sunday?

(A) Try a new menu
(B) Speak with experts
(C) Watch a performance
(D) Get big discounts

---

92. What is the news report mainly about?

(A) An international event
(B) A city election
(C) A selection process
(D) A cleanup project

93. What change is being planned?

(A) More frequent inspections
(B) Developing public land
(C) Additional train services
(D) Changing the date of an event

94. Why does the speaker say, "It might be time to reconsider that decision"?

(A) The town should offer more attractions.
(B) There may not be enough accommodation.
(C) More employment opportunities are needed.
(D) The council has spent too much money.

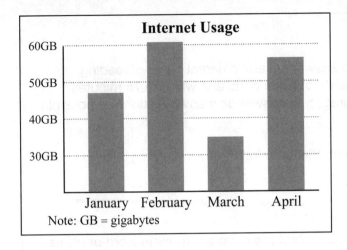

Internet Usage

Note: GB = gigabytes

95. Who is attending the meeting?

(A) Board members
(B) Client representatives
(C) Department heads
(D) Business analysts

96. Look at the graphic. How many times has the company paid additional charges this year?

(A) Once
(B) Twice
(C) Three times
(D) Four times

97. What are employees asked to do?

(A) Stop watching online videos
(B) Upload files to a server
(C) Rely on e-mail more
(D) Attend a workshop

CROUCHING THAI-GER

This voucher entitles the bearer to 25% off!
Lunch —For *group reservations only
Dinner — 5:30 P.M. to 9:00 P.M. daily
(Last order at 8:30 P.M.)

*Six or more people
Expires August 28

98. Who most likely is the speaker?

(A) A chef
(B) A restaurant critic
(C) A journalist
(D) A plumber

99. What does the speaker say about the company cafeteria?

(A) It will be undergoing some maintenance.
(B) It has been closed permanently.
(C) It has been reserved by a large group.
(D) It is not very large.

100. Look at the graphic. Why will the speaker be unable to use the coupon?

(A) He will arrive after 8:30 P.M.
(B) The restaurant is closed on Tuesday.
(C) There are only two people in his group.
(D) The coupon has expired.

This is the end of the Listening Test. Turn to Part 5 in your test book.

GO ON TO THE NEXT PAGE

In this section, you will read a variety of texts and answer several different types of reading comprehension questions. The Reading test consists of three parts and will take 75 minutes. Directions are given for each part. You are encouraged to answer as many questions as possible within the time allowed.

You must mark your answers on your answer sheet. Please refrain from writing anything in your test book.

PART 5

Directions: The following sentences are incomplete. Select the most appropriate word or phrase from the choices (A), (B), (C), and (D), and mark your answer on your answer sheet.

101. Yuka Sano proved to be an excellent ------- to the design team.

(A) add
(B) additional
(C) addition
(D) additionally

102. Humphrey brand soups are popular with health-conscious people because they ------- all natural ingredients.

(A) secure
(B) contain
(C) conclude
(D) propose

103. Managers at Glacier Tools are ------- required to travel internationally.

(A) frequented
(B) frequency
(C) frequently
(D) frequent

104. Kim Salazar opened ------- first bakery on Valencia Street ten years ago.

(A) her
(B) herself
(C) she
(D) hers

105. Using Sue Valtine's recipe book, even beginners can cook delicious meals with -------.

(A) easy
(B) easily
(C) ease
(D) eased

106. ------- to the Woodhill Art Competition must be delivered in person by August 19.

(A) Compositions
(B) Submissions
(C) Establishments
(D) Refunds

107. ------- of an interview Mr. Gaines gave before he became famous were discovered by a local journalist.

(A) Record
(B) Recorded
(C) Recording
(D) Recordings

108. If sales continue at their current pace, we will ------- the year's target by October.

(A) exceed
(B) dictate
(C) anticipate
(D) resolve

109. Inspectors have identified ------- issues that must be rectified before the reopening.
(A) every
(B) neither
(C) several
(D) another

110. Many listeners criticized Hal Winter's latest radio drama, complaining that the plot was too -------.
(A) virtual
(B) ultimate
(C) relative
(D) predictable

111. Most of the trainees were ------- sure that they could operate the machinery after the workshop.
(A) reason
(B) reasonable
(C) reasonably
(D) reasoning

112. The Bellmax store at Hastings Mall is expected to reopen ------- next month.
(A) early
(B) really
(C) mostly
(D) quickly

113. The consultant admitted that the sales team's efforts were -------, but suggested some changes nonetheless.
(A) admiration
(B) admirable
(C) admire
(D) admirably

114. ------- she returned from the marketing conference in Tokyo, Ms. Castro has been pushing for more Internet advertising.
(A) As though
(B) Ever since
(C) Only if
(D) Even when

115. Costing twenty percent less than the next cheapest forklift, the R20 is ------- affordable.
(A) compare
(B) comparison
(C) comparative
(D) comparatively

116. Stan Saunders is ------- the most qualified of all the applicants for the bus driver position.
(A) widely
(B) closely
(C) obviously
(D) punctually

117. The beach cleaning event is staffed by over fifty volunteers, ------- are students from a local university.
(A) most of whom
(B) whereas
(C) notwithstanding
(D) one of which

118. The Mason Library will be closed for a month ------- on June 12.
(A) begin
(B) began
(C) have begun
(D) beginning

119. ------- adequate promotion, Ms. Walker's book should be a national bestseller.
(A) Once
(B) Given
(C) Moreover
(D) According to

120. All requests for information will receive a ------- response from our customer service personnel.
(A) durable
(B) swift
(C) previous
(D) constant

GO ON TO THE NEXT PAGE

121. The ------- of Monday's meeting is to decide on a route for the walkathon.
    (A) objectively
    (B) objecting
    (C) objection
    (D) objective

122. The company has decided to ------- three new staff members ahead of the busy season.
    (A) apply
    (B) employ
    (C) demonstrate
    (D) search

123. When Ms. Juma learned she would be involved in the upcoming sales campaign, she ------- canceling her trip to Spain.
    (A) considered
    (B) considerable
    (C) consideration
    (D) considerably

124. The Hills Cinema is ------- five venues that have expressed interest in hosting the film festival.
    (A) for
    (B) about
    (C) until
    (D) among

125. The company president is extremely ------- to the needs of the various sections.
    (A) attends
    (B) attentively
    (C) attention
    (D) attentive

126. The manufacturer of HGL swimwear is taking ------- so that stores do not run out of stock again.
    (A) valuations
    (B) oppositions
    (C) impressions
    (D) precautions

127. For its new store, Bettina's Grill is looking at three locations ------- five minutes' walk of Rupert Station.
    (A) within
    (B) onto
    (C) before
    (D) toward

128. Any suggestions ------- the office party should be brought up at the regularly scheduled meetings.
    (A) regard
    (B) regarding
    (C) may regard
    (D) are regarded

129. Invitations to the summer banquet will be sent out ------- the guest list is finalized.
    (A) as soon as
    (B) as well as
    (C) in return for
    (D) insofar as

130. West Motors and Brix City will split the cost ------- for the Kelly Park renovation evenly.
    (A) requiring
    (B) is required
    (C) required
    (D) having required

PART 6

Directions: Some of the following sentences are incomplete. Select the most appropriate word, phrase, or sentence from the choices (A), (B), (C), and (D), and mark your answer on your answer sheet.

Questions 131-134 refer to the following e-mail.

To: Steven Rand <srand@speedway.com>

From: FF Internet Customer Service <cs@ffinternet.com>

Date: March 6

Subject: Overdue account

Dear Mr. Rand,

It has come to our attention that payment for your Internet ------- for February is overdue. You
                                                              131.

agreed to have the fee automatically deducted from your bank account on the 1st of every month.

We attempted to make a ------- on March 1. However, the request was denied by your bank. We
                        132.

will try again on March 20 as stipulated in the agreement. Please make sure you have sufficient

funds in the account by then.

If you are ------- using this bank account, you can switch to payment by credit card by changing
            133.

your payment information on your Account page by March 20. -------.
                                                            134.

Sincerely,

Mary Cole

Customer Service — FF Internet

---

131. (A) connective
     (B) connect
     (C) connection
     (D) connectively

132. (A) difference
     (B) concession
     (C) decision
     (D) withdrawal

133. (A) no longer
     (B) still
     (C) just
     (D) at present

134. (A) Please note that the due date for
         payment will be announced soon.
     (B) In this case, we will take payment for
         February and March on April 1.
     (C) You are encouraged to reapply next
         time a vacant position becomes
         available.
     (D) To make things easier, you could
         consider automatic payment in future.

GO ON TO THE NEXT PAGE

The LM55 Printer is the ------- solution for the home office. However, proper ------- is necessary
135.   136.
to ensure that the device is always ready for use. Therefore, the printing heads should be cleaned

at least once a month. This can be done automatically, by pressing the head cleaner button on

the front of the device. Refilling the printer with ink is easy enough for anyone to do. -------. We
137.
suggest scheduling free home delivery of replacement ink from the manufacturer. This will ensure

that you receive the highest quality ink and ------- the lifespan of your printer.
138.

135. (A) perfection
(B) perfect
(C) perfectly
(D) perfecting

136. (A) installation
(B) conversion
(C) maintenance
(D) disposal

137. (A) Using cheap inks from unknown
suppliers is not recommended.
(B) The printer is not suitable for domestic
use.
(C) Staff training is certainly advised for
such complicated procedures.
(D) The device will work for years with no
user intervention.

138. (A) express
(B) develop
(C) widen
(D) extend

Questions 139-142 refer to the following article.

Newcomer in the fast food industry

In just under 12 months, Lin Mian Chinese Food ------- a major competitor in the fast food
139.
industry. This has surprised many of the industry's experts.

Chinese food has always been popular with diners. They have ------- enjoyed dining at Chinese
140.
restaurants or ordering deliveries. On the other hand, fast food has been most commonly

associated with burgers, pizza, and chicken. -------. There are now more than 200 Lin Mian
141.
restaurants nationwide, and that number is growing.

Lin Mian is seen as a tasty healthy option. -------, it has been recognized by the National Healthy
142.
Eating Association. A meal at Lin Mian has around 20 percent less salt and fat than the equivalent

at a hamburger restaurant.

---

139. (A) has become
(B) will become
(C) to become
(D) had become

140. (A) subsequently
(B) traditionally
(C) rarely
(D) creatively

141. (A) Lin Mian will open soon in both
countries.
(B) This was generally expected.
(C) The plan has to be abandoned due to
certain problems.
(D) Lin Mian is changing that.

142. (A) Nevertheless
(B) Instead
(C) In fact
(D) Similarly

GO ON TO THE NEXT PAGE

MEMO

To: All employees

From: Jennifer Wright

Date: September 8

Subject: Rescheduling

Dear all,

Regretfully, I have to ------- the weekly staff meeting as the marketing department is still
                              143.

processing the survey data. The meeting was scheduled for them to deliver a summary of their

findings. -------. As that will not be possible by tomorrow, I would like everyone to attend a
          144.

rescheduled meeting on Thursday afternoon from 4:00 P.M. Your attendance at the meeting is

-------. The information will be extremely valuable and I want everyone's input. Those -------
  145.   **146.**

cannot attend should let me know as soon as possible. I will make alternative arrangements.

---

143. (A) cancel
(B) accompany
(C) postpone
(D) leave

144. (A) I am sure you all learned a lot from their
detailed descriptions.
(B) I had hoped to hold a brainstorming
session after their presentation.
(C) Only select staff members have been
made aware of the meeting.
(D) At the moment, there don't appear to
be any other dates available.

145. (A) optional
(B) considerate
(C) variable
(D) important

146. (A) who
(B) anyone
(C) which
(D) some

PART 7

Directions: In this part, you will read a selection of texts, such as advertisements, e-mails, and instant messages. Each text or set of texts is followed by several questions. Select the most appropriate answer for each question and mark the letter (A), (B), (C), or (D) on your answer sheet.

Questions 147-148 refer to the following advertisement.

Galaxy Plus
127 Vardy Cobb Street, Lipton
Use our super efficient online services to promote your company!

We specialize in:

• Business cards	• Survey forms
• Brochures	• Full-sized posters

Galaxy Plus offers speedy service at affordable prices. Our easy-to-use online design tool can enable you to create the perfect full-color product in minutes. The software automatically calculates the price and even provides an estimated completion time. You can request same-day delivery or even come into the store and pick your order up yourself. Visit www.galaxyplus.com to learn more about our special prices for bulk orders. You can register as a customer for free and take advantage of our 20 percent off introductory offer.

147. What is being advertised?

(A) A printing company
(B) A Web site designer
(C) A courier service
(D) A photography business

148. What is indicated about Galaxy Plus?

(A) It will open in new locations soon.
(B) It has recently changed ownership.
(C) It has a free delivery service.
(D) It offers discounts on large orders.

GO ON TO THE NEXT PAGE

Join the Bronson Wilderness Society (BWS)

Our society of wilderness enthusiasts meets every weekend for a variety of activities around Orchid Bay. These include bushwalks, bird watching, volunteer cleanups, and educational seminars. Our members come from all walks of life and this variation is what helps make the group exciting and fulfilling for all participants. We are currently looking for new members to join and bring more fresh ideas and variety to the society.

Membership costs only $200 annually and it affords members discounts at many local businesses such as Drysdale's Leisure Center, where you can save as much as $10 a month. Other participating businesses include Randolph All Sports, Hooper Health Food, and Kreese Camping Goods.

Before they apply for full membership, interested people are offered a free three-month trial membership to help them make up their minds. The secretary of the society, Philomena Driscoll, provides information sessions about the society at our office in Strathpine. Please call her at 555-8423 to schedule an appointment.

149. What is indicated about BWS members?
(A) They have special skills.
(B) They all own local businesses.
(C) They were all introduced by other members.
(D) They have diverse backgrounds.

150. The word "affords" in paragraph 2, line 1, is closest in meaning to
(A) spares
(B) admits
(C) manages
(D) grants

151. Why are people instructed to call Ms. Driscoll?
(A) To learn more about an association
(B) To apply for membership
(C) To submit to an assessment
(D) To volunteer to help at an event

TERESA CURRY 6:40 P.M.
I forgot to call the clients at Prescot Seafood to let them know that tomorrow's delivery would be late.

ANDY SEDAKA 6:41 P.M.
I'll call them for you now. I have the number in front of me. What time will the delivery arrive?

TERESA CURRY 6:43 P.M.
We can't really say. The ship has been delayed getting into port.

ANDY SEDAKA 6:44 P.M.
What should I tell them, then?

TERESA CURRY 6:45 P.M.
Let them know that it'll be late and that we'll give them an update as soon as we know.

ANDY SEDAKA 6:49 P.M.
I just got off the phone. They say it will cause some trouble, but they thanked us for the warning.

TERESA CURRY 7:02 P.M.
Thanks. I'll call them first thing in the morning. Hopefully, it won't be too late.

Test 2

152. At 6:43 P.M., what does Ms. Curry mean when she writes, "We can't really say"?

(A) She is not authorized to comment.
(B) She does not know the answer.
(C) She does not have time to respond.
(D) She is unable to speak the client's language.

153. Who did Mr. Sedaka most likely call?

(A) A supplier
(B) A trainee
(C) A client
(D) An applicant

GO ON TO THE NEXT PAGE

Venus Fitness Center
Twin Pines Mall
772 Coleman Rd., Seattle, WA 98563

May 2

Mr. Diego Sanchez
63 Gibson Street
Seattle, WA 98112

Dear Mr. Sanchez,

I am happy to announce that next Friday, May 11 is the tenth anniversary of Venus Fitness Center. To celebrate, we are holding a barbecue on the grassed area at the rear of the gym. All members are invited and food and drink will be supplied by the center. You can even bring along a friend to join in the celebrations for free.

All of the trainers will be there to lend a hand and socialize with members. Even Josh Kruger, whose work with several movie stars has made him a minor celebrity, has agreed to attend.

I have been put in charge of organizing the event. People who wish to attend should send me a text message with the words, "I'm in" to my mobile phone at 823 555 3495. Please also mention whether or not you will be bringing a friend.

Sincerely,

Beth Hays

Beth Hays
Member Services — Venus Fitness Center

154. What is the purpose of the letter?
(A) To offer a discount membership
(B) To announce a special event
(C) To recommend a new program
(D) To congratulate a successful candidate

155. Who is Josh Kruger?
(A) A movie star
(B) A founder of a gym
(C) A physical trainer
(D) A customer service agent

E-Mail Message	
To:	Loretta Wang <lwang@simpsonbeverages.com>
From:	Timothy Lennox <tlennox@simpsonbeverages.com>
Subject:	Marketing
Date:	September 17

Dear Loretta,

I have just received some information about the Western Professional Marketing (WPM) Convention in Sacramento. The theme this year is the use of social media for marketing, which is something that will be more and more important in the future. I would like to take a trip to Sacramento from October 12 to October 15 to attend the conference.

I am currently scheduled to train some new salespeople on those dates. However, I have spoken with Ms. Fayed and she has agreed to take care of that while I am away. When I get back from the conference, I will cover any topics that they miss.

The Web site of the event organizers is already offering tickets for the conference at $250 per head. I realize that this is not cheap, but I hope you will approve my application to buy one. Considering the potential for extra sales, I think this is a small expense.

Sincerely,

Timothy Lennox
Marketing Manager

156. Why did Mr. Lennox send the e-mail?

(A) To learn more about an upcoming event
(B) To request permission to attend a conference
(C) To explain the reason for a delay
(D) To ask for a transfer to a different department

157. What has Ms. Fayed agreed to do?

(A) Train some new employees
(B) Accompany Mr. Lennox on a trip
(C) Take care of Mr. Lennox's clients
(D) Try some new marketing techniques

158. What is indicated about Mr. Lennox?

(A) He is being transferred to the sales division.
(B) He has worked for Ms. Wang for many years.
(C) He considers the conference worth the admission fee.
(D) He has attended a WPM Convention in the past.

GO ON TO THE NEXT PAGE

Wilson's Crest Hotel

45 Portman Street
Arlington

The premier place to stay in Arlington

Thank you for choosing to stay at Wilson's Crest Hotel. We hope you enjoyed your visit to Arlington and that we will have an opportunity to serve you again on your return. There are many wonderful places to visit in the area and our staff would be more than happy to recommend things to do on your next visit.

Please take a moment to let us know how we did. While Wilson's Crest Hotel takes great pride in its luxury and customer service, we know there is always room for improvement.

	Unsatisfactory	Satisfactory	Excellent
The helpfulness of front desk		X	
The location		X	
The lobby			X
The room size		X	

Additional comments: I found the room satisfactory. However, I must mention that the décor was hardly fashionable, neither was it quaint nor antique. This was in stark contrast with the lobby, which had obviously been recently refurbished and looked amazing.

Was this your first time staying at Wilson's Crest Hotel? Yes _X_ No ___

What was the purpose of your visit to Arlington? I was born and raised here, but I have been living in Ottawa for the past 20 years. My mother was the architect who designed this building and I wanted to come and admire her work.

Name: Sven Harbor

159. For whom is the survey intended?

(A) Hotel guests
(B) Conference attendees
(C) Travel agents
(D) Front desk staff

160. According to the survey, what can the business provide?

(A) Transportation to the airport
(B) Information about local attractions
(C) Chargers for several devices
(D) Cleaning for guests' clothing

161. What does Mr. Harbor indicate about the room?

(A) Its equipment was out of order.
(B) It was too small.
(C) It was outdated.
(D) Its location was inconvenient.

162. What is true about Mr. Harbor?

(A) He used a discount coupon.
(B) He grew up in Arlington.
(C) He accompanied a group of tourists.
(D) He worked on the building of Wilson's Crest Hotel.

GO ON TO THE NEXT PAGE

Notice:

This area is for Cosmos Financial Services' Staff to have meetings with clients and visitors.

- The area must be kept clean at all times. Please inspect the area after each meeting to ensure that it is ready for unexpected visits.
- The area can be reserved for up to one hour. If you would like to do so, please speak with Curtis Hyde. Check that no other staff member has reserved the room by checking the schedule posted on the door.
- This area is not to be used for discussion of sensitive personal information as it is a shared space. Private talks should be held in either Meeting Room 1 or Meeting Room 2.

163. Why might an employee contact Mr. Hyde?

(A) To request that he restock cleaning supplies
(B) To sign in a visitor to the office
(C) To reserve a meeting area
(D) To schedule an employee evaluation

164. What rule is applied to the use of the room?

(A) The carpets must be cleaned every month.
(B) The furniture must not be moved to another location.
(C) It should only be used if no other option is available.
(D) Sensitive information should not be discussed there.

Mr. Ramon Klukinski
LaTrobe Vocational College
Baltimore, MD 21208

Dear Mr. Klukinski,

I am interested in the position at LaTrobe Vocational College advertised in today's Herald Newspaper. I am currently the head of cleaning and facility maintenance at Goldman Convention Center, where I have been for the last five years. — [1] —. The center is open between the hours of 9:00 A.M. and 11:00 P.M. Therefore, in addition to my maintenance duties, I am required to manage the complicated schedules of people working different shifts.

I would like to work at LaTrobe Vocational College because the position suits my experience and skill set and also because the college is so close to my home. — [2] —. In fact, I am a graduate of the college and even worked there as an assistant to the groundskeeper during my final year of studies. — [3] —.

I have recently obtained an advanced certificate in building maintenance. — [4] —. This qualification will be particularly useful in maintaining the equipment and furnishings of your newly completed auditorium.

Please find enclosed my résumé and contact details.

Sincerely,

Paula Riser
Paula Riser

165. For what position is Ms. Riser most likely applying?

(A) Janitor
(B) Lecturer
(C) Receptionist
(D) Research assistant

166. What does Ms. Riser NOT mention about the college?

(A) It has recently added a performance space.
(B) She lives nearby.
(C) It offers attractive employee benefits.
(D) She has worked there before.

167. In which of the positions marked [1], [2], [3], and [4] does the following sentence best belong?

"It was a six-week course offered online through the National Institute of Adult Learning."

(A) [1]
(B) [2]
(C) [3]
(D) [4]

Col Simms [3:30 P.M.]: We need an article for the May issue. Another magazine has just published an article that's too similar to the one I was going to use. Do any of you have anything suitable?

Janice Rietz [3:31 P.M.]: I have an article on Dan Cross. He's an up-and-coming tennis player from Detroit. I spent a week there researching it. When is the deadline?

Col Simms [3:32 P.M.]: Sounds interesting. The deadline is Friday so you have two days.

Theo Ledbetter [3:35 P.M.]: I have an article, but I can't proofread it that soon. That's not long enough.

Col Simms [3:36 P.M.]: What's it about, Theo? I might be able to help.

Theo Ledbetter [3:37 P.M.]: It's on some rule changes the state basketball league is going to introduce. Would that be any good?

Col Simms [3:40 P.M.]: It's a good idea for an article, but the changes won't take effect until January. Let's consider that again in October.

Donna Papazian [3:42 P.M.]: I am about to write one about the popularity of watching games online. I don't think I could have it done by Friday, though.

Col Simms [3:45 P.M.]: Thanks, there's no flexibility on the deadline, I'm afraid. Janice, could you let me see the article you mentioned? I'll read it and let you know.

Janice Rietz [3:49 P.M.]: Sure thing. I won't be coming into the office today, though. Do you mind if I e-mail it to you?

Col Simms [3:50 P.M.]: Not at all.

168. At what type of business do the writers most likely work?

(A) A ticket agency
(B) A sports arena
(C) A publishing company
(D) A broadcasting studio

169. At 3:35 P.M., what does Mr. Ledbetter mean when he writes, "That's not long enough"?

(A) An article is too short.
(B) He needs more time.
(C) Few people have come to an event.
(D) The wrong items have been delivered.

170. According to the online chat discussion, what will happen next year?

(A) A tournament will be held in Detroit.
(B) An online service will be launched.
(C) Some athletes will retire.
(D) Some rules will be changed.

171. What is Ms. Rietz asked to do?

(A) Evaluate some potential suppliers
(B) Send a story about Dan Cross
(C) Investigate online gaming
(D) Take a business trip

Test 2

GO ON TO THE NEXT PAGE

A New Awareness of Healthy Eating

By Seth Olyphant, lifestyle reporter

In recent years, there have been more and more television shows and books focusing on food, nutrition, and cooking. — [1] —. People are choosing ingredients at the supermarket differently. They are reading up on the health benefits of certain foods and they are becoming more critical of the options available on restaurant menus.

According to Kenny Bates of the Australian Consumer Association, it is having a real effect on which restaurants they choose to eat at and which they avoid. — [2] —. Once popular food chains are experiencing slumps while others are booking out months in advance. Restaurant owners are taking notice, and they are looking at replacing many dishes with more nutritional alternatives.

Nutritionists are finding it hard to keep up with the demand as they are asked to consult with restaurants, hotels, and caterers around the country. None more so than Isabella Scott, who is largely responsible for the change of attitude. — [3] —. Ms. Scott consulted and even shared screen time with celebrity chefs in many of the most popular broadcasts. In an interview for this article, she mentioned a new problem that restaurants are facing.

The trend that started here is now starting to take effect in many other countries and there is a demand for Australian chefs around the world. — [4] —. Becky Harmer from the Australian Restaurant Owners' Association says, "Many chefs at top restaurants are being offered excellent money to work in foreign countries. It is important that our culinary schools and vocational colleges prepare students for the changing expectations of their employers and the dining public."

172. According to the article, what is probably happening in many Australian restaurants?

(A) They are updating their menus.
(B) They are changing their cleaning procedures.
(C) They are advertising for employees internationally.
(D) They are spending more on advertising.

173. Who has appeared on several television shows?

(A) Seth Olyphant
(B) Kenny Bates
(C) Isabella Scott
(D) Becky Harmer

174. What is indicated about the chefs at many top restaurants?

(A) They are returning to culinary schools.
(B) They are making money from online videos.
(C) They are publishing their own recipe books.
(D) They are being offered employment overseas.

175. In which of the positions marked [1], [2], [3], and [4] does the following sentence best belong?

"This has made people take a greater interest in what they are putting in their mouths."

(A) [1]
(B) [2]
(C) [3]
(D) [4]

GO ON TO THE NEXT PAGE

E-Mail Message	
To:	Karina Chow <kchow@choweducation.com>
From:	Daniel Odanaka <dodanaka@dukecorporation.com>
Subject:	Learning Seminar
Date:	1 May
Attachment:	📎 Itinerary

Dear Ms. Chow,

My name is Daniel Odanaka and I have been put in charge of making the arrangements for your visit on 19 and 20 June. Unfortunately, Tim Whatley has had to take some time off work for personal reasons and I am filling in for him. I should let you know that both of the seminars on personal finance have sold out. It seems that the excellent reviews of your latest book on financial planning have also affected ticket sales.

I was able to arrange the station wagon you requested. I wonder if Mr. Whatley mentioned that Duke Corporation can provide a driver and car at no cost to you. Otherwise, considering the lack of parking in the city, you may prefer to rely on our excellent subway service as he proposed in a previous e-mail.

Judging from ticket sales, it appears that we could probably arrange a third appearance and draw a big enough audience to make a healthy profit. I have found an alternative venue, which is available in the afternoon of 21 June. Please let us know if you would like to take advantage of this situation.

You can contact me by e-mail or phone if there is anything else I can do to make your visit to Manchester go more smoothly.

Sincerely,

Daniel Odanaka

Itinerary — Karina Chow

(Revised 1 May)

Friday, 19 June

7:00 A.M. – Depart from Heathrow Airport

8:10 A.M. – Arrive at Manchester Airport (Pick up rental car)

10:00 A.M. - Planning meeting with representatives from Duke Corporation

2:30 P.M. – Check into the Grand Hotel

7:00 P.M. – Speaking engagement at Compton Event Centre

9:30 P.M. – Watch video recording of seminar

Saturday, 20 June

11:00 A.M. – Lunch with Carol Duncan from ARK Publishing

2:00 P.M. – Speaking engagement at Fort Congress Centre

6:00 P.M. – Dinner with Teri Wesley from Portsmouth University

8:45 P.M. – Depart from Manchester Airport (Return rental car)

9:50 P.M. – Arrive at Heathrow Airport

176. Where most likely does Mr. Odanaka work?

(A) At a limousine service
(B) At a convention center
(C) At an accommodation provider
(D) At an event promotions company

177. What did Mr. Whatley recommend that Ms. Chow do?

(A) Use public transportation
(B) Look for a cheaper hotel
(C) Publish another book
(D) Call a travel agent

178. According to the e-mail, why might Ms. Chow want to extend her stay?

(A) To meet with a university professor
(B) To give another seminar
(C) To attend a book signing
(D) To do some sightseeing

179. What time is Ms. Chow scheduled to arrive at her accommodation on June 19?

(A) At 8:10 A.M.
(B) At 10:00 A.M.
(C) At 2:30 P.M.
(D) At 7:00 P.M.

180. What is indicated about the event at Fort Congress Centre?

(A) Its location has been changed.
(B) Ms. Chow will watch a performance there.
(C) Tickets are no longer available.
(D) It was advertised on the radio.

GO ON TO THE NEXT PAGE

E-Mail Message

To:	Gerald Comiskey <gcomiskey@barrontiling.com>
From:	Jane Whitman <jwhitman@clementprojects.com>
Date:	September 28
Subject:	234 Towers Road

Dear Mr. Comiskey,

I am writing with regard to the apartment block at 234 Towers Road in Flinders. Clement Projects hired your company to tile all of the bathrooms. The understanding was that you would start work on September 19 and finish tiling all eight bathrooms by September 23. It was important that you do so because we had other workers coming in after you to fit cabinets, mirrors, and so on.

Your delay in getting started on the work meant that we had other tradespeople waiting for you to finish. We were charged a high hourly rate to have these people wait for you until they could start work themselves. In the end, your employees were not done with the final bathroom until the afternoon of September 26. I have just received your invoice for the full amount of $59,623. As we suffered significant additional expenses as a result of the delays, I am hoping that you will offer us a discount on the work. If we cannot come to an acceptable arrangement, I will not be able to accept bids from Barron Tiling for any future projects. This includes the Montgomery Hotel project, which has more than 120 rooms.

Sincerely,

Jane Whitman

Barron Tiling
27 Longmans Close, Seacrest

Invoice

For work carried out at: 234 Towers Road
Client: Clement Projects
Address: 17 Bloomingdale Street, Brighton

Date of issue: September 30
Payment due: October 31

Item Description	Unit Price	Quantity	Subtotal
Tiling Bathroom (labor)	$3,699	8	$29,592.00
Tiling Bathroom (materials)	$3,399	8	$27,192.00
		Discount (10%)	-$5,678.40
		Tax	$2,555.28
		Total	$53,660.88

All work by Barron Tiling is covered by a ten-year guarantee on materials and workmanship.

Thank you for continuing to rely on Barron Tiling for your tiling needs.

181. What kind of company does Ms. Whitman most likely work for?

(A) A real estate agency
(B) A construction company
(C) A hardware store
(D) An office furniture manufacturer

182. What is one purpose of the e-mail?

(A) To announce the outcome of a bidding
(B) To request an update on a project
(C) To recommend a superior service
(D) To explain the effects of a delay

183. When was the tiling work at 234 Towers Road completed?

(A) On September 19
(B) On September 23
(C) On September 26
(D) On September 28

184. What is probably true about Barron Tiling?

(A) It intends to bid on the Montgomery Hotel project.
(B) It is partially owned by Clement Projects.
(C) It uses locally sourced materials.
(D) It specializes in office buildings.

185. What is implied about the bathrooms in 234 Towers Road?

(A) They are covered by a ten-year guarantee.
(B) They failed to pass a safety inspection.
(C) They are designed for large families.
(D) They do not have any storage space.

GO ON TO THE NEXT PAGE

www.ivebeenthere.com

Welcome to I've been there dot com.

Read reviews of local businesses written by their clients and customers.

Business: Neptune Sports and Leisure at Bay Town Shopping Center
Reviewed by: Rod Barkworth   **Date:** June 18

I was at Neptune Sports and Leisure at Bay Town Shopping Center today. It was the day after opening and there were still a lot of people. It was especially surprising as it was a weekday. We had a great time. I especially enjoyed the climbing wall, the golf simulator, and the batting cage. The range of goods was excellent. Some of the brands I had never heard of, though. So, it is hard for me to comment on their quality. The prices seemed a little higher than I'm used to. Nevertheless, I bought a pair of running shoes and a new sweater.

Bay Town (June 19)—Neptune Sports and Leisure has opened a store in the Bay Town Shopping Center. Neptune Sports and Leisure's success has been attributed to its competitive prices and the many enjoyable experiences on offer to customers. Every Neptune store has a climbing wall, running track and a batting cage, which are freely available to customers. Neptune has been generating a lot of interest through its innovative Internet marketing campaign, and the Bay Town Shopping Center location attracted record crowds to its opening.

In a move that hardly seemed necessary, free lunch vouchers for meals at nearby Gee's Healthy Eating were given to the first 50 people to show up. By 11 A.M., when they stopped counting, some 500 people had passed through the doors. They were there to enjoy the free facilities and check out the amazing variety of products and brands on offer.

Letters to the Editor

June 21 — I read the article about the opening of Neptune Sports and Leisure at Bay Town Shopping Center. The article almost appeared to be an advertisement for the store. I think that as it was intended as a news article, it should have taken a more critical stance. Bay Town already has Foreman Sports, which is an excellent sporting goods store that hires many young locals and has sponsored several of our sporting teams over the years. Neither of these deeds has been covered by the newspaper. Furthermore, the claim that prices are low is hard to accept as I found the prices to be 10 percent higher on average than Foreman Sports'.

— Samantha Riley

186. When was the grand opening of the new Neptune Sports and Leisure store?

(A) On June 17
(B) On June 18
(C) On June 19
(D) On June 20

187. What attraction is most likely unique to the Bay Town Shopping Center location?

(A) The climbing wall
(B) The golf simulator
(C) The batting cage
(D) The running track

188. What is mentioned about the grand opening of the new Neptune Sports and Leisure store?

(A) It was timed to coincide with a popular local sporting event.
(B) The turnout was a disappointment to the organizers of the event.
(C) It had received extensive publicity on various local radio programs.
(D) Coupons for people to use at a local restaurant were provided.

189. What does Ms. Riley indicate about the article?

(A) It should have been published earlier.
(B) It was quite critical of a local business.
(C) It has appeared in another publication.
(D) It seemed to be promoting a business.

190. About what do Mr. Barkworth and Ms. Riley agree?

(A) The job opportunities provided by Foreman Sports
(B) The little-known brands on offer at Neptune Sports and Leisure
(C) The higher prices at Neptune Sports and Leisure
(D) The lack of newspaper coverage of team sponsorship

GO ON TO THE NEXT PAGE ➡

Kramer Construction

Office 7, 78 McDougal Street, Cincinnati 45268

August 5

Ms. Barbara Drazen:

The MacArthur Hotel in downtown Cincinnati has been demolished to make way for an even larger hotel and convention center. Because you previously used the conference rooms there, we thought you might be interested in helping us design an even better event space for the site. We intend to make the New MacArthur Hotel Cincinnati's premier location for large events.

With that end in mind, we have arranged an information session at our head office where we will explain the plans and receive feedback. We will pay for transportation and accommodation for a representative of your organization to take part. Please take a look at the invitation enclosed for details. We are looking forward to seeing you.

Sincerely,

Abramo Jenkins

Abramo Jenkins
Chief Designer — Kramer Construction

Feedback Form
Kramer Construction — New MacArthur Hotel

Name: Wendy Tang   **Company:** Gruber Publishing

Comments: I love the color scheme and layout of the conference center. I think that naming the conference rooms after local celebrities is a nice idea. However, I suggest that you use a numbering system instead. I also love the idea of having screens at the entrance of each room where event organizers can post messages for people arriving. Perhaps it would be nice to have a live video feed of the event broadcast on them so that latecomers can time their entrance.

E-Mail Message

To:	Antonio Damiano <adamiano@riseacademy.net>
From:	Juno Venn <jvenn@newmacarthurhotel.com>
Date:	July 2
Subject:	Availability

Dear Mr. Damiano,

Thank you for coming to see our facilities yesterday. I am glad you have chosen us as the venue for the Rise Academy Cooking Contest. I checked the availability of the two rooms you mentioned in your previous e-mail and found that both are available. I believe that Convention Room 3 would be the perfect choice considering the size of the audience. The adjacent room can seat no more than ninety people. Furthermore, it is equipped with the huge movable platform you need, which you can use at no extra charge. Please let me know if you would like us to reserve the room for you.

Sincerely,

Juno Venn — New MacArthur Hotel

191. What is one purpose of the letter?

(A) To explain a development project
(B) To announce the results of a survey
(C) To recommend an alternative service
(D) To invite prospective clients to a celebration

192. In the letter, the word "end" in paragraph 2, line 1, is closest in meaning to

(A) completion
(B) goal
(C) limitation
(D) side

193. According to the feedback form, where will screens probably be placed?

(A) On the counter at reception
(B) In front of every elevator
(C) At the entrance of the hotel
(D) By the door of each event space

194. What is most likely true about the New MacArthur Hotel?

(A) It adopted Ms. Tang's suggestion.
(B) It was closed at the beginning of July.
(C) It hired a professional videographer.
(D) It has appointed a new general manager.

195. What is NOT indicated about the cooking contest?

(A) It will be held in the city center.
(B) It will require a large platform.
(C) It will be using two rooms.
(D) It will be attended by more than ninety people.

GO ON TO THE NEXT PAGE ➡

July 12

Dear Sir or Madam,

The Mansfield City Council is about to approve the construction of a train line that will pass through the center of Mansfield City. Mayor Noah Chavira, and others arguing in favor of the proposal point out that it will make it easier for tourists to get here. However, there is a compelling argument against the project. In addition to me, there are three other council members who hold that a train line would ruin the atmosphere of our town and make the area less attractive to tourists, who are contributing more and more to our economy. The proposed line is not only for passenger trains. Many freight trains would also be traveling through the town's center at all hours of the night.

We would like people living in the area to write in and put pressure on council members to vote against the plan at their next meeting; July 27. You can do so by filling out the enclosed survey and mailing it to the secretary of Mansfield City Council, Vince Marcel.

Sincerely,

Kendall Tesch

Council Member — Mansfield City Council

Mansfield City Central Train Line Survey

Name: Colleen Donaldson   **Address:** Creek Street, Mansfield City

Are you in favor of creating a railway through the city center?   _____ Yes   _X_ No

Will the decision by council members affect the way you vote at the next election?

_X_ Yes _____ No

A train line would:	_____ Increase the number of visitors	_X_ Decrease the number of visitors	_____ Have no effect on visitor numbers
A better alternative to a train line is:	_____ Shuttle buses from Glendale	_X_ A subway line from Glendale	_____ More parking in the city center

Comments: I think the best solution to the ongoing dispute is to build a subway line to connect Mansfield city center with the suburb of Glendale. Visitors coming from the airport could transfer at Glendale Station. A subway line would be a quieter option, and it would not harm the appearance of our wonderful town.

Thank you for participating in this survey. We also recommend sending an e-mail to the council member for your division.

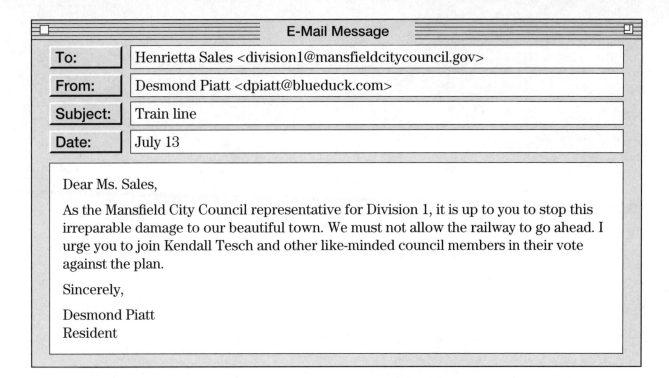

196. What is mentioned about Mansfield City?

(A) Its population has decreased.
(B) Its airport was recently expanded.
(C) It is a growing tourist destination.
(D) It will host an upcoming sporting event.

197. Who is the intended recipient of the letter?

(A) A railway company representative
(B) A city council employee
(C) A member of a construction crew
(D) A resident of Mansfield City

198. What is suggested about Ms. Donaldson?

(A) She addressed an envelope to Vince Marcel.
(B) She wants to attract fewer visitors to Mansfield City.
(C) She attended a public discussion of construction plans.
(D) She is a local business owner.

199. What does Ms. Donaldson propose that Mansfield City do?

(A) Provide additional parking near the airport
(B) Conduct a survey of visitors
(C) Promote some of the city's attractions
(D) Construct a subway line

200. What is probably true about Mr. Piatt?

(A) He is a member of the Mansfield City Council.
(B) He opposes the mayor's argument.
(C) He commutes to work by car.
(D) He had a meeting with Kendall Tesch.

Stop! This is the end of the test. If you finish before time is called, you may go back to Parts 5, 6, and 7 and check your work.

『TOEIC® L&Rテスト　究極の模試600問＋』別冊②

PC：7019067

発行：株式会社アルク

TOEIC® L&Rテスト 究極の模試600問⁺
模擬試験 ③
Test 3

	1回目			2回目			3回目		
受験日	年	月	日	年	月	日	年	月	日
開始時間	時		分	時		分	時		分
Listening Section 終了時間	時		分	時		分	時		分
Reading Section 終了時間	時		分	時		分	時		分

◆Listening Section の音声は、ダウンロードしてご利用ください。詳しくは本冊のp.10に掲載されています。【Test 3】の音声を利用します。所要時間は**約47分**です。

◆解答には本冊巻末のマークシートを使用してください。マークシートA（勘ボックスあり）の使い方は本冊のp.12〜で説明しています。テスト採点センター（本冊p.11）もご利用いただけます。

◆解答一覧は本冊p.260〜にあります。

使用する音声ファイル一覧

Listening Section、Part 1 Directions	129_T3_P1_Dir.mp3
Part 1 No.1〜No.6	130_T3_P1_01.mp3〜136_T3_P1_06.mp3
Part 2 Directions	137_T3_P2_Dir.mp3
Part 2 No.7〜No.31	138_T3_P2_07.mp3〜163_T3_P2_31.mp3
Part 3 Directions	164_T3_P3_Dir.mp3
Part 3 No.32〜No.70	165_T3_P3_32-34.mp3〜179_T3_P3_68-70.mp3
Part 4 Directions	180_T3_P4_Dir.mp3
Part 4 No.71〜No.100	181_T3_P4_71-73.mp3〜191_T3_P4_98-100.mp3

矢印の方向に引くと、この冊子を取り外すことができます。

LISTENING TEST

In this section, your ability to understand spoken English will be shown. The Listening test consists of four parts and will take approximately 45 minutes. Directions will be given for each part. By following the directions you hear, select the best possible answer and mark your answers on your answer sheet. Please refrain from writing anything in your test book.

PART 1

Directions: In this part, you will see a picture in your test book and hear four statements. After hearing each statement, select the one statement you think is the best description for the picture. Then, mark the answer on your answer sheet. You will only hear the statements one time, and they will not be printed in your test book.

Statement (B), "They're sitting side by side," best describes the picture. Therefore, you should choose answer (B) and mark it on your answer sheet.

1.

2.

GO ON TO THE NEXT PAGE

3.

4.

5.

6.

GO ON TO THE NEXT PAGE

PART 2

Directions: In this part, you will hear a question or statement. You will then hear three alternative responses to the question or statement. They will all be spoken in English. You will only hear them one time, and they will not be printed in your test book. Choose the best response to each question and mark the letter (A), (B), or (C) on your answer sheet.

7. Mark your answer on your answer sheet.

8. Mark your answer on your answer sheet.

9. Mark your answer on your answer sheet.

10. Mark your answer on your answer sheet.

11. Mark your answer on your answer sheet.

12. Mark your answer on your answer sheet.

13. Mark your answer on your answer sheet.

14. Mark your answer on your answer sheet.

15. Mark your answer on your answer sheet.

16. Mark your answer on your answer sheet.

17. Mark your answer on your answer sheet.

18. Mark your answer on your answer sheet.

19. Mark your answer on your answer sheet.

20. Mark your answer on your answer sheet.

21. Mark your answer on your answer sheet.

22. Mark your answer on your answer sheet.

23. Mark your answer on your answer sheet.

24. Mark your answer on your answer sheet.

25. Mark your answer on your answer sheet.

26. Mark your answer on your answer sheet.

27. Mark your answer on your answer sheet.

28. Mark your answer on your answer sheet.

29. Mark your answer on your answer sheet.

30. Mark your answer on your answer sheet.

31. Mark your answer on your answer sheet.

Directions: In this part, you will hear conversations between two or more people. You will be asked to answer three questions about what the speakers say in each conversation. You will only hear the conversations one time, and they will not be printed in your test book. Choose the best response to each question and mark the letter (A), (B), (C), or (D) on your answer sheet.

32. What are the speakers discussing?

(A) An exhibit
(B) A film
(C) A contest
(D) A sporting event

33. Where did the woman get the tickets?

(A) On the Internet
(B) From a friend
(C) At a ticket booth
(D) In a competition

34. According to the man, when will the event begin?

(A) In a day
(B) In a week
(C) In a month
(D) In two months

35. Why is the woman calling?

(A) To reserve a vehicle
(B) To ask for directions
(C) To discuss a project
(D) To recommend a business

36. What does the man mean when he says, "those are very popular"?

(A) The price has gone up.
(B) A product is selling well.
(C) An option might be unavailable.
(D) Membership is required.

37. What is the woman asked to do?

(A) Make a payment
(B) Review some paperwork
(C) Choose an insurance package
(D) Provide her contact information

38. What is the purpose of the woman's call?

(A) To explain a procedure
(B) To set up an appointment
(C) To thank the man for some help
(D) To offer some advice

39. What does the woman say about the man's portfolio?

(A) It will be delivered tomorrow.
(B) It is heavier than expected.
(C) It does not contain the required materials.
(D) It will be viewed by a team leader.

40. When will the speakers most likely meet?

(A) On Monday
(B) On Tuesday
(C) On Wednesday
(D) On Friday

41. Who most likely is the man?

(A) A real estate agent
(B) A restaurant owner
(C) A construction worker
(D) A city official

42. What does the woman ask about?

(A) Rental prices
(B) Nearby businesses
(C) Daily specials
(D) Local rules

43. What will the man most likely do next?

(A) Check a menu
(B) Take a reservation
(C) Look at his computer
(D) Explain a system

GO ON TO THE NEXT PAGE

44. Why is the woman going to Madrid?

(A) To take a vacation
(B) To talk about a problem
(C) To inspect a construction
(D) To interview an applicant

45. What does Robert suggest doing?

(A) Contacting a travel agent
(B) Purchasing a guidebook
(C) Asking for a better price
(D) Taking a coworker

46. What does the woman say she will do?

(A) Update a Web site
(B) Speak with a supervisor
(C) Invite a client
(D) Provide her travel schedule

47. Where do the speakers most likely work?

(A) At a sports arena
(B) At a radio station
(C) At a car manufacturer
(D) At an advertising firm

48. What problem does the woman mention?

(A) The weather has been unfavorable.
(B) There is another event on the same day.
(C) Attendance has been low.
(D) Running costs have risen.

49. What does the man imply about this year's motor show?

(A) Some impressive products will be on show.
(B) Some manufacturers will not attend.
(C) It will be smaller than in previous years.
(D) It will be held indoors.

50. What is the purpose of the woman's visit?

(A) To report a problem
(B) To request a manual
(C) To update her address
(D) To purchase a gift

51. What has recently happened at the store?

(A) A change of management
(B) A clearance sale
(C) A policy revision
(D) An opening ceremony

52. What will the woman most likely do next?

(A) Check an online catalog
(B) Obtain proof of purchase
(C) Look at different models
(D) Go to another store

53. Why does the man want to sell his apartment?

(A) He is moving to another town.
(B) It is far from some stores.
(C) There is not enough parking.
(D) It is too small for his family.

54. Why does the woman say, "You live on Davis Avenue"?

(A) To express excitement
(B) To suggest an alternative
(C) To turn down an offer
(D) To show her knowledge

55. What does the man say the woman should do?

(A) Visit his office after work
(B) Make a phone call
(C) Rent a house
(D) Install an app

56. What is the conversation mainly about?

(A) A training workshop
(B) A recruitment plan
(C) A marketing strategy
(D) A company banquet

57. What does the man offer to do?

(A) Prepare some documents
(B) Check some inventory
(C) Review a proposal
(D) Calculate a budget

58. What does the woman say she will do?

(A) Create a shopping list
(B) Complete a report
(C) Evaluate a product
(D) Revise some materials

---

59. Why is the man calling?

(A) To cancel a reservation
(B) To book a seat on a bus
(C) To confirm the time of an appointment
(D) To request an extension to a deadline

60. What problem does the man mention?

(A) Traffic congestion
(B) A computer malfunction
(C) A flight delay
(D) A scheduling error

61. What does the woman say the man can do?

(A) Finalize a plan at a later date
(B) Send a text message to Mr. Collins
(C) Use some space near a building
(D) Borrow a company-owned car

Directory	
Floor 4	Sciences
Floor 3	Architecture
Floor 2	Languages
Floor 1	Travel

62. Who most likely is the woman?

(A) A school teacher
(B) An artist
(C) A shop clerk
(D) A translator

63. What information does the woman request?

(A) The title of a publication
(B) The number of visitors
(C) The date of an event
(D) The address of a building

64. Look at the graphic. Which floor will the man go to next?

(A) Floor 4
(B) Floor 3
(C) Floor 2
(D) Floor 1

GO ON TO THE NEXT PAGE

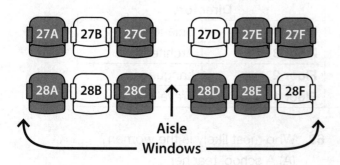

ALOE SOAP	
Size	Volume
Mini	100ml
Small	300ml
Regular	500ml
Large	1L

Aisle

— **Windows** —

65. When will the man's flight leave?

(A) This morning
(B) This evening
(C) Tomorrow morning
(D) Tomorrow afternoon

66. Look at the graphic. Which seat will the man take?

(A) 27B
(B) 27D
(C) 28B
(D) 28F

67. What does the man say about his home?

(A) It is near the airport.
(B) It is in Dallas.
(C) He will not have time to return there.
(D) He does not have an Internet connection.

68. Where does the conversation most likely take place?

(A) At a hotel
(B) At a hair salon
(C) At a supermarket
(D) At a manufacturing plant

69. What does the man say about the supplier?

(A) It has won an award.
(B) It will redesign its logo.
(C) It has raised its prices.
(D) It will terminate a contract.

70. Look at the graphic. Which size will the speakers most likely choose?

(A) Mini
(B) Small
(C) Regular
(D) Large

PART 4

Directions: In this part, you will hear some talks given by a single person. You will be asked to answer three questions about what the speaker says in each talk. You will only hear the talks one time, and they will not be printed in your test book. Choose the best response to each question and mark the letter (A), (B), (C), or (D) on your answer sheet.

71. What has the community center done recently?

(A) Hosted an auction
(B) Undergone renovations
(C) Moved to a new location
(D) Changed its opening hours

72. What has Mr. Broman agreed to do?

(A) Sign a contract
(B) Discuss a book
(C) Make a donation
(D) Answer questions

73. How can listeners obtain tickets?

(A) By buying a magazine
(B) By visiting a Web site
(C) By answering a survey
(D) By calling an organizer

74. Where is the talk taking place?

(A) At a movie trade fair
(B) At a department meeting
(C) At an orientation session
(D) At a press conference

75. What is planned for September 20?

(A) The company will change ownership.
(B) A new line of merchandise will go on sale.
(C) New employees will start work.
(D) A review will be published.

76. What are the listeners asked to do?

(A) Purchase protective clothing
(B) Bid for a contract
(C) Complete a customer survey
(D) Receive a sample as they leave

77. Why will the listener go to Hampton Institute of Technology?

(A) To meet with a candidate
(B) To take a class
(C) To collaborate on some research
(D) To give a presentation

78. What is the listener instructed to bring?

(A) A piece of identification
(B) A travel receipt
(C) An application form
(D) A research paper

79. What does the speaker mean when she says, "Let me address that now"?

(A) She wants to make some plans clear.
(B) She will give the listener her contact details.
(C) She believes there has been a misunderstanding.
(D) She thinks the listener has gone to the wrong location.

80. What is being advertised?

(A) A grand opening
(B) An art competition
(C) An employment opportunity
(D) A catering service

81. What does the card enable people to do?

(A) Use a special room
(B) Obtain additional points
(C) Prove their identification
(D) Get price reductions

82. What does the speaker say about the organization?

(A) It is based in Hobart.
(B) It manufactures its own products.
(C) It has been expanding.
(D) It advertises online.

GO ON TO THE NEXT PAGE ➡

83. Who most likely is the speaker?

(A) A bus driver
(B) A security guard
(C) A tour guide
(D) A museum director

84. Why does the speaker say, "We're leaving at two o'clock"?

(A) To encourage listeners to hurry
(B) To explain a change to the schedule
(C) To advise listeners to stay longer
(D) To draw attention to a closing time

85. What are listeners advised to do?

(A) Buy tickets online
(B) Enjoy a meal
(C) Read a product description
(D) Refrain from taking pictures

---

86. Where is the announcement being made?

(A) At a tourist information counter
(B) At a departure gate
(C) In a hotel lobby
(D) On an airplane

87. What problem does the speaker mention?

(A) Some luggage has been lost.
(B) An aircraft has arrived late.
(C) A tour is overbooked.
(D) A suitcase is too large.

88. Why are listeners asked to wait?

(A) To watch a video
(B) To receive some money
(C) To meet another employee
(D) To hear updated information

---

89. What has the listener most likely ordered?

(A) Cleaning equipment
(B) Food supplies
(C) Stationery items
(D) Car parts

90. Why does the speaker say, "Your department has already gone over its budget"?

(A) Better prices should be negotiated.
(B) A budget has been reduced recently.
(C) A different application process is necessary.
(D) Some goods must be returned to the store.

91. What does the speaker say about Hillside Mart?

(A) It has a delivery service.
(B) It has a new catalog.
(C) Its prices are high.
(D) Its staff are very helpful.

---

92. Who most likely is the speaker?

(A) A sporting goods store owner
(B) A magazine editor
(C) A software engineer
(D) A factory manager

93. What is the speaker's concern?

(A) Some advertising revenue will be lost.
(B) An app is not well designed.
(C) Some items are out of stock.
(D) A client will request a refund.

94. How are the listeners encouraged to show their ideas?

(A) By sending an e-mail
(B) By posting on a bulletin board
(C) By phoning the speaker
(D) By making a presentation

CATERING MENU

Item	Price per platter
Specialty Garden Salad	$49
Vegetarian Casserole	$59
Beef Stroganoff	$79
Herb Roasted Pork	$89

Floor Space Allocation

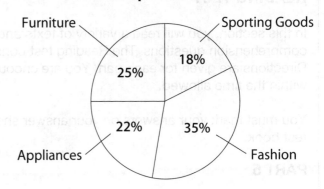

95. What event is Robinson Brothers going to hold?

(A) A company picnic
(B) An awards ceremony
(C) A shareholders' meeting
(D) A retirement party

96. Look at the graphic. Which amount will no longer be charged?

(A) $49
(B) $59
(C) $79
(D) $89

97. What is the listener asked to do?

(A) Send a document
(B) Update a flyer
(C) Waive a fee
(D) Propose a solution

98. What does the speaker say about the company's sales?

(A) They have been improving.
(B) They have not been reported.
(C) They are difficult to anticipate.
(D) They are affected by the seasons.

99. Look at the graphic. What category does the speaker suggest eliminating?

(A) Sporting Goods
(B) Fashion
(C) Appliances
(D) Furniture

100. When does the speaker say they should carry out the change?

(A) In May
(B) In June
(C) In July
(D) In August

This is the end of the Listening Test. Turn to Part 5 in your test book.

GO ON TO THE NEXT PAGE ➤

In this section, you will read a variety of texts and answer several different types of reading comprehension questions. The Reading test consists of three parts and will take 75 minutes. Directions are given for each part. You are encouraged to answer as many questions as possible within the time allowed.

You must mark your answers on your answer sheet. Please refrain from writing anything in your test book.

PART 5

Directions: The following sentences are incomplete. Select the most appropriate word or phrase from the choices (A), (B), (C), and (D), and mark your answer on your answer sheet.

101. Mr. Onoda has recently sold the rights to his ------- to a major manufacturer.

(A) invent
(B) inventive
(C) inventively
(D) invention

102. The equipment used by BFP Pool Care workers is not ------- own.

(A) they
(B) theirs
(C) them
(D) their

103. Once we obtain ------- of the number of guests, we will place an order with a catering company.

(A) supervision
(B) acquisition
(C) permission
(D) confirmation

104. Bradman Software has been conducting research ------- new markets for robotics.

(A) by
(B) into
(C) besides
(D) out of

105. It has been ------- announced that Margaret Smith is the new head of public relations.

(A) official
(B) office
(C) officially
(D) officer

106. Before purchasing an item, please check the product ------- listed on the Web site.

(A) complications
(B) specifications
(C) renovations
(D) destinations

107. Mr. Ford decided to use a conference room at the Central Hotel ------- the Douglas Center.

(A) but also
(B) although
(C) otherwise
(D) instead of

108. The remote-control camera was packaged -------, but the instruction book contained many errors.

(A) attractively
(B) formerly
(C) significantly
(D) conclusively

109. The ------- experience of the design team at G-Clef Cabinetry makes it Brisbane's most popular kitchen maker.

(A) collection
(B) collecting
(C) collective
(D) collectively

110. At the end of the lease, tenants are required to give the apartment a ------- cleaning.

(A) thorough
(B) sizable
(C) diverse
(D) defective

111. Please submit your ------- letter to human resources if you would like reimbursement for evening classes.

(A) acceptance
(B) acceptable
(C) acceptability
(D) accepted

112. Part-time staff should be called ahead of their shift and informed of ------- their goals for the day are.

(A) what
(B) such
(C) why
(D) also

113. Many businesses in Townsville urgently require ------- people due to the labor shortage.

(A) qualifying
(B) qualified
(C) to qualify
(D) to be qualified

114. Remuneration for overtime work expenses is made as a ------- payment from monthly wages.

(A) distinct
(B) separate
(C) nominal
(D) provisional

115. The success of the project is ------- attributable to the hard work of all the people involved.

(A) direction
(B) direct
(C) directly
(D) directed

116. Employment conditions at Fairfield Industries changed ------- the merger took place in March.

(A) so that
(B) wherever
(C) even if
(D) when

117. It is important the customer ------- with the changes before we process the catering order.

(A) agree
(B) agreement
(C) agreeable
(D) agreeably

118. -------, applicants will have more than three years' experience in the hotel industry.

(A) Mutually
(B) Fiercely
(C) Ideally
(D) Majorly

119. There are massive discounts on goods all ------- the store.

(A) against
(B) from
(C) under
(D) throughout

120. Brad Myers is one of the most ------- people in the programming industry and his talks attract large audiences.

(A) celebratory
(B) influential
(C) tentative
(D) confidential

GO ON TO THE NEXT PAGE

121. KJT Software has received a lot of complaints about the ------- of its new accounting package.
(A) stabilize
(B) stably
(C) stability
(D) stable

122. Companywide cost-cutting at Cougar Auto has ------- to a drop in product quality and dependability.
(A) caused
(B) led
(C) invited
(D) proceeded

123. Sherman Gallery provides certificates to prove that each piece is an ------- artwork.
(A) authentic
(B) authentically
(C) authenticate
(D) authenticity

124. There have been discussions ------- the organizing committee and representatives of several potential venues.
(A) during
(B) between
(C) through
(D) underneath

125. Ms. Dunn has ------- offered to share her sound-engineering experience with the theater's technical staff.
(A) grace
(B) gracious
(C) graciously
(D) graciousness

126. Some participants made ------- critical observations about the validity of the health and safety workshop.
(A) its
(B) something
(C) rather
(D) themselves

127. Trinidad brand sweaters are available ------- at Frampton Department Stores.
(A) exclusively
(B) eventually
(C) innovatively
(D) enthusiastically

128. Employees may leave early on Fridays ------- their weekly production quota has been met.
(A) in spite of
(B) provided that
(C) in order that
(D) as much as

129. The gym offers discounts at certain times of day ------- the number of visitors at any one time.
(A) to regulate
(B) has regulated
(C) is regulating
(D) was regulated

130. Before anyone is allowed to operate heavy machinery, they must pass a ------- test.
(A) feasibility
(B) preference
(C) determination
(D) competency

PART 6

Directions: Some of the following sentences are incomplete. Select the most appropriate word, phrase, or sentence from the choices (A), (B), (C), and (D), and mark your answer on your answer sheet.

Questions 131-134 refer to the following information.

There are still tickets available for the ------- performance of *Jardin Verde* at the Lyric Theater in
                                               131.

Hamilton. The popular musical has been playing there for nearly six months and Friday, January

26 will be the last time it will be performed. -------. It is highly recommended that anyone with an
                                                 132.

------- in live entertainment take this opportunity. The cast has won multiple awards for their work
133.

and newspaper reviews have been overwhelmingly positive. ------- January 26, the theater will be
                                                            134.

closed for two weeks while they get ready for the next production — *Los Perros de Homero*.

131. (A) initial
     (B) preview
     (C) partial
     (D) final

132. (A) Tickets can be purchased from the box
         office or through the Web site.
     (B) The show has been canceled due to an
         unfavorable response.
     (C) The film will be available for home
         rental in six months.
     (D) The theater will be torn down the
         following week.

133. (A) interesting
     (B) interest
     (C) interested
     (D) interestingly

134. (A) Until
     (B) On
     (C) After
     (D) At

GO ON TO THE NEXT PAGE →

Questions 135-138 refer to the following advertisement.

Qualified Accountant Needed

-------. We are one of Canada's most successful accounting firms. The ------- retirement of one
135.   **136.**

of the branch's most senior employees puts us in need of a suitable replacement. You will be

working with the accountant you will be replacing until she leaves the company. During that

brief period, you will be expected to learn every aspect of the clients' accounts and come up

with strategies to manage their finances. -------, we are looking for someone capable of making
137.

an immediate start. We ------- interviews between April 7 and April 11. If you would like to be
138.

considered, you should send in an application and résumé by April 1.

---

135. (A) There is currently an entry-level
position available in our organization.
(B) KLH Accounting is looking to hire an
expert accountant for its Miami
Branch.
(C) We are the state's top provider of
certification for accountants.
(D) KLH is the perfect place to advertise
your vacant positions.

136. (A) forthcoming
(B) occasional
(C) recent
(D) questionable

137. (A) Insomuch as
(B) Alternatively
(C) Therefore
(D) In contrast

138. (A) have been holding
(B) held
(C) were held
(D) will be holding

MEMO

To: Sales Managers
From: Pauline Jolly
Date: February 3
Subject: Evaluations

Dear sales managers,

It is time for supervisors to conduct the annual employee evaluation. Between February 6 and

February 12, sales managers should provide ------- to the people on their team using the
139.

downloadable form on the server. Please treat this as an opportunity to encourage salespeople.

If someone on your team is underperforming, you should work with them to find the ------- of the
140.

problem. The company has produced a number of videos on sales techniques which may be of

use in such cases. You can watch ------- online using the links on the company's Web site. -------.
141.   142.

Pauline Jolly

---

139. (A) feedback
(B) directions
(C) registration
(D) services

140. (A) purpose
(B) reasoning
(C) blame
(D) source

141. (A) it
(B) me
(C) them
(D) us

142. (A) Therefore, it is only relevant to people
working in customer service.
(B) It is a requirement that employees fill
out the survey after each viewing.
(C) By doing so, you could lower employee
morale and make the situation worse.
(D) You must complete the entire process
during January this year.

GO ON TO THE NEXT PAGE

Questions 143-146 refer to the following article.

(25 July) — As of 17 August this year, a new set of rules will be applied to all ------- work in the
                                                                                    143.

suburb of Port Melbourne. Existing structures can remain as they are. However, all new and

renovated structures must comply with a set of design standards determined by the city council.

This legislation ------- the cultural identity and atmosphere of the area. The new set of standards
                   144.

lists acceptable construction materials, design elements, and color schemes. -------. To discuss
                                                                             145.

the rules or request an -------, you may call the city planner's office at 555-4834.
                        146.

143. (A) cleaning
     (B) advertising
     (C) building
     (D) consulting

144. (A) will preserve
     (B) has preserved
     (C) has been preserved
     (D) preserved

145. (A) Fortunately, this does not affect homes
         which will be constructed this year.
     (B) All communication regarding the
         regulations must be made in writing.
     (C) People are free to choose any kind of
         architecture they like.
     (D) It is available for download from the
         council website.

146. (A) except
     (B) exception
     (C) exceptional
     (D) exceptionally

Directions: In this part, you will read a selection of texts, such as advertisements, e-mails, and instant messages. Each text or set of texts is followed by several questions. Select the most appropriate answer for each question and mark the letter (A), (B), (C), or (D) on your answer sheet.

Questions 147-148 refer to the following receipt.

McQueen Online Bookstore

Receipt # 99393-834893

Date of Purchase: May 28, 1:28 P.M.
For the amount of: $23.50
Payment for: Download of the eBook, *Getting around Estonia*
Received from: Chadwick Heller
McQueen Points Remaining: 64 *Valid until May 31 (3 days left)

Note: The above title may be downloaded for three years from the date of purchase. You may download it up to three times to any device registered in your name. Purchase of this eBook also entitles the owner to receive 20 percent off on a physical copy of the book from McQueen Online Bookstore. To take advantage of this offer, simply input the above receipt number into the voucher field at the checkout. Offer expires on November 28.

---

147. What is indicated about Mr. Heller?

(A) He may lose some points soon.
(B) He paid with a gift certificate.
(C) He used the store three years ago.
(D) He is waiting for an item to be shipped.

148. How can Mr. Heller obtain a discount?

(A) By sending a copy of the receipt
(B) By registering his name with the seller
(C) By visiting a physical store
(D) By providing the receipt number

GO ON TO THE NEXT PAGE

Test 3

COREY WOLFE	10:50 A.M.

I'm so sorry I missed the meeting. Did Claire tell you about my car problems?

ANTHEA TAUBMAN	10:51 A.M.

Yes, she did. I told you that you need to buy a new car. That one's been causing nothing but trouble.

COREY WOLFE	10:53 A.M.

I have to agree with you now. I'll go to a dealership and have a look today. The mechanic gave me the same advice.

ANTHEA TAUBMAN	10:53 A.M.

I'm sure he did. As for the meeting, Harper Uniforms offered us a 15 percent discount if we stay with them.

COREY WOLFE	10:54 A.M.

So, are you going to take them up on it?

ANTHEA TAUBMAN	10:59 A.M.

We'll see. I have asked some other uniform manufacturers to bid on the contract. I want to look at their offers first.

COREY WOLFE	11:02 A.M.

Good idea. I'll be in the office by noon.

ANTHEA TAUBMAN	11:03 A.M.

Just in time for lunch!

149. What did the mechanic advise Mr. Wolfe do?

(A) Update his contact details
(B) Purchase a new vehicle
(C) Create a customer account
(D) Go to a larger repair shop

150. At 10:59 A.M., what does Ms. Taubman mean when she writes, "We'll see"?

(A) She will take a good look at the product quality.
(B) She wants to get Mr. Wolfe's opinion.
(C) She has not yet made up her mind.
(D) She thinks she has made the right decision.

Randall Skin Care
45 Carlota Way
Mildura VIC 3502

27 June

Dear Shareholders,

Randall Skin Care has always been a market leader, and this has been linked to our increased investment in research and development and the close relationship that exists between that department and marketing, which is also getting extra funds. So, while it pains me to admit that profits are down this quarter, I can assure you that it is not because sales have declined.

In fact, quite the opposite is true. Sales have improved by some 8 percent since April. The profit margin has been affected by an increase in production costs and a massive investment in product development. We believe that this is necessary from time to time in order to ensure the long-term success of our brand.

In the coming quarter, we intend to diversify the business by offering some new products such as deodorants and body soaps. The product development and marketing departments will take a central role and some extra spending there now will surely pay off down the line. We will also be spending a little more on customer service. As online product reviews become more and more important, ensuring customer satisfaction is critical.

I would like to thank you for your patience during this time and assure you that the company's prospects are better than ever.

Sincerely,

Clara Braden

Clara Braden, CEO, Randall Skin Care

151. According to the letter, why have profits dropped?

(A) Manufacturing costs have risen.
(B) Sales are declining.
(C) Advertising costs have risen.
(D) A new office was opened.

152. Which department is NOT mentioned as receiving additional spending?

(A) Research and development
(B) Distribution
(C) Marketing
(D) Customer service

153. What does the company intend to do next quarter?

(A) Reduce unnecessary spending
(B) Hire experts from abroad
(C) Expand into new product ranges
(D) Hold a meeting for shareholders

154. The word "critical" in paragraph 3, line 6, is closest in meaning to

(A) demanding
(B) essential
(C) negative
(D) sensitive

Volunteer at the Ralstow Community Fun Run!

If you are planning on taking part in the Ralstow Community Fun Run, you may be interested to learn that you can register for half price and avoid the selection process. As the event has grown in popularity, organizers now only accept about half of the applications they receive. One way to ensure you are selected is to volunteer. Participants in the three and five-kilometer events will finish before the full and half marathon participants start, so if you take part in one of these runs you will have plenty of time to get to one of the drink stations and help other volunteers dispense water and other drinks for the half and full marathon. We are looking for 100 people to assist us with this work. If you are interested, fill out an online application at www.ralstowcfr.org. It is necessary that you carry a mobile phone as you will be contacted on it by our chief organizer to finalize your application. It will also be used to coordinate your activities on the day of the fun run. Participants in the full and half marathon can also contact organizers to discuss other volunteer opportunities.

155. What is one benefit of volunteering?
(A) Guaranteed entry into the event
(B) Free runner registration
(C) An invitation to an after party
(D) A free T-shirt

156. What is one task volunteers will carry out at the Fun Run?
(A) Helping clean up garbage after the event
(B) Preparing beverages for participants
(C) Recording the runners' finishing times
(D) Directing traffic around the route

157. What condition must applicants satisfy to join the volunteers?
(A) They must supply an e-mail address.
(B) They must live in the Ralstow area.
(C) They must wear an official shirt.
(D) They must have a mobile phone.

Questions 158-159 refer to the following e-mail.

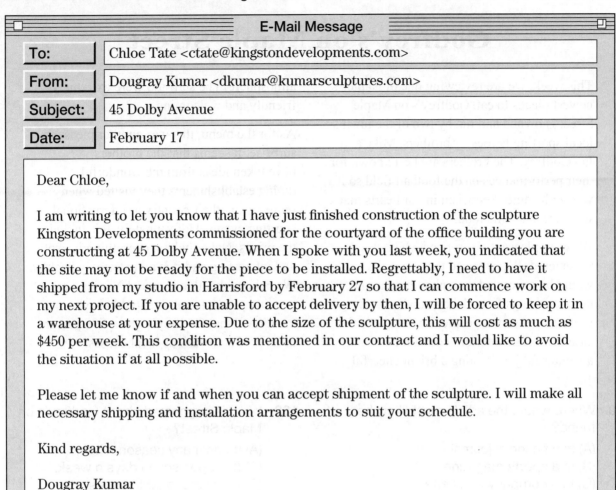

E-Mail Message

To:	Chloe Tate <ctate@kingstondevelopments.com>
From:	Dougray Kumar <dkumar@kumarsculptures.com>
Subject:	45 Dolby Avenue
Date:	February 17

Dear Chloe,

I am writing to let you know that I have just finished construction of the sculpture Kingston Developments commissioned for the courtyard of the office building you are constructing at 45 Dolby Avenue. When I spoke with you last week, you indicated that the site may not be ready for the piece to be installed. Regrettably, I need to have it shipped from my studio in Harrisford by February 27 so that I can commence work on my next project. If you are unable to accept delivery by then, I will be forced to keep it in a warehouse at your expense. Due to the size of the sculpture, this will cost as much as $450 per week. This condition was mentioned in our contract and I would like to avoid the situation if at all possible.

Please let me know if and when you can accept shipment of the sculpture. I will make all necessary shipping and installation arrangements to suit your schedule.

Kind regards,

Dougray Kumar
Kumar Sculptures

158. What is the purpose of the e-mail?

(A) To thank a client for paying a bill
(B) To provide an update on a project
(C) To invoice a customer for a service
(D) To ask for an extension to a deadline

159. What is mentioned in the contract?

(A) The sculpture must be ready by February 27.
(B) The artist must attend an unveiling event.
(C) The purchaser must pay a storage fee if it is incurred.
(D) The payment must be made in full within two months.

Test 3

Godfrey's on Maple Street

This week, we are reviewing one of Napier's newest places to eat. Godfrey's on Maple Street is owned and run by two of the town's local sporting heroes — brothers, Mike and Ian Godfrey. The brothers are best known for their performances on the football field so it was with some skepticism in our hearts that we went to try the food.

We were pleasantly surprised when we entered. We expected that the walls would be decorated with photographs and news clippings from the owners' time as professional sports people. That was not the case at all. The interior decorator has done a wonderful job creating a bright cheerful

atmosphere. The staff too were extremely friendly and welcoming.

As for the menu, this was another pleasant surprise. It seems that the brothers have taken ideas from the wonderful dining establishments they visited when representing their country at international sporting events. Unfortunately, this includes the prices. Nevertheless, everything is exotic and interesting and it is all extremely healthy. We believe that this is one of Napier's most exciting places to eat. It should also be mentioned that Godfrey's gives five percent of its profits to various local causes.

160. Where would the article most likely be found?

(A) In a financial journal
(B) In a sports magazine
(C) In a company newsletter
(D) In a restaurant review

161. What is implied about the Godfrey brothers?

(A) They are not drawing attention to their sporting achievements.
(B) They are at the business every day.
(C) They were interviewed by the writers of the article.
(D) They are currently managing a professional sports team.

162. What is suggested about Godfrey's on Maple Street?

(A) It has many seasonal items.
(B) It is open seven days a week.
(C) It has reasonable prices.
(D) It has made charitable donations.

MEMO

To: All B&T Employees
From: Portia Tuttle
Date: November 17
Subject: December banquet

I just checked the schedule and noticed that the annual employee appreciation banquet is next month. This year, I have been put in charge of entertainment. — [1] —. I have been given a budget to hire an entertainer, but I would much rather put the money toward a lucky door prize and enjoy some entertainment from our colleagues.

— [2] —. If there is anyone who can perform a few songs on stage, I would love to hear from them. You can usually get me on extension 259. If there is more than one person or band interested in providing entertainment, I will either hold auditions or split the assigned time between two acts. — [3] —.

If no one expresses interest in this idea by Friday this week, I will contact Aprikana Talent Agents and ask them to provide a lounge singer for the evening. — [4] —. I think that would be a real disappointment because I had intended to arrange tickets for two for a stay at Astin Resort in Key West.

Sincerely,

Portia Tuttle

163. What is the memo mainly about?

(A) Entertainment options for a company dinner
(B) Company policy with regard to hiring temporary staff members
(C) The following year's tentative work schedule
(D) Suggested themes for a corporate event

164. How should interested people contact Ms. Tuttle?

(A) By calling her on the telephone
(B) By sending her an e-mail
(C) By approaching her at her desk
(D) By sending her a text message

165. In which of the positions marked [1], [2], [3], and [4] does the following sentence best belong?

"As a result, there would be no lucky door prize this year."

(A) [1]
(B) [2]
(C) [3]
(D) [4]

GO ON TO THE NEXT PAGE

ATTENTION

The museum will open its doors later than usual on Wednesday, October 28. Officials from the city's Department of Health and Safety will be inspecting the museum's exits, alarms, and sprinkler system to ensure our compliance with city codes. This is scheduled to take place between 9:00 A.M. and 11:00 A.M. We anticipate being able to welcome guests from 11:30 A.M. instead of the usual 9:30 A.M. If you need to make a special allowance for any tour companies who require access for a group earlier than that, please speak with the museum manager. Keep in mind that requests will be considered on a first come, first served basis. Opening hours will be back to normal on Thursday.

Naveen Prasad — Assistant Manager

166. For whom is the notice intended?

(A) Tourists
(B) City officials
(C) Museum staff
(D) Tour company employees

167. What time will the facility open on October 29?

(A) At 9:00 A.M.
(B) At 9:30 A.M.
(C) At 11:00 A.M.
(D) At 11:30 A.M.

Sunny Castle Amusement Park
Mobile Phones

Employees of Sunny Castle Amusement Park are not allowed to carry their personal mobile phones with them while working in the amusement park grounds. — [1] —. All mobile phones can be kept in the lockers at the administration building. Otherwise, they may be left with the staff at the security desk near the main entrance. — [2] —. The rule only applies to employees who come in direct contact with park visitors. Therefore, the office staff is not obliged to conform.

The park provides all staff members with company-owned mobile phones, which employees are expected to carry with them while on duty. — [3] —. You may not use this phone for personal calls nor may you install any unapproved applications. A list of approved applications is provided on the last page of this document. — [4] —. A more up-to-date version of the employee manual may be posted on the Web site. Check www.sunnycastleap.com/staff for updates.

168. Where would the information most likely be found?

(A) In an employee handbook
(B) In a newspaper article
(C) In a visitor information leaflet
(D) In a travel brochure

169. What is implied about office staff at Sunny Castle Amusement Park?

(A) They can be contacted 24 hours a day.
(B) They cannot arrange group tours without advance notice.
(C) They recharge mobile phone batteries at the end of each shift.
(D) They do not communicate with patrons directly.

170. Why might someone visit the Web site?

(A) To obtain a list of show times
(B) To check changes to company policy
(C) To sign up for an information session
(D) To download the most recent newsletter

171. In which of the positions marked [1], [2], [3], and [4] does the following sentence best belong?

"They are recent models with excellent specifications."

(A) [1]
(B) [2]
(C) [3]
(D) [4]

GO ON TO THE NEXT PAGE

Clyde Kang [3:30 P.M.]: As we discussed at last night's meeting, we have to let a few of our clients go. We're getting too busy to handle them all properly. I'm planning on calling Larusso University this afternoon to let them know. I would like to put them in touch with another reputable firm when I call. Any ideas?

Harry Larkin [3:31 P.M.]: I used to work at Ramsey Images. They were always very professional.

Jang-Mi Sin [3:31 P.M.]: That's true, but I don't think they're in business anymore.

Clyde Kang [3:33 P.M.]: Harry, I'm surprised you didn't know that. It's one of the reasons we've been so busy.

Derek Wilks [3:35 P.M.]: I hear that Galione Studios recently won an award for their work for Macchio Fashion.

Jang-Mi Sin [3:35 P.M.]: I have a friend who works there. He says they're in the same situation as we are. I doubt they're looking for extra work, either.

Harry Larkin [3:37 P.M.]: We haven't gotten any work from Larusso University recently. I don't think they'll be very concerned about the news.

Clyde Kang [3:45 P.M.]: They might. I heard that they have a big job coming up. I really don't want to put them in a difficult position.

Derek Wilks [3:46 P.M.]: Perhaps we should try to keep them as a client. How about hiring a dependable freelance photographer?

Clyde Kang [3:49 P.M.]: You might be right. Harry, can you recommend one of your old colleagues?

172. Why did Mr. Kang start the online chat discussion?

(A) To ask for introductions to job seekers
(B) To announce the signing of a contract
(C) To thank employees for their hard work
(D) To get suggestions for a client referral

173. What is implied about Galione Studios?

(A) It is hiring new staff.
(B) It is very busy.
(C) It took on a new client.
(D) It specializes in fashion photography.

174. At 3:45 P.M., why does Mr. Kang write, "They might"?

(A) He believes Ramsey Images will be interested in an offer.
(B) He sent some equipment away for repairs.
(C) He thinks Larusso University will be affected by a decision.
(D) He heard some news about a photography course.

175. What will Mr. Larkin most likely do next?

(A) Meet the hiring manager at Galione Studios
(B) Inquire about evening courses at Larusso University
(C) Contact a previous employee of Ramsey Images
(D) Renew a contract with Macchio Fashion

GO ON TO THE NEXT PAGE ▶

Software Developer's Monthly
February
Table of Contents

An Interview with Verne Ramirez — founder of Ramirez Solutions
By Carmen Matei
Verne Ramirez recently sat down for an interview with Carmen Matei, one of the staff writers at *Software Developer's Monthly*. Matei arrived at the Skytop Hotel in central Taipei, where Ramirez was staying, and they met in the wonderful Clamshell Restaurant to talk about his exciting career.

Matei: Thank you for agreeing to this interview. Can you tell us why you're so far from home?

Ramirez: Not at all. I'm here to meet with a couple of young developers who are developing a smartphone application that can help you recognize locations from photographs and find them on a map. I'd like to use the technology in one of my company's upcoming software packages.

Matei: It sounds interesting. Can I ask how you got into software development?

Ramirez: Of course. I'm afraid it isn't a very interesting story. In high school, I asked a career counselor what the best paying jobs were. She mentioned medicine, law, and computers. I thought computers sounded the most fun of the three.

Matei: Did you have any experience programming before that?

Ramirez: None at all. Luckily, I was taught by Dr. Joseph Morgan at Kelston University. He really inspired me to try new things.

Matei: What do you wish you had known more about when you were starting out?

Ramirez: Many things, obviously. In particular, I wish I'd known more about choosing a good company to work for. I wasted a lot of time working in jobs where I learned nothing.

Matei: What a coincidence! One of our staff writers is working on an article about that for our February issue.

Ramirez: Well, I think everyone getting started in the industry should probably read it. It's important to plan your career well.

Matei: Speaking of plans, what do you have in mind for the next few years?

Ramirez: I'm getting ready to launch an online college where people from all over the world can learn computer programming. Instruction will be given by my employees, who are some of the most talented programmers in the industry.

176. For whom is the magazine most likely intended?

(A) Computer programmers
(B) Video game enthusiasts
(C) Hardware designers
(D) Appliance salespeople

177. What is indicated about Mr. Ramirez?

(A) He often stays at the Skytop Hotel.
(B) He will give interviews to multiple magazines.
(C) He is negotiating a merger with another company.
(D) He is in Taipei to negotiate a business deal.

178. What attracted Mr. Ramirez to his current field?

(A) Positive experiences from his childhood
(B) The opportunities for extended holidays
(C) The prospect of working with Dr. Morgan
(D) The promise of high financial reward

179. On what page of the magazine is the article Ms. Matei mentions?

(A) Page 7
(B) Page 8
(C) Page 19
(D) Page 22

180. What will Mr. Ramirez do soon?

(A) Publish a book on his life as a company president
(B) Teach a course to university students
(C) Establish an educational institution
(D) Purchase land for a new company headquarters

GO ON TO THE NEXT PAGE

GILMORE (February 10) — Gilmore City has recently cleared and developed a large area of parkland in Mulberry Hills. This land has been used to create a new fashion district known as the Gilmore Fashion District or GFD. Gilmore has been associated with a growing number of fashion labels over the years. City leaders are hoping that fashion design and production will become one of the town's major industries. To encourage businesses to move into the new district and provide them a financial boost, the council has agreed to subsidize the rent for the first five years of every lease. As a result, businesses will be able to save up to 50 percent on rent and benefit from being in one of the most attractive locations businesses in this industry could hope for.

Besides the obvious financial advantages, companies will benefit from a connection with the newly founded Balmoral College of Art. The publicly owned college is located within the GFD and has agreed to provide a space for all of the city's fashion shows. The college's 640 square-meter function hall is available for free for approved events. According to Cheryl Dominic from Zebra Garments, one of the first companies to move to the GFD, the event hall has been an excellent venue for her company's promotional events.

So far, the only way to rent an office in the GFD has been to receive an invitation from the GFD administrators. Soon, however, administrators will be accepting applications from other businesses. There are conditions on the type and size of company that is allowed to move into the GFD and interested people can learn more about them by following the links on the Web site.

Admit One

The Annual Gilmore Fashion Show
See exciting designs created exclusively in the GFD!
7:00 P.M. to 10:00 P.M., June 16

This ticket has been provided for **Noelle Peabody** of **Crisp Fashion**.

This is a free ticket provided for employees of businesses displaying items in the show. Please note that this ticket is non-transferable. As a result, you may be asked to show identification at the entrance. A detailed map of the event's location, as well as contact details of the organizers, are printed on the back.

181. What is most likely true about the GFD?

(A) It was inspired by a project in another town.

(B) The land was previously used for recreation.

(C) The cost of rent there is rising.

(D) It offers excellent views of the city.

182. Why was the GFD created?

(A) To raise funds through charity events

(B) To reduce traffic in the city center

(C) To provide jobs for college graduates

(D) To foster a growing industry

183. What is suggested about Zebra Garments?

(A) It was invited to the district by GFD Administration.

(B) It hires students from Balmoral College of Art.

(C) It provided initial funding for the GFD.

(D) It has submitted an entry to the Gilmore Fashion Show.

184. What is implied about Ms. Peabody?

(A) She will visit Balmoral College of Art.

(B) She works for a business outside the GFD.

(C) She will judge garments in the Gilmore Fashion Show.

(D) She is one of the administrators of the GFD.

185. According to the ticket, what should ticket holders refrain from doing?

(A) Driving to the venue

(B) Selling their tickets

(C) Calling the event organizer

(D) Video recording the show

GO ON TO THE NEXT PAGE ➞

www.hansencc.org

Upcoming Events at the Hansen Community Center (March)

Ikebana — From 3:00 P.M. March 5, 12, 19, and 26 (Wednesdays)
The art of traditional Japanese flower arrangement is not only a lot of fun, it is a great way to add a sense of sophistication to any interior. Come and learn from Ichiho Fukuzaki, an expert certified by the National Ikebana Association of Japan.

Secretarial Skills Classes — From 2:00 P.M. March 6, 8, 13, 15, 20, 22, 27, and 29 (Thursdays and Saturdays)
Participants who complete this month-long course will receive a certificate in Basic Secretarial Skills from Bobson Community College.
Note: The teacher hired to provide this class is no longer available. Unless we can find a very experienced teacher with qualifications in word processing, spreadsheets, office administration, and corporate communications, this course may be canceled. Please contact Hansen Community Center Administration to apply.

Hansen Jazz Club — From 8:00 P.M. March 3 and 17
This popular association meets twice a month to discuss jazz, share information, and enjoy performances by members.

Thorne Gardening Society — From 9:00 A.M. March 2, 9, 16, and 23 (Sundays)
Members of the Thorne Gardening Society gather on Sundays to discuss gardening and organize the Annual Thorne Gardening Competition, a hugely popular event in Hansen. They are always looking for new members. Contact the society at tgs@hopeone.org for details on becoming a member.

If you would like to use the Hansen Community Center for your event, please contact the chief scheduler at 555-2394. Please note it is necessary to submit a photographic identification when reserving a space. Until March 31, programs will be provided on the seventh and eighth floors except the one in the evening, which will be held on the sixth floor. However, due to the renovation work, they will all be conducted on the ninth floor next month.

ONLINE APPLICATION

Position:	Teacher of Secretarial Course
Applicant name:	Travis Waldron
Address:	12 Schreiber Drive, West Vandros
Contact number:	555-4932
Self-introduction:	I graduated from the Mnuchin School of Business last month, so I believe I am well qualified for the position. I have excellent word processing and spreadsheets skills as evidenced by my Level 5 certificates in both. Furthermore, the course I took at Mnuchin School of Business covers the topics of corporate communications and office administration in great depth.

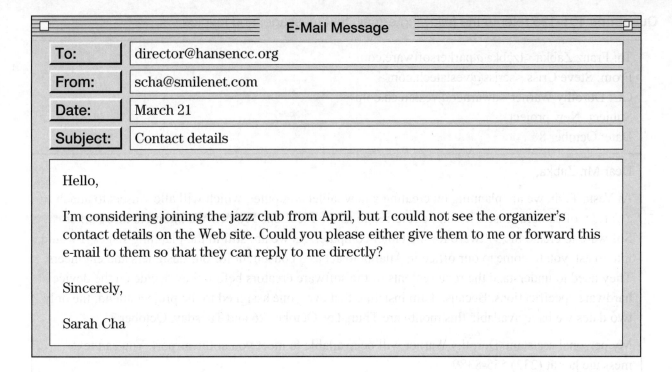

E-Mail Message

To:	director@hansencc.org
From:	scha@smilenet.com
Date:	March 21
Subject:	Contact details

Hello,

I'm considering joining the jazz club from April, but I could not see the organizer's contact details on the Web site. Could you please either give them to me or forward this e-mail to them so that they can reply to me directly?

Sincerely,

Sarah Cha

---

186. According to the schedule, which event is looking to increase its size?

(A) Ikebana
(B) Secretarial Skills Classes
(C) Hansen Jazz Club
(D) Thorne Gardening Society

187. What is implied about Ms. Fukuzaki?

(A) She is training an apprentice.
(B) She advertised her course in a newspaper.
(C) She is the founder of a national association.
(D) She has submitted identification to the community center.

188. What is NOT mentioned about the Hansen Jazz Club?

(A) It has regular meetings.
(B) It is a well-liked club.
(C) It provides free membership.
(D) It hosts performances by members.

189. What is suggested about Mr. Waldron?

(A) He takes part in one of the events at the community center.
(B) He taught a class at the Mnuchin School of Business.
(C) He has insufficient experience for the position.
(D) He was notified of the vacant position by Ms. Cha.

190. Where would Ms. Cha attend her first session?

(A) On the sixth floor
(B) On the seventh floor
(C) On the eighth floor
(D) On the ninth floor

GO ON TO THE NEXT PAGE

To: Franz Zabka <fzabka@parkersoftware.com>
From: Steve Criss <scriss@vestatech.com>
CC: Dorothy Warner <dwarner@vestatech.com>
Subject: New project
Date: October 8

Dear Mr. Zabka,

At Vesta Tech, we are planning on creating a new tablet computer, which will allow users to attach a variety of camera lenses. It will be referred to as the FlexLens Project. We intend to hire Parker Software to create the software for the tablet computer. As we are still in the planning stages, I would like to ask you to come to our office in Atlanta to act as a consultant for our designers and engineers. They need to understand the requirements of the software creators before they decide on the device's hardware specifications. Because I am insisting that everyone assigned to the project attend, the only two dates we have available this month are Thursday, October 26 and Tuesday, October 31.

My personal assistant, Dorothy Warner will be available to meet you at the airport. You can text message her at (232) 555-8389.

According to our agreement, Parker Software does not bill us for this kind of preliminary meeting unless the project is later abandoned and we do not offer you a programming contract. Regardless of whether or not this project goes ahead, I would like to pay for your travel costs. Please pass your receipts to Ms. Warner when you arrive. She will take care of the reimbursement before you leave.

Sincerely,

Steve Criss
President — Vesta Tech

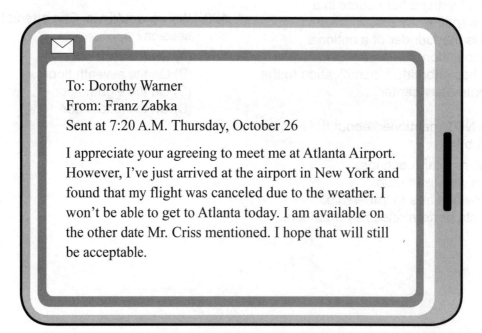

To: Dorothy Warner
From: Franz Zabka
Sent at 7:20 A.M. Thursday, October 26

I appreciate your agreeing to meet me at Atlanta Airport. However, I've just arrived at the airport in New York and found that my flight was canceled due to the weather. I won't be able to get to Atlanta today. I am available on the other date Mr. Criss mentioned. I hope that will still be acceptable.

Parker Software
24 Muriel Lane, Queens, NY
Invoice

Client: Vesta Tech   **Date:** November 30   **Project:** FlexLens

Service	Hourly Rate	Semi Total
Meeting with Vesta Tech Employees (5 hour preliminary meeting in October)	$270	$1,350.00
Transportation and Accommodation	N/A	$0.00
	Tax	$162.00
	Total	$1,512.00

191. What is the purpose of the e-mail?
(A) To provide a sample of a software program
(B) To request an interview with an applicant
(C) To arrange a consultation
(D) To promote a business

192. Whose contact details did Mr. Criss provide to Mr. Zabka?
(A) A company president's
(B) A secretary's
(C) A software developer's
(D) An engineer's

193. In the text message, the word "appreciate" in paragraph 1, line 1, is closest in meaning to
(A) enhance
(B) take account of
(C) feel grateful for
(D) admire

194. When did Mr. Zabka most likely arrive in Atlanta?
(A) On October 8
(B) On October 9
(C) On October 26
(D) On October 31

195. What is implied about Vesta Tech?
(A) It did not go ahead with the FlexLens Project.
(B) It is not recognized as a major brand.
(C) It has an office in New York.
(D) It charged Parker Software for transportation costs.

https://www.colbertcatering.com/faq

Welcome to Colbert Catering

Home	Events	Menus	**FAQ**

What is the largest event you can cater?
We can cater to groups of up to 500. However, it should be noted that not all menus will be available to such large groups. For example, the "deluxe menu" and the "food of the world menu" are only available to groups of under 300 and 200 people respectively.

Do you offer discounts to frequent customers?
We offer discounts for select customers based on the amount they spend at Colbert Catering rather than their frequency. People who spend more than $2,000 in any quarter will receive 10 percent off in the following quarter.

What are Colbert Catering's business hours?
Our office hours are from 9:00 A.M. to 5:00 P.M., Monday to Friday. However, Colbert Catering is able to serve its clients 24 hours a day, seven days a week. Some penalty rates apply on weekends, public holidays, and between the hours of 9:00 P.M. to 9:00 A.M.

How far can Colbert Catering deliver food?
Colbert Catering is based in Vernon. Generally speaking, we only provide catering to addresses within 30 kilometers of our facility.

Are alternatives available for people with allergies?
We can substitute ingredients where necessary. Please fill out a special request form on the Web site.

To: Trish Bryson <tbryson@colbertcatering.com>
From: Abu Markov <amarkov@firecoot.com>
Date: October 11
Subject: Party catering

Dear Ms. Bryson,

Thank you for providing catering for my party so expertly last night. The Colbert Catering staff were all extremely professional and the food and drinks were very high quality. I was also impressed with your value for money. I feel that I received higher quality food for about 10 percent less than the previous caterer charged. Well done! I have recommended your services to my neighbor, who I expect will contact you later today for an appointment.

The real purpose of my e-mail, however, is to let you know that your team has left some equipment behind. This morning I found a silver tray with the Colbert Catering logo on it in my kitchen.

Sincerely,

Abu Markov

E-Mail Message

To:	Trish Bryson <tbryson@colbertcatering.com>
From:	Valerie Yasser <vyasser@swandive.com>
Date:	October 11
Subject:	Appointment request

Dear Ms. Bryson,

I was handed your business card by Abu Markov, who praised your services highly. I would like to set up an appointment to discuss arrangements for a business luncheon I am planning. It will be held in the conference room in my office at 34 Prince Street, Vernon. It will be a group of around 30 business executives and I would like to serve one of your high-end menu plans. I am aware that one of the guests is allergic to shrimp and another to coconut. Can you accommodate special menu requests?

Please contact me on 832-555-3472 to discuss an appointment time.

Sincerely,

Valerie Yasser
President — Swandive Trading

196. Who is eligible for a discount?

(A) People who frequently use Colbert Catering
(B) People who spend over a certain amount
(C) People who sign up for a membership plan
(D) People who recommend Colbert Catering to others

197. According to the Web page, why might Colbert Catering charge an additional fee?

(A) The client lives outside the Vernon central business district.
(B) A combination of two menus is required.
(C) A job is scheduled for a national holiday.
(D) The number of guests is too small.

198. What is implied about Mr. Markov?

(A) He tried to contact a sales representative after 5:00 P.M.
(B) His home is within 30 kilometers of Colbert Catering.
(C) His event attracted over 300 guests.
(D) He ordered more than $2,000 worth of catering in the previous quarter.

199. What is indicated about Ms. Yasser's event?

(A) It will be held in a commercial building.
(B) It has a very restrictive budget.
(C) It was catered by Colbert Catering last year.
(D) It will have the maximum number of guests.

200. What will Ms. Yasser most likely be required to do?

(A) Fill out an online form
(B) Give directions to her company
(C) Amend the number of attendees
(D) Call another branch of Colbert Catering

Stop! This is the end of the test. If you finish before time is called, you may go back to Parts 5, 6, 7 and check your work.

NO TEST MATERIAL ON THIS PAGE

NO TEST MATERIAL ON THIS PAGE

『TOEIC® L&Rテスト 究極の模試600問＋』別冊③

PC：7019067

発行：株式会社アルク

無断複製および配布禁止

TOEIC® L＆Rテスト
究極の模試
600問＋

ヒロ前田 著

「　ま え が き　」

　もともとは、「まえがき」を書くつもりはありませんでした。この次から始まる「はじめに」が本書の出発点としてふさわしいからです。それなのに、このページを書くことにしたのは、タイトル末尾に付いている「＋」（プラス）の意味を説明する必要があると判断したからです。

　タイトルに付けた「＋」（プラス）には、3つの意味があります。

　1つ目は「600問＋200問」の「＋」です。この本には、Test 1からTest 3までの600問だけでなく、Test 4（200問）も収録されています。Test 4は、Test 1からTest 3までのコンテンツをあなたがどれだけモノにしたかを測る「復習仕上がり度チェックテスト」です。Test 4の使い方については、p.12をご覧ください。ということで、1つ目の「＋」は、問題数が600問より多いことを示す「＋」です。

　2つ目は「問題＋動画」の「＋」です。従来の模試本は「問題＋テキストによる解説」がスタンダードですが、本書は国内史上初の試みとして解説をテキストだけでなく動画にもしました。つまり、本書に収録されている600問を全て動画で解説し、無料提供していますので、「自宅で解いて、電車で解説授業を見る」といった学習が可能です。もちろん、紙に印刷された解説も存在するので、「読んで学ぶ」ことも可能です。ということで、2つ目の「＋」は、学習スタイルが増えたことを示す「＋」です。

　3つ目は「目標スコア＋α」の「＋」です。どんな模試でも、ちゃんと使えば成果は出ます。ただ、この本が推奨している「3回チャレンジ法プラス」を忠実に実践していただければ、あなたの期待を大きく超えるスコアを手にすることができます。

　この本は壮大な1つの物語です。ヒロという名の講師が経営するスクールが舞台。そこで開かれるTOEIC対策講座で、本書に収録された模試を使って4人の受講生が学んでいきます。目標や保有スコア、獲得したいスキル、社会的な立場、年齢も性格も異なる彼らは、あなたの鏡です。きっと、共感する部分が多く見つかるでしょう。そして、ドンドン成長していく彼らに負けないよう、あなたも学んでいってください。応援しています。

　では、ページをめくってください。物語の始まりです。

ヒロ前田

「 はじめに 」

20XX年某所
ここは、ある小さなTOEIC対策スクールの1室。
さまざまな理由でTOEIC L&Rテストに挑戦している受講生が集まってくる場所だ。
今回の講座に集まったのは、現在のレベルも目標もバラバラな4人。
模擬試験を使った試験対策が始まる日に、講師が4人の前に立った…。

どうも。講師のヒロです。最初に、ゼミについて説明します。今回のゼミでは、**模試を使ってTOEICを疑似体験**しながら、**効率的なスコアアップ**を目指します。「効率的」と言っても、楽して成果を出すことを目指すわけじゃない。ちゃんと努力して、それに見合う**巨大な成果を出すことを目指す**。短期のゼミだけど、一緒にたくさん学んでいこう。よろしく。

よろしくお願いします。

えっと、名前はサキだったね。受講を決めたんだね。

この前の面談で、弱点を秒で見抜かれたので、ここしかないと思って来ました。

形容詞と副詞をごっちゃにしてたから、文法に弱いって分かったよ。当面は600点を目指すんだよね。

はい。**スコアを就活に活かしたいです。**

サキに先輩たちを紹介する。まず、マイから。

マイです。証券会社で働いています。**英語を使う部門で仕事をしたい**ので、ここに通っています。最初は500点でしたが、今は700点台の後半まで来ました。よろしくね。

マイは半年前に通い始めて、着実に実力が伸びている。で、マイの同期生がダイ。メーカー勤務だよね。

そうです。**会社で昇格するのに470点が必要**になりまして。困った時代です。

家族のために頑張って。では、ゼミの話をする。

ちょっと待ってください。また無視ですか。

あれ、ヤス。いつ来たの?

ずっといましたよ!

ヤスはアパレルショップで働いていて、店に外国人がたくさん来るから英語が必要なんだって。今は適当に単語を並べて話すのが精一杯だけど、**将来は海外へ買い付けに行きたい**らしく、730点が目標。だよね?

そうですけど……。

では、ゼミの目的を確認する。1つ目の目的は**スコアアップ**。全員に150点から200点ほど上げてもらう。もう1つの目的は**学び方を学ぶ**こと。このゼミを通じて、「成果が出る学習スタイル」を習得してもらう。そうすれば、ゼミが終わっても独学で成果を出せるようになるから。

やっぱり、自分で勉強できるのが理想ですね。

次は教材を説明する。この本には本物そっくりの模試が入っている。重たいけれど、問題冊子はバラバラで1つ1つ取り外せる。

解説冊子を取り外せる方が便利だと思いますが。

持ち歩きのためだよね。大丈夫、この本の**解説冊子には電子版があって、無料でゲットできる。**

無料ですか? すげー。

それだけじゃない。解説は、紙と電子だけでなく、動画にもなっている。**全600問分の講義動画が無料**だよ。

動画ってうれしいかも。

😊 電子版と動画については、10ページの「ダウンロード他各種サービスのご案内」を読んでね。

🙂 便利な時代になりましたね。

😊 ちょっと、巻末にあるクリーム色のマークシートを見て。「勘ボックス」が付いているよね。これは「**3回チャレンジ法プラス**」という学習法で使うマークシートで、意外と便利なんだよ。

😊 ここにある数字は何ですか？

😊 それは、モニター受験者のデータだよ。各選択肢をモニターの何パーセントが選んだかが分かる。あと、答え合わせすれば、**予想スコアと自分が苦手な問題タイプを知る**ことができる。本物のTOEICのスコアシートに「項目別正答率」が載っているよね。あれを自分で計算できるようになっている。

😊 こういうの、他の本では見たことがないなぁ。

😊 あれ、Test 4もあるのですね。

😊 実はこの本には**模試が4つ入っている**。Test 4を使うと、**Test 1からTest 3を「モノにした度」を測れる**。

🙂 至れり尽くせりですね。

😊 では、オリエンテーションに入ろう。

登場人物紹介

😊 マイ

証券会社勤務、30代。大学では英文学を専攻していたので、英語力には自信があったが、TOEIC L&Rテストのスコアは700点台後半で伸び悩んでいる。最高は**795点**。海外企業と直接取引する部門への異動を希望している。そのために900点突破と、実用的な英語運用能力の獲得を目標に邁進中。何事も堅実にこなす性格で、TOEICの試験対策はかなりしてきた。しかし英語を話すことには抵抗があり、そのことがコンプレックスになっている。

😊 ヤス

衣料品販売店勤務、20代。海外からのお客さまと接する機会が多く、英語を使うチャンスはそれなりにあるものの、**定型的なやりとりに終始する**。就職活動のときに受けたTOEIC L&Rテストでは470点、その後580点までスコアを伸ばしている。お調子者で、当たって砕けろ精神の持ち主。海外旅行は語学力よりも**身振り手ぶり＆気合で乗り切る**タイプ。TOEICはゲームみたいで好き。目標は、**海外へ1人で買い付けに出る許可が得られる730点**。

😊 ヒロ

TOEIC対策専門の講師。小さいスクールを経営しながらTOEIC L&Rテストを受験し続け、大学生と社会人を対象にスコアアップ指導を行う。努力しない受講者には冷たいが、頑張る人の成果を目標以上に高めることが生きがい。受講者のニーズがあれば、スコア上昇に見合う英語運用力アップの訓練も提供する。今回の講座で、本書を指定教材に採用した。

🙂 ダイ

メーカー勤務、40代。英語とは無縁の仕事のはずが、**会社の方針でどの部門でもTOEIC L&Rテストで470点を取得しないと昇格できない**ことに。この前初めて受けた結果は380点。目標とのギャップにがく然として、ヒロのスクールに駆け込んだ。自分の職分を忠実に守り、成果も出しているものの、**融通がきかない面**も。会社で義務付けられるまでTOEICに一切興味がなかったが、子どもにかかるお金を考えて、昇給・昇格を目指している。

😊 サキ

大学2年生。テレビ局で活躍するバイリンガル・アナウンサーに憧れ、グローバル教養学部を選んだ。しかし英語は得意ではなく、入学時の英語のクラス分けのために受けさせられたTOEIC L&Rテスト（IPテスト）のスコアは**375点**。就職活動中の先輩から、**履歴書に書けるスコアを取得する**ようアドバイスされ、3年生になるまでに600点超えを決意。純朴で素直な性格のためか、問題作成者が仕掛ける**トラップに引っ掛かりやすい**。

5

目 次

Contents

「　別　冊　」

※別冊①〜③は巻頭に、別冊④は巻末にとじ込まれています。

『 オリエンテーション 』

本書の特長

本書には、TOEIC L&R テストの模擬試験4セットが収載されています。各模試には以下のような特長があります。

① TOEIC L&R テストの最新傾向を反映しています。

Test 1〜3は、TOEIC L&R テストの問題作成機関 ETS が制作した公式教材や公開テストを参考に、使用語彙、トピック、難易度、問題タイプのバランスなどを調整して、200問ずつセットにしています。本番のテストの予行演習に最適です。

②復習用の Test 4 があります。

Test 4は、Test 1〜3から問題を抽出し、トピック、難易度、問題タイプのバランスなどを調整して200問にした、復習用の模擬試験です。Test 1〜3の模試それぞれを復習した後に受験してください。

③換算スコアを計算できます。

Test 1〜4の4模試それぞれについて、TOEIC L&R テストのスコアの保有者300人以上を対象としたモニタリングテストを実施し、換算スコアを算出しました。本書の模試の正解数を基に、本番のテストでのスコアを予想できます。

④全問題を Abilities Measured の各項目に分類しています。

Abilities Measured（項目別正答率、以下AM）とは、TOEIC L&R テストのスコアシートに記載されている、リスニング・リーディング各5項目における正答率のことです。本書ではすべての模試の問題を、AM の項目を参考にした「問題タイプ」に分類し、項目ごとの正答率を計算できるようにしました（各模試の「解答・解説」ページに記載）。弱点の発見、強化にお役立ていただけます。

※「問題タイプ」の詳細はp.23でご紹介しています。

⑤自動採点サイトを利用可能。解答を入力すると、自動で結果を表示します。

「テスト採点センター」を利用して解答を入力すると、自動で採点され、換算スコアや問題タイプ別正答率が表示されます。採点結果を自分にメールしたりして保存しておけば、間違えた問題の復習もできます。

⑥丁寧な解説や「ゼミ生中継」などで、さまざまな角度からテストを理解できます。

Test 1〜3の解答・解説には問題も再掲。そのページだけで復習が可能です。本番で活用できる解答する際の心構えや普段の学習法が満載の「TOEICよろず相談所：ヒロの部屋」ではTOEIC L&R テストの受験者から寄せられたさまざまな問題を解決します。

⑦動画解説ほか、復習用コンテンツが充実。

「動画センター」では、Test 1〜3、全600問の解説動画を視聴いただけます。Test 1〜3の解答解説は、音声再生機能付電子書籍（epub）でもご用意。本書を持ち歩かなくても、タブレットやスマートフォンなどを使って空き時間に模試の復習が可能です。

※「動画センター」の詳細はp.11、復習用コンテンツの詳細はp.24をご確認ください。

本書の使い方

本書の模試は、以下のように取り組むことで、学習効果が最大になるよう設計されています。

☐ TOEIC L&R テストの形式を知る

p.16〜の「TOEIC L&R テスト　パート別の試験形式」で、問題形式を確認しましょう。

> 😊 問題形式を把握しておくだけで本番のテストで気持ちに余裕ができる。
>
> 😨 初めて受けたとき、形式も知らずに受験したので後悔しました。
>
> 😣 自分も最初は聞く必要のない「指示」を一生懸命聞いていました。

☐ 必要なものを準備する

巻末のマークシートを切り取り（コピーしても可）、鉛筆またはシャープペンシル、消しゴム、時計またはタイマーを準備しましょう。Listening Section の音声はダウンロードで提供しています。

☐ Test 1〜3に取り組む

本番の試験と同様に、全200問を既定の2時間で解くことから始めましょう。確実に力を付けるために、p.12〜で説明されている「3回チャレンジ法プラス」で取り組んでください。

> 😮 厳密に言えば、リスニングは45分じゃないですよね。
>
> 😊 確かに。本番でも日によって微妙に違う。各テストの表紙に時間が載っているから、それを見てね。

☐ Test 4に取り組む

Test 1〜3の復習を終えたら、全問正解を目指して Test 4に取り組みましょう。

● テスト冊子

本書の巻頭に Test 1〜3、巻末に Test 4が付属しています。これらを外して、表紙に受験日等、必要事項を記入してから始めましょう。

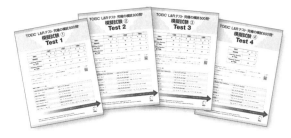

● マークシート

本書の巻末のマークシートを取り外し、必要に応じてコピーしてご利用ください。「マークシートA」は勘ボックス付き、「マークシートB」は勘ボックスなしです。

> 💀 「勘ボックス」が付いたマークシートは、他の教材にも使えそうだなぁ。
>
> 😊 もちろん。たくさんコピーしておくといいよ。

● 音声

ダウンロードで提供しています。p.10の「ダウンロードセンター」に記載された手順に従って準備してください。

● 解答一覧

Listening Section・Reading Section 別の「問題タイプ」付きのものと、正解・不正解が視覚的に分かりやすいマークシート状のものがあります。問題タイプ付きのものは、誤答した問題の問題タイプの集計ができるようになっています。

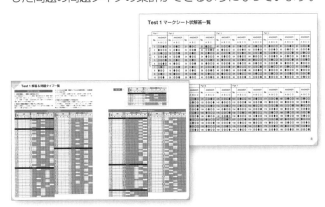

● 解説

解説ページでは各問題の英文や日本語訳、解説の他、モニタリングテストの結果を受けた難易度や各選択肢の選択率などを確認できます。「ゼミ生中継」では、ヒロ・マイ・ヤス・ダイ・サキの5人が登場し、問題に関する疑問や解き方のコツ、正解以外の選択肢が誤りである理由などを話し合っています。

ダウンロード他各種サービスのご案内

本書は、以下のサービスを利用してより快適に学習を進めることができます。

※各サービスの内容は予告なく変更する場合があります。あらかじめご了承ください。

ダウンロードセンター

本書の学習に必要な音声（mp3）や、マークシート（pdf）、解答・解説ページの音声再生機能付き電子書籍（epub）などを提供しています。

アルクのウェブサイト内「ダウンロードセンター」からパソコンにダウンロードする方法と、専用アプリを用いてタブレットやスマートフォンに直接ダウンロードする方法があります。

●パソコンにダウンロードする方法

1. アルクのダウンロードセンター（https://portal-dlc.alc.co.jp/）にアクセスしてください。

2. 商品コード（7019067）で検索してください。

3. 必要なコンテンツをパソコン上にダウンロードし、zip ファイルを解凍してください。

   ※パソコンのOSによっては圧縮ファイルの解凍ソフト（Lhaplus など）が必要な場合があります。

   ※ mp3 ファイルはパソコンで聞くほか、デジタル音楽プレーヤーやスマートフォンに転送して聞くこともできます。

●スマートフォンにダウンロードする方法

1. スマートフォンでApp Store（iPhone）か Google Play（Android）にアクセスし、アルクが提供する語学学習用のアプリ「ALCO for DLC」をダウンロード、インストールしてください。

2. 「ALCO for DLC」からアルクのダウンロードセンターにアクセスしてください。

3. 商品コード（7019067）で検索してください。

4. 該当ページのリンクからzip ファイルをダウンロードしてください。ファイルは自動で解凍され、「ALCO for DLC」で利用できるようになります。

> 👧 私は最近、スマホで音声を聞いています。サキちゃんは？
>
> 👩 私はスマホでしか聞けません。
>
> 👧 ALCO を使うと、試験に必要な音声はもちろん、復習に役立つ便利な音声や電子書籍もダウンロードできるよ。すごく便利。
>
> 👨 この本の解説編の電子版を無料でもらえるんだけど、これもALCO で読める。知らない人が多いから知り合いに勧めてね。

「ALCO for DLC」とは

「ALCO for DLC」は、書籍・通信講座の音声、通信講座の電子版テキストブックをダウンロードして利用するための専用アプリです。便利な機能を多数備えています。「ALCO for DLC」は App Store（iPhone）、Google Play（Android）からダウンロードできます。詳細は https://doc-alco.alc.co.jp/ をご覧ください。

※ダウンロードコンテンツには容量の大きいものが多いため、ダウンロードの際はWi-Fi 環境でのご利用を推奨します。また、スマートフォンの内蔵メモリにファイルサイズ相当の空き容量が必要です。

テスト採点センター

各テストの解答を入力すると、自動で採点され、換算スコアや問題タイプ別正答率が表示される機能がご利用いただけます。採点結果を自分にメールしておけば、復習にも役立ちます。

> 😊 自動採点ができるなんて便利ですね。
> 😮 問題タイプ別正答率の計算まで自動だなんてビックリです。

1. アルクのテスト採点センター（https://saiten. alc-book.jp）にアクセスしてください。個人情報などの登録は不要です。
2. 『TOEIC L&R テスト 究極の模試600問＋』の、採点したい Test 番号を選んでください。
3. 解答内容を入力し、「解答する」ボタンを押してください。
4. テスト結果が表示された後に画面下部の「クリップボードにコピー」ボタンを押すと、結果をテキストでコピーできます。必要に応じてデータを保存したり、自分宛てにメールで送ったりしましょう。

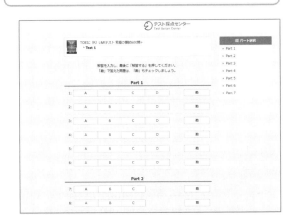

動画センター

各テストの解説をすべて動画でご確認いただけます。文字の説明だけではよく理解できないときなどにご利用ください。

1. アルクの動画センター（https://vc.alc-book. jp）にアクセスしてください。
2. 『TOEIC L&R テスト 究極の模試600問＋』の、解説を確認したい Test 番号を選んでください。パスワードは kk600plus です。
3. 「セクション別再生」「パート別再生」「設問別再生」が選べます。ボタンを選ぶと動画が再生されます。

> 😊 動画だと電車やバスの中で勉強できるのがいいですね。
> 😮 本当だね。私は喫茶店で見ようかな。
> 😊 一体、どれくらいの長さがあるんだろう？
> 😮 さぁ。全問が動画になっているし、本に載っていないおまけコンテンツも数本あるから、とにかく尋常ではない長さだと思う。

【テスト採点センター、動画センター推奨環境】
Google Chrome、Microsoft Edge、Firefox、Safari
（いずれも最新版をご利用ください）

「3回チャレンジ法プラス」は、学習効果を最大限に高める学習法です。受験までに3週間以上ある場合は、少なくとも模試1セット分はこの方法で取り組んでください。ただし、Test 4はTest 1〜Test 3の復習を完璧に仕上げてから取り組んでください。

Test 1〜3ではマークシートA-1、A-2、A-3を、Test 4ではマークシートBを使用します。

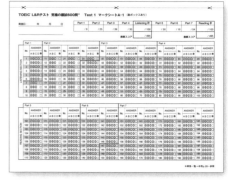

❶-1. 1回目の受験。マークシートA-1を使います。約2時間の制限時間を守って解答してください（リスニング約45分、リーディング75分）。時間内に解けなかった問題や、自分の解答に自信がない問題があれば、解答欄の右端にある「勘ボックス」にチェックを入れておきます。問題冊子への書き込みは常に禁止です（2回目以降の受験でも同じ）。

> 1回目の受験の主な目的は「できること」と「できないこと」を区別すること。模試を使って実力を高めるには2回目以降の受験が大切だよ。

❶-2. ❶-1.の採点をします。この時点ではまだ「解説」と「ゼミ生中継」を読んではいけません。「解答一覧」を見て正答数を数え「スコア換算表」から「換算点A」を、勘で答えたものを含まない正答数から「換算点B」を出します。この「換算点B」は勘に頼らない実力を示します。ここで「問題タイプ別正答率」も把握します。

> 解説を読まずに採点するということは、記号だけをチェックするということか。
>
> だったら、採点も不要じゃないですか？
>
> そうだよ。ただ、受験直後には出来具合を知りたいよね。その気持ちを抑えられる場合は、2回目の受験後に一気に採点すればいい。

❷-1. 2回目の受験。マークシートA-2を使います。制限時間はありません。リスニングセクションでは音声を何度聞いても構いません。全問正解を目指し、じっくり問題に取り組んでください。ただし、現時点の英語力を引き出すことが目的なので、辞書の利用は禁止です。解答に自信がない場合は「勘ボックス」にチェックを入れます。
※この2回目の受験は1回目の直後でなく、数日後でも構いません。1回目の直後に受験する場合は、1回目の採点はせずに2回目の受験をし、その後で2回分の採点をしてください。

> 2回目の受験には何時間かかりますか。
>
> さぁ。5時間かかっても変じゃない。
>
> え。効率が悪いのでは……
>
> 何を言ってるの。その時間は英語にしか触れていないんだから、英語力アップにつながるんだよ。そうすればスコアも伸びる。効率が悪いと言える？
>
> ……
>
> 実力を「測る」より、「伸ばす」ことを重視しようよ。

❷-2. 1回目の答え合わせと同様に、❷-1の採点をし、「換算点A」「換算点B」「問題タイプ別正答率」を出します。この2回目の受験での「換算点B」が、現在の「英語力」が正しく発揮されれば取得可能なスコアです。通常、1回目と2回目の正答数には差があります。その差を完全に埋めるために、さまざまな角度から復習し、さらに良い結果を目指します。

> 現時点での英語力をフルに発揮した状態が2回目の受験ってことですね。
>
> その通り。現時点での「限界点」でもある。もちろん、英語力自体を高めることで、その限界点を上げていくことも大切だよ。

❷-3. 復習。正解した問題も含めて全問の解説を読み、音声（リーディングセクションも含む）を聞き直して復習しましょう。特に「勘ボックス」にチェックを入れた問題は念入りに見直してください。日本語で書かれた「解説」を理解したら、続けて「出題された英語」を理解することに重点を置いた学習をしましょう。「音読する」「書く」などのアウトプット練習を含め、丁寧に英文に触れ、すべての英文を100パーセント理解し、不正解の選択肢が不正解である理由まで説明できるようになることが理想的です。復習の目的は「問題を解く」ことではなく、目の前の英語に没頭し、その英語を完全に自分のモノにすることです。

> 大胆に言えば、日本語解説や訳を読んでも英語力は伸びない。英語力を伸ばすには、英語に没頭する必要がある。当たり前のことだけど、盲点じゃないかな。
> 文法の勉強には日本語が必要な気がします。
> 確かに文法は日本語で学ぶ方が身につきやすい。大事なのは比率だよ。文法問題を15分で30問解くとしよう。解説を読む時間が30分あってもいいけど、その後が問題。解いた30問に再び没頭すれば1時間や2時間はすぐに過ぎる。日本語を介さず、英語に接するんだよ。復習のときは「解く」必要はない。
> 解かずに何をするんですか。
> 英語を観察し、吸収するんだよ。

> **復習期間の目安：1つの模試につき3週間**

● **おすすめ学習法の例**
リスニング
● 音声を聞いてディクテーションや音読、リピート練習、オーバーラッピング、シャドーイング、暗誦などをする
● 会話やトーク、選択肢から知らない語句を探して覚える
リーディング
● すべての英文と文書を精読・音読する
● 選択肢を隠して解答してみる（Part 5／Part 6）
● すべての英文と文書、選択肢から知らない語句を探して覚える

> リピート練習やシャドーイングといった音声を使った復習法は、動画でも説明があるよ。（p.11参照）

本書では、解答には直接関係のない箇所や、不正解の選択肢の中にも、実際のTOEIC L&Rテストでは正解の鍵を握る重要語句がたくさん含まれています。徹底的に復習して本書に掲載された英語を100パーセント理解できるようになれば、間違いなく大きな成果が出ます。

> 何を基準に復習をストップしていいのですか。
> この本の中に「理解できない英文は1つもない」と思い込むことができたら、それが合図だよ。

❸-1. 3回目の受験。マークシートA-3を使います（ここでマークシートAを使うのは、Test 4で全問正解を得るためです）。約2時間の制限時間以内に、本番同様に問題を解いていきます。受験のタイミングは復習期間から数日が過ぎて記憶が薄れかけた時期がお勧めです。

> ちゃんと復習したのなら、3回目の受験は不要だと思うかもしれないけれど、2時間連続で英語と向かい合う経験が多ければ、本番が楽に感じる。
> 集中力も上がりそうですね。
> もちろん。それ以前に、本当に復習できているかどうかは、制限時間を設けた本番形式で試されないと検証できないものだよ。

❸-2. 自己採点をし、間違えた問題や勘ボックスにチェックが入った問題がまだあれば、解説を読まずに再チャレンジします。それでも自信を持って解答できない問題があれば解説や訳を参照して復習します。

> 人は新しく仕入れた知識は忘れるのが普通だよね。広く浅く勉強するより、こうやって狭く深く学習した方が英語がしっかり身について、大きい成果につながるよ。

❹ 1つの模試に対する3回チャレンジが終わってから、同じ要領でTest 2、Test 3に取り組んでください。

❺ -1. Test 4に挑戦。勘ボックスのないマークシートBを使います。3つの模試に対して3回チャレンジが完了したら、Test 4に取り組みます。Test 4は、復習の仕上がり度が完璧であることを証明するテストなので、確実に全問正解できる自信を持てるようになってから挑戦してください。

❺ -2. 自己採点。万が一、間違えた問題や自信をもって答えられなかった問題があった場合は、解説を読まずに英語を聞いたり読んだりするだけできちんと理解できるか確認します。あいまいな問題があったら❸ -2. に戻りましょう。Test 4で全問正解したときに、本書を習得したことになります。

> 🙂 3回目のチャレンジで、600問すべてを正解できた場合は、Test 4をやる必要はない。この本を十分に使い倒したと言える。
>
> 😖 全問正解なんて自信ありません。
>
> 🙂 そんなこと言わずに。大きい成果を出す人は、反復練習を避けない人だよ。

3回チャレンジ法プラス　学習の流れイメージ図

● **Test 1に取り組む**

| 1回目 | 制限時間あり・解答力を知る |
| 解説を読まずに2回目に挑戦 |
| 2回目 | 制限時間なし・現時点での英語力を知る |
| 〈復習（目安：3週間）〉英語力と解答力を高める |
| 数日空けると効果的 |
| 3回目 |

> 🙂 「3回チャレンジ法プラス」の取り組み方は動画でも説明しているから見てみて。(p.11参照)

● **Test 2に取り組む**

| 1回目 | 制限時間あり・解答力を知る |
| 解説を読まずに2回目に挑戦 |
| 2回目 | 制限時間なし・現時点での英語力を知る |
| 〈復習（目安：3週間）〉英語力と解答力を高める |
| 数日空けると効果的 |
| 3回目 |

● **Test 3に取り組む**

| 1回目 | 制限時間あり・解答力を知る |
| 解説を読まずに2回目に挑戦 |
| 2回目 | 制限時間なし・現時点での英語力を知る |
| 〈復習（目安：3週間）〉英語力と解答力を高める |
| 数日空けると効果的 |
| 3回目 |

> 😖 3つの模試×3回にTest 4×1回を加えると、計10回ですね。
>
> 🙂 そう。10種類の模試に1回ずつ取り組むより圧倒的に成果が大きくなる。

● **Test 4に挑戦！**

テストの特徴や構成、スコアが示すコミュニケーション能力の目安を確認しましょう。

● TOEIC® L&Rテストとは？

TOEICとは、Test of English for International Communicationの略で、英語を母語としない人を対象とした、英語によるコミュニケーション能力を測定するためのテストです。アメリカの非営利テスト開発機関ETS（Educational Testing Service）によって開発・制作されています。そのうち、Listening & Reading Test（L&Rテスト）は、Listening（聞く）とReading（読む）の2つの英語力を測定します。
L&Rテストは、世界約160カ国で実施されており、日本では年間約245万人が受験しています（2018年度）。

● TOEIC® L&Rテストの特徴

① Listening（L）とReading（R）の2つのSectionに分かれ、英語コミュニケーション能力が総合的に評価されます。
② テスト結果は合否でなく、10～990点（L、R共に495点満点）のスコアで示されます。
③ 受験者の能力に変化がない限り、何度受験してもスコアが一定に保たれます。
④ テストは、印刷された問題も音声も英語のみで構成されています。
⑤ 受験級のような区別はありません。受験者の英語レベルに関係なく、全員が同じ問題に取り組みます。

😊 受験者の大半は日本人と韓国人だよ。
😮 この前、韓国の本屋さんに行ったら過去問がたくさん売られていて驚きました。
😊 うちの学校のロビーに飾ってあるよ。
😮 え、あれがそうなんですか！

😊 スコアを左右する力は2種類。1つは英語力で、もう1つは受験力。英語力をきっちりスコアに反映させるには、それなりのスキルが必要なんだよ。マイはピンと来るよね。
😮 はい。以前と違って今は、時間の使い方とか難問を捨てる力なんかもスコアを上げるには役立つと強く感じます。

● TOEIC® L&Rテストの利用

① 各自のレベルに合わせた目標スコアの設定が可能です。英語力の成長度の測定に利用できます。
② 企業・団体・学校などが、次のような目的で採用しています。
- ●人事採用や海外部門要員の選定　●昇進・昇格の要件　●英語研修の成果測定
- ●大学などの推薦入試の基準　●大学などの英語課程の単位認定

● TOEIC® L&Rテストのスコアとコミュニケーション能力レベルとの相関表

レベル	スコア	コミュニケーション能力
A	860～	Non-Nativeとして十分なコミュニケーションができる。
B	730～855	どんな状況でも適切なコミュニケーションができる素地を備えている。
C	470～725	日常生活のニーズを充足し、限定された範囲内では業務上のコミュニケーションができる。
D	220～465	通常会話で最低限のコミュニケーションができる。
E	～215	コミュニケーションができるまでに至っていない。

出典：TOEIC Listening & Reading Test 公式データ・資料「TOEICスコアとコミュニケーション能力レベルとの相関表」

● TOEIC® L&Rテストの構成

Listening Section　100問・約45分間		Reading Section　100問・75分間	
Part 1　写真描写問題	6問	Part 5　短文穴埋め問題	30問
Part 2　応答問題	25問	Part 6　長文穴埋め問題	16問
Part 3　会話問題	39問	Part 7　読解問題	54問（　1文書：29問
Part 4　説明文問題	30問		複数文書：25問）

各パートの出題形式の詳細は次ページから ➡

TOEIC L&Rテストでは、Part 1から7までの各パートの出題形式は毎回同じです。
ここで内容を確認しておけば、試験本番で、時間を有効に使うことができます。

Listening Section

会話やナレーションを聞いて設問に解答します。Part 1からPart 4の4つのパートで構成されています。テスト開始と同時にリスニングセクション全体に関する指示事項の放送が始まります（Ⓐ部分）。

Part 1 写真描写問題

形式：1枚の写真について、4つの短い説明文が放送されます。説明文はテスト冊子には印刷されていません。4つの文のうち、写真を最も的確に描写しているものを選び、その記号を解答用紙にマークします。

問題数：6問
選択肢の数：4つ
問題間のポーズの長さ：約5秒

🦉 6枚の写真のうち4枚か5枚に人が写っている。その人の動作や状態に注目しながら音声を聞くといい。ダイ、Part 1は好き？

😎 はい。たまに難問がありますが嫌いではありません。

🦉 TOEICは初級者にも上級者にも同じ問題を出すから、1～2問難しい問題があることは珍しくない。

※下の指示事項、問題はアルクが制作したサンプルです（以下同）。

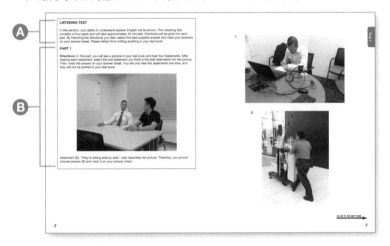

🦉 指示事項の音声は1分半くらい。ヤス、この時間をどう使っている？

😎 一応、写真を全部見ます。

🦉 私は基本的にはPart 3の設問を読みます。特に、意図問題だけは選択肢も全部読みます。一度目を通しておくと、後で読むときのスピードが上がるので。

🦉 何をするかは受験者の自由だけど、事前に自分のやり方を決めて練習しておくことが大事だよ。

😎 リーディングの問題を解いちゃいけないんですか。

🦉 それは禁止されているからやっちゃいけない。

指示事項の内容は常に同じです。内容を知っていれば、本番で読んだり聞いたりする必要はありません。Now Part 1 will begin.（それでは、Part 1が始まります）という放送がPart 1開始の合図です。

問題ごとに、Number 1. Look at the picture marked number 1 in your test book.（1番。テスト冊子にある1番と記された写真を見てください）という指示が流れます。1ページに2枚ずつ掲載された写真を見ながら解答していきます。ページをめくるときは、Go on to the next page.（次のページへ進んでください）という放送が流れ、約5秒のポーズがあります。

指示事項の内容

Ⓐ **リスニングテスト：** リスニングテストでは、話される英語をどれだけよく理解しているかを示すことが求められます。リスニングテストは 全体で約45分続きます。4つのパートがあり、パートごとに指示が与えられます。解答は別紙の解答用紙にマークしなければいけません。テスト冊子には何も書き込まないでください。

Ⓑ **Part 1：** このパートでは問題ごとにテスト冊子中の1枚の写真に関する4つの文を聞きます。文を聞いたら写真から見て取れ

ることを最もよく描写している文を1つ選びます。それから、解答用紙の問題番号を見つけ、解答をマークしてください。
文はテスト冊子には印刷されておらず、一度しか読まれません。
（サンプル問題の読み上げ）
(B)の文「彼らは並んで座っている」が写真に関する最も的確な描写なので、解答(B)を選んで解答用紙にマークします。それでは、Part 1が始まります。
※網掛け部分は音声のみで、テスト冊子に印刷されていません。

Part 2 応答問題

形式：1つの質問または発言と、それに対する3つの応答が、それぞれ1回だけ放送されます。質問・発言と応答は、テスト冊子に印刷されていません。3つの応答のうち、質問・発言に対して最もふさわしいものを選び、その記号を解答用紙にマークします。

問題数：25問
選択肢の数：3つ
問題間のポーズの長さ：約5秒

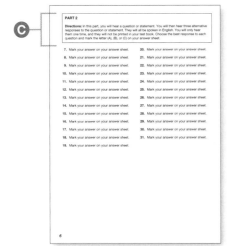

Part 2には例題はありません。指示事項最後のNow let us begin with Question number 7.（では、7番から始めましょう）が、Part 2開始の合図です。問題用紙にはMark your answer on your answer sheet.（解答用紙に解答をマークしてください）とだけ記載されています。

😀 短い設問は4ワードしかない。短い方が簡単だと思いがちだけど、実際はそうとは言えない。1語でも聞き逃したら解けなくなることがあるから。

😀 あるある。

😀 特に質問の最初の1語や2語を聞き逃さないようにすることが大事。マイ、どうして？

😀 WhenとかWhereで始まるWH疑問文が多いからです。

😀 そう。How many ～ ？やHow long ～ ?といった質問も出るから、少なくとも最初の2語は絶対に聞き落とさないように。

😀 Part 2は音声があれば足りるから、問題冊子を見る必要はないよね。ダイ、代わりにどこを見る？

😀 自分は目を閉じるので、まぶたの裏です。

😀 慣れているならそれでOKだけど、基本はマークシートだよ。25問が終わるまでマークシートだけ見ればいい。そういえば、動画センターに効果的なマークの塗り方を教えてくれる動画があるよ。p.11を参照してね。

指示事項の内容

◉ Part 2： 英語で話されている質問または発言と、3つの応答が聞こえてきます。それらはテスト冊子に印刷されておらず、1回しか話されません。質問または発言に対し最も適切な応答を選び、解答用紙の(A)、(B)または(C)にマークしてください。では、7番から始めましょう。

※網掛け部分は音声のみで、テスト冊子に印刷されていません。

Part 3 会話問題

形式：2人または3人による会話が1回だけ放送されます。会話はテスト冊子に印刷されていません。会話を聞いて、テスト冊子に印刷された設問（設問は放送もされます）と4つの選択肢を読み、設問の答えとして最も適切なものを選んで、その記号を解答用紙にマークします。会話の中で聞いたことと、印刷された図などで見た情報を関連付けて解答する設問もあります（E参照）。1つの会話につき、設問は3問ずつです。

問題数：39問（13会話）
選択肢の数：4つ
問題間のポーズの長さ：約8秒
　※グラフィック問題（E参照）は約12秒

😮 Part 3の設問を大まかに分類すると2種類ある。1つはWhat are the speakers discussing?（話者たちは何を話し合っていますか）みたいな、概要を問うタイプ。会話を聞けば聞くほど解きやすくなる。もう1つはWhat does the woman suggest doing?（女性は何をするよう提案していますか）のような、細かい情報を問うタイプで、ヒントは1回しか登場しない。

😐「意図問題」もありますよね。

😮 ある発言について、話者の意図や発言動機が問われる設問だね。詳細は模試を解説する中で話すよ。

😐 3人が登場する会話はいくつですか。

😮 1つか2つであることが多い。会話が聞こえる前に、Questions XX through XX refer to the following conversation with three speakers. と合図が聞こえるよ。

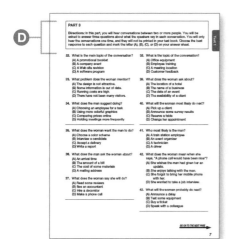

D

指示事項の後、Questions 32 through 34 refer to the following conversation. （32番から34番の問題は、次の会話に関するものです）という放送が流れます。これを合図にPart 3が始まります。会話の後には、3つの設問だけが放送されます。

😮 会話の音声が放送される前に、3つの設問に目を通すことを勧めるよ。そうすれば、ヒントが聞こえたときにそれがヒントだと認識できるから。簡単じゃないけれど、できる限りやった方がいい。

😐 最初の3セットくらいは設問の先読みができるけど、途中でペースが乱れてうまくいかなくなるんだよなぁ。

😮 そうだよね。それは上級者も同じだよ。あとはとにかく実力を高めることが大事。何を聞いても理解できるリスニング力があれば先読みは不要になる。

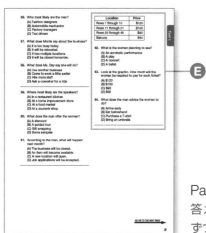

E

Part 3の最後の2～3セットは、図を見て答える設問、「グラフィック問題」が1問ずつ含まれます。

D Part 3：2人、あるいはそれより多い人物が交わす会話が聞こえてきます。それぞれの会話の中で話し手たちが言っていることについて、3つの質問に答えるよう要求されます。それぞれの質問に対し、最も適切な答えを選び、解答用紙の (A)、(B)、(C) または (D) をマークしてください。会話はテスト冊子に印刷されておらず、1回しか話されません。

Part 4 説明文問題

形式：1人によるトークが1回だけ放送されます。トークはテスト冊子に印刷されていません。トークを聞いて、テスト冊子に印刷された設問（設問は放送もされます）と4つの選択肢を読み、設問の答えとして最も適切なものを選び、その記号を解答用紙にマークします。トークの中で聞いたことと、印刷された図などで見た情報を関連付けて解答する設問もあります（**G**参照）。1つのトークにつき、設問は3問ずつです。

問題数：30問（10トーク）
選択肢の数：4つ
問題間のポーズの長さ：約8秒
　※グラフィック問題（**G**参照）は約12秒

> 😎 Part 4のトークは実践的だと思う。公共施設で流れるアナウンスがたくさん登場するからね。慣れておくと、旅行や出張で外国に行ったときに必ず役に立つよ。サキは海外旅行には行く？
>
> 🙂 はい、家族と行きます。ただ、母が英語の先生なので頼りっぱなしですが。

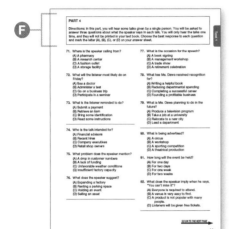

指示事項の後、Questions 71 through 73 refer to the following talk.（71番から73番の問題は、次のトークに関するものです）といった放送が流れます。これを合図に Part 4 が始まります。トークの後には、3つの設問だけが放送されます。

> 😎 Part 4の設問にも概要を問うタイプと詳細を問うタイプがある。Part 3と同じで、音声が放送される前に、設問に目を通すことができれば有利だよ。
>
> 😎 意図問題やグラフィック問題も出ますね。Part 3とPart 4はほとんど同じだと思います。
>
> 😎 確かに問題形式はほぼ同じ。好き嫌いは人によって違うみたいだけど。ダイはどっちが好き？
>
> 😐 どちらかと言えばPart 4です。話が一本道なので理解しやすい気がします。日本語であればもっといいんですが。
>
> 😎 おいおい。それを言っちゃいけない。

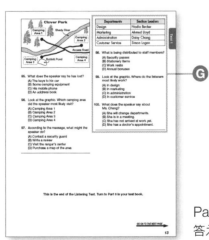

Part 4の最後の2～3セットは、図を見て答える設問が1問ずつ含まれます。

> 😎 Part 3もだけど、グラフィック問題は音声を聞くだけでは解けないように設計されている。図の中の情報と音声中の情報を関連付ける必要があるんだよ。
>
> 🙂 どれがそういう設問か見分けることはできますか。
>
> 😎 そのタイプは必ずLook at the graphic.で始まるから見つけるのは簡単だよ。

指示事項の内容

F **Part 4：**1人の人物によるトークが聞こえてきます。それぞれのトークの中で話し手が言っていることについて、3つの質問に答えるよう要求されます。それぞれの質問に対し、最も適切な答えを選び、解答用紙の (A)、(B)、(C) または (D) をマークしてください。トークはテスト冊子に印刷されておらず、1回しか話されません。

Reading Section

印刷された問題を読んで設問に解答します。Part 5からPart 7の3つのパートから構成されています。Part 4が終わると、「Part 5に進んでください」という放送があり、リーディングセクションの解答時間が始まります。リーディングセクションの指示事項は放送されません。

Part 5 短文穴埋め問題

形式：テスト冊子に空所を1つ含む英文が印刷されています。英文を完成させるために、空所に入れるべき最も適切な語句を4つの選択肢から選び、その記号を解答用紙にマークします。

問題数：30問
選択肢の数：4つ
時間配分の目安：10分以内

リーディングセクションでも指示事項の内容は常に同じです。問題の解き方を知っていれば本番で読む必要はありません。限られた時間の中でできるだけ多くの問題に解答できるよう、どんどん問題に取り組みましょう。

> 😊 Part 5では文法力を試す問題と、語彙力を試す問題がだいたい半々だよ。サキは文法が苦手だったね。
>
> 😊 はい。と言っても、語彙が得意なわけではありません。
>
> 😊 30問の中には、上級者と超上級者を区別するために出題されている難問もある。いくら悩んでも答えを急に思いつくことはないから、時間を浪費しないことが大切だよ。
>
> 😊 どれくらい時間をかけていいんですか。
>
> 😊 だいたいの目安として、Part 5では1問当たり20秒前後で処理することを目指そう。

> 😊 いったん試験が始まったら、文法と語彙の「知識」は増えない。だから、試験開始の時点で、その日にPart 5で稼げるスコアは決まっているんだよ。だけど、「読解」で勝負するPart 7は時間があればあるほど正解数を増やせる。
>
> 😊 なるほど。
>
> 😊 だから、なるべくPart 7に時間を投入したい。そのために、簡単に実行できる方法が1つある。ダイ、何だと思う？
>
> 😊 Part 5と6を捨てる。
>
> 😊 大胆だね（苦笑）
>
> 😊 Part 7を先にやるといいと思います。
>
> 😊 それだよ。Part 7は「読解」で勝負するんだから、時間をたくさん使う価値は高い。
>
> 😊 ということは、解く順番は自分で決めていいんですね。
>
> 😊 そう。自分にとってのベストな順番を知っておくことが大切ってことだよ。

指示事項の内容

Ⓗ リーディングテスト： リーディングテストでは、さまざまな文書を読んで、いくつかの異なるタイプの質問に答えます。リーディングテストは全体で75分続きます。3つのパートがあり、パートごとに指示が与えられます。時間の許す範囲でできるだけ多くの質問に答えてください。解答は解答用紙にマークしなければいけません。テスト冊子には解答を書き込まないでください。

Ⓘ Part 5： 以下の各文は不完全です。文を完成させるのに最も適切な語または語句を (A)、(B)、(C) または (D) から選び、解答用紙にマークしてください。

Part 6 長文穴埋め問題

形式：テスト冊子に、空所を4つ含む英語の文書が印刷されています。文書を完成させるために、空所に入れるべき最も適切な語句あるいは文を4つの選択肢から選び、その記号を解答用紙にマークします。

問題数：16問（4文書）
選択肢の数：4つ
時間配分の目安：10分以内

😀 Part 6の性質は基本的にはPart 5と同じで、文法力と語彙力が問われるけれど、違う点もある。ヤス、それは何？

😀 それくらい知っていますよ。文脈が必要な問題が多いんですよね。1文だけ読んでも解けません。

😀 ま、そうだね。Part 5のように空所を含む1文を読んだだけでは絶対に解けない問題がいくつか出る。

😀 でも、すぐに解ける問題もありますね。

😀 少しはね。Part 6は、Part 5とPart 7を足して2で割ったようなものだよ。

J

```
PART 6
Directions: Some of the following sentences are incomplete. Select the most appropriate word,
phrase, or sentence from the choices (A), (B), (C), and (D), and mark your answer on your answer
sheet.

Questions 131-134 refer to the following information.

                          Training

_____ their previous experience in the finance industry, all consultants are required to take part
   131.
in a two-week training course in New York. There, you _____ about the standards of conduct
                                                    132.
required of all Ogilvy and Horne employees. _____. Accommodation will be provided in a
                                        133.
company-owned apartment for _____ coming from outside New York. Please call chief organizer,
                        134.
Cobie Patel, if you would like to make your own arrangements.

131. (A) In addition to          133. (A) This is only necessary for people who
     (B) With respect for              have never worked in finance.
     (C) Regardless of               (B) The weeklong course is available for
     (D) Along with                       only $250 per person.
                                      (C) The course will be held in the first two
132. (A) learned                          weeks of February.
     (B) learning                     (D) It is necessary for trainees to find
     (C) were learning                    somewhere convenient to stay.
     (D) will learn
                                 134. (A) applicants
                                      (B) participants
                                      (C) judges
                                      (D) customers

                                                GO ON TO THE NEXT PAGE
                                                                    17
```

😀 Part 6も1問20秒で解くべきですか。

😀 いや、それは厳しい。4文書で計8分から10分を目安にすればいい。Part 5とPart 6を合わせると、だいたい20分が目標だよ。

😀 頭で分かっていても、なかなか実行できないんだよなぁ。

😀 試験中は20分が目標だけど、大事なのは試験を迎える前の勉強だよ。文法と語彙の知識を増やせば、必ず解答スピードが上がる。特に、この本に登場する全パートの語彙をきちんと覚えれば解答が格段に速くなるよ。

Part 6では1セットに1問、空所にふさわしい文を選ぶ問題が含まれます。

😀 あと、Part 6の特徴は文を選択する問題があることだね。

😀 私の苦手な問題です。

😀 1文書につき1問だけ出る。詳しいことはゼミの中で話す予定だけど、このタイプは後回しにするといいよ。

指示事項の内容

J **Part 6：** 以下の文書を読んでください。いくつかの文は不完全です。文書を完成させるのに最も適切な語、語句または文を (A)、(B)、(C) または (D) から選び、解答用紙にマークしてください。

Part 7 読解問題

形式：テスト冊子にメールや広告、記事、テキストメッセージやチャットなどの英語の文書、あるいは複数の文書のセット（**L**参照）と、2〜5問の設問・選択肢が印刷されています。文書を読み、各設問に対し最も適切な答えを4つの選択肢から選び、その記号を解答用紙にマークします。

問題数：54問
1文書を読む問題：29問（10文書）
複数文書を読む問題：25問
（2文書2組10問＋3文書3組15問）
選択肢の数：4つ
時間配分の目安：55分

😺 Part 7には23文書が出題されるけれど、本当にいろんな種類の文書がランダムに出題される。あまり規則性がないので、何がよく出るとか出ないとかを気にする必要はない。

😺 結局、正しく読めば解けるようになっているんですよね。

😺 もちろん。英語を読むことを習慣化できている人は、Part 7を厳しいとは思っていないよ。

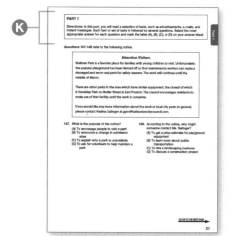

😺 仮に、Part 5とPart 6に20分を使うと、Part 7に使える時間は55分となる。もちろん、55分では足りない人もいるだろうけれど、当面の目標としてはPart 7に55分を投入することを目指そう。

1つの文書を読むセットでは、設問は1セットにつき2〜4問です。

😺 2問付きは簡単で4問付きは難しいみたいな傾向はあるんですか。

😺 緩やかな傾向としてはそう言えるよ。

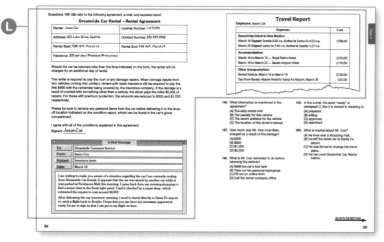

複数の文書を読むセットでは、設問は1セットにつき5問です。複数の文書を読まないと解けない問題もあるので注意が必要です。

😺 前回受けたときは、時間が足りなくて、Part 7の最後の25問が解けませんでした。

😺 複数の文書が出る「マルチプルパッセージ」の問題全部だね。

😺 複数の文書を読まないと解けない問題って難しそうです。

😺 易しい問題も難しい問題もある。試験本番では、Part 7でどれだけ時間を使えるかで勝負が決まる。でもダイとサキは短期間でPart 7を得意にする必要はないよ。まず、リスニングと文法を中心に学習して、基礎固めをしよう。

指示事項の内容

🄺 **Part 7：**このパートでは、広告、メール、そしてインスタントメッセージなど、さまざまな文書を読みます。それぞれの文書、あるいは文書のセットの後には、いくつかの質問が続きます。それぞれの質問に対し最も適切な答えを(A)、(B)、(C)または(D)から選び、解答用紙にマークしてください。

TOEIC® L&Rテスト模擬試験で測れる力、伸ばせる力

TOEIC L&Rテストでは200問を通して、受験者の英語での理解力を測っています。テスト結果や模擬試験を活用することで自分の弱点と伸ばすべきポイントが分かります。

問題タイプ一覧

本書では、TOEIC L&Rテストの「公式認定証」に記載されているAbilities Measured（項目別正答率）を参考に、各問題に「問題タイプ」のタグを付けました。それぞれの問題タイプが測る力は以下の通りです。

Listening Section

L1：短い会話、アナウンス、ナレーションなどの中で明確に述べられている情報をもとに要点、目的、基本的な文脈を推測できる（Part 1、2）

L2：長めの会話、アナウンス、ナレーションなどの中で明確に述べられている情報をもとに要点、目的、基本的な文脈を推測できる（Part 3、4）

L3：短い会話、アナウンス、ナレーションなどにおいて詳細が理解できる（Part 1、2）

L4：長めの会話、アナウンス、ナレーションなどにおいて詳細が理解できる（Part 3、4）

L5：フレーズや文から話し手の目的や暗示されている意味が理解できる（Part 2、3、4）

Reading Section

R1：文書の中の情報をもとに推測できる（Part 7）

R2：文書の中の具体的な情報を見つけて理解できる（Part 7）

R3：1つの文書中、または複数の文書間にちりばめられた情報を関連付けることができる（Part 6、7）

R4：語彙が理解できる（Part 5、6、7）

R5：文法が理解できる（Part 5、6）

※本書で記載している「問題タイプ」は、著者の推測によるもので、ETSが公式発表しているものではありません。
※L1〜L5、R1〜R5は便宜的な呼称です。

模擬試験を受験後、換算スコアだけでなく「問題タイプ別正答率」も算出しましょう。自分の弱点を把握し、弱点に合わせた学習を計画的に行えば、TOEIC L&Rテストのスコアアップや自分の英語の弱点克服に役立ちます。

> 🧑 基本的には1問に対してタグは1つだけど、2つ付く場合もある。
>
> 👧 そうなのですか。
>
> 🧑 L5に分類されているのは、Part 2の約10問と、Part 3とPart 4に出題されている意図問題の計5問なんだよ。だから、いずれもL1からL4のどこかに入っていて、同時にL5にも分類されている。
>
> 👧 へぇ、知らなかった。
>
> 🧑 リーディングについては、もっと複雑。例えば、Part 7に出る「文の入る位置を選ぶ問題」などには複数のタグが付くんだよ。

本書ご購入の特典として、アルクダウンロードセンター（https://portal-dlc.alc.co.jp/）より、下記のコンテンツを無料でダウンロードできます。

「ALCO for DLC」をご利用いただけば、スマートフォンまたはタブレットでご利用いただけます。

※ダウンロードセンターや「ALCO for DLC」について詳しくはp.10をご確認ください。

☐ 特典コンテンツ1：動画内容の音声（mp3）

Test 1～3の全問題の動画解説（p.11参照）から音声をmp3ファイルにして提供します。通勤・通学時などに音声だけで確認したい場合にご利用ください。

> 😮 え、動画があるだけでもすごいのに、動画の音声ももらえるんですか!
>
> 🙂 動画は便利だけど、視線を奪われるから音声だけの方が勉強しやすいかもしれないね。
>
> 😀 確かに。自分は車で通勤しているので、動画は使えないと思っていました。
>
> 🙂 じゃ、この特典は絶対に使ってね。

☐ 特典コンテンツ2：復習用音声（mp3）

以下のパートの復習用音声をmp3ファイルで提供します。リスニングセクションの会話を復習したい場合や、リーディングセクションの英文の音声を聞いて音読やシャドーイングをする場合などにご利用ください。

> 🙂 音読練習をしたり、ひたすらリスニングの練習をするには、この特典が役立つよ。

- **Test 1～3　Part 2**　質問または発言と正解応答のペア音声
- **Test 1～3　Part 3**　ロールプレイ用音声（話者1人の発話が消音されたもの）
- **Test 1～3　Part 5**　正解入り問題文音声
- **Test 1～3　Part 6**　正解入り問題文書音声
- **Test 1～3　Part 7**　問題文書音声

☐ 特典コンテンツ3：特製マークシート（pdf）

Test 1～4と予備のマークシートをpdf形式でダウンロードできます。Test 1～3はマークシートA（勘ボックスあり）が3枚、Test 4にはマークシートB（勘ボックスなし）が1枚、マークシートA、Bの予備が1枚ずつ、計12枚あります。

> 😆 この本以外の教材を使うときにも、このマークシートは使えるからたくさんコピーしておくといいね。

☐ 特典コンテンツ4：音声再生機能付き電子書籍（epub）

Test 1～3の解答・解説を電子書籍でも確認できます。解答・解説を読みながら電子書籍上で該当部分の問題の音声が再生できます。（本書購入者限定特典）

> 😊 電子版がもらえるのは助かります。
>
> 😯 持ち運ぶのに便利だよね。
>
> 🙂 しかも、音声を再生することもできるよ。
>
> 😮 これほど手厚い特典が付いた模試なんて、見たことないなぁ。
>
> 😀 同じく。

※このコンテンツの利用にはALCOのインストールが必須です。ALCO経由でダウンロードセンターにアクセスし、商品コード7019067でコンテンツを検索してください。epubダウンロード用ボタンをタップし、パスワードkk600plusを入力してコンテンツをダウンロードしてください。

※このepubファイルは固定レイアウトで作成されており、文字列のハイライトや、検索、辞書の参照、引用などの機能は使用できません。

Test 1
模擬試験 ①
解答と解説

お役立ちサイトやアプリのご案内

● ダウンロードセンター、ALCO：
模擬試験で使用した音声や復習用の音声をダウンロードできます。　　　　　（利用法は p.10、24）

● テスト採点センター：
簡単に答え合わせができます。（利用法は p.11）

● 動画センター：
全問題の解説が確認できます。（利用法は p.11）

※ QR コードを読み込む際は、他の QR コードを隠してカメラを向けてください。

記号について

【品詞を表す】
名 名詞　　動 動詞　　形 形容詞　　副 副詞
接 接続詞　　前 前置詞　　代 代名詞
※品詞が複数ある場合は、問題文での用法に合うものを1つ表示しています。

【ナレーターの性別や国籍を表す】
M: 男性ナレーター　　W: 女性ナレーター
■ アメリカ人　　■ カナダ人
■ イギリス人　　■ オーストラリア人

Test 1 成長記録シート

「3回チャレンジ法プラス」での正答数などの記録をつけて、成長を振り返りましょう。

1回目（勘を含む）

● 正答数

Part	正答数	
Part 1	／6	Listening 合計正答数
Part 2	／25	
Part 3	／39	
Part 4	／30	／100
Part 5	／30	Reading 合計正答数
Part 6	／16	
Part 7	／54	／100

● 換算スコアA

Listening _____
Reading _____
合 計 _____

● 問題タイプ別正答数と正答率

Listening Section

	正答数	正答数	正答率
L1：	／16	(_____ ÷16)×100 = _____ %
L2：	／21	(_____ ÷21)×100 = _____ %
L3：	／15	(_____ ÷15)×100 = _____ %
L4：	／48	(_____ ÷48)×100 = _____ %
L5：	／15	(_____ ÷15)×100 = _____ %

Reading Section

	正答数	正答数	正答率
R1：	／23	(_____ ÷23)×100 = _____ %
R2：	／15	(_____ ÷15)×100 = _____ %
R3：	／34	(_____ ÷34)×100 = _____ %
R4：	／24	(_____ ÷24)×100 = _____ %
R5：	／20	(_____ ÷20)×100 = _____ %

年 月 日

1回目（勘を除く）

● 正答数

Part	正答数	
Part 1	／6	Listening 合計正答数
Part 2	／25	
Part 3	／39	
Part 4	／30	／100
Part 5	／30	Reading 合計正答数
Part 6	／16	
Part 7	／54	／100

● 換算スコアB

Listening _____
Reading _____
合 計 _____

● 問題タイプ別正答数と正答率

Listening Section

	正答数	正答数	正答率
L1：	／16	(_____ ÷16)×100 = _____ %
L2：	／21	(_____ ÷21)×100 = _____ %
L3：	／15	(_____ ÷15)×100 = _____ %
L4：	／48	(_____ ÷48)×100 = _____ %
L5：	／15	(_____ ÷15)×100 = _____ %

Reading Section

	正答数	正答数	正答率
R1：	／23	(_____ ÷23)×100 = _____ %
R2：	／15	(_____ ÷15)×100 = _____ %
R3：	／34	(_____ ÷34)×100 = _____ %
R4：	／24	(_____ ÷24)×100 = _____ %
R5：	／20	(_____ ÷20)×100 = _____ %

年 月 日

2回目（勘を含む）

● 正答数

Part	正答数	
Part 1	／6	Listening 合計正答数
Part 2	／25	
Part 3	／39	
Part 4	／30	／100
Part 5	／30	Reading 合計正答数
Part 6	／16	
Part 7	／54	／100

● 換算スコアA

Listening _____
Reading _____
合 計 _____

● 問題タイプ別正答数と正答率

Listening Section

	正答数	正答数	正答率
L1：	／16	(_____ ÷16)×100 = _____ %
L2：	／21	(_____ ÷21)×100 = _____ %
L3：	／15	(_____ ÷15)×100 = _____ %
L4：	／48	(_____ ÷48)×100 = _____ %
L5：	／15	(_____ ÷15)×100 = _____ %

Reading Section

	正答数	正答数	正答率
R1：	／23	(_____ ÷23)×100 = _____ %
R2：	／15	(_____ ÷15)×100 = _____ %
R3：	／34	(_____ ÷34)×100 = _____ %
R4：	／24	(_____ ÷24)×100 = _____ %
R5：	／20	(_____ ÷20)×100 = _____ %

年 月 日

2回目（勘を除く）

● 正答数

Part	正答数	
Part 1	／6	Listening 合計正答数
Part 2	／25	
Part 3	／39	
Part 4	／30	／100
Part 5	／30	Reading 合計正答数
Part 6	／16	
Part 7	／54	／100

● 換算スコアB

Listening _____
Reading _____
合 計 _____

● 問題タイプ別正答数と正答率

Listening Section

	正答数	正答数	正答率
L1：	／16	(_____ ÷16)×100 = _____ %
L2：	／21	(_____ ÷21)×100 = _____ %
L3：	／15	(_____ ÷15)×100 = _____ %
L4：	／48	(_____ ÷48)×100 = _____ %
L5：	／15	(_____ ÷15)×100 = _____ %

Reading Section

	正答数	正答数	正答率
R1：	／23	(_____ ÷23)×100 = _____ %
R2：	／15	(_____ ÷15)×100 = _____ %
R3：	／34	(_____ ÷34)×100 = _____ %
R4：	／24	(_____ ÷24)×100 = _____ %
R5：	／20	(_____ ÷20)×100 = _____ %

年 月 日

3回目（勘を含む）

● 正答数

Part	正答数		
Part 1	／6	Listening 合計正答数	
Part 2	／25		
Part 3	／39		
Part 4	／30		／100
Part 5	／30	Reading 合計正答数	
Part 6	／16		
Part 7	／54		／100

● 換算スコアA

Listening ＿＿＿＿＿

Reading ＿＿＿＿＿

合　計 ＿＿＿＿＿

● 問題タイプ別正答数と正答率

Listening Section

	正答数		正答数		正答率
L1：	＿＿＿／16	（＿＿＿	÷16）×100＝	＿＿＿	％
L2：	＿＿＿／21	（＿＿＿	÷21）×100＝	＿＿＿	％
L3：	＿＿＿／15	（＿＿＿	÷15）×100＝	＿＿＿	％
L4：	＿＿＿／48	（＿＿＿	÷48）×100＝	＿＿＿	％
L5：	＿＿＿／15	（＿＿＿	÷15）×100＝	＿＿＿	％

Reading Section

	正答数		正答数		正答率
R1：	＿＿＿／23	（＿＿＿	÷23）×100＝	＿＿＿	％
R2：	＿＿＿／15	（＿＿＿	÷15）×100＝	＿＿＿	％
R3：	＿＿＿／34	（＿＿＿	÷34）×100＝	＿＿＿	％
R4：	＿＿＿／24	（＿＿＿	÷24）×100＝	＿＿＿	％
R5：	＿＿＿／20	（＿＿＿	÷20）×100＝	＿＿＿	％

年　月　日

3回目（勘を除く）

● 正答数

Part	正答数		
Part 1	／6	Listening 合計正答数	
Part 2	／25		
Part 3	／39		
Part 4	／30		／100
Part 5	／30	Reading 合計正答数	
Part 6	／16		
Part 7	／54		／100

● 換算スコアB

Listening ＿＿＿＿＿

Reading ＿＿＿＿＿

合　計 ＿＿＿＿＿

● 問題タイプ別正答数と正答率

Listening Section

	正答数		正答数		正答率
L1：	＿＿＿／16	（＿＿＿	÷16）×100＝	＿＿＿	％
L2：	＿＿＿／21	（＿＿＿	÷21）×100＝	＿＿＿	％
L3：	＿＿＿／15	（＿＿＿	÷15）×100＝	＿＿＿	％
L4：	＿＿＿／48	（＿＿＿	÷48）×100＝	＿＿＿	％
L5：	＿＿＿／15	（＿＿＿	÷15）×100＝	＿＿＿	％

Reading Section

	正答数		正答数		正答率
R1：	＿＿＿／23	（＿＿＿	÷23）×100＝	＿＿＿	％
R2：	＿＿＿／15	（＿＿＿	÷15）×100＝	＿＿＿	％
R3：	＿＿＿／34	（＿＿＿	÷34）×100＝	＿＿＿	％
R4：	＿＿＿／24	（＿＿＿	÷24）×100＝	＿＿＿	％
R5：	＿＿＿／20	（＿＿＿	÷20）×100＝	＿＿＿	％

年　月　日

弱点問題タイプ診断

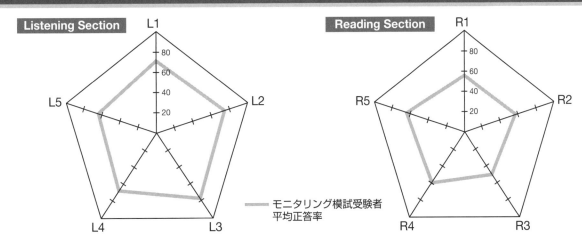

モニタリング模試受験者 平均正答率

参考資料：モニタリング模試実施データ

p.31に掲載された「スコア換算表」を作成するために、TOEIC L&Rテストの公式スコア保持者409名を対象に、Test 1と同じ問題を使用した模擬試験を実施しました。以下はその結果をまとめたものです。

	公式スコア平均	正答数平均	最低正答数	最高正答数	初級者レベル正答数	上級者レベル正答数
Listening	360.2	71.1	41	99	61問以下	80問以上
Reading	295.5	56.8	24	96	46問以下	66問以上

※表中の数字はモニタリング模試受験者409名のうち正常に受験したと認められたモニターの数値を基に算出しています。

※モニタリング模試受験者のうち、Listening Section、Reading Sectionそれぞれにおいて、正答数が少なかった25％を「初級者レベル」、多かった25％を「上級者レベル」と呼んでいます。

Test 1 解答＆問題タイプ一覧

答え合わせの手順

1. 正解を確認し、一覧表に正誤を記入する
自分の解答済のマークシートと解答一覧を突き合わせ、解答一覧内に正誤（○×）を記入しましょう。①～③は3回チャレンジ法プラス（p.12～参照）の1回目～3回目を表します。勘ボックスを利用した場合、勘ボックスの✔も転記します。

2. 間違えた問題の問題タイプ欄にチェックを入れる
間違えた問題もしくは正答したが勘ボックスに✔がある問題の「問題タイプ」欄に✔を記入します。

3. パートごとの正答数・問題タイプごとの正答数を数え、「成長記録シート」に記入する
パートごとの正答数（正誤欄の○の数）と勘を除く正答数（○の数―✔の付いた数）を数え、その数をp.26～の「成長記録シート」に記入しましょう。

4. 予想スコアと弱点問題タイプを算出する
p.31のスコア換算表を参照して実際のTOEIC L&Rテストでの予想スコアを算出し、「成長記録シート」に記入しましょう。また、問題タイプごとに誤答数（「問題タイプ」欄の✔の数）を転記し、正答率を算出して弱点問題タイプ／パートを把握しましょう。

Listing Section

問題番号	正解	問題タイプ
Part 1		
1	C	L3
2	A	L1
3	B	L3
4	D	L1
5	D	L1
6	C	L3
Part 2		
7	B	L3
8	A	L1
9	B	L3
10	C	L1、L5
11	B	L1
12	B	L3
13	C	L3
14	C	L1、L5
15	B	L3
16	A	L3
17	C	L3
18	A	L1、L5
19	A	L1、L5
20	C	L1、L5
21	A	L3
22	C	L3
23	B	L1、L5
24	A	L3
25	B	L3
26	C	L1、L5
27	B	L1、L5
28	B	L1、L5
29	C	L1
30	A	L3
31	A	L1、L5
Part 3		
32	C	L2
33	B	L4
34	A	L4
35	C	L4
36	A	L4
37	D	L2
38	C	L2
39	B	L4
40	C	L4
41	D	L2
42	A	L2、L5
43	D	L4
44	B	L2
45	A	L4
46	D	L4
47	D	L4
48	C	L4
49	A	L4
50	A	L2

問題番号	正解	問題タイプ
51	B	L4
52	C	L4
53	C	L4
54	B	L2、L5
55	C	L4
56	B	L2
57	A	L4
58	D	L4
59	B	L2
60	D	L4
61	B	L4
62	C	L4
63	C	L4
64	A	L4
65	A	L2
66	B	L4
67	D	L4
68	C	L2
69	B	L4
70	D	L4
Part 4		
71	A	L2
72	C	L4
73	C	L4
74	C	L2
75	B	L4
76	D	L4
77	B	L2
78	A	L4
79	D	L4
80	A	L2
81	C	L4
82	B	L2、L5
83	D	L2
84	B	L4
85	D	L4
86	A	L2
87	B	L4
88	A	L2、L5
89	C	L4
90	A	L4
91	D	L4
92	D	L2
93	B	L2、L5
94	A	L4
95	C	L4
96	A	L4
97	C	L4
98	A	L4
99	D	L4
100	B	L4

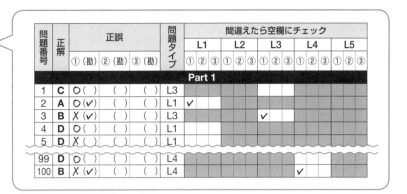

記入例

問題番号	正解	正誤 ①(勘) ②(勘) ③(勘)	問題タイプ	間違えたら空欄にチェック L1 ①②③	L2 ①②③	L3 ①②③	L4 ①②③	L5 ①②③
Part 1								
1	C	○( ) ( ) ( )	L3					
2	A	○(✓) ( ) ( )	L1	✓				
3	B	✗(✓) ( ) ( )	L3			✓		
4	D	○( ) ( ) ( )	L1					
5	D	✗( ) ( ) ( )	L1					
99	D	○( ) ( ) ( )	L4					
100	B	✗(✓) ( ) ( )	L4				✓	

Reading Section

問題番号	正解	正誤 ①(勘) ②(勘) ③(勘)	問題タイプ	R1	R2	R3	R4	R5
Part 5								
101	A	( ) ( ) ( )	R5					
102	B	( ) ( ) ( )	R4					
103	D	( ) ( ) ( )	R5					
104	B	( ) ( ) ( )	R4					
105	C	( ) ( ) ( )	R5					
106	B	( ) ( ) ( )	R4					
107	D	( ) ( ) ( )	R5					
108	B	( ) ( ) ( )	R4					
109	C	( ) ( ) ( )	R5					
110	A	( ) ( ) ( )	R4					
111	C	( ) ( ) ( )	R5					
112	A	( ) ( ) ( )	R4					
113	B	( ) ( ) ( )	R5					
114	B	( ) ( ) ( )	R4					
115	D	( ) ( ) ( )	R5					
116	D	( ) ( ) ( )	R5					
117	A	( ) ( ) ( )	R4					
118	C	( ) ( ) ( )	R4					
119	D	( ) ( ) ( )	R5					
120	A	( ) ( ) ( )	R4					
121	C	( ) ( ) ( )	R5					
122	B	( ) ( ) ( )	R4					
123	D	( ) ( ) ( )	R5					
124	D	( ) ( ) ( )	R4					
125	C	( ) ( ) ( )	R5					
126	D	( ) ( ) ( )	R4					
127	A	( ) ( ) ( )	R4					
128	B	( ) ( ) ( )	R4					
129	A	( ) ( ) ( )	R5					
130	C	( ) ( ) ( )	R5					
Part 6								
131	C	( ) ( ) ( )	R4					
132	D	( ) ( ) ( )	R3,R5					
133	C	( ) ( ) ( )	R3					
134	B	( ) ( ) ( )	R3,R4					
135	A	( ) ( ) ( )	R3,R5					
136	B	( ) ( ) ( )	R3					
137	A	( ) ( ) ( )	R3,R4					
138	D	( ) ( ) ( )	R3,R4					
139	A	( ) ( ) ( )	R3					
140	B	( ) ( ) ( )	R5					
141	D	( ) ( ) ( )	R3,R4					
142	A	( ) ( ) ( )	R3,R4					
143	C	( ) ( ) ( )	R3,R5					
144	B	( ) ( ) ( )	R3,R4					
145	D	( ) ( ) ( )	R3					
146	C	( ) ( ) ( )	R5					
Part 7								
147	C	( ) ( ) ( )	R1					
148	D	( ) ( ) ( )	R3					
149	C	( ) ( ) ( )	R1					
150	D	( ) ( ) ( )	R2					
151	B	( ) ( ) ( )	R1					
152	D	( ) ( ) ( )	R1,R3					
153	B	( ) ( ) ( )	R2					
154	A	( ) ( ) ( )	R2					
155	C	( ) ( ) ( )	R3					
156	A	( ) ( ) ( )	R1					
157	D	( ) ( ) ( )	R2					
158	B	( ) ( ) ( )	R1					
159	D	( ) ( ) ( )	R2					
160	D	( ) ( ) ( )	R3					
161	B	( ) ( ) ( )	R1,R3					
162	D	( ) ( ) ( )	R1					
163	A	( ) ( ) ( )	R3					
164	D	( ) ( ) ( )	R2					
165	A	( ) ( ) ( )	R1					
166	B	( ) ( ) ( )	R2					
167	A	( ) ( ) ( )	R1,R3					
168	A	( ) ( ) ( )	R2					
169	B	( ) ( ) ( )	R2					
170	C	( ) ( ) ( )	R3					
171	D	( ) ( ) ( )	R3					
172	A	( ) ( ) ( )	R1					
173	D	( ) ( ) ( )	R2					
174	C	( ) ( ) ( )	R1					
175	B	( ) ( ) ( )	R1,R3					
176	C	( ) ( ) ( )	R2					
177	D	( ) ( ) ( )	R1					
178	A	( ) ( ) ( )	R3					
179	C	( ) ( ) ( )	R3					
180	C	( ) ( ) ( )	R1					
181	B	( ) ( ) ( )	R1					
182	A	( ) ( ) ( )	R3					
183	D	( ) ( ) ( )	R1,R3					
184	A	( ) ( ) ( )	R2					
185	B	( ) ( ) ( )	R1					
186	B	( ) ( ) ( )	R2					
187	A	( ) ( ) ( )	R3					
188	B	( ) ( ) ( )	R2					
189	A	( ) ( ) ( )	R4					
190	C	( ) ( ) ( )	R1,R3					
191	B	( ) ( ) ( )	R1					
192	C	( ) ( ) ( )	R1					
193	A	( ) ( ) ( )	R3					
194	C	( ) ( ) ( )	R2					
195	D	( ) ( ) ( )	R1,R3					
196	B	( ) ( ) ( )	R3					
197	A	( ) ( ) ( )	R1					
198	C	( ) ( ) ( )	R3					
199	C	( ) ( ) ( )	R4					
200	D	( ) ( ) ( )	R3					

Test 1 マークシート状解答一覧

READING SECTION

Part 5		Part 6		Part 7	

Part 5 — No. 101–130 (ANSWER A B C D)

Part 6 — No. 131–140 (ANSWER A B C D)

Part 7 — No. 141–200 (ANSWER A B C D)

LISTENING SECTION

Part 1 — No. 1–10 (ANSWER A B C D)

Part 2 — No. 11–40 (ANSWER A B C)

Part 3 — No. 41–70 (ANSWER A B C D)

Part 4 — No. 71–100 (ANSWER A B C D)

協力：アルク教育総合研究所

Listening Section

正答数	換算スコア	正答数	換算スコア
0	5	51	285
1	5	52	290
2	5	53	295
3	5	54	295
4	5	55	300
5	5	56	305
6	10	57	305
7	15	58	310
8	25	59	310
9	30	60	315
10	40	61	320
11	45	62	330
12	50	63	335
13	60	64	340
14	65	65	345
15	70	66	345
16	80	67	350
17	85	68	355
18	90	69	360
19	100	70	365
20	105	71	370
21	115	72	375
22	120	73	380
23	130	74	385
24	135	75	390
25	140	76	400
26	150	77	405
27	155	78	415
28	165	79	420
29	170	80	425
30	175	81	435
31	180	82	440
32	190	83	450
33	200	84	455
34	205	85	460
35	210	86	465
36	220	87	470
37	225	88	470
38	235	89	475
39	240	90	475
40	245	91	480
41	245	92	480
42	250	93	485
43	255	94	485
44	260	95	490
45	265	96	490
46	270	97	495
47	270	98	495
48	275	99	495
49	275	100	495
50	280		

Reading Section

正答数	換算スコア	正答数	換算スコア
0	5	51	255
1	5	52	265
2	5	53	270
3	5	54	275
4	5	55	285
5	5	56	290
6	5	57	295
7	5	58	305
8	10	59	310
9	20	60	320
10	25	61	325
11	30	62	330
12	40	63	340
13	45	64	345
14	55	65	355
15	60	66	360
16	65	67	365
17	75	68	370
18	80	69	375
19	85	70	380
20	95	71	385
21	100	72	390
22	100	73	390
23	105	74	395
24	110	75	400
25	120	76	405
26	125	77	410
27	130	78	415
28	135	79	420
29	135	80	425
30	140	81	430
31	140	82	435
32	145	83	440
33	150	84	445
34	155	85	450
35	160	86	455
36	165	87	455
37	170	88	460
38	175	89	465
39	175	90	470
40	180	91	475
41	190	92	480
42	195	93	485
43	200	94	490
44	210	95	495
45	215	96	495
46	220	97	495
47	230	98	495
48	235	99	495
49	245	100	495
50	250		

結果活用アドバイス

本書に登場するマイ、ヤス、ダイ、サキの4人の「換算スコアA」を例に「弱点問題タイプ診断」の活用法をご紹介します。自分に最も近い人物の診断を参考に、今後の学習に役立ててください。

Listening Section

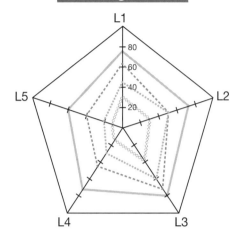

Reading Section

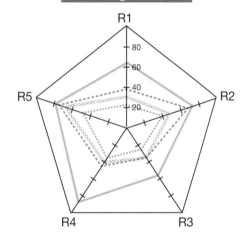

換算スコア

		Listening	Reading	合計
——	マイ	385	390	775
-----	ヤス	295	250	545
∿∿∿	ダイ	150	195	345
⋯⋯⋯	サキ	245	155	400

では、マイから始めよう。マイは英語の運用力を高めていきたいんだよね。だったら、Part 1と2は無視して、Part 3と4に絞って練習すればいい。今回は19問も落としたけれど、これを5問ミスまで減らせるようリスニング力を鍛えていこう。

はい。本当にPart 2を無視していいのですか。

大丈夫。Part 3と4を使って練習すれば、Part 2も自動的に伸びる。リーディングで得意なのはどこ?

Part 7は、時間さえあれば正答率を上げることができると思います。今回は後半でかなり急いだのでミスが多かったです。

じゃ、Part 7を先に解いたらどうかな。それだけで良い結果が出るかもしれないよ。

マークミスしそうで怖いですが、練習してみます。

次は、ヤス。Part 3で25問正答したのに、Part 4では8問だけ? 途中で失神したの?

寝落ちしそうになってました。集中力が続かなくて……。

宿題を出す。Test 1のPart 4を、音声を真似するように音読して。毎日1トークを10回。今日から始めて毎日スマホに録音してLINEで送ってね。きちんとやれば絶対にL2とL4が上がるから。

厳しいなぁ。でも、頑張りヤス。

次はダイ。リスニングが壊滅的だね。Part 2とPart 3の音声を、スクリプトを見ながら聞きまくって。英語を頭から理解する練習にもなる。あと、Part 5の英文をよく見て、単語の品詞と、単語が並んでいる順番をしっかり意識して何度も読んでみて。英語のルールが見えてくるから。できれば、この本の特典音声を聞きながらやってみて。

了解です。

サキも英語の基礎から学び直す必要があるから、ダイと同じようにPart 5を読み込んで。あの30問については誰よりも詳しいと思えるようになるまで、しっかり読み込んでほしい。まずは、それだけでいいよ。

単語も覚えるべきですよね。

そう。ただし、「単語と訳」を丸暗記するより、問題文を見て、その文の意味を言えるかどうかを大事にして。

Part 7を解く時間が全然足りなかったんですが……。

何もしなくていい。Part 7は、英文の集まりだよね。だから、まず、1つ1つの英文を正確に読む練習をしなきゃ。Part 7に特化した勉強は後回しでいい。

分かりました。

では、みんな、それぞれTest 1の復習をきっちりやってね。問題を「解く」ことから離れて、「素材を体内に吸収する」という意識で取り組むことを忘れずに。いいね。

解説を確認し、間違えた問題は二度と間違えないようにきっちり復習しましょう。

Part 1 写真描写問題

1. DL ↓002 🇨🇦 正解：**C** 易▰▰▰▱▱▱▱▱▱難 選択率：(A) 7.9% (B) 6.0% **(C) 85.4%** (D) 0.7%

(A) He's reaching for a jacket.
(B) He's assembling a machine.
(C) He's seated at a table.
(D) He's drinking from a cup.

☐ reach for ～：～に手を伸ばす
☐ assemble：動 ～を組み立てる
☐ be seated at ～：～に座る
☐ drink from ～：～から飲む

(A) 彼は上着に手を伸ばしています。
(B) 彼は機械を組み立てています。
(C) 彼はテーブルに座っています。
(D) 彼はカップから飲んでいます。

▶解説 男性が席に着いている様子をseated at a table（テーブルに座っている）と描写した(C)が正解です。(A)のjacket（上着）や(D)のcup（カップ）は写真にありますが、それぞれの選択肢の動詞が男性の動作と異なります。男性の正面にあるパソコンをmachine（機械）と表現することは可能ですが、組み立て中ではないため、(B)は不正解です。

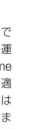

2. DL ↓003 🇬🇧 正解：**A** 易▰▰▱▱▱▱▱▱▱難 選択率：**(A) 91.4%** (B) 6.0% (C) 1.0% (D) 1.7%

(A) A woman is transporting some tools.
(B) A woman is removing a brush.
(C) A woman is reflected in a mirror.
(D) A woman is emptying a bucket.

☐ transport：動 ～を運ぶ、輸送する
☐ tool：名 道具
☐ remove：動 ～を移動させる
☐ reflect：動 ～を映す
☐ mirror：名 鏡
☐ empty：動 ～を空にする
☐ bucket：名 バケツ

(A) 女性がいくつかの道具を運んでいます。
(B) 女性がブラシを移動させています。
(C) 女性が鏡に映っています。
(D) 女性がバケツを空にしています。

▶解説 女性の動作を表す語句がポイントです。女性は道具の乗ったカートを押して運んでいるので、(A)のtransporting some tools（いくつかの道具を運んでいる）が適切に写真を描写しています。カートにはbrush（ブラシ）やbucket（バケツ）が積まれていますが、女性はどちらも扱っていません。また、窓が鏡のように見えるかもしれませんが、女性の姿は映っていないため(C)も不適切です。

(((📻))) ゼミ生中継　　😀Hiro 😊Mai 😎Yasu 😆Dai 😀Saki

😀 お疲れ。では、Part 1から振り返ろう。易しめのパートだけど、全てが楽勝というわけではない。絶対になめちゃいけないよ。

1.
😀 Part 1の学習で特に大切なのは何だと思う？　不正解の選択肢をチェックすることだよ。マイ、どうしてだと思う？

😊 不正解にも大事な単語が入っているからでしょうか。

😀 そう。Part 1の英文は短いから、不正解の選択肢が、そのまま本番で正解として出題されることがある。特に、この本みたいな良い模試を使うとそうなる。

😆 なるほど。

😀 (D)を見て。He's drinking from a cup. だよね。このdrinkとfromの組み合わせは本番に出るよ。似た例として、本を読んでいる人をHe's reading from a book. と描写することもできる。

2.
😆 この人、男だと思ってたのに、womanが聞こえてきて驚きました。

😎 私もです。男女を区別できないといけないんですか。

😀 いや、それは考えなくていい。写真に1人しか写っていなければ、選択肢の中でwomanとmanが混ざることはない。

Part 1 写真描写問題

3. 🔽005 🇺🇸 正解：**B** 易▰▰▰▱▱難 選択率：(A) 4.6% **(B) 63.9%** (C) 13.2% (D) 18.2%

(A) They're waiting in line.
(B) They're looking in different directions.
(C) One of the men is stacking chairs.
(D) One of the men is taking off his cap.

- ☐ wait: 動 待つ
- ☐ in line: 列で、列になって
- ☐ different: 形 異なった、別の
- ☐ direction: 名 方向、向き
- ☐ one of the 〜: 〜の1人
- ☐ stack: 動 〜を積み重ねる
- ☐ take off 〜: 〜を取る、外す
- ☐ cap: 名 帽子

(A) 彼らは列になって待っています。
(B) 彼らは異なる方向を見ています。
(C) 男性の1人が椅子を積み重ねています。
(D) 男性の1人が帽子を脱いでいます。

▶解説 写真に写っている人物の位置関係に注目しましょう。男性2人の様子を looking in different directions（異なる方向を見ている）と描写した(B)が正解です。2人は椅子に座っており、列に並んでいる様子ではないため(A)は不正解です。椅子を積み重ねている人はいないので、(C)は間違っています。1人は帽子をかぶっていますが、脱いでいるところではないため、(D)の taking off his cap（帽子を脱いでいる）も不適切です。

---

4. 🔽006 🇬🇧 正解：**D** 易▰▱▱▱▱難 選択率：(A) 1.7% (B) 0.3% (C) 0.3% **(D) 97.7%**

(A) Some trees are being trimmed.
(B) A janitor is watering some plants.
(C) Flowers have been arranged in pots.
(D) Two people are resting on a bench.

- ☐ trim: 動 〜を刈り込む、手入れする
- ☐ janitor: 名 管理人、用務員
- ☐ water: 動 〜に水をやる、水をまく
- ☐ plant: 名 植物
- ☐ arrange: 動 〜を配置する
- ☐ pot: 名 鉢
- ☐ rest: 動 休憩する、休む

(A) 何本かの木が手入れされています。
(B) 管理人が植物に水をやっています。
(C) 花が鉢に配置されています。
(D) 2人の人物がベンチで休んでいます。

▶解説 写真に写っている2人がベンチに座っている様子は「休憩している」と判断できるので、resting on a bench（ベンチで休んでいる）と表現した(D)が正解です。Part 1 では、このように人物の様子から具体的な動作を推測して描写することもありますので気を付けましょう。(A)と(B)はそれぞれの動詞が示す動作を行っている人物がいないため不正解です。

((📡)) 🔺 ゼミ 🔴中継　　　　　　　　　　(👓)Hiro (😊)Mai (😎)Yasu (😆)Dai (😊)Saki

3.

(😎) 意外と正答率が低いね。

(😆) この人たちはお互いを見ているので、They're facing each other.（彼らはお互いに向かい合っている）を予測していました。ですので、different directions を聞いて迷いました。

(😎) どっちでもいい。互いを見ているということは、確実に異なる方向を見ているのだから、looking in different directions は正しい描写だよ。

(😊) (C)の stacking chairs が sitting in chairs に聞こえて迷っちゃった。

(😎) 重ねて収納できる椅子のことを日本語でスタッキングチェアって言うよね。「スタッキング」はこの stacking だよ。

(😆) 自分は(D)が正解だと思いました。帽子をかぶっていない人がいるので。

(👓) (D)は現在進行形だから、帽子を「今まさに脱ごうとしている」という意味だよ。

4.

(😎) 2人しか写っていない場合は、このように Two people が主語になることがある。Some people が普通だけどね。

(😊) (B)の janitor を知らなくて微妙にパニクりました。

(😆) 同じく。

(😎) janitor は用務員とか管理人のことだよ。この本の後半にも出てくるから覚えておいてね。

(😊) あ〜、janitor ってこういう人ですか。見たことあります。

(😎) お、スマホで画像検索したのか。いいね。

5. DL 007 🇨🇦 正解：**D**　易 ▉▉▉▁▁▁▁ 難　　選択率：(A) 1.7%　(B) 0.3%　(C) 2.3%　**(D) 95.7%**

(A) An aircraft is being followed by a van.
(B) A worker is wiping some windows.
(C) Some passengers are checking in their baggage.
(D) Some people are boarding a flight.

☐ aircraft: 名 飛行機
☐ follow: 動 〜を追う
☐ van: 名 バン（商品運搬用の小型トラック、ワゴン車）
☐ worker: 名 労働者
☐ wipe: 動 〜を拭く
☐ passenger: 名 乗客
☐ check in 〜: （搭乗手続きをして）機内に〜を預ける
☐ baggage: 名 手荷物
☐ board: 動 （飛行機、列車など）に乗り込む

(A) 飛行機が小型トラックに付いてこられています。
(B) 労働者が窓を拭いています。
(C) 何人かの乗客が手荷物を預けています。
(D) 何人かの人々が飛行機に搭乗しています。

▶解説 乗客と思われる人々が飛行機に搭乗している様子を boarding a flight（飛行機に搭乗している）と描写した(D)が正解です。不正解の選択肢には、空港に関連した語句が多く登場していますが、飛行機の後ろにvan（小型トラック）はありませんし、窓を拭いている人物も存在しません。また、乗客が手荷物を預けている場面でもないため、これらは全て不適切な描写です。

---

6. DL 008 🇬🇧 正解：**C**　易 ▁▉▉▉▉▁▁ 難　　選択率：(A) 6.6%　(B) 0.7%　**(C) 59.6%**　(D) 32.8%

(A) Silverware has been set for diners.
(B) Some doors are being held open.
(C) A lounge is being illuminated by lights.
(D) A wooden floor is being swept clean.

☐ silverware: 名 銀器
☐ set: 動 〜を置く
☐ diner: 名 食事をする人、ディナーの客
☐ hold 〜 open: 〜を開け放しにする
☐ lounge: 名 ラウンジ、休憩室、待合室
☐ illuminate: 動 〜を照らす
☐ wooden: 形 木製の、木の
☐ floor: 名 床
☐ sweep: 動 〜を掃除する、掃く　＊swept は過去分詞
☐ clean: 副 きれいになるように

(A) 銀器が食事用にセットされています。
(B) いくつかのドアが開かれています。
(C) ラウンジがライトで照らされています。
(D) 木の床がきれいに掃除されています。

▶解説 写真に写っている物の状態がポイントです。正解は、この空間（ラウンジ）がライトで照らされている様子を being illuminatedと描写した(C)です。テーブルの上に silverware（銀器 [ナイフやフォークなどのこと]）は存在しないため(A)は不正解です。写真にドアは写っていますが、閉じられた状態なので(B)の描写と異なります。また、床を掃除している人もいないため(D)の描写も不適切です。

🗼 ゼミ 生 中継　　😀Hiro 😊Mai 😺Yasu 😎Dai 😆Saki

5.
😀 (D)にあるboardは名詞としても使える。ダイ、意味は何？
😎 ホワイトボードのボードですか。
😀 そう、「板」だね。ただ、TOEICに「板」はあまり出題されない。それより、board meeting の方が大事だよ。取締役会のこと。
😺 Part 4 のトークに出ていました。
😀 よく覚えているね。あと、この本のどこかに commence boarding という表現も登場する。意味を知らなければ調べておくといいことが起きるよ。

6.
😀 これは少し難しかったかな。サキ、どう？
😆 (D)を選びました。床が clean とはっきり聞こえた気がして。
😀 A wooden floor is being swept clean. だね。どこがダメか分かる？
😆 えっと、swept って……何でしたっけ。
😀 そこだよ。being swept は「今まさに掃除中」だからダメなんだよ。

TOEICよろず相談所　ヒロの部屋

①オーストラリアの発音が苦手です

あのー、オーストラリアの発音が苦手なんですが、何か対策はありますか。

まず、英語学習の目的を教えていただけますか。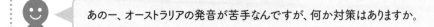

今は大学3年で、もうすぐ就職活動が始まります。とりあえず700点を取るのが目標です。今は580点です。

分かりました。TOEICのスコアを上げることがゴールであれば、公式教材を使ってください。持っていますか?

はい。テストが2つ入っているやつを持っています。

それでOKです。**公式教材に登場するナレーターと、試験本番に登場するナレーターはかなり重複しますよ。**

大学の先生に相談したら、YouTubeにオーストラリアのニュース放送とかがあるから、そういうのを聞けばいいと言っていました。

スコアアップを優先するなら、「オーストラリア人の発音」に慣れることより「TOEICに登場するオーストラリア人ナレーターの発音」に慣れることの方が大事ですよ。なので、公式教材の音声を使うことをお勧めします。

分かりました。

ただし、大事なのは1回聞いて内容を理解するリスニング力を養うことですよね。単に「慣れる」ことは目的ではありません。ですから、①聞いて書き起こす　②聞いて口頭でリピートする　といった積極的な学習をメインにしてください。その方が、効果が大きいはずです。

はい。ありがとうございました。

Part 2 応答問題

7. DL 011 🇬🇧🇨🇦　正解：**B**　易■■■□□□□難　選択率：(A) 6.0%　**(B) 82.1%**　(C) 11.6%

Where did you leave the keys for the cabinet?
(A) To do some research.
(B) On your desk.
(C) I lived there before.

□ leave: 動 ～を置く　□ cabinet: 名 キャビネット
□ research: 名 研究、学術調査　□ before: 副 以前に

キャビネットの鍵をどこに置いたんですか。
(A) 研究をするために。
(B) あなたのデスクの上に。
(C) 私は以前そこに住んでいました。

▶解説 Where ～?で「場所」が問われています。鍵をどこに置いたかを尋ねられ、「あなたのデスクの上」と答えた(B)が正解です。 (A)の「To+動詞」は、目的や理由を述べる際の表現です。(C)は質問文のleaveと似た音のlivedを用いた引っ掛けです。

---

8. DL 012 🇬🇧🇺🇸　正解：**A**　易■■■□□□□難　選択率：**(A) 79.8%**　(B) 7.9%　(C) 11.9%

How much longer should we wait for the bus?
(A) I have no idea.
(B) Just in front of the entrance.
(C) Up to three bags, right?

□ wait for ～: ～を待つ　□ have no idea: まったく分からない
□ just: 副 まさに、ちょうど　□ in front of ～: ～の前に
□ entrance: 名 入り口　□ up to ～: 最大で～まで
□ ～, right?: ～ですよね?

私たちはあとどれくらい長くバスを待つべきですか。
(A) 分かりません。
(B) 入り口のすぐ前です。
(C) バッグは3つまでですよね?

▶解説 待ち時間を尋ねられたのに対し、「分からない」と答えた(A)が正解です。質問に対する答えを知らない場合、「分からない」と述べるのは、Part 2の頻出応答パターンです。他に、I'm not sure. も「分からない」と伝える時によく登場する表現です。

---

9. DL 013 🇨🇦🇨🇦　正解：**B**　易■■■□□□□難　選択率：(A) 9.9%　**(B) 88.4%**　(C) 1.7%

Don't you have any more of this paper in stock?
(A) No, I wasn't surprised.
(B) We've run out, sorry.
(C) Very cheap.

□ stock: 名 在庫品　□ surprised: 形 驚いて
□ run out: 売り切れる　□ cheap: 形 安い、安価な

この紙の在庫はもうないんですか。
(A) いいえ、私は驚きませんでした。
(B) 売り切れてしまったんです、すみません。
(C) とても安いです。

▶解説 「紙の在庫はもうないのか」という問いに対し、「売り切れた」と述べ、「すみません」と謝罪している(B)が正解です。No, we've run out, sorry. のNoが省略されています。(A)のNoには問題ありませんが、その後の内容が質問とかみ合いません。

---

10. DL 014 🇦🇺🇺🇸　正解：**C**　易■■■□□□□難　選択率：(A) 8.3%　(B) 27.8%　**(C) 63.9%**

How much is it going to cost to replace the carpet?
(A) Until next June.
(B) I think that's the best place.
(C) We'll hire a cleaning company this time.

□ cost: 動 ～（の金額）がかかる
□ replace: 動 ～を交換する　□ until: 前 ～まで
□ hire: 動 ～を雇う　□ cleaning company: 清掃会社

カーペットを交換するにはいくらかかりますか。
(A) 次の6月まで。
(B) それが最高の場所だと思います。
(C) 今回は清掃会社を雇います。

▶解説 How much ～?で「値段」が問われています。「値段」を答える代わりに、「今回は（自分たちで張り替えを行わず）清掃会社を雇う」と述べた(C)が自然な応答です。(B)は質問文にあるreplaceと似た音のplaceを用いた引っ掛けです。

((📡)) ゼミ 生中継　😀 Hiro 😀 Mai 😀 Yasu 😀 Dai 😀 Saki

7.

😀 じゃ、Part 2に進もう。

😀 質問が速くてWhereとkeysしか聞き取れませんでした。

😀 それで?

😀 「鍵、どこ?」と意識し続けたら正解できました。

😀 正解を選ぶだけならそれで十分だよ。もちろん、それだけでは対応できない場合もあるけど、そうやって重要情報を意識し続けるのは常にやった方がいい。

10.

😀 これは「質問の前提を否定する」パターンだよ。質問の前提は「カーペットを張り替える」ことだけど、それ自体を否定することで会話が成立している。サキは正解できた?

😀 いいえ。どれもお金の話をしていないので正解がないと思いました。

😀 「カーペットを張り替えない」と答えてくれたら解きやすいですが、「清掃会社を雇う」だと、それが何を意味するか考えなくちゃいけないので難しかったです。

😀 そうだね。発言の意図を見抜く必要がある。難しいけど、このようなタイプの問題は決してレアじゃないよ。

Part 2 応答問題

11. DL↓015 🇬🇧🇦🇺 正解：**B** 易▰▰▱▱▱▱▱難 選択率：(A) 3.3% **(B) 91.1%** (C) 5.6%

Can we meet this afternoon?
(A) This is the only one I have.
(B) I need to check my calendar.
(C) I go there sometimes, too.

☐ check: 動 ～を確認する
☐ calendar: 名 カレンダー、予定表

今日の午後会えますか。
(A) これは私が持っている唯一のものです。
(B) カレンダーを確認する必要があります。
(C) 私も時々そこへ行きます。

▶解説 依頼の表現である Can we ～? を使い、午後に時間を空けてもらえるかを尋ねています。それに対し、「カレンダーを確認する必要がある」と述べ、今すぐには返答できないことを伝えている (B) が自然な応答です。

12. DL↓016 🇦🇺🇨🇦 正解：**B** 易▰▰▰▱▱▱▱難 選択率：(A) 26.8% **(B) 61.9%** (C) 10.9%

Where's the photocopier going to be placed?
(A) Thursday, I guess.
(B) In the hall for now.
(C) Yeah, you're right.

☐ photocopier: 名 コピー機 ☐ place: 動 ～を置く、配置する
☐ guess: 動 ～だと思う、～を予測する
☐ hall: 名 廊下、ホール ☐ for now: 今のところは

コピー機はどこに置かれるんですか。
(A) 木曜日だと思います。
(B) 今のところは廊下に。
(C) ええ、その通りです。

▶解説 Where's (Where is) ～? で「場所」を問われ、具体的な場所を答えている (B) が正解です。(A) は When ～?（いつ～?）に対する応答です。WH疑問文に Yeah (Yes) で答えることはできないため、(C) は不正解です。

13. DL↓017 🇬🇧🇺🇸 正解：**C** 易▰▰▰▱▱▱▱難 選択率：(A) 15.6% (B) 3.6% **(C) 80.8%**

Why are the lights on on the fifth floor?
(A) It's a tall building, isn't it?
(B) Until September 4.
(C) The sales department is in a meeting.

☐ tall: 形 高い ☐ ～, isn't it?: ～ですよね?
☐ until: 前 ～まで ☐ sales department: 営業部
☐ meeting: 名 会議

5階の電気がついているのはなぜですか。
(A) 高い建物ですよね?
(B) 9月4日まで。
(C) 営業部が会議中です。

▶解説 Why ～? で電気がついている「理由」を問われ、「営業部が会議中だ」と説明している (C) が正解です。このように Because なしでも、理由を表す内容を述べたり、事情を説明したりしていれば、Why ～? に対する応答として成立します。

📻((📡)) ゼミ生中継　　　😊 Hiro 😊 Mai 😊 Yasu 🎲 Dai 😊 Saki

12.
😊 質問の出だしを When だと思ってしまうと、(A) を選びたくなる。

😊 最初、Where だと思っていたんですが、(A) を聞いて、急に自分に自信がなくなってしまいました。

😊 それ、分かる。私もよくあるよ。

😊 頭の中で「どこ?」を強く意識し続けることが大事だよ。

13.
😊 この質問はイギリス発音ですよね。7番の質問もそうでしたが、聞き取りにくいです。

😊 試験本番でもイギリス発音はたくさん登場するから、慣れるしかないよ。ところで、この質問は Why で始まるよね。Why に対する正解はたいてい「文」だから、(B) のような「句」は消去していい。

😊 どういうことですか。

😊 (B) の Until September 4. には主語も動詞もない。こういう「前置詞＋名詞」で Why に答えるのはほぼ無理だから正解にならないんだよ。現実世界では、Because of the snow.（雪が原因で）や Due to an accident.（事故のせいで）などは Why への答えになり得るけど、不思議なことに TOEIC では「文」が正解になる。99.9%間違いない。

38

14. DL 018 🇨🇦🇬🇧　正解：**C**　易▰▰▰▰▰▱▱難　選択率：(A) 8.6%　(B) 27.5%　**(C) 63.9%**

It's too warm in here, isn't it?
(A) In London.
(B) Let me know what you think.
(C) I'll turn off the air conditioning.

□ warm: 形 暖かい　□ ～, isn't it?: ～ですよね?
□ Let me know ～.: ～を教えてください。
□ turn off ～: ～を止める、消す
□ air conditioning: 空調、エアコン

この中は暖かすぎますよね?
(A) ロンドンで。
(B) あなたがどう考えているのか教えてください。
(C) エアコンを止めます。

▶解説 付加疑問文で「ここは暖かすぎるよね」と「同意」を求めています。「エアコンを切るよ」と答えることで、相手の発言内容に理解を示し、その状況に対処しようとしている (C) が正解です。(B) は相手の意見や考えを尋ねる時に使う表現です。

---

15. DL 019 🇨🇦🇦🇺　正解：**B**　易▰▰▰▰▱▱▱難　選択率：(A) 10.3%　**(B) 68.2%**　(C) 21.5%

Why's it taking so long to repair the escalator?
(A) Yes, see you later.
(B) It's a big job.
(C) I have a pair.

□ take long: 時間がかかる　□ repair: 動 ～を修理する
□ escalator: 名 エスカレーター
□ See you later.: また会いましょう。

エスカレーターを修理するのになぜそれほど時間がかかっているんですか。
(A) はい、また会いましょう。
(B) 大仕事なんです。
(C) ペアを持っています。

▶解説 Why's (Why is) ～?で「理由」を問うています。「エスカレーターの修理になぜそれほど時間がかかっているのか」に対し、「大仕事だから」と理由を述べた (B) が正解です。(C) は質問文にある repair に似た音の pair を使った引っ掛けです。

---

16. DL 020 🇺🇸🇦🇺　正解：**A**　易▰▱▱▱▱▱▱難　選択率：**(A) 93.7%**　(B) 4.3%　(C) 1.7%

Which conference room should we reserve?
(A) The larger one.
(B) I don't have any more room.
(C) Yes, I think we should.

□ conference: 名 会議
□ room: 名 (可算名詞で) 部屋、(不可算名詞で) 空き場所
□ reserve: 動 ～を予約する

どちらの会議室を予約すべきですか。
(A) 大きい方です。
(B) もう余裕はありません。
(C) はい、そうすべきだと思います。

▶解説 Which ～?で「どの」会議室を予約するべきかを問うています。「大きい方」と会議室の特徴を答えた (A) が正解です。one は代名詞で、質問者が使った room を繰り返すのを避けるために使われています。

Part 2 ▼ Listening Section

📻))) ゼミ生中継　😀 Hiro　😊 Mai　😆 Yasu　📷 Dai　😄 Saki

14.
😆 (B)を選んだ人はいる?
📷 選びました。
😀「暑いね。あなたはどう?」と尋ねるのは自然だから質問者の発言としては問題ない。でも、応答者のセリフとしては変だよ。「暑いね」と言った人に「あなたはどう?」と質問するのはおかしい。
📷 確かに。
😄 これは冬の会話ですね。私は夏だと思い込んで頭が混乱しました。

どうしてエアコンをオフにするのだろうとか考えて……
😆 効き過ぎの暖房を切ろうとしてるんだよ。

16.
😀 (A)を選べたかな。Whichで始まる質問にoneという代名詞を使った応答が正解になることはよくある。あと、(C)はYesで始まるからダメだね。WhichとかHowなどで始まるWH疑問文にYesやNoで答えることはできない。

Part 2 応答問題

---

17. DL 021 🇨🇦 🇬🇧 正解：**C** 易 ▰▰▱▱▱▱▱ 難 選択率：(A) 1.0% (B) 1.0% **(C) 98.0%**

Shall we walk to the hotel, or take a taxi?
(A) This is a nice hotel.
(B) For three nights.
(C) Why don't we just walk?

☐ Shall we ～?: ～しましょうか。 ☐ nice: 形 良い、素敵な
☐ Why don't we ～?: ～しませんか。 ☐ just: 副 ただ

ホテルまで歩いて行きましょうか、それともタクシーに乗りましょうか。
(A) これはいいホテルです。
(B) 3泊です。
(C) ただ歩きませんか。

▶解説 選択疑問文で「歩くか、タクシーに乗るか」と尋ねたのに対し、歩くことを提案している (C) が正解です。Why don't we ～?は、「～するのはどうですか」と自分たちの行動を提案する表現で、他に Let's ～ . や How about –ing?などがあります。

---

18. DL 022 🇨🇦 🇨🇦 正解：**A** 易 ▰▰▱▱▱▱▱ 難 選択率：**(A) 73.5%** (B) 23.8% (C) 2.6%

Who rented this projector?
(A) I didn't know it wasn't needed.
(B) During the board meeting.
(C) $1,000.

☐ rent: 動 ～を借りる ☐ projector: 名 プロジェクター
☐ need: 動 ～を必要とする ☐ during: 前 ～の間に
☐ board: 名 (集合的に) 重役会、役員会
☐ meeting: 名 会議

誰がこのプロジェクターを借りたんですか。
(A) 必要とされていないとは知りませんでした。
(B) 重役会の会議中にです。
(C) 1000ドルです。

▶解説 プロジェクターを借りた人物を尋ねる質問に、「必要ないとは知らなかった」と答えている (A) が正解です。不要な備品を借りた人を探している質問者に対して、借りてしまった人がその理由を説明している場面です。

---

19. DL 023 🇦🇺 🇺🇸 正解：**A** 易 ▰▰▰▱▱▱▱ 難 選択率：**(A) 62.3%** (B) 19.5% (C) 18.2%

Did you send out the invitations as scheduled?
(A) The guest list has yet to be fixed.
(B) Thanks for inviting me.
(C) He'll be back in a few minutes.

☐ send out ～: ～を送る ☐ invitation: 名 招待状
☐ as scheduled: 予定通りに ☐ guest: 名 招待客
☐ yet to be ～: まだ～されていない
☐ fix: 動 ～を決める、確定する ☐ invite: 動 ～を招待する
☐ back: 副 元の場所へ、戻って

予定通り招待状を送りましたか。
(A) 招待客リストがまだ確定されていません。
(B) ご招待いただき、ありがとうございます。
(C) 彼は数分で戻ってきます。

▶解説 「予定通り招待状を送付したのか」と問うています。それに対し、「招待者リストがまだ確定されていない」と言うことで間接的に「招待状をまだ送っていない」と答えている (A) が正解です。(C) は、He が指す人物が質問文に登場していないので正解になり得ません。

📡 ゼミ生中継 😀 Hiro 😊 Mai 😄 Yasu 😎 Dai 😆 Saki

17. ....
😀 質問にある単語が応答で繰り返されたらワナである可能性が高い。例えば、16番の(B)と(C)にあるroomとshouldは質問でも使われているから、不正解である可能性が高い。サキ、この法則を知ってた？

😆 先週、授業で習いました。

😀 え。大学がこんな受験技術を教えているの？

😆 私の大学では、英語の授業イコールTOEIC対策です。

😀 へぇ。で、17番は選択疑問文だから、繰り返された単語がワナとは限らない。「歩くかタクシーに乗るか」と尋ねられて「歩こう」は会話として自然だよね。(C)は文句なしの正解。

😊 でも、(A)にあるhotelはワナですね。

😀 そう。結局、同じ単語が繰り返されても、それだけを根拠に正解か不

正解かを判断するのは危険。最も大切なのは、英語を聞いて一発で内容を理解する力を伸ばすことだよ。

18. ....
😀 正答率が少し低いね。何を選んだ？

😎 消去法で(A)です。(B)と(C)が明らかに変だったので。

😀 ダイは？

😎 消去法を使ったら全部消えました。

😀 まったく。何も理解できなかったってことか。

😎 あ、it was neededじゃなくて it wasn't neededだったのか！

😀 肯定形だと思ったの？　ま、wasn'tのtが聞こえないから仕方ないね。このような音の変化に強くなるには、何度も聞いてモノマネ練習をするのが効果的だよ。

20. DL 024 🇺🇸🇦🇺　正解：**C**　易▮▮▮▯▯▯難　選択率：(A) 2.6%　(B) 39.4%　**(C) 48.0%**

Can't I speak on Tuesday instead of Monday?
(A) Yes, she's the keynote speaker.
(B) By the end of the day.
(C) We've already started publicizing the event.

□ Can't I ～?: ～できませんか。
□ speak: 動 講演する
□ A instead of B: B の代わりに A
□ keynote speaker: 基調講演者
□ already: 副 すでに　□ publicize: 動 ～を宣伝する

私の講演を月曜日の代わりに火曜日にできませんか。
(A) はい、彼女が基調講演者です。
(B) 1日の終わりまでに。
(C) すでにイベントの宣伝を始めてしまっているんです。

▶解説 講演日を火曜日に変更したい質問者に対し、「すでにイベントの告知を始めた」と答えることで、もう変更はできない旨を伝え、相手の要望を断っている (C) が正解です。(A) は Yes の後の内容が質問とかみ合いません。

---

21. DL 025 🇨🇦🇬🇧　正解：**A**　易▮▮▮▯▯▯難　選択率：**(A) 69.2%**　(B) 10.3%　(C) 20.2%

There are a lot of applicants for the receptionist position, aren't there?
(A) Yes, we'll be busy with the interviews.
(B) The personnel director.
(C) We're all looking forward to it.

□ applicant: 名 応募者、候補者
□ receptionist: 名 受付係　□ position: 名 地位
□ interview: 名 面接　□ personnel: 名 人事部、人事課
□ director: 名 部長、指導者
□ look forward to ～: ～を楽しみにしている

受付係への応募者がたくさんいますよね？
(A) はい、面接で忙しくなりますよ。
(B) 人事部長です。
(C) 私たちは皆、楽しみにしています。

▶解説 付加疑問文で「応募者がたくさんいるよね」と「確認」しています。それに対し、Yes で「応募者がたくさんいる」と肯定した上で、「面接で忙しくなる」と追加情報を述べた (A) が正解です。

---

22. DL 026 🇨🇦🇦🇺　正解：**C**　易▮▮▯▯▯▯難　選択率：(A) 6.6%　(B) 7.6%　**(C) 85.8%**

Why haven't any of the commercials been broadcast yet?
(A) No, not yet.
(B) I've already bought one.
(C) Because we're waiting for the product launch.

□ commercial: 名 コマーシャル
□ broadcast: 動 ～を放映する　＊ここでは過去分詞
□ already: 副 すでに
□ buy: 動 ～を買う（bought は過去分詞）
□ wait for ～: ～を待つ　□ product: 名 製品
□ launch: 名 （新製品の）発売

なぜコマーシャルはまだどれも放映されていないんですか。
(A) いいえ、まだです。
(B) 私はすでに1つ買いました。
(C) 製品の発売を待っているからです。

▶解説 Why ～? でコマーシャルがまだ放送されていない「理由」を問われ、「商品の発売を待っているから」と説明している (C) が正解です。(A) は No で始まっているため、Why ～? への答えにはなりません。

📡 ゼミ生中継　😀Hiro 😀Mai 😀Yasu 😀Oai 😀Saki

21.
😀 (C) が少し魅力的だったかな。どう？
😀 はい。選びました。多くの人が応募しているので、会えるのを楽しみにしているのかと思いました。
😀 なるほど。We're all looking forward to it. の it が何を指すか不明だよ。「会うのを楽しみにしている」と言いたいなら、it の代わりに meeting them と具体的に言わないといけない。

22.
😀 Why の質問に Because で答える応答は「引っ掛け」だと本で読んだことがあります。
😀 そんなのウソだよ。普通、Because は正解として登場する。

41

Part 2 応答問題

---

23. DL ⬇027 🇬🇧🇬🇧 　正解：**B**　易 ▰▰▰▱▱▱▱ 難　選択率：(A) 18.2%　**(B) 55.3%**　(C) 26.2%

Are you still on Linden Avenue?
(A) Right after lunch.
(B) I'm running a little late.
(C) No, it's not that new.

☐ still: 副 まだ、今なお　☐ right after 〜: 〜の直後に
☐ run late: （予定より）遅れる　☐ that: 副 それほど、そんなに

あなたはまだLinden Avenueに
いるんですか。
(A) 昼食の直後にです。
(B) 少し遅れています。
(C) いいえ、それはそれほど新し
くありません。

▶解説 「あなたはまだLinden Avenueに
いるのか」と問われ、「少し遅れている」と
自分の状況を説明している (B) が自然な応答
です。(C) は質問文のAvenueの -nueと同
じ発音のnewを使った引っ掛けです。

---

24. DL ⬇028 🇺🇸🇦🇺 　正解：**A**　易 ▰▰▱▱▱▱▱ 難　選択率：**(A) 97.7%**　(B) 1.3%　(C) 1.0%

Whose car is that parked in front of the
entrance?
(A) It's Mr. Peterson's.
(B) If you don't mind.
(C) Just over there.

☐ park: 動 〜を駐車する　☐ in front of 〜: 〜の前に
☐ entrance: 名 入り口　☐ mind: 動 〜を嫌がる、嫌だと思う
☐ just: 副 まさに、ちょうど　☐ over there: あそこに、向こうに

入り口の前に駐車しているのは誰
の車ですか。
(A) Petersonさんのです。
(B) あなたが気にしないのであれ
ば。
(C) ちょうど向こうにです。

▶解説 Whose 〜？で「誰の」車かを尋ね
ているのに対し、「Petersonさんのもの」と
答えた (A) が正解です。(B) のIf you don't
mind. は、「もしよかったら」という意味の
決まり文句です。(C) は「場所」を答えてい
るので不正解です。

---

25. DL ⬇029 🇦🇺🇨🇦 　正解：**B**　易 ▰▰▱▱▱▱▱ 難　選択率：(A) 10.9%　**(B) 79.5%**　(C) 9.3%

How often should we send reports to the
accounting department?
(A) For a couple of years now.
(B) Every Friday.
(C) I haven't read it.

☐ How often 〜?: どれくらいの頻度で〜?
☐ send: 動 〜を送る　☐ report: 名 報告書、リポート
☐ accounting department: 経理部
☐ a couple of 〜: 2、3の〜　☐ every: 形 毎〜

どれくらいの頻度で経理部に報告
書を送るべきですか。
(A) 今ではもう数年間は。
(B) 毎週金曜日に。
(C) まだ読んでいません。

▶解説 How often 〜？で「頻度」が問われ
ているので、「毎週金曜日」と答えた (B) が正
解です。(A) は「期間」を答えているので不
適切です。(C) は it が何を指すか不明で、「頻
度」にも関係ないことを述べているので不正
解です。

((📡)) ゼミ生中継　　　　　🙂Hiro 🙂Mai 🙂Yasu 🙂Dai 🙂Saki

23. ....

🙂 この質問者はどんな気持ちで質問しているか想像してみて。

🙂 驚いている感じがします。

🙂 相手がまだLinden Avenueにいることを期待している。

🙂 絶望している。

🙂 絶望（笑）　ま、どれもあり得る。(B) を聞くと、応答者は遅刻している
ことが分かるから、たぶん質問者は驚いているかイラっときてる。この
ような、質問を聞いても状況を把握しにくい問題はPart2に頻出す
るよ。

24. ....

🙂 質問の出だしがWhoseだと分かっていれば、仮にその後を聞き逃し
ても (A) を選べるはず。このように、文頭をしっかり聞けば簡単に解け
る問題は意外と多いよ。

25. ....

🙂 ヤス、この質問に対して、他にどんな答えが正解になるかな？

🙂 週2日なら、Twice a week. でどうですか。

🙂 いいね。サキ、2日に1回ならどうなる？

🙂 えっと、Two days one time. ですか？

🙂 惜し……くない。Every other day. だよ。

26. DL 030 🇦🇺🇺🇸　正解：**C**　易 ■■■■■□□□ 難　選択率：(A) 9.3%　(B) 51.0%　**(C) 39.4%**

I'm selecting a hotel for the client.
(A) An excellent restaurant.
(B) How long did they stay there?
(C) Cedar Hotel isn't too expensive.

☐ select: 動 〜を選ぶ　☐ client: 名 顧客
☐ excellent: 形 優れた、素晴らしい　☐ stay: 動 滞在する
☐ expensive: 形 高価な、費用のかかる

私は顧客のためにホテルを選んで
います。
(A) 素晴らしいレストランです。
(B) 彼らはどれくらいそこに滞在
　しましたか。
(C) Cedar Hotel はそれほど高く
　ありません。

▶解説 「顧客のためにホテルを選んでいる」
という発言に対し、「Cedar Hotel はそんな
に高くない」と答え、候補となり得るホテル
を提案している (C) が正解です。(A) や (B)
は、「ホテルを選んでいる」という発言とか
み合いません。

---

27. DL 031 🇺🇸🇨🇦　正解：**B**　易 ■■■□□□□□ 難　選択率：(A) 4.6%　**(B) 74.5%**　(C) 20.9%

Traffic is always heavy in the afternoon.
(A) I can't lift it myself.
(B) We should leave soon then.
(C) I've been here all morning.

☐ traffic: 名 交通量　☐ always: 副 いつも
☐ heavy: 形 (交通量が) 多い　☐ lift: 動 〜を持ち上げる
☐ myself: 代 私自身　☐ leave: 動 出発する
☐ then: 副 それなら

午後はいつも渋滞するんです。
(A) 私は自分でそれを持ち上げる
　ことができません。
(B) それではすぐに出発すべきで
　すね。
(C) 私は午前中ずっとここにいま
　した。

▶解説 平叙文で「午後はいつも渋滞が激し
い」という道路情報が述べられています。そ
れに対し、「(それなら) 私たちは早く出発し
た方がいい」と答えることで、「渋滞に巻き
込まれないようにしよう」という気持ちを表
した (B) が自然な応答です。

---

28. DL 032 🇬🇧🇺🇸　正解：**B**　易 ■■■■□□□□ 難　選択率：(A) 33.8%　**(B) 59.6%**　(C) 6.6%

Where is the retirement party being held?
(A) From two o'clock.
(B) I didn't think you'd arrive on time!
(C) If there's enough money.

☐ retirement: 名 退職、引退　☐ hold: 動 〜を開催する
☐ arrive: 動 到着する　☐ on time: 時間通りに
☐ enough: 形 十分な

退職パーティーはどこで開かれて
いますか。
(A) 2時からです。
(B) 時間通りに到着するとは思い
　ませんでした！
(C) 十分お金があれば。

▶解説 退職パーティーの場所を尋ねた相手
に「あなたが時間通りに着くとは思わなかっ
た」と、時間通りに現れたことに対する驚き
を表した (B) が自然な応答です。(A) は
When 〜?(いつ〜?) に対する答えです。

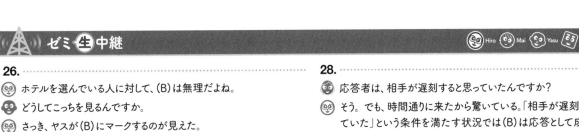

((📡)) ゼミ 生中継　😊 Hiro　😮 Mai　😄 Yasu　😎 Dai　😀 Saki

26.
😄 ホテルを選んでいる人に対して、(B) は無理だよね。
😮 どうしてこっちを見るんですか。
😄 さっき、ヤスが (B) にマークするのが見えた。
😮 見ないでください！ (B) の did they stay there が過去形だと気づ
　かなかったんですよ。内容的にホテルに関係しそうですし。それに、
　(C) に Hotel があったので、ワナだと思って除外しました。
😄 やっぱり。さっき17番で言ったように、繰り返された音がワナだと即
　決するのは危険だよ。このような例外もあるからね。

28.
😀 応答者は、相手が遅刻すると思っていたんですか？
😄 そう。でも、時間通りに来たから驚いている。「相手が遅刻すると思っ
　ていた」という条件を満たす状況では (B) は応答として成立するけ
　ど、満たさなければ、(B) は全くダメ。状況に依存した応答だよ。
😎 それにしても、応答者は失礼な人ですね。
😄 まぁね。TOEIC ワールドには温和な人が多いけど、近年は失礼な人
　や怒る人が増えていることが確認済みらしい。

Part 2 応答問題

---

29. DL 033 🇨🇦🇨🇦 正解：**C** 易▰▰▱▱▱▱難 選択率：(A) 7.6% (B) 9.9% (C) 82.5%

Shall we hire an entertainer, or ask an
employee to perform?
(A) At the performance review.
(B) It was a great time.
(C) Either is fine with me.

□ Shall we 〜?: 〜しましょうか。 □ hire: 動 〜を雇う
□ entertainer: 名 芸人、エンターテイナー
□ ask 〜 to ...: 〜に…するように頼む
□ employee: 名 従業員
□ perform: 動（楽器を）演奏する
□ performance review: 人事考課
□ great: 形 素晴らしい、すごい
□ either: 代（二者のうち）どちらでも
□ fine: 形 結構な、好都合な

芸人を雇いましょうか、それとも
従業員に演奏してくれるよう頼み
ましょうか。
(A) 人事考課で。
(B) 素晴らしい時間でした。
(C) 私はどちらでも結構です。

▶解説 「誰か雇うのか、従業員に頼むのか」
という質問に「どちらでもいい」と返答して
いる (C) が正解です。選択疑問文に対し、ど
ちらかを選ぶだけでなく、「どちらでも可」
「どちらも否」「（AでもBでもなく）C」とい
う返答も正解になります。

---

30. DL 034 🇦🇺🇺🇸 正解：**A** 易▰▰▰▱▱▱▱難 選択率：(A) 74.8% (B) 13.6% (C) 11.3%

Let's ask the caterer for a price estimate.
(A) Sure, I'll take care of that.
(B) I'm certain she is.
(C) I don't like either of them.

□ caterer: 名 仕出し業者 □ ask 〜 for ...: 〜に…を頼む
□ price: 名 値段、価格 □ estimate: 名 見積もり
□ take care of 〜: 〜を担当する □ certain: 形 確信して
□ either: 代（否定で）どちらも〜ない

仕出し業者に金額の見積もりを頼
みましょう。
(A) もちろん、私が担当します。
(B) 私は彼女がそうだと確信して
います。
(C) 私はどちらも好きではありま
せん。

▶解説 Let's 〜は「〜しよう」と相手を誘
う時の表現です。「価格の見積もりを頼も
う」に対し、「私がやる」と相手の提案に応
じた (A) が正解です。take care of 〜は、
「〜を引き受ける」や「〜の面倒を見る」と
いう意味です。

---

31. DL 035 🇬🇧🇦🇺 正解：**A** 易▰▰▰▱▱▱難 選択率：(A) 53.6% (B) 22.5% (C) 23.8%

I think I've booked this conference room.
(A) We're just about done.
(B) At the front desk.
(C) I saw a book on the table.

□ book: 動 〜を予約する □ conference: 名 会議
□ just about: ほとんど、おおむね □ done: 形 終わった
□ front desk: 受付、フロント

私はこの会議室を予約したと思い
ます。
(A) ちょうど終わるところです。
(B) 受付で。
(C) テーブルの上で本を見ました。

▶解説 「この会議室を予約したと思った」
は、予約したはずの部屋を他の人が使用して
いるので、確認する意図で述べられていま
す。その意図をくみ取り、「ちょうど終わる
ところだ」と述べ、場所がすぐに空くことを
伝えた (A) が正解です。

 ((•)) ゼミ 生中継 　　　　　　　　　　　　　😎Hiro 😊Mai 😐Yasu 🎲Dai 😺Saki

31. ·····································

😎 さて、最後の問題。どこが難しかった?

😊 (A)を聞き取れなくて、何となく(C)にしました。

😺 私もです。We're done. なら問題ないと思うのですが、justとabout
が入って聞き取りにくかったです。

😎 これで Part 2 は終わり。本番よりミスが多かったかもしれないけど、リ
スニング力を鍛えれば得意になるよ。Part 2 では文脈からの推測
や文字情報に頼れないから、純粋にリスニング力を伸ばすことが最
も有効な対策になる。この点を忘れちゃいけないよ。

TOEICよろず相談所 ヒロの部屋

②IPテストのスコアは就職活動で使える?

 すみませーん。TOEICについて1つ知りたいことがあります。

 どうぞ。

 大学で受験するIPテストのスコアは就活で使えますか。今は大学2年で、就活準備をしています。

 IPテストのスコアを認めるかどうかは応募先の企業が決めることなので、ここで安易な答えは書けません。ただ、**多くの企業ではIPテストであれ公開テストであれ、区別なく認めているようです。**

 スコアが高く出るのはどっちですか?

 と言いますと?

 IPテストの方が簡単だと先輩から聞いたことがあります。

 あ、そういうことですか。結論は「どちらも同じ」と思ってOKです。**基本的に、IPテストは公開テストと同じなんです。**公開テストで使われた問題が、何年かしてからIPテストに登場すると言われています。

 知りませんでした。

 ただし、受験者が「試験中に感じる難易度」はテストによって異なるのが普通です。だからと言って、それがスコアの上下を意味するわけではありません。

 そうなんですか。

 ですから、しっかり実力を高めることを優先してください。それがスコアアップへの近道です。

 はーい。ありがとうございました!

Part 3 会話問題

DL 037 **Questions 32 through 34** refer to the following conversation.

W: ❶ I've just finished updating the Web site. ❷ I'd appreciate it if you
🇨🇦 could all open up your browsers and take a look.

M: Wow. It looks great. ❸ I love how we can see the latest updates
🇦🇺 about the company on the top page now.

W: Yes. That was requested by Mr. Anderson. ❹ The problem is that
the information isn't very new. We need someone to update it as
often as possible so that the site doesn't look out of date.

M: ❺ Let's assign that job to one employee so that we know who's
responsible. (91w/30 sec.)

問題32-34は次の会話に関するものです。
女：ちょうどウェブサイトの更新が終わったところなの。できれば皆、ブラウザーを開いて見てもらえるとありがたいんだけど。
男：へえ。素晴らしいね。とても気に入ったよ、このトップページにある会社の最新情報の見え方が。
女：ええ。それはAndersonさんに依頼されたの。問題は、情報が大して新しくないことね。誰かに、なるべく頻繁に更新してもらって、サイトが古びて見えないようにしなくちゃ。
男：その仕事は従業員1人に担当してもらおう。責任が明確になるからね。

☐ update: 動 ～を更新する、最新のものにする、名 最新情報 ☐ appreciate: 動 ～を感謝する ☐ take a look: 見てみる ☐ latest: 形 最新の
☐ request: 動 ～を頼む ☐ often: 副 しばしば ☐ out of date: 時代遅れの ☐ assign: 動 ～を割り当てる ☐ responsible: 形 責任のある

---

32. 正解：**C** 易 ▰▰▱▱▱▱▱ 難 選択率：(A) 1.0% (B) 2.6% **(C) 93.4%** (D) 3.0%

What is the main topic of the conversation?
(A) A promotional booklet
(B) A company event
(C) A Web site revision
(D) A software program

この会話の主な話題は何ですか。
(A) 販促用冊子
(B) 会社の行事
(C) ウェブサイトの修正
(D) ソフトウェアのプログラム

▶解説 女性は❶で、ウェブサイトの更新を終えたと言い、さらに❷で、ブラウザーを開いてそれを見るよう依頼しています。男性は❸で会社に関する最新情報の見せ方について感想を述べています。これらから、話題は(C)のウェブサイトの修正だと考えられます。

☐ promotional: 形 販売を促進する ☐ booklet: 名 小冊子 ☐ revision: 名 修正

---

33. 正解：**B** 易 ▰▰▰▱▱▱▱ 難 選択率：(A) 5.6% **(B) 84.1%** (C) 4.6% (D) 5.3%

What problem does the woman mention?
(A) The design is not attractive.
(B) Some information is out of date.
(C) Running costs are high.
(D) There have not been many visitors.

女性はどんな問題を指摘していますか。
(A) デザインが魅力に欠ける。
(B) 情報に古いものがある。
(C) 運用費が高い。
(D) 閲覧者数があまり多くない。

▶解説 通常、「問題」を示すヒントはネガティブな表現です。ここでは、❹で女性が「問題は情報があまり新しくない」と指摘しています。それをout of date（古い）を使って表している(B)が正解です。

☐ mention: 動 ～に言及する ☐ attractive: 形 魅力的な ☐ running cost: 運用費

---

34. 正解：**A** 易 ▰▰▰▱▱▱▱ 難 選択率：**(A) 74.2%** (B) 8.3% (C) 5.3% (D) 11.9%

What does the man suggest doing?
(A) Choosing an employee for a task
(B) Using more colorful graphics
(C) Comparing prices online
(D) Holding meetings more frequently

男性は何をすることを提案していますか。
(A) ある業務のために従業員を選ぶ
(B) もっと多色のビジュアルを用いること
(C) オンラインで価格を比較すること
(D) もっと頻繁に会議を開くこと

▶解説 女性が、ウェブサイト情報の頻繁な更新の必要性に触れ、男性が❺で、責任者が明確になるように、その業務を従業員1名に割り当てることを提案しています。つまり、ある業務のために従業員を選ぶことを意味するため、(A)が正解です。

☐ suggest: 動 ～を提案する ☐ task: 名 仕事、務め
☐ compare: 動 ～を比較する ☐ online: 副 オンラインで
☐ frequently: 副 頻繁に

(((🗼))) ゼミ 生 中継
😀Hiro 😊Mai 😺Yasu 🎲Dai 😄Saki

😀 やってみてどうだった？
😊 たくさん聞いてたくさん読まなきゃいけないので大変です。
🎲 同じく。
😺 でも、解きやすい問題が多かった気がします。
😄 私は、Part 2よりはPart 3の方がやりやすいです。
😀 バラバラだね。では、1つずつ振り返っていこう。受験テクニックもいくつか紹介していくよ。

34.
😀 提案内容を問う設問はPart 3の常連だよ。ここでは設問にsuggestがあるけど、proposeやrecommend、adviseが使われることも多い。で、ヒントは何だったか覚えている？
😺 男性がLet's assign ～と言っていました。
😀 典型的な提案表現を確認しよう。有名なのはWhy don't you ～？とHow about ～？だね。あと、You should ～とか。ほかは？
😄 えっと……
😀 動詞で始まる命令文も提案の一種だよ。Make sure ～とかね。

Part 3 ▼ Listening Section

DL ↓ 038 **Questions 35 through 37** refer to the following conversation.

W: Kyle, I'm going to be out of the office this afternoon, but I have a
🇨🇦 delivery of paper coming in. My assistant called in sick, and you're
the only one I can count on. ❶ <u>Would you mind signing for it?</u>

M: Not at all. ❷ <u>You'd better let me know what time they're coming,</u>
🇨🇦 though. I'll be pretty busy this afternoon, myself.

W: I'm not exactly sure. ❸ <u>I'll give the supplier a call and let you know</u>
<u>what they say.</u>

M: Great. I'll be in my office. Oh, and tell me where to have them
leave the paper.

W: Just put it next to the photocopier over there, please. I'll take care
of it when I get back.   (113w/41 sec.)

問題35-37は次の会話に関するものです。
女：Kyle、今日の午後に外出する予定なんだけど、紙の配達があることになっているの。アシスタントが病欠の電話を入れてきたから、あなたに頼むしかないのよ。受け取っておいてくれない？
男：構わないよ。ただ、何時に届くのか教えておいてくれた方がいいね。僕も今日の午後はとても忙しいんだ。
女：私にもはっきり分からないの。業者に電話してから結果を知らせるわ。
男：分かった。自分の部屋にいるよ。ああ、紙をどこに置いていってもらえばいいか教えて。
女：あそこのコピー機の隣に置いてくれればいいわ。戻ったら自分で処理するから。

□ office: 名 会社、オフィス　□ delivery: 名 配達　□ come in: 入ってくる、入荷する　□ assistant: 名 アシスタント、助手
□ call in sick: 病欠の電話を入れる　□ count on ～: ～に頼る　□ sign for ～: ～を署名して受け取る　□ Not at all.: いいえ少しも。、とんでもない。
□ pretty: 副 かなり、非常に　□ exactly: 副 正確に　□ sure: 形 確信して　□ supplier: 名 供給業者　□ give ～ a call: ～に電話をかける
□ photocopier: 名 コピー機　□ take care of ～: ～を処理する

---

35. 正解：**C**　易 ■■■□□ 難　選択率：(A) 1.3%　(B) 2.6%　**(C) 82.5%**　(D) 13.2%

What does the woman want the man to do?
(A) Choose a color scheme
(B) Interview a candidate
(C) Accept a delivery
(D) Write a report

女性は男性に何をしてもらいたがっていますか。
(A) 配色を選ぶ
(B) 応募者を面接する
(C) 配送物を受け取る
(D) 報告書を書く

▶解説 午後に外出する予定がある女性は、その間に紙が届くことを男性に伝え、さらに❶でその際に「サインをしてもらえないか」と依頼しています。これは受領のサインのことだと推測できますので、(C)のAccept a delivery（配達物を受け取る）が正解です。

□ color scheme: 色彩の設計、配色　□ interview: 動 ～を面接する
□ candidate: 名 候補者、応募者　□ accept: 動 ～を受け取る

---

36. 正解：**A**　易 ■■□□□ 難　選択率：**(A) 82.5%**　(B)5.6%　(C) 5.6%　(D) 6.0%

What does the man ask the woman about?
(A) An arrival time
(B) The amount of a bill
(C) The cost of some materials
(D) A mailing address

男性は女性に、何について尋ねていますか。
(A) 到着時刻
(B) 請求総額
(C) 材料費
(D) 郵送先住所

▶解説 男性は女性の依頼を承諾した後、自分も午後は忙しいことから、❷で「配達物が何時に届くのかを知らせてほしい」と述べています。男性は紙が届く時刻を尋ねているので、それをAn arrival timeと言い換えた(A)が正解となります。

□ arrival: 形 到着の　□ amount: 名 総額
□ bill: 名 請求書　□ cost: 名 費用　□ material: 名 材料

---

37. 正解：**D**　易 ■■□□□ 難　選択率：(A) 17.2%　(B) 19.2%　(C) 3.0%　**(D) 59.9%**

What does the woman say she will do?
(A) Read some reviews
(B) See an accountant
(C) Hire a decorator
(D) Make a phone call

女性は何をすると言っていますか。
(A) 評論を読む
(B) 会計士と会う
(C) 装飾家を雇う
(D) 電話をかける

▶解説 男性に配達時刻を尋ねられ、女性は❸で「業者に電話をして、結果を知らせる」と答えています。よって、女性はこれから電話をかけると考えられますので、正解は(D)です。

□ review: 名 批評　□ accountant: 名 会計士
□ hire: 動 ～を雇う　□ decorator: 名 装飾家

((·)) 📻 ゼミ 生 中継   😎Hiro 😊Mai 😆Yasu 😑Dai 😄Saki

😑 3つの設問を見て。サキ、それぞれの動詞は何？

😄 wantとaskとsayです。

😑 「望む」「尋ねる」「言う」だね。このような設問では、間違いなく主語となっている人物がヒントを言う。つまり、上から順に女性、男性、女性の発言にヒントがある。スクリプトを確認して。

😊 そうなっています。

😎 33番と34番にあったmentionやsuggestも仲間だよ。設問にこれらの「言う」系の動詞を見つけたら主語の人物が言うことに意識を向けると解きやすくなるよ。

Part 3 会話問題

039 **Questions 38 through 40** refer to the following conversation with three speakers.

M1: Susan, ❶ where should we take our clients for dinner?

W: Oh, right. Well, how about Brella's?

M1: I'm afraid it's always so busy, and a bit far from their hotel.

W: Bryan told me that his clients from Oklahoma loved a restaurant when he–oh, hi, Bryan! What perfect timing. ❷ Do you remember the name of that restaurant your clients liked?

M2: You mean Intermezzo on Parkview Avenue?

W: That's the one.

M2: Their service and food are superb and ❸ the private room was perfect for a business meeting.

W: Sounds great. ❹ I'll see if we can book a table. Thanks, Bryan.

(95w/39 sec.)

問題38-40は次の3人の話者による会話に関するものです。

男1：Susan、お客さんたちを夕食にどこへ連れていけばいいかな？

女：あ、そうね。ええと、Brella'sはどう？

男1：あそこはいつも混んでると思うよ。それに、彼らのホテルからちょっと離れてるし。

女：Bryanが言ってたけど、Oklahomaから来たお客さんが、あるレストランをとても気に入ってくれて、彼が――あら、ねえ、Bryan！　絶好のタイミングだわ。あなたのお客さんが気に入ってくれたレストランの名前、覚えてる？

男2：Parkview AvenueのIntermezzoのこと？

女：それだわ。

男2：あそこのサービスと料理は素晴らしいし、個室が商談にもってこいだったよ。

女性：良さそうね。席を予約できるか確かめてみるわ。ありがとう、Bryan。

□ client: 名 顧客　□ a bit: ちょっと、少し　□ perfect: 形 完全な、理想的な　□ remember: 動 ～を覚えている
□ superb: 形 素晴らしい　□ private room: 個室　□ business meeting: 商談　□ book: 動 ～を予約する

38. 正解：C　易 ■■■□□□ 難　選択率：(A) 1.7%　(B) 0.7%　**(C) 96.0%**　(D) 1.7%

What is the topic of the conversation?

(A) Office equipment

(B) Employee training

(C) A meeting location

(D) Customer feedback

この会話の話題は何ですか。

(A) 会社の設備

(B) 従業員研修

(C) 会議の場所

(D) 顧客の反応

▶解説　冒頭❶で男性1が顧客を夕食に連れて行く場所について、どこがいいかと尋ねています。さらに❸で男性2が、自分の薦めるレストランについて「個室が商談に最適だった」と述べており、ミーティングの場所についての会話だと判断できます。

☐ office: 名 会社　☐ equipment: 名 設備　☐ training: 名 研修　☐ meeting: 名 会議
☐ location: 名 場所　☐ feedback: 名 反応、意見

---

39. 正解：B　易 ■■■■■□ 難　選択率：(A) 58.6%　**(B) 25.8%**　(C) 1.3%　(D) 14.2%

What does the woman ask about?

(A) The location of a hotel

(B) The name of a business

(C) The date of an event

(D) The availability of a client

女性は何について尋ねていますか。

(A) ホテルの場所

(B) 店の名前

(C) 行事の日付

(D) 顧客の都合

▶解説　女性は同僚のBryanから得た情報として、顧客が気に入ったレストランがあることを述べています。その後❷でそのレストランの名前をBryanに尋ねていますので、レストランの名前を「店の名前」と言い換えた(B)が正解です。

☐ business: 名 店、会社　☐ availability: 名 利用できること

---

40. 正解：C　易 ■□□□□□ 難　選択率：(A) 2.6%　(B) 0.0%　**(C) 95.7%**　(D) 1.7%

What will the woman most likely do next?

(A) Pick up a client

(B) Announce some survey results

(C) Reserve a table

(D) Change her appointment

女性はこの後何をする可能性が最も高いですか。

(A) 顧客を車で迎えに行く

(B) 調査結果を発表する

(C) 席を予約する

(D) 約束を変更する

▶解説　女性は❹で、レストランに席を予約できるかどうかを確認すると述べています。よって、女性の次の行動はレストランの席を予約することだと判断できます。(C)が正解です。

☐ pick up ～: ～を車で迎えに行く　☐ announce: 動 ～を発表する　☐ survey: 名 調査
☐ result: 名 結果　☐ reserve: 動 ～を予約する　☐ appointment: 名 予約、約束

Part 3 ▼ Listening Section

(((📡))) ゼミ 生 中継　　　　　　　(😊) Hiro (😊) Mai (😊) Yasu (😎) Dai (😊) Saki

39.

(😊) もしかして、(A)を選んだ？

(😊) はい。男性が何かの場所を答えていたので、女性は場所を聞いたと思いました。ただ、hotelかどうかは自信なかったです。

(😊) 女性が聞いたのはホテルじゃなくてレストランの場所だね。

(😊) (B)がThe name of a restaurantだったら選べたのに。businessと言い換えられるかどうかで悩みました。

(😎) 同じく。「商売の名前」って変だと思いました。

(😊) そういうことか。businessは「商売」を意味する場合もあるけれど、もっと具体的に「店」や「会社」を意味する場合もある。(B)は「商売の名前」ではなく「店の名前」と解釈するべきだよ。

(😊) そういうことか～。

(😎) なるほど。

(😊) ところで、この会話の後の数字は何ですか？

(😊) これ？　会話に含まれる単語数と、会話の長さだよ。復習するとき、この数字を目安に「今日は短いのに取り組もう」とか計画を立てるといい。

Part 3 会話問題

Questions 41 through 43 refer to the following conversation.

W: You're finally here. You were supposed to come at 1:00 P.M.

M: Yes, I know. ❶ I had a delivery in Sunnybank before I came here and there was a traffic jam on Holland Bridge.

W: A phone call would have been nice. ❷ If I'd known you were going to be late, I could have been working on something else.

M: Right. I'm sorry about that.

W: Well, the cabinets we need you to take away are over here. ❸ I'll ask one of my employees to give you a hand loading them into the truck.

M: Thanks. That'll be a big help.

W: No problem. Just give me a minute. (103w/34 sec.)

問題41-43は次の会話に関するものです。
女：やっと来てくださったのね。午後1時にいらっしゃるはずだったのに。
男：はい、そうなんです。Sunnybankに配達してからこちらへ回ったのですが、Holland Bridgeが渋滞してまして。
女：1本電話をくださればよかったのに。あなたが遅れそうだと分かっていれば、別の作業にかかっていられたのよ。
男：おっしゃる通りです。それについては申し訳ございません。
女：で、撤去していただきたいキャビネットはあそこにあります。うちの従業員の1人に頼んで、トラックへの積み込みを手伝わせますから。
男：ありがとうございます。それは大変助かります。
女：どういたしまして。ちょっとだけ待ってください。

☐ supposed to ~: ~することになっている ☐ traffic jam: 交通渋滞 ☐ late: 形 時間に遅れる ☐ give ~ a hand: ~を手伝う ☐ load: 動 ~を積み込む

---

41. 正解：D 易 ■■■□□□□ 難 選択率：(A) 4.0% (B) 11.9% (C) 11.9% **(D) 72.2%**

Who most likely is the man?
(A) A train station employee
(B) An event organizer
(C) A technician
(D) A driver

この男性は誰である可能性が最も高いですか。
(A) 駅員
(B) イベント主催者
(C) 技術者
(D) 運転手

▶解説 女性に1時に来るはずだったことを指摘された男性は❶で、前の配達先からの途中渋滞があったことが遅れた理由だと説明しています。その後もトラックに荷物を載せる手はずについて話していることから、男性は(D)の運転手だと推測できます。

☐ organizer: 名 主催者 ☐ technician: 名 技術者

---

42. 正解：A 易 ■■■□□□□ 難 選択率：**(A) 71.9%** (B) 4.0% (C) 14.9% (D) 7.9%

What does the woman mean when she says, "A phone call would have been nice"?
(A) She wishes the man had given her an update.
(B) She enjoys talking with the man.
(C) She forgot to bring her mobile phone with her.
(D) She wanted to take a job interview.

女性は、どんなつもりで「1本電話をくださればよかったのに」と言っていますか。
(A) 彼女は男性が状況報告をしてくれればよかったと思っている。
(B) 彼女は男性と楽しく話している。
(C) 彼女は携帯電話を持ってくるのを忘れてしまった。
(D) 彼女は就職の面接を受けたかった。

▶解説 遅れた理由を述べた男性に対し、女性がA phone call would have been nice「1本電話をもらえたらよかった」と発言しています。そして直後に❷で「遅れると分かっていたら他の仕事ができた」と付け加えていることから、男性からの、遅れるという最新情報がほしかったと判断できます。(A)が正解です。

☐ update: 名 最新情報 ☐ mobile phone: 携帯電話
☐ interview: 名 面接

---

43. 正解：D 易 ■■■■□□□ 難 選択率：(A) 31.5% (B) 15.6% (C) 6.6% **(D) 46.4%**

What will the woman probably do next?
(A) Announce a delay
(B) Test some equipment
(C) Buy a ticket
(D) Speak with a colleague

女性はこの後おそらく何をしますか。
(A) 遅延を報告する
(B) 機器を試用する
(C) チケットを購入する
(D) 同僚と話す

▶解説 女性は撤去すべきキャビネットの場所を指示した後、❸で「トラックへの積み込みの手伝いを従業員の誰かに頼む」と述べて、男性もそれにお礼を言っています。従って、女性の次の行動は(D)の「同僚と話す」ことだと考えられます。

☐ delay: 名 遅れ ☐ equipment: 名 設備 ☐ colleague: 名 同僚

((•)) ゼミ 生 中継
Hiro Mai Yasu Dai Saki

42. ....

これは「意図問題」と呼ぼう。セリフの文字通りの意味ではなく、発言動機や暗示された意図を理解したかどうかを試す設問だよ。抜き出された発言は「ターゲット文」と呼ぶことにする。

私は意図問題が苦手ですが、これは簡単でした。ターゲット文が「電

話をくれたらよかったのに」と仮定法になっていて、(A)がShe wishes ～だったので、同じニュアンスを感じました。

いい勘だね。ただ、これはリスニング問題だから、設問と選択肢を読むだけで解答してはいけないよ。ちゃんと聞いてから答えてね。

DL 042 Questions 44 through 46 refer to the following conversation.

W: ❶ We need to hire a moving company to take all our furniture to the new office. I'm thinking of using JDM Movers. What do you think?

M: I don't know them. ❷ I hope they're not too expensive. ❸ If we need to spend more than five hundred dollars, we're supposed to get permission from the manager. And, Mr. Hammond won't be back until next week.

W: I don't think they'll charge that much. ❹ One of my friends at Klinger Sporting Goods used them to take their summer stock to a storage container. They only charged two hundred dollars for that. (97w/32 sec.)

問題44-46は次の会話に関するものです。

女：うちの備品を全部新しいオフィスへ運ぶのに引っ越し業者を雇わないと駄目ね。JDM Movers を使ったらどうかと思っているの。どうかしら？

男：その業者は知らないな。高すぎなければいいけど。500ドル以上払わなければならない場合、部長に許可をもらうことになってるだろう。しかも、Hammondさんは来週まで戻ってこないよ。

女：あの業者はそこまで請求してこないと思うわ。友達の1人がKlinger Sporting Goodsで働いていて、あの業者を使って夏物の在庫品を保管コンテナへ移したの。それには200ドルしかかからなかったのよ。

□ hire: 動 ～を雇う　□ moving company: 引っ越し業者　□ furniture: 名 家具、備品　□ expensive: 形 高価な、費用のかかる
□ spend: 動 （金）を使う　□ supposed to ～ : ～することになっている　□ permission: 名 許可　□ manager: 名 責任者、長
□ charge: 動 （ある金額）を請求する　□ stock: 名 在庫品　□ storage: 名 保管　□ container: 名 （貨物輸送用）コンテナ

44. 正解：**B**　易■■■□□□□□難　選択率：(A) 3.6%　**(B) 84.8%**　(C) 3.6%　(D) 7.6%

What are the speakers discussing?
(A) Athletic events
(B) A moving company
(C) Employee records
(D) A summer sale

話者たちは何について話していますか。
(A) 競技イベント
(B) 引っ越し業者
(C) 従業員記録
(D) 夏期の売り出し

▶解説 女性は❶で引っ越し業者を雇う必要性について述べた後、具体的な業者名を挙げて男性の意見を求めています。男性もまた引っ越し作業料金について言及していることから、話の内容は (B) の引っ越し業者についてだと推測できます。

□ athletic: 形 競技の、運動の　□ record: 名 記録

45. 正解：**A**　易■■□□□□□□難　選択率：**(A) 90.1%**　(B) 2.3%　(C) 3.3%　(D) 4.0%

What is the man concerned about?
(A) The price of a service
(B) The office's opening hours
(C) Arrangements for a visit
(D) Damage to some merchandise

男性は何を心配していますか。
(A) サービスの料金
(B) オフィスの営業時間
(C) 訪問の準備
(D) 商品の損傷

▶解説 男性は❷で「料金が高すぎないことを望んでいる」と述べています。さらに❸で、高額の場合は上司の許可が必要になる可能性にも触れているので、男性が気にしているのは引っ越し作業の料金のことだと考えられます。正解は (A) です。

□ opening hour: 営業時間　□ arrangement: 名 準備
□ damage: 名 損傷　□ merchandise: 名 商品

46. 正解：**D**　易■■■■□□□■難　選択率：(A) 5.6%　(B) 21.5%　(C) 14.2%　**(D) 58.3%**

What does the woman say one of her friends recently did?
(A) Applied for a position
(B) Transferred to another branch
(C) Got a new qualification
(D) Put some goods in storage

女性は友人の1人が最近何をしたと言っていますか。
(A) ある職に応募した
(B) 別の支店へ異動した
(C) 新たな資格を取った
(D) 商品を倉庫に収めた

▶解説 引っ越し作業の料金はさほど高くないだろうと考える女性は、その理由として❹で、当該引っ越し業者を使い、夏物の在庫品を保管コンテナ、つまり倉庫へ移動させた友人の例を挙げています。それを「商品を倉庫に収めた」と言い換えた (D) が正解です。

□ recently: 副 最近　□ apply for ～ : ～に応募する　□ position: 名 職、地位
□ transfer A to B: AをBへ転任させる　□ branch: 名 支店　□ qualification: 名 資格

(((■))) ゼミ生中継　😀 Hiro　😊 Mai　😎 Yasu　🎲 Dai　😀 Saki

44.

😎 これは、会話のトピックを問う設問。「常連さん」だよ。前半にヒントが登場することが多いけど、設問に複数形のspeakersがあるから、複数の場所にヒントがあるのが通常だよ。

😊 ということは、2人の話を聞くまで答えてはいけないのですか。

😎 いや、いけないわけではない。ただ、会話を聞けば聞くほどヒントに出会う、つまり、解きやすくなるから、急ぐ必要はないんだ。それより、細かい情報を求める2問目と3問目に意識を向けた方がいい。ヒントが1回しか流れないからね。話題を答えるのはその後でも間に合うよ。

Part 3 会話問題

Questions 47 through 49 refer to the following conversation.

M: Hi. Vance Garbage Collection and Disposal. My name is Bob. How can I help you?

W: Hi. Bob. This is Rachel Marsden from Greene Accountants. Every Friday, we have our garbage picked up by your company. ❶ I wanted to ask if you could pay us a visit on Wednesday this week. We have a lot of garbage in front of the office and we'd like it removed.

M: I'm sure we can do that. ❷ There will be an additional charge of fifty dollars because this is an unscheduled visit. Is that OK?

W: That's fine. Please don't cancel our regular Friday pickup, though. ❸ I'm replacing all of our telephones and some old equipment this week so the garbage receptacle should be full again by then.

(122w/44 sec.)

問題47-49は次の会話に関するものです。
男：もしもし。Vance Garbage Collection and Disposal です。Bob と申します。ご用件を承りますが？
女：こんにちは、Bob。Greene Accountants の Rachel Marsden です。毎週金曜日に、御社にごみを収集していただいてるんですが、今週は水曜日に来ていただけるようお願いしたいと思いまして。大量のごみがオフィスの前にあって、それを撤去していただきたいんです。
男：もちろん承れます。追加料金が50ドルかかります。予定外の収集ですから。それでもよろしいですか。
女：それで構いません。ただし、通常の金曜日の収集もお願いしますね。うちのすべての電話機と古い機器を今週入れ替えるので、ごみ置き場がその日までに再びいっぱいになってしまうはずなんです。

□ pay a visit: 訪問する　□ additional: 形 追加の　□ pickup: 名 収集　□ equipment: 名 設備　□ receptacle: 名 置き場

---

47. 正解：D 易 ■■■■□□□ 難　選択率：(A) 5.0% (B) 1.0% (C) 5.6% **(D) 88.4%**

Why did the woman contact the man's company?
(A) To request a replacement invoice
(B) To express thanks for a favor
(C) To announce the cancellation of a product
(D) To have some garbage removed

□ replacement: 名 代替品　□ invoice: 名 請求明細書
□ express: 動 〜を表現する　□ favor: 名 親切

なぜ女性は男性の会社に連絡したのですか。
(A) 代わりの請求明細書を依頼するために
(B) 親切に対して謝意を表明するために
(C) 製品のキャンセルを知らせるために
(D) ごみを撤去してもらうために

▶解説 女性は Vance Garbage Collection and Disposal 社のごみ収集を毎週金曜日に受けていると伝えた後❶で、今週の水曜日に来てほしいと伝えています。その目的は、直後に言及している「多量のごみの撤去」なので、正解は (D) と判断できます。

---

48. 正解：C 易 ■■□□□□□ 難　選択率：(A) 4.6% (B) 2.0% **(C) 93.0%** (D) 0.3%

What does the man say he must do?
(A) Provide a refund
(B) Review some reports
(C) Charge an additional fee
(D) Take a vacation

□ provide: 動 〜を提供する　□ refund: 名 払い戻し　□ review: 動 〜をよく調べる
□ fee: 名 (サービスなどに対する) 料金

男性は何をしなければならないと言っていますか。
(A) 返金する
(B) いくつか報告書を調べる
(C) 追加料金を課す
(D) 休暇を取る

▶解説 ごみ収集の依頼を受けた男性は❷で、それが予定外の業務になることから、追加料金を提示して女性に了承を求めています。男性がしなければいけないと言っているのは (C) の「追加料金を課す」ことだと判断できます。

---

49. 正解：A 易 ■■■□□□□ 難　選択率：**(A) 77.8%** (B) 11.6% (C) 8.9% (D) 1.7%

What will the woman do this week?
(A) Replace some equipment
(B) Speak at a workshop
(C) Take employees on a trip
(D) Watch a movie

女性は今週、何をしますか。
(A) 機器を入れ替える
(B) ワークショップで話す
(C) 従業員を旅行に連れて行く
(D) 映画を見る

▶解説 女性はいつも通り金曜日にもごみ収集に来てほしいと男性に伝え、その理由として❸で、「すべての電話機と古い機器類を今週、入れ替えるつもりだ」と述べています。従って、女性が今週行うのは (A) の「機器を入れ替える」ことだと考えられます。

(((ゼミ生中継

Hiro　Mai　Yasu　Dai　Saki

49.

😀 設問に this weekとある。このような、時を表す語句が設問に入っていたら、ダイ、どうする？

😆 聞き逃さないように頑張ります。

😀 だよね。1つ注意すべきことがある。何だと思う？

😆 ……。

😀 通常、英語ではそのような語句はヒントより後に聞こえる。だから、this week が聞こえた時点で「勝負あり」となる。スクリプトを見て。this week より後を頑張って聞いてもヒントはない。

😆 だから間違えました。

😀 ……。

DL 044 **Questions 50 through 52** refer to the following conversation.

W: Hi, John. ❶ You're using the meeting room behind the patients waiting room for your training session tomorrow, aren't you?

M: ❷ Yes, I'm training the new nurses there. Is everything working?

W: Well, the projector doesn't seem to be working. I've called a technician to take a look at it.

M: Will they be able to fix it in time?

W: I don't know.

M: How about getting a replacement? ❸ I hear the Real Color 90 is a great projector and it's very inexpensive.

W: Sounds good. We can use the old one somewhere else if it can be fixed.

M: Right. ❹ Why don't you go to Dangerfield Electronics in Springfield? They'll give you a good deal. (109w/38 sec.)

問題50-52は次の会話に関するものです。
女：ねえ、John。患者待合室の裏手の会議室を、明日研修会で使う予定なのよね？
男：うん、あそこで新任看護師たちの研修をするんだ。万事問題なさそう？
女：それが、プロジェクターが作動しないみたいなの。修理業者に電話して見てもらうことにしたけど。
男：時間までに直してもらえるのかな？
女：分からないわ。
男：代替品を調達したら？ Real Color 90が優れたプロジェクターで、とても安いそうだよ。
女：良さそうね。古い方は、もし直れば別の場所で使えばいいしね。
男：そうだね。SpringfieldにあるDangerfield Electronicsに行ってみたら？　あそこなら安く買えるよ。

□ patient: 名 患者　□ waiting room: 待合室　□ train: 動 ～を教育する　□ technician: 名 技術者　□ fix: 動 ～を修理する　□ in time: 時間内に
□ replacement: 名 代替品　□ inexpensive: 形 安い　□ give ～ a good deal: ～に良い買い物をさせる

50. 正解：A 易■■■□□□□□□難　選択率：**(A) 71.5%** (B) 18.2% (C) 5.0% (D) 5.3%

Where does the conversation most likely take place?
(A) At a hospital
(B) At a publishing house
(C) At a public library
(D) At a car dealership

この会話はどこで交わされている可能性が最も高いですか。
(A) 病院で
(B) 出版社で
(C) 公共図書館で
(D) 自動車販売店で

▶解説 女性は❶で男性が患者待合室の裏の会議室を使用することを確認しています。また、❷では男性がその会議室を新しい看護師の訓練に使うと述べています。これらから、会話の場所は(A)の病院であると推測できます。

□ publishing house: 出版社　□ public library: 公共図書館　□ car dealership: 自動車販売店

51. 正解：B 易■■■■■□□□□難　選択率：(A) 13.6% **(B) 53.6%** (C) 24.5% (D) 8.3%

What did the man hear about the Real Color 90?
(A) It has advanced software.
(B) It is reasonably priced.
(C) It was released recently.
(D) It is popular with colleges.

男性はReal Color 90についてどんなことを聞きましたか。
(A) 先進的なソフトウェアが組み込まれている。
(B) 価格が手頃だ。
(C) 最近発売された。
(D) 大学でよく使われている。

▶解説 女性がプロジェクターの不具合を伝えると、男性は買い換えを提案しています。さらに❸で具体的な商品名Real Color 90に触れ、この機種はvery inexpensive「とても安価」と聞いていると述べています。それを「価格が手頃である」と言い換えた(B)が正解です。

□ advanced: 形 先進的な　□ reasonably: 副 適度に、程よく　□ price: 動 ～に値をつける　□ release: 動 ～を発売する

52. 正解：C 易■■■■□□□□□難　選択率：(A) 21.9% (B) 9.3% **(C) 42.4%** (D)26.5%

What does the man recommend the woman do?
(A) Ask for a demonstration
(B) Call a manager
(C) Go to a specific store
(D) Set up a meeting room

男性は女性に何をするよう勧めていますか。
(A) 実演を依頼する
(B) 管理者に電話をかける
(C) ある店へ行く
(D) 会議室の準備を整える

▶解説 買い換えに同意した女性に対し男性は、安く商品を購入できるという理由から❹でDangerfield Electronicsに行くことを勧めています。「特定の店へ行く」ことを勧めていると考えられるので、正解は(C)です。give a good dealには「商品を安く提供する」という意味があります。

□ recommend: 動 ～を勧める　□ ask for ～: ～を頼む
□ demonstration: 名 実演　□ specific: 形 特定の

ゼミ生中継　Hiro　Mai　Yasu　Dai　Saki

52.
提案問題だね。recommendとWhy don't you ～?の組み合わせは34番で話した通り。ところで、上位グループでは正答率が高いけど、それ以外では低め。どうしてだろう？

言い換えが原因だと思います。後半で聞こえる固有名詞がお店の

名前に聞こえなくて、(C)のspecific storeを選びにくかったです。

その後にThey'll give you a good deal.のTheyを聞いて「人に会うんだ」と思いました。だから誰かと会議を開くのかと思って、(D)を選びました。

Theyは会社や組織を指すことができる。ここではお店だね。

Part 3 会話問題

Questions 53 through 55 refer to the following conversation.

M: ❶ I'm going to visit the clients in Glen Ridge tomorrow.

W: How are you getting there?

M: I'm flying down and staying overnight. ❷ The only problem is that I can't find any accommodation at such late notice.

W: Ah... I know what that's like. ❸ I almost canceled a recent trip because I couldn't find a hotel room. I ended up calling a few hotels directly. Sometimes there are cancellations, but they haven't gotten around to updating the Web site.

M: Great idea. I'll give a few a call then.

W: ❹ Check the map and make sure the hotel is near the client's address, though. Glen Ridge doesn't have a very good transportation system. (108w/40 sec.)

問題53-55は次の会話に関するものです。
男: 明日、Glen Ridge の顧客を訪問する予定なんだ。
女: どうやってそこへ行くの？
男: 飛行機で行って1泊してくる。唯一の問題は、話が急すぎて宿が見つからないことなんだ。
女: ああ……その状況は分かるわ。私なんて、ホテルの部屋が見つからなくて最近、危うく出張を取りやめるところだったもの。結局、2、3のホテルに直接電話したの。たまにキャンセルが出ても、ホテルは手が回らなくてウェブサイトを更新してなかったりするのよ。
男: なるほどね。じゃ、何カ所かに電話してみるよ。
女: でも、地図を調べて、ホテルが客先に近いことを確かめてね。Glen Ridge は交通の便があまり良くないから。

□ fly: 動 (飛行機で) 飛ぶ　□ stay overnight: 1泊する　□ end up -ing: 最後には～する羽目になる　□ transportation system: 交通網

---

53. 正解：C　易 ■■■■□□□□ 難　選択率：(A) 8.9% (B) 6.3% **(C) 82.1%** (D) 2.3%

What is the purpose of the man's trip?
(A) To inspect a facility
(B) To negotiate with a supplier
(C) To meet with a client
(D) To visit a family member

男性の出張の目的は何ですか。
(A) 設備を視察すること
(B) 納入業者と交渉すること
(C) 顧客に会うこと
(D) 家族を訪ねること

▶解説 男性は❶で、明日客先を訪問すると述べています。続けてその訪問先の宿泊手配について話していることから、男性は出張に行くと分かります。目的は顧客に会うためだと判断できるので、正解は (C) です。

□ inspect: 動 ～を視察する　□ facility: 名 設備　□ negotiate: 動 交渉する　□ supplier: 名 供給業者

---

54. 正解：B　易 ■■■□□□□□ 難　選択率：(A) 5.3% **(B) 85.1%** (C) 3.0% (D) 6.6%

Why does the woman say, "I know what that's like"?
(A) She has to meet with some new clients.
(B) She has had trouble finding accommodation.
(C) She does not want to visit Glen Ridge.
(D) She has made the necessary preparations.

女性はなぜ「その状況は分かるわ」と言ってるのですか。
(A) 彼女は新しい顧客に会わなければならない。
(B) 彼女は宿泊施設を見つけるのに苦労したことがある。
(C) 彼女は Glen Ridge を訪問したくない。
(D) 彼女は必要な準備を終えている。

▶解説 男性は❷で宿泊施設を探せないのではないかと懸念しています。そこで女性がI know what that's likeと言い、❸で「ホテルの部屋が見つからずに出張を取りやめかけた」と続けています。宿泊先の確保に苦労した同様の経験があることを伝えているので (B) が正解です。

□ necessary: 形 必要な　□ preparation: 名 準備

---

55. 正解：C　易 ■■□□□□□□ 難　選択率：(A) 3.3% (B) 4.6% **(C) 78.5%** (D) 13.6%

What does the woman suggest the man do?
(A) Secure a seat
(B) Cancel a trip
(C) Check a map
(D) Request a change

女性は男性に何をするよう勧めていますか。
(A) 座席を確保する
(B) 出張を取りやめる
(C) 地図を調べる
(D) 変更を要請する

▶解説 女性は後半で、Glen Ridge は交通の便が良くないと述べ、❹で「地図で調べて、ホテルが客先に近いことを確かめるよう」に男性に伝えています。よって、正解は (C) です。

□ suggest: 動 ～を提案する　□ secure: 動 ～を確保する

ゼミ生中継　　Hiro　Mai　Yasu　Dai　Saki

55.

😮 あれ、また提案問題だ。提案はPart 3に頻出するんですか？

😎 試験によって差はあるけどね。ここで登場しているヒント表現は命令形だね。Check the map ～とmake sure ～が提案を表している。

😮 あの～、命令と提案は同じなのですか？

😎 厳密には違う。ただ、動詞の原形で始まる発言を日本人は「命令形」と呼んでいるだけで、実際にネイティブスピーカーが話す際は命令しているとは限らない。この会話のように、相手に提案や依頼をする場合にも命令形が使われるんだ。同様に、You should ～も提案表現だけど、多くの日本人が思い浮かべる「～すべきだ」というニュアンスが込められているとは限らない。

😮 それは知りませんでした。

DL 046 **Questions 56 through 58** refer to the following conversation with three speakers.

W: Hi, my name's Gina Day. ❶ I brought my car in earlier for a routine service.

M1: Yes, Ms. Day. ❷ We've changed the oil and water, but there're a few other issues that need to be fixed. Just a moment. ❸ Morris, can you talk to Ms. Day about the problems you found?

M2: Hello, Ms. Day. Unfortunately, ❹ you need to have your brakes replaced. It would be dangerous to drive around on them as they are for much longer.

W: OK, Morris. Can you do it today?

M2: ❺ I'm afraid we have a bit too much work today. Can you come back tomorrow morning?

W: I can't come back. Can I just leave the car with you overnight? ❻ I'll have one of my colleagues pick me up here. (122w/42 sec.)

□ routine: 形 定期的な □ issue: 名 問題 □ fix 動 ～を修理する □ brake: 名 ブレーキ □ replace: 動 ～を交換する □ colleague: 名 同僚

問題56-58は次の3人の話者による会話に関するものです。
女：こんにちは、Gina Dayと申します。さっき、車を定期点検に持ち込んだんですが。
男1：はい、Dayさん。オイルと冷却水の交換は済んでいるんですが、他に2、3問題がありまして、修理が必要です。ちょっとお待ちください。Morris、Dayさんに見つけた問題点について説明して。
男2：どうも、Dayさん。あいにく、ブレーキを交換しなければなりません。これ以上、現状のまま運転するのは危険です。
女：分かったわ、Morris。今日、やっていただけるのかしら？
男2：今日はうち、ちょっと立て込んでまして。明朝、出直してきていただけますか。
女：出直してくるわけにはいかないわ。車を一晩、こちらにお預けしていいかしら。同僚の1人に、車で迎えに来てもらいます。

56. 正解：**B** 易■■■□□□□難 選択率：(A) 1.0% **(B) 78.5%** (C) 10.6% (D) 9.6%

Who most likely are the men?
(A) Fashion designers
(B) Automobile mechanics
(C) Factory managers
(D) Taxi drivers

□ automobile: 形 自動車の □ mechanic: 名 修理工

男性たちは誰である可能性が最も高いですか。
(A) ファッションデザイナー
(B) 自動車修理工
(C) 工場の管理者
(D) タクシーの運転手

▶解説 ❶で「定期点検のため車を預けた」という女性に、男性1が❷で作業内容と問題があることを伝え、❸で男性2であるMorrisにその問題の説明を求めています。男性2は❹でブレーキに問題があり運転するのは危険だと述べています。これらから、男性2人は(B)の自動車修理工だと推測できます。

57. 正解：**A** 易■■□□□□□難 選択率：**(A) 83.8%** (B) 3.6% (C) 7.0% (D) 5.0%

What does Morris say about the business?
(A) It is too busy today.
(B) It will be relocated.
(C) It has multiple locations.
(D) It will be closed tomorrow.

□ business: 名 会社 □ relocate: 動 ～を移転させる □ multiple: 形 多数の □ location: 名 店

Morrisはこの会社について何と言っていますか。
(A) 今日は忙しすぎる。
(B) 移転するだろう。
(C) 店が複数ある。
(D) 明日は休業する。

▶解説 女性に、今日中のブレーキ交換作業が可能かどうかを尋ねられたMorris（男性2)は、❺で「あいにく今日は仕事が多すぎます」と答えています。それを「今日は忙しすぎる」と言い換えた(A)が正解です。

58. 正解：**D** 易■■■■■□□難 選択率：(A) 6.6% (B) 22.5% (C) 5.3% **(D) 65.2%**

What does Ms. Day say she will do?
(A) Use another business
(B) Come to work a little earlier
(C) Hire more staff
(D) Ask a coworker for a ride

□ hire: 動 ～を雇う □ coworker: 名 同僚

Dayさんは何をすると言っていますか。
(A) 別の業者を使う
(B) 少し早めに出勤する
(C) もっと人材を雇用する
(D) 同僚に車に乗せてくれるよう頼む

▶解説 翌日の再来店を求められた女性は、その代わりに車を置いていくことを提案します。そのために❻で「同僚に迎えに来てもらう」と述べていることから、正解は(D)です。colleagueとcoworkerの言い換えはTOEICに頻出です。

ゼミ生中継 Hiro Mai Yasu Dai Saki

- 3人の会話が出るのはこれが2回目だけど、気づいていた？
- はい。3人の会話が3つ入ったテストを受けたことがあります。
58.
- これは少し難しいかな。
- 間違えました。pick me upは聞こえた気がしますが、意味が分かりませんでした。

- 同じく。ピックアップは「選ぶ」ですよね。
- pick upには多くの意味があるけど、日本語の「ピックアップ」は和製英語だよ。英語のpick upは「選ぶ」を意味しない。pick someone upは、その人を「車で迎えに行く」を意味することが多い。文脈によるけど。
- 知りませんでした。

Part 3 会話問題

⬇ 047 Questions 59 through 61 refer to the following conversation.

W: Hi. ❶ I was just in the appliance section looking for a water filter. They told me that you had them with the kitchenware. Is that right?

M: Yes. We have a few models. ❷ Would you like to sample the water from each one and see how well they work?

W: That's interesting. I was looking for one that connects to the water supply, so I don't have to refill it all the time.

M: Um... none of these work like that. ❸ We have a new model from one of the makers coming in next month. That should be what you're looking for. 　　　　　　　　　(99w/32 sec.)

問題59-61は次の会話に関するものです。
女：すみません。家電品売り場で浄水器を探していたんですが、店員さんに台所用品売り場にあると言われました。そうなんですか。
男：ええ。2、3の機種をそろえております。それぞれから取った水を試飲して、どの程度の性能かチェックなさいますか。
女：それは面白いわね。でも、私が探しているのは水道につなぐタイプのものなんです。しょっちゅう水をつぎ足さなくても済むようにね。
男：うーん……ここにあるのはどれもそういう働きはしませんね。メーカーの1つから来月新機種が出ます。それが、探していらっしゃるものでしょう。

☐ appliance: 图 電気製品　☐ section: 图 部門　☐ kitchenware: 图 台所用品　☐ model: 图 型、機種　☐ sample: 動 ～の味を見る
☐ work: 動 機能する　☐ connect to ～: ～につながる　☐ water supply: 水道　☐ refill: 動 ～を補充する

---

59. 正解：B 易▰▰▰▱▱▱▱難　選択率：(A) 21.2% **(B) 71.9%** (C) 2.0% (D) 4.6%

Where most likely are the speakers?
(A) In a restaurant kitchen
(B) At a home improvement store
(C) At a food market
(D) At a souvenir shop

話者たちはどこにいる可能性が最も高いですか。
(A) レストランの厨房に
(B) ホームセンターに
(C) 食品市場に
(D) 土産物店に

▶解説 ❶から、女性が浄水器を探し、家電品売り場から台所用品売り場に移動してきたと分かります。また、男性は台所用品売り場の商品について説明していることから、話し手たちはそれらの売り場を持つホームセンターにいると判断できますので、正解は(B)です。

☐ home improvement store: ホームセンター
☐ souvenir: 图 土産

---

60. 正解：D 易▰▰▰▱▱▱▱難　選択率：(A) 10.9% (B) 7.6% (C) 5.0% **(D) 76.5%**

What does the man offer the woman?
(A) A discount
(B) A guided tour
(C) Gift wrapping
(D) Some samples

男性は女性に何を申し出ていますか。
(A) 値引き
(B) 案内ツアー
(C) 贈答用の包装
(D) サンプル

▶解説 男性は女性に、浄水器の機種をいくつか扱っていると伝えた後、❷で各機種が浄水したサンプルを試してみることを勧めています。つまり、男性が女性に提供するのはサンプルだと判断できます。従って正解は(D)です。

☐ offer: 動 ～を申し出る　☐ discount: 图 値引き

---

61. 正解：B 易▰▰▰▱▱▱▱難　選択率：(A)1.0% **(B) 86.1%** (C) 9.9% (D) 2.6%

According to the man, what will happen next month?
(A) The business will be closed.
(B) An item will become available.
(C) A new location will open.
(D) Job applications will be accepted.

男性によると、来月何がありますか。
(A) 閉店する。
(B) ある商品が手に入るようになる。
(C) 新しい店舗が開く。
(D) 仕事の応募書類が受理される。

▶解説 水道に直接つなぐ浄水器を探している女性に、男性は、在庫品はどれもそのタイプではないと説明した後❸で、来月そのタイプの新しい機種が発売されることを付け加えています。それを「商品が手に入るようになる」と言い換えた(B)が正解です。

☐ according to ～: ～によると　☐ happen: 動 起こる　☐ business: 图 店
☐ available: 形 入手可能な　☐ location: 图 店　☐ application: 图 申し込み　☐ accept: 動 ～を受け取る

((∙)) ゼミ生中継　　😀Hiro 😀Mai 😀Yasu 😀Dai 😀Saki

59.
😀 (A)を選んだ人はいる？
😀 はい、選びました。kitchen が聞こえた気がします。
😀 会話にあるのはkitchenware だね。(A)にkitchen が入っているの

はなぜだと思う？
😀 私みたいな人を「釣る」ためですか。
😀 そう。著者の性格が悪いんだよ。

56

TOEICよろず相談所 ヒロの部屋

③先読みが間に合わない!

「先読み」のコツってありますか?　会話を聞く前に問題冊子を読むよう頑張っていますが、3つ目の設問を読む前に会話が始まってしまうんです。

なるほど。設問だけを先読みしていますか。それとも選択肢も読んでいますか。

設問だけ読むようにしています。

それでOKです。3つの設問を速く読む練習をしていますか?

え、練習は……。やっていません。

試験中に思い通りにいかないことがあるのは当然です。それは誰にでも起きます。大事なのは、対策を考えて普段から練習すること。**設問を読むのが遅いなら、速く読む練習をする**のが当たり前の解決策ですよね。

なるほど…そうですね。どんな練習をすればいいですか。

重要情報を素早く拾う練習がいいと思います。例えば、What does the woman suggest the man do?という設問の重要情報はwomanとsuggestです。理由は、その2つの単語により、ヒントが登場する場所を予測できるからです。女性の発言の中、しかも、提案を示す表現の直後にヒントが聞こえると予測できます。さらに、これが1問目なら会話の前半に、3問目なら中盤以降にヒントがありそうだと推測できます。

わ、すごい!

問題集や模試のPart 3を使って、**設問を一瞬だけ見て重要な情報を拾う練習**を1問ずつやってみてください。これをすることで、設問に頻出する単語に慣れますし、重要な情報とそうでない情報を区別する目が養われます。結果的に、読むスピードが上がります。

やってみます!

Part 3 会話問題

Questions 62 through 64 refer to the following conversation and price list.

W: ❶ Are there any seats available for tonight's concert?

M: Not many, I'm afraid. We have two in Row 16 and four on the balcony.

W: ❷ I need four, so we'll take the balcony.

M: Sure. ❸ I recommend that you get here early. Balcony seats are not assigned. So, the earlier you get here, the closer you can get to the front.

W: Thanks for the advice. How can I pay?

M: You can either give me your credit card details, or you can log on to the Web site and pay there. (87w/28 sec.)

問題62-64は次の会話と価格表に関するものです。
女：今夜のコンサートの席は残っていますか。
男：たくさんはないと思います。16列に2席と、バルコニーに4席ありますね。
女：4席必要なので、バルコニー席をお願いします。
男：かしこまりました。早めにご来場されることをお勧めします。バルコニー席は座席指定されていませんので、ご来場が早ければ早いほど前列に近いところに座れます。
女：ご案内をありがとう。支払いはどうすればいいですか。
男：クレジットカードの詳細情報をご提供いただいても、ウェブサイトにログオンしてそこでお支払いいただいても結構です。

☐ available: 形 入手可能な　☐ balcony: 名 バルコニー席（劇場の2階以上の席）　☐ recommend: 動 ～を勧める　☐ assign: 動 ～を割り当てる
☐ details: 名 詳しい情報　☐ log on to ～ : ～にログオンする

Location	Price
Rows 1 through 10	$120
Rows 11 through 21	$100
Rows 22 through 45	$90
❹ Balcony	$60

場所	値段
1列～10列	120ドル
11列～21列	100ドル
22列～45列	90ドル
バルコニー	60ドル

62. 正解：**C**　易 ■■■□□□ 難　選択率：(A) 2.6%　(B) 11.9%　**(C) 80.1%**　(B) 5.3%

What is the woman planning to see?
(A) An acrobatic performance
(B) A play
(C) A concert
(D) A ballet

女性は何を見ることを計画していますか。
(A) 曲芸公演
(B) 演劇
(C) コンサート
(D) バレエ

▶解説 女性は冒頭❶で、コンサートの空席の有無を尋ねています。その後もその座席についての話が続いていることから、女性が予定しているのはコンサートだと判断できます。よって、正解は (C) です。

□ acrobatic：形 軽業の、曲芸的な　□ performance：名 公演　□ play：名 演劇　□ ballet：名 バレエ

---

63. 正解：**D**　易 ■■□□□□ 難　選択率：(A) 12.3%　(B) 8.6%　(C) 6.6%　**(D) 72.5%**

Look at the graphic. How much will the woman be required to pay for each ticket?
(A) $120
(B) $100
(C) $90
(D) $60

図表を見てください。女性はチケット1枚につきいくら請求されますか。
(A) 120ドル
(B) 100ドル
(C) 90ドル
(D) 60ドル

▶解説 バルコニー席が4席空いていると聞き、女性は❷でバルコニー席のチケットを4枚購入しています。価格表の最下段❹に、バルコニー席の料金は60ドルと書かれています。これらから、女性が支払うチケット1枚の金額は60ドルだと分かります。正解は (D) です。

□ require：動 ～を要求する

---

64. 正解：**A**　易 ■■□□□□ 難　選択率：**(A) 78.5%**　(B) 9.3%　(C) 5.0%　(D) 6.6%

What does the man advise the woman to do?
(A) Arrive early
(B) Eat beforehand
(C) Purchase a T-shirt
(D) Bring an umbrella

男性は女性に何をするよう忠告していますか。
(A) 早く到着する
(B) あらかじめ食事をする
(C) Tシャツを購入する
(D) 傘を持ってくる

▶解説 バルコニーは指定席ではなく、早く来るほど前方の席が取りやすいことから、男性は❸で、女性に早く会場へ行くことを勧めています。男性から女性へのアドバイスは (A) の「早く到着する」ことだと考えられます。

□ advise：動 ～を忠告する　□ beforehand：副 あらかじめ　□ purchase：動 ～を購入する

((📡)) ゼミ🔴中継　　😀Hiro 😊Mai 😄Yasu 😑Dai 😆Saki

😄 63番のように Look at the graphic. で始まる設問を「グラフィック問題」と呼ぼう。

63.
😀 価格が問われているけれど、ヒントがズバリ音で聞こえてくるとは期待できない。もし聞こえてきたら表を見なくても解けるからね。「音情報と文字情報を関連付けて解く」のがグラフィック問題の特徴だよ。

64.
😆 やっぱり間違った。痛いなぁ。

😄 63番を意識し過ぎて、64番のヒントを聞き逃したの?

😆 その通りです。なんで分かったんですか。

😄 この2問のヒントが互いに近いから。著者が仕掛けたワナだよ。Balconyとか60ドルを意識しているうちに、男性の I recommend you get here early. を聞き逃したんだよね。

😑 これも「釣り」の一種ですね。著者は本当に性格が悪いですね。

😄 その通りだね。

050 **Questions 65 through 67** refer to the following conversation and list.

M: ❶ We need to advertise on television to attract more shoppers. ❷ Keating Mall in Cambridge has been advertising a lot and some of the store owners here have been complaining that our visitor numbers are down.

W: I see. Well, I'll leave it with you. We produced a new commercial last month. ❸ I think that will cost about five thousand dollars per showing between 7:00 P.M. and 8:00 P.M.

M: OK. I'll ask Channel 7 to run it once a night for a week.

W: ❹ Send an e-mail to the tenants letting them know what we are doing. I want them to see that we are making an effort.

(105w/36 sec.)

問題65-67は次の会話と表に関するものです。

男：テレビに広告を出して、もっと買い物客を呼び寄せる必要があります。CambridgeのKeating Mallはかなり広告を打っていて、うちの出店者の間で苦情が出てるんです、こっちへの来店者数が減っていると言ってね。

女：なるほど。じゃあ、その件はあなたにお任せします。うちで先月、新しい広告を作りました。放映するごとに5000ドルくらいかかると思います、午後7時から8時の間であれば。

男：分かりました。Channel 7に掛け合って、一晩に1回、1週間流してもらいます。

女：メールをテナントに送って、私たちがやっていることを伝えてください。こちらが努力していることを分かってほしいので。

☐ advertise: 動 広告を出す　☐ attract: 動 ～を引き付ける　☐ shopper: 名 買い物客　☐ complain: 動 苦情を言う　☐ visitor: 名 来客
☐ down: 形 落ち込んで　☐ leave ~ with ...: ～を…に任せる　☐ produce: 動 ～を制作する　☐ cost: 動 ～（の金額）がかかる　☐ per: 前 ～ごとに
☐ showing: 名 放映、上映　☐ run: 動 ～を放映する　☐ tenant: 名 テナント　☐ make an effort: 努力する

7:00 P.M. ~ 8:00 P.M. Advertising Rates	
5 seconds	$3,000
❺10 seconds	$5,000
15 seconds	$7,000
20 seconds	$10,000

午後7時～午後8時 コマーシャル料金	
5 秒	3000ドル
10 秒	5000ドル
15 秒	7000ドル
20 秒	1万ドル

65. 正解：A 易 ■■■■□□□ 難　選択率：**(A) 59.9%**　(B) 17.2%　(C) 10.3%　(D) 12.6%

What kind of business do the speakers most likely work for?
(A) A shopping mall
(B) A construction company
(C) A clothing manufacturer
(D) An insurance firm

話者たちは何の会社で仕事をしている可能性が最も高いですか。
(A) ショッピングモール
(B) 建設会社
(C) 衣料品メーカー
(D) 保険会社

▶解説 男性が冒頭❶で、買い物客を増やすためのテレビ広告の必要性に触れ、さらに❷でKeating Mallとの比較や、来店者数減少を訴える店主たちからの不満について言及しています。これらの情報から、彼らが勤務していると考えられるのは(A)のショッピングモールです。

□ business: 名 会社　□ construction: 名 建設　□ clothing: 名 衣類　□ manufacturer: 名 製造業者、メーカー　□ insurance : 名 保険
□ firm: 名 会社

---

66. 正解：B 易 ■■■□□□□ 難　選択率：(A) 4.3%　**(B) 87.7%**　(C) 6.6%　(D) 1.0%

Look at the graphic. How long is the advertisement the speakers plan to broadcast?
(A) 5 seconds
(B) 10 seconds
(C) 15 seconds
(D) 20 seconds

図表を見てください。話者たちはどのくらいの時間、広告を流すつもりですか。
(A) 5秒
(B) 10秒
(C) 15秒
(D) 20秒

▶解説 女性は新しく制作したコマーシャルについて言及し、❸で1回の放映にかかる費用は5000ドルくらいだと概算しています。表を見ると❺で、その金額が10秒間の広告費用だと分かります。正解は(B)です。

□ advertisement: 名 広告　□ broadcast: 動 ～を放映する

---

67. 正解：D 易 ■■■■□□□ 難　選択率：(A) 3.3%　(B) 7.3%　(C) 21.5%　**(D) 67.9%**

What does the woman ask the man to do?
(A) Correct a mistake
(B) Lead a meeting
(C) Make a presentation
(D) Send out an e-mail

女性は男性に何をするよう頼んでいますか。
(A) 誤りを正す
(B) 会議を取り仕切る
(C) 発表する
(D) メールを送る

▶解説 広告手配を男性に依頼した後、女性は❹でショッピングモールの店主たちにその旨をメールで知らせるよう男性に指示しています。女性が男性に依頼したのはメールを送ることだと判断できますので、(D)が正解です。

□ correct: 動 ～を訂正する　□ lead: 動 ～を率いる、リードする

Part 3 ▼ Listening Section

((•)) ゼミ 生中継　😀Hiro 😊Mai 😎Yasu 😐Dai 😀Saki

65.
😀 意外とモニターの正答率が低い。ヤス、難しかった？
😎 消去法で正解を選びましたが、あまり自信なかったです。
😐 同じく。
😀 このような集客の話はビジネスと切っても切れないから、テストによく出るよ。関連して、広告やクーポン券の話も頻出する。サキはクーポン券って何のことか分かる？
😀 はい。よくLINEでファミレスのクーポンをもらいます。
😀 そういう体験はTOEICで役立つよ。実際、Test 2にレストランのクーポン券が登場する。
😀 楽しみです。

66.
😀 マイ、どうやって解いた？
😊 5000ドルが聞こえたので、隣の10秒が正解だと思って(B)を選びました。こんな単純な解き方でいいのでしょうか。
😀 そのような方法で解けてしまう問題が多い。ただ、そうでないケースもある。69番を見てみよう。

Part 3 会話問題

DL 051 **Questions 68 through 70** refer to the following conversation and catalog.

M: Which one of these clocks should we buy for the weight room? We only have a budget of forty dollars.

W: ❶ This will be the main clock for the fitness center, won't it?

M: ❷ That's right. It'll go above the mirror in the weight room.

W: In that case, ❸ I think we should get the big square digital one. That way, gym users will be able to see the time from anywhere in the gym.

M: Good point. I'll order it now. ❹ The Web site says they can deliver it tomorrow afternoon. (88w/28 sec.)

問題68-70は次の会話とカタログに関するものです。

男：これらの時計のうちのどれを買えばいいかな、ウェートルーム用なんだけど。予算はたったの40ドルなんだ。

女：フィットネスセンターのメインの時計にするんでしょ？

男：その通り。ウェートルームの鏡の上に設置される。

女：それなら、その大きくて四角いデジタル時計を買えばいいと思うわ。そうすれば、ジムの利用者がジム内のどこからでも時間を確認できるでしょ。

男：いい指摘だね。すぐにそれを注文しよう。ウェブサイトによると、明日の午後には配送してもらえる。

□ budget: 名 予算 □ order: 動 ～を注文する □ deliver: 動 ～を配達する

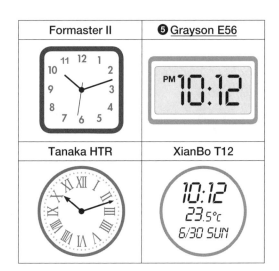

Formaster II	❺ Grayson E56
	PM 10:12
Tanaka HTR	XianBo T12
	10:12 23.5°C 6/30 SUN

68. 正解：C 易 ■■■□□□□ 難 選択率：(A) 7.6% (B) 11.6% **(C) 77.2%** (D) 3.3%

Where do the speakers most likely work?
(A) In a grocery store
(B) In a medical office
(C) In a health club
(D) In a cafeteria

□ grocery store: 食料雑貨店 □ medical office: 診療所 □ health club: スポーツクラブ

話者たちはどこで働いている可能性が最も高いですか。
(A) 食料雑貨店で
(B) 診療所で
(C) スポーツクラブで
(D) カフェテリアで

▶解説 女性が❶で、購入しようとしている時計がフィットネスセンターのメインの時計となることを確認し、男性も❷でそれに同意して時計の設置場所を述べています。よって、2人の職場はフィットネスセンターだと考えられます。それを health club と言い換えた (C) が正解です。

69. 正解：B 易 ■■■□□□□ 難 選択率：(A) 7.6% **(B) 80.1%** (C) 1.3% (D) 10.9%

Look at the graphic. Which clock does the woman recommend?
(A) Formaster II
(B) Grayson E56
(C) Tanaka HTR
(D) XianBo T12

□ recommend: 動 〜を勧める

図表を見てください。女性はどの時計を勧めていますか。
(A) Formaster II
(B) Grayson E56
(C) Tanaka HTR
(D) XianBo T12

▶解説 男性から時計の設置場所を聞いた女性は、❸で大型で四角いデジタルタイプのものを提案し、ジムのどの場所からも見えるから、と付け加えています。カタログによると、その描写に合う時計は❺の Grayson E56 だと判断できます。従って正解は (B) です。

70. 正解：D 易 ■■□□□□□ 難 選択率：(A) 0.7% (B) 7.6% (C) 18.2% **(D) 73.2%**

When will the delivery most likely arrive?
(A) This morning
(B) This afternoon
(C) Tomorrow morning
(D) Tomorrow afternoon

□ delivery: 名 配達物 □ arrive: 動 到着する

いつ配送される可能性が最も高いですか。
(A) 今日の午前中
(B) 今日の午後
(C) 明日の午前中
(D) 明日の午後

▶解説 女性の意見を聞いた男性はそれに同意し、すぐに注文をすると言った後に❹で明日午後の配達が可能であることを女性に伝えています。よって、商品が届けられるのは明日の午後である可能性が高いので正解は (D) です。

Part 3 ▼ Listening Section

((•)) ゼミ 生中継 (😊)Hiro (😊)Mai (😊)Yasu (😑)Dai (😊)Saki

69.

(😊) この問題は 66 番とは少し違う。マイ、分かる?

(😊) 私は (D) にしました。digital がヒントだと思いましたが、(B) と (D) のどちらが正解か分かりませんでした。

(😊) ヒントはもう 1 つあったよ。ダイ、分かった?

(😑) square です。うちの会社は (B) のような時計を作っています。

(😊) 2 つの条件があったのですね。

(😊) そう。(B) と (D) を選んだモニターが多いから、マイのように square を聞き逃した人が多かったんだろうね。では、次は Part 4。

Part 4 説明文問題

Questions 71 through 73 refer to the following telephone message.

M: ❶ Hi, it's Gael Ortega from Dalton Chemists in West Miami. Um... I'm calling about the order you made yesterday. ❷ We've got all the items on your prescription. There's a lot more than you usually get, but ❸ I understand you'll be on a business trip from Friday and you won't be back for a couple of months. It's more than we usually like to give out at once, so I strongly recommend keeping it in the refrigerator. You said you'd be coming in on Friday. Unfortunately, I won't be here then, so ❹ you'd better have your driver's license or some other identification to show the pharmacist.

(105w/36 sec.)

問題71-73は次の電話メッセージに関するものです。
男：もしもし、West MiamiにあるDalton ChemistsのGael Ortegaです。ええと……お電話差し上げておりますのは、昨日のご発注についてです。あなたの処方箋にあるものは全てご用意いたしました。いつもお受け取りいただいているよりもだいぶ分量が多くなっていますが、金曜日から出張に行かれて、2カ月戻られないご予定と承知しております。通常一回にお渡しする分量を超えておりますので、冷蔵庫に保管なさることを強くお勧めします。金曜日にお見えになるとおっしゃっていましたが、あいにく私がその時、不在の予定ですので、運転免許証など何らかの身分証明書をお持ちいただき、薬剤師にお見せいただく方がよろしいでしょう。

□ call: 動 電話をかける □ order: 名 注文 □ item: 名 品目 □ prescription: 名 処方箋 □ usually: 副 普段は □ business trip: 出張 □ give out 〜: 〜を出す □ at once: 一度に □ strongly: 副 強く □ keep: 動 〜をしまっておく □ refrigerator: 名 冷蔵庫 □ driver's license: 運転免許証 □ identification: 名 身分証明書 □ pharmacist: 名 薬剤師

---

71. 正解：A 易 ■■■□□ 難 選択率：**(A) 65.2%** (B) 11.3% (C) 3.0% (D) 19.5%

Where is the speaker calling from?
(A) A pharmacy
(B) A research center
(C) A fashion outlet
(D) A storage facility

□ outlet: 名 小売店

話者はどこから電話をかけていますか。
(A) 薬局
(B) 研究所
(C) ファッション関係の販売店
(D) 貯蔵施設

▶解説 ❶から、話者はDalton Chemists（薬局）で働いており、❷で聞き手の処方箋を元に品物を用意したことが分かります。❹では、聞き手に身分証をpharmacist（薬剤師）に見せる必要があることを伝えていることからも、正解は(A)の「薬局」です。

---

72. 正解：C 易 ■■□□□ 難 選択率：(A) 9.3% (B) 3.6% **(C) 81.8%** (D) 4.6%

What will the listener most likely do on Friday?
(A) See a doctor
(B) Administer a test
(C) Go on a business trip
(D) Participate in a seminar

□ participate in 〜: 〜に参加する

聞き手は金曜日に何をする可能性が最も高いですか。
(A) 医者にかかる
(B) 検査を行う
(C) 出張に行く
(D) セミナーに出席する

▶解説 話者は❸で、「あなたが金曜日から出張に行くと分かっている」と述べています。よって、聞き手は金曜日から出張に行くと考えられるので、正解は(C)です。

---

73. 正解：C 易 □□□□□ 難 選択率：(A) － (B) － (C) － (D) －

What is the listener reminded to do?
(A) Submit a payment
(B) Cancel an appointment
(C) Bring some identification
(D) Read some instructions

□ submit: 動 〜を提出する、提示する □ instruction: 名 指示

聞き手は何をするよう念を押されていますか。
(A) 支払いをする
(B) 約束をキャンセルする
(C) 身分証明書を持参する
(D) 指示を読む

▶解説 話者は❹でyou'd better 〜（あなたは〜をした方がいいです）と相手に物事を勧める時の表現を使い、「driver's license（運転免許証）やsome other identification（その他の身分証明書）があった方がいい」と述べています。よって、(C)が正解です。

((・)) ゼミ 生 中継

Hiro Mai Yasu Dai Saki

71.

😺 「製薬会社」を英語で何て言う？ pharmacyに似た単語を使うんだけど。

🐱 ドラッグストア！

😺 それはdrugstoreだよ。薬を売る店だからpharmacyと同じ。マイは知ってる？

😺 確か、ファーマスーなんとかですね。

😺 そう。pharmaceutical companyだよ。

😺 発音もスペルも難しくて覚えられません。

😺 まぁね。発音はGoogle翻訳に入れれば一発で分かる。今、やってごらん。

DL 054 **Questions 74 through 76** refer to the following talk.

W: ❶Let's get today's board meeting started. First, we'll talk about the new parking garage at our headquarters. We all know that additional parking is urgently needed, but ❷the construction company says that it can't honor the original estimate because material prices have risen. I think it's a valid reason. Basically, ❸we really need to get some extra funding. I don't want to raise our prices or reduce the size of the parking garage. So, ❹I propose that we sell the land we purchased at 19 Goldberg Street. It was originally intended for a parking garage, anyway.　　(96w/40 sec.)

問題74-76は次のトークに関するものです
女：今日の役員会議を始めましょう。まずは、本社の新しい駐車場についての話です。皆さんご承知のとおり、追加の駐車スペースが早急に必要なのですが、建設会社が当初の見積価格ではできないと言っています。材料費が高騰したからです。もっともな理由だと思います。そもそも、追加の資金が本当に必要なのです。当社の販売価格を引き上げたくはありませんし、駐車場の規模を縮小したくもありません。そこで、19 Goldberg Street に購入した土地の売却を提案いたします。あそこは、どのみち元々駐車場に充てるつもりだった所です。

☐ board meeting: 取締役会議　☐ parking garage: 駐車場　☐ headquarters: 名 本社　☐ urgently: 副 至急
☐ construction company: 建設会社　☐ honor: 動（取り決めなど）を守る　☐ original: 形 最初の　☐ estimate: 名 見積もり
☐ material: 名 材料　☐ rise: 動 上昇する　＊risen は過去分詞　☐ valid: 形 正当な　☐ reason: 名 理由
☐ basically: 副 基本的に言えば　☐ funding: 名 資金　☐ raise: 動（価格）を引き上げる　☐ originally: 副 もとは

---

74. 正解：**C**　易 ■■■■□□□ 難　選択率：(A) 16.9%　(B) 8.3%　**(C) 60.3%**　(D) 14.2%

Who is the talk intended for?
(A) Financial advisors
(B) Recent hires
(C) Company executives
(D) Retail shop owners

このトークは誰に向けられていますか。
(A) 財務顧問たち
(B) 最近雇われた人たち
(C) 会社の重役たち
(D) 小売店の店主たち

▶解説 ❶でboard meeting（役員会議）が始まることが伝えられ、話の後半では、駐車場を作るための予算の話をしていることからも、この話は (C)「会社の役員」に向けて行われているものだと言えます。

☐ financial: 形 金融の　☐ hire: 名 雇用
☐ executive: 名 役員　☐ retail shop: 小売店

---

75. 正解：**B**　易 ■■■■□□□ 難　選択率：(A) 6.3%　**(B) 53.0%**　(C) 4.6%　(D) 35.4%

What problem does the speaker mention?
(A) A drop in customer numbers
(B) A lack of funding
(C) Unfavorable weather conditions
(D) Insufficient factory capacity

話者はどんな問題に触れていますか。
(A) 顧客数の減少
(B) 資金不足
(C) 好ましくない気象条件
(D) 不十分な工場の生産能力

▶解説 ❷で「建設会社が材料費の高騰により当初の見積価格ではできない」と述べられています。これは、駐車場を作る費用が予定より大きくなることを示しています。そのため話者は❸で、追加の資金が必要だと述べています。よって、それを「資金不足」と表した (B) が正解です。

☐ mention: 動 〜に言及する　☐ drop: 名 下落　☐ lack: 名 不足
☐ unfavorable: 形 不都合な、不利な　☐ weather condition: 気象条件
☐ insufficient: 形 不十分な　☐ capacity: 名（工場などの）生産力

---

76. 正解：**D**　易 ■■■■■□□ 難　選択率：(A) 5.0%　(B) 68.9%　(C) 1.0%　**(D) 25.2%**

What does the speaker suggest?
(A) Expanding a factory
(B) Renting a parking space
(C) Holding an event
(D) Selling an asset

話者は何を提案していますか。
(A) 工場を拡張すること
(B) 駐車スペースを借りること
(C) イベントを開催すること
(D) 資産を売却すること

▶解説 話者は❹で、以前購入した土地を売ることを提案しています。よって、the land（土地）を an asset（資産）と言い換えた (D) が正解です。

☐ expand: 動 〜を拡大する　☐ hold: 動 〜を開催する　☐ asset: 名 資産、財産

((·A·)) ゼミ 生 中継　😮 Hiro 😊 Mai 😀 Yasu 🎲 Dai 😄 Saki

74.
😮 この言い換えは重要。例えば、Part 7 で Who is Tony Suzuki? と問われたとしよう。Suzuki さんが会社の社長だったら、正解は A company executive と表現されがち。覚えておいてね。

75.
😮 (D) を選んだ人は？
😄 選びました。additional とか extra とかが聞こえたので、とにかく

「何かが足りない」と分かりました。
😮 そっか。(D) の Insufficient は「不十分な」だから、魅力的に見えたのか。でも、その後ろがダメだね。factory capacity は生産能力だから関係ない。
😄 それ以前に、お金のことを funding と言うのを知りませんでした。だから、extra funding を聞き取れなかったんです。
😮 失敗からの学びだね。

Part 4 説明文問題

DL 055 **Questions 77 through 79** refer to the following excerpt from a speech.

W: ❶ We'll be starting today's workshop on team management with a very special speaker. I'd like to introduce you all to Claudia Dawe. Some of you may have seen her on television talking about group dynamics and workplace morale. ❷ She's been making a lot of public appearances since winning the Cochran Award for Non-fiction Writing. ❸ The book has helped many famous companies improve both morale and productivity. This is a very rare opportunity as ❹ Ms. Dawe has accepted a job at Howerton Technology, where she'll head up their human resources department. This will probably be her last freelance speaking engagement for some time.

(102w/42 sec.)

問題77-79は次のスピーチの一部に関するものです。
女：今日のチーム管理研修会は、大変特別な講演者と共に始めます。皆さんにClaudia Daweさんを紹介したいと思います。中には、テレビで彼女が集団力学や職場における士気に関して話されるのを、見たことがある人もいるかもしれません。彼女は、Cochran Award for Non-fiction Writingを受賞なさってから、何度も公の場に姿を見せていらっしゃいます。その本は、多くの有名企業が労働意欲と生産性の両面を改善する上での一助となっています。Daweさんは Howerton Technologyで職に就くことを決め、人事部を率いる任に当たられることになるので、今回は非常に貴重な機会です。おそらく今回をもって、フリーランスの立場でお話しくださるのは当面、終わりとなるでしょう。

□ dynamics: 名 力学 □ workplace: 名 職場 □ morale: 名 士気 □ make a public appearance: 公の場に姿を現す □ productivity: 名 生産性
□ head up ～ : ～を率いる □ human resources department: 人事部 □ freelance: 形 フリーランスの □ engagement: 名 (活動などへの) 関与

---

77. 正解：B 易 ■■■□□□□ 難 選択率：(A) 12.9% **(B) 76.2%** (C) 5.6% (D) 5.0%

What is the occasion for the speech?
(A) A book signing
(B) A management workshop
(C) A trade show
(D) A retirement celebration

どのような場で、このスピーチが行われていますか。
(A) 本のサイン会
(B) 管理研修会
(C) 見本市
(D) 退職祝賀会

▶解説 ❶から、チーム管理研修会が行われることが分かるので、(B)が正解です。本の紹介はされていますが、サイン会が行われているわけではないので、(A)は誤りです。

---

78. 正解：A 易 ■■■■□□□ 難 選択率：**(A) 58.9%** (B) 5.3% (C) 23.2% (D) 11.3%

What has Ms. Dawe received recognition for?
(A) Writing a helpful book
(B) Reducing departmental spending
(C) Completing a successful career
(D) Founding a profitable business

Daweさんはどのようなことで知られていますか。
(A) 役立つ本を書くこと
(B) 部門別支出を削減すること
(C) 輝かしい経歴を完遂すること
(D) 高収益企業を創設すること

▶解説 ❷から、Daweさんの本が賞を受賞したことが分かります。その本は「多くの有名企業の労働意欲と生産性を改善する一助となった」と❸で紹介されています。これらの彼女の実績を「役に立つ本を書いたこと」と表現した(A)が正解です。

□ recognition: 名 認められること □ departmental : 形 部門の □ spending: 名 支出
□ found: 動 ～を設立する □ profitable: 形 もうけの多い

---

79. 正解：D 易 ■■■■■■□ 難 選択率：(A) 30.1% (B) 34.8% (C) 10.3% **(D) 23.8%**

What is Ms. Dawe planning to do in the future?
(A) Produce a television program
(B) Take a job at a university
(C) Relocate to a new city
(D) Lead a department

Daweさんは、この先何をする予定ですか。
(A) テレビ番組を制作する
(B) 大学で職に就く
(C) 新たな都市へ移住する
(D) ある部署を率いる

▶解説 Daweさんの今後については❹から、これから入社するHowerton Technologyで人事部を率いることが分かります。それを「ある部署を率いる」と言い換えた(D)が正解です。

□ relocate: 動 移転する □ lead: 動 ～を率いる、リードする

ゼミ生中継 ⊙⊙Hiro ⊙⊙Mai ⊙⊙Yasu ⊙⊙Dai ⊙⊙Saki

78.
⊙⊙ (D)を選ぶモニターが意外と多かったけど、どうしてかな？
⊙⊙ Daweさんの本のおかげで、多くの会社がもうかったと思いました。だから、(D)のprofitableとかbusinessが良さそうに見えました。
⊙⊙ 同じく。
⊙⊙ その理解は悪くないけど、(D)はFoundingで始まっているから、Daweさんがもうかる会社を設立したという意味だよ。

79.
⊙⊙ Daweさんはもうすぐ企業で働くよね。Ms. Dawe has accepted a job ～と聞こえるから、(B)を選びたくなった？
⊙⊙ 一瞬そう思いましたが、大学には行かないので違うと思いました。ただ、引っ越しすると勝手に妄想して、(C)にしてしまいました。
⊙⊙ 私も同じです。(D)のleadの意味を知りませんでした。
⊙⊙ このleadは「率いる」だよ。head upの言い換えになっている。

DL 056 **Questions 80 through 82** refer to the following advertisement.

M: They're back in town! ❶ Anton's Circus is now preparing to amaze audiences here in Brisbane. They've brought some incredible entertainers from all over the world, so it really is a rare opportunity. ❷ It's here for one week only before it moves on to Sydney and Canberra. ❸ They've set up their enormous new tent at Graham Park in Chirnside. It's right in front of the station. You can't miss it. There's plenty of parking available and trains and buses every few minutes. Be sure to catch this fantastic show.

(88w/37 sec.)

問題80-82は次の宣伝に関するものです。
男：またやって来ました！　Anton's CircusがここBrisbaneで観客を驚かせようと、ただ今準備中です。同団は世界中から最高のエンターテイナーたち数名を帯同してきていますので、まさにめったにないチャンスです。当地で1週間だけ公演した後に、SydneyやCanberraへ移動する予定です。同団はChirnsideのGraham Parkに巨大な新しいテントを張っています。駅の真ん前です。一目で分かります。十分な駐車スペースをご利用いただけますし、鉄道やバスも数分おきに運行しています。ぜひとも、この素晴らしいショーをお見逃しなく。

□amaze: 動 ～をひどくびっくりさせる　□audience: 名 聴衆　□incredible: 形 驚くべき　□set up: (テントを) 張る　□enormous: 形 巨大な
□right: 副 ちょうど　□plenty of ～: 十分な～　□fantastic: 形 素晴らしい

80. 正解：**A**　易■■■□□□□難　選択率：**(A) 86.4%** (B) 2.3% (C) 1.7% (D) 7.3%

What is being advertised?
(A) A circus
(B) A workshop
(C) A sporting competition
(D) A theatrical production

何が宣伝されていますか。
(A) サーカス
(B) 研修会
(C) スポーツの競技会
(D) 演劇作品

▶解説 Part 4のadvertisement (宣伝) では、たいてい冒頭で「何の宣伝か」が述べられるので、その情報を聞き逃さないようにしましょう。❶からAnton's Circusというサーカス団がBrisbaneに来ることが分かるので、正解は(A)です。

□advertise: 動 ～を広告する　□competition: 名 競技会
□theatrical: 形 演劇の　□production: 名 製作

81. 正解：**C**　易■■■□□□□難　選択率：(A) 2.3% (B) 1.7% **(C) 89.1%** (D) 5.0%

How long will the event be held?
(A) For one day
(B) For two days
(C) For one week
(D) For two weeks

この催事はどのくらいの期間、行われますか。
(A) 1日
(B) 2日間
(C) 1週間
(D) 2週間

▶解説 話者は❷で「サーカス団は1週間だけここ (Brisbane) にいる」と述べています。よって、正解は(C)です。

82. 正解：**B**　易■■■■□□□難　選択率：(A) 35.1% **(B) 46.4%** (C) 6.0% (D) 10.6%

What does the speaker imply when he says, "You can't miss it"?
(A) Everyone is required to attend.
(B) A venue is very easy to find.
(C) A product is not popular with many people.
(D) Listeners will be given free tickets.

話者はどのような意味を込めて「一目で分かります」と言っているのですか。
(A) 全員が参加を求められている。
(B) ある会場が非常に簡単に見つかる。
(C) ある製品が多くの人に支持されているわけではない。
(D) 聞き手たちが無料のチケットをもらえる。

▶解説 話者は❸でサーカス団が公園内にテントを立てたと伝え、「駅のすぐ目の前」と説明しています。その直後にYou can't miss it. が続いているので、この発言は「とても見つけやすい場所にある」を意味するものだと解釈できます。よって、(B)が正解です。

□imply: 動 ～を暗に意味する　□require: 動 ～を要求する
□attend: 動 ～に出席する　□venue: 名 会場
□product: 名 製品　□popular: 形 人気のある、評判の良い
□listener: 名 (ラジオの) 聴取者　□free: 形 無料の

ゼミ生中継　Hiro　Mai　Yasu　Dai　Saki

82.
やっぱり、間違えた。(A)じゃなかった。

(A)を選んだモニターは多い。 You can't miss it. は文脈によっては「欠席できない」「出席必須」と解釈できるから、トークを誤解すると選びたくなっても無理はない。ただ、このトークはサーカスの宣伝だから、80番で(A)を選べていたのなら、82番で(A)を選ぶのは変だけど。

そうか、そんな発想があったのですね。

一番大切なのは「英語を聞いて理解する力」だよ。忘れないでね。

Part 4 説明文問題

058 Questions 83 through 85 refer to the following talk.

W: Thank you for gathering at such short notice. ❶I'm happy to announce that Joe Baxter has been appointed as the new director of marketing. As you know, Joe is a son of Russel Baxter, who retired ten years ago. ❷Joe is going to be in charge of marketing our clothing to younger generations through social network services– a job he's far more qualified for than anyone else here. ❸He has acquired his knowledge and expertise working at Fielding Research Institute, where he pioneered many of the techniques now used by leading technology companies around the world. ❹Joe, would you mind coming up here and saying a few words?

(108w/40 sec.)

問題83-85は次のトークに関するものです。
女：急なお知らせにもかかわらずお集まりいただきまして、ありがとうございます。Joe Baxter が新たな営業部長に就任いたしましたことを、ここに発表いたします。ご承知のとおり、Joe は10年前に引退した Russel Baxter 氏のご子息です。Joe は当社の若年層向け衣料品の、SNSを通じたマーケティングを担当する予定です――この職務は、ここにいる他の誰よりもはるかに彼に適任です。彼が今の知識や専門技術を身に付けたのは、Fielding Research Institunte での業務を通じてです。そこで彼は、今世界中の大手テクノロジー企業で用いられている技術の多くを、他に先駆けて開発しました。Joe、こちらへ来て一言いただけますか。

□ gather: 動 集まる　□ appoint: 動 ～を任命する　□ director: 名 部長、指導者　□ market: 動 ～を市場に出す、売る　□ clothing: 名 衣類
□ generation: 名 同世代の人々　□ qualified: 形 資格のある　□ acquire: 動 ～を学ぶ、得る　□ knowledge: 名 知識
□ expertise: 名 専門的知識、ノウハウ　□ pioneer: 動 (新分野)を開く、率先する　□ technique: 名 技術　□ leading: 形 主要な

---

83. 正解：D 易■■■□□□□難　選択率：(A) 1.3% (B) 12.9% (C) 28.1% **(D) 55.6%**

What is the topic of the talk?
(A) A schedule update
(B) A company merger
(C) A marketing campaign
(D) A personnel change

このトークの話題は何ですか。
(A) スケジュールの更新
(B) 会社の合併
(C) 販売キャンペーン
(D) 人員の変更

▶解説 ❶から、Joe Baxter さんが営業部長に就任したことが分かります。彼の担当業務や職務経歴を説明する発言が続いていることからも、正解は (D) です。

□ update: 名 最新化、更新　□ merger: 名 合併　□ personnel: 名 社員

---

84. 正解：B 易■■■■□□□難　選択率：(A) 11.9% **(B) 64.2%** (C) 16.9% (D) 5.3%

What is Joe Baxter's area of expertise?
(A) Audio engineering
(B) Social network services
(C) Personnel administration
(D) Corporate financing

Joe Baxter の専門分野は何ですか。
(A) 音響技術
(B) SNS
(C) 人事
(D) 企業財務

▶解説 ❷で、Joe Baxter さんの担当は「若年層向け衣料品の、SNSを通じたマーケティング」だと述べられています。❸でも、彼が前職での業務を通してテクノロジー分野での先駆者であることが述べられているので、正解は (B) です。

□ administration: 名 本部、管理者側　□ corporate: 形 法人の
□ finance: 動 資金を調達する

---

85. 正解：D 易■■■■□□□難　選択率：(A) 4.6% (B) 9.3% (C) 45.7% **(D) 38.4%**

What does the speaker ask Joe Baxter to do?
(A) Register for a course
(B) Join a luncheon
(C) Explain a technology
(D) Address an audience

話者は Joe Baxter に何をするよう求めていますか。
(A) ある講座へ登録する
(B) 昼食会に参加する
(C) ある技術について説明する
(D) 聴衆に話をする

▶解説 話者は❹でJoe と呼び掛け、would you mind -ing?（～していただけませんか）と相手に依頼する表現に続けて、簡単なあいさつをすることを頼んでいます。この内容を「聴衆に話をする」と表した (D) が正解です。

□ luncheon: 名 昼食　□ address: 動 ～に話し掛ける　□ audience: 名 聴衆

ゼミ生中継

Hiro　Mai　Yasu　Dai　Saki

83.
Part 3と同じで、トピックが問われたらトークを聞けば聞くほど解きやすくなるよ。

85.
サキ、どれを選んだ？

(C)と(D)で迷って、(D)にしました。

ナイス。address もaudienceもトークには登場しないけど、内容的に問題ない。(C)のtechnologyはトーク後半ではっきり聞こえるから、それを利用した「釣り」だよ。今回は釣られなかったんだね。

はい。

見事に釣られました。

DL 059　Questions 86 through 88 refer to the following announcement.

M: ❶Good morning shoppers and welcome to Fairway Supermarket, where you get the best food at the lowest prices every single day. ❷We have specials in dairy, fruit and vegetables, and the frozen foods' sections. Talk to the staff members there to learn more. ❸In a few moments, staff from our award-winning in-store bakery will be delivering freshly baked loaves of bread to the display tables set up at the front of the store. ❹These are always popular items and they sell out in no time at all. If you're interested, get over there fast. You really don't want to be last in line.

(103w/38 sec.)

問題86-88は次のお知らせに関するものです。

男：おはようございます、ご来店の皆さま、ようこそFairway Supermarketへ。当店では最良の品を最安値で、毎日お買い求めいただけます。乳製品、果物と野菜、および冷凍食品の売り場で特価品を販売しております。詳しくは売り場の係員にお尋ねください。数分後に、受賞実績を持つ店内ベーカリーの店員が焼きたてのパンを塊ごと、店舗正面の陳列台に並べます。これは常に人気商品で、あっという間に売り切れてしまいます。ご興味を持たれたお客さまは、急いでお越しください。列の最後尾に並ぶのは本当にやめた方がいいですよ。

□ shopper: 名 買い物客　□ dairy: 名 乳製品　□ frozen food: 冷凍食品　□ section: 名 部門　□ staff member: 職員、社員
□ in a few moments: 間もなく　□ in-store: 形 店内の　□ bakery: 名 パン屋、ベーカリー　□ deliver: 動 ～を届ける　□ freshly: 副 新しく
□ loaf: 名 パンの1斤　＊loavesは複数形　□ display tables: 陳列台　□ sell out: 売り切れる　□ interested: 形 興味を持った

---

86. 正解：A　易 ■■■□□□□□ 難　選択率：**(A) 95.7%** (B) 0.3% (C) 1.3% (D) 1.0%

Where is the announcement being made?
(A) In a supermarket
(B) In a sporting goods store
(C) In a hardware store
(D) In an electronics shop

このお知らせはどこで行われていますか。
(A) スーパーマーケットで
(B) スポーツ用品店で
(C) ホームセンターで
(D) 電器店で

▶解説　❶のFairway Supermarketというスーパーマーケットの店名が決定的なヒントです。ここを聞き逃しても話者は❷で「乳製品、果物と野菜、そして冷凍食品の売り場に特価品がある」と発言していることから、スーパーマーケットだと推測することができます。(A)が正解です。

□ hardware: 名 金物類　□ electronics: 名 電子装置、電子機器

---

87. 正解：B　易 ■■■■□□□□ 難　選択率：(A) 9.6% **(B) 15.9%** (C) 61.6% (D) 10.3%

What does the speaker say about the business?
(A) It is open until late.
(B) It has won an award.
(C) It is holding a seasonal sale.
(D) It is employing new staff.

話者はこの店について何と言っていますか。
(A) 遅くまで営業している。
(B) 受賞したことがある。
(C) 季節ごとのセールを開催している。
(D) 新しいスタッフを採用している。

▶解説　話者は❸で、our award-winning in-store bakery（受賞実績を持つ当店内のベーカリー）と述べています。この発言をwon an award（受賞した）と言い換えた(B)が正解です。季節ごとにセールが開かれているとは述べられていないため、(C)は不正解です。

□ seasonal: 形 季節の　□ employ: 動 ～を雇う

---

88. 正解：A　易 ■■■□□□□□ 難　選択率：**(A) 62.3%** (B) 20.9% (C) 2.6% (D) 11.6%

Why does the speaker say, "You really don't want to be last in line"?
(A) There is a limited number of the goods available.
(B) It will take a long time to serve customers.
(C) The store will close very soon.
(D) The line will extend outdoors.

なぜ話者は「列の最後尾に並ぶのは本当にやめた方がいいですよ」と言っていますか。
(A) 手に入る商品の数に限りがある。
(B) 客に出すのに時間がかかる。
(C) 店はまもなく閉店する。
(D) 列は店外にまで伸びるだろう。

▶解説　❹で「パンは人気商品であっという間に売り切れる」と述べられ、「興味を持った人は急いで行くように」と促しています。この流れから、設問の発言は「商品の数に限りがある」ことを伝えるための発言だと判断できるので、正解は(A)です。

□ limited: 形 限られた、わずかな　□ serve: 動 （店の人が客の）注文を聞く
□ extend: 動 ～に伸びる　□ outdoors: 副 戸外へ、屋外へ

((・)) ゼミ生中継　Hiro　Mai　Yasu　Dai　Saki

87.

😀 上級グループの5割近くが(C)を選び、中級と初級グループでは、なんと6割以上が(C)を選んでいる。

😺 私も(C)に引き寄せられました。トーク全体がバーゲンセールの雰囲気でしたので。

😈 ですよね～。

😎 同じく。ただ、(B)のヒントに気づかなかった自分が悪いのですが。

😆 お、分かっているじゃないか。そう、すべては自己責任だよ。

Part 4　Listening Section

Part 4 説明文問題

060 **Questions 89 through 91** refer to the following telephone message.

W: Hi. It's Kate Sunderland from Astrax Motors. This is a message for customer service staff. I've been checking the confirmations for our event on the conference center Web site and ❶ it looks like you have the wrong reservation date– June 10 instead of June 11. I really hope the conference center isn't fully booked on that day. ❷ If it is, we'll have to look at finding another venue for our product launch. We are flexible on the size of the hall. At the moment, we've booked the largest of the event halls. We could go with the second largest if that's all that's available. Anyway, ❸ please give me an e-mail with any updated information as soon as possible.

(118w/49 sec.)

問題89-91は次の電話メッセージに関するものです。

女：もしもし。Astrax MotorsのKate Sunderlandです。このメッセージは顧客サービス担当の方々へ向けたものです。会議場のウェブサイトで当社のイベントに関する確認情報を調べていたのですが、どうやら間違った日に予約が入ってしまっているようです——6月11日ではなく6月10日に。会議場がその日に埋まっていないことを切に望みますが、埋まっていた場合には、当社の商品発表へ向けて別の会場を見つけなければならなくなります。会場の規模にはこだわりません。今のところは、最大規模の催事場を押さえています。利用できる会場がなければ、これに次ぐ規模の場所でも構わないでしょう。いずれにしても、私宛てにメールで、できるだけ早く最新の状況を報告してください。

☐ customer service: 顧客サービス ☐ confirmation: 名 確認 ☐ conference center: 会議場 ☐ wrong: 形 誤った
☐ A instead of B: Bの代わりにA ☐ hope: 動 (〜であれば良い)と思う ☐ fully: 副 完全に ☐ book: 動 〜を予約する
☐ look at 〜: 〜を検討する ☐ venue: 名 会場 ☐ launch: 名 (新製品の)発売 ☐ flexible: 形 融通の利く ☐ updated: 形 最新の

---

89. 正解：**C** 易■■■■■■難 選択率：(A) 6.6% (B) 15.9% **(C) 70.2%** (D) 2.3%

What problem does the speaker report?
(A) A speaker will be unavailable.
(B) A venue is too small.
(C) A reservation may be wrong.
(D) A prototype is not ready.

話者はどんな問題を報告していますか。
(A) 講演者の都合がつかなくなるだろう。
(B) 会場が小さ過ぎる。
(C) 予約に間違いがあるかもしれない。
(D) 試作品ができていない。

▶解説 話者はイベント会場の予約確認を行っていると述べた後、❶で「間違った日に予約がしてあるようだ」と伝えています。よって、(C)が正解です。

☐ report: 動 〜を報告する ☐ prototype: 名 プロトタイプ、試作品 ☐ ready: 形 準備ができて

---

90. 正解：**A** 易■■■■■■難 選択率：**(A) 66.2%** (B) 15.9% (C) 4.0% (D) 9.3%

What kind of event is the speaker planning?
(A) A product launch
(B) A company banquet
(C) A farewell party
(D) A weekend workshop

話者はどのような催事を計画していますか。
(A) 商品発表会
(B) 会社の宴会
(C) 送別会
(D) 週末の研修会

▶解説 話者は❷で、予定していた会議場が使えない場合の対応を「別の場所を見つける必要がある」と言い、「for our product launch (当社の商品発表のため)」と続けています。よって、話者が計画しているイベントは、(A)です。

☐ banquet: 名 晩餐会、(正式な)宴会 ☐ farewell: 名 別れ

---

91. 正解：**D** 易■■■■■■難 選択率：(A) 0.7% (B) 1.3% (B) 3.6% **(D) 89.7%**

What does the speaker request?
(A) An agenda
(B) A telephone number
(C) An invitation
(D) A confirmation e-mail

話者は何を求めていますか。
(A) 予定表
(B) 電話番号
(C) 招待状
(D) 確認のメール

▶解説 話者が依頼していることを示すヒントは、依頼表現と共に聞こえてきます。❸にpleaseで始まる依頼表現があり、話者は「最新の状況をメールする」よう頼んでいます。これを「確認のメール」と言い換えた(D)が正解です。

☐ agenda: 名 予定表 ☐ invitation: 名 招待状

((📡)) ゼミ生中継　　　😀 Hiro 😀 Mai 😀 Yasu 😀 Dai 😀 Saki

90. ......

😀 (A)のlaunchという単語は重要だよ。基本的には「始める」とか「売り出す」ことを意味する。名詞としても動詞としても試験に出るよ。

😀 よく、ランチと見間違えるんですよね〜。

😀 どんな名詞が目的語になりそうか教えて、マイ。

😀 campaignとかproductでしょうか。

😀 いいね。ダイは何か知っている？

😀 ミサイルです。

😀 確かにそれもある。ただ、TOEICワールドにはミサイルは存在しないけどね。

DL 061 **Questions 92 through 94** refer to the following excerpt from a meeting.

M: As of tomorrow, we'll be adopting new hours of operation. I'm sure you're all well aware of this. ❶A lot of our patients have been too busy to see the dentists during the day and we've been getting more and more appointments in the evenings. We can't stay open any later at night so we're now offering early morning consultations. ❷From tomorrow, we're opening the doors at 7:00 A.M. This means that the first shift will start at 6:30 A.M. ❸Grazer Dental Clinic trialed the same thing last year, and, they're staying with it. So, ❹it appears to be a viable option. ❺It'll mean having two shifts of dentists and dental hygienists, but I'm sure they'll be happy to work slightly different hours.　(123w/49 sec.)

問題92-94は次の会議の一部に関するものです。
男：明日付けで、新たな診療時間を導入します。皆さん、これについてはすでにご存じのはずです。当院の患者さんの多くが大変多忙で、昼間に歯科医の診療を受けられず、夕刻の予約がどんどん増えてきています。これ以上、夜遅くまで診療できませんので、これからは早朝の診療を実施していきます。明日から、午前7時に診療を開始します。これはつまり、最初のシフトが午前6時30分に始まるということです。Grazer Dental Clinic が昨年、同様の試みを行い、今も続けています。つまりは、うまくいく方策なのだろうと思われます。結果的に、歯科医と歯科衛生士には2交代制を取ってもらうことになりますが、きっと彼らは就業時間が少し変わることを喜んでくれるでしょう。

□as of 〜：〜以後は　□adopt: 動 〜を採用する　□aware of 〜：〜に気づいて　□patient: 名 患者　□dentist: 名 歯科医
□during: 前 〜の間に　□consultation: 名 相談　□trial: 動 〜を試用する　□stay with 〜：（仕事など）を続ける　□appear: 動 〜のように見える
□viable: 形 （計画などが）実行可能な　□option: 名 選択肢　□dental hygienist: 歯科衛生士　□slightly: 副 わずかに、少し

---

92. 正解：**D**　易▰▰▱▱▱▱▱難　選択率：(A) 1.0%　(B) 2.3%　(C) 0.7%　**(D) 89.1%**

Where does the speaker most likely work?
(A) At a movie theater
(B) At a warehouse
(C) At a garage
(D) At a dental clinic

話者はどこで働いている可能性が最も高いですか。
(A) 映画館で
(B) 倉庫で
(C) 自動車修理工場で
(D) 歯科医院で

▶解説　話者は❶で、our patients（私たちの患者）がdentist（歯医者）に来るには忙しすぎると述べています。また、❺でdentists and dental hygienists（歯医者と歯科衛生士）の勤務時間に関する話をしていることからも、正解は(D)です。

---

93. 正解：**B**　易▰▰▰▱▱▱▱難　選択率：(A) 13.2%　**(B) 76.2%**　(C) 2.0%　(D) 2.0%

What time will the facility open tomorrow?
(A) At 6:30 A.M.
(B) At 7:00 A.M.
(C) At 8:30 A.M.
(D) At 9:00 A.M.

この施設は明日、何時に開きますか。
(A) 午前6時30分に
(B) 午前7時に
(C) 午前8時30分に
(D) 午前9時に

▶解説　話者は❷で「明日から午前7時から診療を開始する」と述べているので、正解は(B)です。open the doorは、ここでは患者に対してのドアを開ける、つまり「診療を始める」という意味で使われています。

---

94. 正解：**B**　易▰▰▰▰▱▱▱難　選択率：(A) 13.6%　**(B) 39.7%**　(C) 23.2%　(D) 14.9%

What does the speaker mean when he says, "they're staying with it"?
(A) The company has chosen some accommodations.
(B) A plan seems to be successful.
(C) A client cannot change an appointment.
(D) Prices have been kept the same.

話者はどのような意味で「今も続けています」と言っているのですか。
(A) その事業者は宿泊施設を選んだ。
(B) 計画が成功しそうに思われる。
(C) 顧客が面会の約束を変更できない。
(D) 物価が変わっていない。

▶解説　❸から、他の歯科医院も試しに診療時間を早くしたことが分かり、その直後に設問の発言をし、続く❹でそれは実行可能な案のようだと述べています。この流れから、話者は「この案はうまくいきそうだ」と思っていること分かるので、(B)が正解です。

□accommodation: 名 宿泊施設
□successful: 形 成功した　□facility: 名 施設

(((📡))) ゼミ 生 中継　😀Hiro 😊Mai 😶Yasu 😎Dai 😄Saki

94.
😊 ターゲット文にあるthey って誰？
😈 トライアルって聞こえたから、彼ら自身が去年「お試し」でやったんじゃないですか。
😊 それなら、自分たちをtheyと呼ばないよ。
😎 早朝シフトで働いた人たちでしょうか。

😊 いや、違う。サキはどう思う？
😄 グレーザーとかいう名前が聞こえました。
😊 惜しい。Grazer Dental Clinicだよ。別の歯科医院の名前だね。
😄 そうだったのか〜。
😊 このように、theyは組織や団体で働いている人を漠然と想定して使えるんだよ。

Part 4 説明文問題

062 Questions 95 through 97 refer to the following telephone message and map.

M: Hi. My name's Burt Ridgely. I recently went camping at Clover Park, and ❶ I seem to have left my phone at the campsite. I don't remember which area, but I had to cross the bridge on Shady River to get there. Um... ❷ and the campsite was completely surrounded by trees. I don't know if that helps. I'm just hoping that someone has turned it in at the Park Ranger's Center. It's a black YMJ– the battery has probably run out by now. Anyway, ❸ if it does turn up, I'd appreciate it if you could give me a call at 273-555-8489. I'll come to the ranger center and pick it up in person.

(112w/40 sec.)

問題95-97は次の電話メッセージと地図に関するものです。

男：もしもし。Burt Ridgelyといいます。最近、Clover Parkへキャンプに行ったのですが、キャンプ場に携帯電話を忘れてきたようなのです。どの区域か覚えていないのですが、その場所へ行くにはShady Riverに架かる橋を渡らなければなりませんでした。ええと、それから、キャンプ場はすっかり木で囲まれていました。これが役に立つかどうか分かりませんが。どなたかがPark Ranger's Centerに携帯電話を届けてくださっていることを願うばかりです。黒いYMJ製——バッテリーはおそらくもう切れているでしょう。いずれにせよ、もし見つかりましたら、273-555-8489へお電話いただけるとありがたく存じます。公園管理者センターへ、直接取りに伺いますので。

□ leave: 動 ～を置き忘れる　＊leftは過去分詞　□ campsite: 名 キャンプ場　□ remember: 動 ～を覚えている　□ cross: 動 ～を渡る、横断する　□ completely: 副 完全に　□ surround: 動 ～を囲む　□ help: 動 役に立つ　□ turn ～ in: ～を届ける　□ run out: 切れる、流れ出る　□ by now: そろそろ　□ turn up: 見つかる　□ appreciate: 動 ～を感謝する　□ ranger: 名 公園管理者　□ in person: 本人が直接に

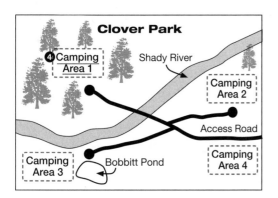

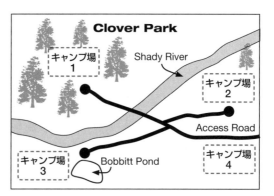

95. 正解：C 易 ■■■■□□□□ 難　選択率：(A) 7.6%　(B) 16.9%　**(C) 59.6%**　(B) 3.0%

What does the speaker say he has lost?
(A) The keys to his car
(B) Some camping equipment
(C) His mobile phone
(D) An address book

話者は何をなくしたと言っていますか。
(A) 自分の車のキー
(B) キャンプ用具
(C) 自分の携帯電話
(D) 住所録

▶解説 話者は❶で「電話を置いてきたようだ」と述べています。よって、正解は(C)です。

☐ lose: 動 ～をなくす ＊lost は過去形
☐ equipment: 名 用品　☐ address book: 住所録

96. 正解：A 易 ■■■□□□□□ 難　選択率：**(A) 68.9%**　(B) 7.9%　(C) 6.3%　(D) 2.6%

Look at the graphic. Which camping area did the speaker most likely visit?
(A) Camping Area 1
(B) Camping Area 2
(C) Camping Area 3
(D) Camping Area 4

図表を見てください。話者はどのキャンプ場を訪れた可能性が最も高いですか。
(A) キャンプ場1
(B) キャンプ場2
(C) キャンプ場3
(D) キャンプ場4

▶解説 選択肢は「キャンプ場名」なので、地図上でそれ以外の「川」や「池」や「道路」などの目標物を確認しておきましょう。❷から、話者が訪れたキャンプ場は木に囲まれていたことが分かります。地図内の❹からキャンプ場1のみが両方の条件に合致するので、(A)が正解です。

97. 正解：C 易 ■■■□□□□□ 難　選択率：(A) 23.5%　(B) 0.3%　**(C) 57.0%**　(D) 5.3%

According to the message, what might the speaker do?
(A) Contact a security guard
(B) Write a review
(C) Visit the ranger's center
(D) Purchase a map of the area

このメッセージによると、話者は何をする可能性がありますか。
(A) 警備員に連絡する
(B) 批評を書く
(C) 公園管理者センターへ行く
(D) その区域の地図を買う

▶解説 話者は❸で、探している電話が見つかった場合の対応を伝えています。まず「電話をくれたらありがたい」と言い、続けてI'll come to the ranger center（私が公園管理者センターに行く）と言っています。in person は「本人が直接」という意味です。つまり、「話者本人がキャンプ場を訪れる」ことになるので、正解は(C)です。

☐ according to ～：～によると　☐ contact: 動 ～に連絡する
☐ security guard: 警備員　☐ review: 名 批評、レビュー
☐ purchase: 動 ～を購入する

Part 4 ▼ Listening Section

📡 ゼミ 生 中継　　　　😊Hiro 😊Mai 😊Yasu 🎲Dai 😊Saki

😊 このような地図も頻出するよ。

95.

😊 トークの中にcamping やcampsite があるから、(B)を選んだモニターがいたみたい。

🎲 自分も(B)を選びました。音にだまされました。

😊 あれ？　どうして選択率を足しても100%にならないんですか。

😊 モニター用の模試はオンラインで実施されたんだけど、リスニングとリーディングそれぞれに制限時間があって、制限時間以後はマークもできないようになってたらしい。それで、Part 4の最後の方では何もマークできなかった人がいたみたい。

96.

😊 サキ、これは解けたよね？

😊 ヒントが2つあったので簡単でした。「橋を渡った」と「木に囲まれていた」が聞こえたので、(A)にしました。

😊 Access Roadは、特定区域に行くための連絡道路のことだから、どのキャンプ場に行く場合でも右側から左側に向かってAccess Roadを使うことになる。この人は橋を渡ったのだから、Camping Area 1に行ったと判断できるよ。もちろん、「木に囲まれていた」も分かりやすいヒントだけどね。

Part 4 説明文問題

Questions 98 through 100 refer to the following announcement and list.

W: OK. Could I have your attention, please? We've updated the building security system, and ❶ we're handing out new security passes today. Employees are required to pick up their passes from the supervisor before they leave the office this evening. Anyone who fails to do so won't be able to get back in tomorrow morning. ❷ In our case, we'll have to pick them up from Mr. Logan's office. However, you'll have to wait until just after three o'clock because ❸ Mr. Logan and Ms. Chang are having a meeting now, and it won't finish until then. The security system will scan your eye to verify your identity, so when you pick up your pass, you'll have to take an eye scan. It'll only take a couple of minutes and it won't hurt at all.

(132w/49 sec.)

問題**98-100**は次のお知らせと表に関するものです。
女：それでは、ちょっと聞いていただけますか。このビルの保安システムが新しくなりまして、新たな入館許可証を本日、配布しています。従業員は上長から許可証を受け取ったうえで、今晩、退出するように求められています。そうしないと、明朝、職場に入れなくなります。うちの部署の場合、許可証をLoganさんのオフィスへ取りに行く必要があります。ただし、3時過ぎまで待たなければなりません。LoganさんとChangさんが今、会議中で、その時刻まで終わらないからです。今度の保安システムでは、各自の瞳を読み取って本人確認を行いますので、自分の許可証を受け取ったら、瞳の読み取り作業をする必要があります。ほんの2、3分で終わりますし、痛みは全くありません。

☐ attention: 名 注意、注目　☐ security system: 保安システム　☐ hand out ～ : ～を配る　☐ security pass: 入館証　☐ employee: 名 従業員
☐ supervisor: 名 監督者、上司　☐ fail to ～ : ～し損なう　☐ case: 名 事例、場合　☐ scan: 動 ～をスキャンする、名 スキャン
☐ verify: 動 ～を確かめる　☐ identity: 名 本人であること　☐ hurt: 動 痛む

Departments	Section Leaders
Design	Nadia Becker
Marketing	Ahmed Lloyd
Administration	Daisy Chang
❹ Customer Service	Simon Logan

部　署	部門長
設計部	Nadia Becker
マーケティング部	Ahmed Lloyd
管理部	Daisy Chang
顧客サービス部	Simon Logan

98. 正解：A 易■■■□□□ 難　選択率：(A) 80.5% (B) 1.3% (C) 1.0% (D) 0.0%

What is being distributed to staff members?
(A) Security passes
(B) Stationery items
(C) Work vests
(D) Annual bonuses

職員に何が配布されていますか。
(A) 入館許可証
(B) 事務用品
(C) 作業用ベスト
(D) 年次ボーナス

▶解説 話者は❶で「新しい入館許可証を配布している」と述べているので、(A) が正解です。設問の distribute（配る）は、トークでは hand out という表現を使って述べられています。

☐ distribute A to B: A を B に配布する
☐ staff member: 職員、社員　☐ stationery: 名 文房具
☐ annual: 形 年1回の

99. 正解：D 易■■■□□□ 難　選択率：(A) 5.3% (B) 7.6% (C) 24.8% **(D) 40.7%**

Look at the graphic. Where do the listeners most likely work?
(A) In design
(B) In marketing
(C) In administration
(D) In customer service

図表を見てください。聞き手たちはどこで働いている可能性が最も高いですか。
(A) 設計部で
(B) マーケティング部で
(C) 管理部で
(D) 顧客サービス部で

▶解説 入館許可証の受取場所について、話者は❷で「私たちの場合、Logan さんのオフィスに行かないといけない」と説明しています。表から、Logan さんのオフィスで許可証を受け取る部署は❹の「顧客サービス部」であることが分かるので、正解は (D) です。

100. 正解：B 易■■■□□□ 難　選択率：(A) 9.6% **(B) 53.0%** (C) 13.6% (D) 2.3%

What does the speaker say about Ms. Chang?
(A) She will change departments.
(B) She is in a meeting.
(C) She has not arrived at work yet.
(D) She has a doctor's appointment.

話者は Chang さんについて何と言っていますか。
(A) 彼女は部署を異動するだろう。
(B) 彼女は会議中だ。
(C) 彼女はまだ出社していない。
(D) 彼女は医師の診療予約を取っている。

▶解説 話者は、Logan さんのオフィスには3時以降に行くよう伝えた後、❸で「Logan さんと Chang さんは今、会議をしている」と述べています。このトークで Chang さんの名前が出てくるのはここだけなので、正解は (B) です。

Part 4 ▼ Listening Section

(((📡))) ゼミ 生 中継　　　(👓)Hiro (👦)Mai (👦)Yasu (🎲)Dai (👧)Saki

99.

(👓) 意外と正答率が低いけど、何が難しかったかな？

(👦) 人の名前がたくさんあると、パニックになります。

(👓) 下手な言い訳だな。聞こえた名前は2人だけだったよね。

(🎲) 通常、このような許可証は IT 部門か総務部が配ります。

(👓) ん？　そうかもしれないけど、このトークでは各部署の責任者が持っているんだよ。余計な妄想をしちゃダメ。

(👓) リスニングセクションの結果はどう？

(👦) 74問正解です。換算スコアは385のようです。

(👦) 54問で295だ。いつもと同じくらいだなぁ。

(🎲) 自分は26問だけです。換算スコアは150です。

(👧) 私は正解数が41問で、スコアは245です。

(👓) それがみんなの現在地だよ。これからガンガン伸ばしていけばいい。よし、次は Part 5 に行こう。

④固有名詞が聞き取れなくてパニックに…

 リスニングセクションで固有名詞が聞こえるとパニックになっちゃうんです。そうすると、知ってる単語も分からなくなって落ち込みます…。

会社名とか人の名前がイヤなんですね。

 はい。実際には、それが固有名詞であることに気づくのは答え合わせの後です。解説を読んでいるときに気づきます。

なるほど。解いているときは、自分が知らない単語だと思って焦るのですか。

 そうです。

1つ目の対策はシンプルです。聞き取れない名前があっても、**文法的な観点からそれが会社名か人名だろうと推測する**ことです。例えば、I called XXX XXXX this morning and ～と聞こえたら、そこに会社名か人名があると推測し、それ以上は意識しない。それでOKです。その名前がHilltop Suppliesであれ、Gavin Ortegaであれ重要ではないと割り切りましょう。

 それでいいのですか。

はい。パニックになるよりマシです。2つ目の対策もシンプルで、これが理想だと思います。固有名詞以外の英語を全部聞き取れるよう、リスニング力を鍛えることです。

 それはそうだと思いますが……

考えてみてください。固有名詞はほぼ無限にありますし、わざわざ暗記するようなものではありません。われわれ**英語学習者が優先するべきなのは、固有名詞の前後を正確に理解するよう努力する**ことではないでしょうか。固有名詞で悩むなんて、時間がもったいないですよ。

 確かにそうですね。ありがとうございました。

Part 5 短文穴埋め問題

101. 正解：**A** 易 ■■■■□□ 難　選択率：**(A) 64.9%** (B) 10.4% (C) 18.7% (D) 5.6%

Employees should come to the ------- office to receive a windshield sticker for their vehicle.
(A) administration
(B) administrator
(C) administrate
(D) administer

☐ receive: 動 ～を受け取る
☐ windshield: 名 （自動車の）フロントガラス
☐ sticker: 名 シール
☐ vehicle: 名 車両、乗り物

従業員は管理事務所に出向き、各自の車両のフロントガラスに貼るシールを受け取ることになっている。
(A) 名 管理
(B) 名 管理者
(C) 動 ～を管理する
(D) 動 ～を施行する

▶解説 コロケーションの問題です。(A) を入れると administration office で「管理事務所」を意味する複合名詞が成り立ちます。(B) は「管理者」などの人を表す名詞で、所有格の administrator's なら空所に入れることができます。

---

102. 正解：**B** 易 ■■■□□□ 難　選択率：(A) 9.3% **(B) 64.9%** (C) 1.9% (D) 23.9%

The section meeting was ------- to finish at 5:00 P.M. but carried on for two hours longer.
(A) forced
(B) supposed
(C) refused
(D) postponed

☐ section: 名 部門
☐ carry on: 続く

課内会議は午後5時に終わる予定だったが、2時間超過して行われた。
(A) 動 強制された
(B) 動 予定だった
(C) 動 断られた
(D) 動 延期された

▶解説 語彙の問題です。後半は「2時間延長して続いた」なので、(B) の supposed を用いれば、前半は「午後5時に終わる予定だった」という意味になり、後半と逆接の関係が成り立ちます。

---

103. 正解：**D** 易 ■■■□□□ 難　選択率：(A) 11.9% (B) 18.3% (C) 8.6% **(D) 61.2%**

Rules have been put in place which ------- the number of visitors to the national park each month.
(A) restrictively
(B) restrictive
(C) restriction
(D) restrict

☐ put ～ in place: ～を制定する

1カ月あたりの国立公園への来訪者数を制限する規則が制定された。
(A) 副 制限的に
(B) 形 制限の
(C) 名 制限
(D) 動 制限する

▶解説 品詞が問われています。前後に関係代名詞の which と名詞句の the number of visitors があり、空所にはこれらを主語と目的語にとる動詞が入るので、正解は (D) です。which の先行詞は直前の place ではなく文頭の Rules です。

Part 5 ▸ Reading Section

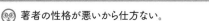

ゼミ生中継
Hiro　Mai　Yasu　Dai　Saki

101.

😆 前半は易しめだったかな。101番はどう？

😅 悩みました。the と office の間には形容詞が入ると思ったんですが……

😊 いきなり複合名詞だったね。

😆 サキが言ったように形容詞を入れることはできる。administrative office も管理事務所を表すからね。ただ、選択肢にないから選べない。

😅 意地悪な問題ですね。

😆 著者の性格が悪いから仕方ない。

102.

😊 ダイ、どれを選んだ？

😆 (D) です。会議が延期されるのは日常茶飯事です。空所の後ろを読まずに選びました。

😆 後ろも読んで。「5時まで延期された」のであれば、postponed until 5:00 P.M. だよ。それに、後半に「しかし、さらに2時間続いた」とあるから変な内容になる。

😆 確かに……。

77

Part 5 短文穴埋め問題

104. 正解：**B**　易 ■■■□□□ 難　選択率：(A) 13.8% **(B) 70.1%** (C) 11.9% (D) 4.1%

Hotel guests are given a coconut juice drink immediately ------- arrival.
(A) over
(B) upon
(C) beyond
(D) across

ホテルの宿泊客は、到着次第すぐにココナツジュースをもらえる。
(A) 前 ～を超えて
(B) 前 ～に際して
(C) 前 ～を超えて
(D) 前 ～を横切って

▶解説 前置詞の用法が問われています。(B) のuponは、upon arrivalで「到着すると」という意味になり、「ジュースが提供される」タイミングの説明として文意が通ります。よって、(B) が正解です。

□ immediately: 副 ただちに、すぐに　□ arrival: 名 到着

---

105. 正解：**C**　易 ■■■■□□ 難　選択率：(A) 27.6% (B) 9.0% **(C) 52.6%** (D) 10.8%

The changes to the film's production schedule were ------- a result of unforeseeable weather conditions.
(A) large
(B) largeness
(C) largely
(D) larger

その映画の製作スケジュールの変更は、主に予測不能の気象条件がもたらしたものだった。
(A) 形 大きな
(B) 名 大きさ
(C) 副 主に
(D) 形 より大きな（比較級）

▶解説 空所には何も入れなくても問題文は「スケジュールの変更は予測不能の気象条件がもたらしたものだった」の意味で成立するため、空所には修飾語が入ります。空所前後はbe動詞と補語なので、「主に」を意味する副詞である (C) のlargelyが正解です。

□ film: 名 映画　□ production: 名 製作
□ unforeseeable: 形 予想できない　□ weather condition: 気象条件

---

106. 正解：**B**　易 ■■■■□□ 難　選択率：(A) 6.3% **(B) 61.6%** (C) 31.0% (D) 1.1%

None of the plans can be carried out ------- additional funds are provided.
(A) only
(B) unless
(C) without
(D) again

さらなる資金が投入されない限り、どの計画も実行できない。
(A) 副 わずか
(B) 接 ～でない限り
(C) 前 ～なしで
(D) 副 再び

▶解説 空所前の「どの計画も実行できない」と、後ろの「さらなる資金が投入される」を結ぶのは、接続詞である (B) のunless（～でない限り）のみです。(A) と (D) は副詞、(C) は前置詞なので、2つの節をつなぐことはできません。

□ carry out ～: ～を実行する　□ additional: 形 追加の
□ fund: 名 資金　□ provide: 動 ～を提供する

---

107. 正解：**D**　易 ■■□□□□ 難　選択率：(A) 7.8% (B) 10.8% (C) 4.9% **(D) 76.1.%**

Products ------- on the shelves to attract the attention of shoppers.
(A) are arranging
(B) have arranged
(C) arranged
(D) are arranged

買い物客の注意を引くように、商品が棚の上に並べられている。
(A) ～を並べている
(B) 並べ終わった
(C) 並べた
(D) 並べられている

▶解説 空所には、直前の名詞Productsを主語にする動詞が入ります。arrange（～を並べる）は、主語の「製品」と受け身の関係になればいいので、受動態である (D) のare arrangedが正解です。

□ shelf: 名 棚　□ attract: 動 ～を引き付ける
□ attention: 名 注意、注目　□ shopper: 名 買い物客

((•A•)) ゼミ生中継　　(ﾟoﾟ)Hiro (ﾟoﾟ)Mai (ﾟoﾟ)Yasu (ﾟoﾟ)Dai (ﾟoﾟ)Saki

105. ⋯⋯⋯⋯⋯⋯⋯⋯⋯⋯⋯⋯⋯⋯⋯⋯⋯
(ﾟoﾟ) 主語は複数形だね。The changes ～ were largely a result of ... と単数形のa result が続くことに違和感を覚えるかもしれないけど、これは問題ない。「スケジュールがあちこち変更されたこと」をまとめて「1つの結果」ととらえているから単数形でいい。

106. ⋯⋯⋯⋯⋯⋯⋯⋯⋯⋯⋯⋯⋯⋯⋯⋯⋯
(ﾟoﾟ) withoutは「～なしで」を意味するから使えそうだけど不正解。前置詞だからね。～ without additional funds.のように文が終わっていれば大丈夫だけど。

108. 正解：B 易■■■■■□□□難　選択率：(A) 8.6% **(B) 68.7%** (C) 8.6% (D) 13.8%

Updating the car's design will increase costs ------- but the changes will result in long-term savings.
(A) accessibly
(B) initially
(C) maturely
(D) negatively

車の設計を更新すると初期費用が増えるが、変更すれば結果として長期的な節約につながるだろう。
(A) 副 利用しやすく
(B) 副 初期に
(C) 副 成熟して
(D) 副 逆に

▶解説 前後の節がbutでつながっています。前半は、後半「変更は結果的に長期的な節約になる」と逆接の関係なので、経費がかさむのは「初期段階」だと考えるのが妥当です。よって、正解は(B)です。(D)のnegativelyはincreaseを修飾できません。仮に空所に入れると、「費用が逆に増える（＝減る）」ことを示唆するため不適切です。

□ update: 動 ～を更新する、最新のものにする　□ result in ～: ～という結果になる
□ long-term: 形 長期の　□ saving: 名 節約

109. 正解：C 易■■□□□□□□難　選択率：(A) 0.0% (B) 0.7% **(C) 95.1%** (C) 4.1%

As no one else was qualified to operate the machinery, Rafael Barros took on the task -------.
(A) he
(B) his
(C) himself
(D) him

他の誰にもその機械を操作する資格がなかったので、Rafael Barros が自らその業務を引き受けた。
(A) 代 彼が
(B) 代 彼の
(C) 代 彼自身
(D) 代 彼を

▶解説 代名詞の問題です。空所を含む節は「Rafael Barros はその仕事を引き受けた」の意味が完成しているので、空所には「自分自身で」と主語を強調する再帰代名詞が入ります。従って、正解は(C)です。

□ qualified: 形 資格のある　□ operate: 動 ～を操作する　□ machinery: 名 機械
□ take on ～: ～を引き受ける　□ task 名 仕事、務め

110. 正解：A 易■■■□□□□□難　選択率：**(A) 73.5%** (B) 12.7% (C) 9.3% (D) 4.5%

Glasgow Catering has always provided ------- levels of food quality for our in-flight meals.
(A) satisfactory
(B) protective
(C) periodical
(D) lengthy

Glasgow Catering は、当社の機内食向けに満足のいく水準の品質の食べ物を常に提供してきた。
(A) 形 満足のいく
(B) 形 保護の
(C) 形 定期的な
(D) 形 長い

▶解説 空所の直前に動詞 provided、直後にその目的語 levels があります。(A)を入れると、satisfactory levels で「満足のいくレベル」という意味が成り立ち、文意が通ります。

□ quality: 名 品質　□ in-flight: 形 機内の

111. 正解：C 易■■■□□□□□難　選択率：(A) 17.2% (B) 10.8% **(C) 69.0%** (D) 3.0%

Additional ticket sellers have been hired to ensure that lines for admission to the gallery are -------.
(A) tolerate
(B) toleration
(C) tolerable
(D) tolerably

美術館への入場者の列の長さを確実に許容範囲内に抑えるために追加のチケット販売員が雇われた。
(A) 動 ～を許容する
(B) 名 許容
(C) 形 許容できる
(D) 副 許容できる程度に

▶解説 空所には、lines を主語にとる動詞 are の補語が入ります。人員の追加は美術館への入場列を「許容できるものにするため」とすると文意が通るので、形容詞の(C) tolerable が正解です。accurate（正確な）など -rate で終わる形容詞はありますが、(A) の tolerate は動詞です。

□ ensure: 動 ～を確実にする　□ admission: 名 入場　□ gallery: 名 美術館

((•)) ゼミ生中継　　　　　(••) Hiro (••) Mai (••) Yasu (••) Dai (••) Saki

108.
(••) initially のニュアンスは「最初は」だよ。英語力が高い人は、initially を目にした時点で「次はどうなるの？」と展開を予測しながら英語を読んでいる。同じニュアンスを持つフレーズは何？ at で始まる。
(••) at first ですね!
(••) その通り。

110.
(••) food quality は「食べ物の質」だけど、良いか悪いかどっち？
(••) どちらでもないです。
(••) そうだね。では、quality food は？
(••) あ、それだと良い質ですね。
(••) ピンポーン。quality は形容詞としても使える。

Part 5 短文穴埋め問題

---

112. 正解：A 易 ▬▬▬□□□□ 難　選択率：**(A) 77.6%** (B) 13.4% (C) 2.2% (D) 6.7%

Customers should ------- the instructions for Greyson teeth whitening gel.
(A) follow
(B) undertake
(C) establish
(D) convey

□ whitening: 形 美白用の

顧客は Greyson 社の歯の美白用ジェルを使うにあたり、使用説明書の指示に従う必要がある。
(A) 動 〜に従う
(B) 動 〜を引き受ける
(C) 動 〜を確立する
(D) 動 〜を運ぶ

▶解説 文頭の Customers を主語に、空所直後の the instructions を目的語にして文意の通る動詞を選びます。(A)の follow を入れると「顧客は使用説明書の指示に従う必要がある」という文意が成り立ちます。

---

113. 正解：B 易 ▬▬▬▬▬□□ 難　選択率：(A) 35.4% **(B) 45.9%** (C) 16.0% (D) 2.6%

Attractions at Megaworld Theme Park have ------- inspections for safety issues.
(A) regularly
(B) regular
(C) regulate
(D) regulation

□ inspection: 名 点検　□ safety: 名 安全

Megaworld Theme Park のアトラクションは、安全上の問題から定期的な検査を受けている。
(A) 副 定期的に
(B) 形 定期的な
(C) 動 〜を規制する
(D) 名 規則

▶解説 空所直後の名詞 inspections は直前の動詞 have の目的語で、空所にはこの名詞を修飾する形容詞が入ります。よって、形容詞の(B)が正解です。have regular inspections で「定期的な検査を受ける」の意味になり、文意が通ります。

---

114. 正解：B 易 ▬▬▬▬□□□ 難　選択率：(A) 10.1% **(B) 43.7%** (C) 13.1% (D) 33.2%

------- the updates are installed, users should be able to start using the software.
(A) Whether
(B) Now that
(C) So
(D) As far as

□ update: 名 更新データ　□ install: 動 〜をインストールする

これで更新データがインストールされたので、ユーザーはソフトウェアを使い始められるはずだ。
(A) 接 〜かどうか
(B) 〜であるからには
(C) 接 だから
(D) 〜である限り

▶解説 前半「更新データがインストールされている」は、後半「ソフトウェアを使い始められるはず」と判断する理由を示しているので、(B)が正解です。(D)は程度や範囲を示す語句ですが、「更新データがインストールされている限り〜できる」のように条件を示すことはできません。

---

115. 正解：D 易 ▬▬▬□□□□ 難　選択率：(A) 6.3% (B) 9.0% (C) 4.5% **(D) 80.2%**

Pear Tree devices are ------- more expensive than other manufacturers'.
(A) generalization
(B) generalize
(C) general
(D) generally

□ device: 名 装置　□ expensive: 形 高価な、費用のかかる　□ manufacturer: 名 メーカー

Pear Tree 社の装置は、概して他のメーカーのものよりも値が張る。
(A) 名 一般化
(B) 動 〜を一般化する
(C) 形 一般的な
(D) 副 一般的に

▶解説 空所直後にある比較級の形容詞 more expensive は動詞 are の補語です。空所にはこの形容詞を修飾する副詞が入ります。選択肢の中で、副詞は -ly で終わる(D)の generally です。

((･)) ゼミ 生 中継　　　Hiro　Mai　Yasu　Dai　Saki

113.

😎 上級グループの正答率は高いけど、初級グループでは意外と24%しか正答できていない。間違えた人は？

😊 (A)にしちゃいました。

😎 名詞の前に副詞を置いたの？

😵 まず、have が現在完了の have だと勘違いしました。そのせいで、inspections が inspected に見えてしまって。

😑 同じく。

😎 なるほど。Attractions 〜 have regularly inspected だと思い込んだのか。もっと落ち着いて読まなきゃ。

114.

😎 選択肢は接続詞の役割を持つ語句が4つだから、<u>全文を読んだ方が解きやすい</u>。そして、登場する2つの情報の関係をチェックするといい。

😵 接続詞は解くのに時間がかかりますよね？

😎 それは仕方がない。空所に1つ1つ選択肢を当てはめて、スムーズに理解できるものを選ぶしかないよ。

116. 正解：D　易 ■■■□□□□□ 難　選択率：(A) 7.1%　(B) 7.8%　(C) 9.3%　**(D) 75.0%**

When ------- a delivery vehicle, aside from size, efficiency is usually an important factor.
(A) chose
(B) choose
(C) chosen
(D) choosing

□ delivery: 图 配達　□ vehicle: 图 車両、乗り物
□ aside from 〜: 〜は別として　□ efficiency: 图 効率
□ factor: 图 要因、要素

配送車両を選ぶに当たっては、大きさを別にすれば、普通、効率が重要な要素だ。
(A) 動 選んだ（過去形）
(B) 動 選ぶ
(C) 動 選ばれた（過去分詞）
(D) 動 選んでいる（現在分詞）

▶解説 動詞の形が問われています。空所の前に主語がないのでWhenで始まる節は分詞構文だと判断します。空所直後に目的語となるa delivery vehicleがあるので、(D)のchoosingが正解です。

---

117. 正解：A　易 ■■■□□□□□ 難　選択率：**(A) 79.9%**　(B) 0.7%　(C) 4.1%　(D) 14.9%

Ms. Carter met a number of renowned architects ------- she was stationed in France.
(A) while
(B) seldom
(C) afterward
(D) so that

□ renowned: 形 有名な　□ architect: 图 建築家
□ station: 動 〜を駐在させる

Carter さんは、フランスに駐在中に大勢の有名な建築家に会った。
(A) 接 〜の間に
(B) 副 めったに〜ない
(C) 副 後に
(D) 〜できるように

▶解説 前後の節をつなぐ接続詞を選びます。(A)のwhileを入れると「フランス駐在中に大勢の有名な建築家に会った」の意味が成り立ちます。(D)に続く節には、通常助動詞か現在形の動詞が使われます。そのため、空所後がshe would be stationed 〜であれば、(D)は空所に入れることができます。

---

118. 正解：C　易 ■■■■□□□□ 難　選択率：　(A) 13.8%　(B) 30.2%　**(C) 38.1%**　(D) 17.5%

Greg Silva is the chief editor of the ------- acclaimed magazine *Indoor Outdoor*.
(A) mindfully
(B) personally
(C) critically
(D) virtually

□ chief editor: 編集長　□ acclaim: 動 〜を称賛する

Greg Silva は、高く評価されている雑誌『Indoor Outdoor』の編集長だ。
(A) 副 注意深く
(B) 副 個人的に
(C) 副 非常に
(D) 副 事実上

▶解説 空所後ろの形容詞acclaimed（称賛されている）を修飾する副詞を選択します。(C)のcriticallyは「非常に、とても」という意味で、この語を入れると「高く評価されている」という意味になり、文意が通ります。

((•)) ゼミ 生中継　　　　😊Hiro 😊Mai 😊Yasu 😊Dai 😊Saki

116. ....
😊 中盤にaside fromがあるよね。ここが空所になって問われても解けるようしっかり覚えておいてね。重要フレーズだから。
😊 「〜を除いて」ですよね。
😊 そう。「冗談はさておき」の「さておき」もaside fromだよ。

118. ....
😊 中級と初級グループの正答率は30％前後で、不正解の(B)が人気だったみたい。サキとダイはどうやって解いた？
😊 personallyしか知らなかったので、(B)にしました。
😊 完全にお手上げです。白旗を上げました。

😊 ヤスは？
😊 criticallyは何か厳しいイメージがあるので消してmindfullyを選びました。
😊 私は消去法でcriticallyを選びましたが、acclaimedとセットでどんな意味になるか知りません。
😊 critically acclaimedは「高く評価されている」という意味だよ。この2語は相性の良い組み合わせだから忘れないで。ところで、criticalが重要な役割を果たす問題が後でまた登場するから辞書でcriticalについて予習しておくといいよ。

Part 5 短文穴埋め問題

119. 正解：**D** 易 ■■■■■ 難　選択率：(A) 2.6% (B) 38.4% (C) 31.3% **(D) 27.6%**

------- at this year's summer concert was higher than organizers had expected.
(A) Attend
(B) Attending
(C) Attendees
(D) Attendance

□ organizer: 名 主催者　□ expect: 動 ～を予期する

今年の夏のコンサートの参加者数は、主催者側が予想したよりも多かった。
(A) 動 ～に参加する
(B) 動 ～に参加している（現在分詞）
(C) 名 参加者
(D) 名 参加者数

▶解説 空所には動詞wasの主語が入ります。主催者の予想を上回ったのはコンサートの「参加者数」だと考えるのが自然です。従って、単数形で「参加者数」を意味する(D)のAttendanceが正解です。(B)を用いると、直後のatが不要な上、Attending ～ was higher では意味を成しません。

120. 正解：**A** 易 ■■■■■ 難　選択率：**(A) 70.2%** (B) 12.7% (C) 6.3% (D) 9.0%

A range of ------- priced laptop computers has recently come onto the market.
(A) affordably
(B) constructively
(C) immensely
(D) completely

□ range of ～：～の範囲　□ laptop computer: ノートパソコン

手頃な価格のノートパソコンが、最近いろいろ市場に出回っている。
(A) 副 手頃な価格に
(B) 副 建設的に
(C) 副 大いに
(D) 副 完全に

▶解説 空所直前に前置詞ofがあるので、直後の形容詞pricedを修飾する副詞を選択します。(A)を入れると、affordably pricedで「手頃な価格の」という意味が成り立つので、これが正解です。

121. 正解：**C** 易 ■■■■■ 難　選択率：(A) 23.5% (B) 16.8% **(C) 55.2%** (D) 4.5%

Lime Sky is far ------- to receive an award than any other music video in the competition.
(A) most likely
(B) likely
(C) more likely
(D) likelihood

□ far: 副 はるかに　□ award: 名 賞　□ competition: 名 コンテスト

「Lime Sky」はそのコンテストで受賞する可能性が他の音楽ビデオよりもはるかに高い。
(A) 最も見込みがあって
(B) 形 見込みがあって
(C) より見込みがあって
(D) 名 見込み

▶解説 直前に副詞farがあるので、形容詞を選択します。空所の後に前置詞than（～より）があることから、空所には比較級が入ることが分かります。従って、moreを含む(C)が正解です。

122. 正解：**B** 易 ■■■■■ 難　選択率：(A) 72.8% **(B) 18.7%** (C) 3.7% (D) 4.9%

Details of the advertisement's production schedule will be ------- to the crew by the director.
(A) informed
(B) distributed
(C) suspended
(D) advised

□ details: 名 詳しい情報　□ production: 名 制作　□ crew: 名 （共同の仕事をする）班、チーム

広告制作スケジュールの詳細は、ディレクターからスタッフに配られるだろう。
(A) 動 知らされた
(B) 動 配られた
(C) 動 停止された
(D) 動 忠告された

▶解説 空所直後に前置詞のtoがあります。＜distribute ～ to 人＞で「～を（人）に配る」の意味を表すので、(B)が正解です。(A)は＜inform 人 of /about ～＞で「（人）に～を知らせる」を表します。従って人を主語にした受動態なら成立しますが、ここでは「詳細」が主語なので(A)は使えません。

((•)) ゼミ 生 中継　⊙Hiro ⊙Mai ⊙Yasu ⊙Dai ⊙Saki

119. ······················
😈 あ、動詞がwasだったのか。仮に動詞がwereだったら、Attendeesが正解ですよね。

😺 その場合、コンサートの参加者が、主催者の想像を超えてhighだったことになる。

😈 highって……？

😺 クスリでハイになっていたってこと。TOEICワールドでは起きそうになりね。

122. ······················
😺 簡潔に言えば、主語が人じゃないから(A)はダメ。

😈 どういうことですか。

😺 informを単に「知らせる」と解釈すると、「詳細が知らされる」でOKな気がするよね。

😈 はい、そう考えました。

😺 でも、informは正確に言うと「人に知らせる」だから、受動態だと「人が知らされる」という形にする必要がある。ところが、この文の主語は人じゃない。

😈 ということは、The crewが主語ならOKですか。

😺 そう。The crew will be informed about details ～という形なら文法的に成立する。

123. 正解：**D**　易 ■■■■■□□□ 難　選択率：　(A) 17.5%　(B) 6.7%　(C) 34.4%　**(D) 41.4%**

Patients wishing to see Dr. Park must receive a ------- from their family physician before making an appointment.
(A) refer
(B) referred
(C) referring
(D) referral

☐ see: 動 (医者に) 診てもらう　☐ receive: 動 〜を受け取る
☐ family physician: 家庭医、かかりつけ医

Park医師の診察を希望する患者は、予約をする前にかかりつけの医師に紹介状をもらわなければならない。
(A) 動 〜を参照する
(B) 動 参照された (過去分詞)
(C) 動 〜を参照している
　　（現在分詞）
(D) 名 紹介状

▶解説 空所前後にそれぞれ冠詞aと前置詞fromがあるので、空所には名詞が入ります。医者の診察を受けるのに必要なのは「紹介状」とすると文意が通るので、(D)のreferralが正解です。

---

124. 正解：**D**　易 ■■■□□□□□ 難　選択率：　(A) 16.0%　(B) 4.5%　(C) 6.0%　**(D) 73.5%**

Mr. Brown was offered an important position ------- his lack of experience.
(A) in
(B) around
(C) above
(D) despite

☐ position: 名 職、地位　☐ lack: 名 不足

Brownさんは経験が無いにもかかわらず要職を提示された。
(A) 前 〜の中に
(B) 前 〜の周囲に
(C) 前 〜より上に
(D) 前 〜にもかかわらず

▶解説 空所後ろのhis lack of experience (経験不足)は、前の「要職を提示された」に対して逆接の内容です。従って、(D)のdespite (〜にもかかわらず)を選ぶと文意が通ります。

---

125. 正解：**C**　易 ■■■□□□□□ 難　選択率：(A) 3.7%　(B) 8.6%　**(C) 81.7%**　(D) 6.0%

Companies must obtain written ------- before disposing of waste at public garbage processing sites.
(A) authorize
(B) authorized
(C) authorization
(D) authorizing

☐ obtain: 動 〜を手に入れる　☐ dispose of 〜: 〜を捨てる　☐ waste: 名 廃棄物
☐ public: 形 公営の　☐ process: 動 〜を処理する　☐ site: 名 用地

公営ごみ処理場に廃棄物を捨てる前に、事業所は許可証を取得しなければならない。
(A) 動 〜を承認する
(B) 動 承認された (過去分詞)
(C) 名 承認
(D) 動 〜を承認している
　　（現在分詞）

▶解説 空所には動詞obtainの目的語となる名詞が入ります。(C)を選ぶとwritten authorizationで「文書による承認」の意味になり文意が通るので、これが正解です。

---

126. 正解：**D**　易 ■■■■□□□□ 難　選択率：　(A) 5.2%　(B) 10.1%　(C) 24.6%　**(D) 60.1%**

Applicants to the Dunham Auto Club must read all of the ------- explained in the members' agreement before signing.
(A) allocations
(B) circumstances
(C) qualifications
(D) regulations

☐ applicant: 名 応募者、申込者　☐ agreement: 名 同意書

Dunham Auto Clubへの入会希望者は、署名する前に会員同意書に書かれたすべての規則を読まなければならない。
(A) 名 割り当て
(B) 名 環境
(C) 名 資格
(D) 名 規則

▶解説 動詞readの目的語として文意の通る語を選びます。「Dunham Auto Clubへの入会希望者は〜を読まなければならない」という文意から、(D)のregulations (規則)が正解です。

((🗼)) ゼミ生中継　　　　　　　😮Hiro 😊Mai 😀Yasu 🎲Dai 😄Saki

123.
😮 これ、(B)も(C)も(D)も正解かと思いました。どれも形容詞として使えそうなので、formの前に置けそうです。
😀 ちょっと待った。空所の後ろはformじゃなくてfromだよ。だから空所には名詞が入る。
😮 しまった〜。
😀 referralは形容詞に見えるけど名詞だね。TOEIC受験者にとって重要語の1つだよ。

126.
😄 もしかすると、(C)が魅力的かな。どう?
😊 はい。「応募資格を読む必要がある」と思って、(C)にしました。
😀 文の後半によれば、空所に入るものは会員同意書の中で説明されている。その同意書には、会員の役割とか規則などが書かれていると考えられるよね。応募資格は「応募に必要な条件」という意味だから、応募前に読むべきものだよ。会員同意書に書かれているものじゃない。それに、応募に必要な条件はrequirementsだよ。

Part 5 短文穴埋め問題

---

127. 正解：**A**　易 ■■■□□□□□ 難　選択率：**(A) 76.1%**　(B) 7.5%　(C) 13.1%　(D) 3.4%

Business Plus magazine is full of articles that modern business leaders should find both ------- and entertaining.
(A) beneficial
(B) actual
(C) objectionable
(D) portable

『Business Plus』誌には、現代の
ビジネスリーダーたちが有益かつ
楽しめると感じる記事が満載され
ている。
(A) 形 有益な
(B) 形 実際の
(C) 形 不愉快な
(D) 形 持ち運べる

▶解説 both A and Bで「AとBの両方」
の意味を表すので、空所に入る語は形容詞
entertaining と並列の関係です。雑誌の掲
載記事を修飾する語として文意に合うのは
(A)のbeneficial（有益な）です。(C)は「不
愉快な」を意味するため、entertaining とは
両立しません。

□ modern: 形 現代の　□ entertaining: 形 面白い、楽しい

---

128. 正解：**B**　易 ■■■■□□□□ 難　選択率：(A) 14.6%　**(B) 63.4%**　(C) 4.1%　(D) 17.5%

An up-to-date understanding of social networking technology is becoming ------- important for advertisers.
(A) responsibly
(B) increasingly
(C) adversely
(D) promptly

ソーシャル・ネットワーキング技
術に関する最新の理解が、広告主
にとってますます重要になってき
ている。
(A) 副 責任を持って
(B) 副 ますます
(C) 副 逆に
(D) 副 即座に

▶解説 空所直後のimportantを修飾する副
詞を選びます。「広告主にとってソーシャル・
ネットワーキング技術の最新の理解が重要
になっている」という文意から、正解は(B)
のincreasingly（ますます）です。(B)以外
の副詞はいずれもimportantを修飾できま
せん。

□ up-to-date: 形 最新の　□ understanding: 名 理解
□ technology: 名 技術　□ advertiser: 名 広告主

---

129. 正解：**A**　易 ■■■■□□□□ 難　選択率：**(A) 51.1%**　(B) 6.7%　(C) 11.2%　(D) 31.0%

The president of Dixon Foods praises divisions ------- successfully reduce their use of paper.
(A) that
(B) if
(C) whom
(D) how

Dixon Foodsの社長は、紙の使用
削減に成功した部署を称賛する。
(A) 代 （関係代名詞のthat）
(B) 接 もしも
(C) 代 （関係代名詞whoの目的格）
(D) 副 どうやって

▶解説 空所前後をつなぐ語を選択します。
後ろの動詞reduceの主語がないので、空所
には直前の名詞divisionsを先行詞とする主
格の関係代名詞である(A)のthatが入りま
す。reduceの主語がないため、(D)のhow
を空所に入れて名詞句を作ることはできま
せん。

□ president: 名 社長　□ praise: 動 ～を称賛する
□ division: 名 （会社などの）部、課　□ successfully: 副 首尾よく、うまく

---

130. 正解：**C**　易 ■■■□□□□□ 難　選択率：(A) 5.6%　(B) 5.2%　**(C) 85.1%**　(D) 4.1%

Harrison Concrete ------- as the leader in concrete production in Melbourne.
(A) is acknowledging
(B) acknowledges
(C) is acknowledged
(D) acknowledged

Harrison Concrete社はMelbourne
におけるコンクリート生産のトッ
プ企業として認知されている。
(A) 認知している（現在進行形）
(B) 動 認知する
(C) 認知されている（受け身）
(D) 動 認知された（過去形）

▶解説 Harrison Concreteを主語にとる
動詞の形を選びます。acknowledge（～を
認める）は他動詞です。空所の後ろに目的語
が存在しないので、受動態である(C)のis
acknowledgedが正解です。

□ production: 名 生産

((•)) ゼミ 生 中継　😀 Hiro　😀 Mai　😀 Yasu　😎 Dai　😀 Saki

😀 Part 5を解くのにどれくらい時間を使った？

😀 9分でした。

😀 スピードだけは1人前だね。

😀 12分前後です。

😀 私は15分かかったと思います。

😈 記憶にありません。

😀 単に速ければ良いというわけではないけれど、Part 5に使う時間は
10分を目標にしよう。1問平均20秒だよ。よし、次はPart 6に進もう。

TOEICよろず相談所　ヒロの部屋

⑤文法の問題集をやってもモノにならない

相談に乗っていただけますか。高校時代から英語が苦手で、特に英文法がダメなんです。どうすればいいのでしょうか。

まず確認しますが、英語を学ぶ必要があるのですか。

会社でTOEICのIPテストを受けないといけないんです。今年中に600点を取らないとヒドイ目に遭うぞって上司に脅されました。一応、有名な文法の問題集をやりましたが、全然モノになった感じがしません。

文法はルールです。ルールを身につけるには、「理解」することから始めて、頭に「定着」させる必要があります。その問題集をどのように使いましたか？

問題を解いて解説を読みました。一応、最後まで行きました。

それは「理解」のステージです。読んで理解しただけの情報は、脳内に定着したとは限りません。むしろ、忘れるのが普通です。

そう、忘れちゃうんです…。

情報を知識として定着させるには、反復練習とアウトプットが有効です。問題集を1回やっても足りません。繰り返してください。

アウトプットとはどういうことですか？

自分で自分に口頭で解説することをお勧めします。例えば、ある問題の解き方を講師みたいに説明するのです。そうすれば、自分が理解できている部分と、まだ理解できていない部分に気づきます。**学習テーマを設定しながら1つずつ進める**といいでしょう。今週は「関係代名詞」、来週は「動詞の時制」のように。そうすれば短期間で類似問題に繰り返し取り組むことになって身につきやすいです。

ありがとうございます。今日からやってみます。

Part 5 ▼ Reading Section

Part 6 長文穴埋め問題

Questions 131-134 refer to the following information.

Training

------- their previous experience in the finance industry, all consultants are required to take part
131. ❶

in a two-week training course in New York. There, you ------- about the standards of conduct
132.

required of all Ogilvy and Horne employees. -------. Accommodation will be provided in a
133. ❷

company-owned apartment for ------- coming from outside New York. Please call chief organizer,
134.

Cobie Patel, if you would like to make your own arrangements.

(83w)

問題131-134は次の情報に関するものです。
研修
金融業界での過去の経験の有無にかかわらず、コンサルティング業務の
従事者は全員、New Yorkでの2週間の研修コースへ参加する必要があ
ります。研修会では、Ogilvy and Horneの全従業員に求められる行動
規範について学ぶ予定です。このコースは2月の最初の2週間を使って
行われます。宿泊施設として、New York市外からの参加者には会社所
有のアパートが提供されます。ご自身での手配を希望される場合には、
主任担当者のCobie Patelまでお電話ください。

☐ previous: 形 前の　　☐ finance: 名 財政、財務　☐ industry: 名 ～業　☐ consultant: 名 コンサルタント、顧問
☐ take part in ～: ～に参加する　☐ standard: 名 基準　☐ conduct: 名 振る舞い、（業務などの）遂行、処理　☐ accommodation: 名 宿泊施設
☐ provide: 動 ～を提供する　☐ organizer: 名 世話人、まとめ役　☐ arrangement: 名 手配

131. 正解：C 易■■■■□難 選択率：(A) 24.6% (B) 7.5% **(C) 48.9%** (D) 18.7%

(A) In addition to
(B) With respect for
(C) Regardless of
(D) Along with

(A) 〜に加えて
(B) 〜に敬意を表して
(C) 〜にかかわらず
(D) 〜とともに

▶解説 空所後のtheir previous experience（彼らの過去の経験）と、カンマ後にあるall consultants are required to 〜（コンサルタント全員が〜する必要がある）が必要です。(C) Regardless of（〜にかかわらず）を入れると、「経験の有無にかかわらず全員が〜」となり、文意が通ります。

132. 正解：D 易■■■□□難 選択率：(A) 5.6% (B) 2.6% (C) 3.0% **(D) 88.4%**

(A) learned
(B) learning
(C) were learning
(D) will learn

(A) 動 学んだ（過去形）
(B) 動 学んでいる（現在分詞）
(C) 学んでいた（過去進行形）
(D) 学ぶだろう（未来形）

▶解説 動詞の時制が問われています。文頭のThereは、前文で言及された研修を指します。前文の動詞はare requiredなので、その研修はまだ開かれていません。よって、未来を表す (D) will learn が正解です。

133. 正解：C 易■■■■□難 選択率：(A) 8.6% (B) 12.3% **(C) 40.7%** (D) 38.1%

(A) This is only necessary for people who have never worked in finance.
(B) The weeklong course is available for only $250 per person.
(C) The course will be held in the first two weeks of February.
(D) It is necessary for trainees to find somewhere convenient to stay.

(A) これが必要なのは、金融業界で働いたことのない人たちだけです。
(B) この1週間コースは、1人当たりたったの250ドルで利用できます。
(C) このコースは2月の最初の2週間を使って行われます。
(D) 受講者は、どこか便利な滞在場所を見つける必要があります。

▶解説 (A)は❶の「全員参加」に合致しません。研修は2週間続くため、(B)にあるweeklong（1週間）も誤りです。(D)は❷の「宿泊施設が提供される」から間違っていると判断できます。(C)には研修の時期が記載されており、空所前の研修内容に続く情報として自然です。

□weeklong: 形 1週間にわたる　□available: 形 入手可能な
□trainee: 名 訓練を受ける人　□convenient: 形 便利な

134. 正解：B 易■■■□□難 選択率：(A) 28.0% **(B) 59.0%** (C) 3.4% (D) 9.3%

(A) applicants
(B) participants
(C) judges
(D) customers

(A) 名 応募者たち
(B) 名 参加者たち
(C) 名 審査員たち
(D) 名 顧客たち

▶解説 宿泊施設が誰に提供されるかが問われています。❶でコンサルタント全員がtake part in a two-week training（2週間の研修に参加する）ことが求められています。よって宿泊施設を利用できるのは、(B) participants（参加者）だと判断できます。研修は申込制ではなく参加必須なので、(A)は不適切です。

Part 6 ▼ Reading Section

📡 ゼミ生中継
😀 Hiro 😀 Mai 😀 Yasu 😀 Dai 😀 Saki

131.
😀 誰か (A) を選んだ?
😀 一瞬、選びそうになりました。
😀 私は選びました。コンサルタントは金融業界での経験に加えて、研修を受ける必要があると思って、In addition to にしました。
😀 その日本語が少しおかしいことに気づかない?
😀 え……?
😀 じゃあ、「スープだけでなく、サラダも食べなさい」はどう?
😀 サラダは食べるものですが、スープは飲むものです。
😀 そう、それと同じ。研修を受ける必要があるとは言えるけれど、経験を受ける必要があるとは言えないよね。この英文の中でtheir previous

experienceはどの動詞の目的語にもならないんだよ。
😀 あ、なるほど。分かりました。

133.
😀 文を選ばせる設問を「文選択問題」と呼ぼう。文書を正確に理解していれば解きやすいけれど、単語を拾い読みしてストーリーを勝手に作る人は解けない。つまり、ヤスは解けない。
😀 何ですか、いきなり?　まぁ、(D) を選んで間違えたけど……。
😀 ほらね。空所の後に宿泊関連の情報が続いているから、(D) が正しいと思ったんだよね。
😀 はい。ちくしょう、悔しいなぁ。

Part 6 長文穴埋め問題

Questions 135-138 refer to the following e-mail.

To: Laurence Keen <lkeen@bradleygroup.com>

From: Stephanie Dion <sdion@portlandprojects.com>

Date: June 23

Subject: July gathering

Thank you for agreeing to attend our two-day presentation for prospective investors in the ❶

Moreton Island Sterling Hotel and Resort project. ------- have arranged a variety of entertainment
135.

for you to enjoy after you have attended the project information sessions and toured the proposed ❷

building location. -------.
136.

You will be staying in luxury rooms at the Daydream Hotel on the Gold Coast. That, your meals,

and your helicopter transportation between the ------- and our project offices will all be provided
137.

courtesy of Portland Projects. Please note that representatives of other ------- investors will also
138.

be visiting at the same time.

Sincerely,

Stephanie Dion

Investor Relations — Portland Projects

(134w)

問題135-138は次のメールに関するものです。
宛先：Laurence Keen <lkeen@bradleygroup.com>
送信者：Stephanie Dion <sdion@portlandprojects.com>
日付：6月23日
件名：7月の会合

当社の2日にわたる、Moreton Island Sterling Hotel and Resort 計画
への投資家候補向けプレゼンテーションへのご参加を承諾くださいまし
て、どうもありがとうございます。プロジェクト説明会へのご出席と、
建設予定地の視察が終わりましたら、当社が手配したさまざまなエンタ
ーテインメントをお楽しみいただけます。それにより、当該地区がどれ
ほど観光事業にとって有望か、ご理解いただけると思います。

ご宿泊いただく予定なのは、Gold Coast にある Daydream Hotel の豪
華なお部屋です。このお部屋やお食事、それに現場と当社のプロジェク
トオフィスの往復でご利用いただくヘリコプターは、全て Portland
Projects 社の取り計らいでご用意させていただきます。他の投資家候補
の方々にも同時にご来訪いただくことになっておりますので、ご了承く
ださい。

よろしくお願い申し上げます。

投資家向け広報担当——Portland Projects
Stephanie Dion

☐ gathering: 图 集会、集まり　☐ prospective: 形 見込みの、予期される　☐ investor: 图 投資者　☐ a variety of 〜: 種類豊富な〜
☐ attend: 動 〜に出席する　☐ session: 图 会合、集い　☐ tour: 動 〜を周遊する　☐ propose: 動 〜を提案する
☐ location: 图 場所　☐ luxury: 形 豪華な、ぜいたくな　☐ transportation: 图 交通機関、乗り物　☐ provide: 動 〜を提供する
☐ courtesy of 〜: 〜の好意によって　☐ representative: 图 代表者、代理人　☐ investor relations: 投資家向け広報活動

135. 正解：**A**　易■■■■■難　選択率：**(A) 93.3%** (B) 3.4% (C) 3.4% (D) 0.0%

(A) We
(B) You
(C) They
(D) Ours

(A) 代 私たちが
(B) 代 あなたが
(C) 代 彼らが
(D) 代 私たちのもの

▶解説 ❶の our two-day presentation（私たちの2日間のプレゼン）から、メールの書き手はこの会合の主催者側だと判断できます。よって、「（読み手のために）エンターテインメントを用意している」の主語として適切なのは (A) We です。

---

136. 正解：**B**　易■■■■■難　選択率：(A) 12.7% **(B) 53.7%** (C) 5.2% (D) 27.6%

(A) Please remember to make your own arrangements in this regard.
(B) I hope it will help you understand how promising the area is for tourism.
(C) Unfortunately, we will not have time for any recreational activities.
(D) This opportunity is only available to frequent guests.

(A) つきましては、必ずご自分でご手配いただくようお願いします。
(B) それにより、当該地区がどれほど観光事業にとって有望か、ご理解いただけると思います。
(C) あいにく、レクリエーション活動に割く時間はありません。
(D) この機会をご利用いただけるのは、常連のお客さまだけです。

□arrangement: 名 手配　□in this regard: この点については
□promising: 形 将来有望な　□tourism: 名 観光事業
□recreational activity: レクリエーション活動
□opportunity: 名 機会　□available: 形 利用できる
□frequent: 形 頻繁な

▶解説 空所前の情報によれば、メールの受信者はある地区への投資家候補に向けたプレゼンテーションに出席すること、説明会への出席と視察を終えたら、さまざまなエンターテインメントを体験することが分かります。これらの内容を it で受けた (B) を入れると、「プレゼンの内容や（観光客向けの）エンターテインメントを実際に体験することで、当該地区が有望だと分かるだろう」という自然な文脈になります。

---

137. 正解：**A**　易■■■■■難　選択率：**(A) 80.6%** (B) 9.7% (C) 4.1% (D) 4.9%

(A) site
(B) factory
(C) bank
(D) stadium

(A) 名 現場
(B) 名 工場
(C) 名 銀行
(D) 名 競技場

▶解説 ❷から、投資家らは2日間のイベントの間に、建設予定地などを見て回ることが分かります。ヘリコプター移動の区間として考えられるのは、その予定地とオフィスの間だと考えられるので、その場所を site と表した (A) が正解です。

---

138. 正解：**D**　易■■■■■難　選択率：(A) 26.9% (B) 14.2% (C) 7.8% **(D) 50.7%**

(A) confirmed
(B) reluctant
(C) defined
(D) potential

(A) 形 確認済みの
(B) 形 消極的な
(C) 形 明白な
(D) 形 見込みのある

▶解説 文脈に合う形容詞を選択します。❶で、この会合は prospective investors（見込みのある投資家）が対象だと述べられているので、メールの読み手の他にも、同様の投資候補者が参集すると考えられます。従って、空所には prospective の類語である (D) potential（見込みのある）が入ります。

((◦)) ゼミ 生中継　😀Hiro 😀Mai 😀Yasu 😀Dai 😀Saki

136.

😀 当たり前だけど、文選択問題の正解は (A) から (D) までいろいろあり得る。だから、正解を見て正解だと気づくのと同じくらい、<u>不正解が不正解であることに気づくことも大事</u>。では、ストーリーを少しだけ読んだ状態と、全部読んだ状態を比べよう。ダイ、不正解が不正解だと判断しやすいのは、どっち？

😀 全部読んでからです。

😀 そう。だから、文選択問題は最後に回した方が解きやすい。途中で出会っても「既読スルー」しよう。選択肢を読む必要もない。

😀 だったら「未読スルー」ですね。

😀 確かに（笑）

😀 136番の場合、最後まで読んだころには前半の内容を忘れていそうで怖いのですが。

😀 その不安があるなら、<u>文選択問題を含む段落の最後まで読んでから解く</u>という方針でもいい。1つの段落を全て読めば1つのトピックについてまとまりのある情報を読むことになるから、不正解の選択肢を消去しやすくなるよ。実際、(B) 以外は第1段落を理解できていれば消去できる。

Part 6 ▼ Reading Section

Part 6 長文穴埋め問題

Questions 139-142 refer to the following excerpt from a report.

-------. In accordance with a company-wide push to reduce spending, every department was set
139.

a goal of ten percent, which ------- except one were able to achieve. The accounting department
140. ❶

did manage to cut spending a little. However, their expenses were ------- so low that the goal may
141.

have been unrealistic. Their modest achievement was made by switching their paper supplier.
❷

The new supplier, Ascot Paper offered to undercut the price of the previous supplier by five
❸

percent. According to our calculations, the ------- will result in a saving of around €1,600 per year.
142.

(98w)

問題139-142は次の報告書の一部に関するものです。
今四半期、支出は減っている。全社的な支出削減の後押しに呼応して、各部門に10パーセント削減の目標が設定され、1つを除き全部門がこれを達成した。経理部はわずかながらも支出削減を成し遂げた。ただし、同部署の支出額はもともと非常に低かったので、設定目標が非現実的な

ものだった可能性がある。同部署のささやかな功績の背景には、用紙供給業者の変更があった。新たな業者、Ascot Paper 社は、以前の業者の価格よりも5パーセント値下げしてきた。当方の見積もりによると、この変化は結果的に1年につき1600ユーロの節減となるだろう。

☐ in accordance with 〜 : 〜に従って　☐ company-wide: 形 全社的な　☐ push: 名 後押し、攻勢　☐ reduce: 動 〜を減らす
☐ spending: 名 支出、費用　☐ department: 名 部門、部　☐ achieve: 動 〜を成し遂げる　☐ accounting department: 経理部
☐ manage to 〜: どうにかして〜する　☐ expense: 名 費用　☐ unrealistic: 形 非現実的な　☐ modest: 形 あまり多くない
☐ achievement: 名 達成、業績　☐ switch: 動 〜を切り替える　☐ supplier: 名 供給業者　☐ undercut: 動 （相手より）商品の価格を下げる
☐ previous: 形 前の　☐ according to 〜 : 〜によると　☐ calculation: 名 計算、見積もり　☐ result in 〜 : 〜という結果になる

139. 正解：**A** 易 ■■■■■ 難 選択率：**(A) 31.3%** (B) 48.9% (C) 6.7% (D) 12.3%

(A) Expenditure is down this quarter.
(B) Running costs should increase as the company grows.
(C) No objectives have been met since last year.
(D) We are no longer using paper.

(A) 今四半期、支出は減っている。
(B) 会社が成長するにつれて維持費が膨らむはずだ。
(C) 昨年来、1つの目標も達成されていない。
(D) 当社では、もはや紙を使用していない。

▶解説 この文書では、全部門が支出削減に取り組んだことや、その取り組みが成功していることを、具体例を交えて報告しています。よって、(A)の「今四半期、支出は減っている」が結論であり、それを説明するために後続の情報があると考えるのが自然です。(B)は文書の趣旨と逆なので不適切です。仮に(B)を空所に入れると、その後に維持費が増える理由や支出増の例などが続くべきです。

□ expenditure: 名 支出、経費 □ quarter: 名 四半期 □ running cost: 維持費
□ increase: 動 増える □ objective: 名 目的、目標 □ no longer ～ : もはや～でない

---

140. 正解：**B** 易 ■■■■ 難 選択率：(A) - (B) - (C) - (D) -

(A) each
(B) all
(C) neither
(D) other

(A) 代 各自
(B) 代 すべて
(C) 代 どちらも～ない
(D) 形 他の

▶解説 主語に対応する動詞がwereであることから、主語は複数形だと判断できます。よって、(B) all が空所に入ります。all except one were able to achieve. (1つを除いてすべての部署が達成できた) となり文全体の意味が通ります。

---

141. 正解：**D** 易 ■■■■■ 難 選択率：(A) 11.9% (B) 43.3% (C) 23.9% **(D) 20.1%**

(A) likewise
(B) quite
(C) indeed
(D) already

(A) 副 同様に
(B) 副 非常に
(C) 副 確かに
(D) 副 すでに

▶解説 文脈に合う副詞を選択します。❶で、経理部は支出の削減幅が少なかったとあります。空所に(D) already を補うと、「しかし、経理部は支出がもともと非常に低かったので、目標が非現実的だったかもしれない」となり、前文と自然につながります。

---

142. 正解：**A** 易 ■■■■■ 難 選択率：**(A) 59.3%** (B) 21.3% (C) 15.3% (D) 3.0%

(A) change
(B) campaign
(C) program
(D) closure

(A) 名 変化
(B) 名 キャンペーン
(C) 名 制度
(D) 名 閉鎖

▶解説 ❷の情報から、経理部が紙の供給業者を変更したこと、また、❸からは、前の供給業者と比べて価格が5パーセント下がったことが分かります。この値下げが年1600ユーロの節約につながると考えられるので、空所に入るのは「変化」を意味する(A)のchangeです。

(((▲))) ゼミ 生中継   Hiro   Mai   Yasu   Dai   Saki

141. ....
魅力的な不正解は(B)のquiteだけど、文法的にダメ。「かなり低かった」と言いたければ、quite so lowじゃなくquite lowでいい。

soが邪魔ですね。

そう。

😮😮😮😮……。

えっと、ここではsoとthatがセットで使われているから、仮にquiteを使うなら、～ their expenses were quite low, so the goal may ... という形にすれば大丈夫。(A)と(C)は「同様に」「確かに」だから文法的にはOKだけど、文脈的にアウト。

Part6

Reading Section

Part 6 長文穴埋め問題

Questions 143-146 refer to the following notice.

Attention

On Friday, a company called Sensible Security Solutions ------- the security system at the main
143.

entrance. The work is scheduled to take place between 7:00 P.M. and 10:00 P.M. because that is
❶

when we have the least -------. While the work is being carried out, you will not be able to use the
144.

automatic card reader. You will not be able to unlock the exterior doors using the electric buzzers
❷

in the offices, either. -------. If you have a guest to whom you would like to grant entry, you should
145.

provide the building team with the name and the ------- arrival time in advance.
146.

(118w)

問題143-146は次のお知らせに関するものです。
お知らせ
金曜日に、Sensible Security Solutionsという会社が正面玄関の保安
システムの更新作業を行います。作業は午後7時から午後10時の間に
行われる予定です。これは、その時間帯に人の出入りが最も少ないから

です。作業中は、自動カード読み取り機が使えません。また、オフィス
内の電動ブザーを使って外の扉を解錠することもできなくなります。代
わりに、玄関に警備員を1名配置します。入館を許可したい来訪者がい
る場合には、あらかじめ建物の管理担当班に来訪者の氏名と到着予定時
刻を連絡しておいてください。

□ notice: 名 お知らせ　□ attention: 名 注意　□ security system: 保安システム　□ main entrance: 正面玄関　□ schedule: 動 ～を予定する
□ take place: 行われる　□ carry out ～: ～を実行する　□ automatic: 形 自動の　□ unlock: 動 ～を開錠する　□ exterior: 形 外の、外部の
□ electric: 形 電動の　□ buzzer: 名 ブザー　□ grant: 動 ～を承諾する　□ provide: 動 ～を提供する　□ arrival time: 到着時間
□ in advance: あらかじめ

143. 正解：**C**　易 ■■■□□□ 難　選択率：(A) 5.2%　(B) 15.3%　**(C) 69.4%**　(D) 8.6%

(A) was upgrading
(B) have upgraded
(C) will be upgrading
(D) is upgraded

(A) 更新していた（過去進行形）
(B) 更新し終わった（現在完了形）
(C) 更新されるだろう（未来形）
(D) 更新されている（受け身）

▶解説 ❶の部分で、作業を実施する予定の時間について触れられています。このことから、作業はまだ行われていない未来の事柄だと判断できます。よって、未来を表す (C) will be upgrading が正解です。

---

144. 正解：**B**　易 ■■□□□□ 難　選択率：(A) 16.0%　**(B) 48.9%**　(C) 8.6%　(D) 25.7%

(A) confidence
(B) traffic
(C) evidence
(D) reference

(A) 名 自信
(B) 名 往来
(C) 名 証拠
(D) 名 言及

▶解説 空所に自然に入る語彙が問われています。選択肢のうち、「人の往来」という意味の (B) traffic を入れると、「最も人通りが少ない時間帯を選んで、夜に工事を行う予定を組んでいる」という意味になり、文意が通ります。

---

145. 正解：**D**　易 ■□□□□□ 難　選択率：(A) 14.6%　(B) 22.4%　(C) 29.5%　**(D) 32.5%**

(A) Unfortunately, no one will be allowed to enter until the work is complete.
(B) However, it will be possible to allow access remotely.
(C) Therefore, you should have all employees leave before 7:00 P.M.
(D) Instead, we will have a security guard standing at the front door.

(A) あいにく、作業が完了するまで誰も入館を許可されません。
(B) ただし、遠隔でのアクセス許可は可能です。
(C) 従って、全従業員を午後7時前に退社させた方がいいでしょう。
(D) 代わりに、玄関に警備員を1名配置します。

▶解説 文選択問題です。❷の部分で、作業中は外のドアを（オフィス内から）解錠できなくなると注意喚起されています。その内容を受けて「代わりに、警備員を配置する予定だ」と述べている (D) が続くと話の展開が自然になります。

☐ unfortunately: 副 あいにく　☐ allow: 動 ～を許す　☐ complete: 形 完成して
☐ however: 副 しかしながら　☐ access: 名 出入り　☐ remotely: 副 遠く離れて
☐ therefore: 副 従って　☐ instead: 副 その代わりに　☐ security guard: 警備員

---

146. 正解：**C**　易 ■■■□□□ 難　選択率：(A) 23.5%　(B) 13.4%　**(C) 53.4%**　(D) 9.0%

(A) expecting
(B) expectation
(C) expected
(D) expectedly

(A) 動 予想している（現在分詞）
(B) 名 予想
(C) 動 予想される（過去分詞）
(D) 副 予想されて

▶解説 空所前に冠詞 the、後に名詞 arrival time（到着時刻）があるので、空所に入るのは名詞を修飾する語です。選択肢のうち、名詞を修飾できるのは、分詞の (A) か (C) です。時刻は「予想されるもの」なので、(C) の expected が適切です。

Part 6 ▶ Reading Section

((A)) ゼミ 生 中継　　Hiro　Mai　Yasu　Dai　Saki

145.

😀 不正解が不正解である理由を確認しよう。空所の後に、訪問客を入館させる手順が続いている。つまり、従業員も訪問客も出入り可能ということだから、(A) と (C) は間違った情報と言える。

🐵 (B) は大丈夫な気がします。スマホで遠隔操作してドアを開けられるんじゃないですか？

😀 妄想しちゃダメ。直前を読んで。オフィスにあるブザーを使っての開錠ができないんだ。その直後に「しかし、遠隔でのアクセス許可は可能だ」と書くと、矛盾する。

🐵 あ、ブザーも遠隔操作の1つか。じゃあ、(B) も間違った情報だ。

😀 そう。文選択問題の不正解は「間違った情報」か、139番の (B) みた

いな「場違いな情報」なんだよ。覚えておいて。

🐱 私は「場違いな情報」が苦手です。Part 7 に文の位置を問う設問が出ますよね。あれがダメなんです。

😀 あれはまさに「場違い」かどうかを純粋に問うているから、悩む人が多い。ただ、攻略法はあるから、後で話すよ。

146.

😀 「見込んでいる到着時刻」と和訳すると、何となく「～している」を意識して -ing を使いたくなるよね。

🎲 まさにその通りです。(A) にしました。

😀 でも、時刻は人によって「見込まれる」ものなので、過去分詞が必要だ。では、いよいよ Part 7 だね。

Part 7 読解問題

Questions 147-148 refer to the following notice.

<hr>

Attention Visitors

Walbran Park is a favorite place for families with young children to visit. Unfortunately, **❶** the popular playground has been fenced off so that maintenance workers can replace damaged and worn-out parts for safety reasons. The work will continue until the middle of March.

There are other parks in the area which have similar equipment, the closest of which is Vandelay Park on Butler Street in East Preston. The council encourages residents to make use of that facility until the work is complete.

❷ If you would like any more information about the work or local city parks in general, please contact Nadine Salinger at gpm@haliburtoncitycouncil.com.

<hr>

(106w)

問題**147-148**は次のお知らせに関するものです。

来園者の皆さま

Walbran Parkは、お子さま連れのご家族にぴったりの場所です。あいにく、この人気の遊び場が柵で囲われた状態になっています。これは安全上の理由から保守作業員が損傷や老朽化の進んだ設備品の交換作業に携われるようにするための措置です。作業は3月中旬まで継続される予定です。

この地域には同様の設備を擁する公園が他にもあり、最も近隣のものはEast PrestonのButler Street沿いにあるVandelay Parkです。市では住民の皆さまに、作業が完了するまでそちらの施設をご利用になるようお勧めしています。

この作業や市内の公園全般に関する情報をさらにご希望でしたら、gpm@haliburtoncitycoucil.comのNadine Salinger宛てにご連絡ください。

☐ notice: 图 通知、お知らせ ☐ attention: 图 注意、注目 ☐ visitor: 图 来客 ☐ favorite: 形 お気に入りの ☐ unfortunately: 副 あいにく
☐ popular: 形 人気のある、評判の良い ☐ playground: 图 遊び場 ☐ fence off 〜: 〜を柵で囲う ☐ maintenance worker: 保守作業員
☐ replace: 動 〜を交換する ☐ damage: 動 〜を害する、傷つける ☐ worn-out: 形 使い古した ☐ safety: 图 安全 ☐ continue : 動 続く
☐ similar : 形 類似した ☐ equipment : 图 設備 ☐ council : 图 評議会 ☐ encourage 〜 to ...: 〜に…するよう働き掛ける
☐ resident: 图 居住者 ☐ make use of 〜: 〜を使用する ☐ facility: 图 設備 ☐ complete: 形 完成して ☐ local: 形 地元の
☐ in general: 一般の

147. 正解：**C**　易 ■■□□□□□ 難　選択率：(A) 4.9%　(B) 3.0%　**(C) 90.7%**　(D) 0.7%

What is the purpose of the notice?
(A) To encourage people to make a donation
(B) To announce a change in admission rates
(C) To explain why a park is unavailable
(D) To ask for volunteers to help maintain a park

このお知らせの目的は何ですか。
(A) 人々に寄付を促すこと
(B) 入園料の変更を発表すること
(C) なぜ公園が利用できないかを説明すること
(D) 公園の整備を手伝うボランティアを募集すること

▶解説 ❶で、メンテナンス作業のために現在 Walbran Park が柵で囲まれていると述べられています。従ってこのお知らせの目的は、(C) の公園が利用できない理由を説明するためと考えられます。

☐ purpose: 名 目的　☐ donation: 名 寄付
☐ admission rate: 入場料　☐ explain: 動 ～を説明する
☐ unavailable: 形 利用できない
☐ maintain: 動 ～を整備する、保全する

---

148. 正解：**D**　易 ■□■■■□□□ 難　選択率：(A) 9.7%　(B) 27.6%　(C) 4.1%　**(D) 57.5%**

According to the notice, why might someone contact Ms. Salinger?
(A) To get a price estimate for playground equipment
(B) To learn more about public transportation
(C) To hire a landscaping business
(D) To discuss a construction project

このお知らせによると、誰かが Salinger さんに連絡を取るとしたら、それはなぜですか。
(A) 遊び場の設備の価格見積もりを取るために
(B) 公共交通機関についてさらに知るために
(C) 造園業者を雇うために
(D) 建設計画について話し合うために

▶解説 Ms. Salinger は❷に登場します。❷で、公園での作業についての情報がさらに必要であれば Salinger さんに連絡をするよう求めていることから、本文中の the work を construction project と言い換えた (D) が正解となります。

☐ according to ～: ～によると
☐ contact: 動 ～に連絡する　☐ estimate: 名 見積もり
☐ public transportation: 公共交通機関　☐ hire: 動 ～を雇う
☐ landscaping: 名 造園　☐ business: 名 店、会社
☐ discuss: 動 ～を話し合う　☐ construction: 名 建設
☐ project: 名 計画、事業

📡 ゼミ 生 中継　

😊 さて、最後の Part 7 だけど、54 問もある。とにかく、最初から見ていこう。

148. ⋯⋯⋯⋯⋯⋯⋯⋯⋯⋯⋯⋯⋯⋯⋯⋯⋯⋯⋯

😊 誰か (B) を選んだ?

😊 私は (B) にしました。Vandelay Park に行きたい人が交通手段を問い合わせするかもしれないと思って。

😊 公共交通機関に関する情報は文書にある?

😊 ないです。でも、誰かが問い合わせる可能性はありそうです。

😊 設問に According to the notice とあるよね。「かもしれない」とか「可能性はある」といった想像を根拠にしちゃいけない。

😊 え、それが理由ですか?

😊 まだある。(B) の learn more ～は「もっと知る」だよ。この文書に「電車の駅は遠いが、近くにバス停がある。詳細はお問い合わせください」と書かれていれば、(B) は文句なしの正解だけど、そんな情報はないから、(B) はダメ。

😊 私は (D) の discuss が大げさだと思ったのですが、「議論する」とは限らないのですね。

😊 そう。軽く話し合うのも discuss だよ。余談だけど、独りで何かを説明することも discuss と言えるから、Part 4 でトークの目的が To discuss ～と表現されることだってある。

Questions 149-150 refer to the following article.

Drummond (September 6) — Blake Hawthorne, the president of Zeno Pharmaceuticals, announced today that he had finished negotiations for a takeover of Omicron Corporation. He stated that Zeno Pharmaceuticals would completely absorb the smaller company and that all their products would simply be rebranded.

Both companies have their headquarters and production facilities in Drummond so the change is not expected to have a very profound effect on staff members, who should be able to continue in their current positions albeit at a different address.

"I'll be retiring as soon as the deal is formalized" said Melissa Raver, the current CEO of Omicron Corporation. "I am very happy with the arrangement and expect the company to experience even greater prosperity as a result" she added.

(123w)

問題149-150は次の記事に関するものです。
Drummond（9月6日）——Zeno Pharmaceuticals 社社長の Blake Hawthorne 氏は本日、Omicron Corporation の買収交渉を終えたことを明らかにした。同氏によると、Zeno Pharmaceuticals 社はより規模の小さい Omicron 社を完全吸収し、同社の全商品が単純に商標を変更することになるという。

両社共が本社と生産施設を Drummond に構えていることから、今回の変更が従業員に与える影響はさほど大きなものではないと予想されており、従業員は、勤務地の変更はあっても現在の職位にとどまれることになっている。

「私は、この協定が正式なものになったらすぐに退くつもりです」と Omicron Corporation の現 CEO、Melissa Raver は話した。「今回の合意について非常にうれしく思っており、会社は結果的に今まで以上の繁栄を享受するだろうと予想しています」と同氏は付け加えた。

☐ president: 图 社長　☐ announce: 動 〜を発表する　☐ negotiation: 图 交渉　☐ takeover: 图 乗っ取り、企業取得　☐ state: 動 〜を述べる
☐ completely: 副 完全に　☐ absorb: 動 〜を吸収合併する　☐ simply: 副 単に　☐ rebrand: 動 〜をリブランドする（ブランド名やロゴなどを変更すること）　☐ headquarters: 图 本社　☐ facility: 图 施設　☐ expect to 〜: 〜することを予期する　☐ profound: 形 重大な　☐ effect: 图 影響
☐ staff member: 職員、社員　☐ current: 形 現在の　☐ position: 图 地位　☐ albeit: 接 〜にかかわらず　☐ retire: 動 退役する
☐ deal: 图 取引、計画　☐ formalize: 動 〜を正式なものにする　☐ arrangement: 图 取り決め、協定　☐ experience: 動 〜を経験する
☐ prosperity: 图 繁栄　☐ as a result: 結果として

149. 正解：C　易 ■■■□□□□□ 難　選択率：(A) 4.9%　(B) 3.4%　(C) 88.1%　(D) 3.4%

What is the article mainly about?
(A) A new product
(B) A temporary closure
(C) A corporate merger
(D) An advertising strategy

この記事は、主に何に関するものですか。
(A) 新製品
(B) 一時的な撤退
(C) 企業合併
(D) 広告戦略

▶解説　❶に、Zeno Pharmaceuticals 社の社長がOmicron Corporation 社の買収に関する交渉を終えたと述べた、とあります。それ以降も完全吸収合併であることなどが説明されていることから、この記事は(C)の A corporate merger ついてのものであることが分かります。merger は「合併」という意味です。

□ temporary: 形 一時的な　□ closure: 名 休業　□ corporate: 形 法人の
□ merger: 名 合併　□ advertising: 名 広告　□ strategy: 名 戦略

150. 正解：D　易 ■■■□□□□□ 難　選択率：(A) 4.9%　(B) 6.3%　(C) 13.8%　(D) 74.6%

What is indicated about Omicron Corporation?
(A) It has recently reported record profits.
(B) It has received an industry award.
(C) It is moving away from Drummond.
(D) It will have a change in leadership.

Omicron Corporation について何が示されていますか。
(A) 最近、記録的な利益を上げたと報じられている。
(B) 業界の賞を受けた。
(C) Drummond から離れた場所へ移転する。
(D) トップが交代するだろう。

▶解説　❷にOmicron Corporation 社の現 CEOである Raver 氏が、この交渉が正式なものになり次第辞任すると述べた、とあることから、同社の leadership（指導者）が交代することが分かります。(D)が正解です。

□ indicate: 動 ～を暗に示す　□ recently: 副 最近
□ report: 動 ～を報告する　□ record: 形 記録的な
□ profit: 名 利益　□ receive: 動 ～を受け取る
□ industry: 名 産業界　□ award: 名 賞
□ move away from ～: ～から移転する
□ leadership: 名 指導者

 ゼミ 生中継　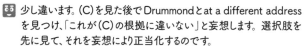 Hiro　Mai　Yasu　Dai　Saki

150.
 意外と多くのモニターが(C)を選んだのは、拾い読みが原因だね。第2段落にある Drummond と at a different address から、会社の移転を妄想すると、(C)が魅力的に見える。

😠 少し違います。(C)を見た後で Drummond と at a different address を見つけ、「これが(C)の根拠に違いない」と妄想します。選択肢を先に見て、それを妄想により正当化するのです。

😀 真面目に解説しなくていいよ！　とにかく妄想は禁止。

Part 7 読解問題

Questions 151-152 refer to the following text-message chain.

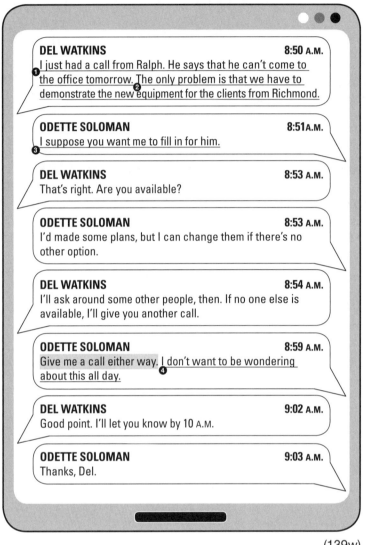

(139w)

問題151-152は次のテキストメッセージのやりとりに関するものです。

DEL WATKINS 午前8時50分
たった今Ralphから電話があった。彼は明日出社できないって言ってる。唯一の問題は、Richmondから来るお客さんたちに、新しい装置の実演説明をしなければならないことなんだ。

ODETTE SOLOMAN 午前8時51分
私に彼の代役を務めてほしいということね。

DEL WATKINS 午前8時53分
その通り。都合は大丈夫?

ODETTE SOLOMAN 午前8時53分
予定があったんだけど、変更してもいいわ、もし他に誰もいないなら。

DEL WATKINS 午前8時54分
じゃあ、周りの人に聞いてみる。もし誰も都合がつかなければ、あらためて君に電話するよ。

ODETTE SOLOMAN 午前8時59分
どちらにしても電話して。この件はどうなったんだろうって1日中考えていたくないから。

DEL WATKINS 午前9時02分
そうだよね。午前10時までに知らせる。

ODETTE SOLOMAN 午前9時03分
よろしく、Del。

☐ text-message chain: テキストメッセージのやりとり（携帯電話同士のショートメッセージのこと） ☐ demonstrate: 動（商品など）を実物宣伝する
☐ equipment: 名 設備 ☐ client: 名 顧客 ☐ suppose: 動 ～だと思う ☐ fill in for ～: ～の代わりをする ☐ available: 形 手が空いていて
☐ option: 名 選択肢 ☐ ask around: （周囲の人々に）聞いて回る ☐ wonder about ～: （進行形で）～について知りたいと思う

151. 正解：**B**　易 ■■■■■■■ 難　選択率： (A) 6.7%　**(B) 86.2%**8　(C) 6.3%　(D) 0.4%

Who most likely is Ralph?
(A) A client
(B) A work colleague
(C) A supplier
(D) A safety inspector

☐ colleague: 图 同僚　☐ supplier: 图 供給業者
☐ inspector: 图 検査官

Ralphとは誰である可能性が最も高いですか。
(A) 顧客
(B) 職場の同僚
(C) 納入業者
(D) 安全検査官

▶解説 ❶でRalphは明日欠勤の旨を伝えてきた人物だと分かります。また❷から、Ralphは顧客に実演をする予定だったと分かります。❸でSolomanさんは、Ralphの代役をしてほしいということかと確認しています。これらのことから、RalphはWatkinsさんとSolomanさんの同僚だと判断でき、(B)が正解に決まります。

152. 正解：**D**　易 ■■■■■■■ 難　選択率： (A) 7.8%　(B) 6.7%　(C) 20.5%　**(D) 64.9%**

At 8:59 A.M., why does Ms. Soloman write, "Give me a call either way"?
(A) She does not mind how Mr. Watkins calls her.
(B) She hopes that Mr. Watkins will not use another supplier.
(C) She is very eager to solve a problem.
(D) She wants to know whether or not she is needed.

☐ eager to ～ : しきりに～したがっている
☐ solve: 動 ～を解決する
☐ whether or not ～ : ～であろうとなかろうと

午前8時59分に、なぜSolomanさんは「どちらにしても電話して」と書いていますか。
(A) 彼女は、Watkinsさんがどのように彼女に電話しようと構わない。
(B) 彼女は、Watkinsさんが別の納入業者を使わなければいいと思っている。
(C) 彼女はぜひとも問題を解決したいと望んでいる。
(D) 彼女は、自分が必要とされているかどうかを知りたがっている。

▶解説 いずれにしても電話がほしいと言うSolomanさんは、続く❹で自分が出勤になるのかどうか1日中、心配していたくない、と述べています。このことから、彼女は自分が明日必要かどうか知りたいから電話がほしいのだと分かります。(D)が正解です。

📡 ゼミ 生 中継　😀Hiro 😊Mai 😎Yasu 🤖Dai 😀Saki

152.
😀 意図問題だね。ヤス、どれを選んだ？
👤 (C)です。Solomanさんは協力しようとしていますから。
😀 でも、問題解決に対してvery eagerとは言えない。本気で協力する

気があるなら、8時53分のAre you available? にYes. と答えるはずだよ。でも、態度を保留しているよね。彼女はあまり乗り気じゃない。
👤 確かに「自分はやりたくない」感を出していますね。

Part 7 読解問題

Questions 153-155 refer to the following notice.

Help Save the Odeon Theater

On May 19, the Doraville Historical Society will host a screening of *Free Hearts* at the Odeon Theater on Cordon Street, Doraville. The Odeon Theater building is listed as a heritage asset of Doraville and has been protected from demolition by an order of the town council. The current owners have been unable to find a tenant and therefore, the building is not generating an income. As a result, little has been spent on its upkeep. The historical society hopes to generate interest in the old building and to find people willing to invest in a business there. Unless there is some investment and restoration work soon, the building may become unsalvageable. All money raised from admission fees for the event on May 19 will be used to carry out some emergency repairs on the roof and a couple of the exterior walls. Visit www.doravillehs.org/odeontheater for further details about the film screening and to purchase tickets for the May 19 event.

(166w)

問題153-155は次のお知らせに関するものです。

Odeon Theater 保存にお力添えを

5月19日に、Doraville Historical Society は『Free Hearts』の上映会を主催します。場所は、Doraville の Cordon Street にある Odeon Theater です。Odeon Theater の建物は Doraville の遺産物件に登録されており、町当局の要請に基づいて取り壊されないよう保護されています。現在の建物の所有者は借り主を見つけられず、そのため建物から収入を得られない状況です。結果的に、ほとんど維持費が投じられていません。当歴史協会はこの古い建造物への興味を喚起し、そこでの事業に積極的に投資しようという方々を見つけたいと考えています。ある程度の費用の確保と修復工事を早急に実現しない限り、建物は取り壊しを免れなくなるかもしれません。5月19日に当催しの入場料として集められる全額が、緊急修復工事に使われる予定です。工事の対象は、屋根と外壁数カ所です。www.doravillehs.org/odeontheater へアクセスして、5月19日の催しの上映内容やチケットの購入に関する詳細をご確認ください。

☐ host: 動 ～を主催する　☐ screening: 名 上映　☐ list: 動 ～を目録に載せる　☐ heritage: 名 遺産　☐ asset: 名 資産、財産
☐ protect: 動 ～を守る、保護する　☐ demolition: 名 (建物などの) 取り壊し　☐ town council: 町議会　☐ current: 形 現在の
☐ tenant: 名 テナント　☐ generate: 動 ～をもたらす、発生させる　☐ income: 名 収入　☐ as a result: 結果として　☐ upkeep: 名 維持
☐ historical: 形 歴史の　☐ society: 名 会、協会、学会　☐ interest: 名 興味、関心　☐ willing to ～: ～する意思がある　☐ invest: 動 投資する
☐ business: 名 事業　☐ unless: 接 ～でない限り　☐ investment: 名 投資、出資　☐ restoration: 名 修復　☐ unsalvageable: 形 救助不可能な
☐ raise: 動 (資金など) を集める　☐ admission fee: 入場料　☐ carry out ～: ～を実行する　☐ emergency: 形 緊急の　☐ repair: 名 修理
☐ a couple of ～: 2、3の～　☐ exterior: 形 外の、外部の　☐ further: 形 それ以上の　☐ details: 名 詳しい情報　☐ purchase: 動 ～を購入する

153. 正解：**B**　易▬▬▬▭▭難　選択率：(A) 7.5%　**(B) 75.4%**　(C) 11.6%　(D) 4.9%

What is true about the Odeon Theater?
(A) It is scheduled for demolition.
(B) It has historical value.
(C) It has recently changed ownership.
(D) It is popular with local residents.

☐ value: 图 価値　☐ ownership: 图 所有権、所有者であること
☐ resident: 图 居住者

Odeon Theater について正しいものはどれですか。
(A) 取り壊しが予定されている。
(B) 歴史的価値がある。
(C) 最近、所有者が代わった。
(D) 地元の住民たちに人気がある。

▶解説　❶で Odeon Theater は遺産として登録されており、町議会の命令により取り壊しから保護されていると述べられています。この記述から、この劇場には歴史的価値があるのだと分かります。(B) が正解です。

---

154. 正解：**A**　易▬▬▬▭▭▭難　選択率：**(A) 66.4%**　(B) 14.2%　(C) 10.4%　(D) 7.8%

Why will the event most likely be held?
(A) To attract attention to an important building
(B) To provide a networking opportunity for business people
(C) To celebrate the foundation of a business
(D) To welcome new members to a community group.

☐ attract: 動 ～を引き付ける　☐ attention: 图 注意、注目
☐ network: 動 人脈を保つ、他の人と関わりを持つ
☐ opportunity: 图 機会　☐ celebrate: 動 ～を祝う
☐ foundation: 图 設立
☐ community: 图 コミュニティー、共同体

どのような理由でこの催しが開かれる可能性が最も高いですか。
(A) ある重要な建物への関心を引くために
(B) ビジネスに携わる人たちに交流の機会を提供するために
(C) ある事業所の設立を祝うために
(D) 地域の団体に新しく加入するメンバーを歓迎するために

▶解説　イベント（映画の上映）については、❷で人々にその建物への興味を持ってもらうために歴史協会が行うものであると述べられています。よって to generate interest を to attract attention と言い換えて表現している (A) が正解です。

---

155. 正解：**C**　易▬▭▬▭▭▭難　選択率：(A) 10.8%　(B) 7.8%　**(C) 77.6%**　(D) 2.6%

What is suggested about the tickets?
(A) They can be purchased at the theater.
(B) The price was determined by council employees.
(C) The revenue will be used to pay for repairs.
(D) They cannot be refunded within 24 hours of the event.

☐ determine: 動 ～を決定する　☐ revenue: 图 収益
☐ refund: 動 ～を払い戻す

チケットについて何が示されていますか。
(A) 劇場で購入できる。
(B) 価格は自治体の職員によって決められた。
(C) 収益は修理費の支払いに充てられるだろう。
(D) 催しまで24時間を切ったら払い戻しできない。

▶解説　❸に、催しの入場料から得られたお金は屋根と外壁の一部の緊急補修に充てられる、とあることから、チケットの売上金は修理に使われることが分かります。(C) が正解です。revenue は「収入、収益」の意です。

((📡)) ゼミ 生中継　

153.

（Hiro）設問タイプの話をしよう。153番と155番を見て。このゼミでは「選択肢照合型」と呼ぶことにする。サキ、印象は？

（Saki）ヤな感じです。選択肢が長いし、どこまで読めば解けるか分からないです。

（Dai）そうだね。各選択肢を文書と照合させないと解きようがない。

（Mai）ということは、選択肢を先に読んだ方がいいですか。

（Yasu）個人差がある。何度か試して、自分に合うならそれでいい。ただ、選択肢の内容はバラバラだから記憶に残りにくいと思うよ。短めの文書なら、4～5割読めば1～2問は解けるから、とにかく文書を読んでから正解の選択肢を探せばいい。文書はどっちみち全部読むのが鉄則だからね。下手に省エネする必要はないよ。

Part 7 読解問題

Questions 156-157 refer to the following text message.

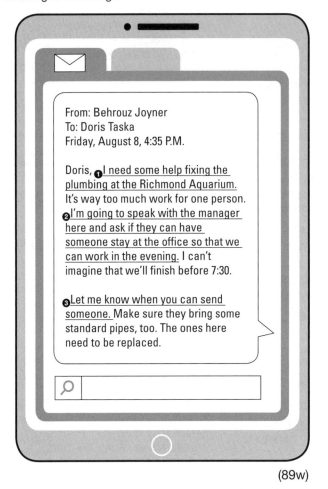

From: Behrouz Joyner
To: Doris Taska
Friday, August 8, 4:35 P.M.

Doris, ❶I need some help fixing the plumbing at the Richmond Aquarium. It's way too much work for one person. ❷I'm going to speak with the manager here and ask if they can have someone stay at the office so that we can work in the evening. I can't imagine that we'll finish before 7:30.

❸Let me know when you can send someone. Make sure they bring some standard pipes, too. The ones here need to be replaced.

(89w)

問題156-157は次のテキストメッセージに関するものです。
送信者：Behrouz Joyner
宛先：Doris Taska
8月8日、金曜日、午後4時35分

Doris、Richmond Aquarium の配管修理に手伝いが必要なんだ。とても1人でできる仕事量じゃない。こちらの管理者と話して、誰か事務所に残ってもらい、夜に作業できるようにしてもらうつもりだ。7時30分より前に終わるとはとうてい思えないからね。

いつごろ人をよこしてもらえるか教えて。それと、必ず標準のパイプを何本か持ってきてもらいたいんだ。ここのを交換しなければならないだよ。

☐ fix: 動 〜を修理する　☐ plumbing: 名 配管　☐ aquarium: 名 水族館　☐ way: 副 はるかに、ずっと　☐ imagine: 動 〜と思う
☐ make sure 〜: 確実に〜する　☐ standard: 形 標準の　☐ replace: 動 〜を交換する

156. 正解：A 易 ■■■□□□□ 難　選択率：**(A) 91.0%** (B) 1.9% (C) 3.4% (D) 2.6%

Why did Mr. Joyner send the text message?
(A) To request assistance with a job
(B) To announce the date of an interview
(C) To comment on the price of some materials
(D) To apply for a position at an aquarium.

□ assistance: 名 手伝い　□ interview: 名 面接
□ comment: 動 論評する　□ material: 名 材料
□ apply: 動 申し込む、出願する　□ position: 名 職

なぜJoynerさんはテキストメッセージを送りましたか。
(A) 仕事の補助を依頼するために
(B) 面接の日取りを知らせるために
(C) いくつかの資材の価格について意見を述べるために
(D) 水族館の職に応募するために

▶解説 Joynerさんは❶で、Richmond Aquariumでの配管修理に手伝い(help)が必要だと述べています。また❸では人を送り込んでくれるのはいつなのか知らせてほしい、と依頼していることから、仕事の応援を頼んでいることが分かります。よってhelpをassistanceと言い換えている(A)が正解です。

---

157. 正解：D 易 ■■■□□□□ 難　選択率：(A) 6.7% (B) 14.6% (C) 6.0% **(D) 72.4%**

What will Mr. Joyner do?
(A) Purchase some new equipment
(B) Deliver some supplies to a client
(C) Apply for a position at a manufacturing plant
(D) Make arrangements to work in the evening

□ equipment: 名 設備　□ supply: 名 供給品　□ manufacturing plant: 製造工場
□ arrangement: 名 手配

Joynerさんは何をするつもりですか。
(A) 新しい設備を購入する
(B) 補充品を顧客に届ける
(C) 製造工場の職に応募する
(D) 夜に作業する手はずを整える

▶解説 自分1人では7時30分までに作業を終えられないと悟ったJoynerさんは、❷で夜間作業ができるよう水族館に依頼すると述べています。このことから、正解は(D)です。make arrangementsは「手配(用意)をする」の意です。

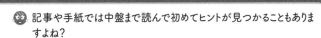

(((📡)))ゼミ生中継　　　Hiro　Mai　Yasu　Dai　Saki

156.

Hiro: これは実質的には文書の目的を問うている。147番のように、What is the purpose of ～?という表現が使われることもある。この設問タイプを「文脈型」と呼ぼう。多くの場合、目的が問われたらヒントは最初の段落で見つかる。

Mai: 記事や手紙では中盤まで読んで初めてヒントが見つかることもありますよね？

Hiro: 詳しいね。たまにそういうことも起きるけれど、1回のテストにつき1問あるかないか程度だよ。文脈型には目的を問うもの以外に、登場人物の勤務先を問うものもある。ちょうど、次のセットにある。158番に進もう。

Part 7 読解問題

Questions 158-161 refer to the following online chat discussion.

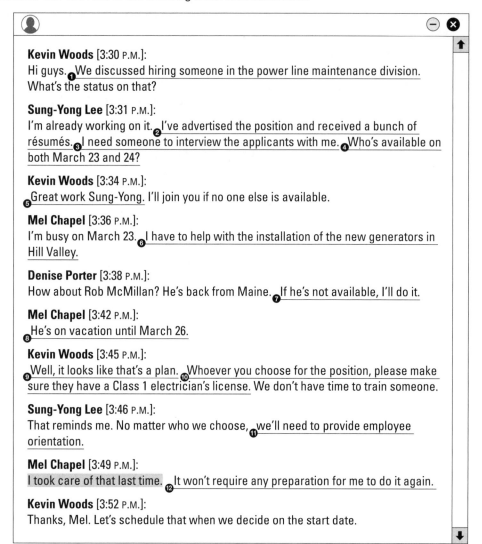

Kevin Woods [3:30 P.M.]:
Hi guys. ●We discussed hiring someone in the power line maintenance division. What's the status on that?

Sung-Yong Lee [3:31 P.M.]:
I'm already working on it. ●I've advertised the position and received a bunch of résumés. ●I need someone to interview the applicants with me. ●Who's available on both March 23 and 24?

Kevin Woods [3:34 P.M.]:
●Great work Sung-Yong. I'll join you if no one else is available.

Mel Chapel [3:36 P.M.]:
I'm busy on March 23. ●I have to help with the installation of the new generators in Hill Valley.

Denise Porter [3:38 P.M.]:
How about Rob McMillan? He's back from Maine. ●If he's not available, I'll do it.

Mel Chapel [3:42 P.M.]:
●He's on vacation until March 26.

Kevin Woods [3:45 P.M.]:
●Well, it looks like that's a plan. ●Whoever you choose for the position, please make sure they have a Class 1 electrician's license. We don't have time to train someone.

Sung-Yong Lee [3:46 P.M.]:
That reminds me. No matter who we choose, ●we'll need to provide employee orientation.

Mel Chapel [3:49 P.M.]:
I took care of that last time. ●It won't require any preparation for me to do it again.

Kevin Woods [3:52 P.M.]:
Thanks, Mel. Let's schedule that when we decide on the start date.

(215w)

問題158-161は次のオンライン会議に関するものです。

Kevin Woods［午後3時30分］：
やあ、みんな。送電線保守課に人を雇うことについて話したけど、あの件、どうなってる？

Sung-Yong Lee［午後3時31分］：
すでに取り掛かっています。求人広告を出して、多数の履歴書を受け取っています。どなたかに、私と一緒に応募者を面接していただく必要があります。3月23日と24日にご都合のよろしい方はいらっしゃいますか。

Kevin Woods［午後3時34分］
ご苦労さま、Sung-Yong。私が行くよ、もし他に誰も都合がつかないのなら。

Mel Chapel［午後3時36分］
私は3月23日が駄目です。新しい発電機をHill Valleyに設置する手伝いをしなければなりません。

Denice Porter［午後3時38分］
Rob McMillanはどうですか。彼はMaineから戻ってきています。もし彼の都合がつかなければ、私がやりますよ。

Mel Chapel［午後3時42分］
彼は3月26日にならないと出社しません。

Kevin Woods［午後3時45分］
まあ、どうやら何とかなりそうだね。今回の職に誰を選ぶにせよ、必ず1級電気技師の資格を持っていることを確認してくれよ。われわれには採用者を研修している暇はないんだ。

Sung-Yong Lee［午後3時46分］
それで思い出しました。誰を採用するにしても、新入社員オリエンテーションは受けてもらわなければなりません。

Mel Chapel［午後3時49分］
前回、私が担当しました。私なら、何も準備せずにもう一度できますよ。

Kevin Woods［午後3時52分］
よろしく頼むよ、Mel。開始日を決めたら、スケジュールを組むことにしよう。

☐ guy：图 みんな、連中　＊Hi guys. は「やあみんな」と大勢に呼び掛ける言葉　☐ discuss：動 ～を話し合う　☐ hire：動 ～を雇う
☐ power line：電気系統、送電線　☐ maintenance：图 整備、メンテナンス　☐ division：图（会社などの）部、課　☐ status：图 状態、現状
☐ advertise：動 ～を広告する　☐ position：图 職、地位　☐ receive：動 ～を受け取る　☐ a bunch of ～：たくさんの～　☐ résumé：图 履歴書
☐ interview：動 ～と面接する　☐ applicant：图 応募者、候補者　☐ available：形 手が空いていて　☐ installation：图 取り付け、架設
☐ generator：图 発電機　☐ whoever：代 ～する人は誰でも　☐ make sure ～：確実に～する　☐ electrician：图 電気技師
☐ license：图 免許　☐ train：動 ～を教育する　☐ remind：動 ～に思い出させる　☐ no matter ～：たとえ～でも　☐ provide：動 ～を提供する
☐ employee：图 従業員　☐ orientation：图 オリエンテーション　☐ take care of ～：～を担当する　☐ require：動 ～を必要とする
☐ preparation：图 準備　☐ schedule：動 ～を予定に組み込む　☐ decide on ～：～を決める

Part 7 読解問題

158. 正解：**B**　易 ■■■■■■■■ 難　選択率：(A) 2.6%　(B) 91.4%　(C) 1.9%　(D) 3.4%

Where do the writers most likely work?
(A) At a fitness center
(B) At an electric company
(C) At a department store
(C) At a financial institution

□ fitness center: フィットネスセンター　□ electric: 形 電気の
□ department store: デパート、百貨店
□ financial: 形 金融の　□ institution: 名 協会、機関

書き手たちはどこで働いている可能性が最も高いですか。
(A) フィットネスセンターで
(B) 電気会社で
(C) 百貨店で
(D) 金融機関で

▶解説 ❶で送電線保守課に人を雇う話題が、❻で新しい発電機の話題が出ていること、また❿で1級電気技師資格を持っている人を雇うようにとの指示がなされているところから、このオンライン会議の参加者は電気会社に勤めていることが分かります。正解は (B) です。

---

159. 正解：**D**　易 ■■■■■■■■ 難　選択率：(A) 13.8%　(B) 10.4%　(C) 20.9%　(D) 54.5%

Why does Mr. Woods praise Mr. Lee?
(A) He helped train some new employees.
(B) He has received a new qualification.
(C) He made a useful suggestion.
(D) He has made progress on a task.

□ praise: 動 ～を称賛する　□ qualification: 名 資格
□ useful: 形 役に立つ　□ suggestion: 名 提案
□ progress: 名 前進、経過

なぜWoodsさんはLeeさんを褒めていますか。
(A) 彼は何人かの新入社員の研修を手伝った。
(B) 彼は新たな資格を取得した。
(C) 彼は有益な提案をした。
(D) 彼は業務を前進させた。

▶解説 ❺でWoodsさんはLeeさんを褒めています。その理由は、すでに求人活動のために広告を打ち、❷から履歴書が多く届いていることを、❸、❹から面接日時まで設定したことを知り、仕事をどんどん進めていることが分かったからです。これを「業務を前進させた」とまとめた (D) が正解です。

---

160. 正解：**B**　易 ■■■■■■■■ 難　選択率：(A) 7.1%　(B) 27.2%　(C) 27.2%　(D) 37.7%

Who will most likely assist Mr. Lee with the interview?
(A) Rob McMillan
(B) Denise Porter
(C) Mel Chapel
(D) Kevin Woods

□ assist: 動 ～を手伝う

誰が面接でLeeさんを手伝う可能性が最も高いですか。
(A) Rob McMillan
(B) Denise Porter
(C) Mel Chapel
(D) Kevin Woods

▶解説 ❸、❹で面接の手伝いを求めたLeeさんに対して、Porterさんは❼で「彼」が無理なら自分が行う、と述べています。「彼」とは❼の直前に登場するMcMillanさんですが、❽で休暇中だと明らかになったため、❾でWoodsさんは何とかなりそうだと発言しています。つまり、面接の手伝いはPorterさんが行うことに決まったと判断できます。(B) が正解です。

---

161. 正解：**B**　易 ■■■■■■■■ 難　選択率：(A) 13.4%　(B) 62.3%　(C) 17.5%　(D) 5.2%

At 3:49 P.M., why does Ms. Chapel write, "I took care of that last time"?
(A) She thinks it is another staff member's turn.
(B) She is ready to conduct an orientation.
(C) She has a lot of projects to complete.
(D) She would like to try something new.

□ staff member: 職員、社員　□ turn: 名 順番、番
□ conduct: 動 ～を実施する　□ complete: 動 ～を仕上げる

午後3時49分に、なぜChapelさんは「前回、私が担当しました」と書いていますか。
(A) 彼女は、今回は別の従業員の番だと考えている。
(B) 彼女はオリエンテーションを担当できる状況にある。
(C) 彼女は数多くのプロジェクトを完遂してきた。
(D) 彼女はなにか新しいことを試したいと思っている。

▶解説 ターゲット文の直前⓫で新入社員にはオリエンテーションを行う必要があるという発言がありますが、ターゲット文直後の⓬でChapelさんは、もう一度行うための準備は不要だ、と述べていることから、彼女はいつでもオリエンテーションを行うことができる状態であることが分かります。正解は (B) です。

((◦)) ゼミ 生 中継

(◦) Hiro (◦) Mai (◦) Yasu (◦) Dai (◦) Saki

158. ....

(◦) これも156番で紹介した文脈型の一種。チャットの書き手がどこで働いているかが問われている。文書の目的は前半に登場しがちだけど、158番は少し性質が違う。サキ、どう違うと思う?

(◦) えっと、設問にwritersがあるので、たくさん読んだ方が解きやすくなるんじゃないですか。Part 3で似た話が出た気がします。

(◦) そう、44番だった。会話の話題が問われたら、聞けば聞くほど解きやすくなるという話。この158番は複数の書き手の勤務先が問われているから、読めば読むほどヒントに出会えるはずだよ。よって、いったん158番を忘れていいから、159番を意識しながら文書を読めばいい。158番は後回しにした方が解きやすいはずだからね。

160. ....

(◦) (D)のKevinを選んだ人に聞きたい。なぜ選んだの?

(◦) 3時34分にKevinが I'll join you if no one else is available. と言ったので、きっと彼が正解だと思いつつ読み進めたら、直後にMelが無理だと言ったので、Kevinで確定しました。

(◦) そこで確定? Deniseを無視したのか。それにKevinは3時45分で Whoever you choose for the position ～と言っている。自分が面接するならyouと言うはずがないでしょ。じゃ、Melを選んだ人は?

(◦) 3時46分でLeeさんがオリエンテーションの話をした後、すぐにMelが名乗り出ています。ということは、MelがLeeさんを助けることになります。

(◦) ん? オリエンテーションは関係ない。誰が面接を手伝うかが問われているんだよ。

(◦) ……。

(◦) まったく。設問はちゃんと読まなきゃ。

161. ....

(◦) (A)は間違いだけど、誰かの依頼に対する「前回は私がやった」はPart 2で正解として使われることがある。「だから次は別の人にやってほしい」という意図なのか、Melみたいに「だから自分がやる」という意図なのかは不明だけどね。

Part 7 読解問題

Questions 162-164 refer to the following information.

For more than 30 years, Cameron Associates has been helping our clients in the business world grow their companies and develop mutually beneficial relationships with people and organizations in both the public and private sectors.

❶Our vast network of connections enables us to put our clients together with both suppliers and clients whose needs and capabilities are a perfect match. ❷Our clients also have complete access to the database of résumés on our job search Web site, ZipJobs.com, which is the most popular and highly rated in the country. ❸Our team of consultants are also excellent motivational speakers and can be relied on to give your workforce the boost it needs when things are not going as well as they should. Please view the testimonials from our many satisfied customers on our Web site at www.cameronassociates.com.

❹We have just expanded our business, which means we now have the means to take on new clients. ❺If you think your company could use the services of the United States' top consultancy firm, why not give us a call? One of our representatives will be happy to thoroughly explain our services and pricing structure so that you can make an informed decision. Call 405-555-8489 to arrange a free consultation.

Cameron Associates

(208w)

問題162-164は次の情報に関するものです。
30年以上にわたり、Cameron Associatesはビジネス界におけるお客さま方が企業として成長し、公共部門・民間部門の両方で個人や法人と相互に有益な関係を築くお手伝いをしてまいりました。

当社の膨大な個人・法人間ネットワークによって、お客さまを、納入業者と発注者の双方の立場でニーズと受注能力が完璧に合致するよう、結び付けることが可能です。お客さまにはまた、当社の求人サイトZipJobs.comの履歴書のデータベースへの完全なアクセス権をご提供します。このサイトは国内で最も人気があり、高く評価されています。当社のコンサルタント陣はまた、人の意欲を導き出すことにたけた優秀な話し手で、物事が思ったほどうまくいかないときに従業員の方々への

必要な後押しをお任せいただけます。当社のウェブサイトwww. cameronassociates.comで、当社のたくさんのお客さまのご推薦の声をご確認ください。

当社では先ごろ事業規模を拡大し、新たなお客さまにご奉仕させていただける体制を用意いたしました。もし、貴社が全米一のコンサルティング会社のサービスを必要とされる場合は、当社へご一報ください。当社の担当者が喜んでサービスの概要や価格体系をご説明いたしますので、ご理解の上ご判断いただけます。405-555-8489へお電話くだされば、無料のご相談会を手配いたします。

Cameron Associates

- [ ] client: 名 顧客 - [ ] grow: 動 〜を成長させる - [ ] develop: 動 〜を発展させる - [ ] mutually: 副 相互に - [ ] beneficial: 形 有益な
- [ ] relationship: 名 関係 - [ ] organization: 名 団体 - [ ] public: 形 公的な - [ ] private: 形 私的な - [ ] sector: 名 部門、分野 - [ ] vast: 形 広大な
- [ ] network: 名 ネットワーク - [ ] connection: 名 (通例複数形で) 取引先、得意先 - [ ] enable 〜 to …: 〜に…することを可能にさせる
- [ ] put 〜 together with …: 〜を…と結び付ける - [ ] supplier: 名 供給業者 - [ ] capability: 名 能力、手腕 - [ ] perfect: 形 完全な、理想的な
- [ ] match: 名 ふさわしい相手 - [ ] complete: 形 全部の、完璧な - [ ] access: 名 アクセス - [ ] database: 名 データベース - [ ] résumé: 名 履歴書
- [ ] highly: 副 大いに、高く - [ ] rate: 動 〜を評価する - [ ] consultant: 名 コンサルタント、顧問 - [ ] excellent: 形 優れた、素晴らしい
- [ ] motivational: 形 やる気を起こさせる - [ ] rely on 〜: 〜を信頼する、〜を当てにする - [ ] workforce: 名 全従業員 - [ ] boost: 名 押し上げ、励まし
- [ ] view: 動 〜を見る - [ ] testimonial: 名 推薦状 - [ ] satisfied: 形 満足した - [ ] expand: 動 〜を拡大する
- [ ] have the means to 〜: 〜する手段がある - [ ] could use 〜: 〜を必要としている - [ ] consultancy: 名 コンサルタントの仕事 - [ ] firm: 名 会社
- [ ] why not 〜: 〜してはどうですか - [ ] give 〜 a call: 〜に電話をかける - [ ] representative: 名 担当者 - [ ] thoroughly: 副 徹底的に
- [ ] pricing structure: 価格体系 - [ ] informed: 形 情報に通じた - [ ] decision: 名 決定、決断 - [ ] free: 形 無料の - [ ] consultation: 名 相談

162. 正解：**D**　易 ■■■■□□□□ 難　選択率：(A) 5.6%　(B) 25.0%　(C) 15.7%　**(D) 51.9%**

What is the purpose of the information?
(A) To notify current clients of a change in pricing structure
(B) To describe a company's standards of customer service
(C) To advertise career opportunities
(D) To promote a company's services

この情報の目的は何ですか。
(A) 現在の顧客に価格体系の変更を伝えること
(B) ある企業の顧客サービスの基準を説明すること
(C) 雇用機会を広告すること
(D) ある企業のサービスを売り込むこと

▶解説　第1段落、第2段落でCameron Associatesが自社の概要とサービスについて紹介した後、❺でこれらのサービスを利用したければ電話をかけるよう促しています。よって、この情報の目的は(D)の宣伝であることが分かります。

☐ notify: 動 〜を通知する　☐ current: 形 現在の　☐ describe: 動 〜を説明する
☐ standard: 名 基準　☐ advertise: 動 〜を広告する　☐ career opportunity: 就業のチャンス
☐ promote: 動 〜を宣伝する

---

163. 正解：**A**　易 ■■■□□□□□ 難　選択率：**(A) 50.4%**　(B) 16.4%　(C) 19.0%　(D) 12.7%

What is NOT provided by Cameron Associates?
(A) Financial advice
(B) Professional introductions
(C) Recruitment services
(D) Employee motivational talks

Cameron Associates 社で提供されないことは何ですか。
(A) 財務上の助言
(B) 事業関係者の紹介
(C) 求人サービス
(D) 従業員の意欲を高めるための講演

▶解説　❶から(B)が、❷から(C)が、❸から(D)がそれぞれCameron Associatesの業務の1つであると分かるので正解候補から消去できます。財務系のサービスに関しては記述が全くないので、(A)が正解です。

☐ recruitment: 名 人員補充

---

164. 正解：**D**　易 ■■■□□□□□ 難　選択率：(A) 28.0%　(B) 4.9%　(C) 8.6%　**(D) 57.1%**

What has Cameron Associates done recently?
(A) It has launched a new service.
(B) It has changed its address.
(C) It has won an award.
(D) It has grown.

Cameron Associates 社は最近何をしましたか。
(A) 新たなサービスを立ち上げた。
(B) 所在地を変更した。
(C) 賞を取った。
(D) 規模を大きくした。

▶解説　❹でCameron Associatesは業務を拡大したと述べられています。それをIt has grown.と表現している(D)が正解です。(D)以外の内容は言及されていません。

☐ launch: 動 〜を売り出す　☐ address: 名 住所、所在地
☐ award: 名 賞

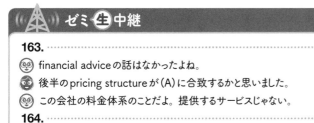

((((())))) ゼミ 生中継　　　　　　　😊Hiro 😊Mai 😊Yasu 😊Dai 😊Saki

163.
😊 financial advice の話はなかったよね。
😊 後半の pricing structure が(A)に合致するかと思いました。
😊 この会社の料金体系のことだよ。提供するサービスじゃない。

164.
😊 (A)が人気なんだけど、どうしてだろう？
😊 (B)と(C)は根拠がないので消去できましたが、(D)のgrownがWe have just expanded 〜の言い換えだと気づかず、(A)と(D)で迷いました。

😊 それで？
😊 第3段落に会社の最近の状況が書かれていますし、servicesという単語も登場するので、何となく(A)を選んだだけです。
😊 そうやって迷った時は、特に具体的な単語を含む選択肢を消去するといい。(A)のlaunchedとnewは割と具体的で意味が狭い。問題作成者は、不正解の選択肢を確実に不正解にするために具体的な言葉を入れる傾向があるんだよ。ま、必ず有効だとは言わないけど、こういう発想を持っておけば悩む時間を短縮できる。

Questions 165-167 refer to the following e-mail.

To: Fred Wilcox <fwilcox@essexprime.com>
From: Vanessa Zhi <vzhi@essexprime.com>
Subject: Dover
Date: 6 November

We have hired contractors to build a studio at the new office in Dover. ❶They have encountered a problem that may cause us to delay the opening. — [1] — . ❷It is going to be quite demanding in terms of both time and cost. Therefore, we need a company executive to go down there, authorize the work and oversee its completion. — [2] — .

❸I know you were supposed to spend some time there in December, but I would like you to go there immediately. It is important that everything go according to plan. We already have clients there and it would be a disaster if this were allowed to affect their businesses. — [3] — .

I will ask Silvia Durant to fill in for you here while you're gone. — [4] — . ❹She has a good knowledge of the production schedule for the Pure Shine toothpaste commercial. I am sure she is qualified to complete that project.

Sincerely,

Vanessa Zhi

(171w)

問題165-167は次のメールに関するものです。
宛先：Fred Wilcox <fwilcox@essexprime.com>
送信者：Vanessa Zhi <vzhi@essexprime.com>
件名：Dover
日付：11月6日

私たちは建築業者を雇い、Doverの新オフィスにスタジオを造ろうとしています。その業者が問題に突き当たっており、スタジオの開業が遅れるかもしれません。建物の基礎部分に大きな欠陥があるのです。そのため、時間と費用の両面で非常に厳しい事態になりそうです。そこで、会社の幹部が現地に赴いて、作業を監督し、完成を見届ける必要があります。

あなたが12月に一定期間、現地へ赴く予定でいたことは承知していますが、早急に現地へ行ってもらいたいのです。全て計画通りに進むことが重要です。当社はすでに現地に顧客を抱えており、もしも本件が顧客の事業に影響を及ぼすことになれば最悪の事態です。

Silvia Durantに頼んで、出張中のあなたの代役を務めてもらおうと思います。彼女は、Pure Shine歯磨き粉のコマーシャルの制作スケジュールについてよく分かっています。彼女なら間違いなく、そのプロジェクトをやり遂げてくれるはずです。

よろしくお願いします。

Vanessa Zhi

☐ hire: 動 ～を雇う　☐ contractor: 名 請負人、土建業者　☐ studio: 名 スタジオ　☐ encounter: 動 ～に遭遇する、（困難など）に直面する
☐ cause: 動 ～を引き起こす　☐ delay: 動 ～を遅れさせる　☐ quite: 副 (思ったより) かなり、なかなか　☐ demanding: 形 (仕事などが)過酷な、きつい
☐ in terms of ～：～の観点から　☐ therefore: 副 従って　☐ executive: 名 役員　☐ authorize: 動 ～を認可する、許可する
☐ oversee: 動 (仕事)を監督する　☐ completion: 名 完了、完成　☐ supposed to ～：～することになっている　☐ immediately: 副 ただちに、すぐに
☐ according to ～：～に従って　☐ client: 名 顧客　☐ disaster: 名 大惨事　☐ allow ～ to ...：～に…することを許す
☐ affect: 動 ～に悪影響を及ぼす　☐ business: 名 事業　☐ fill in for ～：～の代わりをする　☐ production: 名 制作　☐ toothpaste: 名 歯磨き粉
☐ qualified: 形 資格のある

165. 正解：**A** 易 ■■■■■□□□ 難　選択率：**(A) 50.7%** (B) 19.4% (C) 15.7% (D) 13.1%

Why is Ms. Zhi sending the e-mail?
(A) To explain a change in plans
(B) To ask for an extension to a deadline
(C) To comment on the quality of some work
(D) To introduce a new member of staff

☐ explain: 動 ～を説明する
☐ extension: 名 繰り延べ、延期　☐ deadline: 名 締め切り
☐ comment: 動 論評する、批評する　☐ quality: 名 品質
☐ introduce: 動 ～を紹介する

なぜZhiさんは、このメールを送っていますか。
(A) 計画の変更について説明するために
(B) 締め切りの延長を依頼するために
(C) ある業務の質について意見を述べるために
(D) 新しいスタッフを紹介するために

▶解説 第1段落で工事の完成が遅れるかもしれないと知らせた後、Zhiさんは❸でWilcoxさんに、12月ではなく直ちにDoverに向かうように依頼しています。また第3段落ではWilcoxさんがするはずだった仕事の代役についても述べられていることからも、予定に変更があることが分かります。これをa change in plansとまとめた(A)が正解です。

---

166. 正解：**B** 易 ■■■■□□□□ 難　選択率：(A) 17.9% **(B) 32.8%** (C) 11.2% (D) 36.6%

What will Ms. Durant most likely be asked to do?
(A) Attend a conference
(B) Produce a commercial
(C) Reduce department spending
(D) Meet with a prospective client

☐ attend: 動 ～に出席する　☐ conference: 名 会議　☐ produce: 動 ～を制作する
☐ spending: 名 支出、費用　☐ prospective: 形 見込みの、予期される

Durantさんは何をするよう依頼される可能性が最も高いですか。
(A) 会議に出席する
(B) コマーシャルを制作する
(C) 部署の経費を削減する
(D) 見込み客と会う

▶解説 Durantさんの名前は第3段落1文目に登場した後、❹で彼女は歯磨き粉のコマーシャル制作予定について十分な知識を持っていると述べられています。よって、Durantさんはコマーシャル制作を依頼されると判断でき、正解は(B)となります。

---

167. 正解：**A** 易 ■■■■■□□□ 難　選択率：**(A)67.9%** (B) 18.7% (C) 9.0% (D) 3.0%

In which of the positions marked [1], [2], [3], and [4] does the following sentence best belong?

"There is a large fault in the building's foundation."
(A) [1]
(B) [2]
(C) [3]
(D) [4]

☐ fault: 名 欠陥　☐ foundation: 名 （建物の）基礎

次の文を当てはめるには、[1]、[2]、[3]、[4]と印が付けられた箇所のうちのどこが最もふさわしいですか。

「建物の基礎部分に大きな欠陥があるのです」
(A) [1]
(B) [2]
(C) [3]
(D) [4]

▶解説 「建物の基礎部分に大きな欠陥が見つかった」の意のターゲット文なので、建物と工事についての記述があった第1段落を見てみましょう。❶にあるa problemを具体的に表したのがターゲット文の内容です。❷の時間的・費用的に大きな影響がある、という内容ともつながります。❶と❷の間に入れるのが適切で、正解は(A)です。

((( ))) ゼミ 生 中継　😀 Hiro 😀 Mai 😀 Yasu 😀 Dai 😀 Saki

166.
😀 (D)を選ぶモニターが多かったけど、見込み客の話はどこにもない。第2段落に登場するclientsに会う可能性があるのはZhiさんであって、Durantさんは無関係だね。

167.
😀 Part 6の「文選択問題」と区別するために、うちのゼミではこれを「位置選択問題」と呼んでいる。文選択問題に出る「場違いな情報」が苦手だってマイは言ってたね。
😀 はい。ですから、「場」を問う位置選択問題はもっと苦手です。
😀 5つの視点を持てば解きやすくなるよ。「代名詞」「副詞」「接続副詞」「the＋名詞」「言い換え」の5つ。167番のターゲット文に「the＋

名詞」がある。the buildingと書くだけで、書き手も読み手もそれがどの建物か分かるってこと。ということは、ターゲット文の前に関連情報があるはずだね。
😀 1行目のthe new office in Doverですね。
😀 そう。Doverのオフィスが入っている建物のことをthe buildingと言っているから、「言い換え」の一種だね。似た現象は次の文とターゲット文でも起きている。ヤス、分かる？
😀 problemとfaultですか。
😀 ナイス。「問題が見つかった」→「建物の基礎に欠陥がある」と、似た単語を使って情報を詳しくしている。
😀 慎重に読めば意外と簡単に解ける気がしてきました。

Questions 168-171 refer to the following Web page.

https://www.comstockcitygardens.com

Comstock
25th Annual Arts and Crafts Festival
Comstock City Gardens
Saturday, May 17

9:00 A.M. – 6:00 P.M.

Arts and Crafts Demonstrations

Local artists will be demonstrating their methods to audiences. Admission to seminars with hands-on learning opportunities can be purchased in advance from the festival Web site at www.comstockfest.org.

11:00 A.M. – 11:30 A.M.

Charity Auction

Artworks donated by participating artists will be auctioned off in the main tent. The proceeds will be divided among a number of worthy causes. The auction will be conducted by Matt Hunt from the popular television show, Art Under the Hammer.

11:00 A.M. – 2:00 P.M.

Riverside Lunch

A variety of local vendors will be offering meals, drinks, and snacks from stalls set up on the path along the Regent River. Food items will be priced fairly at between $1 and $12.

9:00 A.M. – 4:00 P.M.

Comstock Annual Art Exhibit and Competition

The popular annual art competition will be held in the main tent. Anyone can submit paintings, sculptures or pottery to the event, which will be judged by a panel of local experts. View the Web site to learn more about the submission process.

www.comstockaac.com

Winners will be announced at the end of the lunch services.

There is limited parking in the area so visitors are encouraged to come by public transportation. Click here to view the area map.

For more information, visit the festival headquarters at Comstock City Hall on Dwyer Street.

(239w)

問題168-171は次のウェブページに関するものです。

Comstock
第25回年次美術工芸祭
Comstock City Gardens
5月17日 土曜日

午前9時〜午後6時　美術工芸実演会

地元の芸術家たちが自らの手法を観覧者の前で披露します。実践的な学びの機会を伴うセミナーへの入場券は、この催事のウェブサイトwww.comstockfest.orgで事前にお求めいただけます。

午前11時〜午前11時30分　チャリティーオークション

参加する芸術家たちから寄付された作品が、中央テントでオークションに掛けられます。収益は、さまざまな価値ある目的に分配される予定です。オークションは人気テレビ番組 Art Under the Hammer の Matt Hunt によって執り行われます。

午前11時〜午後2時　川辺でのランチ

さまざまな地元の販売業者が、料理や飲み物、軽食を屋台で提供します。

屋台は Regent River 沿いの小道に設営されます。飲食物はどれも1ドルから12ドルの間の適正な価格で販売されます。

午前9時〜午後4時　Comstock 年次芸術展とコンテスト

人気の年次芸術コンテストが、中央テントで行われます。誰でも、絵画、彫刻、陶芸作品をこの催しに出品でき、地元の専門家委員会によって審査されます。ウェブサイトをご覧になり、出品手続きの詳細をご確認ください。

www.comstockaac.com
入賞者は、ランチサービス時間の終わりに発表されます。

会場付近の駐車スペースには限りがありますので、公共交通機関でのご来場をお勧めします。ここをクリックすると、周辺の地図が表示されます。
さらに情報が必要でしたら、Dwyer Street の Comstock City Hall 内の催事本部をお訪ねください。

☐ annual: 形 年1回の　☐ arts and crafts: 美術工芸　☐ local: 形 地元の　☐ artist: 名 芸術家　☐ demonstrate: 動 〜を説明する
☐ method: 名 方法　☐ audience: 名 聴衆　☐ admission: 名 入場　☐ hands-on: 形 実地の、実践の　☐ opportunity: 名 機会
☐ purchase: 動 〜を購入する　☐ in advance: あらかじめ　☐ charity: 名 慈善　☐ auction: 名 競売、オークション
☐ artwork: 名 手工芸品　☐ donate: 動 〜を贈与する、寄付する　☐ participate: 動 〜に参加する　☐ auction off 〜: 〜を競売にかける
☐ proceed: 名 収入、利益　☐ divide: 動 〜を配分する　☐ worthy: 形 価値のある　☐ cause: 名 目的　☐ conduct: 動 〜を運営する
☐ riverside: 形 川岸の　☐ a variety of 〜: 種類豊富な〜　☐ vendor: 名 販売者　☐ offer: 動 〜を売りに出す　☐ stall: 名 屋台、露店
☐ food item: 食品　☐ fairly: 副 公正に　☐ competition: 名 コンテスト　☐ hold: 動 〜を開催する（held は過去分詞）
☐ submit: 動 〜を提出する　☐ sculpture: 名 彫刻　☐ pottery: 名 焼き物、陶器類　☐ judge: 動 〜を審査する　☐ a panel of 〜: 〜の一団
☐ expert: 名 専門家　☐ submission: 名 提出　☐ process: 名 手順、方法　☐ limited: 形 限られた
☐ encourage 〜 to ...: 〜に…するよう働き掛ける　☐ public transportation: 公共交通機関　☐ headquarters: 名 本社

---

168. 正解：**A**　易 ■■■□□□□ 難　選択率：(A) 60.1% (B) 31.0% (C) 5.2% (D) 2.6%

According to the Web page, what can people buy online?
(A) Tickets to practical workshops
(B) Artworks by local artists
(C) Vouchers for meals
(D) Parking permits

このウェブページによると、人々はオンラインで何を買えますか。
(A) 実体験ができるワークショップへの入場券
(B) 地元の芸術家が手掛け芸術作品
(C) 食事券
(D) 駐車許可証

▶解説 ❷で、Web site で地元の芸術家によるセミナーの入場券を事前に買うことができると述べられています。「実践的な学びの機会を伴うセミナー」を practical workshop と表している (A) が正解です。

□ practical: 形 実践的な　□ permit: 名 許可証

---

169. 正解：**B**　易 ■■■■□□□ 難　選択率：(A) 5.2% (B) 69.4% (C) 10.8% (D) 13.4%

At which event can visitors meet a celebrity?
(A) The Arts and Crafts Demonstrations
(B) The Charity Auction
(C) The Riverside Lunch
(D) The Comstock Annual Art Exhibit and Competition

来場者はどの催しで著名人に会えますか。
(A) 芸術工芸実演会
(B) チャリティーオークション
(C) 川辺でのランチ
(D) Comstock 年次芸術展コンテスト

▶解説 ❸で人気テレビ番組の出演者、Matt Hunt さんがチャリティーオークションの進行を務めると述べられています。人気番組に出演している Hunt さんは celebrity とみなすことができ、(B) が正解です。

□ celebrity: 名 有名人

---

170. 正解：**C**　易 ■■■■■□□ 難　選択率：(A) 7.1% (B) 6.3% (C) 73.9% (D) 11.6%

When will the competition winners be announced?
(A) At 11:00 A.M.
(B) At 1:00 P.M.
(C) At 2:00 P.M.
(D) At 6:00 P.M.

コンテストの入賞者はいつ発表されますか。
(A) 午前11時に
(B) 午後1時に
(C) 午後2時に
(D) 午後6時に

▶解説 ❺にランチサービス終了時に入賞者が発表されと述べられているので、❹で Riverside Lunch の時間を確かめます。ランチサービスの終了は午後2時なので、(C) が正解です。

---

171. 正解：**D**　易 ■■■■■■□ 難　選択率：(A) 13.1% (B) 13.8% (C) 9.0% (D) 63.1%

What is suggested about Comstock City Gardens?
(A) It will be sold to a local business.
(B) It has some historical landmarks.
(C) The opening hours will be extended.
(D) There are few places to leave private vehicles.

Comstock City Gardens について何が示されていますか。
(A) 地元の企業に売却されるだろう。
(B) いくつかの歴史的な史跡がある。
(C) 開園時間が延長される。
(D) 自家用車を置く場所がほとんどない。

▶解説 Comstock City Gardens はこのイベントが行われる場所であることが❶で述べられています。❻の、近辺には駐車できる場所が限られているという内容を言い換えている (D) が正解です。

□ landmark: 名 史跡　□ extend: 動（期間など）を延長する
□ few: 形 ほとんどない　□ private: 形 私的な

(((▲))) ゼミ 生 中継　　😊 Hiro　😊 Mai　😊 Yasu　😎 Dai　😊 Saki

169.
😊 サキ、設問内のどの情報を文書で探したくなる?
😊 celebrity です。かなり具体的なので。
😊 ヒントは何カ所にあると予想する?
😎 1カ所です。
😊 そうだね。このような設問を「ピンポイント型」と呼ぼう。具体的な情報を元にピンポイント攻撃するタイプだよ。じゃあ、次の170番を見よう。

170.
😊 こっちはどう?　どの情報を探したくなるかな、ダイ?
😎 winners です。具体的ですし、言い換えにくいので簡単に見つかりそ

うです。
😊 お、その感覚はナイスだよ。で、実際はどうだった?
😎 winners は見つかりましたが、ヒントは離れていました。
😊 これが「情報分散型」で、複数のヒントを見つける必要がある。
😊 こっちの方が意地悪な問題ですね。
😊 そう。著者の性格の悪さが表れている。ただし、実際の試験にも「情報分散型」はたくさんある。どれくらい出ると思う?
😊 さぁ、10問くらいですか?
😊 いや、Part 7 だけで20問前後。
😊 そんなにあるのですか。多いですね。

TOEICよろず相談所　ヒロの部屋

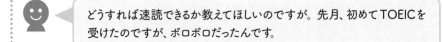

⑥スコアアップのために速読力をつけたい

どうすれば速読できるか教えてほしいのですが。先月、初めてTOEICを受けたのですが、ボロボロだったんです。

なるほど。リーディングセクションのスコアはどうでしたか。

リーディングは215で、合計は500です。

分かりました。TOEICのスコアを上げることが目的ですね。速読するとスコアが下がりますが、それでいいですか。

え、、、どういうことですか?

日本語を勉強中のアメリカ人を想像してください。語彙も文法もミスだらけです。その人が日本語でメールを読むとき、速読すると理解度は上がりますか。

いえ、下がるでしょうね、、、

ですよね。TOEICに置き換えて考えましょう。

いえ、もう分かりました。**基礎力が足りなければ、速読しても逆効果**ということですね。

はい。英語を正確に理解できる人が速読の練習をすれば効果があると思いますが、そうでない人が速読を求めてもうまくいきません。あえて言えば「速読する資格がない」ということです。

分かりました。まず、基本をしっかり勉強します。

TOEICは理解度を試すテストであることを忘れないでくださいね。お問い合わせありがとうございました。

Questions 172-175 refer to the following letter.

Supreme Furniture
267 North Fernanda Avenue
Aurora IL 60509

July 7

Madeline Asaba
356 Rinehart Road
Victoria BC V8P 4R7
Canada

Dear Ms. Asaba,

❶I am pleased to be able to inform you that your application for the position as the regional manager of our Portsmouth branch has been approved. — [1] — . As we discussed at your interview, ❷the annual salary will start at $135,000 per year. ❸This will increase in line with the Supreme Furniture pay scale, which you will find in ❹the welcome package I mailed to you this morning. — [2] — . ❺There are also some forms for you to fill out and turn in to us before you can start work. They should be fairly straightforward, but ❻if there is anything you do not understand, please call Tony Burton in human resources.

We would like you to begin work as soon as possible. However, I understand that ❼you will need some time to move from your current home in Victoria. — [3] — . Please let me know if there is anything I can do to make that transition go more smoothly. We have a company apartment near the office which you may use until your permanent accommodation is finalized. — [4] — . ❽Please keep any receipts for the shipping of your belongings and your travel. Send them to the accounting department at head office by August 31. They will reimburse you with your first paycheck.

I look forward to having you on the team.

Sincerely,

Lynn Delany

Lynn Delany
President — Supreme Furniture

(253w)

問題172-175は次の手紙に関するものです。

Supreme Furniture
267 North Fernanda Avenue
Aurora IL 60509

7月7日

Madeline Asabaさま
356 Rinehart Road
Victoria BC V8P 4R7
Canada

前略　Asabaさま

ご応募いただいた当社Portsmouth支社の地域担当管理者の職へのご就任が承認されたとお知らせできることを、うれしく思います。面接の場でお話した通り、初任給は年額13万5000ドルです。これは、Supreme Furniture社の給与体系にのっとって増額されることになります。この情報は、今朝ほど当方が郵送した入社案内資料一式の中に含まれています。それは明日か、遅くとも木曜日にはお手元に届くはずです。また、

勤務開始前にご記入・ご提出していただく書類があります。ごく簡単なものではありますが、もし何かご不明な点があれば、人事部のTony Burtonまでお電話ください。

できるだけ早く、ご着任いただきたく存じます。とはいえ、今お住まいのVictoriaからの転居にお時間が必要でしょう。転居を少しでも円滑に進めるために何か必要なことがあれば、お知らせください。当社では、オフィスの近隣に社宅アパートを所有しているので、お住まいが最終確定するまでそちらをお使いいただくことも可能です。引っ越し荷物の発送費や交通費の領収書を保管しておいてください。本社の経理部宛てに8月31日までにお送りいただけば、最初の給与の支払時に精算されます。

あなたを私どものチームにお迎えするのを楽しみにしております。

草々

Lynn Delany
Supreme Furniture社長

□ pleased to ～: 喜んで～する、～してうれしい　□ inform: 動 ～に知らせる　□ application: 名 申し込み　□ position: 名 地位
□ regional: 形 地域の　□ manager: 名 責任者、長　□ branch: 名 支店　□ approve: 動 ～を承認する　□ discuss: 動 ～を話し合う
□ interview: 名 面接　□ annual: 形 年1回の　□ salary: 名 給料　□ in line with ～: ～に従って　□ pay scale: 給与体系　□ mail: 動 郵送する
□ form: 名 記入用紙　□ fill out ～: ～に記入する　□ turn in ～: ～を提出する　□ fairly: 副 かなり　□ straightforward: 形 複雑でない、簡単な
□ human resources: 人事部　□ however: 副 しかしながら　□ current: 形 現在の　□ transition: 名 移行　□ smoothly 副 円滑に
□ company apartment: 社宅　□ permanent: 形 永久の　□ accommodation: 名 宿泊施設　□ finalize: 動 ～に決着をつける
□ receipt: 名 領収書　□ shipping: 名 輸送料　□ belonging: 名 (複数形で) 所有物、所持品　□ accounting department: 経理部
□ head office: 本社　□ reimburse: 動 (費用などを) ～に払い戻す　□ paycheck: 名 給料　□ president: 名 社長

Part 7 読解問題

---

172. 正解：**A** 易 ■■■■■□□ 難　選択率：(A) 63.8%　(B) 8.6%　(C) 20.1%　(D) 6.3%

Why did Mr. Delany send the letter?
(A) To confirm the details of a contract
(B) To request an update on the progress of a project
(C) To thank a colleague for introducing a job applicant
(D) To announce the opening of a new branch office

なぜDelanyさんはこの手紙を送りましたか。
(A) 契約の詳細を確認するために
(B) プロジェクトの進捗状況の報告を求めるために
(C) 同僚に、求人への応募者を紹介してくれたことへの謝意を伝えるために
(D) 新しい支社の開業を知らせるために

▶解説 手紙やメールの目的は冒頭部分で述べられるのが普通です。この場合も冒頭の❶で採用が承認されたこと、❷で初年度の年俸、❸で昇給が言及されていることから、雇用契約の詳細を述べた手紙であることが分かります。よって、正解は (A) です。

☐ confirm: 動 ～を確認する　☐ details: 名 詳しい情報
☐ contract: 名 契約　☐ update: 名 最新情報
☐ progress: 名 前進、経過　☐ colleague: 名 同僚
☐ introduce: 動 ～を紹介する
☐ applicant: 名 応募者、候補者

---

173. 正解：**D** 易 ■■■■■□□ 難　選択率：(A) 14.6%　(B) 20.9%　(C) 11.6%　(D) 51.1%

According to the letter, why might Ms. Asaba contact Mr. Burton?
(A) To suggest ways to manage a project
(B) To find out more about a pricing policy
(C) To ask for an extension to a deadline
(D) To get assistance completing a form

この手紙によると、Asabaさんはどのような理由でBurtonさんに連絡を取る可能性がありますか。
(A) プロジェクトの管理方法を提案するために
(B) 価格決定の方針についてさらに詳しく調べるために
(C) 締め切りの延長を依頼するために
(D) 書類への記入を補助してもらうために

▶解説 ❻に分からないことがあればBurtonさんに電話するようにという指示があります。さかのぼって❺に、Asabaさんが記入するべき書類があることが述べられています。つまり彼女は、用紙の記入方法について手助けを求めるためにBurtonさんに連絡を取るかもしれないと考えられ、(D) が正解です。

☐ contact: 動 ～に連絡する　☐ manage: 動 ～を管理する、統率する　☐ pricing policy: 価格決定方針
☐ extension: 名 繰り延べ、延期
☐ deadline: 名 締め切り　☐ assistance: 名 手伝い
☐ complete: 動 ～を仕上げる

---

174. 正解：**C** 易 ■■■■□□□ 難　選択率：(A) 9.7%　(B) 9.7%　(C) 66.8%　(D) 11.9%

What is implied about Supreme Furniture?
(A) It has relocated its head office to Victoria.
(B) Its employees are paid at the end of every month.
(C) It will cover the costs of Ms. Asaba's move.
(D) Its new recruits are required to attend a company retreat.

Supreme Furnitureについて、何が示唆されていますか。
(A) 本社をVictoriaへ移転した。
(B) 従業員の給与が毎月の月末に支払われる。
(C) Asabaさんの転居費用を肩代わりする。
(D) 新入社員が社員旅行への参加を求められる。

▶解説 Supreme Furnitureで勤務を開始するにあたって、Asabaさんは引っ越す必要があると❼で明らかにされています。❽の3文から、領収書を保管しておき、それらを8月末までに本社に提出すると、初回の給与と共に発送費と交通費が支払われることが分かります。つまり、引っ越し費用は同社が負担するので (C) が正解です。

☐ imply: 動 ～を暗に意味する
☐ relocate: 動 ～を移転させる　☐ recruit: 名 新入社員
☐ require: 動 ～を要求する　☐ attend: 動 ～に出席する
☐ company retreat: 社員旅行

---

175. 正解：**B**　易 ■■■■■ ■ ■ 難　選択率：(A) 3.4% **(B) 67.5%** (C) 15.3% (D) 12.7

In which of the positions marked [1], [2], [3], and [4] does the following sentence best belong?

"That should arrive by tomorrow or Thursday at the latest."

(A) [1]
(B) [2]
(C) [3]
(D) [4]

次の文を当てはめるには、[1]、[2]、[3]、[4]と印が付けられた箇所のうちのどこが最もふさわしいですか。
「それは明日か、遅くとも木曜日にはお手元に届くはずです」
(A) [1]
(B) [2]
(C) [3]
(D) [4]

▶解説　「明日か木曜日に届く物」に言及されている部分がヒントです。❹にあるDelanyさんが今朝発送した荷物がThatが指すもので、それが明日か木曜日に届くと考えると話がつながります。従って正解は (B) です。

((( ))) ゼミ生中継　　Hiro　Mai　Yasu　Dai　Saki

173.
😀 あの〜、設問の why might 〜？ってどういう意味ですか？
😎 これは、何かが起きるとすればどんな場合かを問うている。ここでは、AsabaさんがBurtonさんに連絡するかどうかは不明だけど、もし、連絡するなら、どんな場合かが問われている。だから、if がヒントになることが多いんだよ。
😀 本当だ！　確かに if there is anything 〜と書かれていますね。
😎 実は148番にも Why might があったよ。
😀 ありましたね。しかも、if がヒントになっていました。
😎 絶対に if がヒントになるとは限らないけど、知っておけば役立つことが

多い。「Why might のヒントは if にアリ」だね。

175.
😎 位置選択問題だね。167番で紹介した5つの視点のうち、ここで使える視点はどれ？
😀 代名詞ですか？　That が何を指すか知りたくなります。
😎 その通り。正解となる空所の直前に、ターゲット文の先頭にあるThatが指す名詞が必ず存在する。このような視点を持って文書を読めば、正解の場所を特定しやすくなるはずだよ。マイ、どう？
😀 だんだん自信がついてきました。

Part 7 ▼ Reading Section

Part 7 読解問題

Questions 176-180 refer to the following advertisement and e-mail.

Beaudesert Regional Fair

❶The annual Beaudesert Regional Fair will be held this November 12 and 13 at the Beaudesert Showgrounds on Alice Street. There are prizes to be won for submissions to a number of exhibition categories. ❷As this is a rural fair, many of the categories are agricultural in nature. The following list features the most popular exhibition categories. Only a limited number of entries will be accepted. If you would like to make a submission, you should apply by October 31 at the latest.

❸
- Funniest Pumpkin Carving
- Juiciest Tomato
- Tastiest Yogurt
- Best Cheese
- Most Delicious Cherry Pie

❹An extensive list of exhibition categories is available on the Web page. ❺Everyone submitting agricultural items must be registered with the State Board of Farmers. Furthermore, ❻entrants in categories judged on flavor must submit a minimum of two samples.

❼All applications must be made in person at the administration office. Please note that the office at the showgrounds is only a temporary office and it will not be staffed until October 25. Until that date, we will be located on the third floor of the Beaudesert City Hall. You may contact chief organizer Harold Cake at hcake@beaudesertrfoc.org.

(201w)

問題**176-180**は次の広告とメールに関するものです。
Beaudesert Regional Fair

年 次 Beaudesert Regional Fair が 11月12日 と 13日 に Alice Street の Beaudesert Showgrounds で開催されます。多数の出品部門があり、出品品には賞が授与されます。これは農村の見本市なので、多くの部門が事実上、農業関連のものです。以下のリストにあるのは、最も人気の高い出品部門です。限られた件数しか受け付けられません。出品をお考えでしたら、遅くとも10月31日までにお申し込みください。

・最も面白いカボチャの彫刻
・一番ジューシーなトマト
・最高においしいヨーグルト
・最高のチーズ
・どこのものよりもおいしいチェリーパイ

ウェブページでは、全ての出品部門を示したリストをご覧いただけます。農産物を出品なさる方は全員、必ず State Board of Farmers にご登録いただいています。また、風味で審査される部門への出品者には、少なくとも2品をご出品いただく必要があります。

お申し込みは全て、必ず事務局へ直接お越しの上、行ってください。催し物会場の事務所は一時的なものにすぎず、10月25日になるまでは無人であることをご承知おきください。同日より前は、Beaudesert City Hall の3階に事務局を設けています。事務局長の Harold Cake へのご連絡は、hcake@beaudesertrfoc.org までお願いいたします。

□ regional: 形 地域の　□ prize: 名 賞　□ submission: 名 提出　□ a number of ～: 多くの～　□ exhibition: 名 展示、公開
□ category: 名 部門、カテゴリー　□ rural: 形 田舎の、田園の　□ agricultural: 形 農業の　□ in nature: 実際は、事実上
□ feature: 動 ～を特徴づける、～の特色となる　□ limited: 形 限られた、わずかな　□ accept: 動 ～を受け取る　□ apply: 動 申し込む、出願する
□ carving: 名 彫り物　□ extensive: 形 広範囲の、膨大な　□ available: 形 入手可能な　□ submit: 動 ～を提出する　□ register: 動 ～を登録する
□ furthermore: 副 なお、さらに　□ entrant: 名 参加者　□ judge: 動 ～を審査する　□ minimum: 名 最低限　□ application: 名 申し込み
□ in person: 本人が直接に　□ administration office: 管理事務所　□ showground: 名 (野外の) 催し物会場　□ temporary: 形 一時的な
□ staff: 動 ～に職員を置く　□ organizer: 名 主催者

```
┌─────────────────────────────────────────────────────────────┐
│                       E-Mail Message                          │
├──────────┬──────────────────────────────────────────────────┤
│ To:      │ Harold Cake <hcake@beaudesertrfoc.org>           │
├──────────┼──────────────────────────────────────────────────┤
│ From:    │ Alexi Smirnoff <asmirnoff@novaduck.com>          │
├──────────┼──────────────────────────────────────────────────┤
│ Subject: │ Beaudesert Regional Fair                          │
├──────────┼──────────────────────────────────────────────────┤
│ Date:    │ November 3                                        │
└──────────┴──────────────────────────────────────────────────┘
```

Dear Mr. Cake,

I have already had my application accepted. I submitted it to the Giant Watermelon category, which I understand is new this year. Unfortunately, I misplaced the literature that the office staff handed to me so I am unclear about a couple of things. I did not deliver the watermelon with my application on October 27 as it is still on the vine. This is because I want to keep it fresh for as long as possible and because it is still growing. I understand that I must deliver it to a refrigerated warehouse at 19 James Street, but I would like to know the latest possible date on which I can do so.

Sincerely,

Alexi Smirnoff

(136w)

宛先：Harold Cake <hcake@beaudesertrfoc.org>
送信者：Alexi Smirnoff <asmirnoff@novaduck.com>
件名：Beaudesert Regional Fair
日付：11月3日

Cakeさま

当方は、すでに申し込みを受け付けていただいています。「巨大スイカ」の部門に申し込みました。この部門は、今年新たに設けられたものと存じます。あいにく、事務局の方からいただいた資料をどこかになくして

しまったため、少々不明な点があります。10月27日の申込時にスイカを持ち込まなかったのですが、それはスイカがまだつるに付いたままだからです。この理由は、なるべく長期間スイカを新鮮に保っておきたいことと、スイカがまだ成長の途上にあることです。James Street 19番地の冷蔵倉庫に搬入しなければならないことは承知していますが、最大限遅らせるといつまでに搬入すればいいか知りたく存じます。

よろしくお願いいたします。

Alexi Smirnoff

☐ misplace: 動 ～を置き忘れる　☐ literature: 名 文献、資料　☐ unclear: 形 はっきりしない、不確かな　☐ vine: 名 つる　☐ refrigerate: 動 ～を冷蔵する
☐ warehouse: 名 倉庫

---

176. 正解：**C** 易 ■■■■□□ 難　選択率：(A) 13.4%　(B) 13.1%　(C) 63.4%　(B) 7.1%

What is indicated about the Beaudesert
Regional Fair?
(A) It is sponsored by local businesses.
(B) It is staffed by volunteers.
(C) It is held once a year.
(D) It is growing in popularity.

□ indicate: 動 ～を暗に示す　□ sponsor: 動 ～を後援する
□ business: 名 店、会社

Beaudesert Regional Fair について何が示されていますか。
(A) 地元の企業が後援している。
(B) ボランティアによって運営されている。
(C) 年に1回、開かれている。
(D) 人気が上がっている。

▶解説　❶の annual（年に1度の、毎年恒例の）から、Beaudesert Regional Fair は毎年1回開催されるイベントであることが分かります。従って、正解は(C)です。It is held every year. と表すことも可能です。

---

177. 正解：**D** 易 ■■■■□□ 難　選択率：(A) 7.8%　(B) 22.8%　(C) 14.6%　(D) 52.6%

What is most likely true about the Beaudesert
region?
(A) It advertises the fair on television.
(B) It has a new administrative building.
(C) It attracts many tourists.
(D) It has a farming economy.

□ region: 名 地域　□ advertise: 動 ～を広告する
□ administrative building: 管理棟
□ attract: 動 ～を引き付ける　□ tourist: 名 観光客
□ farming economy: 農業経済

Beaudesert 地区に、どれが当てはまる可能性が最も高いですか。
(A) この催しをテレビで宣伝している。
(B) 新しい管理棟がある。
(C) 多くの旅行者が訪れている。
(D) 農業で経済が成り立っている。

▶解説　❷から、この Beaudesert Regional Fair には農業関連の部門が多いことが分かります。また、❸の箇条書きにしてある品目（カボチャ、トマトなど）からも、そのことが読み取れます。よって、この地区では農業を中心とした経済が成り立っていると推測でき、(D)が正解です。他の選択肢の内容は述べられていません。

---

178. 正解：**A** 易 ■■■■■□ 難　選択率：(A) 42.9%　(B) 21.6%　(C) 17.2%　(D) 15.3%

In which category are competitors expected
to submit a single item?
(A) Funniest Pumpkin Carving
(B) Tastiest Yogurt
(C) Best Cheese
(D) Most Delicious Cherry Pie

□ competitor: 名 競争者

出品者が出展品を1つ持ち込めばいいのは、どの部門ですか。
(A) 最も面白いカボチャの彫刻
(B) 最高においしいヨーグルト
(C) 最高のチーズ
(D) どこのものよりもおいしいチェリーパイ

▶解説　広告の❻の部分で、味を競うものは2個以上の見本を提出するようにと指示されています。選択肢の中で(B)、(C)、(D)は味を競う種類のものです。よって、見本を1つ出品すればいいのは(A)です。

---

179. 正解：**C** 易 ■■■■■□ 難　選択率：(A) 13.4%　(B) 22.0%　(C) 41.4%　(D) 18.3%

What is NOT suggested about Ms. Smirnoff?
(A) She has viewed the Web page.
(B) She is registered with the State Board of
Farmers.
(C) She has submitted items in more than one
category.
(D) She obtained documents at the
showgrounds.

□ obtain: 動 ～を手に入れる　□ document: 名 書類

Smirnoff さんについて示唆されていないのは何ですか。
(A) 彼女はすでにウェブページを見た。
(B) 彼女は State Board of Farmers に登録されている。
(C) 彼女は複数の部門に出品している。
(D) 彼女は会場で書類を受け取った。

▶解説　Smirnoff さんはメールの❽で自分が提出したカテゴリーを述べていますが、広告の❸のリストにそのカテゴリーはありません。ただし❹にウェブページで詳細なリストが確認できるとあるので、Smirnoff さんはウェブページを確認したと考えられ、(A)は消去できます。コンテストに出品するには、State Board of Farmers への登録が必要だと❺で分かるので、(B)も消去できます。また、❾で Smirnoff さんはすでに書類を入手した（そして紛失した）と分かりますが、入手日は申し込みをした10月27日です（❽❿）。広告の❼で会場の事務所が営業を開始するのは10月25日だと分かるので、(D)も消去できます。Smirnoff さんが出品した部門の数は述べられていないので(C)が正解です。

180. 正解：**C**　易 ■■■■■■ 難　選択率：(A) 11.6%　(B) 24.3%　**(C) 47.8%**　(D) 12.7%

Why did Ms. Smirnoff write to Mr. Cake?
(A) To ask for assistance planning an event
(B) To complain about a mistake
(C) To inquire about a date
(D) To announce a change to a plan

☐ assistance: 名 手伝い　☐ complain: 動 苦情を言う
☐ inquire: 動 尋ねる

なぜSmirnoffさんはCakeさんに連絡しましたか。
(A) 催しの計画の手伝いを依頼するために
(B) 間違いに苦情を言うために
(C) 日付を尋ねるために
(D) 計画の変更を知らせるために

▶解説 メールや手紙の目的は冒頭に述べられることが多いですが、このように最後で目的を問われるということは、正解のヒントが少なくとも冒頭にはないと予測できます。メールの中でSmirnoffさんは状況説明を行った後、❶で最も遅い搬入可能日を尋ねているので正解は (C) です。

(((📡 ゼミ 生 中継

👤 ダブルパッセージのことはDPと呼ぼう。DPには5つの設問がある。そのうち1問は「2文書参照型」と言って、ヒントが2文書に分散している設問がある。

👤 1問だけですか。

👤 絶対とは断言しないけど、ほぼ間違いなく1問だけだよ。

179. ⋯⋯⋯⋯⋯⋯⋯⋯⋯⋯⋯⋯

👤 NOTを含む設問は「NOT型」と呼ぼう。基本的に、3つの選択肢を消去して解く。設問にNOTがないと仮定した時に、設問に合致

する情報が文書に3つあって、残りの1つが正解となる。4つの選択肢を読んでから文書を読むと、消去法を使いやすくなるよ。

👤 私はマークミスをしがちです。消去する3つの情報のうち最後の1つが離れた場所に見つかることがあるんです。その最後の1つが見つかったら、うれしくなって塗ってしまうんです。消去しなきゃいけないのに。

👤 あるある。

👤 それは「TOEICあるあるランキング第6位」だよ。次は注意してね。

Questions 181-185 refer to the following letter and e-mail.

Roman Rossi
Rossi Modeling Agency
Office 2, Level 19, Gibraltar Office Building
10 Well Street,
Wellington, 6011

16 January

Dear Mr. Rossi,

❶ I would like to hire two of your models for a photography shoot on 27 January. I recently founded a company that imports various fashion items from manufacturers around the world and ❷ I am putting together a new catalog of our products that I will mail to customers. ❸ I was given your contact details by Michelle Leeds. She mentioned that she used your company exclusively in the past and that she found you and your employees extremely reliable.

We would require the models to come to a studio at 257 Barkley Street. ❹ The shoot should take about four hours from 2:00 P.M. to 6:00 P.M. However, I would appreciate it if the models could arrive one hour early. We require a male and a female model as we stock garments for both genders. ❺ I am sure you will be pleased to know that the photographer is Milo Milano. He was also introduced to us by Ms. Leeds. My e-mail address is on my business card, which you will find enclosed along with last year's catalog.

Sincerely,

Harriett Clutterbuck

Harriett Clutterbuck
CEO — Clutterbuck Fashion

(205w)

問題181-185は次の手紙とメールに関するものです。
Roman Rossiさま
Rossi Modeling Agency
Office 2, Level 19, Gibraltar Office Building
10 Well Street,
Wellington, 6011

1月16日

前略　Rossiさま

1月27日に撮影会があり、貴社のモデルさんを2名ご手配いただきたく存じます。私が近年設立した会社では、さまざまなファッション関連商品を世界中のメーカーから輸入しています。弊社で取り扱う商品の新しいカタログを編集しているところで、それを顧客に郵送する予定です。そちらさまの連絡先の詳細は、Michelle Leedsさんから聞きました。

話によると、彼女はかつて貴社と専属契約を結んでいたことがあり、貴殿や貴社のスタッフが非常に信頼できると感じたそうです。

モデルさんたちには、257 Barkley Streetのスタジオにお越しいただけるよう、お願いいたします。撮影時間はおよそ4時間で、午後2時から午後6時までの予定です。ただし、できましたらモデルさんに1時間早くおいでいただけると幸いです。男性モデル1名と女性モデル1名が必要です。弊社で在庫する衣類には、男女どちら向けのものもありますので。きっと、カメラマンがMilo Milanoさんだと聞けば、喜ばれるでしょう。彼もLeedsさんからの紹介です。私のメールアドレスは、昨年のカタログとともに同封した名刺に記してあります。

草々
Harriett Clutterbuck
最高経営責任者——Clutterbuck Fashion

☐ hire: 動 ～を雇う　☐ shoot: 名 撮影　☐ found: 動 ～を設立する　☐ import: 動 ～を輸入する　☐ various: 形 さまざまな
☐ manufacturer: 名 製造業者、メーカー　☐ around the world: 世界中の　☐ put together ～ : ～を編集する　☐ mail: 動 郵送する
☐ contact detail: 詳細な連絡先　☐ mention: 動 ～をちょっと言う　☐ exclusively: 副 もっぱら　☐ extremely: 副 とても
☐ reliable: 形 頼りになる、信頼できる　☐ require: 動 ～を要求する　☐ appreciate: 動 ～を感謝する　☐ stock: 動 ～を店に置く
☐ garment: 名 衣服　☐ gender: 名 性別　☐ business card: 名刺　☐ enclose: 動 ～を同封する

To: Harriett Clutterbuck <hclutterbuck@clutterbuckfashion.com>
From: Roman Rossi <rrossi@rossima.com>
Date: 21 January
Subject: Request

Dear Ms. Clutterbuck,

Thank you for contacting me. ❻I am happy to hear that Ms. Leeds is still in the industry. For many years she was my best client and the models all loved her designs. ❼Ordinarily, we only accept appointments made at least a month in advance. However, I realize you are new to the business and I will do what I can to accommodate you. You can contact my secretary at 555-2423 to set up an appointment to look at the profiles of the people we represent.

By the way, ❽our models will be happy with your choice of photographer. Mr. Milano's reputation in the industry is unmatched.

I look forward to meeting you when you come to our office.

Sincerely,

Roman Rossi

(138w)

宛先：Harriett Clutterbuck <hclutterbuck@clutterbuckfashion.
　　com>
送信者：Roman Rossi <rrossi@rossima.com>
日付：1月21日
件名：ご要望

Clutterbuck さま

ご連絡いただきまして、どうもありがとうございます。Leeds さんがまだ業界にいらっしゃると伺い、うれしく思います。長年にわたり、彼女は私の最良のお客さまでしたし、モデルたちは皆、彼女のデザインを大変気に入っていました。本来、弊社では少なくとも1カ月前までのご予約しか承っておりません。しかし、御社はこのビジネスには新規参入のようですので、できる限りの便宜を図らせていただきます。555-2423の私の秘書宛てにご連絡いただき、ご予約いただいた上で、弊社がご紹介する人物のプロフィールをご確認にいらしてください。

ところで、弊社のモデル陣は、御社が起用なさるカメラマンに喜ぶことでしょう。Milano さんの評判は、この業界で比類なきものですから。

弊社にてお待ち申し上げております。

よろしくお願いいたします。

Roman Rossi

□ industry: 名 産業界　□ ordinarily: 副 通常、たいていは　□ in advance: あらかじめ　□ realize: 動 ～を理解する　□ business: 名 業種、業界
□ accommodate: 動 ～のために便宜を図る　□ secretary: 名 秘書　□ set up an appointment: （面会などの）約束を取る
□ represent: 動 ～の代理をしている　□ reputation: 名 評判　□ unmatched: 形 無比の、並ぶ者のない

181. 正解：**B**　易 ■■■■■■ 難　選択率：(A) 17.5%　**(B) 43.7%**　(C) 14.2%　(D) 20.1%

Why did Ms. Clutterbuck contact Mr. Rossi?
(A) She would like to work as a model.
(B) She is creating a brochure.
(C) She wants to interview him for an article.
(D) She is organizing a fashion show.

☐ create: 動 ～を作る　☐ brochure: 名 パンフレット
☐ article: 名 記事　☐ organize: 動 ～を催す

なぜ Clutterbuck さんは Rossi さんに連絡しましたか。
(A) 彼女はモデルとして働きたい。
(B) 彼女はパンフレットを制作している。
(C) 彼女は記事を書くために彼を取材したがっている。
(D) 彼女はファッションショーを催している。

▶解説　Clutterbuck さんは1文書目の手紙の中で、❶Rossi さんのところのモデルを雇いたいこと、❷新しい製品カタログを作成中であることを説明しています。Rossi さんに連絡した理由はカタログ用のモデルを雇たいということですから、❷の put together を create に、catalog を brochure に 言い換えた (B) が正解です。

182. 正解：**A**　易 ■■■■■■ 難　選択率：**(A) 64.2%**　(B) 15.7%　(C) 14.2%　(D) 2.2%

At what time should the models arrive on January 27?
(A) 1:00 P.M.
(B) 2:00 P.M.
(C) 5:00 P.M.
(D) 6:00 P.M.

モデルたちは1月27日の何時に到着すればいいですか。
(A) 午後1時
(B) 午後2時
(C) 午後5時
(D) 午後6時

▶解説　1月27日に行われるカタログ用の撮影は、❹の1文目で午後2時からだと分かりますが、続く文でモデルには1時間早く来てもらいたいと述べられています。従って正解は (A) の「午後1時」です。

183. 正解：**D**　易 ■■■■■■ 難　選択率：(A) 9.3%　(B) 21.3%　(C) 32.8%　**(D) 29.9%**

Who gave Ms. Clutterbuck Mr. Rossi's contact details?
(A) An apparel importer
(B) A fashion model
(C) An advertising executive
(D) A clothing designer

☐ apparel: 名 衣服　☐ importer: 名 輸入業者
☐ executive: 名 役員

誰が Clutterbuck さんに Rossi さんの詳しい連絡先を教えましたか。
(A) 衣料品の輸入業者
(B) ファッションモデル
(C) 広告会社の役員
(D) 衣料品のデザイナー

▶解説　手紙の❸で、Rossi さんの連絡先を教えたのは Leeds さんだと述べられています。Leeds さんの名前はメールの❻で再び登場し、モデルたちは彼女のデザインをとても気に入っていたと説明されているため、Leeds さんはデザイナーであると判断できます。正解は (D) です。

184. 正解：**A**　易 ■■■■■■ 難　選択率：**(A) 42.9%**　(B) 16.0%　(C) 18.7%　(D) 16.8%

Why does Mr. Rossi make an exception for Ms. Clutterbuck?
(A) She has limited experience in the fashion industry.
(B) She is paying for a premium service.
(C) Another client canceled unexpectedly.
(D) She requires only a little assistance.

☐ exception: 名 例外　☐ limited: 形 限られた、わずかな
☐ premium: 形 (値段などが) 割り増し付きの
☐ unexpectedly: 副 突然　☐ assistance: 名 手伝い

なぜ Rossi さんは Clutterbuck さんを例外扱いしますか。
(A) 彼女のファッション業界での経験は限られている。
(B) 彼女は特別サービス料を支払っている。
(C) 別の顧客が思いがけずキャンセルした。
(D) 彼女はごくわずかな援助しか求めていない。

▶解説　Rossi さんはメールの❼で、「通常なら少なくとも1カ月前までの予約しか受けないが、あなた (＝ Clutterbuck さん) は新規参入なので便宜を図る」と述べています。また、手紙の内容や署名から、Clutterbuck さんはファッション業界の人だと分かります。これらのことから正解は (A) です。

185. 正解：**B**　易 ■■■■□□□ 難　選択率：(A) 10.1%　(B) 52.6%　(C) 26.1%　(D) 6.3%

What is suggested about Mr. Milano?
(A) He primarily works at 257 Barkley Street.
(B) He is an experienced fashion photographer.
(C) He helped create Clutterbuck Fashion's previous catalog.
(D) He charges extra for assignments outside Wellington.

☐ primarily: 副 主に　☐ experienced: 形 経験を積んだ
☐ previous: 形 前の　☐ charge extra: 追加料金を請求する
☐ assignment: 名 仕事

Milano さんについて何が示唆されていますか。
(A) 彼 は 主 に 257 Barkley Street で仕事をしている。
(B) 彼は経験豊かなファッション写真家だ。
(C) 彼は Clutterback Fashion の昔のカタログの制作を手伝った。
(D) 彼は Wellington 以外の場所での仕事には特別料金を要求する。

▶解説 カメラマンである Milano さんの名前は手紙の❺に登場します。ただし彼については メールの方で詳しく述べられており、❽でモデルたちは彼が撮影するなら喜ぶだろう、業界での彼の名声は並ぶものがない、と説明されています。つまり彼はファッション業界で長い経験を持つことが示唆されています。正解は (B) です。

((🔊)) ゼミ🅖中継　　　(😊)Hiro (😊)Mai (😊)Yasu (🎲)Dai (😊)Saki

183. ⋯⋯⋯⋯⋯⋯⋯⋯⋯⋯⋯⋯⋯⋯⋯⋯

(😊) これは正答率が意外と低いけど、間違えた人いる?

(😊) 正解は Leeds さんだと思ったのですが、選択肢に職業が並んでいたので焦りました。Rossi さんの会社と取引があったことは分かったので、何となく (B) を選びましたが、根拠はありません。

(😊) 下の文書に Leeds さんが登場した時点で、彼女自身がモデルじゃないことに気づいたでしょ?

(😊) いえ、意識が 184 番に移動したので気づきませんでした。

185. ⋯⋯⋯⋯⋯⋯⋯⋯⋯⋯⋯⋯⋯⋯⋯⋯

(😊) メールの後半に、Milano さんの評判は業界で unmatched と書か

れている。この単語を知っていたかな。ダイ、どう?

(🎲) いいえ。ただ、印象が悪いと思いました。

(😊) え、どうして?

(🎲) un で始まる単語に良いイメージがありません。

(😊) ですよね!　unimportant とか unrealistic とか、悪そうです。

(😊) おいおい、ひどい思い込みだな。unmatched は「並ぶ人がいないくらい良い」という意味だよ。直前の文で、Milano さんが撮影するならモデルがハッピーだと言っているじゃないか。

Part 7 読解問題

Questions 186-190 refer to the following agreement, e-mail, and expense report.

Dreamride Car Rental – Rental Agreement

Renter: *Jason Cox*	License Number: *16172334*
Address: *622 Lake Drive, Seattle*	Contact Number: *832-555-8348*
Rental Start: *9:00 A.M. March 16*	Rental End: *9:00 A.M. March 19*
Insurance: *$35 per day (Premium Protection)*	

❶

❷ Should the car be returned later than the time indicated on the form, the renter will be charged for an additional day of rental.

The renter is required to pay the cost of any damage repairs. **❸** When damage results from two vehicles coming into contact, renters with basic insurance will be required to pay the first $990 with the remainder being covered by the insurance company. If the damage is a result of contact with something other than a vehicle, the driver pays the initial $5,000 of repairs. **❹** For those with premium protection, the amounts are reduced to $300 and $1,000 respectively.

❺ Please be sure to remove any personal items from the car before delivering it to the drop-off location indicated on the condition report, which can be found in the car's glove compartment.

I agree with all of the conditions explained in this agreement.
Signed: *Jason Cox*

(185w)

問題186-190は次の契約書、メールと経費報告書に関するものです。

Dreamride Car Rental——レンタル契約書

借受人：Jason Cox	登録番号：16172334
住所：662 Lake Drive, Seattle	連絡先電話番号：832-555-8348
レンタル開始日時：3月16日 午前9時	返却日時：3月19日 午前9時
保険：一日35ドル（プレミアム保険）	

車両の返却が本状の記載時刻よりも遅れた場合、借受人は1日分の追加料金を支払うものとします。

借受人は、いかなる損傷の修理費用をも負担することを求められます。損傷が車両2台の接触によって生じた場合、基本保険に加入した借受人は990ドルまでの負担を求められ、残分が保険会社によって負担されます。損傷が車両以外のものとの接触によるものである場合、5000ドルまでが運転者の負担となります。プレミアム保険の加入者については、

負担金額がそれぞれ300ドル、1000ドルまで減額されます。

必ずあらゆる私物を撤去した上で、状態報告書に記載された返却所へ車両をお届けください。書類は車内のグローブボックスに収められています。

私はこの契約書に記載されたあらゆる条項に同意いたします。
署名：Jason Cox

☐ agreement: 图 契約書　☐ renter: 图 借り手　☐ license: 图 免許　☐ contact number: 連絡先電話番号　☐ insurance: 图 保険
☐ premium: 形 (値段などが) 割り増し付きの　☐ protection: 图 保護、保証　☐ indicate: 動 ~を暗に示す　☐ form: 图 形式、記入用紙
☐ charge: 動 (ある金額を) 請求する　☐ additional: 形 追加の　☐ require: 動 ~を要求する　☐ damage: 图 損傷　☐ repair: 图 修理
☐ result: 图 結果　☐ come into ~: ~の状態になる　☐ contact: 图 接触　☐ remainder: 图 残り　☐ initial: 形 最初の　☐ amount: 图 金額
☐ reduce: 動 ~を減らす　☐ respectively: 副 それぞれ　☐ remove: 動 ~を取り除く　☐ personal items: 私物、身の回り品
☐ drop-off location: (レンタカーの) 乗り捨て場所　☐ condition: 图 状態、条件
☐ glove compartment: グローブボックス　＊自動車のダッシュボードにある小物入れ

```
┌─────────────────────────────────────────────────────────┐
│                      E-Mail Message                       │
├──────────┬──────────────────────────────────────────────┤
│ To:      │ Dreamride Customer Service                    │
├──────────┼──────────────────────────────────────────────┤
│ From:    │ Jason Cox                                     │
├──────────┼──────────────────────────────────────────────┤
│ Subject: │ Insurance issue                               │
├──────────┼──────────────────────────────────────────────┤
│ Date:    │ March 18                                      │
└──────────┴──────────────────────────────────────────────┘
```

I am writing to make you aware of a situation regarding the car I am currently renting from Dreamride Car Rental. ❻It appears that the car was struck by another car while it was parked at Newhaven Mall this morning. ❼I came back from my morning shopping to find a minor dent in the front right panel. ❽I had it checked by a repair shop, which estimated the repairs to cost around $2,000.

❾After delivering the car tomorrow morning, I need to travel directly to Santa Fe airport to catch a flight back to Seattle. ❿I hope that you can have any necessary paperwork ready for me to sign so that I can get to my flight on time.

(134w)

宛先：Dreamride 顧客サービス課
送信者：Jason Cox
件名：保険の件
日付：3月18日
現在 Dreamride Car Rental からレンタルしている車の状況についてお知らせしたく、連絡を差し上げました。どうやら、今朝 Newhaven Mall に駐車している間に車をぶつけられてしまったようなのです。朝の買い物から戻ってみると、右前の車体に小さなくぼみがありました。修理工場で見てもらったところ、修理費が2000ドルほどかかるだろうとの見積もりでした。

明朝、車を返却した後、私はそのまま Santa Fe 空港へ行って Seattle へ戻る飛行機に乗らなければなりません。飛行機に間に合うよう、必要書類をご用意の上、サインするばかりにしておいていただければ幸いです。

☐ make ~ aware of ...: ~に…を知らせる　☐ regarding: 前 ~に関して　☐ currently: 副 現在、今　☐ strike: 動 ~に衝突する　＊struck は過去分詞
☐ minor: 形 小さい、目立たない　☐ dent: 名 くぼみ、へこみ　☐ front panel: フロントパネル　☐ estimate: 動 ~を見積もる
☐ necessary : 形 必要な　☐ paperwork: 名 書類事務

Travel Report

Employee: Jason Cox

Expenses	Cost
Round trip ticket to New Mexico: March 16 **Depart** Seattle 9:20 A.M. **Arrive in** Santa Fe 4:55 P.M. ⓫March 20 **Depart** Santa Fe 7:40 A.M. **Arrive in** Seattle 1:27 P.M.	$789.00
Accommodation: March 16 to March 19 — Royal Palms Hotel	$570.00
⓬March 19 to March 20 — Barato Airport Hotel	$110.00
Other transportation: Rental Vehicle, March 16 to March 19	$720.00
⓭Taxi from Barato Airport Hotel to Santa Fe Airport, March 20	$35.00

(79w)

出張報告書

従業員：Jason Cox

支出内容	金額
New Mexico との往復旅費： 3月16日　Seatle 発 午前9時20分　Santa Fe 到着 午後4時55分 3月20日　Santa Fe 発 午前7時40分　Seatle 到着 午後1時27分	789ドル
宿泊費： 3月16日から3月19日——Royal Palms Hotel 3月19日から3月20日——Barato Airport Hotel	570ドル 110ドル
その他の交通費： レンタカー、3月16日から3月19日 タクシー、3月20日に Barato Airport Hotel から Santa Fe 空港	720ドル 35ドル

☐ round trip: 往復　☐ accommodation: 名 宿泊施設　☐ transportation: 名 交通機関、乗り物

---

186. 正解：**B**　易 ■■■■■ 難　選択率：(A) 29.1%　**(B) 43.7%**　(C) 17.2%　(D) 3.0%

What information is mentioned in the agreement?
(A) The daily rental cost
(B) The penalty for late returns
(C) The return address for the vehicle
(D) The location of the driver's manual

☐ mention: 動 ～に言及する　☐ daily: 形 1日計算の
☐ penalty: 名 罰則　☐ location: 名 場所

契約書には何の情報が記されていますか。
(A) 日割りのレンタル料金
(B) 返却遅延時の違約条項
(C) 車両返却所の所在地
(D) 運転者マニュアルの在りか

▶解説　1文書目の契約書の❷で、車の返却が指定時刻より遅れた場合は1日分多くレンタル料を請求される旨が述べられています。これに合致する (B) が正解です。

---

187. 正解：**A**　易 ■■■■■ 難　選択率：**(A) 17.5%**　(B) 29.9%　(C) 29.5%　(D) 13.8%

How much was Mr. Cox most likely charged as a result of the damage?
(A) $300
(B) $990
(C) $1,000
(D) $5,000

☐ as a result of ～：～の結果として

Cox さんは損傷について結果的にいくら請求される可能性が最も高いですか。
(A) 300ドル
(B) 990ドル
(C) 1000ドル
(D) 5000ドル

▶解説　2文書目のメールの❻と❼で Cox さんは他車に車をぶつけられたことが分かり、その修理費用は❽で2000ドルだと述べられています。しかしこの金額は選択肢にありません。1文書目の契約書内❸に、基本保険の場合、他車との事故による損害には990ドルを支払う必要があり、残額は保険会社が負担すると述べられています。ただし❹で、プレミアム保険の場合、負担額は300ドルまでだと説明されています。❶でCoxさんはプレミアム保険に加入していることが分かるので、Coxさんの負担は (A) の300ドルです。(C) と (D) は、車以外のものとの接触事故の際に借り主が負担する最大額です。

188. 正解：**B** 易■■■■■□難　選択率：(A) 12.3% **(B) 44.4%** (C) 20.9% (D) 11.6%

What is Mr. Cox reminded to do before returning the vehicle?
(A) Refill the car's fuel tank
(B) Take out his personal belongings
(C) Fill out an online form
(D) Call the rental company office

Coxさんは車を返却する前に、何をするように言われていますか。
(A) 車を満タンにする
(B) 私物を撤去する
(C) オンラインで書式に記入する
(D) レンタカー会社に電話をかける

▶解説　1文書目の契約書の❺で、「車の返却前に必ず私物を撤去するように」と述べられているので、正解は(B)です。delivering it to the drop-off location が車の返却を意味することに気づくことが解答のポイントです。

□ remind ~ to ...: ~に…するよう言い聞かせる　□ refill: 動 ~を補充する
□ fuel tank: 燃料タンク　□ belonging: 名（複数形で）所有物、所持品
□ fill out ~: ~に記入する

---

189. 正解：**A** 易■■■■□□難　選択率：**(A) 54.9%** (B) 13.8% (C) 15.3% (D) 6.0%

In the e-mail, the word "ready" in paragraph 2, line 3, is closest in meaning to
(A) prepared
(B) willing
(C) approved
(D) examined

メールの第2段落3行目にある「ready」に最も意味が近いのは
(A) 用意された
(B) （~するのを）いとわない
(C) 承認された
(D) 検査された

▶解説　2文書目のメールの❿でCoxさんは「予定通りの飛行機に乗れるよう書類をreadyの状態にしておいてほしい」と述べています。よって、(A)のpreparedが「準備ができている」の意味でreadyに最も似ています。これが正解です。

---

190. 正解：**C** 易■■■■□□難　選択率：(A) 6.0% (B) 45.1% **(C) 30.2%** (D) 7.5%

What is implied about Mr. Cox?
(A) He lives near a shopping mall.
(B) He left the rental car at Santa Fe airport.
(C) He was forced to change his travel plans.
(D) He has used Dreamride Car Rental before.

Coxさんについて何が示唆されていますか。
(A) 彼はショッピングモールのそばに住んでいる。
(B) 彼はレンタカーをSanta Fe空港で乗り捨てた。
(C) 彼は出張計画の変更を余儀なくされた。
(D) 彼はかつてDreamride Car Rentalを利用したことがある。

▶解説　メールの❾から、Coxさんが空港に行く予定だったのは3月19日だと分かります。ところが、報告書の⓫、⓬、⓭によれば、3月19日にはホテルに宿泊し、3月20日にタクシーで空港に行き、飛行機に乗っています。よって、彼は何らかの事情で予定を変更せざるを得なかったと判断でき、正解は(C)に決まります。空港にはタクシーで行ったので、(B)は正しくありません。

□ imply: 動 ~を暗に意味する
□ force ~ to ...: ~に余儀なく…させる

　ゼミ生中継　Hiro Mai Yasu Dai Saki

187.
これは2文書参照型だね。気づいた？
いいえ。実は時間が足りなくてトリプルパッセージはできませんでした。
そっか。ダイは？
同じく時間がなくて。
どうしたの？
990が魅力的だったので、(B)にしました。
同じだ！
……。

189.
このタイプを「同義語問題」と呼ぶことにする。わずか1文だけ見て解くタイプだから、絶対に「塗り絵」しちゃダメだよ。

190.
魅力的な不正解はどれかな？
私は(B)にしました。レンタカーで空港まで行ったと思ったのですが、違うのですか？
第3文書の最後を見て。空港にはタクシーで行ったんだよ。だから、(B)は間違い。(A)と(D)の内容は、否定はできないけれど肯定するための証拠が全然ないから正解にはならない。

Questions 191-195 refer to the following letter, e-mail, and schedule.

SANDER'S PRODUCTIONS
772 Rockatanski Road • Boise • ID 83644

March 23

Ms. Lawrence,

❶ Thank you so much for putting me in touch with Todd Jensen. We were having difficulty finding someone with his qualifications and it felt like a miracle when you suddenly contacted us and explained his situation. He has been doing an excellent job on the Francis Inn television commercials. ❷ The project reminds me of the time we worked together on the Heathcliff Hotel advertising campaign.

If there is anything we can do to repay the favor, do not hesitate to let me know. I look forward to seeing you at this year's Producers' Conference in Boulder. ❸ I hear that Freda Watts is presenting. We attended her lectures at Kamloops University. It is great to see that she is finally getting the industry recognition she deserves.

Sincerely,

Reg Garibaldi

Reg Garibaldi

(142w)

問題**191-195**は次の手紙、メールと予定表に関するものです。
SANDER'S PRODUCTIONS
772 Rockatanski Road · Boise · ID 83644

3月23日

Lawrence さま

Todd Jensen とお引き合わせくださり、どうもありがとうございました。彼のような能力を持った人物がなかなか見つからない状況だったので、あなたが突然連絡をくださり、彼の状況をご説明くださったときには、まるで奇跡のように感じました。彼は Francis Inn のテレビコマーシャルで素晴らしい働きを見せてくれています。このプロジェクトは、われわれが共に手掛けた Heathercliff Hotel の広告キャンペーンをほうふつとさせてくれます。

今回のご親切に当方で何か報いられることがあれば、ご遠慮なくお知らせください。今年の Boulder での Producers' Conference でお目に掛かるのを楽しみにしております。Freda Watts が発表を行う予定だそうです。我々は Kamloops University で彼女の講義に出席しましたね。彼女がついに業界で相応の評価を受けるようになっているのを目の当たりにするのは、素晴らしいことです。

よろしくお願いいたします。

Reg Garibaldi

☐ put ~ in touch with ...: ~に…と連絡を取らせる　☐ qualification: 图 資格　☐ miracle: 图 奇跡　☐ suddenly: 副 突然に
☐ contact: 動 ~に連絡する　☐ situation: 图 状態、境遇　☐ excellent: 形 優れた、素晴らしい　☐ remind ~ of ...: ~に…を思い出させる
☐ repay: 動 ~に恩返しをする　☐ favor: 图 親切、好意　☐ hesitate to ~: ~するのをためらう　☐ present: 動 発表する　☐ attend: 動 ~に出席する
☐ lecture: 图 講義　☐ industry: 图 産業界　☐ recognition: 图 認められること　☐ deserve: 動 ~を受けるに足る

To: Reg Garibaldi <rgaribaldi@sandersproductions.com>
From: Carrie Lawrence <clawrence@eaglevl.com>
Subject: Instructional videos
Date: June 17

Dear Reg,

I have been communicating with Mr. Jensen of late and he informs me that you have secured a contract to shoot a series of instructional videos and need a second crew to cover the workload. While we have not received a formal invitation, I would like to offer our services as a subcontractor. I remember that our previous collaboration was regarded as a great success, and I hope that we can repeat that this time.

Best regards,

Carrie
Eagle Video Labs

(97w)

宛先：Reg Garibaldi <rgaribaldi@sandersproductions.com>
送信者：Carrie Lawrence <clawrence@eaglevl.com>
件名：教育用動画
日付：6月17日

親愛なる Reg

このところ Jensen さんと連絡を取り合っているのですが、彼の話によると、貴社は教育用の動画シリーズを撮影する契約を取り、その仕事を担当する撮影班がもう一組必要だそうですね。弊社に正式なご依頼をいただいてはいませんが、委託業者として弊社のサービスを提供させていただきたいと思います。思い返せば、私たちのかつての協業は大成功との評判を取りました。今回、再び同じようにできれば幸いです。

よろしくお願いいたします。

Carrie
Eagle Video Labs

□ instructional: 形 教育の　□ communicate with ～: ～と連絡を取る　□ of late: 最近　□ inform: 動 ～に知らせる　□ secure: 動 ～を確保する
□ contract: 名 契約　□ crew: 名（共同の仕事をする）班、チーム　□ workload: 名 仕事量　□ formal: 形 正式の　□ invitation: 名 勧誘
□ subcontractor: 名 下請け人　□ previous: 形 前の　□ collaboration: 名 協業　□ regard ～ as ...: ～を…とみなす

ACVPA

Annual Corporate Video Production Awards Ceremony
Event Schedule (Confidential Information for Committee Members ONLY)
Chandler Plaza Hotel, December 2

Time	Event	Presenter
7:00 P.M.–7:10 P.M.	**Opening Speech** **By:** ACVPA President Sam Whitehall	
7:10 P.M.–7:40 P.M.	**Dinner Service**	
7:40 P.M.–7:50 P.M.	Award for Best Regional Advertisement **Recipient:** Voorhees Video	Presented by: Creed Norris
7:50 P.M.–8:00 P.M.	Award for Best Public Service Announcement **Recipient:** Undecided	Presented by: Undecided
8:00 P.M.–8:10 P.M.	Award for Best Instructional Video **Recipient:** Sanders Productions/Eagle Video Labs	Presented by: Luke Moore
8:10 P.M.–8:20 P.M.	Award for Best Memorial Video **Recipient:** Undecided	Presented by: Undecided
8:20 P.M.–8:40 P.M.	**Closing Speech** **By:** ACVPA Founder Cindy DuPont	

(111w)

ACVPA

Annual Corporate Video Production Awards Ceremony
開催予定表（委員会関係者のみの部外秘情報）
12月2日、Chandler Plaza Hotel にて

午後7時〜午後7時10分	**開会の辞** 登壇者：ACVPA 代表 Sam Whitehall	
午後7時10分〜午後7時40分	**夕食サービス**	
午後7時40分〜午後7時50分	最優秀地域広告賞 **受賞者**：Voorhees Video	贈呈者： Creed Norris
午後7時50分〜午後8時	最優秀公共広告賞 **受賞者**：未定	贈呈者：未定
午後8時〜午後8時10分	最優秀教育動画賞 **受賞者**：Sanders Productions / Eagle Video Labs	贈呈者： Luke Moore
午後8時10分〜午後8時20分	最優秀記念動画賞 **受賞者**：未定	贈呈者：未定
午後8時20分〜午後8時40分	**閉会の辞** 登壇者：ACVPA 創設者 Cindy DuPont	

□ annual: 形 年1回の　□ corporate: 形 法人の　□ confidential: 形 機密の　□ committee: 名 委員会　□ regional: 形 地域の
□ public service: 公共事業　□ undecided: 形 未決定の　□ memorial: 形 記念の　□ founder: 名 創設者

---

191. 正解：**B**　易 ■■■■■■□□ 難　選択率：(A) 12.3%　**(B) 48.5%**　(C)18.7% (D)8.6%

Why did Mr. Garibaldi write to Ms. Lawrence?
(A) To offer a suggestion for a title
(B) To express appreciation for an introduction
(C) To remind her of a condition in her contract
(D) To suggest she submit her work for evaluation

□ suggestion: 名 提案　□ express: 動 〜を表現する
□ appreciation: 名 感謝　□ introduction: 名 紹介
□ condition: 名 条件　□ submit: 動 〜を提出する
□ evaluation: 名 評価

なぜ Garibaldi さんは Lawrence さんに手紙を書きましたか。
(A) 題名の案を提供するために
(B) 人を紹介してくれたことへの謝意を表すために
(C) ある契約条件を彼女に思い出してもらうために
(D) 彼女に作品を提出して評価を受けるよう勧めるために

▶ 解説　❶ で「Jensen さんと引き合わせてくれてありがとう」と述べられていることから、この手紙は紹介に対して礼を言うためだと考えられます。正解は (B) です。メールや手紙の目的は冒頭に書かれていることが多いです。

---

192. 正解：**C**　易 ■■■■■□□□ 難　選択率：(A) 20.9%　(B) 23.5%　**(C) 35.4%**　(D) 8.6%

Who most likely is Ms. Watts?
(A) A conference organizer
(B) A software engineer
(C) A university lecturer
(D) A factory manager

□ conference: 名 会議　□ organizer: 名 主催者
□ lecturer: 名 講師

ワッツさんはどんな人物である可能性が最も高いですか。
(A) 会議の主催者
(B) ソフトウエア技術者
(C) 大学講師
(D) 工場長

▶ 解説　Watts さんの名前は手紙の ❸ で登場します。この手紙を書いた Garibaldi さんと手紙の受取人である Lawrence さんの2人は、大学で Watts さんの講義を受けていたことが分かります。従って、Watts さんは (C) の A university lecturer（大学講師）だと推測できます。

193. 正解：**A**　易 ■■■■■■ 難　選択率：(A) **28.0%** (B) 22.8% (C) 16.4% (D) 18.7%

What is indicated about the Heathcliff Hotel advertising campaign?
(A) It was considered a success.
(B) It will be completed in March.
(C) It has had its budget reduced.
(D) It is being managed by Mr. Jensen.

□ indicate: 動 〜を暗に示す　□ consider: 動 〜だとみなす
□ budget: 名 予算　□ reduce: 動 〜を減らす

Heathcliff Hotel の広告キャンペーンについて何が示されていますか。
(A) 成功とみなされた。
(B) 3月に完了するだろう。
(C) 予算を削減されている。
(D) Jensen さんに管理されている。

▶解説 Heathcliff Hotel の広告キャンペーンは手紙の❷で言及されています。この文から、Garibaldi さんと Lawrence さんは協働したことが分かります。2文書目のメールの❼で Lawrence さんは「前回の協業は大成功だった」と述べているので、Heathcliff Hotel の広告キャンペーンは成功したと考えられます。よって、正解は (A) です。

---

194. 正解：**C**　易 ■■■■■■ 難　選択率：(A) 6.0% (B) 30.6% (C) **41.4%** (D) 8.6%

What will happen on December 2?
(A) Transportation will be provided for guests.
(B) Mr. Norris will receive an award.
(C) Chandler Plaza Hotel will host a ceremony.
(D) A committee member will greet the audience.

□ transportation: 名 交通機関、乗り物
□ host: 動 〜の会場になる
□ greet: 動 〜にあいさつする、〜を出迎える
□ audience: 名 聴衆

12月2日に何がありますか。
(A) 招待客に交通手段が供給される。
(B) Norris さんが受賞する。
(C) Chandler Plaza Hotel で式典が開かれる。
(D) ある委員が聴衆にあいさつする。

▶解説 December 2は3文書目の予定表の❾に Chandler Plaza Hotel の名前と共に登場しています。❽でこの予定表が授賞式のものであることが示されているので、正解は (C) だと判断できます。President（代表）が開会の辞を、Founder（創設者）が閉会の辞を担当しますが、彼らは委員会の代表的な立場であり、(D) にある A committee member（ある委員）ではありません。

---

195. 正解：**D**　易 ■■■■■■ 難　選択率：(A) 15.7% (B) 23.9% (C) 26.5% (D) **20.1%**

What is suggested about Mr. Garibaldi?
(A) He is a member of the awards committee.
(B) He will provide training to Mr. Jensen.
(C) He will give a presentation at ACVPA.
(D) He accepted Ms. Lawrence's business proposal.

□ accept: 動 〜を受け入れる　□ proposal: 名 提案

Garibaldi さんについて何が示唆されていますか。
(A) 彼は授賞委員会の委員だ。
(B) 彼は Jensen さんを研修するだろう。
(C) 彼は ACVPA で発表するだろう。
(D) 彼は Lawrence さんのビジネスの提案を受け入れた。

▶解説 メールで Lawrence さんは、Garibaldi さんの会社が instructional video（教育用動画）の仕事を獲得したことを知り（❹❺）、❻で「委託業者としてサービスを提供したい」と申し出ています。そして❿に、教育用動画部門の受賞者として Garibaldi さんの Sanders Productions 社と Lawrence さんの Eagle Video Labs 社の名が記載されています。これらから、Garibaldi さんは Lawrence さんの申し出を受け入れたと推測でき、正解は (D) です。

📡 ゼミ 生 中継

😺 Hiro 😺 Mai 😺 Yasu 😺 Dai 😺 Saki

193.

😺 過去に、Lawrence さんと Garibaldi さんが一緒にこのホテルの宣伝活動をしたことは読み取れたかな。ヤス？

😺 はい、そこは何とか。でも、Heathcliff Hotel が第1文書にしか登場しなかったので、ヒントが第2文書にあるとは思わず、適当に (D) にしました。

😺 (D) は現在進行形だよ？　宣伝活動は過去だから、(D) はおかしい。

😺 正直、疲れていたので集中力が切れました。

194.

😺 Chandler Plaza Hotel は授賞式の会場ですよね。その場合でも host という動詞を使えるのですか。host するのは主催者で、ホテルではないと思って、(C) を選べませんでした。

😺 ナイスな疑問だね。実はどちらの場合でも host を使える。

😺 そうでしたか。変だと思いながら、(B) にしました。

😺 Norris さんはプレゼンターだね。受賞者じゃない。

195.

😺 Lawrence さんの提案を Garibaldi さんが受け入れたんだね。気づいた？

😺 Garibaldi さんは実は反対して、彼の同僚か誰かが受け入れたから仕方なくコラボした可能性もありますよね。だから、(D) が正しいとは確定できませんでした。

😺 なるほどね。ただ、設問は What is suggested 〜? だよ。つまり、「正しい情報」ではなく、「暗示されている情報」が問われている。だから、文書中の根拠に基づく、正しいであろう情報を選べばいい。さて、次はいよいよ最後のセットだよ。

Part 7 読解問題

Questions 196-200 refer to the following receipt, e-mail, and warranty.

www.frontierwear.com/receipt9783903

FRONTIER WEAR ONLINE STORE

❶ **Customer name:** Cliff Spence
Account number: 783834
Date: October 2

Quantity	Description	Price
1	Mountain Climbing Boots (GB839)	$125.00
2	Knitted Hat Blue (NH739)	$38.00
2	❷60L Backpack (ER331)	$178.00
1	Winter Socks Black (HB949)	$18.00
	Subtotal	$359.00
	Shipping	$12.00
	❸**Amount Paid**	**$371.00**

❹You will receive a hard copy of this receipt with your order. ❺Frontier Wear will provide a full refund or exchange for any defective item for a period of 12 months from the date of purchase. Returns and exchanges can be made within 28 days of purchase if there is a discrepancy between the description and the actual article.

❻By spending over $100 at Frontier Wear you are automatically eligible to take part in our yearly hiking adventure. Click HERE for details.

(130w)

問題196-200は次の領収書、メールと保証書に関するものです。

www.frontierwear.com/receipt9783903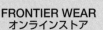

FRONTIER WEAR オンラインストア

お客さまのお名前：Cliff Spence
アカウント番号：783834
日付：10月2日

数 量	品 目	価 格
1	登山ブーツ (GB839)	125ドル
2	ニット帽 青 (NH739)	38ドル
2	60リットル バックパック (ER331)	178ドル
1	冬物靴下 黒 (HB949)	18ドル
	小計	359ドル
	送料	12ドル
	お支払金額	**371ドル**

ご注文品と一緒に本領収書を印刷したものをお送りいたします。Frontier Wearは、お買い上げ日以降12カ月間、不良品について全額返金または交換を行います。商品説明と実際の品物の間に相違があった場合には、お買い上げ後28日以内であれば返品や交換に応じます。

Frontier Wearで100ドル以上お買い物をしていただくと、当店が年1回催すハイキング大会への参加資格が自動的に付与されます。「ここ」をクリックして詳細をご確認ください。

□ account number: 会員番号　□ quantity: 图 数量
□ description: 图 種類、明細、説明　□ knitted: 形 ニットの
□ backpack: 图 バックパック、リュックサック
□ subtotal: 图 小計　□ shipping: 图 輸送料
□ amount paid: 支払額
□ hard copy: ハードコピー (データを印刷したもの)
□ full refund: 全額返金　□ exchange: 图 交換
□ defective: 形 欠陥のある　□ period: 图 期間
□ purchase: 图 購入　□ return: 图 返品
□ discrepancy: 图 不一致　□ actual: 形 実際の
□ automatically: 副 自動的に　□ eligible to ~: ~の資格がある
□ take part in ~: ~に参加する　□ yearly: 形 年1回の
□ adventure: 图 冒険

To: Cliff Spence <cspence@youngpanda.com>
From: Holly Waters <hwaters@frontierwear.com>
Date: October 7
Subject: Your order
Attachment: 📎 careinstructions

Dear Mr. Spence,

I'm sorry to hear that the care instructions for the mountain climbing boots were not enclosed in the box. We source our footwear from overseas. Therefore, having instructions sent from the manufacturer would take a long time. Fortunately, I was able to find care instructions on the manufacturer's Web site. I have downloaded them and had them translated by a member of our staff. I can confirm that all of the items mentioned in the instructions are available from our online store. Please see the attachment to this e-mail. Should you require a paper copy, please let me know and I will have the store nearest to your home print one out.

Sincerely,

Holly Waters
Customer Service Officer — Frontier Wear

(139w)

宛先：Cliff Spence <cspence@youngpanda.com>
送信者：Holly Waters <hwaters@frontierwear.com>
日付：10月7日
件名：ご注文
添付書類：careinstructions

Spence さま

登山ブーツの取扱説明書が箱に同梱（どうこん）されていなかったとのこと、申し訳ございませんでした。当店では履物類を海外から仕入れております。そのため、説明書をメーカーから取り寄せるには時間がかかってしまいます。運よく、取扱説明書をメーカーのウェブサイトで見つけました。それをダウンロードし、当店の従業員に翻訳させました。間違いなく、説明書に記載されている全商品が当店のオンラインストアで購入可能です。本メールの添付書類をご確認ください。もし紙に印刷したものをご希望でしたら、お知らせいただければ、お客さまのご自宅の最寄りの店舗に印刷させるようにいたします。

よろしくお願い申し上げます。

Holly Waters
顧客サービス担当役員—— Frontier Wear

□ attachment: 图 添付 □ instruction: 图 説明書 □ enclose: 動 ～を同封する □ source: 動（他の会社から製品など）を得る
□ footwear: 图 履物類 □ manufacturer: 图 製造業者、メーカー □ fortunately: 副 幸いにも □ translate: 動 ～を翻訳する
□ confirm: 動 ～を確証する □ mention: 動 ～に言及する □ available: 形 入手可能な □ require: 動 ～を必要とする
□ paper copy: 印刷物、紙のコピー □ customer service: 顧客サービス □ officer: 图 役員

Manufacturer's Warranty

The Bradbury 60L Backpack (ER331) is the top of the line in backpacks for serious hikers. Whether you are climbing mountains, crossing deserts, or navigating glaciers, this sturdy backpack will keep your belongings safe and dry there and back. In fact, we are so sure about our product quality that we will guarantee it for five years. If you have any issues with the construction or materials used in this item, call our customer service hotline at 321-555-7838.

(80w)

メーカー保証書

Bradbury 60L Backpackは、本格的なハイキング愛好者向けの最高級バックパックです。登山でも、砂漠の横断でも、氷河を踏破するときでも、この頑丈なバックパックは全行程でお客さまの荷物を安全で乾燥した状態に保ちます。事実、当社は自社製品の品質について大きな自信を持っており、保証期間を5年間としています。もし、本製品の構造や使用素材に何か問題がありましたら、当社のお客さまサービス直通番号321-555-7838までお電話ください。

□ warranty: 图 保証書 □ top of the line:（同一種類の製品の中で）最高の商品 □ serious: 形 本気の、真剣な
□ cross: 動 ～を渡る、横断する □ desert: 图 砂漠 □ navigate: 動（雑踏など）を通り抜ける □ glacier: 图 氷河 □ sturdy: 形 丈夫な、頑丈な
□ belonging: 图（複数形で）所有物、所持品 □ there and back: 往復で □ in fact: 実は □ sure: 形 確信して □ quality: 图 品質
□ guarantee: 動（商品など）を保証する □ issue: 图 問題 □ construction: 图 構造 □ material: 图 材料 □ hotline: 图 電話相談サービス

196. 正解：**B** 易 ■■■■■■ 難 選択率：(A) 27.2% **(B) 32.1%** (C) 15.3% (D) 10.4%

What is indicated about Mr. Spence?
(A) He is a frequent customer of Frontier Wear.
(B) He is eligible to take part in a store-run event.
(C) He has planned an international trip.
(D) He made the payment in installments.

☐ indicate: 動 ～を暗に示す ☐ frequent: 形 頻繁な
☐ international: 形 国際的な、国家間の
☐ installment: 名 分割払いの1回分

Spence さんについて何が示されていますか。
(A) 彼は Frontier Wear の常連客である。
(B) 彼には店が主催するイベントへの参加資格がある。
(C) 彼は海外旅行を計画している。
(D) 彼は分割払いを行った。

▶解説 Spence さんは1文書目の領収書の❶に出てくる、商品の購入者です。❻で「100ドルを超える購入をした人はハイキング大会への参加資格が付与される」と述べられています。❸から Spence さんは371ドル支払っていると分かるので、Frontier Wear 主催のイベントに参加可能です。正解は (B) です。

---

197. 正解：**A** 易 ■■■■■■ 難 選択率：**(A) 18.3%** (B) 41.8% (C) 13.1% (D) 11.6%

Why most likely is Ms. Waters sending the e-mail?
(A) To accommodate a customer's request
(B) To apologize for a defective product
(C) To provide updates on a project
(D) To inform staff of a shipping error

☐ accommodate: 動 ～のために便宜を図る
☐ apologize: 動 謝る ☐ provide: 動 ～を提供する
☐ update: 名 最新情報
☐ inform ～ of ...: ～に…のことを知らせる
☐ shipping: 名 (貨物の) 発送 ☐ error: 名 誤り、間違い

Waters さんは、どんな理由でメールを送っている可能性が最も高いですか。
(A) 顧客の要望に応えるために
(B) 不良品について謝罪するために
(C) プロジェクトの進捗状況を報告するために
(D) 従業員に配送ミスを知らせるために

▶解説 Waters さんはメールの送信者です (❼)。Waters さんは❽で「登山ブーツの使用説明書が箱に入っていなかったと聞いたと」述べています。Waters さんは事情を説明し、❿でサイトで見つけた説明書をスタッフに訳させ、⓫でそれをメールに添付したと書いています。これらから、客である Spence さんの要望に応じるためにメールを送ったと判断できるので、(A) が正解です。不良品への言及はないため、(B) は不適切です。

---

198. 正解：**C** 易 ■■■■■■ 難 選択率：(A) 12.3% (B) 27.6% **(C) 32.1%** (D) 11.6%

What is NOT mentioned about Frontier Wear?
(A) It sells imported items.
(B) It operates stores in several locations.
(C) It has a translating team.
(D) It ships orders with a printed receipt.

☐ mention: 動 ～に言及する ☐ imported: 形 輸入された
☐ operate: 動 ～を経営する ☐ location: 名 場所、店
☐ ship: 動 ～を送る

Frontier Wear について述べられていないことは何ですか。
(A) 輸入品を販売している。
(B) 数カ所に店舗を構えている。
(C) 翻訳チームがある。
(D) 印刷された領収書を付けて注文品を出荷する。

▶解説 (A) はメールの❾にあります。また、⓬で店舗が複数あると分かるので (B) も不正解です。領収書の❹にある hard copy は「印刷物」という意味があるので、(D) も述べられています。Frontier Wear に翻訳チームがあるとは示されておらず、Spence さんへ送る説明書も、スタッフの1人が訳したと述べられているだけです。よって、(C) が正解です。

199. 正解：**C**　易 ▪▪▪▪▪▪▪ 難　選択率：(A) 8.2%　(B) 27.2%　**(C) 33.2%**　(D) 14.2%

In the warranty, the word "serious" in paragraph 1, line 2, is closest in meaning to
(A) affordable
(B) urgent
(C) passionate
(D) cautious

保証書の第1段落2行目にある「serious」に最も意味が近いのは
(A) 手頃な
(B) 緊急の
(C) 熱心な
(D) 注意深い

▶解説 serious hikers とは「本気の」「真剣な」ハイカーのことです。(C)の passionate には「熱心な」の意味があるので、serious とほぼ同意と考えることができます。

---

200. 正解：**D**　易 ▪▪▪▪▪▪▪ 難　選択率：(A) 11.2%　(B) 22.4%　(C) 19.4%　**(D) 28.4%**

What is true about the Bradbury 60L Backpack?
(A) It comes with some accessories.
(B) The price is higher than many of its competitors'.
(C) It can be converted into different shapes.
(D) The manufacturer's warranty exceeds the seller's.

☐ accessory: 名 付属品　☐ competitor: 名 競争相手
☐ convert ～ into ...: ～を…に改装する、改造する
☐ exceed: 動 ～を超える

Bradbury 60L Backpack について何が当てはまりますか。
(A) いくつか付属品がある。
(B) 多くの競合他社の製品よりも価格が高い。
(C) 異なる形に変えることができる。
(D) メーカーの保証が販売業者のそれを上回っている。

▶解説 Bradbury 60L Backpack は、3文書目のメーカーによる保証書に記載があり（⓭）、その品番 ER331 は領収書の❷にもあります。⓮ からメーカーによる保証は5年間だと分かります。一方、販売者 Frontier Wear による保証は、❺ に「不良品の全額返金や交換は購入日から12カ月」とあります。つまり、メーカーの保証期間が販売者のそれを上回っていることが分かるので(D)が正解です。

((•)) ゼミ 生 中継

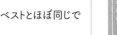

198.
😀 (D)がどこに書かれているか分かった?
😮 いいえ。hard copy の意味を知りませんでした。
😎 こんな終盤にNOT型は厳しいです。ここで時間切れになりました。
😀 それは惜しい。199番の同義語問題は短時間で解けるのに。
😮 1つ1つ順番に解いていくクセが抜けないんです。

199.
😀 ヤス、どう?　この問題は解けそう?
😎 正解は(C)ですね。しまった～。198番をさっさと捨てるべきだった!

😀 お疲れサマー。結果はどうだった?
😮 72問で390点でした。合計775点なので自己ベストとほぼ同じです。
😀 ちょうど半分です。50問で250点なので、1問5点といううわさは本当だったんですね。
😀 いや、ただの偶然だね。ダイは?
😑 42問で195点です。合計345点なので470点は厳しいですね。
😀 大丈夫。すでに射程圏内だよ。サキは?
😊 33問正解で、155点です。合計400点なので、入学時の375点を超えました。
😀 いいね。さ、これで Test 1 は終わり。ちゃんと「3回チャレンジ法プラス」を実践してね。やり方は12ページで確認できるよ。

Test 2
模擬試験 ②
解答と解説

お役立ちサイトやアプリのご案内

● ダウンロードセンター、ALCO：
模擬試験で使用した音声や復習用の音声をダウンロードできます。 （利用法は p.10、24）

● テスト採点センター：
簡単に答え合わせができます。（利用法は p.11）

● 動画センター：
全問題の解説が確認できます。（利用法は p.11）

※ QR コードを読み込む際は、他の QR コードを隠してカメラを向けてください。

記号について

【品詞を表す】
名 名詞　動 動詞　形 形容詞　副 副詞
接 接続詞　前 前置詞　代 代名詞

※品詞が複数ある場合は、問題文での用法に合うものを1つ表示しています。

【ナレーターの性別や国籍を表す】
M: 男性ナレーター　W: 女性ナレーター

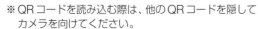 アメリカ人　　カナダ人
イギリス人　　オーストラリア人

Test 2 成長記録シート

「3回チャレンジ法プラス」での正答数などの記録をつけて、成長を振り返りましょう。

1回目（勘を含む）　年　月　日

● 正答数

Part	正答数	
Part 1	／6	Listening 合計正答数
Part 2	／25	
Part 3	／39	
Part 4	／30	／100
Part 5	／30	Reading 合計正答数
Part 6	／16	
Part 7	／54	／100

● 換算スコアA

Listening ＿＿＿＿＿＿

Reading ＿＿＿＿＿＿

合　計 ＿＿＿＿＿＿

● 問題タイプ別正答数と正答率

Listening Section

正答数	正答率
L1： ＿＿＿／16	(＿＿＿ ÷16)×100＝ ＿＿＿ %
L2： ＿＿＿／21	(＿＿＿ ÷21)×100＝ ＿＿＿ %
L3： ＿＿＿／15	(＿＿＿ ÷15)×100＝ ＿＿＿ %
L4： ＿＿＿／48	(＿＿＿ ÷48)×100＝ ＿＿＿ %
L5： ＿＿＿／15	(＿＿＿ ÷15)×100＝ ＿＿＿ %

Reading Section

正答数	正答率
R1： ＿＿＿／21	(＿＿＿ ÷21)×100＝ ＿＿＿ %
R2： ＿＿＿／19	(＿＿＿ ÷19)×100＝ ＿＿＿ %
R3： ＿＿＿／34	(＿＿＿ ÷34)×100＝ ＿＿＿ %
R4： ＿＿＿／24	(＿＿＿ ÷24)×100＝ ＿＿＿ %
R5： ＿＿＿／20	(＿＿＿ ÷20)×100＝ ＿＿＿ %

1回目（勘を除く）　年　月　日

● 正答数

Part	正答数	
Part 1	／6	Listening 合計正答数
Part 2	／25	
Part 3	／39	
Part 4	／30	／100
Part 5	／30	Reading 合計正答数
Part 6	／16	
Part 7	／54	／100

● 換算スコアB

Listening ＿＿＿＿＿＿

Reading ＿＿＿＿＿＿

合　計 ＿＿＿＿＿＿

● 問題タイプ別正答数と正答率

Listening Section

正答数	正答率
L1： ＿＿＿／16	(＿＿＿ ÷16)×100＝ ＿＿＿ %
L2： ＿＿＿／21	(＿＿＿ ÷21)×100＝ ＿＿＿ %
L3： ＿＿＿／15	(＿＿＿ ÷15)×100＝ ＿＿＿ %
L4： ＿＿＿／48	(＿＿＿ ÷48)×100＝ ＿＿＿ %
L5： ＿＿＿／15	(＿＿＿ ÷15)×100＝ ＿＿＿ %

Reading Section

正答数	正答率
R1： ＿＿＿／21	(＿＿＿ ÷21)×100＝ ＿＿＿ %
R2： ＿＿＿／19	(＿＿＿ ÷19)×100＝ ＿＿＿ %
R3： ＿＿＿／34	(＿＿＿ ÷34)×100＝ ＿＿＿ %
R4： ＿＿＿／24	(＿＿＿ ÷24)×100＝ ＿＿＿ %
R5： ＿＿＿／20	(＿＿＿ ÷20)×100＝ ＿＿＿ %

2回目（勘を含む）　年　月　日

● 正答数

Part	正答数	
Part 1	／6	Listening 合計正答数
Part 2	／25	
Part 3	／39	
Part 4	／30	／100
Part 5	／30	Reading 合計正答数
Part 6	／16	
Part 7	／54	／100

● 換算スコアA

Listening ＿＿＿＿＿＿

Reading ＿＿＿＿＿＿

合　計 ＿＿＿＿＿＿

● 問題タイプ別正答数と正答率

Listening Section

正答数	正答率
L1： ＿＿＿／16	(＿＿＿ ÷16)×100＝ ＿＿＿ %
L2： ＿＿＿／21	(＿＿＿ ÷21)×100＝ ＿＿＿ %
L3： ＿＿＿／15	(＿＿＿ ÷15)×100＝ ＿＿＿ %
L4： ＿＿＿／48	(＿＿＿ ÷48)×100＝ ＿＿＿ %
L5： ＿＿＿／15	(＿＿＿ ÷15)×100＝ ＿＿＿ %

Reading Section

正答数	正答率
R1： ＿＿＿／21	(＿＿＿ ÷21)×100＝ ＿＿＿ %
R2： ＿＿＿／19	(＿＿＿ ÷19)×100＝ ＿＿＿ %
R3： ＿＿＿／34	(＿＿＿ ÷34)×100＝ ＿＿＿ %
R4： ＿＿＿／24	(＿＿＿ ÷24)×100＝ ＿＿＿ %
R5： ＿＿＿／20	(＿＿＿ ÷20)×100＝ ＿＿＿ %

2回目（勘を除く）　年　月　日

● 正答数

Part	正答数	
Part 1	／6	Listening 合計正答数
Part 2	／25	
Part 3	／39	
Part 4	／30	／100
Part 5	／30	Reading 合計正答数
Part 6	／16	
Part 7	／54	／100

● 換算スコアB

Listening ＿＿＿＿＿＿

Reading ＿＿＿＿＿＿

合　計 ＿＿＿＿＿＿

● 問題タイプ別正答数と正答率

Listening Section

正答数	正答率
L1： ＿＿＿／16	(＿＿＿ ÷16)×100＝ ＿＿＿ %
L2： ＿＿＿／21	(＿＿＿ ÷21)×100＝ ＿＿＿ %
L3： ＿＿＿／15	(＿＿＿ ÷15)×100＝ ＿＿＿ %
L4： ＿＿＿／48	(＿＿＿ ÷48)×100＝ ＿＿＿ %
L5： ＿＿＿／15	(＿＿＿ ÷15)×100＝ ＿＿＿ %

Reading Section

正答数	正答率
R1： ＿＿＿／21	(＿＿＿ ÷21)×100＝ ＿＿＿ %
R2： ＿＿＿／19	(＿＿＿ ÷19)×100＝ ＿＿＿ %
R3： ＿＿＿／34	(＿＿＿ ÷34)×100＝ ＿＿＿ %
R4： ＿＿＿／24	(＿＿＿ ÷24)×100＝ ＿＿＿ %
R5： ＿＿＿／20	(＿＿＿ ÷20)×100＝ ＿＿＿ %

左側（3回目（勘を含む））

● 正答数

Part	正答数		
Part 1	／6	Listening 合計正答数	
Part 2	／25		
Part 3	／39		
Part 4	／30		／100
Part 5	／30	Reading 合計正答数	
Part 6	／16		
Part 7	／54		／100

● 換算スコアA

Listening _____
Reading _____
合 計 _____

● 問題タイプ別正答数と正答率

Listening Section

	正答数	正答数	正答率
L1 :	_____／16	(_____ ÷16)×100 = _____ %	
L2 :	_____／21	(_____ ÷21)×100 = _____ %	
L3 :	_____／15	(_____ ÷15)×100 = _____ %	
L4 :	_____／48	(_____ ÷48)×100 = _____ %	
L5 :	_____／15	(_____ ÷15)×100 = _____ %	

Reading Section

	正答数	正答数	正答率
R1 :	_____／21	(_____ ÷21)×100 = _____ %	
R2 :	_____／19	(_____ ÷19)×100 = _____ %	
R3 :	_____／34	(_____ ÷34)×100 = _____ %	
R4 :	_____／24	(_____ ÷24)×100 = _____ %	
R5 :	_____／20	(_____ ÷20)×100 = _____ %	

3回目（勘を含む）
年 月 日

右側（3回目（勘を除く））

● 正答数

Part	正答数		
Part 1	／6	Listening 合計正答数	
Part 2	／25		
Part 3	／39		
Part 4	／30		／100
Part 5	／30	Reading 合計正答数	
Part 6	／16		
Part 7	／54		／100

● 換算スコアB

Listening _____
Reading _____
合 計 _____

● 問題タイプ別正答数と正答率

Listening Section

	正答数	正答数	正答率
L1 :	_____／16	(_____ ÷16)×100 = _____ %	
L2 :	_____／21	(_____ ÷21)×100 = _____ %	
L3 :	_____／15	(_____ ÷15)×100 = _____ %	
L4 :	_____／48	(_____ ÷48)×100 = _____ %	
L5 :	_____／15	(_____ ÷15)×100 = _____ %	

Reading Section

	正答数	正答数	正答率
R1 :	_____／21	(_____ ÷21)×100 = _____ %	
R2 :	_____／19	(_____ ÷19)×100 = _____ %	
R3 :	_____／34	(_____ ÷34)×100 = _____ %	
R4 :	_____／24	(_____ ÷24)×100 = _____ %	
R5 :	_____／20	(_____ ÷20)×100 = _____ %	

3回目（勘を除く）
年 月 日

弱点問題タイプ診断

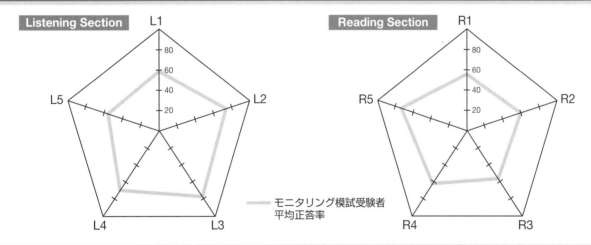

Listening Section — L1, L2, L3, L4, L5
Reading Section — R1, R2, R3, R4, R5
モニタリング模試受験者平均正答率

参考資料：モニタリング模試実施データ

p.147に掲載された「スコア換算表」を作成するために、TOEIC L&Rテストの公式スコア保持者392名を対象に、Test 2と同じ問題を使用した模擬試験を実施しました。以下はその結果をまとめたものです。

	公式スコア平均	正答数平均	最低正答数	最高正答数	初級者レベル正答数	上級者レベル正答数
Listening	351.0	74.3	42	99	65問以下	84問以上
Reading	300.2	61.5	26	97	50問以下	73問以上

※表中の数字はモニタリング模試受験者392名のうち正常に受験したと認められたモニターの数値を基に算出しています。
※モニタリング模試受験者のうち、Listening Section、Reading Sectionそれぞれにおいて、正答数が少なかった25%を「初級者レベル」、多かった25%を「上級者レベル」と呼んでいます。

Test 2 解答＆問題タイプ一覧

答え合わせの手順

1. 正解を確認し、一覧表に正誤を記入する

自分の解答済のマークシートと解答一覧を突き合わせ、解答一覧内に正誤（○×）を記入しましょう。①～③は3回チャレンジ法プラス（p.12～参照）の1回目～3回目を表します。勘ボックスを利用した場合、勘ボックスの✔も転記します。

2. 間違えた問題の問題タイプ欄にチェックを入れる

間違えた問題もしくは正答したが勘ボックスに✔がある問題の「問題タイプ」欄に✔を記入します。

3. パートごとの正答数・問題タイプごとの正答数を数え、「成長記録シート」に記入する

パートごとの正答数（正誤欄の○の数）と勘を除く正答数（○の数―✔の付いた数）を数え、その数をp.142～の「成長記録シート」に記入しましょう。

4. 予想スコアと弱点問題タイプを算出する

p.147のスコア換算表を参照して実際のTOEIC L&Rテストでの予想スコアを算出し、「成長記録シート」に記入しましょう。また、問題タイプごとに誤答数（「問題タイプ」欄の✔の数）を転記し、正答率を算出して弱点問題タイプ／パートを把握しましょう。

Listening Section

問題番号	正解	①(勘)	②(勘)	③(勘)	問題タイプ
Part 1
1	D	( )	( )	( )	L3
2	B	( )	( )	( )	L1
3	A	( )	( )	( )	L3
4	C	( )	( )	( )	L1
5	D	( )	( )	( )	L1
6	B	( )	( )	( )	L3
Part 2
7	B	( )	( )	( )	L3
8	C	( )	( )	( )	L3
9	B	( )	( )	( )	L3
10	A	( )	( )	( )	L3
11	A	( )	( )	( )	L1、L5
12	B	( )	( )	( )	L3
13	C	( )	( )	( )	L1
14	A	( )	( )	( )	L3
15	A	( )	( )	( )	L1、L5
16	C	( )	( )	( )	L3
17	A	( )	( )	( )	L1、L5
18	C	( )	( )	( )	L1
19	B	( )	( )	( )	L1、L5
20	A	( )	( )	( )	L3
21	B	( )	( )	( )	L1、L5
22	A	( )	( )	( )	L1
23	C	( )	( )	( )	L1、L5
24	B	( )	( )	( )	L1、L5
25	B	( )	( )	( )	L3
26	A	( )	( )	( )	L1、L5
27	B	( )	( )	( )	L1、L5
28	C	( )	( )	( )	L3
29	C	( )	( )	( )	L3
30	C	( )	( )	( )	L3
31	A	( )	( )	( )	L1、L5
Part 3
32	C	( )	( )	( )	L4
33	B	( )	( )	( )	L4
34	A	( )	( )	( )	L4
35	B	( )	( )	( )	L2
36	A	( )	( )	( )	L4
37	D	( )	( )	( )	L4
38	D	( )	( )	( )	L4
39	A	( )	( )	( )	L4
40	D	( )	( )	( )	L4
41	C	( )	( )	( )	L2
42	C	( )	( )	( )	L2、L5
43	B	( )	( )	( )	L4
44	A	( )	( )	( )	L2
45	A	( )	( )	( )	L4
46	D	( )	( )	( )	L4
47	C	( )	( )	( )	L2
48	B	( )	( )	( )	L4
49	D	( )	( )	( )	L4
50	D	( )	( )	( )	L4

問題番号	正解	①(勘)	②(勘)	③(勘)	問題タイプ
51	C	( )	( )	( )	L4
52	A	( )	( )	( )	L4
53	B	( )	( )	( )	L2
54	B	( )	( )	( )	L4
55	C	( )	( )	( )	L2、L5
56	C	( )	( )	( )	L2
57	D	( )	( )	( )	L4
58	A	( )	( )	( )	L4
59	B	( )	( )	( )	L2
60	A	( )	( )	( )	L4
61	A	( )	( )	( )	L4
62	A	( )	( )	( )	L4
63	A	( )	( )	( )	L4
64	D	( )	( )	( )	L4
65	C	( )	( )	( )	L2
66	D	( )	( )	( )	L4
67	B	( )	( )	( )	L4
68	A	( )	( )	( )	L4
69	C	( )	( )	( )	L4
70	B	( )	( )	( )	L4
Part 4
71	D	( )	( )	( )	L2
72	B	( )	( )	( )	L4
73	C	( )	( )	( )	L4
74	C	( )	( )	( )	L4
75	A	( )	( )	( )	L4
76	D	( )	( )	( )	L4
77	A	( )	( )	( )	L2
78	B	( )	( )	( )	L4
79	D	( )	( )	( )	L4
80	D	( )	( )	( )	L2
81	D	( )	( )	( )	L2、L5
82	B	( )	( )	( )	L4
83	B	( )	( )	( )	L2
84	C	( )	( )	( )	L4
85	D	( )	( )	( )	L4
86	A	( )	( )	( )	L2
87	B	( )	( )	( )	L4
88	A	( )	( )	( )	L2、L5
89	A	( )	( )	( )	L2
90	C	( )	( )	( )	L4
91	C	( )	( )	( )	L4
92	A	( )	( )	( )	L2
93	C	( )	( )	( )	L4
94	B	( )	( )	( )	L2、L5
95	C	( )	( )	( )	L4
96	B	( )	( )	( )	L4
97	B	( )	( )	( )	L4
98	C	( )	( )	( )	L2
99	A	( )	( )	( )	L4
100	C	( )	( )	( )	L4

間違えたら空欄にチェック（L1／L2／L3／L4／L5、各①②③）

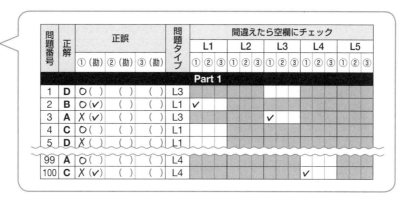

記入例

問題番号	正解	正誤 ①(勘)	②(勘)	③(勘)	問題タイプ	間違えたら空欄にチェック L1 ①②③	L2 ①②③	L3 ①②③	L4 ①②③	L5 ①②③
					Part 1					
1	D	○( )	( )	( )	L3					
2	B	○(✓)	( )	( )	L1	✓				
3	A	✗(✓)	( )	( )	L3			✓		
4	C	○( )	( )	( )	L1					
5	D	✗	( )	( )	L1					
99	A	○( )	( )	( )	L4					
100	C	✗(✓)	( )	( )	L4				✓	

Reading Section

問題番号	正解	正誤 ①(勘)	②(勘)	③(勘)	問題タイプ	R1 ①②③	R2 ①②③	R3 ①②③	R4 ①②③	R5 ①②③
					Part 5					
101	C	( )	( )	( )	R5					
102	B	( )	( )	( )	R4					
103	C	( )	( )	( )	R5					
104	A	( )	( )	( )	R5					
105	C	( )	( )	( )	R5					
106	B	( )	( )	( )	R4					
107	D	( )	( )	( )	R5					
108	A	( )	( )	( )	R4					
109	C	( )	( )	( )	R5					
110	D	( )	( )	( )	R4					
111	C	( )	( )	( )	R5					
112	A	( )	( )	( )	R4					
113	B	( )	( )	( )	R5					
114	B	( )	( )	( )	R4					
115	D	( )	( )	( )	R5					
116	C	( )	( )	( )	R4					
117	A	( )	( )	( )	R5					
118	D	( )	( )	( )	R5					
119	B	( )	( )	( )	R4					
120	B	( )	( )	( )	R4					
121	D	( )	( )	( )	R5					
122	B	( )	( )	( )	R4					
123	A	( )	( )	( )	R5					
124	D	( )	( )	( )	R4					
125	D	( )	( )	( )	R5					
126	D	( )	( )	( )	R4					
127	A	( )	( )	( )	R4					
128	B	( )	( )	( )	R5					
129	A	( )	( )	( )	R4					
130	C	( )	( )	( )	R5					
					Part 6					
131	C	( )	( )	( )	R5					
132	D	( )	( )	( )	R3、R4					
133	A	( )	( )	( )	R3、R4					
134	B	( )	( )	( )	R3					
135	B	( )	( )	( )	R5					
136	C	( )	( )	( )	R3、R4					
137	A	( )	( )	( )	R3					
138	D	( )	( )	( )	R4					
139	A	( )	( )	( )	R3、R5					
140	B	( )	( )	( )	R3、R4					
141	D	( )	( )	( )	R3					
142	C	( )	( )	( )	R3、R4					
143	C	( )	( )	( )	R3、R4					
144	B	( )	( )	( )	R3					
145	D	( )	( )	( )	R3、R4					
146	A	( )	( )	( )	R5					
					Part 7					
147	A	( )	( )	( )	R1					
148	D	( )	( )	( )	R2					
149	D	( )	( )	( )	R2					
150	D	( )	( )	( )	R4					

問題番号	正解	正誤 ①(勘)	②(勘)	③(勘)	問題タイプ	R1 ①②③	R2 ①②③	R3 ①②③	R4 ①②③	R5 ①②③
151	A	( )	( )	( )	R2					
152	B	( )	( )	( )	R1、R3					
153	C	( )	( )	( )	R3					
154	B	( )	( )	( )	R1					
155	C	( )	( )	( )	R2					
156	B	( )	( )	( )	R1					
157	A	( )	( )	( )	R2					
158	C	( )	( )	( )	R2					
159	A	( )	( )	( )	R1					
160	B	( )	( )	( )	R2					
161	C	( )	( )	( )	R2					
162	B	( )	( )	( )	R2					
163	C	( )	( )	( )	R2					
164	D	( )	( )	( )	R2					
165	A	( )	( )	( )	R1					
166	C	( )	( )	( )	R3					
167	D	( )	( )	( )	R1、R3					
168	C	( )	( )	( )	R1					
169	B	( )	( )	( )	R1、R3					
170	D	( )	( )	( )	R3					
171	B	( )	( )	( )	R3					
172	A	( )	( )	( )	R2					
173	C	( )	( )	( )	R2					
174	D	( )	( )	( )	R2					
175	A	( )	( )	( )	R1、R3					
176	D	( )	( )	( )	R1					
177	A	( )	( )	( )	R3					
178	B	( )	( )	( )	R3					
179	C	( )	( )	( )	R2					
180	C	( )	( )	( )	R1、R3					
181	B	( )	( )	( )	R1					
182	D	( )	( )	( )	R1					
183	C	( )	( )	( )	R3					
184	A	( )	( )	( )	R1、R3					
185	A	( )	( )	( )	R3					
186	A	( )	( )	( )	R3					
187	B	( )	( )	( )	R1、R3					
188	D	( )	( )	( )	R3					
189	D	( )	( )	( )	R2					
190	C	( )	( )	( )	R3					
191	A	( )	( )	( )	R1					
192	B	( )	( )	( )	R4					
193	D	( )	( )	( )	R2					
194	A	( )	( )	( )	R1、R3					
195	C	( )	( )	( )	R3					
196	C	( )	( )	( )	R2					
197	D	( )	( )	( )	R1					
198	A	( )	( )	( )	R1、R3					
199	D	( )	( )	( )	R2					
200	B	( )	( )	( )	R1、R3					

Test 2 マークシート状解答一覧

LISTENING SECTION

Part 1

No.	A	B	C	D
1			●	
2			●	
3			●	
4	●			
5		●		
6	●			
7			●	
8		●		
9				●
10	●			

Part 2

No.	A	B	C
11	●		
12			●
13		●	
14			●
15		●	
16	●		
17			●
18		●	
19	●		
20			●
21			●
22		●	
23	●		
24			●
25		●	
26	●		
27			●
28		●	
29			●
30		●	
31	●		
32		●	
33			●
34		●	
35	●		
36			●
37		●	
38	●		
39			●
40		●	

Part 3

No.	A	B	C	D
41			●	
42		●		
43	●			
44				●
45		●		
46	●			
47			●	
48		●		
49	●			
50				●
51		●		
52	●			
53			●	
54		●		
55				●
56	●			
57			●	
58		●		
59	●			
60				●
61		●		
62	●			
63			●	
64		●		
65	●			
66				●
67			●	
68		●		
69	●			
70				●

Part 4

No.	A	B	C	D
71		●		
72	●			
73			●	
74		●		
75	●			
76				●
77			●	
78		●		
79	●			
80				●
81		●		
82	●			
83			●	
84		●		
85	●			
86				●
87			●	
88		●		
89	●			
90				●
91		●		
92	●			
93			●	
94		●		
95	●			
96				●
97			●	
98		●		
99	●			
100				●

READING SECTION

Part 5

No.	A	B	C	D
101		●		
102	●			
103				●
104			●	
105		●		
106	●			
107			●	
108				●
109		●		
110	●			
111			●	
112		●		
113	●			
114				●
115			●	
116		●		
117	●			
118				●
119		●		
120			●	
121		●		
122	●			
123			●	
124		●		
125				●
126	●			
127			●	
128		●		
129				●
130	●			

Part 6

No.	A	B	C	D
131		●		
132	●			
133				●
134			●	
135		●		
136	●			
137			●	
138		●		
139				●
140	●			

Part 7

No.	A	B	C	D
141	●			
142			●	
143		●		
144	●			
145				●
146			●	
147		●		
148			●	
149	●			
150				●
151	●			
152			●	
153		●		
154	●			
155				●
156			●	
157		●		
158	●			
159				●
160			●	
161			●	
162		●		
163	●			
164				●
165			●	
166		●		
167	●			
168			●	
169		●		
170	●			
171		●		
172	●			
173			●	
174				●
175		●		
176	●			
177			●	
178		●		
179				●
180	●			
181		●		
182	●			
183			●	
184				●
185		●		
186	●			
187			●	
188		●		
189				●
190	●			
191		●		
192	●			
193			●	
194				●
195		●		
196	●			
197			●	
198		●		
199				●
200	●			

Test 2 スコア換算表

協力：アルク教育総合研究所

Listening Section

正答数	換算スコア		正答数	換算スコア
0	5		51	215
1	5		52	220
2	5		53	230
3	5		54	235
4	5		55	240
5	10		56	250
6	20		57	255
7	25		58	260
8	30		59	265
9	40		60	265
10	45		61	270
11	50		62	280
12	50		63	285
13	55		64	290
14	60		65	300
15	70		66	300
16	75		67	305
17	80		68	310
18	85		69	315
19	85		70	320
20	90		71	330
21	95		72	335
22	95		73	340
23	100		74	350
24	105		75	355
25	105		76	360
26	110		77	370
27	115		78	380
28	115		79	385
29	120		80	390
30	125		81	400
31	125		82	410
32	130		83	415
33	135		84	415
34	135		85	420
35	140		86	425
36	145		87	430
37	150		88	435
38	155		89	440
39	160		90	445
40	165		91	450
41	170		92	455
42	170		93	460
43	175		94	465
44	175		95	470
45	180		96	480
46	185		97	485
47	190		98	490
48	195		99	495
49	205		100	495
50	210			

Reading Section

正答数	換算スコア		正答数	換算スコア
0	5		51	235
1	5		52	245
2	5		53	250
3	5		54	255
4	5		55	260
5	5		56	270
6	10		57	275
7	15		58	280
8	15		59	285
9	20		60	295
10	25		61	300
11	30		62	305
12	30		63	315
13	35		64	320
14	35		65	325
15	40		66	330
16	45		67	340
17	50		68	345
18	55		69	350
19	60		70	355
20	65		71	365
21	70		72	370
22	75		73	375
23	75		74	380
24	80		75	385
25	80		76	390
26	85		77	395
27	90		78	400
28	90		79	405
29	95		80	410
30	105		81	415
31	110		82	415
32	115		83	420
33	120		84	425
34	130		85	430
35	135		86	435
36	140		87	440
37	145		88	445
38	155		89	450
39	160		90	455
40	165		91	460
41	175		92	465
42	180		93	475
43	185		94	480
44	190		95	485
45	200		96	495
46	205		97	495
47	210		98	495
48	215		99	495
49	225		100	495
50	230			

結果活用アドバイス

本書に登場するマイ、ヤス、ダイ、サキの4人の「換算スコアA」を例に「弱点問題タイプ診断」の活用法をご紹介します。自分に最も近い人物の診断を参考に、今後の学習に役立ててください。

Listening Section

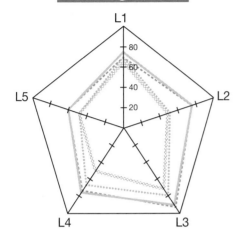

Reading Section

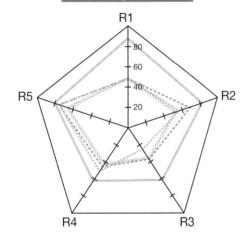

換算スコア

		Listening	Reading	合計
———	😊 マイ	380	395	775
- - - -	😮 ヤス	360	260	620
～～～	😐 ダイ	240	225	465
·········	😊 サキ	300	250	550

😊 マイはR1とR2が伸びたね。Part 7でどんな工夫をしたの?

😊 Part 7をPart 5の次にやったのが良かったのかもしれません。パニックにならずに最後まで解けました。

😊 46問も正答できたのはナイスだね。Part 3と4の練習はやってるの?

😊 はい。音読しています。効果はなかったみたいですが。

😊 それでいいよ。学習のタイミングと、効果が出るタイミングにはズレがあるのが普通だよ。今後も続けてね。次は、ヤス。ちゃんと宿題をやってたから、予想通りL2とL4が激変したね。

😮 はい。換算スコアが65点アップです。

😊 その調子。本番で730点を狙うには、文法をもっと鍛える必要がある。今後しばらく集中的に文法に取り組んで。ただし、しつこいくらいの反復練習と、自分で解説することを忘れずに。

😮 「自分で解説」ってどういうことですか。

😊 いくら解説を読んで理解したつもりでも、知識として定着しているとは限らない。定着させるには、自分で自分に解説することが効果的なんだよ。詳しいことはp.85の「TOEICよろず相談所」を読めば分かるよ。じゃ、次はダイ。リスニングの正答数が激増したね。

😐 はい。解きやすくなったのを実感しました。ただ、Part 5はあまり変わりませんでした。

😊 そうだけど、Part 7で伸びたよね。英語そのものに慣れてきたんだと思うよ。Part 5の読み込みは続けてね。必ずR4とR5が伸びるから。

😐 了解です。

😊 サキもかなりスコアが伸びたね。

😊 Part 6で時間を使うのはもったいないと分かったので、文を選ぶ問題を捨てて、Part 7に使う時間を増やしたんです。

😊 なるほど。それは賢いね。1問あたりの価値は同じだから、「易しい問題を全部見つけて解く」のが作戦として正しい。リスニングも正答数が25問も増えたね。

😊 はい。リスニングは楽しいです。ALCOを使うのが面白いんです。スピードを少し遅くして聞くことができるので、私に合っていると思います。

😊 なるほど。そうやって、自分が好きな学習が見つかると強いよ。これからも続けてね。

😊 大学の試験が近づいているので不安ですが、頑張ります。

😊 みんな忘れないでね。試験本番は2時間連続で英語を聞いたり読んだりする。普段、それと同じくらいのことをやっておけば、試験本番が楽になる。日本語の解説と訳を読みまくるより、英語を聞いたり読んだりすることの方が大事だよ。

解説を確認し、間違えた問題は二度と間違えないようにきっちり復習しましょう。

Part 1 写真描写問題

1. DL ↓066 🇨🇦 正解：**D**　易■■□□□□□難　選択率：(A) 4.2% (B) 2.1% (C) 2.5% (D) 90.8%

(A) She's putting up a sign.
(B) She's holding some flowers.
(C) She's mounting a wall clock.
(D) She's wearing glasses.

☐ put up 〜：〜を提示する
☐ sign: 名 看板、標識
☐ hold: 動 〜を持つ
☐ mount: 動 〜を据え付ける
☐ wall clock: 掛け時計
☐ wear: 動 〜を身に着ける
☐ glass: 名 (複数形で) 眼鏡

(A) 彼女は看板を掲示しています。
(B) 彼女は何本かの花を持っています。
(C) 彼女は掛け時計を据え付けています。
(D) 彼女は眼鏡をかけています。

▶解説 女性は眼鏡を掛けています。それをストレートに描写した(D)が正解です。(A)、(B)、(C)にあるsign（看板）、flowers（花）、wall clock（掛け時計）は写っていますが、それぞれの描写で使われている動詞が女性の動作と一致しません。

2. DL ↓067 🇬🇧 正解：**B**　易■■□□□□□難　選択率：(A) 3.2% (B) 72.8% (C) 21.9% (D) 1.4%

(A) He's strolling along a wall.
(B) He's working at the rear of a vehicle.
(C) He's loading luggage onto a truck.
(D) He's examining a motorbike.

☐ stroll: 動 散歩する
☐ along: 前 〜に沿って
☐ rear: 名 後ろ、後部
☐ vehicle: 名 車両、乗り物
☐ load: 動 〜を積む
☐ luggage: 名 手荷物
☐ examine: 動 〜を調査する、検査する
☐ motorbike: 名 バイク、オートバイ

(A) 彼は壁に沿って散歩しています。
(B) 彼は車両の後部で働いています。
(C) 彼はトラックに手荷物を積んでいます。
(D) 彼はバイクを検査しています。

▶解説 男性がトラック後部の荷台で作業しています。その様子をworking at the rear of a vehicle（車両の後部で働いている）と描写した(B)が正解です。男性は、荷物を積む作業を行なっていないため(C)は不正解です。truck（トラック）という単語に惑わされず、選択肢の動詞が表す動作が写真の男性を正しく描写しているかを確認しましょう。(D)のバイクは写真に写っていません。

📡))) ゼミ生中継

🙂Hiro 🙂Mai 🙂Yasu 🙂Dai 🙂Saki

🙂 お疲れ。では、Part 1から振り返ろう。易しめのパートだけど、全てが楽勝というわけではない。絶対になめちゃいけないよ。

1.

🙂 ダイ、(C)のmountingは聞き取れた?

😀 はい。山は写っていないので消去しました。

🙂 それはmountainでしょ。mountingは動詞のmountに-ingが付いたもの。受け身の完了形のA wall clock has been mounted. だったら正解になる。

😀 了解です。

2.

😀 あ、(A)はstrollingだったのか。全然分からなくてパニくった。

🙂 私は(B)のat the rear ofの部分が聞き取れなくて。

🙂 で、どうした?

🙂 (C)で、トラックとか荷物とかが聞こえました。それで、ワンチャンいけるんじゃないかと思って、(C)にしました。

🙂 惜しい。(C)はloadingが間違っている。

Part 1 写真描写問題

3. DL 069 🇦🇺 正解：**A** 易 ■■□□□□□ 難 選択率：**(A) 65.4%** (B) 7.4% (C) 14.8% (D) 12.0%

(A) Shadows are being cast on the pathway.
(B) A man is ascending the steps.
(C) Some lampposts are being fixed.
(D) Some railings are being installed.

☐ shadow: 名 影
☐ cast: 動（影）を投じる
☐ pathway: 名 歩道、通路
☐ ascend: 動 ～を上る
☐ step: 名（複数形で）階段
☐ lamppost: 名 街灯
☐ fix: 動 ～を修理する
☐ railing: 名 手すり、欄干
☐ install: 動 ～を取り付ける

(A) 影が歩道に投じられています。
(B) 男性が階段を上っています。
(C) いくつかの街灯が修理されています。
(D) いくつかの手すりが取り付けられています。

▶解説 pathway（歩道）には影が伸びています。その様子を描写した(A)が正解です。写真中央に男性がいますが、階段を上っているところ（ascending the steps）ではないため(B)は不正解です。また、lamppost（街灯）やrailing（手すり）が見えますが、それぞれ修理中でも設置中でもないため、描写が不適切です。受動態の進行形に注意しましょう。

---

4. DL 070 🇬🇧 正解：**C** 易 ■□□□□□□ 難 選択率：(A) 0.0% (B) 0.4% **(C) 98.9%** (D) 0.4%

(A) They're leaning against a bench.
(B) They're taking off their glasses.
(C) They're looking at a laptop computer.
(D) They're entering the room.

☐ lean against ～ : ～に寄り掛かる
☐ take off ～ : ～を取る、外す
☐ glass: 名（複数形で）眼鏡
☐ look at ～ : ～を見る
☐ laptop computer: ノートパソコン、ラップトップ型コンピューター
☐ enter: 動 ～に入る

(A) 彼らはベンチに寄り掛かっています。
(B) 彼らは眼鏡を外しています。
(C) 彼らはノートパソコンを見ています。
(D) 彼らは部屋に入るところです。

▶解説 2人の男性の動作がポイントです。パソコン画面を見ている様子を描写した(C)が正解です。laptop computerは「ノートパソコン」のことですが、laptopだけでも表現することができます。(A)はベンチがないため、(D)は彼らがすでに部屋の中にいるため、それぞれ不正解です。また、2人とも眼鏡を掛けていますが、取り外しているところではないため(B)も不適切です。

((📡)) ゼミ 生 中継　　　　　　　　😀Hiro 😀Mai 😀Yasu 😎Dai 😀Saki

3.

😀 どうしてこの写真でsendingが聞こえるのかと思ったら、ascendingだったのですね。

😀 そういうこと。それと、lamppostsやrailingsはPart 1が好きな単語だから、知らなかったらまずいよ。(C)と(D)にbeingがあるね。beingが聞こえたら「今まさに」をイメージして。手すりは写っているけれど、今まさに設置されているところではないから正解にならない。6番にも似た例がある。

4.

😀 これは簡単。99パーセント近くのモニターが正解を選んだみたい。ところで、Part 1にこういう簡単な問題が出ると、正解が流れた時点で近くに座っている受験者がマークを塗り始めることがあるね。

😀 ありますね。音が聞こえるので少し気になります。

😎 その音に合わせて自分も塗ります。

😀 勇気があるなぁ。

😀 合ってるとは限らないのにね。これからは自力で解答するように。

5. DL 071 🇺🇸 正解：**D**　易 ■■■□□□□ 難　選択率： (A) 24.4% (B) 3.5% (C) 1.1% **(D) 70.7%**

(A) Food items are stored on shelves.
(B) Some people are setting up a canopy.
(C) A customer is paying some money.
(D) A vendor is selling some merchandise.

☐ food item: 食品
☐ store: 動 ～を入れる、収容する
☐ shelf: 名 棚
☐ set up ～: ～を据え付ける、組み立てる
☐ canopy: 名 天蓋型のひさし
☐ customer: 名 客
☐ pay: 動 ～を払う
☐ vendor: 名 売り主
☐ merchandise: 名 商品

(A) 食品が棚に入れられています。
(B) 何人かの人々がひさしを取り付けています。
(C) 客がいくらかお金を払っています。
(D) 商人がいくつかの商品を売っています。

▶解説 vender（商人）と思われる男性が merchandise（商品）を売っている様子を描写した(D)が正解です。food items（食物）が客に見えるように置かれていますが、棚にないため(A)は不正解です。写真の上の方に canopy（ひさし）がありますが、それを設置している様子ではありません。また、客と思われる人物がいますが、支払いの場面ではありません。

---

6. DL 072 🇦🇺 正解：**B**　易 ■■■□□□□ 難　選択率： (A) 0.4% **(B) 83.0%** (C) 15.5% (D) 0.4%

(A) A rug is being measured.
(B) Cushions are placed on the sofa.
(C) Some frames are being hung on the wall.
(D) The armchairs are facing the paintings.

☐ rug: 名 じゅうたん
☐ measure: 動 ～を測る
☐ place: 動 ～を置く、配置する
☐ frame: 名 額縁
☐ hang: 動 ～をつるす　＊hung は過去分詞
☐ armchair: 名 肘掛け椅子
☐ face: 動 ～に向く
☐ painting: 名 絵

(A) じゅうたんが測られています。
(B) クッションがソファに置かれています。
(C) いくつかの額縁が壁に掛けられています。
(D) 肘掛け椅子が絵に向いています。

▶解説 部屋に設置されている物の位置や状態がポイントです。正解は、クッションがソファの上に置かれている様子を描写した(B)です。床に rug（じゅうたん）があったり、壁に frame（額縁）があったりしますが、選択肢で使われている動詞の表現が写真と合致しないため不正解です。(D)の armchairs は「肘置き付きの椅子」のことですが、写真にありません。

((📡)) ゼミ 生中継　　😀Hiro 😊Mai 😺Yasu 🙂Dai 😆Saki

5.

😺 ちょっとスマホでcanopyを画像検索して。

😆 やってます。

😺 canopyはテントみたいだよね。じゃあ、tentも検索して。

😆 ほぼ同じです。

😺 そう。最後にawningも調べて。こっちはどう?

😊 微妙に違います。

😀 全部ナナメってますね。

😺 awningだけ建物から突き出しているよね。こうやって似た物を画像検索で比べると違いが見えやすいし、記憶に残りやすい。この3つは Part 1 頻出の「日よけ3兄弟」だから忘れないで。

😀 ほかにも3兄弟がいるんですか。

😺 いる。Test 3 で紹介するよ。

6.

😺 (C)はかなり魅力的だから上級者がミスしてもおかしくない。動詞が are hungだったら正解になる。

😆 やっぱり、(C)にはbeingがあったんですね……。最初は(B)が正解だと思っていましたが、(C)を聞いて不安になって、(C)を塗ってしまいました。

😺 いったん決めた答えを変えると間違える。「TOEICあるあるランキング第1位」だよ。

Part 2 応答問題

---

7. DL 075 🇨🇦 🇬🇧 **正解：B** 易 ■■■■■□□□□□ 難 　選択率：(A) 6.0% **(B) 65.7%** (C) 27.9%

Where will the banquet be held?
(A) I'm going to the bank in a minute.
(B) At Brando's Seafood Restaurant.
(C) On the way.

☐ banquet: 名 宴会
☐ hold: 動 ～を開催する ＊held は過去分詞
☐ in a minute: すぐに　☐ on the way: 途中で

宴会はどこで開催されますか。
(A) 私はすぐに銀行へ行きます。
(B) Brando's Seafood
　　Restaurant で。
(C) 途中なんです。

▶解説 Where ～? で宴会が開かれる「場所」を問うています。それに対し、具体的なレストラン名を答えた (B) が正解です。(A) は質問文の banquet に似た音の bank を引っ掛けに用いています。(C) の On the way. は、「途中で」という意味の表現です。

---

8. DL 076 🇦🇺 🇨🇦 **正解：C** 易 ■■□□□□□□□□ 難 　選択率：(A) 7.1% (B) 2.1% **(C) 90.5%**

What do you think of the fitness center?
(A) A special membership.
(B) An hour or two.
(C) It's in a nice location.

☐ fitness center: フィットネスセンター
☐ special: 形 特別な　☐ membership: 名 会員であること
☐ nice: 形 良い、素敵な　☐ location: 名 場所、店

フィットネスセンターについてどう思いますか。
(A) 特別会員です。
(B) 1、2時間です。
(C) いい場所にありますよね。

▶解説 What do you think ～? でフィットネスセンターへの「意見」を尋ねています。それに対し、「いい場所にある」と答えている (C) が正解です。(A) の「特別会員」という発言や、(B) の「時間」に関する発言では会話が成立しません。

---

9. DL 077 🇨🇦 🇬🇧 **正解：B** 易 ■□□□□□□□□□ 難 　選択率：(A) 3.9% **(B) 92.9%** (C) 2.8%

When did we last clean the refrigerator?
(A) In the main office.
(B) A couple of months ago.
(C) No, I use a dry cleaner.

☐ last: 副 最後に　☐ refrigerator: 名 冷蔵庫
☐ main office: 本社　☐ a couple of ～: 2、3の～
☐ dry cleaner: ドライクリーニング店

最後に冷蔵庫を掃除したのはいつですか。
(A) 本社で。
(B) 2、3カ月前。
(C) いいえ、私はドライクリーニング店を利用します。

▶解説 When ～? で最後に冷蔵庫を掃除した「時」が問われているので、「2、3カ月前」と答えている (B) が正解です。(A) は「場所」を答えているので不正解です。WH で始まる疑問文に Yes/No で答えることはできないので、(C) も不正解です。

---

10. DL 078 🇺🇸 🇺🇸 **正解：A** 易 ■■■□□□□□□□ 難 　選択率：**(A) 82.0%** (B) 3.2% (C) 14.5%

Where should I leave these pizzas?
(A) There's a dining room over there.
(B) If you have to.
(C) Just what I ordered.

☐ leave: 動 ～を置く　☐ dining room: 食堂
☐ over there: あそこに、向こうに
☐ have to ～: ～しなければならない
☐ just: 副 まさに、ちょうど　☐ order: 動 ～を注文する

これらのピザをどこに置けばいいですか。
(A) あちらに食堂があります。
(B) そうしなければいけないなら。
(C) まさに私が注文したものです。

▶解説 Where ～? で「場所」を尋ねています。ピザを置いておく場所を問われ、「あちらに食堂があります」と答えている (A) が正解です。(B) や (C) では、「場所」を尋ねた質問への答えにはなっていないので、いずれも不適切です。

((📡)) ゼミ 生 中継　　　　　　　😀 Hiro 😀 Mai 😀 Yasu 😀 Dai 😀 Saki

7.
😀 これは簡単だよね。間違えるとすれば (C) かな？

😀 On the way. は大学の英会話の授業で習いました。「家に帰るところ」は、確か I'm on the way home. ですよね？

😀 その通り。英会話を中心に英語を学べば、Part 2 が得意になるよ。

8.
😀 What do you think ～? は「～についてどう思う？」だから、絶対に

主語と動詞を含む「節」で答えることになるよね。だから、(A) と (B) のような「句」は聞いた瞬間に消去できる。

10.
😀 しまった～。(C) の Just を聞き間違えて、That's what I ordered. だと思い込んじゃった。

😀 ん？　「ピザをどこに置くか？」に「私が注文した」では会話が成立しないよ。

11. ^{DL} 079 正解：**A**　易 ■■■■■■□ 難　選択率：**(A) 21.2%** (B) 29.7% (C) 48.8%

Don't you want a microwave for the kitchen?
(A) I'm waiting for approval.
(B) At an electronics store.
(C) No, I'm in the kitchen now.

□ microwave: 名 電子レンジ
□ kitchen: 名 台所、キッチン
□ wait for 〜: 〜を待つ　□ approval: 名 承認
□ electronics store: 電器店

キッチンに電子レンジが欲しくないですか。
(A) 承認を待っているんです。
(B) 電器店で。
(C) いいえ、私は今キッチンにいます。

▶解説 否定疑問文で「電子レンジが欲しくないのか」と相手の意向を尋ねています。「承認を待っている」と答えることで、「欲しいと思ったので、その意向は既に伝達した」ということを述べている (A) が自然な応答です。

---

12. ^{DL} 080 正解：**B**　易 ■■■□□□□ 難　選択率：(A) 3.5% **(B) 89.4%** (C) 6.4%

Where is the key to the storage room?
(A) That's correct.
(B) In my drawer.
(C) This evening.

□ storage room: 貯蔵室、倉庫
□ correct: 形 正しい　□ drawer: 名 引き出し

倉庫の鍵はどこですか。
(A) それは正しいです。
(B) 私の引き出しの中です。
(C) 今晩です。

▶解説 Where 〜? で「場所」が問われています。それに対し、「私の引き出しの中」と答えた (B) が正解です。(C) の「今晩」では、会話が成立しません。

---

13. ^{DL} 081 正解：**C**　易 ■■■■□□□ 難　選択率：(A) 28.3% (B) 9.2% **(C) 61.8%**

I'm not expected to work extra hours today, am I?
(A) Let me know, then.
(B) It was one and a half meters.
(C) You can go home now.

□ expect 〜 to ...: 〜が…することを期待する
□ work extra hours: 残業する　□ then: 副 それなら

私は今日、残業することを期待されてはいませんよね？
(A) それなら、私に教えてください。
(B) 1.5メートルでした。
(C) もう帰っていいですよ。

▶解説 付加疑問文で「私は今日、残業をしなくてもいいよね」と「確認」がなされています。直接的に Yes/No では答えず、「もう家に帰っていい」と答えることで、「残業をしなくていい」ということを伝えている (C) が正解です。

(((♦))) ゼミ 生 中継　 😀Hiro 😊Mai 😀Yasu 😎Dai 😀Saki

11. ....

😀 モニターの正答率が低い。サキ、これはどうだった？

😀 (A)を聞いて「違う」、(B)を聞いて「違う」、(C)を聞いて「これも違う」だったので「はぁ？」となりました。

😀 それ、「TOEICあるあるランキング第5位」だよ。

😊 「承認を待っている」ってどういうことですか。

😎 学生だとピンと来ないか。ダイ、教えてあげて。

😎 会社に「電子レンジを買いたい」と申請して返事を待っているという

こと。キッチンの備品の話です。

😊 会社にキッチンがあるとは知りませんでした。

😀 よっぽど小さい会社以外には、キッチンはあるよ。

13. ....

😀 (A)を選んだのか。Let me know, then. をどう解釈したの？

😀 「残業するべきかどうか分かったら教えて」みたいな。

😎 それは質問者のセリフでしょ？

😀 え……。あ、そうか。試験中はそこまで頭が働かないな〜。

153

Part 2 応答問題

---

14. DL 082 🇨🇦🇦🇺 正解：**A** 易▬▬□□□□ 難 選択率：**(A) 91.5%** (B) 7.1% (C) 0.7%

Which floor tiles would you like to use in the lobby?
(A) The blue ones.
(B) In front of the reception.
(C) I agree with you.

☐ floor tile: 床タイル ☐ lobby: 图 ロビー
☐ in front of 〜：〜の前に ☐ reception: 图 受付
☐ agree: 動 賛成する、意見が合う

ロビーにどの床タイルを使いたいですか。
(A) 青いやつです。
(B) 受付の前です。
(C) 私はあなたに賛成です。

▶解説 Which 〜？で「どの」床タイルを使いたいかを問うています。質問文の floor tiles を代名詞 ones に言い換えて「青いの」と答えた(A)が正解です。

---

15. DL 083 🇬🇧🇺🇸 正解：**A** 易▬▬▬□□□ 難 選択率：**(A) 52.7%** (B) 14.1% (C) 32.5%

This building has a parking garage in the basement.
(A) Most of my employees drive to work.
(B) I went to an airport.
(C) The park is beautiful this time of year.

☐ parking garage: 駐車場 ☐ basement: 图 地下
☐ most of 〜：ほとんどの〜 ☐ employee: 图 従業員
☐ drive to 〜：車で〜へ行く ☐ airport: 图 空港
☐ this time of year: この季節

この建物は地下に駐車場があります。
(A) うちのほとんどの従業員は車で仕事に来ます。
(B) 私は空港へ行きました。
(C) この季節、公園はとても美しいです。

▶解説 「この建物の地下に駐車場がある」に対し、「ほとんどの従業員が車で来る」と返答することで、「駐車場があるのは助かる」という気持ちを述べた(A)が正解です。(B)の「空港」や(C)の「公園」の話はしていないので、それぞれ不正解です。

---

16. DL 084 🇬🇧🇨🇦 正解：**C** 易▬▬□□□□ 難 選択率：(A) 13.8% (B) 12.0% **(C) 73.1%**

Aren't you going to inspect the factory today?
(A) We're already at full capacity.
(B) I know they're coming.
(C) Yes, I'll be there in a few minutes.

☐ inspect: 動 〜を視察する、立ち入り検査する
☐ factory: 图 工場 ☐ already: 副 すでに
☐ at full capacity: 最大生産能力で、フル稼働で
☐ in a few minutes: すぐに、数分で

今日、工場を視察するんではないんですか。
(A) すでにフル稼働しています。
(B) 彼らが来ることは知っています。
(C) はい、数分後に着きます。

▶解説 今日、工場の視察をするのかを尋ねています。Yesで「視察する」と答え、「数分後に着く」と情報を追加した(C)が正解です。Aren't you 〜？のような否定疑問文に対する応答は、Are you 〜？と聞かれた場合と変わりません。

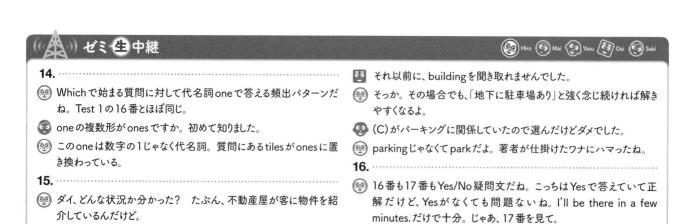

((∙)) ゼミ生中継 😎Hiro 😀Mai 😁Yasu 😵Dai 😆Saki

14.

😎 Whichで始まる質問に対して代名詞 one で答える頻出パターンだね。Test 1の16番とほぼ同じ。

😀 one の複数形が ones ですか。初めて知りました。

😁 この one は数字の1じゃなく代名詞。質問にある tiles が ones に置き換わっている。

15.

😆 ダイ、どんな状況か分かった？ たぶん、不動産屋が客に物件を紹介しているんだけど。

😵 それ以前に、building を聞き取れませんでした。

😎 そっか。その場合でも、「地下に駐車場あり」と強く念じ続ければ解きやすくなるよ。

😵 (C)がパーキングに関係していたので選んだけどダメでした。

😎 parking じゃなくて park だよ。著者が仕掛けたワナにハマったね。

16.

😆 16番も17番も Yes/No 疑問文だね。こっちは Yes で答えていて正解だけど、Yes がなくても問題ないね。I'll be there in a few minutes. だけで十分。じゃあ、17番を見て。

17. DL 085 🇦🇺 🇺🇸　正解：**A**　易 ▰▰▱▱▱▱▱▱ 難　選択率：(A) **71.4%** (B) 9.9% (C) 18.0%

Does Geoff Bowden still work here?
(A) He's the branch manager now.
(B) I try to walk at least once a day.
(C) Yes, anytime you like.

☐ still: 副 まだ、今なお　☐ branch: 名 支店
☐ manager: 名 責任者、長　☐ at least: 少なくとも
☐ anytime: 副 いつでも

Geoff Bowdenはまだこちらで働いていますか。
(A) 彼は今は支店長です。
(B) 私は少なくとも1日に1回歩くようにしています。
(C) はい、いつでもお好きなときに。

▶解説 「Geoffがまだここで働いているか」という問いに対し、「今は支店長をしている」と答えることで、「まだ働いている」と伝えている (A) が正解です。(C) はYesの後の内容が質問への答えになっていないので不正解です。

---

18. DL 086 🇨🇦 🇨🇦　正解：**C**　易 ▰▰▰▰▰▱▱▱ 難　選択率：(A) 11.7% (B) 19.1% (C) **68.6%**

Would you like me to come with you to Paris, or will you take someone else?
(A) No, it was me.
(B) I liked it very much.
(C) I'm going alone.

☐ alone: 副 1人で

あなたと一緒に私がパリに行きましょうか、それとも別の人を連れていきますか。
(A) いいえ、それは私でした。
(B) 私はそれをとても気に入りました。
(C) 私は1人で行きます。

▶解説 選択疑問文で「一緒に来てほしいか、別の人を連れて行くのか」と尋ねています。「AかB」かと聞かれても、直接どちらかを答えるとは限りません。ここでは「1人で行く」と答えた (C) が正解です。

---

19. DL 087 🇦🇺 🇬🇧　正解：**B**　易 ▰▰▰▱▱▱▱▱ 難　選択率：(A) 9.9% (B) **79.5%** (C) 10.2%

Who can help me set up the large screen?
(A) That should be helpful.
(B) The instructor won't use it.
(C) Much smaller than that.

☐ set up ～: ～を据え付ける、設置する
☐ large: 形 大きな　☐ screen: 名 スクリーン
☐ helpful: 形 役立つ
☐ instructor: 名 インストラクター

誰が大きなスクリーンを設置するのを手伝ってくれますか。
(A) それはとても助かります。
(B) インストラクターはそれを使いません。
(C) あれよりももっと小さいです。

▶解説 Who ～?でスクリーンの設置を手伝える「人物」が問われています。ここでは「インストラクターはそれを使わない」と答えることで、「スクリーンは使わないので、設置する必要はない」ということを伝えた (B) が自然な応答です。

📡))) ゼミ 生 中継　

17.
😀 16番と違って、正解にYesはない。でも、会話は成立する。結局、YesやNoがあるかどうかに関係なく、大事なのは答えている内容だね。(C) は会話が成立しないけれど、選びたくなった？

😮 質問者はGeoffに会いに来ているっぽいので、「会える時間を知りたいはず」と応答者が察して「はい、何時でも大丈夫です」と言っていると思いました。

😀 ナイス妄想だけど、Geoffに会いたいとは言っていない。Yes. の後に、You can see him anytime if you like.と言えば大丈夫。

18.
😀 選択疑問の応答パターンは限られている。大まかに言って、「どちらかを選ぶ」か「どちらも選ばない」の2種類だよ。ここでは後者。他の可能性として「質問返し」もある。この質問に質問を返すとすれば、

どうなる？

😮 「一体、何の話？」

😀 そう、そんな感じ。「あなたはムンバイに行くよね？」とかね。

19.
😀 難問だと思ったけど、モニターの正答率は高い。初級から上級まで全グループで約8割が (B) を選んでいる。ダイは何を選んだ？

😎 質問がWhoで、(B) だけ人を答えていたので即決しました。

😊 私もです。講師が手伝うんですよね。

😀 そうだっけ？　講師が自分でスクリーンを設置するんでしょ。

😮 違う違う。スクリーンは不要なんだよ。そうか、The instructorだけ聞いて選んだら、たまたま正解だったのか。

😊 その通り。

Part 2 応答問題

---

20. DL 088 🇬🇧 🇺🇸　正解：**A**　易 ▰▰▰▱▱▱▱▱ 難　選択率：**(A) 70.0%** (B) 14.1% (C) 15.2%

You should download a travel app for your trip.
(A) Thanks, I'll try that.
(B) An online form.
(C) In August, this year.

☐ download: 動 〜をダウンロードする
☐ app: 名 アプリ ＊application program の略

旅行用に旅行アプリをダウンロードすべきですよ。
(A) ありがとう、試してみます。
(B) オンラインフォームです。
(C) 今年の8月に。

▶解説 You should 〜は、相手に提案する表現です。「アプリをダウンロードするべきだ」という提案に対し、お礼を述べ、「試してみる」と答えた (A) が正解です。(B) の「オンラインフォーム」や(C)の「今年の8月」では提案の内容とかみ合いません。

---

21. DL 089 🇦🇺 🇦🇺　正解：**B**　易 ▰▰▰▱▱▱▱▱ 難　選択率：(A) 33.6% **(B) 55.1%** (C) 10.6%

When does the train leave?
(A) From Platform Seven.
(B) You still have time to buy something.
(C) I'd appreciate it.

☐ leave: 動 出発する
☐ still: 副 まだ、今なお
☐ appreciate: 動 〜を感謝する

電車はいつ出発しますか。
(A) 7番線からです。
(B) まだ何かを買う時間はありますよ。
(C) 感謝します。

▶解説 When 〜？で電車の発車「時刻」を問うことで、発車までの残り時間を確認しようとしています。その意図をくみ取り、「まだ買い物する時間はあるよ」と答えることで、発車時刻までまだ余裕があることを伝えている (B) が正解です。

---

22. DL 090 🇨🇦 🇬🇧　正解：**A**　易 ▰▰▰▰▰▰▱▱ 難　選択率：**(A) 29.3%** (B) 41.7% (C) 28.6%

Michael has been working a bit too hard lately, hasn't he?
(A) I asked him to take some time off.
(B) It's not as hard as it looks.
(C) He's usually here on time.

☐ a bit: ちょっと、少し　☐ work hard: 一生懸命に働く
☐ lately: 副 最近、このごろ
☐ take time off: 休みを取る
☐ usually: 副 たいてい、普段は
☐ on time: 時間通りに

Michaelは最近、ちょっと一生懸命働き過ぎですよね。
(A) 彼に少し休みを取るよう頼みました。
(B) 見た目ほど難しくはありません。
(C) 彼はたいてい時間通りにここにいます。

▶解説 付加疑問文で「最近、Michaelは少し働き過ぎだよね」と「同意」を求めています。「彼に少し休むように言った」ということで、「働き過ぎだ」と感じている男性の意見に同意を示している (A) が正解です。

(((📻 ゼミ 生中継　😀Hiro 😀Mai 😀Yasu 😀Dai 😀Saki

20.
😀 アプリは英語でappだけど、「プ」はほとんど聞こえない。何度も聞いて慣れておいてね。TOEICにappは頻出するから。

21.
😀 (A)を選んだ？　質問がWhereだと思ったのかな。

😀 と言うか、WhereかWhenか分からないまま聞いたら、(A)が場所を答えたので、質問がWhereだったんだろうって逆算しました。

😀 なるほど。で、(B)を聞いても時刻を言っていないから、質問がWhenだったとは逆算できなかったんだな。

22.
😀 え、全員が(B)にしたの？　どうして？

😀 「彼は見た目ほどには働いていない」だと思いました。

😀 私も同じ理由です。

😀 それを言うなら、He hasn't been working as hard as it appears. のように、hardを副詞として使わなきゃ。(B)のhardは形容詞だから意味が違うし、文頭のItが何を指すか不明だよ。(B)を積極的に選ぶ人は、文法が弱い。あと、スピーキングも弱いだろうね。

😀 まるで英作文の試験みたい。

😀 もちろん。アウトプット力も間接的に測定されていることが分かったでしょ。

23. 🔽091 🇨🇦🇨🇦　正解：**C**　易▰▰▰▰▰▰難　選択率：(A) 13.8%　(B) 60.1%　**(C) 25.4%**

How long is it gonna be before I can leave for the day?
(A) I did it yesterday.
(B) It wasn't too long.
(C) We're understaffed today.

☐ gonna: ＊going to の口語表現
☐ leave for the day: 1日の仕事を終えて帰る
☐ understaffed: 形 人員不足の

私が1日の仕事を終えて帰るまで、あとどれくらいかかるんですか。
(A) 私は昨日それをやりました。
(B) それほど長くはなかったですよ。
(C) 今日は人員不足なんです。

▶解説 残りの勤務時間を問うことによって、「長く勤務しているのにまだ帰れないのか」というら立ちを表しています。その意図をくみ取り、「今日はスタッフが足りない」と勤務時間が長くなっている理由を述べた (C) が正解です。

---

24. 🔽092 🇺🇸🇦🇺　正解：**B**　易▰▰▰▰▰▰難　選択率：(A) 20.1%　**(B) 63.3%**　(C) 16.3%

I'm planning on entering the design competition.
(A) We should look at our prices again.
(B) The guidelines are on our Web site.
(C) I like the new sign.

☐ plan on -ing: ～する計画である　☐ enter: 動 ～に応募する
☐ competition: 名 コンテスト　☐ look at ～: ～を検討する
☐ guideline: 名 ガイドライン　☐ sign: 名 看板、標識

デザインコンテストに応募する予定です。
(A) もう一度わが社の価格を検討するべきです。
(B) ガイドラインはわが社のウェブサイトに載っています。
(C) 私は新しい看板が好きです。

▶解説 平叙文で「デザインのコンテストに応募しようと思っている」と意思が表明されています。それに対し、「（応募するのなら）ガイドラインがウェブサイトに載っている」とコンテストに関する情報を伝えた (B) が正解です。

---

25. 🔽093 🇨🇦🇨🇦　正解：**B**　易▰▰▰▰▰▰難　選択率：(A) 6.4%　**(B) 83.7%**　(C) 9.5%

Would you mind checking this article for errors?
(A) It didn't take me long at all.
(B) No problem.
(C) I didn't expect so many.

☐ Would you mind ～?: ～してくださいませんか。
☐ take long: 時間がかかる
☐ at all: まったく～ない　☐ expect: 動 ～を予期する

この記事に間違いがないか確認してくださいませんか。
(A) それはまったく時間がかかりませんでした。
(B) いいですよ。
(C) それほどたくさんだとは予期していませんでした。

▶解説 Would you mind ～? は「～してくださいませんか」という依頼表現です。記事の内容確認を依頼され、「いいよ」と返答した (B) が正解です。Would you mind ～? に対し、承諾する場合の返事に Not at all.（まったく構いません）もあります。

---

26. 🔽094 🇦🇺🇺🇸　正解：**A**　易▰▰▰▰▰▰難　選択率：**(A) 88.7%**　(B) 7.4%　(C) 3.5%

How many name tags did you bring?
(A) I thought we'd have a lot of guests.
(B) Twenty years ago.
(C) Yes, that's yours.

☐ name tag: 名札　☐ a lot of ～: たくさんの～

いくつ名札を持ってきたんですか。
(A) 多くのゲストが来ると思ったんです。
(B) 20年前です。
(C) はい、それはあなたのものです。

▶解説 How many ～? で持ってきた名札の「数」を尋ねることで、「いったい何個あるのか」という驚きを表しています。その意図をくみ取り、「多くのゲストが来ると思った」と名札を多く持参した理由を説明した (A) が自然な応答です。

📻 ゼミ生中継　😀Hiro 😀Mai 😀Yasu 😀Dai 😀Saki

23.
😀 初級グループの7割、上級でも5割が (B) を選んでいる。It won't be too long. なら正解になるけれど、過去形は絶対に変だよ。
😀 (C) が正解に聞こえなかったのが敗因です。
😀 どのように聞こえたの？
😀 We're under staff today. に聞こえました。
😀 同じです。場所を答えていると思いました。
😀 そういうことか。under staff ってスタッフの下？
😀 頭が混乱して、仕方なく (B) にしただけです。

26.
😀 少し高度な応答だけど、消去法で解いたのかな。
😀 はい。How many を意識して解きました。
😀 質問者は名札の数を正確に知りたいわけじゃない。例えば、名札は30個しか必要ないのに、研修室にあまりにもたくさんあるからキレている。だから、仮に、答える人がバカ正直に「56個です」とか言ったら、もっとキレる。
😀 間違いない。
😀 「ごめんなさい」の方がマシですね。
😀 いいこと言うね。(A) の頭に Sorry. を付けても正解だよ。

Part 2 ▶ Listening Section

Part 2 応答問題

27. DL 095 🇦🇺 🇬🇧 正解：**B** 易 ▰▰▰▱▱▱▱ 難 選択率：(A) 26.1% **(B) 54.8%** (C) 18.4%

It looks like the bus will be ten minutes late.
(A) I haven't seen it before.
(B) We'll have some coffee and wait.
(C) No later than Friday.

□ look like 〜：〜のように見える、〜のようだ
□ late: 形 時間に遅れる、遅れた
□ wait: 動 待つ
□ no later than 〜：〜よりも遅れることなく

バスは10分遅れるようです。
(A) 私は今までそれを見たことが
　　ありません。
(B) コーヒーを飲みながら待ちま
　　しょう。
(C) 金曜日までに。

▶解説 平叙文で「バスが遅れるようだ」と報告しています。それに対し、「(バスが遅れるなら) コーヒーを飲みながら待とう」と返している (B) が自然な応答です。「バスの遅延」が話題なので、(A) と (C) では話がかみ合いません。

---

28. DL 096 🇺🇸 🇬🇧 正解：**C** 易 ▰▰▰▱▱▱▱ 難 選択率：(A) 10.2% (B) 15.5% **(C) 73.5%**

Why haven't the judges announced the winner of the contest yet?
(A) She must be so happy.
(B) Yes, it's getting colder and colder.
(C) They're reviewing the rules.

□ judge: 名 審査員　□ announce: 動 〜を発表する
□ winner: 名 優勝者、受賞者　□ contest: 名 コンテスト
□ yet: 副 まだ　□ review: 動 〜をよく調べる

審査員たちはなぜまだコンテストの受賞者を発表していないんですか。
(A) 彼女は幸せに違いありません。
(B) はい、だんだん寒くなっています。
(C) 彼らはルールをよく調べているんです。

▶解説 コンテストの受賞者がまだ発表されていない理由が問われているのに対し、「ルールを調べている」と事情を説明している (C) が正解です。WH疑問文にYes/Noで答えることはできないので、Yesと聞こえた瞬間に (B) は不正解だと判断できます。

---

29. DL 097 🇬🇧 🇨🇦 正解：**C** 易 ▰▰▱▱▱▱▱ 難 選択率：(A) 12.7% (B) 13.1% **(C) 73.9%**

Are you leading the tour of the museum today?
(A) It's just won an award.
(B) The cost of admission.
(C) Yes, the university group is coming at noon.

□ lead: 動 〜を案内する　□ tour: 名 ツアー
□ museum: 名 博物館、美術館　□ just: 副 まさに、ちょうど
□ win: 動 〜に勝つ　＊won は過去分詞　□ award: 名 賞
□ cost: 名 費用　□ admission: 名 入場
□ university: 名 大学

今日、博物館のツアーを案内するんですか。
(A) それはちょうど賞を取りました。
(B) 入場料です。
(C) はい、大学のグループが正午に来ます。

▶解説 Yes/No疑問文で「ツアーを案内するのか」と問うています。Yesで「案内する」と肯定し、「大学のグループが正午に来る」と追加情報を述べた (C) が正解です。(A) は賞を受賞したことを、(B) は「入場料」と述べているので、いずれも不正解です。

((🗼)) ゼミ 生 中継　　　　　　　　　😊Hiro 🙂Mai 😺Yasu 😎Dai 😊Saki

27. ⋯⋯⋯⋯⋯⋯⋯⋯⋯⋯⋯⋯⋯⋯⋯⋯⋯⋯⋯⋯⋯⋯⋯⋯

😺 (A) をどう解釈した？

😊 「バスが遅れたことなんてない」と言っているかと思いました。

😺 それを言うなら It has never happened before. だよ。

😎 10分遅れるだけでコーヒーを飲んで待つとは妙ですね。

😺 ま、いいじゃないか。

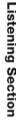

30. 🇦🇺 🇨🇦 正解：**C** 易 ▬▬▬▬▬ 難 選択率：(A) 29.0% (B) 7.1% **(C) 63.6%**

Should we ask the suppliers for a discount, or raise our prices?
(A) About twenty percent.
(B) In the supplies closet.
(C) Let's talk to them first.

☐ supplier: 名 供給業者
☐ discount: 名 値引き、割引
☐ raise: 動 (価格を) 引き上げる
☐ supply: 名 (複数形で) 生活用品
☐ closet: 名 戸棚、押し入れ

供給業者に値引きを頼みましょうか、それともわが社の価格を引き上げましょうか。
(A) 約20パーセントです。
(B) 生活用品の棚の中に。
(C) 最初に彼らに話をしましょう。

▶解説 選択疑問文で「供給業者に値引きを頼むべきか、値段を上げるべきか」と尋ねています。質問文のsuppliers (供給業者) を代名詞themに言い換えて、「まずは彼らに話そう」と答えた (C) が正解です。

---

31. 🇬🇧 🇺🇸 正解：**A** 易 ▬▬▬▬▬ 難 選択率：**(A) 33.9%** (B) 52.3% (C) 12.7%

Are we going to take a subway from here?
(A) A parade is about to begin downtown.
(B) Yes, it's taken a while.
(C) Only a few passengers.

☐ subway: 名 地下鉄
☐ parade: 名 パレード、行進
☐ about to 〜: まさに〜しようとしている
☐ downtown: 副 商業地区で、都心部で
☐ take a while: しばらく時間がかかる
☐ only a few: ほんのわずかだけ
☐ passenger: 名 乗客

ここから地下鉄を使いますか。
(A) 都心部でまさにパレードが始まろうとしています。
(B) はい、しばらく時間がかかりました。
(C) ほんのわずかな乗客です。

▶解説 地下鉄に乗るのかどうかを問うています。「都心部でパレードが始まる」と答えることで、地下鉄に乗ろうと思った事情を間接的に説明している (A) が正解です。(B) はYesの後の内容が質問とかみ合っていません。

Part 2 ▼ Listening Section

((📡)) **ゼミ 生 中継** 😀 Hiro 😊 Mai 😎 Yasu 🙂 Dai 😄 Saki

30.

😊 18番でもやった選択疑問だね。「どちらかを選ぶ」か「どちらも選ばない」か。どっちだった?

😎 値引きを頼むことを選んでいます。

😀 そう。Let's talk to them first. は ask the suppliers for a discount を別の言葉で表現しただけだよ。ただ、firstと言っているから、値引きが断られたら、自分たちの売値を上げる可能性が高い。つまり、片方だけを選んでいるわけじゃなくて、両方を選んでいるとも言える。ところで、supplier って誰のことか分かる?

😊 聞いたことありません。

😀 簡単に言えば仕入れ先のこと。例えば、喫茶店はコーヒー豆やパンをどこかの会社から買っているはずだよね。売っている会社がsupplierと呼ばれる。

😎 (A) が不正解なのは「約20パーセント」だけでは意味が通じないからですか。

😀 そう。何を言いたいか分からない。2割引きのことを言いたいのか、2割値上げすると言いたいのか、それ以外なのか。言葉が足りない。

31.

😀 (B) は「しばらく時間がかかった」だから、正解になり得ない。マイはどうして選んだの?

😊 (A) のparade が「パレード」に聞こえなくて……。

😀 それで、(B) のYesに釣られた?

😊 答えがないと思いながら適当に塗りました。

😀 「パレードのせいで車では行けないから、地下鉄で行く」みたいな状況で成立する会話だね。

😎 聞いた瞬間にそこまで判断できないな〜。

🙂 同感。

😀 よし、Part 2は終わり。ちゃんと復習してね。消去法に頼ることなく全問をスラスラ解答できる状態を目指すこと。では、Part 3に進もう。

TOEICよろず相談所　ヒロの部屋

⑦日本では過去問を買えないの?

質問があります。韓国では過去問が販売されているそうですが、日本では売っていないのでしょうか。

日本の書店では買えないはずです。ただし、韓国の本を専門的に扱っている書店は日本にもあります。オンラインで検索してみてください。

分かりました。過去問はやはり買った方がいいでしょうか。

過去問を使って勉強するのは悪くはないですが、**日本語の解説と訳が全く載っていないので使いにくい**かもしれません。

そうですよね。そこが心配です。

でも、**日本語が載っていないからこそ、英語に集中できて良い**と言う人もいます。

なるほど。そういう効果はありそうです。

ただし、日本では「公式教材」がたくさん売られているので、わざわざ韓国の本を買う必要はないと思いますよ。趣味としてTOEIC本を集めたいなら止めませんが、スコアアップのための勉強ツールとしては、買う必要はありません。それより、**手元にある問題集や模試の中身をしっかり吸収することの方がよっぽど大事**です。

そうですね。ありがとうございました。

Part 3 会話問題

DL 101 **Questions 32 through 34** refer to the following conversation.

M: Hi, Greta. Um... ❶ I was hoping to talk with you about our plans for the sales trip.

W: Sure thing, Greg. We'll have to finish by eleven o'clock, though. ❷ I've got a meeting with a client in Runcorn this afternoon. We'll be inspecting the building site.

M: You know there's a football game at Runcorn Stadium this afternoon, don't you? There will be a lot of traffic.

W: Oh. I didn't think about that. ❸ I'd better call the client and see if we can reschedule. (84w/35 sec.)

問題32-34は次の会話に関するものです。
男：やあ、Greta。ええと、君と話したいと思ってたんだよ、営業の出張計画について。
女：いいわよ、Greg。でも、11時までには終わらせなくちゃ。私、午後にRuncornでお客さんと会うことになってるの。建設現場を視察するのよ。
男：午後にRuncorn Stadiumでサッカーの試合があるって知ってるよね？　かなり道が混むだろうね。
女：ああ。それは考えなかったわ。お客さんに電話して、予定を変更できないか聞いた方がいいわね。

□ inspect: 動 ～を視察する　□ site: 名 用地　□ football: 名 サッカー　□ reschedule: 動 ～の計画を変更する

---

32. 正解：**C**　易 ■■■■□□□□ 難　選択率：(A) 8.8% (B) 2.1% **(C) 86.9%** (D) 1.8%

What does the man want to discuss?
(A) Deadlines for sales reports
(B) The location of some furniture
(C) Plans for a business trip
(D) The cost of some upgrades

男性は何について話したいのですか。
(A) 営業報告書の締め切り
(B) 備品の置き場所
(C) 出張の計画
(D) 改良の費用

▶解説 男性が話し合いたい内容は男性の発言にヒントがあると考えられます。❶で男性は、営業目的の出張計画について話し合いたいと述べています。sales trip を business trip（出張）と言い換えた (C) が正解です。

□ sales report: 営業報告書　□ furniture: 名 備品、家具　□ upgrade: 名 （品質の）向上

---

33. 正解：**B**　易 ■■■■■□□□ 難　選択率：(A) 15.2% **(B) 34.6%** (C) 42.8% (D) 7.1%

What does the woman say she will be doing in the afternoon?
(A) Attending a game
(B) Looking at a building site
(C) Meeting an auditor
(D) Dealing with some problems

女性は午後に何をするつもりだと言っていますか。
(A) 試合を見に行く
(B) 建設現場を見る
(C) 監査人と会う
(D) いくつかの問題に対処する

▶解説 設問から、女性が午後の予定に言及することが推測できます。❷から女性の予定は、午後Runcornの顧客と会い、一緒に建設用地を視察することだと分かります。正解は inspect（～を視察する）を look at（～を調べる）と言い換えた (B) です。

□ attend: 動 ～に出席する　□ auditor: 名 監査役　□ deal with ～: ～を処理する

---

34. 正解：**A**　易 ■■■□□□□□ 難　選択率：**(A) 92.9%** (B) 1.4% (C) 1.1% (D) 4.2%

Why will the woman call a client?
(A) To reschedule a meeting
(B) To give a progress report
(C) To introduce a coworker
(D) To request an extension to a deadline

女性はなぜ顧客に電話をかけようとしているのですか。
(A) 会合の予定を変更するために
(B) 進捗報告をするために
(C) 同僚を紹介するために
(D) 期日の延長を依頼するために

▶解説 サッカーの試合で交通渋滞が予想されることを知らされた女性は、予定が変更できるかどうか電話で聞いた方がいいと考えていることが❸で分かります。電話をかける理由は会合の予定を変更するためだと言えます。正解は (A) です。

□ progress report: 進捗報告　□ coworker: 名 同僚　□ extension: 名 延期

ゼミ 生中継

🙂Hiro 🙂Mai 🙂Yasu 🎲Dai 🙂Saki

33. ....

🙂 女性は中盤で meeting にも building site にも触れている。だから、多くのモニターが (B) か (C) を選んだんだね。マイはどれを選んだ？

🙂 会話を聞く前に設問を読んだので、afternoon を待ち伏せしました。afternoon のような時を示す副詞が設問にある場合、その言葉よりも前にヒントが出ることが多いですよね。

🙂 そうだね。Test 1の47番で説明した通りだよ。

🙂 なので、afternoon の前に聞こえた meeting がヒントだと思って、(C) にしてしまいました。

🙂 発想は悪くない。でも、auditor の意味を知らなかった？

🙂 知っていますが、自分が聞き逃したと思いました。

🙂 なるほど。サキは？

🙂 私もマイさんと同じで、afternoon を聞こうと思っていました。それで、afternoon の直後に聞こえた building site を頼りに、(B) を選びました。ラッキーでした。

🙂 Part 3とPart 4では、聞こえた単語やフレーズがそのまま正解の選択肢に入っていることがよくある。ただ、大事なのは選択肢が丸ごと正しいかどうかを判断することだよ。この設問で言えば、auditor が間違っているから、(C) は違う。

161

Part 3 会話問題

DL 102 **Questions 35 through 37** refer to the following conversation with three speakers.

M1: Hi, ❶ we're from GeoSun Solar Panels. We're here to install some solar panels on your roof.

W: Oh, right. Will you be here long?

M1: ❷ I think we'll be here all afternoon. What do you think, Paul?

M2: ❸ I'm afraid so, but you don't need to be at home.

W: That's good.

M2: By the way, ❹ we're offering additional panels at half price this week. Would you like us to add a few more panels? We can give you a free price estimate on installation.

W: Well, I'd like to hear the estimate, but I'll be out until 7 P.M. ❺ Can you send me a text message with the price?

M1: Certainly. I think we have your number. But just in case, can you give it to us again?

W: Sure. Here's my business card.   (127w/40 sec.)

問題35-37は次の3人の話者による会話に関するものです。

男1：こんにちは、私たち、GeoSun Solar Panelsの者です。お宅の屋根にソーラーパネルを設置するために参りました。

女：ああ、分かりました。長くかかりそうですか。

男1：午後一杯かかると思いますが。どうかな、Paul？

男2：そうなると思いますが、ご在宅いただく必要はありません。

女：よかったわ。

男2：ところで、弊社では今週、追加のパネルを半額でご提供しています。あと数枚パネルを追加いたしましょうか。設置料を無料でお見積もりできますが。

女：そうね、見積もっていただきたいけど、午後7時まで戻らないのよ。携帯メールで価格を送ってくださらない？

男1：かしこまりました。お客さまの電話番号を承知していると思うのですが、念のためにもう一度教えていただけますか。

女：いいですよ。名刺をどうぞ。

□ install: 動 ～を取り付ける　□ solar panel: 太陽電池パネル、ソーラーパネル　□ roof: 名 屋根　□ I'm afraid so: 残念ですがそのようです
□ need to ～ : ～する必要がある　□ at home: 在宅して　□ by the way: ところで　□ offer: 動 ～を申し出る　□ additional: 形 追加の
□ add: 動 ～を追加する　□ estimate: 名 見積もり　□ installation: 名 取り付け、架設　□ until: 前 ～まで
□ text message: テキスト・メッセージ、携帯メッセージ　□ certainly: 副 （要求に対する返答で）もちろんです、承知しました
□ number: 名 番号　＊ここでは「電話番号」のこと　□ just in case: 念のため　□ business card: 名刺

35. 正解：B 易 ■■■■■ 難　選択率：(A) 1.4%　**(B) 92.9%**　(C) 3.9%　(D) 1.1%

What kind of business do the men work for?
(A) A cleaning service
(B) A solar power company
(C) A construction firm
(D) An Internet service provider

男性たちはどのような企業に勤めていますか。
(A) 清掃サービス会社
(B) 太陽電力会社
(C) 建設会社
(D) インターネットサービス業者

▶解説 男性1が❶で、GeoSun Solar Panelsからソーラーパネルの設置に来たと伝えています。男性2の発言❹も、追加パネル割引の申し出であることから、2人は(B)の太陽電力の会社で働いていると考えられます。

☐ business: 图 店、会社　☐ solar power：太陽電力　☐ construction: 图 建設
☐ firm: 图 会社　☐ provider: 图 供給者

---

36. 正解：A 易 ■■■■■ 難　選択率：**(A) 35.3%**　(B) 39.2%　(C) 10.2%　(D) 14.8%

What do the men imply about the job?
(A) It will take a long time.
(B) It will be carried out on another day.
(C) It has been assigned to a different team.
(D) It was requested by a company executive.

男性たちは作業について何を示唆していますか。
(A) 長時間かかるだろう。
(B) 別の日に行われるだろう。
(C) 別の班に割り当てられている。
(D) 会社の役員に依頼された。

▶解説 滞在は長時間になるかと尋ねられた男性1が❷で「午後いっぱいかかると思う」と述べ、男性2も❸で同意しています。パネル設置の仕事は時間がかかることを暗に伝えており、正解は(A)です。他の日に実施するとは言っておらず、(B)は不正解です。

☐ imply: 動 ～を暗に意味する　☐ carry out ～：～を実行する　☐ assign: 動 ～を割り当てる
☐ request: 動 ～を要請する、頼む　☐ executive: 图 役員

---

37. 正解：D 易 ■■■■■ 難　選択率：(A) 2.5%　(B) 2.8%　(C) 1.4%　**(D) 92.6%**

What does the woman ask the men to do?
(A) Lock the door
(B) Return her keys
(C) Take out some garbage
(D) Send a text message

女性は男性たちに何をするよう頼んでいますか。
(A) 扉を施錠する
(B) 彼女に鍵を返す
(C) ごみを出す
(D) 携帯メールを送る

▶解説 ❺で女性は、パネルの価格を携帯メールで送ってほしいと頼んでおり、(D)が正解です。他の選択肢については全く言及がありません。男性の発言にも依頼表現Can you ～?がありますが、問われているのは設問の主語である女性が依頼する内容です。

☐ lock: 動 鍵を掛ける　☐ return: 動 ～を返す　☐ take out ～：～を出す　☐ garbage: 图 ごみ

(((📡 ゼミ 生 中継　　　　　　　　😎Hiro 😊Mai 😎Yasu 😐Dai 😎Saki

36.
😎 2問目の正答率が極端に低い。何を選んだ？
😊 (B)です。「午後7時まで外出している」とか何とか聞こえたので、作業が別の日に延期されたと思いました。
😎 確かに女性はI'll be out until 7 P.M.と言っているけど、ソーラーパネルの設置する男性の仕事は今日の午後に終わる。設問にある主語はmenだから、男性のセリフにヒントがあると考えなきゃ。
😎 あ、そうか。「言う」系の動詞が設問にある場合は、主語の人物がヒントを言うんですよね。

37.
😎 ダイ、正解にあるtext messageって何？
😐 メールのことですか？
😎 惜しい。日本語で言えばメールと同じようなものだけど、英語のtext messageは、携帯電話で送るメールのことだよ。
😐 LINEもそうですか。
😎 そう。PC以外でやりとりするテキスト情報はtext messageだよ。

163

Part 3 会話問題

Questions 38 through 40 refer to the following conversation.

M: ❶ The next interviewee is Jules Martinez. Um... He has taken pictures for a number of major magazines and advertising campaigns. Shall I show him in?

W: Well, just a moment. ❷ He was supposed to send us some samples of the photographs he took in previous assignments. ❸ I contacted him earlier in the week to remind him, but we haven't received them.

M: I see. What should I do?

W: We can't interview him today. I'm interviewing some other applicants on Thursday. ❹ Please ask him to e-mail me the work samples and invite him to come back then. (94w/35 sec.)

問題38-40は次の会話に関するものです。

男：次に面接するのは Jules Martinez さんです。ええと……。彼はたくさんの一流雑誌や宣伝キャンペーン向けに写真を撮ってきました。入ってもらいましょうか。

女：いえ、ちょっと待って。彼はこれまでの仕事で撮影した写真のサンプルをいくつか送ってくれることになってたわよね。今週の前半に私から彼に連絡して、その件を念押ししたんだけど、まだ届いてないわ。

男：なるほど。どうしましょうか。

女：今日は彼を面接できないわ。木曜日に他の何名かと面接する予定なの。彼に、作品のサンプルを私宛てにメールで送るよう頼んで、その日に出直してくるよう伝えてちょうだい。

☐ interviewee: 图 面接を受ける人　☐ major: 形 主要な　☐ advertising: 图 宣伝　☐ show ~ in: ~を（部屋などに）通す
☐ previous: 形 前の　☐ assignment: 图 仕事　☐ receive: 動 ~を受け取る　☐ interview: 動 ~と面接する　☐ applicant: 图 応募者、候補者

---

38. 正解：**D**　易 ▮▮▮▯▯▯▯▯ 難　選択率：(A) 8.5% (B) 6.0% (C) 0.7% **(D) 84.5%**

Who is Jules Martinez?
(A) A guest speaker
(B) A sales representative
(C) A council inspector
(D) A photographer

Jules Martinez とは誰ですか。
(A) 来賓講演者
(B) 営業担当者
(C) 議会監査官
(D) 写真家

▶解説 冒頭❶で、面接を受けに来た Jules Martinez について言及しています。これまでに大手の雑誌や宣伝キャンペーンの写真を撮った経験があると紹介されていることから、(D) の「写真家」であると判断できます。

---

39. 正解：**A**　易 ▮▮▮▮▯▯▯▯ 難　選択率：**(A) 62.5%** (B) 1.8% (C) 27.6% (D) 7.8%

What problem does the woman mention?
(A) A portfolio has not been submitted.
(B) A kitchen has not been cleaned.
(C) Some information is inaccurate.
(D) Some equipment is out of order.

女性はどんな問題を指摘していますか。
(A) 作品が提出されていない。
(B) 台所が掃除されていない。
(C) 情報の一部が不正確だ。
(D) 機器の一部に不具合がある。

▶解説 女性は❷で、Martinez さんがこれまでの仕事で撮った写真のサンプルを送ってくるはずだったことに触れています。さらに❸の「念押ししたにもかかわらずまだ届いていない」との発言から、問題は作品集がまだ提出されていないことだと分かります。(A) が正解です。

☐ portfolio: 图（代表作を収めた紙挟み式の）作品集、写真集　☐ submit: 動 ~を提出する
☐ inaccurate: 形 不正確な　☐ out of order: 故障して

---

40. 正解：**D**　易 ▮▮▮▮▮▮▮▯ 難　選択率：(A) － (B) － (C) － (D) －

What is the man asked to do?
(A) Request some repairs
(B) Fill out a form
(C) Purchase a replacement
(D) Change an appointment

男性は何をするよう頼まれていますか。
(A) 修理を依頼する
(B) 用紙に記入する
(C) 代替品を購入する
(D) 面会の約束を変更する

▶解説 ❹で女性は男性に、Martinez さんに作品集の提出を求め、その後彼を面接に呼ぶように言っています。つまり男性は約束の変更を依頼されていると言えるので、正解は (D) です。

☐ fill out ~: ~に記入する　☐ replacement: 图 代替品

((🗼)) ゼミ生中継 ⓐHiro ⓑMai ⓒYasu ⓓDai ⓔSaki

39.

🙂 魅力的な不正解は (C) かな？

🙂 選びました。写真のサンプルが届いていないと言っていたので、それが Some information に言い換えられていると思いました。でも、inaccurate に自信がなかったです。

🙂 言い換えを意識したのはナイスだけど、inaccurate は「不正確な」だよ。accurate の反対。ところで、(A) にある portfolio は重要語。いくつか意味があるけれど、TOEIC に登場したら「作品集」だと思って

間違いない。

40.

🙂 面接の日を変えることを repairs と言え……ないですね？

🙂 言えない。repairs は修理だから (A) は間違っている。

😊 正答率が書かれていないのはなぜですか。

🙂 もともと (A) は違う内容だったけれど、難易度調整のために易しく変えたらしい。著者がそう言っていた。

(104) **Questions 41 through 43** refer to the following conversation.

M: Helen. ❶I bought a new vacuum cleaner for the lobby, but it doesn't seem to be working. I'm thinking of sending it back.

W: ❷Do you know if they'll give us our money back?

M: I only bought it a week ago.

W: ❸There should be no problem, then. I'm sure they'll accept the return, but we'll need a replacement anyway. So, I hope they'll exchange it with a new one. ❹Before doing anything, though, let me take a look at it. It might not be set up right.

M: Thanks. I was worried that that might be the case. I'll go get it now, and try to find the instruction manual, too.   (109w/37 sec.)

問題41-43は次の会話に関するものです。
男：Helen。ロビーで使う新しい掃除機を買ったんだけど、動かないみたいなんだ。返品しようと思って。
女：返金してくれるかどうか分かる？
男：買ったのはほんの1週間前だから。
女：なら、大丈夫なはずね。きっと返品を受け入れてくれると思うけど、いずれにせよ代替品が必要だから、新しいものと交換してくれるといいんだけど。でも、何か手を打つ前に、私にそれを見せてくれる？きちんと設定されてないのかもしれないわ。
男：助かるよ。僕もそうかもしれないと疑ってたんだ。今取ってくる。ついでに、取扱説明書も見つけてくるよ。

☐ vacuum cleaner: 掃除機 ☐ work: 動 機能する ☐ accept: 動 ～を受け入れる ☐ return: 名 返品 ☐ replacement: 名 代替品
☐ set ～ up: ～を設定する ☐ that might be the case: そうかもしれない ☐ instruction manual: 取扱説明書

---

41. 正解：C 易 ■■■■□□ 難 選択率：(A) 5.3% (B) 0.4% **(C) 56.5%** (D) 36.7%

What are the speakers mainly discussing?
(A) A marketing strategy
(B) A news story
(C) An appliance
(D) A product description

話者たちは、主に何について話していますか。
(A) マーケティング戦略
(B) 報道記事
(C) 電気製品
(D) 商品説明

▶解説 男性は❶で、新しく購入した掃除機の話をしています。さらに、その調子が悪いことを伝え、会話全体を通して対策を話し合っていることから、vacuum cleaner を appliance（電気製品）と言い換えた (C) が正解です。

---

42. 正解：C 易 ■■■■□□ 難 選択率：(A) 11.0% (B) 16.3% **(C) 58.0%** (D) 14.1%

What does the man mean when he says, "I only bought it a week ago"?
(A) He is not familiar with a procedure.
(B) He needs more time to test a product.
(C) He thinks he is eligible for a refund.
(D) He is certain a product works well.

男性はどんな意味で「買ったのはほんの1週間前だから」と言っていますか。
(A) 彼は手続きに不慣れだ。
(B) 彼には商品を試す時間がもっと必要だ。
(C) 彼は自分に返金を受ける資格があると思っている。
(D) 彼は商品がうまく作動すると確信している。

☐ familiar with ～: ～になじみがある
☐ procedure: 名 手順 ☐ eligible for ～: ～の資格がある
☐ refund: 名 返金 ☐ certain: 形 確信して

▶解説 女性が❷で返金してくれるか分かるかと尋ねたのに対し、男性がI only bought it a week ago. と言っています。それを受けて女性は❸で「それなら大丈夫なはず。返品を受け入れてくれるだろう」と述べています。これは、男性が暗に「返金してくれるだろう」と考えていることを言語化している発言です。正解は (C) です。

---

43. 正解：B 易 ■■■■□□ 難 選択率：(A) 4.6% **(B) 66.1%** (C) 23.0% (D) 5.7%

What does the woman ask the man to do?
(A) Make a presentation
(B) Show her a product
(C) Send her some research data
(D) Delay a product launch

女性は男性に何をするよう頼んでいますか。
(A) プレゼンテーションをする
(B) 自分に商品を見せる
(C) 自分に調査データを送る
(D) 商品の発売を遅らせる

▶解説 ❹で女性は、何か行動を起こす前にそれを見せてほしいと頼んでいます。きちんと設定されていないだけかもしれないとの発言、また話の流れからも、it（それ）は掃除機を指すため、正解は (B) です。掃除機を product（製品）と言い換えています。

☐ research data: 調査データ ☐ delay: 動 ～を遅らせる ☐ launch: 名 （新製品の）発売

(((㊙))) ゼミ生中継 😀Hiro 😊Mai 😄Yasu 🎲Dai 😁Saki

41.
😊 (D) が間違っている理由は何？
😁 2人が product を describe している気がして、(D) は正解だと思っちゃいました。
😀 A product description は、製品の説明書きのことですよね。2人は製品について話していますが、説明書きについて話しているわけではありません。
😄 その通り。

😁 あ、そういうことか。了解です。

42.
😄 意図問題。どうだった？
😁 私はI only bought it a week ago. を「1週間前に買っただけ」と解釈してしまい、意味を理解できませんでした。
😀 この only は「ほんの1週間前に買った」の「ほんの」だよ。掃除機が新しいことを伝えている。ちなみに、このターゲット文に似た表現が、Test 3のどこかに出る。正解か不正解かは言えないけどね。

Part 3 会話問題

DL 106 **Questions 44 through 46** refer to the following conversation.

W: ❶ <u>Welcome to the Castanza Art Gallery.</u> We have a private exhibition this evening. It starts in about 30 minutes and it's for invited guests only. ❷ <u>Do you have an invitation?</u>

M: Um... yes. I confirmed that I would be attending the art exhibition a week ago using the gallery Web page. But, I can't find the invitation now.

W: That's fine. We will have a record of it because you must be a registered member. ❸ <u>If you show me some identification, I can print out a pass for you.</u>　　　　(88w/32 sec.)

問題44-46は次の会話に関するものです。
女：ようこそ、Castanza Art Galleryへ。今夜は個展を開催しております。あと30分ほどで開場ですが、ご招待したお客さま限定です。招待状をお持ちでしょうか。
男：ええと……あります。この美術展を観覧する確認は取ったんです、1週間前に画廊のウェブページで。でも、今手元に招待状が見つからなくて。
女：結構ですよ。登録会員でいらっしゃるはずですので、記録を確認いたします。身分証明書をお見せいただければ、入場券を印刷いたします。

☐ private: 形 私的な　☐ exhibition: 名 展示　☐ invitation: 名 招待状　☐ confirm: 動 ～を確認する　☐ attend: 動 ～に出席する
☐ gallery: 名 画廊　☐ record: 動 ～を記録する　☐ register: 動 ～を登録する　☐ identification: 名 身分証明書　☐ pass: 名 入場券

---

44. 正解：**A**　易 ▰▰▱▱▱▱ 難　選択率：**(A) 96.5%** (B) 1.1% (C) 1.1% (D) 0.7%

Where most likely are the speakers?
(A) In an art gallery
(B) In a theater
(C) At the airport
(D) At a taxi stand

話者たちは、どこにいる可能性が最も高いですか。
(A) 画廊に
(B) 劇場に
(C) 空港に
(D) タクシー乗り場に

▶解説 ❶の「Castanza Art Galleryへようこそ」という女性の発言から、話者たちは画廊にいると判断できます。(A) が正解です。ここを聞き逃しても、今夜は個展を行っているとの情報や、男性が美術展への参加について言及していることからも他の選択肢を消去できます。

---

45. 正解：**A**　易 ▰▰▱▱▱▱ 難　選択率：**(A) 96.5%** (B) 2.1% (C) 1.1% (D) 0.0%

What does the woman ask about?
(A) An invitation
(B) A travel time
(C) Seating capacity
(D) Traffic conditions

女性は何について尋ねていますか。
(A) 招待状
(B) 移動時間
(C) 席数
(D) 交通の状況

▶解説 女性が何かについて尋ねることが、設問から分かります。招待客限定の個展だと述べた女性は❷で、招待状を持っているかと男性に問うています。正解は (A) です。

☐ seating: 名 座席　☐ capacity: 名 収容能力
☐ traffic: 形 交通の　☐ condition: 名（複数形で）状況

---

46. 正解：**D**　易 ▰▰▱▱▱▱ 難　選択率：(A) 2.1% (B) 4.6% (C) 1.8% **(D) 90.8%**

What will the man most likely do next?
(A) Go to a train station
(B) Buy a bus pass
(C) Make a phone call
(D) Take out some identification

男性はこの後何をする可能性が最も高いですか。
(A) 駅へ行く
(B) バスの定期券を買う
(C) 電話をかける
(D) 身分証明書を取り出す

▶解説 招待状を求められた男性は、それを持っていません。❸の「身分証明書の提示があれば入場券を印刷できる」との女性の言葉を受け、男性はおそらく身分証明書を取り出すであろうと推測できるため、(D) が正解です。

☐ bus pass: バスの定期券　☐ take out ～: ～を出す

📡 ゼミ 生 中継　　　😀Hiro 😀Mai 😀Yasu 😑Dai 😀Saki

😀 なぜか知らないけれど、美術館とか博物館はTOEICに頻出する。

46. ....

😀 設問内の主語は男性だけど、女性がヒントを言ったね。

😑 最後に男性の発言を待っていたら、会話が終わったので焦りました。

😀 登場人物の次の行動が問われたら、通常、ヒントは「未来」か「依頼」にある。ここでは、女性が男性に身分証明書を見せるよう頼んでいて、それがヒントになっている。

😑 「未来」はどんなヒントですか？

😀 本人の次の行動を示す未来表現だよ。Let me ～とか、I'll ～といった表現はヒントになる可能性が高い。

DL 107 **Questions 47 through 49** refer to the following conversation.

M: Hi, Margaret. Are you ready for your trip to Toronto? ❶ Your designs for the new TGM Bank building are great. I'm sure you'll win the contract for us.

W: Yeah, ❷ I hope they'll accept my design proposal. I'm almost ready to leave now.

M: Can I help you with anything?

W: I'm just making sure I haven't forgotten anything. ❸ I can't find the printout of the construction cost estimates.

M: Don't waste time looking for it. There's a copy on the server. ❹ If you talk to Ted, he'll give you the password so that you can download it when you get there.

W: Great idea. Thanks. (101w/35 sec.)

問題47-49は次の会話に関するものです。
男：やあ、Margaret。Torontoへの出張の準備はできた？　新しいTGM Bankビルの君の設計はすごいよ。君なら絶対に契約を取ってきてくれる。
女：ええ、先方が私の設計案を受け入れてくれるといいんだけど。そろそろ出発しようかと思ってるの。
男：何か手伝えること、ある？
女：忘れ物がないか確かめてるところなんだけど、建設費の見積書のプリントアウトが見つからないのよ。
男：探す時間がもったいないよ。サーバーにコピーがある。Tedに言えば、パスワードを教えてくれるから、現地に着いたらダウンロードできるよ。
女：いい考えだわ。ありがとう。

□ ready: 形 準備ができて　□ design: 名 設計　□ win: 動（賞など）を勝ち取る　□ contract: 名 契約　□ printout: 名 プリントアウト、印刷物
□ construction: 名 建設　□ estimate: 名 見積もり　□ waste: 動 ～を無駄にする

---

47. 正解：**C** 易■■■□□□ 難　選択率：(A) 5.3% (B) 1.1% **(C) 88.3%** (D) 4.9%

Who most likely is the woman?
(A) An author
(B) A lawyer
(C) An architect
(D) A financial advisor

□ financial: 形 金融の

女性は誰である可能性が最も高いですか。
(A) 作家
(B) 法律家
(C) 建築家
(D) 投資顧問

▶解説 ❶で男性は、女性の設計図を評価しており、「契約を取れるはずだ」と考えていることが分かります。❷で女性自身も「私の設計案」と発言しており、選択肢の中で建物の設計図を作成するのはarchitect（建築家）のみなので、正解は(C)です。

---

48. 正解：**B** 易■■□□□□ 難　選択率：(A) 24.7% **(B) 70.7%** (C) 2.5% (D) 1.8%

What is the woman looking for?
(A) A computer
(B) A document
(C) An empty desk
(D) Her luggage

□ empty: 形 空の

女性は何を探していますか。
(A) パソコン
(B) 書類
(C) 空いている机
(D) 自分の荷物

▶解説 ❸で女性は、「建設費の見積書のプリントアウトが見つからない」と言っています。この発言から、探しているのは見積書だと分かります。選択肢ではcost estimates（見積書）がdocument（書類）と抽象的な言葉に言い換えられています。(B)が正解です。

---

49. 正解：**D** 易■■■■□□ 難　選択率：(A) 7.1% (B) 8.8% (C) 18.7% **(D) 65.0%**

Why does the man suggest speaking with Ted?
(A) To discuss a strategy
(B) To learn about a product
(C) To ask for directions
(D) To get a password

□ strategy: 名 戦略　□ learn about ～: ～について知る　□ ask for ～: ～を頼む　□ direction: 名 道順の案内

男性はなぜTedと話すことを勧めていますか。
(A) 戦略について話し合うために
(B) 商品知識を身に付けるために
(C) 道順を尋ねるために
(D) パスワードを教えてもらうために

▶解説 見積書を探す女性に対し男性は、サーバーにコピーがあるからと女性を安心させ、❹で「Tedと話せばダウンロード用のパスワードをもらえる」と伝えています。これが提案の理由だと言えるので、(D)が正解です。

((•)) ゼミ生中継　　😀Hiro 😀Mai 😀Yasu 😀Dai 😀Saki

48.
😀 人気ナンバーワンの不正解が(A)だよ。サキは？
😀 (A)にしました。後半でサーバーとかパスワードとかが聞こえたので、パソコンを連想しました。
😀 でも、その話をしたのは男性だよ。設問は女性が何を探しているか問うているから、女性の発言に注意した方がいい。
😀 設問にあるlooking forを言ったのが男性だから、その後の情報を意識しちゃったんです。

😀 そっか。でも、そこは49番のヒントだから混乱しなかった？
😀 いえ。パスワードが(D)にあったので選べました。
😀 結果オーライってことか。

49.
😀 あ、(C)のdirectionsは道案内ですね。うっかり、説明とか指示とかをイメージしました。
😀 普通、それはinstructionsだよ。どっちみち、Tedはパスワードを教えてくれるだけだから正解にならない。

Part 3　▼ Listening Section

108 **Questions 50 through 52** refer to the following conversation.

M: We're about to start work on the interior walls of the store now. ❶I was counting the wood panels and it looks like we didn't order enough.

W: How many short are you?

M: Ten, I think—not enough to finish the job.

W: I'm ordering some more materials this afternoon. Can you wait until then?

M: Probably not. ❷I was planning to get the walls done before lunch so that we could do the painting this afternoon.

W: In that case, ❸why don't you take my van to the hardware store and pick up some more panels yourself?

M: That might be the safest way to go. Thanks.　　　(104w/35 sec.)

問題50-52は次の会話に関するものです。

男：これから店内の壁面の作業を始めるんだけど、木製パネルの枚数を数えたら、どうやら十分な数を発注しなかったらしい。

女：何枚足りないの？

男：10枚だと思う――これだと作業が完了しない。

女：今日の午後に追加で材料を発注するの。それまで待てる？

男：たぶん駄目だね。壁面は昼食前に終える予定だったんだ。そうすれば、午後に塗装に入れるからね。

女：それなら、私のワンボックス車でホームセンターへ行って、自分で追加のパネルを調達してきたら？

男：それが一番確実なやり方かもしれないね。ありがとう。

☐ about to ～: まさに～しようとしている　☐ interior: 形 内部の　☐ count: 動 ～を数える　☐ wood: 形 木製の　☐ order: 動 ～を注文する
☐ enough: 副 十分に　☐ short: 形 不足して　☐ material: 名 材料　☐ wait: 動 待つ　☐ probably: 副 おそらく　☐ plan: 動 ～を計画する
☐ in that case: その場合　☐ why don't you ～?: ～したらどうですか。　☐ van: 名 バン、ワンボックス車　☐ hardware: 名 金物類
☐ pick up ～: ～を買う　☐ safe: 形 安全な

50. 正解：D　易 ■■■□□□□□ 難　選択率：(A) 11.3%　(B) 5.3%　(C) 10.6%　**(D) 71.7%**

Why is the man concerned?
(A) A client is dissatisfied.
(B) Bad weather was forecast.
(C) A supplier is closed.
(D) An order was incorrect.

男性はなぜ心配していますか。
(A) 顧客が満足していない。
(B) 悪天候が予報された。
(C) 納入業者が休業している。
(D) 発注に間違いがあった。

▶解説 男性の発言❶から、木製パネルの注文数が不十分だったと分かります。男性は次の発言で、今のままでは作業を完了できないと述べているため、これが、彼が心配していることです。その原因として適切なのは(D)です。

□ concerned: 形 心配して　□ client: 名 顧客　□ dissatisfied: 形 不満な
□ bad weather: 悪天候　□ forecast: 動 ～と予報する　＊ここの forecast は過去分詞
□ supplier: 名 供給業者　□ order: 名 注文　□ incorrect: 形 間違った

---

51. 正解：C　易 ■■■□□□□□ 難　選択率：(A) 15.9%　(B) 2.5%　**(C) 79.5%**　(D) 1.4%

What is the man planning to do later today?
(A) Take the afternoon off
(B) Evaluate employee performance
(C) Paint some walls
(D) Photograph a garden

男性は今日、後で何をする予定ですか。
(A) 午後に休みを取る
(B) 従業員の仕事ぶりを査定する
(C) 壁を塗装する
(D) 庭を撮影する

▶解説 later today は、「今日この後の時間帯」を指します。男性は❷で、「昼前に壁の作業を終わらせ午後から塗装作業に入る予定だった」と述べており、(C) Paint some walls（壁を塗装する）が唯一適切な選択肢です。

□ take ～ off: ～を休む　□ evaluate: 動 ～を評価する　□ employee: 名 従業員
□ performance: 名 成績、実績　□ photograph: 動 ～の写真を撮る

---

52. 正解：A　易 ■■■■■□□□ 難　選択率：**(A) 39.9%**　(B) 13.8%　(C) 16.6%　(D) 29.3%

What does the woman propose the man do?
(A) Borrow a van
(B) Wear protective clothing
(C) Check a telephone directory
(D) Use a staffing agency

女性は男性に何をするよう提案していますか。
(A) ワンボックス車を借りる
(B) 防護服を着る
(C) 電話帳を調べる
(D) 人材派遣会社を使う

▶解説 ❸で女性は、「自分の車でホームセンターへ行って、パネルを調達してきてはどうか」と提案しています。Why don't you ～ ？は、提案する際の定番表現です。How about -ing?、Let's ～と併せて覚えておきましょう。正解(A)では、take my van が Borrow a van（ワンボックス車を借りる）となっています。

□ propose: 動 ～を提案する　□ borrow: 動 ～を借りる　□ protective: 形 保護する
□ clothing: 名 衣類　□ telephone directory: 電話帳　□ staffing agency: 人材派遣会社

📡)) ゼミ 生中継　　　　　　　　　😀 Hiro　😀 Mai　😀 Yasu　😀 Dai　😀 Saki

50.
😀 パネルが足りないのは注文側のミスだったのですか。

😀 納品した業者が間違えた可能性もあります。

😀 私もそう思いました。注文通りに配達されないのは、いかにも TOEIC ワールドで起きそうです。

😀 何を言っているの。男性は we didn't order enough と言っているじゃないか。業者がミスしていたのなら、そんなこと言わないよ。

52.
😀 意外とモニターの正答率が低い。ヒントを聞き取れなかった？

😀 最初に聞いたときは全然聞こえませんでしたが、復習したときは不思

議なくらいにクリアに聞こえました。

😀 2回目に聞こえたということは、失敗の原因はリスニング力不足じゃない。意識が音に集中していなかったんだよ。51番の答えをマークしていたとか。

😀 そうです。51番の(C)を塗っていました。塗るのと聞くのがなかなか両立できません。

😀 だったら、グリグリ塗る代わりにチョンと印を付けるだけでいい。そうすれば、すぐに意識を音に戻せる。

😀 そんな技があるんですね。次からやってみます。

Part 3 会話問題

Questions 53 through 55 refer to the following conversation.

M: ❶ I'm afraid we've had an accident at the shipping center. ❷ A box
🇨🇦 fell from a truck and the contents have broken.

W: I'm sure the insurance will cover it. So, just fill out a claim form
🇨🇦 and put it on my desk. I'll send it out before I leave this afternoon.

M: ❸ Can I do that tomorrow? We're really busy at the moment.
❹ There are still a lot of deliveries to make this afternoon.

W: They won't like that. ❺ One of the insurance company's conditions
is that incidents must be reported as they occur. ❻ I'll send someone to help load the trucks.　　　　　　　　　　　(99w/34 sec.)

問題53-55は次の会話に関するものです。
男: まずいことに出荷センターで事故がありました。箱が1つトラックから落ちて、中身が破損しています。
女: 保険の適用を受けられるはずよ。とにかく保険金請求書に記入して、私の机の上に置いておいて。今日の午後に出る前に、発送するから。
男: 明日でもいいですか。今はとても忙しいんです。まだ、今日の午後に配送するものがたくさんあるので。
女: それは嫌がられるわね。保険会社の条件の1つに、事故は発生と同時に報告しなければならない、とあるの。誰かを回して、トラックの荷積みを手伝わせるわ。

☐ I'm afraid 〜 : 残念ですが〜　☐ accident: 图 事故　☐ fall: 動 落ちる ＊fell は過去形　☐ content: 图 中身、内容物
☐ break: 動 壊れる ＊broken は過去分詞　☐ insurance: 图 保険　☐ cover: 動 （費用など）を賄う、〜をカバーする
☐ claim form: 保険金請求書　☐ send 〜 out: 〜を送り出す　☐ condition: 图 条件　☐ incident: 图 出来事、事件
☐ report: 動 〜を報告する　☐ occur: 動 発生する　☐ load: 動 〜を積む

---

53. 正解：B 易■■■□□□□□□ 難　選択率：(A) 5.7% **(B) 88.7%** (C) 4.2% (D) 1.1%

Where do the speakers most likely work?
(A) At an assembly plant
(B) At a shipping facility
(C) At a legal office
(D) At a hotel

話者たちはどこで働いている可能性が最も高いですか。
(A) 組立工場で
(B) 出荷施設で
(C) 法律事務所で
(D) ホテルで

▶解説 男性は❶で出荷センターでの事故について話しており、❹から午後も配送作業に追われる状況だと分かります。さらに❻の「トラックの荷積みを手伝う」という表現からも、職場は (B) の「出荷施設」だと推測できます。

---

54. 正解：B 易■■■□□□□□ 難　選択率：(A) 6.0% **(B) 83.4%** (C) 0.4% (D) 9.9%

What problem does the man mention?
(A) Some guests will arrive late.
(B) Some products have been broken.
(C) A machine is too expensive.
(D) A deadline has passed.

☐ pass: 動 過ぎ去る

男性はどんな問題について話していますか。
(A) 顧客の中に遅れて到着する者がいる。
(B) いくつかの製品が壊れている。
(C) 機械の値段が高すぎる。
(D) 締め切りが過ぎている。

▶解説 ❷で男性は、「箱がトラックから落ちて中の物が壊れた」と伝えています。ネガティブな内容なので、これが男性の言及する問題だと考えられます。contents を Some products（いくつかの製品）と言い換えた (B) が正解です。

---

55. 正解：C 易■■■■□□□ 難　選択率：(A) 9.9% (B) 18.4% **(C) 51.2%** (D) 20.1%

What does the woman mean when she says, "They won't like that"?
(A) Product quality has dropped.
(B) Extra work will be assigned.
(C) A request is unacceptable.
(D) A warranty will expire.

女性はどんな意味で「それは嫌がられるわね」と言っていますか。
(A) 品質が低下した。
(B) 余計な仕事が割り振られるだろう。
(C) 要望が受け入れられない。
(D) 保証期間が過ぎた。

▶解説 保険請求書の作成を指示された男性は❸で「明日でも構わないか」と尋ねています。女性は They won't like that. に続けて❺で、事故は発生後すぐに報告する必要があると述べています。すぐに保険金請求書を作成してほしいとの考えが推測でき、それを言い換えた (C) が正解です。

☐ quality: 图 品質　☐ drop: 動 下落する　☐ extra: 形 余分の　☐ assign: 動 〜を割り当てる
☐ unacceptable: 形 受け入れられない　☐ warranty: 图 保証　☐ expire: 動 終了する

(((♪))) ゼミ 生中継　　　😊 Hiro 😊 Mai 😊 Yasu 😊 Dai 😊 Saki

54.

😊 もう気づいていると思うけど、Part 3 では様々な問題が勃発して、それを解決するために登場人物が話し合う。これが1つのパターンだよ。だから、54番みたいな設問もよく出る。今回の broken や wrong、incorrect のように悪いことを連想させる単語がヒントになることが多い。あと、最初にある I'm afraid 〜 も大事なヒントだよ。その直後に必ず悪いことを言うからね。

55.

😊 意図問題は苦手だな〜。選択肢が長いし。

😊 54番も55番も文ばっかりだから、苦しいよね。

😊 リーディングのテストみたいです。

😊 お、いいこと言うね。速く正確に英語を読む力は、Part 3 と Part 4 の対策には絶対に必要だよ。

DL 110 Questions 56 through 58 refer to the following conversation.

W: Hi, Bill. ❶ I remember you were saying that you wanted to join a gym.

M: That's right. I just haven't gotten around to it. ❷ I was thinking of joining that gym you go to.

W: Well, that's why I brought it up. ❸ Fitnow Gym is running a campaign from tomorrow. ❹ If I introduce a new member, we both get two months membership for free.

M: Sounds great. ❺ I'll bring my gym clothes tomorrow, then. What time were you planning on working out? (79w/26 sec.)

□ join: 動 ～に入る　□ get around to ～: ～する暇ができる　＊gotten は get の過去分詞
□ bring ～ up: ～を持ち出す　＊brought は bring の過去形
□ membership: 名 会員であること　□ for free: 無料で　□ plan: 動 計画する　□ work out: 運動をする

問題56-58は次の会話に関するものです。
女：ねえ、Bill。あなた、ジムに入会したいって言ってたわよね。
男：その通り。これまで時間がなかっただけでね。君が通っているジムに入ろうかと思ってるんだけど。
女：そう、だからこの話をしたのよ。Fitnow Gym が明日からキャンペーンを始めるの。新しい会員を紹介すると、紹介した方もされた方も2カ月間会費が無料になるのよ。
男：良さそうだね。なら、明日ジム用のウエアを持ってくるよ。何時からトレーニングしようと思ってるの？

---

56. 正解：**C**　易 ■■■■□□□□ 難　選択率：(A) 1.1%　(B) 3.5%　**(C) 92.9%**　(D) 1.8%

What is the conversation mainly about?
(A) A photography club
(B) An office cleanup
(C) A fitness center
(D) Transportation routes

□ photography: 名 写真撮影　□ cleanup: 名 大掃除

会話は主に何に関するものですか。
(A) 写真撮影クラブ
(B) 職場大掃除
(C) フィットネスセンター
(D) 交通経路

▶解説 ❶で女性は、男性がジムに入りたがっていたことを確認しています。さらに❷、❸で具体的なジムについて話しており、全体の流れからもジムの入会についての会話だと分かります。正解 (C) では gym を fitness center（フィットネスセンター）と言い換えています。

---

57. 正解：**D**　易 ■■■□□□□□ 難　選択率：(A) 6.7%　(B) 2.1%　(C) 6.4%　**(D) 84.5%**

What does the woman say will happen tomorrow?
(A) Entries for a contest will be accepted.
(B) A truck will come to pick up garbage.
(C) Some cleaners will do some work.
(D) A discount will become available.

□ happen: 動 起こる　□ entry: 名 出場
□ accept: 動 ～を受け入れる

女性は明日、何があると言っていますか。
(A) コンテストへの参加が受け入れられる。
(B) トラックが来てごみを収集する。
(C) 清掃業者が作業を行う。
(D) 割引価格を利用できるようになる。

▶解説 女性の発言にヒントがあります。❸で女性は「明日キャンペーンが始まる」と述べ、❹ではキャンペーンの内容を「新メンバーの入会で紹介者も2カ月間会費が無料になる」と伝えています。明日起きるのは「割引価格が利用できるようになる」ことだと言えるので、(D) が正解です。

---

58. 正解：**A**　易 ■■■■■□□□ 難　選択率：**(A) 32.2%**　(B) 7.8%　(C) 25.1%　(D) 34.6%

What does the man say he will bring?
(A) Some appropriate clothing
(B) Some cleaning products
(C) His employee card
(D) A copy of a certificate

□ appropriate: 形 ふさわしい　□ certificate: 名 証明書

男性は何を持ってくると言っていますか。
(A) ふさわしい衣類
(B) 洗浄剤
(C) 自分の従業員証
(D) 証明書の写し

▶解説 ❺から、男性は明日、ジム用の服を持ってくることが分かります。ジムに行く話をしている中での発言なので、持ってくるのは「運動にふさわしい衣類」と言えます。よって、正解は (A) です。

((•)) ゼミ 生 中継　😀Hiro 😊Mai 😎Yasu 😐Dai 😄Saki

56.
😎 フィットネスセンターは、リスニングにもリーディングにも頻出する。TOEICワールドの住人は健康志向なんだよ。

😀 そう言えば、重たい病気になる人はいないですね。

58.
😎 Part 3 の中でモニターの正答率が最も低い。どれを選んだ？

😀 (D) です。gym clothes を聞き落としたので、ジムに入会する人が持

っていきそうな物を想像しました。

😐 同じく。

😎 そういうことか。ただ、(D) の certificate は、通常は免状とか修了証を指す。そんな物をジムに持っていかないよね。

😄 本人確認のための身分証明書を想像していました。

😎 あぁ、普通それは identification って言うんだよ。

Part 3 ▼ Listening Section

Part 3 会話問題

111 Questions 59 through 61 refer to the following conversation.

W: Glen, ❶ I have a couple of tickets for the Steel Rose concert on Friday night. I can't use them so I thought you might be interested.

M: Really? ❷ Yeah, I'd love to go. Why can't you use them?

W: I have a party to go to. I forgot all about it. ❸ Anyway, it starts at six o'clock. You'll have to leave work a little early. Oh, and there are two tickets, so you'd better invite someone along.

M: Fantastic! ❹ I'll give Adam Turner from accounting a call. ❺ Steel Rose is his favorite band. (90w/34 sec.)

問題59-61は次の会話に関するものです。

女：Glen、Steel Roseのコンサートのチケットが2枚あるの、金曜日の夜の。私、行けないから、あなたなら興味があるかなと思って。

男：本当？　ああ、ぜひ行きたいよ。どうして君は行けないの？

女：パーティーに出なければならないのよ。すっかり忘れてて。とにかく、開演は6時よ。ちょっと早めに退社しなくちゃいけないわ。あ、それでチケットは2枚あるから、誰かを誘った方がいいよ。

男：すごいな！　経理部のAdam Turnerに電話するよ。Steel Roseは彼のお気に入りのバンドなんだ。

□ interested: 形 興味を持った　□ I'd love to ～: ぜひ～したい　□ anyway: 副 とにかく　□ along: 副 一緒に
□ fantastic: 形 素晴らしい　□ accounting: 名 経理　□ give ～ a call: ～に電話をかける　□ favorite: 形 お気に入りの

---

59. 正解：**B** 易 ▰▰▰▱▱ 難　選択率：(A) 1.8% **(B) 84.8%** (C) 6.4% (D) 6.7%

What are the speakers discussing?
(A) A building opening
(B) A musical performance
(C) A client dinner
(D) A film premiere

話者たちは何について話していますか。
(A) 建物の開館
(B) 音楽の公演
(C) 接待
(D) 映画の特別封切り

▶解説 女性は❶でSteel Roseのコンサートチケットに言及しており、興味があるか問われた男性は❷で、「ぜひ行きたい」と答えています。その後もチケットや開始時刻についての会話が続き、❺でSteel Roseはバンドだと分かることからも、(B)の音楽の公演に関する会話だと言えます。

□ performance: 名 公演
□ client dinner: (取引先に食事を提供する) 接待
□ premiere: 名 (映画の) 特別封切り、プレミア試写会

---

60. 正解：**D** 易 ▰▱▱▱▱ 難　選択率：(A) 1.4% (B) 1.4% (C) 0.7% **(D) 96.1%**

What time will the event start?
(A) At 2:00 P.M.
(B) At 4:00 P.M.
(C) At 5:00 P.M.
(D) At 6:00 P.M.

イベントは何時に始まりますか。
(A) 午後2時に
(B) 午後4時に
(C) 午後5時に
(D) 午後6時に

▶解説 女性が❸で「開演は6時だ」と伝えています。その直後で男性に早めの退社を促しているので、6時に始まるのは男性が行くコンサートです。よって、正解は(D)です。

---

61. 正解：**A** 易 ▰▰▱▱▱ 難　選択率：**(A) 83.7%** (B) 4.6% (C) 3.9% (D) 7.4%

What does the man say he will do?
(A) Invite a colleague
(B) Hire a catering company
(C) Send out a memo
(D) Have his suit cleaned

男性は何をすると言っていますか。
(A) 同僚を招待する
(B) 仕出し業者を雇う
(C) 連絡票を送る
(D) 自分のスーツを洗濯してもらう

▶解説 「チケットは2枚あるから誰か誘うべきだ」と女性に言われ、男性は❹で「経理のAdam Turnerに電話をする」と発言しています。会話の流れから、電話は同僚をコンサートに誘うためだと推察でき、(A)が正解です。

□ catering: 名 仕出し、ケータリング
□ send out ～: ～を送る　□ memo: 名 (社内の) 連絡票

((( ))) ゼミ生中継　😮 Hiro 😊 Mai 😮 Yasu 😎 Dai 😮 Saki

59.
😮 サキ、59番のようなトピック問題の特徴を覚えている？
😊 会話を聞けば聞くほど解きやすくなることです。
😮 では、60番と61番を見て、何を予測できる？
😊 両方とも、細かい情報を聞き取る必要がありそうです。2問目のヒント

は誰が言うか分かりません。3問目は男性が言います。
😮 よし、合格。実際、最後に聞こえたbandは59番のヒントだったね。ダイ、いきなりだけど、接待を英語で何て言う？
😎 client dinnerです。(C)にあります。
😮 さすがベテランサラリーマンだね。

TOEICよろず相談所　ヒロの部屋

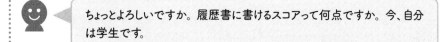

 ちょっとよろしいですか。履歴書に書けるスコアって何点ですか。今、自分は学生です。

 お問い合わせありがとうございます。「履歴書に書ける」というのは、どのような意味でしょうか。

 低いスコアを書くと、就職活動でマイナスになると思うんですが。

 企業がプラス評価をするスコアをお知りになりたいのですね。絶対的な答えはありませんが、**600点以上であればマイナスにはならない**と思います。新入社員の平均が500点くらいと言われていますので。

 自分はまだ450点なんですが、書かない方がいいですか。

 率直に言って、何とも言えません。それは採用する側が判断することですからね。どんな企業を希望しているんですか。

 総合商社がいいなと思っています。

 それなら、もっと高いスコアを取っておく方が良いと思います。入社後に700点を必須にしている商社がありますよ。それに、商社では、TOEICのスコアだけでなく、**実際の英語運用力が重視される**ので、スピーキング力を高めておくといいでしょう。

 スピーキングのテストも受けた方がいいですか。

 そうですね。TOEICにもスピーキングテストがあるので、受験してみてください。あのテストを受ける学生はそれほど多くないので、履歴書に書けば積極性を評価されるかもしれませんよ。

 なるほど、分かりました。

Part 3 会話問題

Questions 62 through 64 refer to the following conversation and map.

W: Hi Jack. It's Fiona. ❶ Thanks for lending me your car to go shopping. I can't seem to find it, though. ❷ You said it would be in the parking lot on Aiden Avenue, didn't you?

M: Yeah, but there are two. ❸ My car is in the one next to Sleeman Sports Center. The one beside Dean's Café was full.

W: OK, I'll head over there now. As I said, I'll be back by three o'clock. Do you need me to get anything on the way back?

M: ❹ Just fill the car with fuel.

W: Sure thing. (91w/35 sec.)

問題62-64は次の会話と地図に関するものです。
女：もしもし、Jack。Fionaよ。買い物に行くのに車を貸してくれてありがとう。でも、車が見つからないのよ。Aiden Avenue の駐車場にあるって言ってたわよね？
男：うん、でも駐車場は2つあるんだ。僕の車は Sleeman Sports Center の隣の方に入れてある。Dean's Café のそばの方が満車だったんだ。
女：分かった、今からそこへ行くわ。言ったとおり、3時までには戻るけど、帰りに何か買ってほしいもの、ある？
男：車のガソリンを満タンにしてきてくれればいいよ。
女：もちろん。

□ lend: 動 ～を貸す　□ seem to ～: ～のようだ　□ though: 副 でも、やっぱり　□ parking lot: 駐車場　□ next to ～: ～の隣に
□ beside: 前 ～のそばに　□ full: 形 いっぱいで　□ head over there: そちらに向かう　□ on the way back: 帰ってくる時に
□ fill: 動 ～をいっぱいにする　□ fuel: 名 燃料　□ Sure thing.: もちろん。

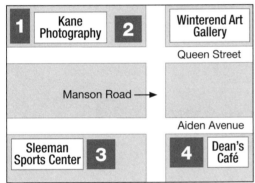

62. 正解：**A**　易 ■■■□□□□□ 難　選択率：**(A) 89.4%**　(B) 5.7%　(C) 2.1%　(D) 2.5%

Why will the woman borrow the man's car?
(A) To go shopping
(B) To meet a client
(C) To make a delivery
(D) To return home

☐ borrow: 動 〜を借りる　☐ return: 動 帰る

女性はなぜ男性の車を借りますか。
(A) 買い物に行くために
(B) 顧客に会うために
(C) 配送するために
(D) 帰宅するために

▶解説　設問から、女性が男性の車を借りることが分かります。❶で女性は男性にお礼を述べており、「買い物に行くために車を貸してくれて」とその理由を明確に述べているので、正解は (A) です。顧客、配送、帰宅に関しては言及がなく、他は不適切です。

---

63. 正解：**C**　易 ■■■■□□□□ 難　選択率：(A) 0.0%　(B) 12.7%　**(C) 64.3%**　(D) 22.6%

Look at the graphic. In which parking lot does the man say he left the car?
(A) Parking Lot 1
(B) Parking Lot 2
(C) Parking Lot 3
(D) Parking Lot 4

☐ leave: 動 〜を置く　＊left は過去形

図表を見てください。男性はどちらの駐車場に車を置いたと言っていますか。
(A) 駐車場1
(B) 駐車場2
(C) 駐車場3
(D) 駐車場4

▶解説　選択肢は駐車場番号なので、地図にある番号以外の情報がヒントになります。女性の❷の発言で車は Aiden Avenue の駐車場にあると分かりますが、男性は❸で、Sleeman Sports Center に隣接する駐車場に停めたと伝えています。従って正解は (C) です。

---

64. 正解：**D**　易 ■■■■□□□□ 難　選択率：(A) 3.9%　(B) 27.2%　(C) 19.1%　**(D) 49.5%**

What does the man ask the woman to do?
(A) Have the car washed
(B) Pay the parking fee
(C) Bring back a receipt
(D) Refill the fuel tank

☐ parking fee: 駐車料金　☐ bring back 〜: 〜を持ち帰る
☐ receipt: 名 領収書　☐ refill: 動 〜を補充する
☐ fuel tank: 燃料タンク

男性は女性に何をするよう頼んでいますか。
(A) 洗車してもらう
(B) 駐車料金を払う
(C) 領収書を持ち帰る
(D) 燃料タンクを補充する

▶解説　男性の依頼内容は、男性の発言にヒントがあります。何か必要な物があるかと聞かれた男性は❹で「ガソリンを満タンにしてくれればいい」と答えており、それが依頼内容だと言えます。Refill the fuel tank（燃料タンクを補充する）と言い換えられている (D) が正解です。

((•)) 🗼 ゼミ 生 中継　　😀 Hiro　😮 Mai　😊 Yasu　🤓 Dai　😄 Saki

63.

😀 人気の不正解は (D) と (B) だね。ダイはどうやって解いた？

🤓 男性が two と言ったので、2番が怪しくて (B) にしました。

😀 冷静に考えて。two が聞こえて (B) が正解だったら、地図がなくても解ける。でも、グラフィック問題は音情報だけでは解けないように作られている。だから、two はヒントじゃない。(D) を選んだ人は？

😄 スポーツセンターとカフェが聞こえて、どっちがヒントか分からず、(D) にしました。カフェにダマされました。

😀 こうやって、グラフィック内のどうでもいい情報をわざわざ会話に入れるのが「ダマシのテクニック」だよ。頭が混乱するよね。

😊 ヒントが2つあって助かりましたが……？

😀 実はそうだよね。スポーツセンターの隣という情報を聞ければ正解を選べるけど、仮にそれを逃しても、カフェの隣が満車だったことを理解できれば、(D) を消去できる。それぞれがヒントだから、親切な問題なんだよ、実は。ちゃんと文単位で情報を理解できる人が得をするってこと。では、66番に進もう。問題作成者が使う、別のテクニックを紹介する。

Part 3 会話問題

Questions 65 through 67 refer to the following conversation and schedule.

W: ❶ What time are you leaving for the bookkeeping conference 🇨🇦 tomorrow?

M: I can't leave here until 11:30 because ❷ I have to help Don check 🇺🇸 his financial report.

W: Oh, really? That's too bad. ❸ You'll miss a few of the presentations by well-known accountants, won't you?

M: Yeah. ❹ I'll only catch the final one, I'm afraid. Thankfully the important ones for me are on day two. They'll be talking about financial predictions for next year and the latest market news.

W: Well, I'm looking forward to hearing about it when you get back. Are you going to stay in a hotel?

M: No, ❺ I'll come home and take an early train in the morning on Friday. (110w/43 sec.)

問題65-67は次の会話と予定表に関するものです。
女：明日、何時に簿記会議に行くの？
男：11時半までは出られないんだ、Don が会計報告書をチェックするのを手伝わないといけないから。
女：え、本当？　それは残念ね。有名な会計士のプレゼンのいくつかを聞き逃すことになるんじゃない？
男：うん。最後のプレゼンしか見られないと思う。ありがたいことに、僕にとって重要なプレゼンは2日目にあるんだ。講演者が話すのは、来年の財務予測と最新の市場の動向についてだ。
女：じゃあ、あなたが戻ってきてから話を聞かせてもらうのを楽しみにしてるわ。ホテルに泊まる予定なの？
男：いや、家に帰って、金曜日の早朝の列車で行くよ。

☐ bookkeeping: 名 簿記　☐ conference: 名 会議　☐ leave: 動 ～を出る、出発する　☐ financial report: 会計報告書　☐ miss: 動 ～を逃す
☐ well-known: 形 有名な　☐ accountant: 名 会計士　☐ catch: 動 （講演など）を見る　☐ final: 形 最後の　☐ I'm afraid: 残念だけど
☐ thankfully: 副 ありがたいことに　☐ important: 形 重要な　☐ prediction: 名 予測、予言　☐ latest: 形 最近の、最新の　☐ market: 名 市場
☐ look forward to ～: ～を楽しみにしている　☐ stay: 動 滞在する

Day 1	
Start Time	**Speaker**
10:00 A.M.	Miles Jones
11:30 A.M.	Calvin Lin
2:00 P.M.	Edgar Burns
4:00 P.M.	Freda Salvatore

1日目	
開始時刻	**講演者**
午前10時	Miles Jones
午前11時30分	Calvin Lin
午後2時	Edgar Burns
午後4時	Freda Salvatore

65. 正解：C　易 ■■■■□□□ 難　**選択率：** (A) 10.2%　(B) 16.6%　**(C) 59.0%**　(D) 13.1%

What type of business do the speakers most likely work for?
(A) A utility company
(B) An advertising agency
(C) An accounting firm
(D) A printing company

☐ business: 名 会社

話者たちはどんな会社で働いている可能性が最も高いですか。
(A) 公共事業会社
(B) 広告代理店
(C) 会計事務所
(D) 印刷会社

▶解説　女性の❶や❸の発言から、男性は著名な会計士がプレゼンを行う簿記会議に出席予定だと分かります。男性は❷で「会計報告書のチェックを手伝う」と述べています。会話の後半で、来年の財務予測に関するプレゼンに参加希望だと述べていることからも、2人は(C)の「会計事務所」に勤務していると推測できます。

---

66. 正解：D　易 ■■■■■□□ 難　**選択率：** (A) 7.4%　(B) 33.6%　(C) 11.7%　**(D) 47.0%**

Look at the graphic. Which presentation will the man attend?
(A) Miles Jones'
(B) Calvin Lin's
(C) Edgar Burns'
(D) Freda Salvatore's

☐ attend: 動 ～に出席する

図表を見てください。男性はどのプレゼンテーションに出席しますか。
(A) Miles Jones の
(B) Calvin Lin の
(C) Edgar Burns の
(D) Freda Salvatore の

▶解説　選択肢には人の名前があるので、ヒントは開始時刻にあります。❸で女性から「プレゼンのいくつかを聞き逃すことになるのでは」と言われ、男性は❹で「最後のプレゼンしか見られない」と答えています。表によれば最後のプレゼンは Freda Salvatore のものなので、(D)が正解です。

---

67. 正解：B　易 ■■■□□□□ 難　**選択率：** (A) 14.8%　**(B) 72.4%**　(C) 7.1%　(D) 5.3%

What does the man say he will do on Friday?
(A) Stay in a hotel
(B) Take a train
(C) Introduce a speaker
(D) Attend a reception desk

☐ introduce: 動 ～を紹介する
☐ attend: 動 （職務として）～の世話をする
☐ reception desk: 受付

男性は金曜日に何をすると言っていますか。
(A) ホテルに泊まる
(B) 電車に乗る
(C) 講演者を紹介する
(D) 受付で働く

▶解説　女性からホテルに滞在するのかと尋ねられた男性は❺で「自宅に戻って金曜日早朝の電車に乗る」と答えています。よって、正解は(B)です。(C)と(D)については全く言及されていません。

Part 3 ▼ Listening Section

(((🗼))) ゼミ 生中継　　　　　🙂Hiro 🙂Mai 🙂Yasu 🎲Dai 🙂Saki

66. ……………………………
🙂 ヒントは何だった？
🙂 11時30分が「ダマシ」だと気づきましたが、解答のヒントが何か分かりません。
🙂 マイは気づいた？
🙂 たぶん、final だと思います。

🙂 そう。午後4時と言う代わりに情報をあいまいにしたよね。これが「ボカシのテクニック」だよ。抽象化された情報が音で聞こえる。
🙂 聞き取れなかったなぁ。2時か4時が聞こえると思い込んだのがマズかった……。
🙂 63番で紹介した「ダマシ」とこの「ボカシ」は実際のテストにもよく現れるから慣れておこう。

Part 3 会話問題

115 **Questions 68 through 70** rrefer to the following conversation and information.

W: Oh, no! Look at that. Our flight's been delayed. ❶ We'd better call Jim and let him know we're going to be late. He's picking us up, isn't he?

M: ❷ Jim or someone else from the office will come. I'll call the manager and find out who's coming.

W: ❸ It says the plane will depart at 6:30. We still have a lot of time.

M: ❹ Why don't we get something to eat? There's a restaurant by the escalators over there.

W: Sounds good. I hope they have some nice vegetarian dishes.

M: I'm sure they do.   (90w/31 sec.)

問題68-70は次の会話と情報に関するものです。

女：ああ、ひどい！　あれを見て。私たちの乗る飛行機が遅れてるわ。Jim に電話して、到着が遅れるって伝えた方がいいわね。彼が迎えに来てくれるんでしょ？

男：Jim か、誰か別の人が会社から来てくれることになってる。部長に電話して、誰が来る予定か聞いてみるよ。

女：飛行機が出発するのは6時30分だって。まだだいぶ時間があるわね。

男：何か食べない？　あそこのエスカレーターのそばにレストランがあるよ。

女：いいわね。おいしいベジタリアン料理があるといいんだけど。

男：きっとあるよ。

☐ flight: 图 飛行便、フライト　☐ delay: 動 ～を遅らせる　＊受け身で用いて「遅れる」の意味　☐ let ～ know: ～に知らせる

☐ pick ～ up: ～を車で迎えに行く　☐ manager: 图 責任者、長　☐ depart: 動 出発する

☐ Why don't we ～?: ～しませんか。　☐ over there: あそこに、向こうに

☐ vegetarian: 形 菜食主義者の、野菜ばかりの　☐ dish: 图 料理　☐ to be advised: 未定

Destination	Status	Departs
Paris	Delayed	To be advised
New York	On Time	4:30 P.M.
London	Delayed	6:30 P.M.
Tokyo	On Time	7:00 P.M.

目的地	状態	出発時刻
パリ	遅延	未定
ニューヨーク	定刻	午後4時30分
ロンドン	遅延	午後6時30分
東京	定刻	午後7時

68. 正解：**A**　易 ▬▬▬ ░░░░ 難　選択率：**(A) 80.9%**　(B) 9.5%　(C) 4.2%　(D) 4.6%

What does the woman suggest doing?
(A) Calling a coworker
(B) Reserving a hotel room
(C) Renting a car
(D) Charging their phones

☐ charge: 動 ～を充電する

女性は何をすることを提案していますか。
(A) 同僚に電話すること
(B) ホテルの部屋を予約すること
(C) 車を借りること
(D) 彼らの携帯電話を充電すること

▶解説 女性の提案は設問の主語である女性の発言に登場します。女性は❶で「Jimに電話をして遅れることを伝えた方がいい」と述べています。男性が❷で「ジムか、事務所の別の人が迎えに来るはず」と言っているのでJimは同僚だと推測でき、(A)が正解です。had betterは「そうしないと困ったことになる」状況で使う、「～した方がいい」を表す表現です。

---

69. 正解：**C**　易 ▬▬ ░░░░ 難　選択率：(A) 10.6%　(B) 2.8%　**(C) 85.2%**　(D) 1.1%

Look at the graphic. Where are the speakers most likely headed?
(A) To Paris
(B) To New York
(C) To London
(D) To Tokyo

☐ head: 動 (～に向かって) 進む

図表を見てください。話者たちはどこへ行こうとしている可能性が最も高いですか。
(A) Parisへ
(B) New Yorkへ
(C) Londonへ
(D) 東京へ

▶解説 選択肢には行き先が並んでいるので、表のDestination以外の項目に注目します。女性が❸で「飛行機は6時30分に出発する」と言っています。表によると6時30分のフライトはLondon行きだと分かります (❺)。従って話者たちは(C)のLondonに向かっていると考えられます。

---

70. 正解：**B**　易 ▬▬ ░░░░ 難　選択率：(A) 2.1%　**(B) 93.3%**　(C) 3.5%　(D) 0.7%

What will the speakers most likely do next?
(A) Change their flight
(B) Have a meal
(C) Postpone a meeting
(D) Submit some forms

☐ postpone: 動 ～を延期する
☐ submit: 動 ～を提出する
☐ form: 名 形式、記入用紙

話者たちはこの後、何をする可能性が最も高いですか。
(A) 航空便を変更する
(B) 食事を取る
(C) 会議を延期する
(D) 記入用紙を提出する

▶解説 出発まで時間があると知って男性は❹で「食事をしよう」と提案しています。女性もSounds good. (いいわね) と同意し、自分の好みに合う食事が提供されているか気にしていることから、2人はこの後レストランで食事をすると考えられます。従って、正解は(B)です。

（((📡))) ゼミ 🅖生中継　😺Hiro 🙂Mai 😺Yasu 😎Dai 😀Saki

69.

😺 これは易しいはず。サキはどうやって解いた？

😀 6時30分が聞こえたので、ロンドンを選びました。

😺 そう。女性の最初の発言にあるdelayedも一応ヒントだけど、パリ行きもDelayedだから、決定打にならない。6時30分がヒントだよ。

😺 グラフィック問題を解くコツが分かってきたかな。選択肢とグラフィックに共通する情報を見つけて、それ以外の情報に注目することが大事。69番で言えば、StatusとDepartsの欄を見るってこと。実際に視線を向けてね。ヒントが聞こえたらすぐに気づくから。グラフィック内の情報は、リスニングを助けてくれることを忘れずに。

TOEICよろず相談所 ヒロの部屋

⑨スキマ時間を活用したい

あの、スキマ時間を利用してTOEIC対策をしたいのですが、何か良い案をいただけませんか。半年後に100点アップが目標です。

では、どれだけスキマをお持ちか調べましょう。朝、家から会社まで何分かかりますか。

50分です。徒歩が15分、残りの35分は電車の中です。往復で70分が電車なので、この時間を利用したいです。

きちんと使えば平日だけで週5時間を超えますね。月に20時間、年240時間です。90分授業に換算すると、なんと160回分。

数値化すると、やる気が出ますね。

今は電車でスマホをいじってるだけじゃないですか。

よく分かりますね（苦笑）

まず、電車でやることを1つに決めましょう。1つに決めれば習慣化しやすいので。小さめの問題集を持っていますか。

はい。文法問題が100問入った本を持っています。

では、これから2カ月、40時間はその本だけやりましょう。100問に繰り返し取り組むのです。電車を道場だと思ってください。

道場…何か注意することはありますか。

最初のうちは日本語の解説をじっくり読んでOKですが、徐々にその時間を減らして、その分、英文を読む時間を増やしてください。必ず文頭から文末まで目を通してくださいね。そして、**解答に関係ない部分に登場している単語も全部覚えてください。**その本について誰よりも詳しくなるつもりで、没頭しましょう。狭く深く学習すれば、そこに出てくる単語や構文が記憶に刻み込まれるはずです。

Part 4 説明文問題

^{DL} 117 **Questions 71 through 73** refer to the following introduction.

M: ❶ Welcome to the annual Rosebank Career fair. I'm Joe Seaver and I'm the head organizer of the fair. ❷ I'm very excited to announce the lineup of speakers we have here to help with today's seminar on choosing a career and learning how to identify the most relevant qualifications. ❸ All of them are career counselors from major educational institutions from Florida and interstate. Each speaker will talk for about 30 minutes, after which I will give the audience an opportunity to ask questions. So, ❹ if you have something you want to ask, don't hesitate. (93w/34 sec.)

問題71-73は次の紹介に関するものです。
年次 Rosebank Career フェアへようこそ。私は Joe Seaver、このフェアの事務局長です。この場で本日のセミナーにお力添えくださる講演者の方々をご紹介できて、大変喜ばしく思います。セミナーのテーマは、キャリアの選択および最も確実な適性の見極め方を知ることについてです。講演者の方々はいずれも、Florida やその他の州をまたぐ主要な教育機関のキャリアカウンセラーです。お1人当たり約30分間お話しいただき、その後で参加者の皆さんからの質疑の時間を設ける予定です。何か尋ねたいことがあれば、ご遠慮なくどうぞ。

☐ annual: 形 年1回の　☐ head organizer: 事務局長　☐ announce: 動 ~を発表する　☐ lineup: 名 (講演者の) 顔触れ、陣容
☐ help with ~: ~を手伝う、力添えする　☐ career: 名 職業　☐ identify 動 ~を見極める　☐ relevant: 形 関連のある、適切な
☐ qualification: 名 資質、適性　☐ major: 形 一流の　☐ educational: 形 教育の　☐ institution: 名 機関　☐ interstate: 形 各州間の
☐ opportunity: 機会　☐ hesitate: 動 遠慮する、行動をためらう

71. 正解：**D**　易 ▭▭▭▭▭ 難　選択率：(A) 6.4% (B) 5.7% (C) 0.0% **(D) 87.6%**

What is about to take place?
(A) A sales presentation
(B) A college introduction
(C) A book reading
(D) A seminar

何が始まろうとしていますか。
(A) 販売のプレゼンテーション
(B) 大学の紹介
(C) 本の読み聞かせ
(D) セミナー

▶解説 話者は❶で「毎年恒例の Rosebank Career Fair (就職フェア) へようこそ」と聴衆に呼び掛け、❷で「本日のセミナーにお力添えくださる講演者」に言及しているので、(D) が正解です。

☐ about to ~: まさに~しようとしている　☐ take place: 起きる

72. 正解：**B**　易 ▭▭▭▭▭ 難　選択率：(A) 17.3% **(B) 78.1%** (C) 1.1% (D) 3.2%

Who is scheduled to speak?
(A) College professors
(B) Career counselors
(C) Artists
(D) Journalists

誰が話す予定ですか。
(A) 大学教授
(B) キャリアカウンセラー
(C) 芸術家
(D) ジャーナリスト

▶解説 話者は❷で、セミナーの講演者と講演内容を今から発表することを伝えています。❸で、その講演者全員が career counselors (キャリアカウンセラー) だと紹介されています。よって、正解は (B) です。

☐ schedule: 動 ~を予定する

73. 正解：**D**　易 ▭▭▭▭▭ 難　選択率：(A) 1.4% (B) 2.8% (C) 1.4% **(D) 93.6%**

What are the audience members encouraged to do?
(A) Take notes
(B) Complete evaluation forms
(C) Open brochures
(D) Ask questions

聴衆は何をするよう促されていますか。
(A) メモを取る
(B) 評価表を埋める
(C) パンフレットを開く
(D) 質問する

▶解説 「聞き手の行動」が問われているので、you を主語にした内容がヒントになります。最終文❹で、何か質問があればためらわずに尋ねるよう、聞き手に促しています。この部分を簡潔に「質問する」と表現した (D) が正解です。

☐ encourage ~ to ...: ~に…するよう勧める、促す　☐ complete: 動 ~に記入する　☐ evaluation form: 評価表　☐ brochure: 名 パンフレット

((📡)) ゼミ 生 中継　　😀 Hiro 😊 Mai 😀 Yasu 😎 Dai 😀 Saki

😀 Part 4の全体的な印象はどうだった？　マイ？

😊 Test 1と比べると解きやすかったです。

😀 では、中身を順に見ていこう。

72.

😀 (A)を選んだ人は？

😀 はい、選びました。career counselors ってちゃんと言っていたんですね。聞き逃しました。

😀 で、educationalという単語を聞いて、(A)にしたのか。

😀 そうです。College professors は教育に関係するので、たぶん正解だと思って。

😀 サキは、どれを選んだ？

😀 educationalは聞き取れなかったのですが、career counselors が聞こえたので、(B)を選びました。ヒントがそのまま選択肢にあると解きやすいです。

Part 4 説明文問題

DL 118 **Questions 74 through 76** refer to the following telephone message.

W: Hi. It's Rhonda Bruce from the Winds Hotel on Carmichael Street. ❶ We ordered some large flowerpots for our lobby. ❷ They have just been delivered but one of them is badly damaged. It's not a big problem for us because we'd actually ordered one too many. ❸ If you could just amend the invoice to one less, that would be great. We'll pay as soon as we get the updated invoice. Also, let me know what you'd like us to do with the broken one. I could have our janitor take care of it. Otherwise, you are welcome to come and pick it up. (102w/36 sec.)

問題74-76は次の電話メッセージに関するものです。もしもし。Carmichael StreetにあるWinds HotelのRhonda Bruceです。当館内ロビーに置くための大型の植木鉢を数点発注しました。今、配送されたところなのですが、そのうちの1つがひどく破損しています。こちらにとっては、大きな問題ではありません。というのも、実は1つ多く発注していたからです。そちらで請求書を修正し、品数を1つ減らしていただければ、大変助かります。新しい請求書を受け取り次第、お支払いします。それから、壊れた植木鉢をどうすればいいかお知らせください。こちらの清掃担当者に処分させることは可能です。あるいは、お引き取りにいらっしゃっても結構です。

□ flowerpot: 名 植木鉢　□ badly: 副 ひどく　□ damaged: 形 破損している　□ too many: 多い、余分な　□ amend: 動 〜を修正する
□ invoice: 名 請求書　□ one less: 1つ減らして、1つ少なく　□ updated: 形 最新の　□ broken: 形 壊れた　□ janitor: 名 管理人、用務員
□ take care of 〜: 〜を処理する　□ otherwise: 副 あるいは、できなければ

---

74. 正解：**C** 易 ▓▓░░░░ 難　選択率：(A) 1.1% (B) 1.1% **(C) 97.2%** (D) 0.4%

What has been ordered?
(A) Tablecloths
(B) A sofa
(C) Flowerpots
(D) Pamphlets

何が発注されましたか。
(A) テーブルクロス
(B) ソファ
(C) 植木鉢
(D) パンフレット

▶解説 注文された物が問われています。❶から、話者は large flowerpots（大きな植木鉢）を注文したことが分かります。よって、正解は (C) です。

---

75. 正解：**A** 易 ▓▓░░░░ 難　選択率：**(A) 94.3%** (B) 1.8% (C) 2.1% (D) 1.4%

What problem does the speaker mention?
(A) An item was damaged.
(B) A delivery was late.
(C) The color was wrong.
(D) The address has changed.

話者はどんな問題に触れていますか。
(A) ある品物が壊れていた。
(B) 配送が遅れた。
(C) 色が間違っていた。
(D) 所在地が変わった。

▶解説 話者は❷で、「配達された植木鉢のうちの1つがひどく破損している」と述べています。よって、正解は (A) です。「配達された」とは述べられていますが、「配達が遅れた」という発言はないので、(B) は不適切です。

---

76. 正解：**D** 易 ░░░░░░ 難　選択率：(A)　-　(B)　-　(C)　-　(D)　-

What is the listener asked to do?
(A) Send a replacement
(B) Take another route
(C) Pay for some repairs
(D) Update an invoice

聞き手は何をするよう求められていますか。
(A) 代替品を送る
(B) 別の道を通る
(C) 修理費用を払う
(D) 請求書を更新する

▶解説 話者は❸で、「amend the invoice（請求書を修正する）してもらえたらとても助かる」と述べています。この内容を「請求書を更新する」と表した (D) が正解です。❸の文末の that would be great（そうしてもらえたら助かる）は感謝の気持ちを伝える際に使う表現です。

□ replacement: 名 代替品　□ repair: 名 修理　□ update: 動 〜を更新する

((↯)) ゼミ 生 中継

🧑 Hiro 👧 Mai 😺 Yasu 🎲 Dai 😀 Saki

76.

😺 難しかった？　ダイ、どれを選んだ？

🎲 (A)です。お客様に納品した植木鉢が壊れていたのであれば、新しいものに交換するのが常識です。

😺 それを言うんだったら、請求書を修正するのも常識だから、(D)でもいいんじゃない？

🎲 (A)を見て即決したので、(D)は読みませんでした。

😺 この問題には難しい点2つある。1つはヒントが早めに登場すること。

もう1つは、Could you 〜 ?のような典型的な依頼表現がないことだよ。ヒントは中盤のIf you could just amend the invoice 〜という発言なんだけど、実はこのifは依頼表現なんだよ。知っていた？

😀 初めて聞きました。

😺 実は日本語でも同じだよ。「請求書を修正していただければ、大変助かります」と取引先が言ってきたら、どう思う？　「だから何？」とは思わないよね。請求書を修正するよう頼まれたと思うよね。

😀 本当ですね。気づきませんでした。

DL 119 **Questions 77 through 79** refer to the following announcement.

M: ❶Since you are all here at the monthly residents' meeting, I have a short announcement to make. At the previous residents' meeting, ❷it was decided that we should have the grounds cleaned up and some minor landscaping carried out. Since then, we have spoken with a landscaper, and ❸they will carry out the work starting next Monday. There is likely to be a lot of noise. Also, as several trees will be removed, we expect a lot of dust. ❹I advise you to keep your windows closed until the work is finished.

(92w/36 sec.)

問題77-79は次のお知らせに関するものです。
皆さん月1回の住民集会にご出席いただきましたので、簡単な報告をさせていただきます。前回の住民集会で、敷地内の清掃と、ちょっとした造園作業を行うことが決まりました。以来、ある造園業者と話を進めており、来週の月曜日に業者が作業を開始する予定です。結構な騒音が出そうです。また、何本か木が伐採されるので、かなりのほこりが予想されます。作業が終了するまで窓を閉めておくことをお勧めします。

☐ resident: 图 居住者　☐ ground: 图 土地　☐ minor: 形 小さい、小規模な　☐ landscaping: 图 造園　☐ carry out 〜: 〜を実施する
☐ landscaper: 图 造園業者　☐ remove: 動 〜を取り除く　☐ expect: 動 〜を予想する　☐ dust: 图 ほこり、粉塵

---

77. 正解：**A** 易■■■□□□□□ 難　選択率：(A) 81.6% (B) 7.4% (C) 4.6% (D) 5.3%

Who is the announcement intended for?
(A) Residents
(B) Tour participants
(C) Hotel guests
(D) Store clerks

このお知らせは誰に向けられたものですか。
(A) 住民
(B) ツアーの参加者
(C) ホテルの客
(D) 店員

▶解説 話者は❶で the monthly residents' meeting（月1回の住民集会）と述べ、簡単な報告をすると言っています。続く内容も前回の住民集会で決められた内容で、住民向けの説明が続くことから(A)の「住民」に向けて行われていると判断できます。

☐ intend A for B: AをBに提供するよう意図する

---

78. 正解：**B** 易■■■■□□□□ 難　選択率：(A) 0.7% (B) 87.3% (C) 4.2% (D) 6.7%

What will happen next week?
(A) An attraction will be closed.
(B) Landscaping will be carried out.
(C) A festival will commence.
(D) A decision will be announced.

来週、何がありますか。
(A) ある集客施設が閉鎖される。
(B) 造園作業が行われる。
(C) 祭りが始まる。
(D) 決定事項が告知される。

▶解説 話者は❷で「敷地内の清掃とちょっとした造園作業をすることが決まった」と述べ、❸で「作業は来週の月曜日から始まる」と伝えています。よって、正解は(B) です。

☐ attraction: 图 観光名所、集客施設
☐ commence: 動 始まる　☐ decision: 图 決定、決断

---

79. 正解：**D** 易■□□□□□□□ 難　選択率：(A) 1.4% (B) 2.8% (C) 3.5% (D) 90.8%

What does the speaker recommend listeners do?
(A) Check their mail
(B) Obtain tickets for an event
(C) Attend a meeting
(D) Keep windows closed

話者は聞き手たちに何をするよう勧めていますか。
(A) 郵便物を調べる
(B) 催事のチケットを手に入れる
(C) 会議に出席する
(D) 窓を閉めておく

▶解説 ❹から、話者が聞き手に推奨しているのは、keep your windows closed（窓を閉めておく）ことだと分かります。従って、(D) が正解です。

☐ recommend: 動 〜を勧める
☐ obtain: 動 〜を手に入れる　☐ attend: 動 〜に出席する

📡))) ゼミ 生中継

😀 Hiro 🙂 Mai 😆 Yasu 😎 Dai 😊 Saki

😀 このトークがどんな状況で行われているかイメージできる？ ヤスは分かった？

😆 いいえ。住人が集まる会議って何ですか？

😀 ヤスみたいに1人暮らしだとピンと来ないよね。サキは学生だからなおさら分からないか。

😎 たぶん、マンションの管理組合の定例会ですよね。最近、うちの父が理事になったので、たまに会議に出ています。

😀 そうなの？ じゃ、ピンと来た？

😎 はい。しかも最近、「明日、除草剤をまくから洗濯物を干すのも窓を開けるのもダメ」って言っていたので、79番は楽勝でした。

😀 ガチで？ ラッキーだったね。

😀 TOEICはビジネス英語だから大学生は不利と言われることがあるけど、そうじゃない。TOEICワールドはビジネスパーソンの「日常」であって、飛び交う英語はビジネス特化じゃない。専門用語や特殊な知識は必要ないから、大学生でも英語力だけで勝負できる。実際、900点以上を取る学生だってたくさんいる。

Part 4 説明文問題

120 **Questions 80 through 82** refer to the following excerpt from a meeting.

W: Thanks for coming to this meeting at short notice. ❶ I've called it so that I can introduce you all to Doreen Gordon. ❷ She's going to be working in our marketing department from today. Ms. Gordon has a long history in television advertising. ❸ I am sure she will be able to give some pointers after we have watched our latest advertisement together. I think the marketing team has been doing amazing work in radio and print media, but television and Internet really seem to be our weakness. ❹ The focus group I commissioned claimed that our most recent television commercial didn't inspire them to buy milk at all. (106w/43 sec.)

問題80-82は次の会議の一部に関するものです。急な知らせにもかかわらずこの会議に集まってくれてありがとう。会議を招集したのは、皆さんをDoreen Gordonさんに紹介できればと思ったからです。彼女は今日からマーケティング部で働きます。Gordonさんにはテレビ広告の分野での長い経験があります。きっと彼女なら、当社の最新の広告を一緒に見た後で何らかの助言をくれると思います。マーケティング部は、ラジオや印刷媒体向けには素晴らしい仕事をしてきたと思いますが、テレビとインターネットは実際、当社の弱みだと思われます。私が集めたフォーカスグループの人たちは、当社の直近のテレビコマーシャルを見ても、ミルクを買う気など全く起きなかったと主張したのです。

- ☐ at short notice: 急な知らせで ☐ introduce A to B: AをBに紹介する ☐ pointer: 名 助言、アドバイス ☐ latest: 形 最新の
- ☐ amazing: 形 素晴らしい ☐ print media: 印刷媒体 ＊新聞や書籍などを指す ☐ weakness: 名 弱み
- ☐ focus group: フォーカスグループ ＊市場調査のために抽出された消費者グループのこと
- ☐ commission: 動 ～に委託する、依頼する ☐ claim: 動 ～だと主張する ☐ inspire: 動 ～の意欲をかき立てる

80. 正解：**D**　易 ■■□□□□□ 難　選択率：(A) 9.5%　(B) 6.0%　(C) 12.0%　**(D) 70.7%**

What is the purpose of the meeting?
(A) To suggest buying some new equipment
(B) To ask people to volunteer on a project
(C) To update a reporting procedure
(D) To introduce a new employee

□ equipment: 名 設備
□ volunteer: 動 自ら進んで行う、手助けを申し出る
□ procedure: 名 手順

この会議の目的は何ですか。
(A) 新たな設備の購入を提案すること
(B) あるプロジェクトにボランティアで関わるよう人々に頼むこと
(C) 報告の手順を変えること
(D) 新しい従業員を紹介すること

▶解説 話者は会議に来てくれたことのお礼に続けて、❶で「皆さんを Doreen Gordon さんに紹介するために会議を開いた」と述べています。続く❷で、「彼女は今日からマーケティング部で働く」と説明しています。つまり、新しい部員である Gordon さんを紹介することが会議の目的なので、正解は (D) です。

81. 正解：**D**　易 ■■□□□□□ 難　選択率：(A) 7.1%　(B) 19.1%　(C) 9.2%　**(D) 63.3%**

What does the speaker mean when she says, "Ms. Gordon has a long history in television advertising"?
(A) She thinks Ms. Gordon's knowledge is outdated.
(B) She hopes Ms. Gordon has connections with many experts.
(C) She has known Ms. Gordon for a long time.
(D) She believes Ms. Gordon has valuable experience.

□ knowledge: 名 知識
□ outdated: 形 時代遅れの、古い
□ connection: 名 (通例複数形で) 人脈
□ expert: 名 専門家　□ valuable: 形 貴重な、有益な

話者はどんな意味を込めて「Gordon さんにはテレビ広告の分野での長い経験があります」と言っていますか。
(A) 彼女は Gordon さんの知識が時代遅れだと思っている。
(B) 彼女は Gordon さんが多くの専門家との人脈を持っていることを望んでいる。
(C) 彼女は Gordon さんと旧知の仲だ。
(D) 彼女は Gordon さんが貴重な経験を積んでいると考えている。

▶解説 設問に引用されているターゲット文の直後、❸で「きっと彼女なら最新の広告に対して助言をくれると思う」と伝えています。この流れからターゲット文は、彼女のマーケティングにおける経験の豊富さを伝えるために述べられたと判断できるため、(D) が正解です。

82. 正解：**B**　易 ■■□□□□□ 難　選択率：(A) 37.5%　**(B) 51.2%**　(C) 1.8%　(D) 8.5%

What did the focus group say about the commercial?
(A) It was very interesting.
(B) It was not inspiring.
(C) It had too much music.
(D) It had confusing dialogue.

□ confusing: 形 紛らわしい、ややこしい
□ dialogue: 名 対話

フォーカスグループはコマーシャルについてどんなことを言いましたか。
(A) それはとても面白かった。
(B) それは意欲をそそられるものではなかった。
(C) それには音楽が多過ぎた。
(D) それには分かりにくい対話が使われていた。

▶解説 設問は focus group（フォーカスグループ）の発言を問うているので、focus group を主語とした発言が手掛かりになるはずです。❹で「フォーカスグループはテレビコマーシャルを見ても、購買意欲が全く起きなかったと主張した」と述べられています。よって、(B) が正解です。

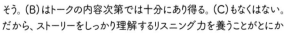

((●)) ゼミ 生中継　　　　😀 Hiro　🙂 Mai　😊 Yasu　😎 Dai　😀 Saki

81.
😊 意図問題の選択肢が全て魅力的であることは少ない。音を聞く前に、ターゲット文と比べるだけでいきなり消せる選択肢がある。ここでは、(A) が魅力ゼロだよ。

😀 やっぱりそうですか。ターゲット文はポジティブな感じなので、(A) は違うと思いました。

😊 正解と同じ程度に魅力的な選択肢もあるけどね。

😎 (B) ですか。

そう。(B) はトークの内容次第では十分にあり得る。(C) もなくはない。だから、ストーリーをしっかり理解するリスニング力を養うことがとにかく大事。

82.
😀 4割近くのモニターが (A) を選んだ。魅力的だった？

😎 81番を解くのに時間がかかり過ぎて、82番まで手が回らなかったんだと思います。私はそうでした。

Part 4 説明文問題

DL 122 Questions 83 through 85 refer to the following broadcast.

M: ❶Today, we have a wonderful talent in the studio — George Wallace! ❷You all know him best as the writer of the popular children's book, *Magic Train,* but he has also written countless other novels and short stories. He's here in Washington to promote his latest project, which is a conversion of one of his novels into a feature-length animation. We'll have a contest first, though. ❸The first person to call the station and name Mr. Wallace's most recent publication will be the winner. And ❹that person will receive a ticket to a writing workshop he is providing about becoming a successful writer.　　　　　　　　　　(102w/36 sec.)

問題83-85は次の放送に関するものです。
今日は、スタジオに素晴らしい才能の持ち主をお招きしています——George Wallaceさんです！　皆さんにとって彼は何よりも、人気の児童書『Magic Train』の作者として有名ですが、他にも数え切れないほどの小説や短編作品を著されています。彼はここWashingtonを訪れ、最新プロジェクトのプロモーションを行っていらっしゃいます。それは、ご自身の小説の1つを長編アニメ化するというものです。さて、まずはコンテストから始めましょう。一番乗りで局に電話をかけ、Wallaceさんの最新作の書名を言い当てた方が勝者です。その方には、彼が主催する、作家として成功するための文章講座の参加チケットが進呈されます。

□ talent: 图 才能のある人　□ countless: 形 数え切れない、無数の　□ promote: 動 ～を宣伝する　□ latest: 形 最新の
□ conversion ～ into ...: ～の…への変換　□ feature-length: 形 長編の　□ animation: 图 アニメーション　□ station: 图 放送局
□ publication: 图 出版物　□ provide: 動 ～を提供する　□ successful: 形 成功した

---

83. 正解：B 易 ■■□□□ 難　選択率：(A) 2.5% **(B) 95.1%** (C) 0.7% (D) 0.4%

Who is George Wallace?
(A) A producer
(B) A writer
(C) A singer
(D) A videographer

George Wallaceとは誰ですか。
(A) プロデューサー
(B) 作家
(C) 歌手
(D) 映像作家

▶解説 話者は❶で、スタジオに来ている人物がGeorge Wallaceさんだと紹介しています。その直後の❷で、彼のことを「人気の児童書の作家として知られている」と言い、彼の書籍名や数多くの小説や短編を書いた経歴を述べています。よって、(B)が正解です。

---

84. 正解：C 易 ■■■■□ 難　選択率：(A) 5.7% (B) 30.4% **(C) 52.3%** (D) 9.9%

What are listeners asked to do when they call?
(A) Suggest a title for a song
(B) Talk about an experience
(C) Name one of George Wallace's works
(D) Guess the location of a film set

聞き手たちは、電話をかけたら何をするよう求められていますか。
(A) 歌のタイトルを提案する
(B) ある体験について語る
(C) George Wallaceの作品を1つ挙げる
(D) 映画の撮影場所を推測する

▶解説 話者は❸で、「一番乗りで局に電話をかけ、Wallaceさんの最新作の書名を言い当てた人が勝者だ」と述べています。この内容を「George Wallaceさんの作品名を1つ挙げる」と表した(C)が正解です。

□ location: 图 ロケ地、野外撮影地　□ film: 映画

---

85. 正解：D 易 ■■■■■ 難　選択率：(A) 17.0% (B) 9.5% (C) 5.7% **(D) 66.4%**

What will the winner be given?
(A) A copy of a new book
(B) An invitation to a party
(C) An autographed album
(D) A ticket to a workshop

勝者には何が与えられますか。
(A) 新刊書1冊
(B) パーティーへの招待状
(C) サイン入りのアルバム
(D) 講座への参加チケット

▶解説 ❹から、勝者は「文章講座の参加チケット」がもらえることが分かります。よって、正解は(D)です。

□ autograph: 動 ～にサインする

(((📡))) ゼミ 生中継　　　　😀Hiro 😀Mai 😀Yasu 😀Dai 😀Saki

84.

😀 ヤス、どれを選んだ?

😀 (B)ですが、正直、勘です。

😀 おかしいな。(B)を選んだモニターが3割もいる。

😀 83番で(B)を選んだ人は、84番で(A)のsongと、(D)のfilmが変だと気づいて消去するはずです。結果、(B)と(C)で迷います。

😀 なるほど。それで思い出した。問題作成者は不正解を利用して偽のシナリオを作るから注意して。

😀 どういうことですか。

😀 83番から順に、(C)と(A)と(C)を見て。どれも歌に関係しているよね。

😀 本当だ！　どうしてこうなるんですか?

😀 問題作成者は、誰にとっても魅力のない選択肢は作らない。もし、84番と85番の選択肢が全て本や著者から連想されるものだったら、83番の正解が(B)だとバレる。だから、そうならないように、異なる設問に対する選択肢が互いに関連するように作るんだ。

123 Questions 86 through 88 refer to the following telephone message.

W: Hi. It's Glenda Rosen from Akimoto Publishing. I've signed up for the annual publishers' conference, but ❶ I haven't received any information about the schedule. I must say, ❷ I'm very disappointed. That was a month ago and ❸ I was informed that a conference agenda and introductions of the speakers and workshop topics would be posted online within a couple of weeks. ❹ I'm still waiting. I would like to plan ahead, so ❺ when will that information be available? I hope this isn't a repeat of last year. ❻ I had to wait until the week before to find out anything. (97w/37 sec.)

問題86-88は次の電話メッセージに関するものです。
もしもし。Akimoto PublishingのGlenda Rosenです。年次出版社会議に申し込んだのですが、スケジュールに関する情報をまだいただいていません。大変がっかりしていると言わざるを得ません。申し込んだのは1カ月前で、その時のお話では、会議の議題や講演者の紹介、セミナーのテーマなどが2週間以内にオンラインで発表されるだろうということでした。いまだに私は待っている状況です。前もって計画を立てたいのですが、いつそうした情報が開示されるのでしょうか。これが昨年の二の舞にならないことを願っています。情報を得るには1週間前まで待たなければいけなかったのですから。

☐ annual: 形 年1回の ☐ publisher: 名 出版社 ☐ conference 名 会議 ☐ disappointed: 形 失望した ☐ agenda: 名 議題、予定
☐ introduction: 名 紹介 ☐ workshop: 名 セミナー、ワークショップ ☐ post: 動 ～を掲載する ☐ within: 前 ～以内に
☐ ahead: 副 これから先に、前もって ☐ repeat: 名 繰り返し

---

86. 正解：A 易■■■■■□□ 難 **選択率：(A) 45.9%** (B) 38.2% (C) 5.7% (D) 8.1%

What is the purpose of the message?
(A) To make a complaint
(B) To announce a schedule
(C) To request a change
(D) To explain a delay

☐ delay: 名 遅延

このメッセージの目的は何ですか。
(A) 苦情を言うこと
(B) スケジュールを発表すること
(C) 変更を求めること
(D) 遅延について説明すること

▶解説 話者は❶で会議のスケジュールを受け取っていないこと、❷でそのせいで失望していることを伝えています。さらに❹で、「まだ待っている」と言っています。これらから、話者は不満を伝えるために電話をかけたと判断できるので、正解は(A)です。

---

87. 正解：B 易■■□□□□□ 難 (A) 1.8% **(B) 81.6%** (C) 2.8% (D) 12.4%

What does the speaker ask about?
(A) Ticket prices
(B) Workshop topics
(C) Parking allocation
(D) Accommodation options

話者は何について尋ねていますか。
(A) チケットの値段
(B) セミナーのテーマ
(C) 駐車場の割り当て
(D) 宿泊施設の選択肢

▶解説 ❸から「会議の議題、講演者の紹介、セミナーのテーマ」の3点がウェブサイトに掲載される予定だったことが分かり、話者は❺で、「いつそれらの情報を得られるのか」と尋ねています。よって、3点のうちの1つに該当する(B)が正解です。

☐ allocation: 名 割り当て ☐ accommodation: 名 宿泊施設 ☐ option: 名 選択肢

---

88. 正解：A 易■■■■■□□ 難 **選択率：(A) 49.8%** (B) 23.0% (C) 19.4% (D) 6.4%

What does the speaker imply when she says, "I hope this isn't a repeat of last year"?
(A) The same problem occurred in the past.
(B) The schedule looks similar to the previous year's.
(C) She did not receive an invitation to a prior event.
(D) Few people are showing interest in an event.

話者はどんな意味を込めて「これが昨年の二の舞になら無いことを願っています」と言っているのですか。
(A) 同じ問題が過去に起きた。
(B) スケジュールが前年のものと同じに思える。
(C) 彼女は事前イベントへの招待状を受け取らなかった。
(D) 催事に興味を示している人がほとんどいない。

▶解説 不満や疑問を伝えた後に、設問で引用された文を言い、❻で「（昨年は）会議の1週間前にならないと情報が得られなかった」と続けています。この流れから、ターゲット文は「今年も昨年と同じ状況になるのでは」という懸念を伝えるための発言だと考えられるので、(A)が正解です。

☐ occur: 動 発生する ☐ similar: 形 類似した ☐ prior: 形 事前の ☐ few: 形 ほとんどない

((ゼミ 生中継 Hiro Mai Yasu Dai Saki

86.
😮 (B)を選びたくなった？ (B)を選んだモニターは、上級グループだと25.5%だけど、初級と中級グループでは40%以上もいる。
😎 前半でscheduleが聞こえたので、思わず選びました。
😮 TOEICは「聞こえた単語を選ぶテスト」じゃない。文単位で情報を理解することが重要だよ。

88.
😮 こちらも(B)を選んだモニターが多いけれど、話者はスケジュールが未発表であることに苦情を言っているのだから、(B)は正解にならない。今年のスケジュールが昨年のスケジュールに似ているかどうかは不明だからね。
😎 確かに。

Part 4 ▼ Listening Section

Part 4 説明文問題

DL 124 **Questions 89 through 91** refer to the following advertisement.

W: For almost 30 years, ❶Rudolph's weekend market has been a popular place for families to spend time in Blackwood. So much so, that we have outgrown our location at 199 Beach Road. ❷From this weekend, Rudolph's will be at a new far more expansive location. You'll find us at 234 Dunhill Street next to the Gregory Library. We have almost twice as much space and, therefore, ❸twice as many stalls and a huge variety of goods for sale. ❹The grand opening is on Sunday, and to celebrate, we've asked performers from the Gilhooley Dance Troop to perform on the main stage between two and three o'clock. Fine weather is forecast and there is plenty of parking, so why not come and spend the day at the markets? (127w/47 sec.)

問題89-91は次の宣伝に関するものです。
30年近くもの間、Rudolph's週末市場は家族連れがBlackwoodで過ごす人気スポットでした。その人気の高さゆえBeach Road 199番地は私たちにとって狭くなりすぎました。今週末からRudolph'sは、従来よりもはるかに広い新たな場所へ移転します。Dunhill Street 234番地、Gregory Libraryの隣です。ほぼ2倍のスペースがあり、そのため、2倍の数の露店が出店し、多種多様な商品を販売します。グランドオープンは日曜日で、これを記念して、Gilhooley Dance Troopのパフォーマーたちに依頼して2時から3時までメインステージでダンスを披露してもらいます。晴天が予報されており、豊富な駐車スペースをご用意していますので、ぜひ当日は市場へ来てお過ごしください。

□ so much so: 非常にそうなので □ outgrow: 動 成長してはみ出す ＊outgrownは過去分詞 □ far: 副（程度を表す比較級を強調して）はるかに
□ expansive: 形 広々としている □ stall: 名 売店 □ celebrate: 動 ～を祝う □ troop: 名 一団 □ forecast: 動 ～を予報する ＊ここでは過去分詞

---

89. 正解：**A** 易■■■□□■■ 難　選択率：**(A) 69.6%** (B) 6.0% (C) 19.1% (D) 3.2%

What kind of business is Rudolph's?
(A) An outdoor market
(B) A restaurant
(C) A grocery store
(D) A vocational school

Rudolph'sはどんな種類の事業者ですか。
(A) 屋外市場
(B) レストラン
(C) 食料雑貨店
(D) 専門学校

▶解説 ❶から、Rudolph'sは週末に開かれるmarket（市場）だと分かります。さらに、❸のstallsは「露店」なので、屋外の市場であることが明らかです。(A)が正解です。

□ outdoor: 形 野外の □ vocational: 形 職業訓練の

---

90. 正解：**C** 易■■■□□■■ 難　選択率：(A) 7.8% (B) 7.4% **(C) 80.9%** (D) 1.4%

According to the speaker, what has Rudolph's done recently?
(A) Started a new course
(B) Changed its opening hours
(C) Moved to a new location
(D) Hired more staff

話者によると、Rudolph'sは最近何をしましたか。
(A) 新たな講座を始めた
(B) 営業時間を変えた
(C) 新たな場所へ移転した
(D) より多くの従業員を雇った

▶解説 設問は「最近、何をしたか」を問うているので、「最近」を示す表現に注意して聞くのがポイントです。❷の文はFrom this weekend（今週から）で始まり、市場が新しい場所で開かれると述べられていることから、(C)が正解です。

---

91. 正解：**C** 易■■■□□■■ 難　選択率：(A) 3.5% (B) 2.8% **(C) 76.3%** (D) 14.8%

What can listeners do on Sunday?
(A) Try a new menu
(B) Speak with experts
(C) Watch a performance
(D) Get big discounts

聞き手たちは日曜日に何ができますか。
(A) 新しい料理を試食する
(B) 専門家たちと話す
(C) パフォーマンスを見る
(D) 大幅な値引きを受ける

▶解説 設問にあるSundayという具体的な曜日を待ち伏せして聞くようにしましょう。❹から、日曜日はグランドオープンの日で、Gilhooley Dance Troopがダンスを披露することが分かります。よって、(C)が正解です。

□ menu: 名 料理 □ expert: 名 専門家

((( ))) ゼミ生中継　😊Hiro 😊Mai 😊Yasu 😊Dai 😊Saki

89.

😊 冒頭のweekend marketを画像検索すれば明らかだね。正解は(A)に決まる。Rudolph'sは店舗じゃなく市場だよ。

😊 この店が売っているのが食料品なのかアウトドア用品なのか分かりませんでした。

😊 え、アウトドアは関係ないよ。

😊 An outdoor marketは「青空市場」のこと。屋外でいろんな店が集まっている場所だけど、イメージできる？

😊 できます。実家がある高知市に「日曜市」という市場がありますので。あ、そっか。(C)は1つの食料品店だから間違いですね。

😊 Part 1の5番は青空市場ですか。

😊 そう、あのような店が集まる場所だよ。中盤のstallsも決定的なヒントだし、最後に聞こえるfine weather is forecastもヒントだね。天気を理由に来場を促しているから、Rudolph'sは屋外にある。

😊 確かに。

DL 125 **Questions 92 through 94** refer to the following news report.

M: Good evening listeners. This is Vin Singh, and I'm here with the evening news for today. ❶ Gladstone is busily getting ready to be in the world's spotlight as it hosts the Gladstone Comedy Festival. ❷ Thousands of visitors will be pouring into the city from all over the world. ❸ To keep up with demand, the city council is putting on additional train services between the suburbs and the city center. ❹ The big concern, however, is the amount of accommodation. ❺ Last year they rejected a petition to build a 500-room hotel on Camden Street. It might be time to reconsider that decision. And, if possible, consider an even larger construction.

(108w/41 sec.)

問題92-94は次のニュース報道に関するものです。こんばんは、リスナーの皆さん。Vin Singhがお送りする、今日の夕方のニュースです。Gladstone市は、世界の注目を浴びるための準備に余念がありません。Gladstone Comedy Festivalを主催するからです。大勢の来訪者が、世界中から市へ押し寄せてくることでしょう。この需要に応えようと、市議会は郊外と市の中心部を結ぶ追加の列車の運行を実施する意向です。しかしながら大きな懸念事項は、宿泊施設の受け入れ規模です。昨年、市議会はCamden Streetに500室規模のホテルの建設を求める請願を退けました。この決定を再考すべき時期が来ているのかもしれません。そして、できれば、さらに大規模な施設の建築を検討すべきところです。

□ busily: 副 盛んに、熱心に　□ be in the world's spotlight: 全世界の注目の的になる　□ demand: 名 需要
□ city council: 市議会　□ put on ～:（サービス）を特別に提供する　□ accommodation: 名 宿泊施設　□ reject: 動 ～を却下する
□ petition: 名 請願　□ reconsider: 動 ～を再考する　□ consider: 動 ～を検討する　□ even: 副（程度を表す比較級を強調して）なお一層

---

92. 正解：**A**　易 ■■■■□□□ 難　選択率：**(A) 76.0%**　(B) 12.4%　(C) 4.9%　(D) 3.2%

What is the news report mainly about?
(A) An international event
(B) A city election
(C) A selection process
(D) A cleanup project

このニュース報道の主題は何ですか。
(A) 国際イベント
(B) 市の選挙
(C) 選考過程
(D) 浄化計画

▶解説 ❶から、GladstoneでComedy Festivalが開かれ、世界中の注目を集めること、❷で世界中から観光客が訪れることが分かります。その後も、Comedy Festivalのために行われる対策や懸念事項が述べられていることから、(A)が正解です。

---

93. 正解：**C**　易 ■■■■□□□ 難　選択率：(A) 9.5%　(B) 19.4%　**(C) 63.3%**　(D) 4.9%

What change is being planned?
(A) More frequent inspections
(B) Developing public land
(C) Additional train services
(D) Changing the date of an event

どのような変更が計画されていますか。
(A) より頻繁な検査
(B) 公有地の開発
(C) 追加の列車運行
(D) 催事の日付の変更

▶解説 ❷で観光客が増えることが分かり、その需要に応えるために、「追加の列車の運行（additional train services）」を実施すると❸で述べられています。よって、(C)が正解です。

---

94. 正解：**B**　易 ■■■■□□□ 難　選択率：(A) 16.6%　**(B) 67.1%**　(C) 6.4%　(D) 6.7%

Why does the speaker say, "It might be time to reconsider that decision"?
(A) The town should offer more attractions.
(B) There may not be enough accommodation.
(C) More employment opportunities are needed.
(D) The council has spent too much money.

なぜ話者は「この決定を再考すべき時期が来ているのかもしれません」と言っていますか。
(A) この町はもっと集客施設を提供した方がよい。
(B) 十分な宿泊施設がないかもしれない。
(C) より多くの雇用機会が必要だ。
(D) 議会が費用を使い過ぎている。

▶解説 ❹と❺から、宿泊施設の不足が心配されるにもかかわらず、大規模ホテルが建設されなかったことが分かります。この後にターゲット文が続くので、「ホテルの建設を却下したことを再考すべき」と話者は考えています。その理由は宿泊施設の不足なので、(B)が正解です。

Part 4　▼ Listening Section

((ᴀ)) ゼミ 生 中継　😀 Hiro　😺 Mai　😼 Yasu　🙂 Dai　😸 Saki

93.

😺 やっぱり、(C)か～。

🙂 additional train servicesはそのままトークにあるけど、気づかなかった？

😀 耳に入ったはずなのに気づかないのは悔しいなぁ。ホテル建設の話があったから、土地の開発が進んでいるのかと思いました。

😸 52番でサキに言ったように、ヒントを聞き取れない原因はリスニング力不足とは限らない。意識を音に集中させていなかったの？

😼 94番の意図問題が気になっていました。

😸 分かります。意図問題は選択肢が長いので不安ですよね。

😸 対策として、意図問題の選択肢を早めに読むのはどうかな。Part 4が始まる前にDirectionsが30秒くらいある。あの時間を使って「先読み」する人は結構いる。同じことがPart 3にも言えるね。

🙂 私はPart 1の前に意図問題を全部読みます。

😺 それは「超先読み」だな～。

😸 いろいろ試して、自分に合う「マイベスト」を見つけるのが大事だよ。

Part 4 説明文問題

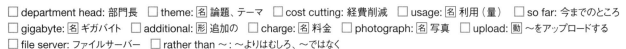

126 **Questions 95 through 97** refer to the following excerpt from a meeting and graph.

M: ❶Thanks for coming to the monthly meeting of department heads.
As I explained in the e-mail, the theme of today's meeting is cost cutting. First, I'd like to draw your attention to this graph, which shows our monthly Internet usage so far this year. ❷When we use over 50 gigabytes, we are required to pay an additional charge. It's happening because employees are e-mailing photographs and videos to each other when they come back from business trips. In the future, ❸I would like you all to upload them onto the office file server rather than sending them by e-mail.　　　　(99w/39 sec.)

問題95-97は次の会議の一部とグラフに関するものです。

月例部長会議に出席いただき、ありがとうございます。メールでお知らせした通り、今日の会議のテーマは経費の削減です。まずは、このグラフをご覧いただきたいと思います。これが示しているのは、今年、これまでの当社の月別インターネットの利用量です。50ギガバイトを超えて使うと、追加料金の支払いを求められます。このような事態が生じているのは、出張から戻った従業員の間で、メールによる画像や動画の授受が行われているからです。将来的には、全員がこの種のファイルを会社のファイルサーバーにアップロードし、メールで送ることのないようにしていただきたいと思います。

☐ department head: 部門長　☐ theme: 名 論題、テーマ　☐ cost cutting: 経費削減　☐ usage: 名 利用（量）　☐ so far: 今までのところ
☐ gigabyte: 名 ギガバイト　☐ additional: 形 追加の　☐ charge: 名 料金　☐ photograph: 名 写真　☐ upload: 動 ～をアップロードする
☐ file server: ファイルサーバー　☐ rather than ～ : ～よりはむしろ、～ではなく

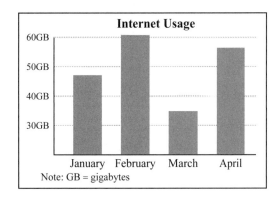

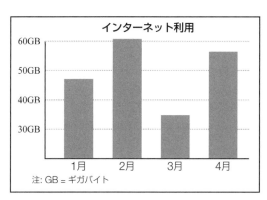

95. 正解：C 易 ■■■□□□□ 難　選択率：(A) 11.7%　(B) 4.9%　**(C) 66.4%**　(D) 13.1%

Who is attending the meeting?
(A) Board members
(B) Client representatives
(C) Department heads
(D) Business analysts

誰が会議に出席していますか。
(A) 役員
(B) 顧客の担当者
(C) 部長
(D) 経営アナリスト

▶解説 ❶で聞き手に対し、department headsの月例会議に来てくれたことへのお礼が述べられています。よって、この会議には (C) の「部長」が参加していると判断できます。

□ attend: 動 ～に出席する　□ board member: 役員会
□ client representative: 顧客担当者
□ analyst: 名 分析家、アナリスト

---

96. 正解：B 易 ■■□□□□□ 難　選択率：(A) 3.9%　**(B) 80.2%**　(C) 9.2%　(D) 2.5%

Look at the graphic. How many times has the company paid additional charges this year?
(A) Once
(B) Twice
(C) Three times
(D) Four times

図表を見てください。この会社は今年、何回追加料金を支払っていますか。
(A) 1回
(B) 2回
(C) 3回
(D) 4回

▶解説 話者は❷で、「50ギガバイトを超えて使用した時は、追加料金を払わないといけない」と述べています。グラフを見ると、2月と4月が該当するため、正解は (B) の「2回」です。

---

97. 正解：B 易 ■■■□□□□ 難　選択率：(A) 9.9%　**(B) 66.4%**　(C) 17.0%　(D) 2.5%

What are employees asked to do?
(A) Stop watching online videos
(B) Upload files to a server
(C) Rely on e-mail more
(D) Attend a workshop

従業員たちは何をするよう求められていますか。
(A) オンラインでの動画の閲覧をやめる
(B) ファイルをサーバーにアップロードする
(C) メールにもっと依存する
(D) 研修会に参加する

▶解説 インターネットの使用量が多い原因を「画像や動画をメールで送っているから」と説明した後、話者は❸でI would like you to ～（～していただきたい）という依頼表現を使い、「それらをサーバーにアップロードする」よう求めています。よって、正解は (B) です。

□ rely on ～: ～に頼る

((📡)) ゼミ 生 中継　😊Hiro 😊Mai 😊Yasu 😎Dai 😊Saki

96.

😊 出張から戻った社員が写真や動画をメールで送りまくっているらしいけれど、実際、そういうことある？

😊 あります。展示会に行くとたくさん写真を撮りますし。

😎 2月に出張が多いのは変ですね。会社は普通、2月は暇です。

😊 そんなことを言っても仕方ない。TOEICワールドは独特なんだよ。

97.

😊 トークがby e-mailで終わっていて、(C) にe-mailがある。明らかな

「釣り」だよ、これは。Test 2でも著者の性格の悪さがにじみ出ている。

😊 本当ですね。でも、今回は釣られませんでした。

😊 ファイルをサーバーにアップロードするって意味が分かる？

😊 はい。社員用のクラウドにスマホから直でアップするんですよね。そういうのはイメージしやすいです。

😊 ……。時代は変わりましたね。

😎 同感。

Part 4 説明文問題

DL 127 **Questions 98 through 100** refer to the following telephone message and coupon.

M: Hi Mary. It's Naoto. I'm calling about lunch on August 7. ❶ We were planning on meeting for lunch so that we could discuss the plans for the magazine article. I heard that the magazine is trying to attract younger readers. ❷ I'd like some advice about how to write articles that interest them. Anyway, ❸ the company cafeteria is closed for some maintenance work apparently. So, Um... I have a coupon for a restaurant called Crouching Thai-Ger. It's just down the road and it looks like a fun place. So, how about meeting there? ❹ It's just you and me so we shouldn't have any trouble making a reservation. (106w/40 sec.)

問題98-100は次の電話メッセージとクーポンに関するものです。

もしもし Mary。Naoto です。8月7日のランチの件で電話しているんだけど。雑誌の記事について話し合うためにお昼に会おうという計画だよね。聞いたところでは、その雑誌は若めの読者層を引き付けようとしているそうなんだ。その層の興味を引く記事の書き方について、助言が欲しいんだ。それはそうと、どうやら社員食堂が保守作業で閉鎖されているみたい。なので、ええと……手元に Crouching Thai-Ger というレストランのクーポンがあるんだけど。通りの先にあって、良さそうな店だよ。そこで会うのはどう？ 僕たち2人だけだから、簡単に予約が取れるはず。

□ article: 名 記事　□ attract: 動 〜を引き付ける　□ interest: 動 〜の興味を引く　□ cafeteria: 名 食堂　□ maintenance work: 保守作業
□ apparently: 副 どうやら〜のようだ　□ coupon: 名 割引券、優待券　□ down the road: この道の先に　□ how about 〜?: 〜はいかが。
□ voucher: 名 クーポン券　□ bearer: 名 持参者　□ expire: 動 有効期限が切れる

CROUCHING THAI-GER

This voucher entitles the bearer to 25% off!

Lunch —For *❺group reservations only

Dinner — 5:30 P.M. to 9:00 P.M. daily

(Last order at 8:30 P.M.)

*❻Six or more people

Expires August 28

CROUCHING THAI-GER

このクーポン持参者は25%割引！

昼食 —— グループ*予約のみ

夕食 —— 毎日午後5時30分から午後9時

(ラストオーダー午後8時30分)

*6人以上

有効期限8月28日

---

98. 正解：C 易▮▮▮▮▯▯▯難　選択率：(A) 6.4%　(B) 19.1%　**(C) 64.0%**　(D) 5.7%

Who most likely is the speaker?
(A) A chef
(B) A restaurant critic
(C) A journalist
(D) A plumber

話者は誰である可能性が最も高いですか。
(A) 調理師
(B) レストラン評論家
(C) ジャーナリスト
(D) 配管工

▶解説　話者は❶で、「雑誌の記事について話し合うために昼に会う」と述べています。❷から、話者は記事の書き方についてのアドバイスを求めていることが分かります。これらの発言から、話者は(C)の「ジャーナリスト」だと考えられます。

---

99. 正解：A 易▮▮▮▮▯▯▯難　選択率：**(A) 51.9%**　(B) 29.7%　(C) 8.8%　(D) 3.9%

What does the speaker say about the company cafeteria?
(A) It will be undergoing some maintenance.
(B) It has been closed permanently.
(C) It has been reserved by a large group.
(D) It is not very large.

□ undergo: 動 ～を受ける
□ permanently: 副 恒久的に、ずっと

話者は社員食堂について何と言っていますか。
(A) 保守作業が行われているだろう。
(B) 恒久的に閉鎖された。
(C) 大勢の集団に予約されている。
(D) あまり広くない。

▶解説　話者は❸で社員食堂について、「保守作業が行われている」と述べています。(A)が正解です。社員食堂がpermanently（恒久的に）閉鎖されたとは述べられていないので、(B)は不正解です。

---

100. 正解：C 易▮▮▮▮▮▯▯難　選択率：(A) 10.6%　(B) 9.9%　**(C) 56.9%**　(D) 15.9%

Look at the graphic. Why will the speaker be unable to use the coupon?
(A) He will arrive after 8:30 P.M.
(B) The restaurant is closed on Tuesday.
(C) There are only two people in his group.
(D) The coupon has expired.

図表を見てください。なぜ話者はこのクーポンを使えないのですか。
(A) 彼は午後8時30分以降に到着する。
(B) このレストランは火曜日に営業していない。
(C) グループに2人しかいない。
(D) クーポンの有効期限が切れている。

▶解説　最終文❹から、話者と聞き手の2人でレストランを利用しようとしていることが分かります。しかし、クーポンの❺と❻から、「6人以上」で利用した場合のみクーポンが使えることが分かります。よって、話者がクーポンを使えない理由は、(C)です。

Part 4　▼ Listening Section

 ゼミ 生 中継　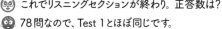

99. ……………………………………………………

😀 company cafeteria の直後に closed が聞こえるから、(B) が魅力的なのは分かる。ただ、その後に for some maintenance work があるから、一時的に閉鎖しているだけ。だから(B)は違う。

😶 その work の次の apparently が permanently に聞こえてしまったので、(B)にしました。

😀 これでリスニングセクションが終わり。正答数は？

😀 78問なので、Test 1とほぼ同じです。

🐵 やった。76問だ。

🎲 55問。

😶 66問でした。Test 1より20問以上増えました！

😀 ナイス。では、Part 5に進もう。

101. 正解：**C** 易 ■■■□□□□□ 難　選択率：(A) 6.3% (B) 5.5% **(C) 83.5%** (D) 4.3%

Yuka Sano proved to be an excellent ------- to the design team.
(A) add
(B) additional
(C) addition
(D) additionally

☐ prove to be 〜：〜であることが判明する
☐ excellent: 形 優れた、素晴らしい

Yuka Sanoは、デザイン班にとっての優れた補強人材であることが明らかになった。
(A) 動 〜を付け加える
(B) 形 追加の
(C) 名 補強
(D) 副 付加的に

▶解説 前後にan excellent とto があるので、be の補語となる名詞を選択します。名詞を作る接尾辞-tion で終わる(C)のaddition が正解です。prove to be 〜の形で「〜であることが判明する」の意味です。

---

102. 正解：**B** 易 ■■■□□□□□ 難　選択率：(A) 5.9% **(B) 75.3%** (C) 7.5% (D) 11.4%

Humphrey brand soups are popular with health-conscious people because they ------- all natural ingredients.
(A) secure
(B) contain
(C) conclude
(D) propose

☐ health-conscious: 形 健康を意識した
☐ natural: 形 自然の　☐ ingredient: 名 原料、材料

Humphrey ブランドのスープが、健康に気を使う人たちに人気が高いのは、天然原料だけで作られているからだ。
(A) 動 〜を確保する
(B) 動 〜を含む
(C) 動 〜と結論づける
(D) 動 〜を提案する

▶解説 語彙の問題です。空所直前の代名詞they は soups を指します。スープは natural ingredients（天然原料）を「含む」とすると人気の理由が成り立つので、(B)のcontain が正解です。

---

103. 正解：**C** 易 ■■□□□□□□ 難　選択率：(A) 0.4% (B) 5.1% **(C) 92.2%** (D) 2.4%

Managers at Glacier Tools are ------- required to travel internationally.
(A) frequented
(B) frequency
(C) frequently
(D) frequent

☐ internationally: 副 国際的に

Glacier Tools 社の管理職は、海外出張することを頻繁に求められる。
(A) 動 よく行った（過去形）
(B) 名 頻度
(C) 副 頻繁に
(D) 形 頻繁な

▶解説 空所は are と required に挟まれているので、空所には「どのように求められるか」を表す副詞が入ります。従って、(C)のfrequently が正解です。形容詞の語尾に付く-ly は、原則として副詞を作る接尾辞です。

---

104. 正解：**A** 易 ■■■□□□□□ 難　選択率：**(A) 83.1%** (B) 11.0% (C) 0.0% (D) 5.9%

Kim Salazar opened ------- first bakery on Valencia Street ten years ago.
(A) her
(B) herself
(C) she
(D) hers

☐ bakery: 名 パン屋

Kim Salazar は、自身の最初のパン屋を10年前に Valencia Street に開いた。
(A) 代 彼女の
(B) 代 彼女自身
(C) 代 彼女が
(D) 代 彼女のもの

▶解説 代名詞の格が問われています。空所からbakery までが直前の動詞opened の目的語となる名詞句です。パン屋は Kim Salazar さんのものなので、所有格である(A)のher が正解です。

((•)) ゼミ 生中継　(😀)Hiro (😀)Mai (😀)Yasu (😀)Dai (😀)Saki

(😀) 正答率が低い問題や、注意が必要な語句に注目していこう。

102.

(😀) 上級グループの正答率は93.8％だけど、初級グループでは48.4％まで下がる。特に、(C)と(D)を選ぶ人が、上級グループにはほぼいないのに対して、初級グループには43.7％もいる。

(😀) 私は they が people を指すと思って (D) を選びました。

(😀) 同じく。propose に「好き」という意味があることを祈っていました。

(😀) 勝手に単語の意味を増やさないで。

103.

(😀) この品詞問題はシンプルなタイプだから正答率が高い。同じ品詞問題でも105番は正答率が6割を切っているから、105番を見よう。

105. 正解：C 易 ■■■■□□□ 難　選択率：(A) 12.9% (B) 25.9% **(C) 59.2%** (D) 2.0%

Using Sue Valtine's recipe book, even beginners can cook delicious meals with -------.
(A) easy
(B) easily
(C) ease
(D) eased

□ recipe book: レシピ本、料理本　□ beginner: 名 初心者

Sue Valtine の料理本を使うことで、たとえ初心者でもおいしい料理を簡単に作れる。
(A) 形 簡単な
(B) 副 簡単に
(C) 名 容易さ
(D) 形 緩めた

▶解説 空所直前の前置詞 with の目的語となるのは名詞である (C) の ease のみです。<前置詞＋抽象名詞>の形で副詞と同じ意味を表し、with ease は easily と同じく「簡単に」の意味です。

106. 正解：B 易 ■■■■□□□ 難　選択率：(A) 13.3% **(B) 61.2%** (C) 11.4% (D) 13.7%

------- to the Woodhill Art Competition must be delivered in person by August 19.
(A) Compositions
(B) Submissions
(C) Establishments
(D) Refunds

□ in person: 本人が直接に

Woodhill Art Competition への提出物は、8月19日までに直接届けなければならない。
(A) 名 構成
(B) 名 提出物
(C) 名 組織
(D) 名 返金

▶解説 語彙の問題です。述語である must be delivered の主語になる語を選びます。Art Competition に送られるのは (B) の Submissions（提出物）だと考えると文意が通ります。従って、正解は (B) です。

107. 正解：D 易 ■■■■□□□ 難　選択率：(A) 19.6% (B) 3.1% (C) 45.5% **(D) 31.8%**

------- of an interview Mr. Gaines gave before he became famous were discovered by a local journalist.
(A) Record
(B) Recorded
(C) Recording
(D) Recordings

□ give an interview: インタビューを受ける
□ discover: 動 ～を発見する　□ local: 形 地元の

Gaines さんが有名になる前に受けたインタビューの録音音源が、地元のジャーナリストの手で発見された。
(A) 名 記録
(B) 形 記録した
(C) 名 録音
(D) 名 録音されたもの

▶解説 直後に前置詞句が続くので、空所には述語 were discovered の主語になる名詞が入ります。選択肢のうち were の主語になれるのは、複数形の名詞である (D) の Recordings です。

Part 5 ▼ Reading Section

105.

😊 上級グループの正答率は98.4%なのに、初級グループでは28.1%まで下がる。初級グループでは、正解の代わりに (B) を選ぶ人が48.4%もいた。

😎 with が邪魔だと思いましたが、意味的に easily がベストだと思いました。

😊 確かに with が邪魔だけど、問題文は変えられない。with と一緒に名詞形の ease を使えばいい。「前置詞の後には名詞」が原則だからね。他の例を1つ考えよう。「注意深く」は carefully だけど、with を使うならどうする？

😎 with care ですか。

😊 ナイス。

106.

😊 サキはどれにした？

😊 (D) です。お金をどこかに届ける話だと思いました。

😊 お金を届けるのは可能だけど、届け先がコンテストだからダメなんだよ。コンテストに返金を届けるって意味不明だよね。

107.

😊 これは本当に基本的な知識だけを試している。でも、いくら知識があっても、そそっかしい人は間違える。だよね？

😐 はい……。

😊 (C) と (D) の違いは単数か複数かだから、動詞の形を見てから判断しなきゃいけない。

😊 (A) の Record も名詞として使えますよね。単数形だからここでは正解にはなりませんが。

😊 そうだね。名詞としても動詞としても使える単語は意外と多いし、TOEIC でもよく見掛ける。Part 5 で出題されるとミスしやすいから注意してね。

Part 5 短文穴埋め問題

108. 正解：A 易 ▰▰▰▱▱▱▱ 難　選択率：(A) 74.1% (B) 6.3% (C) 9.0% (D) 10.2%

If sales continue at their current pace, we will ------- the year's target by October.
(A) exceed
(B) dictate
(C) anticipate
(D) resolve

□ continue: 動 続く　□ current: 形 現在の
□ target: 名 目標

現在のペースで売り上げが続けば、10月までに年間目標を上回るだろう。
(A) 動 ～を上回る
(B) 動 ～を指図する
(C) 動 ～を期待する
(D) 動 ～を解決する

▶解説 文意に合う動詞を選びます。前半「現在のペースで売り上げが続く」の結果、後半「10月までに年間目標を～する」という内容から、(A)のexceed（～を上回る）が正解です。

---

109. 正解：C 易 ▰▰▱▱▱▱▱▱ 難　選択率：(A) 9.8% (B) 1.6% (C) 81.6% (D) 7.1%

Inspectors have identified ------- issues that must be rectified before the reopening.
(A) every
(B) neither
(C) several
(D) another

□ inspector: 名 検査官　□ identify: 動 ～を特定する
□ issue: 名 問題　□ rectify: 動 ～を修正する　□ reopening: 名 再開

検査官らは、業務再開前に修正されるべき問題をいくつか特定した。
(A) 形 全ての
(B) 形 どちらも～ない
(C) 形 いくつかの
(D) 形 別の

▶解説 空所の後ろにある複数形のissuesを修飾できるのは(C)のseveralのみです。(A)のeveryが「～ごとに」を意味する場合は、every ten minutes（10分ごとに）のように数詞に合わせて複数形が続きますが、「あらゆる」を意味する場合は単数形が続きます。

---

110. 正解：D 易 ▰▰▰▰▱▱▱▱ 難　選択率：(A) 18.4% (B) 12.5% (C) 10.2% (D) 58.8%

Many listeners criticized Hal Winter's latest radio drama, complaining that the plot was too -------.
(A) virtual
(B) ultimate
(C) relative
(D) predictable

□ criticize: 動 ～を酷評する　□ latest: 形 最近の、最新の
□ complain: 動 苦情を言う　□ plot: 名 筋書き

多くの聴取者が、あまりにも筋書きがありきたりだと不満を述べ、Hal Winterの最新のラジオドラマを酷評した。
(A) 形 実質上の
(B) 形 究極の
(C) 形 関連する
(D) 形 ありきたりな

▶解説 that節の前にcomplaining（不満を言う）とあることから、plot（筋書き）はマイナスの評価を受けたはずです。よって空所に適切なのは(D)のpredictable（ありきたりな）です。

ゼミ生中継　Hiro Mai Yasu Dai Saki

109.
- もし、この問題文が「もう1つ別の問題を特定した」と伝えているのであればanother issueとなる。
- 追加で見つかった問題が3つだったら、何と言うんですか？
- その場合はanother three issuesと複数形を使う。
- え、「anotherの後ろは単数」だと聞いたことがあります。
- 名詞が直接続く場合はね。ただ、「another＋数字＋複数形」というパターンもある。

110.
- 迷うとすれば(A)かな。

- ドラマの展開がバーチャル過ぎるのかと。
- それ、どんな意味？　virtualは「実質上の」だから、何かが本物に近いことを表すんだよ。例えばインターネット上の店舗は実店舗に対してvirtualな店舗と呼ばれる。でも、virtualな筋書きだと意味が通じない。何と比べてvirtualなのか不明だね。
- ラジオドラマの筋書きがありきたりというのは、酷評の理由になりますか？
- 水戸黄門やドラえもん型ですよね。私は結構好きです。
- 空所の前にtooがあるから、筋書きが「ありきたり過ぎる」と不満を持ったリスナーがいたんだよ。それに、個人的な好みは関係ない。TOEICワールド内の話だから。

111. 正解：**C**　易 ■■■■□□□□ 難　選択率：(A) 1.2%　(B) 23.1%　**(C) 70.2%**　(D) 5.5%

Most of the trainees were ------- sure that they could operate the machinery after the workshop.
(A) reason
(B) reasonable
(C) reasonably
(D) reasoning

□ trainee: 图 訓練を受ける人
□ operate: 動 ～を操作する　□ machinery: 图 機械

大半の訓練生が、研修が終わればその機械を操作できるようになるとかなり確信していた。
(A) 图 理由
(B) 形 合理的な
(C) 副 かなり
(D) 图 推論

▶解説 空所は動詞 were と形容詞 sure に挟まれているので、空所には sure を修飾する副詞が入ります。従って、副詞を作る接尾辞 -ly で終わる (C) の reasonably が正解です。

---

112. 正解：**A**　易 ■■□□□□□□ 難　選択率：**(A) 91.4%**　(B) 0.4%　(C) 5.1%　(D) 3.1%

The Bellmax store at Hastings Mall is expected to reopen ------- next month.
(A) early
(B) really
(C) mostly
(D) quickly

□ expect to ～ : ～することを期待する　□ reopen: 動 （店が）再び開く

Hastings Mall にある Bellmax の店舗は、来月初めに営業を再開すると予想されている。
(A) 副 早期に
(B) 副 実際に
(C) 副 ほとんど
(D) 副 素早く

▶解説 文意に合う副詞を選びます。early next month で「来月初め」の意味を表すため、この形を作る (A) が正解です。(D) の quickly は1回の動作の瞬間的な速さを表すので、この空所には不適切です。

---

113. 正解：**B**　易 ■■■□□□□□ 難　選択率：(A) 5.5%　**(B) 84.7%**　(C) 5.5%　(D) 4.3%

The consultant admitted that the sales team's efforts were -------, but suggested some changes nonetheless.
(A) admiration
(B) admirable
(C) admire
(D) admirably

□ admit: 動 ～を認める　□ sales team: 販売チーム
□ effort: 图 努力　□ nonetheless: 副 それでもなお

そのコンサルタントは、販売チームの努力が見事なものだったと認めたものの、それでもなおいくつかの改善点を指摘した。
(A) 图 称賛
(B) 形 見事な
(C) 動 ～を称賛する
(D) 副 見事に

▶解説 空所は that 節の動詞 were に続く補語です。主語の the sales team's efforts（販売チームの努力）を説明するのにふさわしいのは、形容詞である (B) の admirable（見事な）です。

---

114. 正解：**B**　易 ■■■■□□□□ 難　選択率：(A) 17.6%　**(B) 54.1%**　(C) 7.5%　(D) 20.8%

------- she returned from the marketing conference in Tokyo, Ms. Castro has been pushing for more Internet advertising.
(A) As though
(B) Ever since
(C) Only if
(D) Even when

□ conference: 图 会議、協議会
□ push for ～ : ～を強く求める

東京でのマーケティング協議会から戻って以来、Castro さんはもっとインターネット広告を推進するよう強く求めている。
(A) まるで～であるかのように
(B) ～以来
(C) ～の場合に限って
(D) ～の時でさえ

▶解説 2つの節の時制は、過去形と現在完了形です。(B) の Ever since を入れると「会議から戻って以来、もっとインターネット広告を推進するよう強く求めている」となり、文の意味が通ります。

⚡ ゼミ生中継　😀Hiro 😀Mai 😀Yasu 🎲Dai 😀Saki

111.
😀 このような「be動詞＋副詞＋形容詞」はパート5の常連だよ。X is surprisingly high.（驚くほど高い）とか X is remarkably accurate.（非常に正確）のように、いくらでも例がある。

114.
😀 あっ。(A) は As though だったんですね。Although だと思って選んでしまいました。

😀 Although だと「東京で開かれた、あのマーケティング会議に出たのに、ネット広告を推している」というニュアンスになる。一体どんな会議か知らないけれど、まぁ、成立はする。だけど、As though は「まるで～のように」だからダメ。ダイはどれにした？

🎲 (D) です。

😀 カンマの前が過去形で、後ろが現在完了形だから when は使えない。when は「～の時」だから、前後は同じ時制になるはずだよ。

197

Part 5 短文穴埋め問題

---

115. 正解：D 易 ■■■ □□□ 難　選択率：(A) 2.0% (B) 2.7% (C) 10.6% **(D) 84.7%**

Costing twenty percent less than the next cheapest forklift, the R20 is ------- affordable.
(A) compare
(B) comparison
(C) comparative
(D) comparatively

2番目に安いフォークリフトよりも20パーセント低価格なので、R20は比較的手が届きやすい。
(A) 動 ～を比較する
(B) 名 比較
(C) 形 比較の
(D) 副 比較的

▶解説 空所は動詞isと形容詞affordableの間にあるので、affordableを修飾する副詞が入ります。従って、(D)のcomparativelyが正解です。

□ cost: 動 ～（の金額）がかかる　□ affordable: 形 手頃な

---

116. 正解：C 易 ■■■ □□□ 難　選択率：(A) 16.1% (B) 15.3% **(C) 63.1%** (D) 5.5%

Stan Saunders is ------- the most qualified of all the applicants for the bus driver position.
(A) widely
(B) closely
(C) obviously
(D) punctually

バスの運転手の職に応募してきた全員の中で明らかにStan Saundersが最も適任だ。
(A) 副 広く
(B) 副 しっかり
(C) 副 明らかに
(D) 副 時間に正確に

▶解説 空所には、直後にある最上級の形容詞the most qualifiedを修飾する副詞が入ります。「バスの運転手の職に最も適任だ」という文意から、正解は(C)のobviously（明らかに）です。

□ qualified: 形 資格のある
□ applicant: 名 応募者、候補者　□ position: 名 職

---

117. 正解：A 易 ■■ □□□□ 難　選択率：**(A) 89.4%** (B) 1.6% (C) 3.1% (D) 5.9%

The beach cleaning event is staffed by over fifty volunteers, ------- are students from a local university.
(A) most of whom
(B) whereas
(C) notwithstanding
(D) one of which

海岸の清掃イベントには50人を超えるボランティアが参加するが、その大半が地元の大学の学生たちだ。
(A) その大半
(B) 接 ～の一方で
(C) 前 ～にもかかわらず
(D) そのうちの1人

▶解説 カンマの前後をつなぐ語句を選びます。空所を含む後半の節に主語がないので、areの主語を補う(A)のmost of whomが正解です。先行詞はover fifty volunteersです。

□ staff: 動 ～に職員を置く

---

118. 正解：D 易 ■■ □□□□ 難　選択率：(A) 12.5% (B) 4.3% (C) 7.8% **(D) 75.3%**

The Mason Library will be closed for a month ------- on June 12.
(A) begin
(B) began
(C) have begun
(D) beginning

Mason Libraryは6月12日から1カ月間、閉鎖される。
(A) 動 始まる（原形）
(B) 動 始まった（過去形）
(C) 動 始まっている（現在完了形）
(D) 動 始まる予定の（現在分詞）

▶解説 動詞の形が問われています。主語に対応する動詞はすでに存在し、かつ接続詞や関係詞はありません。従って(A)、(B)、(C)は使えず、現在分詞である(D)のbeginningが入ります。

(((📡))) ゼミ 生 中継　　　　　　　　　　　　😀Hiro 😊Mai 😺Yasu 🎲Dai 😄Saki

115.
😺 ほら、111番で話した「be動詞＋副詞＋形容詞」のパターンだよ。このような問題は5秒で解いて時間を節約しよう。

116.
😺 正答率は63.1%だけど、初級グループでは37.5%、上級グループでは92.2%と大きい差がついている。語彙力の差だね。
😊 (B)のcloselyを問題集で何度も見かけるので思わず選んでしまいました。
😺 closelyは重要語だよ。closely examineの意味は?
😊 うーん……「しっかり調べる」ですか。

😺 その通り。

118.
😺 ヤス、(A)が不正解である理由は?
😺 えっと、この文にはすでに動詞が存在するからです。
😺 そう。will be closedがあるから、図書館が閉まることが分かる。仮に2つ目の動詞としてbeginを使うなら、関係詞か、andやbutみたいな接続詞が必要だけど、どちらもない。だから、beginは主語に対応する動詞としてではなく、「いつから」を示すおまけ情報として使うしかない。このbeginning ～は出来事の起点を表す表現だよ。onを省略してbeginning June 12と言うこともできる。

119. 正解：**B**　易 ■■■■■□ 難　選択率：(A) 9.0% **(B) 34.5%** (C) 3.9% (D) 52.5%

------- adequate promotion, Ms. Walker's book should be a national bestseller.
(A) Once
(B) Given
(C) Moreover
(D) According to

十分な販売促進が施されれば、Walkerさんの著書は全国的なベストセラーになるはずだ。
(A) 接 いったん
(B) 前 ～があれば
(C) 副 さらに
(D) ～によると

▶解説 空所とカンマの間にあるのは名詞句のみなので、前置詞を選択します。(B)のGiven（～があれば）を入れると、後半の「ベストセラーになるはず」と自然につながります。

□ adequate: 形 十分な　□ promotion: 名 販売促進キャンペーン
□ national: 形 全国的な　□ bestseller: 名 ベストセラー

---

120 正解：**B**　易 ■■■■■□ 難　選択率：(A) 16.5% **(B) 26.7%** (C) 18.0% (D) 38.8%

All requests for information will receive a ------- response from our customer service personnel.
(A) durable
(B) swift
(C) previous
(D) constant

情報を求めるあらゆるご要望には、当社の顧客サービス担当者が迅速に対応いたします。
(A) 形 丈夫な
(B) 形 迅速な
(C) 形 以前の
(D) 形 恒常的な

▶解説 コロケーションが問われています。(B)を入れて swift response とすると、「迅速な対応」の意味になります。従って、(B)が正解です。swiftの同義語であるquickやimmediateを入れることも可能です。

□ response: 名 応答、反応　□ personnel: 名 社員

---

121. 正解：**D**　易 ■■■■■□ 難　選択率：(A) 1.6% (B) 2.7% (C) 74.5% **(D) 21.2%**

The ------- of Monday's meeting is to decide on a route for the walkathon.
(A) objectively
(B) objecting
(C) objection
(D) objective

月曜日の会議の目的は、長距離ウオーキング大会のルートを決めることだ。
(A) 副 客観的に
(B) 動 反対している（現在分詞）
(C) 名 反対
(D) 名 目的

▶解説 空所には文の主語となる名詞が入ります。to decide ～ walkathon（長距離ウオーキング大会のルートを決めること）の意味から、主語は「会議の目的」とするのが妥当なので、(D)のobjectiveが正解です。(C)も名詞ですが、「反対」を意味するため不適切です。

□ walkathon: 名 長距離ウオーキング大会　＊walk+marathon の造語。
慈善事業の寄付集めを目的に行われることが多い。

((🗼))) ゼミ 生 中継　　😊Hiro 😊Mai 😊Yasu 😊Dai 😊Saki

119. ……………………………………
😊 サキ、前置詞としてのGivenを知っていた？
😊 いいえ。カンマの前に動詞がないので、(D)にしました。
😊 この文では、Givenは「～があれば」と仮定の意味を加えているけれど、Given the circumstances, は「状況を考えると」だよ。

120. ……………………………………
😊 constantがダメな理由は何ですか？
😊 スマホで類義語を調べてごらん。
😊 あれ、endlessやcontinuousが出ました。

😊 そりゃ、ダメですね。
😊 そう。constantのニュアンスは「絶えず続く」だよ。

121. ……………………………………
😊 theとofの間に空所がある。それだけ見て(C)を選んだ人は？
😊😊😊😊 はい。
😊 ダイは正解を選んだの？
😊 全文をきっちり読んでから、(C)です。
😊 なんだ、全滅か。-tiveで終わる名詞は意外と多いよ。例えば……representative（代表者）とか。

Part 5 短文穴埋め問題

---

122. 正解：B 易 ■■□□□□□ 難 　選択率：(A) 9.8% **(B) 85.1%** (C) 1.2% (D) 3.5%

The company has decided to ------- three new staff members ahead of the busy season.
(A) apply
(B) employ
(C) demonstrate
(D) search

□ staff member: 職員、社員
□ ahead of 〜：〜より前に

会社は、繁忙期に先立ち新たな従業員を3名雇用することを決めた。
(A) 動 〜を適用する
(B) 動 〜を雇用する
(C) 動 〜を実演する
(D) 動 〜を探す

▶解説 空所直後にあるthree new staff membersを目的語にする動詞を選択します。「繁忙期を前に新たな従業員をどうするか」を考えると、(B)のemploy（〜を雇用する）が適切です。

---

123. 正解：A 易 ■■□□□□□ 難 　選択率：**(A) 91.8%** (B) 2.4% (C) 0.0% (D) 5.5%

When Ms. Juma learned she would be involved in the upcoming sales campaign, she ------- canceling her trip to Spain.
(A) considered
(B) considerable
(C) consideration
(D) considerably

□ involved 〜 in ...：〜を…に巻き込む
□ upcoming: 形 やがてやってくる
□ sales campaign: 販売キャンペーン

Jumaさんは自分が今度の販売キャンペーンに関与することになると知り、スペイン旅行をキャンセルすることを考えた。
(A) 動 考えた（過去形）
(B) 形 かなりの
(C) 名 考慮
(D) 副 かなり

▶解説 カンマの後ろにsheに対応する動詞が存在しないため、(A)のconsideredが正解です。このように、適切な品詞を選ぶ問題を解くヒントは、たいてい空所の近くにあります。

---

124. 正解：D 易 □□□□□□ 難 　選択率：(A) 　-　 (B) 　-　 (C) 　-　 (D) 　-

The Hills Cinema is ------- five venues that have expressed interest in hosting the film festival.
(A) for
(B) about
(C) until
(D) among

□ venue: 名 会場
□ express interest in 〜：〜に興味を示す
□ host: 動 〜の会場となる
□ film festival: 映画祭

Hills Cinemaは、映画祭を開催することに興味を示している5会場の1つだ。
(A) 前 〜のために
(B) 前 〜について
(C) 前 〜まで
(D) 前 〜の中の1つで

▶解説 (D)のamongには「〜の中の1つ」という意味があります。これを選ぶと「映画祭を開催することに興味を示した5つの候補地のうちの1つ」という意味が成り立ちます。

((⚡)) ゼミ 生中継 　　　　　　😊 Hiro 😊 Mai 😊 Yasu 😊 Dai 😊 Saki

124.

😊 サキ、amongの使い方を知らなかった？

😊 私は「〜の中で」と覚えていました。

😊 X is popular among Y.という形ならピンと来ます。

😊 be動詞の直後にamongを置く形に慣れていない？　でも、X is among Y.という形はTOEICに出る。解くコツがある。空所にone

ofを入れて成立するならamongを使えると思っていい。

😊 え、どういうことですか。

😊 The Hills Cinema is one of five venues 〜 festival. ってこと。これで「〜のうちの1つ」と理解できるよね。だからamongを使える。

😊 便利ですね。

125. 正解：**D** 易 ■■■□□□□ 難 選択率：(A) 9.8% (B) 3.1% (C) 16.9% **(D) 70.2%**

The company president is extremely ------- to the needs of the various sections.
(A) attends
(B) attentively
(C) attention
(D) attentive

その会社の社長は、さまざまな部署の要望に対して大変よく耳を傾ける。
(A) 動 〜に参加する
(B) 副 注意深く
(C) 名 注意
(D) 形 注意深い

▶解説 空所の前に is extremely があるため、is の補語となる形容詞を選択します。形容詞は (D) の attentive のみなので、これが正解です。be attentive to 〜で「〜に耳を傾ける」の意味です。

☐ president: 名 社長　☐ extremely: 副 とても
☐ various: 形 さまざまな　☐ section: 名 部門

---

126 正解：**D** 易 ■■■■□□ 難 選択率：(A) 23.1% (B) 11.4% (C) 18.0% **(D) 47.5%**

The manufacturer of HGL swimwear is taking ------- so that stores do not run out of stock again.
(A) valuations
(B) oppositions
(C) impressions
(D) precautions

HGL ブランドの水着の製造元は、また店舗から在庫切れにならないように予防策を講じている。
(A) 名 査定
(B) 名 反対
(C) 名 印象
(D) 名 予防策

▶解説 taking の目的語として文意に合う名詞を選びます。後半が示す「在庫切れにならないように」する目的で、メーカーがとるのは「予防策」だとすると文意が通るので、正解は (D) の precautions です。

☐ manufacturer: 名 製造業者、メーカー
☐ swimwear: 名 水着　☐ run out of 〜 : 〜を切らす
☐ stock: 名 在庫品

---

127. 正解：**A** 易 ■■■□□□ 難 選択率：**(A) 88.2%** (B) 3.9% (C) 2.7% (D) 5.1%

For its new store, Bettina's Grill is looking at three locations ------- five minutes' walk of Rupert Station.
(A) within
(B) onto
(C) before
(D) toward

新規出店に備えて、Bettina's Grill は Rupert Station から徒歩5分以内にある3つの候補地を検討している。
(A) 前 〜以内に
(B) 前 〜の上に
(C) 前 〜の前に
(D) 前 〜へ向かって

▶解説 新しい店舗の立地について「駅から徒歩5分以内の場所を検討している」とすれば文意が成立します。従って (A) の within が正解です。

☐ look at 〜 : 〜を検討する
☐ location: 名 場所

(((A))) ゼミ 生 中継　😺Hiro 😺Mai 😺Yasu 🎲Dai 😺Saki

125. ....
😺 また出た。111番と115番で話した「be動詞＋副詞＋形容詞」のパターン。これは形容詞の部分が問題になっているパターンだね。

126. ....
😺 上級グループでは正答率が78.1％あるけれど、初級グループでは28.1％しかない。不正解の中では、(A) を選ぶモニターが多かった。valuations の意味を知っていた？ 「評価」とか「査定額」を意味する単語なんだけど。

😺 知りませんでした。(B) と (C) は絶対に違うので、知らない (A) と (D) で迷って、何となく (A) にしました。

😺 caution は「注意」なので、pre- が付くと「事前の注意」だと推測して選びました。文の内容に合う気がしました。

😺 その発想はナイスだよ。preview とか prepaid から想像できるように、pre- は「前」を意味する接頭辞だね。

Part 5 短文穴埋め問題

---

128. 正解：B 易 ■■■■□□□ 難　選択率：(A) 6.3% **(B) 64.7%** (C) 7.1% (D) 21.6%

Any suggestions ------- the office party should be brought up at the regularly scheduled meetings.
(A) regard
(B) regarding
(C) may regard
(D) are regarded

職場のパーティーに関する提案があれば、定期的に開かれる会議の場で出すといいだろう。
(A) 動 ～と見なす（原形）
(B) 前 ～に関する
(C) 見なすかもしれない
(D) 見なされている（受け身）

▶解説 空所直前の Any suggestions が主語、should be brought up が述語なので、直後の the office party を伴って主語を修飾する語を選択します。従って、前置詞である (B) の regarding（～について）が正解です。

- □ suggestion: 名 提案
- □ bring up ～: (問題など) を持ち出す
- □ regularly: 副 定期的に
- □ scheduled: 形 予定された

---

129. 正解：A 易 ■■■□□□□ 難　選択率：**(A) 81.6%** (B) 5.1% (C) 8.6% (D) 4.7%

Invitations to the summer banquet will be sent out ------- the guest list is finalized.
(A) as soon as
(B) as well as
(C) in return for
(D) insofar as

夏の宴会への招待状は、招待客のリストが完成したらすぐに発送されるだろう。
(A) ～するとすぐに
(B) ～と同様に
(C) ～への見返りに
(D) ～する限り

▶解説 空所前後の節をつなぐ語句が入ります。招待状が送られるのは「リストが完成された後」と判断できることから、時を表す副詞節を作る (A) の as soon as が正解です。

- □ invitation: 名 招待状
- □ banquet: 名 晩餐会、（正式な）宴会
- □ send out ～: ～を送る
- □ guest list: 招待客リスト
- □ finalize: 動 ～を確定する

---

130. 正解：C 易 ■■■■□□□ 難　選択率：(A) 27.1% (B) 11.8% **(C) 52.9%** (D) 8.2%

West Motors and Brix City will split the cost ------- for the Kelly Park renovation evenly.
(A) requiring
(B) is required
(C) required
(D) having required

West Motors 社と Brix City が、Kelly Park の改修にかかる費用を折半するだろう。
(A) 動 必要としている（現在分詞）
(B) 必要とされている（受け身）
(C) 動 必要とされる（過去分詞）
(D) 必要としてきた

▶解説 動詞 split の目的語である cost を後ろから修飾する分詞を選択します。require（～を必要とする）は他動詞で、cost は必要とされるものなので、正解は過去分詞の (C) です。

- □ split: 動 ～を分ける
- □ cost: 名 費用
- □ renovation: 名 修復、改築
- □ evenly: 副 平等に

ゼミ生中継
😀Hiro 😀Mai 😀Yasu 😀Dai 😀Saki

128.

😀 上級グループの正答率は98.4%だけど、初級グループでは28.1%まで下がる。文法力の差だね。文頭から読むと、すぐに空所が目に入る。たぶん、初級グループの人はこの時点で正解を探したんだろうね。上級グループの人は、この時点では解こうとしない。マイ、どうして？

😀 まだ動詞を見つけていないからです。

😀 そう。should be brought up まで読むことで、空所に入るのは suggestions に対応する動詞ではないと気づく。関係詞や接続詞なしで動詞を2つ使ってはいけないから。この時点で、(B) に決まる。

130.

😀 (A) の requiring を選びたくなったかな。お金は公園の改修に必要とされるものだから過去分詞が必要。だから、(A) はダメ。

😀 お金は公園の改修に必要とすると考えて、(A) にしました。

😀 もっと正確に。お金が何かを必要とするわけじゃない。改修がお金を必要とするんだから、お金は必要とされる側だよ。分詞を考える時は、「誰が」「何を」「どうする」といった情報を厳密に考えなきゃ。

😀 日本語から鍛えます。

😀 では、Part 6 に進もう。

TOEICよろず相談所　ヒロの部屋

⑩効率的な語彙力アップの方法は?

 語彙力が低いのが自分の弱点だと分かっていますが、どうしても単語を覚えられません。何か良い方法はありますか。TOEIC用の単語集を買って1つずつ暗記しましたが、すぐに忘れてしまいます。

 単語の覚え方に関しては個人差が大きいので、いくつかの方法を試すことをお勧めします。多くの人が単語集を使っているようですが、使い方には工夫の余地があります。声に出すとか、ノートに書いてみるとか。

 私は電車の中で読んでいただけですね。

 では、次からは音声を利用してはいかがですか。何種類かのやり方を試して、自分に合う方法を発見するのが理想です。単語集を使わないのもアリですよ。

 え!? 何を使うんですか。

 英語で書かれたものなら何でもOKです。Part 5の問題文でもいいですし、Part 3などのリスニング教材でも構いません。つまり、**問題集や模試に取り組む中で見つけた単語を調べながら学んでいけばいいんです。** すでに1回出会った単語ですし、場合によってはその単語のせいでミスしたり悩んだりしたでしょうから、記憶に残りやすいはずですよ。

 単語を覚えてから英語を読もうと思っていましたが、そういう順番じゃないのですね。

 「単語力が低いから英語を読めない」と言う人をたくさん見てきましたが、それは甘えです。**実際は、英語を読まないから単語力が低いのです。**

 耳が痛いです。いろいろ挑戦してマイベストを見つけます!

Part 6 長文穴埋め問題

Questions 131-134 refer to the following e-mail.

To: Steven Rand <srand@speedway.com>
From: FF Internet Customer Service <cs@ffinternet.com>
Date: March 6
Subject: Overdue account

Dear Mr. Rand,

It has come to our attention that payment for your Internet ------- for February is overdue. You
131.
agreed to have the fee automatically deducted from your bank account on the 1st of every month.

We attempted to make a ------- on March 1. However, the request was denied by your bank. We
132.
will try again on March 20 as stipulated in the agreement. Please make sure you have sufficient

funds in the account by then.

If you are ------- using this bank account, you can switch to payment by credit card by changing
133.
your payment information on your Account page by March 20. -------.
134.

Sincerely,

Mary Cole
Customer Service — FF Internet

(141w)

問題**131-134**は次のメールに関するものです。
宛先：Steven Rand <srand@speedway.com>
送信者：FF Internet Customer Service <cs@ffinternet.com>
日付：3月6日
件名：お支払期限超過のアカウント

Randさま

お客さまの2月分のインターネット接続料金のお支払期限が過ぎていることが分かりました。お客さまには、料金がお客さまの銀行口座から毎月1日に自動引き落としされることに同意いただいております。弊社で3月1日に引き落としの手続きを行いました。しかし、お客さまの銀行に、引き落とし依頼が拒否されました。契約書上の規定に基づき、3月

20日に再度引き落とし手続きを行う予定です。同日までに十分な金額を口座にご用意いただけるよう、ご確認ください。

もし、当該の銀行口座のご利用を終えられているようでしたら、3月20日までにお客さまのアカウントページでお支払い情報を変更していただき、クレジットカード払いに変更していただくことも可能です。その場合は、2月分と3月分のお支払いを4月1日にお受けすることになります。

よろしくお願い申し上げます。

顧客サービス部――FF Internet
Mary Cole

☐ overdue: 形 期限の過ぎた ☐ account: 名 アカウント、顧客 ☐ come to one's attention: 判明する ☐ payment: 名 支払い
☐ agree: 動 同意する ☐ automatically: 副 自動的に ☐ deduct ～ from ...: ～を…から引き落とす ☐ bank account: 銀行口座
☐ attempt to ～: ～しようと試みる ☐ request: 名 要請 ☐ deny: 動 ～を拒否する ☐ stipulate: 動 ～を明記する
☐ agreement: 名 契約書 ☐ make sure ～: 確実に～する ☐ sufficient: 形 十分な ☐ fund: 名 資金 ☐ switch to ～: ～に切り替える

204

131. 正解：**C**　易 ■■■□□□□ 難　選択率：(A) 2.4%　(B) 7.5%　**(C) 88.6%**　(D) 1.6%

(A) connective
(B) connect
(C) connection
(D) connectively

(A) 形 結合の
(B) 動 ～を接続する
(C) 名 接続
(D) 副 結び付いて

▶解説 空所には、forに続くべき名詞が必要です。(C)を入れてInternet connectionと複合名詞を作れば「インターネット接続」を意味し、支払いの対象として成立します。

132. 正解：**D**　易 ■■■■□□□ 難　選択率：(A) 4.3%　(B) 11.0%　(C) 27.8%　**(D) 56.9%**

(A) difference
(B) concession
(C) decision
(D) withdrawal

(A) 名 違い
(B) 名 譲歩
(C) 名 決断
(D) 名 引き落とし

▶解説 ❶の情報から、毎月1日に銀行口座から自動引き落としが行われることが分かります。従って、FF Internetは3月1日にも引き落としを試みたと考えるのが自然です。空所に(D)のwithdrawalを入れるとmake a withdrawal（預金を引き出す）となり、意味が通ります。

133. 正解：**A**　易 ■■■■□□□ 難　選択率：**(A) 68.6%**　(B) 23.9%　(C) 3.9%　(D) 3.1%

(A) no longer
(B) still
(C) just
(D) at present

(A) もはや～ない
(B) いまだに
(C) ちょうど
(D) 現在

▶解説 空所を含む文の後半で、クレジットカード払いへの変更方法を説明しています。これは、銀行引き落としが不可能な場合の代替手段なので、空所には否定を表す(A) no longerを入れるのが適切です。もし(B)のstillを入れると支払方法を変える必要がないため、文の後半が不自然になります。

134. 正解：**B**　易 ■■■■□□□ 難　選択率：(A) 26.3%　**(B) 38.8%**　(C) 7.1%　(D) 27.5%

(A) Please note that the due date for payment will be announced soon.
(B) In this case, we will take payment for February and March on April 1.
(C) You are encouraged to reapply next time a vacant position becomes available.
(D) To make things easier, you could consider automatic payment in future.

(A) お支払いの期限をすぐにお知らせいたしますので、ご留意ください。
(B) その場合は、2月分と3月分のお支払いを4月1日にお受けすることになります。
(C) 次回、職に空きが生じたら再応募なさることをお勧めします。
(D) お手続きをより簡単にするために、将来的に自動払いをご検討いただくことも可能です。

▶解説 Randさんがクレジットカード払いに変更する場合は、その手続きは遅くて3月20日に行われます。この場合、2月分に加えて3月分の料金も未払いであり、クレジットカードで支払うことになります。よって、その決済が実行されるのが4月1日であると伝える(B)を入れると自然です。

□ note: 動 ～に留意する　□ due date: 支払期限　□ take payment: 支払いを受ける
□ encourage ～ to ...: ～に…を勧める　□ reapply: 動 再応募する　□ vacant: 形 空いている
□ position: 名 職　□ consider: 動 ～を検討する　□ automatic payment: 自動支払い

((•))ゼミ生中継　Hiro　Mai　Yasu　Dai　Saki

間違えた問題や難しい問題を中心に見ていこう。

133.
なぜかstillが人気だけど、カンマの後にカード払いに切り替える話が続くから変だね。(B)を入れたら、Randさんがやるべきことは、口座にお金を入れることになるよ。

134.
Randさんは毎月1日に口座からの自動引き落としで払う契約を結んでいるから、(A)と(D)は明らかに間違っている。でも、(A)と(D)は

魅力的な不正解。なぜ？
どっちにもpaymentが入っているから。
そう。特にこの空所の直前にpaymentが2回登場している。こうやって、問題作成者は文書にある単語を再利用して不正解を作ることが多い。ヤスのように、単語を拾い読みしてストーリーを妄想する人が選びたくなるようにね。
耳が痛いなぁ……。

Part 6 長文穴埋め問題

Questions 135-138 refer to the following instructions.

The LM55 Printer is the ------- solution for the home office. However, proper ------- is necessary
135. **136.**
to ensure that the device is always ready for use. ❶Therefore, the printing heads should be cleaned
at least once a month. This can be done automatically, by pressing the head cleaner button on
the front of the device. ❷Refilling the printer with ink is easy enough for anyone to do. -------. ❸We
137.
suggest scheduling free home delivery of replacement ink from the manufacturer. This will ensure
that you receive the highest quality ink and ------- the lifespan of your printer.
138.

(105w)

問題135-138は次の指示書に関するものです。

LM55 Printerは、ホームオフィス向きの理想的なツールです。ただし、本機を間違いなくいつでも使える状態にしておくには、適切なメンテナンスが不可欠です。そのため、プリンターヘッドを少なくとも月に1度はクリーニングするといいでしょう。これは自動的に行うことができます。本機の前面にあるヘッド・クリーニング・ボタンを押してくださ

い。本プリンターのインクの補充は非常に簡単で、どなたでも行えます。無名ブランドの安価なインクのご使用は、推奨されません。当メーカーからご自宅へ、交換用インクの定期的な無料配送をご提案しています。これによって、確実に最高品質のインクをお届けできるとともに、お使いのプリンターの製品寿命が延びることでしょう。

---

135. 正解：**B**　易 ■■■□□□□ 難　選択率：(A) 0.8% **(B) 85.1%** (C) 7.8% (D) 5.9%

(A) perfection
(B) perfect
(C) perfectly
(D) perfecting

(A) 名 完全性
(B) 形 完璧な
(C) 副 完璧に
(D) 動 仕上げている（現在分詞）

▶解説 適切な品詞が問われています。空所直前に冠詞theがあり、空所後に名詞のsolution（解決策）があることから、空所には形容詞として機能する語が入ります。よって、(B) perfect（完璧な）が正解です。

---

136. 正解：**C**　易 ■■□□□□□ 難　選択率：(A) 23.5% (B) 3.5% **(C) 72.2%** (D) 0.8%

(A) installation
(B) conversion
(C) maintenance
(D) disposal

(A) 名 設置
(B) 名 変換
(C) 名 保守管理
(D) 名 廃棄

▶解説 空所を含む1文のみを読むと、(A) installation（設置）と(C) maintenance（メンテナンス、保守）の両方が正解の候補に挙がりますが、次の❶で、プリンターヘッドの手入れに関して適切な清掃頻度が述べられています。よって、(C) maintenanceが正解だと判断できます。

---

137. 正解：**A**　易 ■■■□□□□ 難　選択率：**(A) 72.5%** (B) 5.1% (C) 6.7% (D) 15.3%

(A) Using cheap inks from unknown suppliers is not recommended.
(B) The printer is not suitable for domestic use.
(C) Staff training is certainly advised for such complicated procedures.
(D) The device will work for years with no user intervention.

(A) 無名ブランドの安価なインクのご使用は、推奨されません。
(B) 本プリンターは家庭での使用には向きません。
(C) そうした複雑な手続きに対応するよう、確かに担当者研修が勧められています。
(D) 本機は使用者の手を煩わすことなく、何年間も作動するでしょう。

▶解説 空所前❷で、インク交換の手軽さが紹介されており、空所後❸でもインクの話が続いています。❸はメーカーから純正インクを買うことを勧めているため、その対比として直前で「無名ブランドのインクは推奨しない」ことを伝えるのは自然です。よって、(A)が適切です。

☐ cheap: 形 安い　☐ unknown: 形 無名の　☐ supplier: 名 供給業者　☐ recommend: 動 ～を勧める　☐ suitable: 形 適切な　☐ domestic: 形 家庭の　☐ certainly: 副 確かに　☐ advise: 動 ～を勧める　☐ complicated: 形 複雑な　☐ procedure: 名 手続き　☐ intervention: 名 介入

---

138. 正解：**D**　易 ■■□□□□□ 難　選択率：(A) 6.3% (B) 8.2% (C) 6.7% **(D) 78.8%**

(A) express
(B) develop
(C) widen
(D) extend

(A) 動 ～を表現する
(B) 動 ～を発展させる
(C) 動 ～を広げる
(D) 動 ～を延ばす

▶解説 空所後の目的語the lifespan of your printerに呼応する動詞を選びます。the lifespan（寿命）と相性が良いのは(D)で、extend the lifespanは「寿命を延ばす」という意味になります。extendはextend a deadline（締め切りを延ばす）など、期間や期限を延ばすという意味で用いられます。

Part 6 ▶ Reading Section

((📡)) ゼミ 生 中継　😊Hiro 😊Mai 😊Yasu 😎Dai 😊Saki

136.

😎 間違えた人は?

😊 はい。installationは、どうしてダメなのですか。

😎 次の文にThereforeがあるから、この空所を含む文は、「プリンターヘッドの掃除を毎月するべき」という結論を導く理由として機能する。だからinstallationはダメ。このように、Part 6では情報と情報の論理的な関係を考えないと解けないことが多い。

137.

😎 (D)が魅力的な不正解のようだけど、これは間違った情報だよ。ユーザーが何もせずに自動で何年も作動するはずがない。直前で、インク交換は簡単だって言っているからね。簡単だとしても人が交換しなくちゃいけないでしょ。

😊 そういうことですか。(D)は耐久年数が長いことを言っているのかと思っていました。

Part 6 長文穴埋め問題

Questions 139-142 refer to the following article.

Newcomer in the fast food industry

In just under 12 months, Lin Mian Chinese Food ------- a major competitor in the fast food
139.
industry. ❶This has surprised many of the industry's experts.

Chinese food has always been popular with diners. They have ------- enjoyed dining at Chinese
140.
restaurants or ordering deliveries. ❷On the other hand, fast food has been most commonly

associated with burgers, pizza, and chicken. -------. There are now more than 200 Lin Mian
141.
restaurants nationwide, and that number is growing.

❸Lin Mian is seen as a tasty healthy option. -------, it has been recognized by the National Healthy
142.
Eating Association. A meal at Lin Mian has around 20 percent less salt and fat than the equivalent

at a hamburger restaurant.

(129w)

問題139-142は次の記事に関するものです。
ファストフード業界の新星

ほんの12カ月もたたないうちに、Lin Mian Chinese Foodはファスト
フード業界で大きな競争力を獲得した。このことは、業界の多くの専門
家らを驚かせた。

中華料理は常に、食事のメニューとして人気を博してきた。皆、昔から
中華料理店で食事をしたり、出前を取ったりすることを楽しんできた。

一方で、ファストフードと言えば、たいていはハンバーガーやピザ、チ
キンが思い浮かぶ。Lin Mianは、これを変えつつあるのだ。現在、200
店を超えるLin Mianの店舗が全国にあり、その数はさらに増えている。

Lin Mianは、おいしく健康的な選択肢と見なされている。実際、
National Healthy Eating Associationに高く評価されているのだ。Lin
Mianの料理は、ハンバーガー店で出される同等の料理と比べて、含まれ
る塩分と脂肪が約20パーセント少ない。

☐ newcomer: 图 新参者、新規参入　☐ fast food: ファストフード　☐ industry: 图 産業界　☐ become a major competitor: 競争力を身につける
☐ surprise: 動 ～を驚かす　☐ expert: 图 専門家　☐ diner: 图 食事をする人、ディナーの客　☐ dine: 動 食事をする　☐ delivery: 图 配達
☐ on the other hand: 一方で　☐ commonly: 副 共通して　☐ associate ～ with ...: ～を…に関連付けて考える　☐ nationwide: 副 全国的に
☐ grow: 動 成長する　☐ tasty: 形 味の良い　☐ option: 图 選択肢　☐ recognize: 動 ～を評価する　☐ around: 副 およそ、約　☐ fat: 图 脂肪
☐ equivalent: 图 同等物

139. 正解：**A** 易 ■■■□□□□ 難　選択率：(A) 78.4% (B) 7.8% (C) 0.8% (D) 12.9%

(A) has become
(B) will become
(C) to become
(D) had become

(A) なった
(B) なるだろう
(C) なるために
(D) なっていた

▶解説 空所を含む文に続く❶が現在完了形で書かれているので、Lin Mian は現在すでにファストフード業界で競争力を持つ存在となっていることが分かります。従って空所には過去形か現在完了形が入りますが、過去形は選択肢にないため、(A)のhas becomeが正解です。

140. 正解：**B** 易 ■■□□□□□ 難　選択率：(A) 34.9% **(B) 53.7%** (C) 4.7% (D) 6.7%

(A) subsequently
(B) traditionally
(C) rarely
(D) creatively

(A) 副 その後
(B) 副 昔から
(C) 副 めったに
(D) 副 創造的に

▶解説 空所直前で、「中華料理は人気を博してきた」と現在完了で書かれています。よって、空所に(B)のtraditionallyを入れて、人々はレストランや出前を利用して中華料理を「昔から」楽しんでいると考えると自然です。よって、(B)が正解です。

141. 正解：**D** 易 ■■■■□□□ 難　選択率：(A) 9.0% (B) 27.8% (C) 7.5% **(D) 55.7%**

(A) Lin Mian will open soon in both countries.
(B) This was generally expected.
(C) The plan has to be abandoned due to certain problems.
(D) Lin Mian is changing that.

(A) Lin Mian は、程なく両国で開店するだろう。
(B) これは広く予想されていた。
(C) その計画は、ある問題が原因で破棄されなければならない。
(D) Lin Mian は、これを変えつつあるのだ。

□ generally: 副 一般に、多くの人に　□ abandon: 動 〜を破棄する　□ due to 〜 : 〜が原因で

▶解説 Lin Mian は中華料理の店で、fast food を提供していることが第1段落で分かります。第2段落は、一般的な中華料理の楽しみ方の話です。❷で On the other hand, を使って、これまでの fast food（ファストフード）のイメージは「ハンバーガーやピザ、チキンなどで、中華ではなかった」とあります。それを受けて (D) の「Lin Mian はこれを変えつつある」を入れると、Lin Mian がこれまでのファストフードのイメージを変える中華料理店であるという流れになります。

142. 正解：**C** 易 ■□□□□□□ 難　選択率：(A) 7.1% (B) 3.1% **(C) 83.9%** (D) 5.9%

(A) Nevertheless
(B) Instead
(C) In fact
(D) Similarly

(A) 副 それにもかかわらず
(B) 副 代わりに
(C) 実際に
(D) 副 同様に

▶解説 空所前❸で、「おいしくて健康的」という Lin Mian のイメージが述べられています。空所を含む文では、協会に評価されている事実が挙げられています。従って、空所には前に示された内容を論証するために用いられる、(C) In fact（実際に）が入ります。

Part 6　▶ Reading Section

((◢)) ゼミ 生 中継　　　　　　　　　　　 Hiro　Mai　Yasu　Dai　Saki

140.

😀 ダイ、(A)を選んだよね。(B)のtraditionallyを消去した理由は？

😠 人々が中華料理を楽しんでいると言いたいだけなのに、「伝統的に」は違和感を覚えます。

😀 なるほど。それで意味を知らない(A)に賭けたのか。でも、「従来」とか「以前から」と考えれば違和感ないよね。

141.

😀 (B)が人気みたいだけど、「これは広く予想されていた」の「これ」は何？

😼 「ファストフードと言えば、ハンバーガー、ピザ、チキンのこと」ということ

です。

😼 「和食と言えば寿司」と同じ。長い年月を経てそういう文化が作られてきたんだよね。

😾 人が予想したことではないですね……。

😼 直後に Lin Mian が成長中という情報が続いているけど、これも(B)とは関係ない。でも、(D)なら問題ない。ファストフードと言えば今までは3種類だったけど、そこに Lin Mian が参入し、成長している、という話の流れは理解できるよね。サキ、どう？

😺 大丈夫です。ちゃんと読めれば簡単ですね。

😼 正確に英文を読むことが、最も効果的なスコアアップ法だよ。

209

Part 6 長文穴埋め問題

Questions 143-146 refer to the following memo.

MEMO

To: All employees
From: Jennifer Wright
Date: September 8
Subject: Rescheduling

Dear all,

Regretfully, I have to ------- the weekly staff meeting as the marketing department is still
      143.

processing the survey data. ❶The meeting was scheduled for them to deliver a summary of their

findings. -------. As that will not be possible by tomorrow, ❷I would like everyone to attend a
      144.

rescheduled meeting on Thursday afternoon from 4:00 P.M. Your attendance at the meeting is

-------. ❸The information will be extremely valuable and I want everyone's input. Those -------
145.   **146.**

cannot attend should let me know as soon as possible. ❹I will make alternative arrangements.

(114w)

問題143-146は次の連絡票に関するものです。
連絡票

宛先：全従業員
発信者：Jennifer Wright
日付：9月8日
件名：予定変更

皆さま

残念ながら、週例従業員会議を延期しなければなりません。マーケティング部がまだ調査データの処理を終えていないからです。この会議は、同部が調査結果のまとめを発表できるように日程調整されていました。私としては、同部の発表の後に意見交換の場を設けたかったのです。それが、明日までにはかないそうもないので、会議の予定を木曜日の午後4時からに変更し、皆さんにご出席いただきたいと思います。会議への出席は重要です。情報は極めて有用なものになるでしょうし、皆さんからご意見をいただきたいのです。出席できない方は、なるべく早く、その旨私にお知らせください。別の形で調整を図ります。

□ employee: 名 従業員　□ rescheduling: 名 予定変更　□ regretfully: 副 残念にも、遺憾ながら　□ weekly: 形 毎週の、週1回の
□ staff: 名 職員、部員　□ department: 名 部門、部　□ process: 動 ～を処理する　□ survey: 名 調査　□ schedule: 動 ～を予定する
□ deliver: 動 ～を伝える、～を説明する　□ summary: 名 まとめ　□ findings: 名 結果　□ attend: 動 ～に出席する
□ reschedule: 動 ～の予定を変更する　□ attendance: 名 出席　□ extremely: 副 とても　□ valuable: 形 大切な
□ input: 名 意見、アドバイス　□ alternative: 形 代わりの　□ arrangement: 名 手配

143.　正解：C　易 ▭▭▭▭▭▭ 難　選択率：(A) 13.7%　(B) 2.7%　**(C) 81.6%**　(D) 1.6%

(A) cancel
(B) accompany
(C) postpone
(D) leave

(A) 動 ～を中止する
(B) 動 ～に同行する
(C) 動 ～を延期する
(D) 動 ～を出発する

▶解説　空所を含む1文から、マーケティング部の調査データの処理が間に合わず、会議が予定通り行えないことが分かります。❷の部分で、連絡票の発信者は、別の日時で会議に参加するよう従業員に呼び掛けています。従って、空所には (C) postpone (～を延期する) が入ると判断できます。

144. 正解：**B**　易 ■■■■■■ 難　選択率：(A) 19.2%　**(B) 23.9%**　(C) 12.2%　(D) 43.9%

(A) I am sure you all learned a lot from their detailed descriptions.
(B) I had hoped to hold a brainstorming session after their presentation.
(C) Only select staff members have been made aware of the meeting.
(D) At the moment, there don't appear to be any other dates available.

(A) きっと皆さんが彼らの詳細な説明から多くを学んだに違いないと思います。
(B) 私としては、同部の発表の後に意見交換の場を設けたかったのです。
(C) 選ばれた従業員だけが、会議のことを知らされてきました。
(D) 今のところ、他に都合のつく日がないようです。

▶解説　❶で、会議ではマーケティング部が報告を行う予定だったと述べられています。しかしながら、実際には予定通りにならず、「マーケティング部の発表の後、意見交換の場を設けたかった（ができなかった）」という内容の(B)を空所に入れると適切です。(D)が正しいと仮定すると、❷の内容に矛盾するため不正解です。

□ detailed: 形 詳細な　□ description: 名 説明　□ brainstorming: 名 アイデアを出し合うこと
□ session: 名 会合、集い　□ select: 形 えりぬきの
□ make 〜 aware of ...: 〜に…を知らせる　□ at the moment: 今のところ
□ appear: 動 〜のように見える

---

145. 正解：**D**　易 ■■■□□□□ 難　選択率：(A) 12.5%　(B) 7.5%　(C) 7.5%　**(D) 71.8%**

(A) optional
(B) considerate
(C) variable
(D) important

(A) 形 任意の
(B) 形 思いやりのある
(C) 形 変わりやすい
(D) 形 重要な

▶解説　連絡票の発信者は❸で、「会議で得る情報は極めて有用なものになるだろうし、皆から意見をもらいたい」と述べ、❹では「（参加できない人がいる場合は）別の調整を図る」とまで言っています。これらのことから、会議への参加は非常に重要であると判断できます。よって、(D)が適切です。任意参加を示唆する情報はなく、❷と❸にeveryoneとあるため(A)は不適切です。

---

146. 正解：**A**　易 ■■□□□□□ 難　選択率：**(A) 79.2%**　(B) 15.3%　(C) 4.3%　(D) 1.2%

(A) who
(B) anyone
(C) which
(D) some

(A) 〜する人
(B) 誰でも
(C) 〜であるもの
(D) いくつかの

▶解説　空所は、those と cannot attend に挟まれています。those は people と同様に、不特定多数の人々やものを表す代名詞として機能します。空所に(A) who を補えば、those who cannot attend（出席できない人たち）となり意味が通ります。

((・)) ゼミ生中継

👦Hiro 👧Mai 👦Yasu 👦Dai 👧Saki

144. ....

👦 これは難しかったです。

👧 文書をいい加減に読むから難しいと思うんだよ。空所に(D)を入れると、話の流れが「会議は延期するが、代わりの日がない」となる。

👦 自然だと思いました。

👧 じゃ、なぜ「木曜の午後4時に来て」と直後に言うの？　(D)は200％間違った情報だよ。(C)も、この会議は全員対象だからダメ。マーケティング部が準備できていないから会議を延期するのに、(A)は

彼らの説明を聞いたことを前提にしているから全然ダメ。(B)以外はどれも激しく間違っている。

👦 (A)の all learned が will learn に見えました。

👧 私もです。まさか、will に見た目が似ている all がワナとして使われているのですか。

👧 そんな低次元のワナは……、あの著者ならやりかねないなぁ。でも、そんなことはどうでもいい。今後は正確に選択肢を読むよう注意して。

Part 7 読解問題

Questions 147-148 refer to the following advertisement.

Galaxy Plus
127 Vardy Cobb Street, Lipton
Use our super efficient online services to promote your company!

❶We specialize in:

· Business cards	· Survey forms
· Brochures	· Full-sized posters

Galaxy Plus offers speedy service at affordable prices.❷Our easy-to-use online design tool can enable you to create the perfect full-color product in minutes. The software automatically calculates the price and even provides an estimated completion time. You can request same-day delivery or even come into the store and pick your order up yourself.❸Visit www.galaxyplus.com to learn more about our special prices for bulk orders. You can register as a customer for free and take advantage of our 20 percent off introductory offer.

（111w）

問題**147-148**は次の広告に関するものです。

Galaxy Plus
127 Vardy Cobb Street, Lipton
当店の非常に効率的なオンラインサービスを利用して、あなたの会社を宣伝してください！

当店の専門は：

・名刺	・アンケート用紙
・パンフレット	・大判ポスター

Galaxy Plus は迅速なサービスを手頃な価格で提供します。当店の使いやすいオンラインのデザインツールで、完璧なフルカラーの製品をほんの数分でお作りいただけます。このソフトは自動的に料金を計算し、予想完成時刻までお知らせするのです。当日配送をご依頼いただけますし、店舗へお越しになり、品物をお引き取りいただくことも可能です。www.galaxyplus.com へアクセスして、大量注文時の特別価格について詳細をご確認ください。無料でお客さま登録が可能で、20パーセント引きの初回提供価格をご利用いただけます。

☐ super: 副 ものすごく ☐ efficient: 形 効率的な ☐ promote: 動 ～を宣伝する ☐ specialize in ～: ～を専門にする ☐ business card: 名刺
☐ brochure: 名 パンフレット ☐ survey form: アンケート用紙 ☐ full-sized: 形 大型の ☐ offer: 動 ～を提供する ☐ speedy: 形 迅速な
☐ affordable: 形 手頃な ☐ easy-to-use: 形 使いやすい ☐ enable ～ to ...: ～が…できるようにする ☐ create: 動 ～を作り出す
☐ full-color: 形 フルカラーの ☐ product: 名 製品 ☐ in minutes: 数分で ☐ automatically: 副 自動的に ☐ calculate: 動 ～を計算する
☐ provide: 動 ～を提供する ☐ estimated: 形 推測の、予測される ☐ completion: 名 完成 ☐ same-day: 形 同日の、即日の
☐ delivery: 名 配達 ☐ bulk order: 大量注文、大口発注 ☐ register: 動 登録する ☐ for free: 無料で ☐ take advantage of ～: ～を利用する
☐ introductory: 形 最初の

147. 正解：**A**　易 ■■■□□□□ 難　選択率：**(A) 76.5%** (B) 16.9% (C) 3.9% (D) 2.7%

What is being advertised?
(A) A printing company
(B) A Web site designer
(C) A courier service
(D) A photography business

何が宣伝されていますか。
(A) 印刷業者
(B) ウェブサイトのデザイナー
(C) 宅配便サービス
(D) 写真業者

▶解説 ❶は、Galaxy Plus 社の業務内容のリストです。このリストから、この会社が名刺やパンフレットなどの印刷物を扱っていることが分かります。さらに、❷に「ツールを使ってフルカラーの製品を作れる」が提供するサービスについての記述があります。これらの情報から、(A)の印刷業者が宣伝されていると判断できます。

---

148. 正解：**D**　易 ■■■□□□□ 難　選択率：(A) 2.0% (B) 2.7% (C) 12.5% **(D) 82.7%**

What is indicated about Galaxy Plus?
(A) It will open in new locations soon.
(B) It has recently changed ownership.
(C) It has a free delivery service.
(D) It offers discounts on large orders.

☐ ownership: 图 所有権、所有者であること
☐ discount: 图 値引き、割引

Galaxy Plus について何が示されていますか。
(A) もうじき新しい場所で開業する。
(B) 最近、オーナーが変わった。
(C) 無料の配送サービスがある。
(D) 大量注文には割引価格が提供される。

▶解説 ❸で、「大量注文時の特別価格」に関する情報がウェブサイトで入手できると述べられています。従って、bulk orders を large orders と言い換えた (D) が正解です。(A) と (B) は述べられていません。配送に関する情報はありますが、無料とは書かれていないため、(C) も不適切です。

🗼))) ゼミ 生中継　　😀 Hiro 😁 Mai 😄 Yasu 😎 Dai 😊 Saki

😀 Part 7 はどうだった？　今は時間のことより、ちゃんと考えて解いた問題の正答率を気にすればいい。時間が余るのは超上級者だけだから。大事なのは、自分が犯したミスから原因を学び、同じミスを繰り返さないことだよ。まぁ、正確な読解さえできれば、ミスの99%は防げるけど。

😊 そう思います。今回、Part 7 から解いてみたら、かなり楽でした。気持ちに余裕がある状態で長文を読んだので、頭に内容がスッと入ってきました。

😎 なるほど。それで Part 6 を雑に解いてミスしていたのか。

😊 そうです。

148.

😎 これは言い換えられた情報に気づけば簡単。

😊 special prices と discounts は同じですか？

😎 同じだよ。特別価格は特別に高い価格じゃなく、特別に安い価格のことだから、意味は「割引」と同じ。

Part 7 読解問題

Questions 149-151 refer to the following brochure.

Join the Bronson Wilderness Society (BWS)

Our society of wilderness enthusiasts meets every weekend for a variety of activities around Orchid Bay. These include bushwalks, bird watching, volunteer cleanups, and educational seminars. Our members come from all walks of life and this variation is what helps make the group exciting and fulfilling for all participants. We are currently looking for new members to join and bring more fresh ideas and variety to the society.

Membership costs only $200 annually and it affords members discounts at many local businesses such as Drysdale's Leisure Center, where you can save as much as $10 a month. Other participating businesses include Randolph All Sports, Hooper Health Food, and Kreese Camping Goods.

Before they apply for full membership, interested people are offered a free three-month trial membership to help them make up their minds. The secretary of the society, Philomena Driscoll, provides information sessions about the society at our office in Strathpine. Please call her at 555-8423 to schedule an appointment.

(167w)

問題149-151は次のパンフレットに関するものです。

Bronson Wilderness Society (BWS) へご参加ください

当原生地愛好者協会は、毎週末にOrchid Bay周辺に集まり、さまざまな活動に従事しています。例えば、森林ハイキングやバードウオッチング、ボランティアでの清掃、教育セミナーといった活動です。当協会は、さまざまな職業や立場の人たちで構成されており、この多様性のおかげで協会が全ての参加者にとって楽しく充実したものとなっています。当協会では現在、新たに加わっていただける方々を求めています。当協会に、さらなる新しい考えや多様性をもたらしてください。

会費は年間たったの200ドルです。この会費で、会員は多くの地元の施設・店舗で割引を受けることができます。例えばDrysdale's Leisure Centerでは、月に10ドルも引かれます。他に割引の適用される店舗として、Randolph All Sports、Hooper Health Food、Kreese Camping Goodsがあります。

正規会員へのお申し込みの前に、興味をお持ちの方には無料で3カ月間の仮会員権を提供していますので、ご判断の参考としていただけます。協会の書記Philomena Driscollが、Strathpineの事務所で説明会を開いています。555-8423の彼女宛てにお電話いただき、予約を入れてください。

☐ wilderness: 图 原生地　☐ enthusiast: 图 愛好家、ファン　☐ bushwalk: 图 （低木地帯の）ハイキング　☐ cleanup: 图 清掃
☐ walk of life: 職業、社会的地位　☐ variation: 图 多様性　☐ fulfilling: 形 充実した　☐ participant: 图 参加者　☐ currently: 副 現在、今
☐ fresh: 形 新鮮な、新しい　☐ membership: 图 会員であること　☐ annually: 副 毎年、年1回　☐ afford: 動 ～が得られる
☐ local business: 地元企業　☐ apply for ～: ～に申し込む　☐ trial: 形 試験的な、お試しの　☐ make up one's mind: 決心する、決める
☐ secretary: 图 （団体などの）書記、幹事　☐ provide: 動 ～を提供する

149. 正解：**D**　易 ■■■■■■□□□ 難　選択率：(A) 14.5%　(B) 14.5%　(C) 15.3%　**(D) 54.9%**

What is indicated about BWS members?
(A) They have special skills.
(B) They all own local businesses.
(C) They were all introduced by other members.
(D) They have diverse backgrounds.

□ diverse: 形 多様な　□ background: 名 経歴、背景

BWSの会員について何が示されていますか。
(A) 彼らは特別な技能を持っている。
(B) 彼らは皆、地元の事業主だ。
(C) 彼らは皆、他の会員に紹介された。
(D) 彼らの経歴は多岐にわたる。

▶解説 ❶の all walks of life は、「あらゆる職業や社会的地位」という意味です。この文で、BWSの会員は、さまざまな職業や社会的地位出身者であると分かります。従って、それを diverse backgrounds（多様な経歴）と言い換えた (D) が正解です。

---

150. 正解：**D**　易 ■■■■■■□□□ 難　選択率：(A) 10.2%　(B) 40.0%　(C) 9.0%　**(D) 40.4%**

The word "affords" in paragraph 2, line 1, is closest in meaning to
(A) spares
(B) admits
(C) manages
(D) grants

第2段落1行目にある「affords」に最も意味が近いのは
(A) 〜を割く
(B) 〜を認める
(C) 〜を管理する
(D) 〜を与える

▶解説 問われている語、affords には「〜を提供する」という意味があります。❷で、年会費についての情報に加え、地元で割引サービスが受けられる旨について述べられています。(D)の grants にも「〜を与える」という意味があり、置き換えると「（メンバーに）割引サービスを与える」となり、これが同義語として適切です。

---

151. 正解：**A**　易 ■■■■□□□□□ 難　選択率：**(A) 63.5%**　(B) 28.2%　(C) 3.1%　(D) 5.1%

Why are people instructed to call Ms. Driscoll?
(A) To learn more about an association
(B) To apply for membership
(C) To submit to an assessment
(D) To volunteer to help at an event

□ association: 名 協会　□ submit: 動 おとなしく従う
□ assessment: 名 評価
□ volunteer to 〜: 進んで〜しようと申し出る

なぜ人々はDriscollさんへ電話をかけるよう指示されていますか。
(A) 協会についてもっと詳しく知るために
(B) 会員に申し込むために
(C) 判断に従うために
(D) イベントの手伝いを申し出るために

▶解説 ❸で、書記の Driscoll さんの役割について述べた後、❹で、彼女に電話をして、説明会の予約を入れるようにと述べています。よって、(A) が正解です。彼女に電話をするのはBWSに申し込むためではないので、(B) は不正解です。

150.

🦉 (B) が魅力的なのかな。

🐵 選びました。会員は割引してもらえるんですよね。それが「認められる」のイメージに近いので、admitを選びました。

🦉 admit が持つ「認める」は、人が何かに入ることを認めるというイメージか、ミスしたことを認めるというイメージだよ。割引を与えるという意

味での「認める」とは全く違う。

🐵 そうなのかぁ。

🦉 あと、語法が不適切。この affords は give のように「members に discounts を与える」という形で使われている。でも、admit にはそんな用法はない。

Part 7 読解問題

Questions 152-153 refer to the following text-message chain.

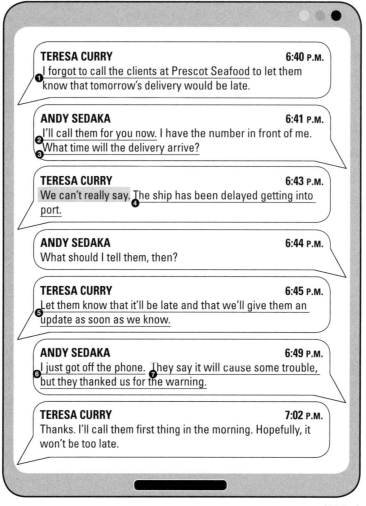

TERESA CURRY   6:40 P.M.
❶ I forgot to call the clients at Prescot Seafood to let them know that tomorrow's delivery would be late.

ANDY SEDAKA   6:41 P.M.
❷ I'll call them for you now. I have the number in front of me.
❸ What time will the delivery arrive?

TERESA CURRY   6:43 P.M.
We can't really say. ❹ The ship has been delayed getting into port.

ANDY SEDAKA   6:44 P.M.
What should I tell them, then?

TERESA CURRY   6:45 P.M.
❺ Let them know that it'll be late and that we'll give them an update as soon as we know.

ANDY SEDAKA   6:49 P.M.
❻ I just got off the phone. ❼ They say it will cause some trouble, but they thanked us for the warning.

TERESA CURRY   7:02 P.M.
Thanks. I'll call them first thing in the morning. Hopefully, it won't be too late.

(139w)

問題152-153は次のテキストメッセージのやりとりに関するものです。

TERESA CURRY 　午後6時40分
Prescot Seafoodのお客さんへ電話するのを忘れたの、明日の配送が遅れることを知らせなくちゃいけなかったのに。

ANDY SEDAKA 　午後6時41分
僕が今、代わりに電話するよ。目の前に電話番号がある。何時に配送されるの？

TERESA CURRY 　午後6時43分
はっきりしないの。船の入港が遅れているのよ。

ANDY SEDAKA 　午後6時44分
じゃあ、先方に何と言えばいい？

TERESA CURRY 　午後6時45分
配送が遅れそうで、分かり次第新たな情報を伝えますって言っておいて。

ANDY SEDAKA 　午後6時49分
今電話を切ったところ。先方は、困ったことになるだろうって言ってるけど、事前に伝えたことには感謝してくれたよ。

TERESA CURRY 　午後7時02分
ありがとう。私から朝一番に電話する。遅れがひどくなり過ぎないといいんだけど。

☐ port: 图 港　☐ update: 图 最新情報　☐ get off the phone: 電話を切る　☐ cause trouble: 問題を引き起こす　☐ warning: 图 通知
☐ first thing in the morning: 朝一番に　☐ hopefully: 副 願わくば〜だといいのだが

152. 正解：**B**　易 ■■■□□□□ 難　選択率：(A) 9.0%　**(B) 81.6%**　(C) 9.0%　(D) 0.4%

At 6:43 P.M., what does Ms. Curry mean when she writes, "We can't really say"?
(A) She is not authorized to comment.
(B) She does not know the answer.
(C) She does not have time to respond.
(D) She is unable to speak the client's language.

☐ be authorized to 〜：〜する権限を与えらえている
☐ respond: 動 返事する

午後6時43分に、どのような意味でCurryさんは「はっきりしないの」と書いていますか。
(A) 彼女には発言する権限がない。
(B) 彼女は答えを知らない。
(C) 彼女には答える時間がない。
(D) 彼女は顧客の使う言葉を話せない。

▶解説 問われているのは、配送時間についての質問 (❸) に対する応答です。ターゲット文の発言の後、❹で船の入港が遅れていること、❺で最新情報は後で伝えるので、配送が遅れることを相手に伝えてほしいと述べています。これらからCurryさんは、配送時間を知らないと判断できます。よって、(B)が正解です。

---

153. 正解：**C**　易 ■■■□□□□ 難　選択率：(A) 26.3%　(B) 5.1%　**(C) 66.3%**　(D) 2.4%

Who did Mr. Sedaka most likely call?
(A) A supplier
(B) A trainee
(C) A client
(D) An applicant

Sedakaさんは誰に電話をかけた可能性が最も高いですか。
(A) 納入業者
(B) 研修生
(C) 顧客
(D) 応募者

▶解説 ❶で、Curryさんが顧客であるPrescot Seafood社に電話をかけ忘れたことを述べ、❷でSedakaさんが代わりに電話をすると申し出ています。その後、❻で、Sedakaさんが電話をかけ終えたこと、❼で顧客からの返事を伝えています。これらのことから、Sedakaさんが電話をしたのはPrescot Seafood社、つまり、(C)の顧客であると判断できます。

(((●))) ゼミ 生 中継　　　😎 Hiro　😎 Mai　😎 Yasu　😎 Dai　😎 Saki

152.
😎 Part 7の意図問題は時刻で始まる。ここでは午後6時43分だね。ただ、いきなりその時刻を探しちゃいけない。なぜだと思う？

😎 もっと前の情報も大事だからですか。

😎 その通り。状況を説明する発言が最初にあるから、そこを読まないとチャット全体の概要を把握しにくい。それに、意図問題を解くにはタ

ーゲット文だけでなく、その前後も読む必要があるからね。最初から狭く読んで解こうとするのは得策じゃない。

😎 なるほど。

😎 人の名前は覚えなくていいですか？

😎 覚える必要はない。名前と時刻を読まなくても、チャットの内容は把握できる。だから、名前に注意するのは設問を解く時でいい。

Questions 154-155 refer to the following letter.

Venus Fitness Center
Twin Pines Mall
772 Coleman Rd., Seattle, WA 98563

May 2

Mr. Diego Sanchez
63 Gibson Street
Seattle, WA 98112

Dear Mr. Sanchez,

❶ I am happy to announce that next Friday, May 11 is the tenth anniversary
of Venus Fitness Center. ❷ To celebrate, we are holding a barbecue on the
grassed area at the rear of the gym. All members are invited and food and
drink will be supplied by the center. You can even bring along a friend to
join in the celebrations for free.

❸ All of the trainers will be there to lend a hand and socialize with members.
❹ Even Josh Kruger, whose work with several movie stars has made him a
minor celebrity, has agreed to attend.

I have been put in charge of organizing the event. People who wish to
attend should send me a text message with the words, "I'm in" to my
mobile phone at 823 555 3495. Please also mention whether or not you
will be bringing a friend.

Sincerely,

Beth Hays

Beth Hays
Member Services — Venus Fitness Center

(179w)

問題**154-155**は次の手紙に関するものです。

Venus Fitness Center
Twin Pines Mall
772 Coleman Rd., Seattle, WA 98563

5月2日

Diego Sanchez さま
63 Gibson Street
Seattle, WA 98112

前略　Sanchez さま

以下についてお知らせできますことを、喜ばしく存じます。来週の金曜日、5月11日は、Venus Fitness Center の開業10周年記念日です。これを祝して、ジムの裏手の芝生エリアでバーベキューを催す予定です。

会員の皆さまをご招待し、飲食物は当センターでご用意します。ご友人をお連れくださっても、祝賀会に無料でご参加いただけます。

全トレーナーが、会場で運営を手伝いながら会員との交流を図る予定です。何人かの映画スターとの仕事でちょっとした有名人の仲間入りをしている Josh Kruger も、参加を表明しています。

私がこの催しの運営を担当しております。参加をご希望の方は、「参加します」の言葉を添えて私宛てにショートメールを送信してください。私の携帯電話の番号は823-555-3495です。ご友人をお連れになるか否かについても、併せてお知らせください。

草々

Beth Hays
会員サービス担当——Venus Fitness Center

☐ announce: 動 ～を発表する　☐ anniversary: 名 記念日　☐ celebrate: 動 ～を祝う　☐ supply: 動 ～を提供する
☐ bring along ～: ～を連れていく　☐ join in ～: ～に加わる　☐ celebration: 名 祝うこと、お祝い　☐ lend a hand: 手を貸す、手伝う
☐ socialize with ～: ～と交流する　☐ celebrity: 名 有名人　☐ in charge of ～: ～を任されて　☐ organize an event: イベントを企画する
☐ text message: テキスト・メッセージ、携帯メッセージ　☐ I'm in.: やります。、参加します。　☐ whether: 接 ～かどうか

154. 正解：**B**　易 ■■□□□□ 難　選択率：(A) 0.4%　**(B) 98.0%**　(C) 0.4%　(D) 1.2%

What is the purpose of the letter?
(A) To offer a discount membership
(B) To announce a special event
(C) To recommend a new program
(D) To congratulate a successful candidate

□ membership: 名 会員であること
□ congratulate: 動 ～を祝う　□ successful: 形 成功した
□ candidate: 名 候補者

この手紙の目的は何ですか。
(A) 割引会員権を提供すること
(B) 特別な催しについて伝えること
(C) 新しいプログラムを勧めること
(D) 成功した候補者を祝うこと

▶解説 ❶で、5月11日がVenus Fitness Centerの10周年記念日であることを述べ、❷でそれを祝うためのバーベキューを行うことを伝えています。このバーベキューを a special eventと言い換えた(B)が正解です。

---

155. 正解：**C**　易 ■■■■□□ 難　選択率：(A) 52.9%　(B) 3.5%　**(C) 39.2%**　(D) 4.3%

Who is Josh Kruger?
(A) A movie star
(B) A founder of a gym
(C) A physical trainer
(D) A customer service agent

Josh Krugerとは誰ですか。
(A) 映画スター
(B) あるジムの創設者
(C) 身体トレーナー
(D) 顧客サービス代理業者

▶解説 このイベントには全てのトレーナーが手伝いに来て会員と交流する、と❸で述べられています。また、❹で、Josh Krugerも参加に同意したと続いていることから、Krugerさんもトレーナーであると考えられます。よって、(C)が正解です。(A)の映画スターはKrugerさんが一緒に仕事をしたことがあると述べられているだけです。

📻 ゼミ🈟中継　　　　　　　　　😀Hiro 😊Mai 😁Yasu 😎Dai 😄Saki

😎 第1段落の3行目にat the rear of the gymとあるけど、見覚えないかな？

😊 Part 1の2番です。at the rear of a vehicleでした。

😄 ピンポーン。

155.

😎 正解の(C)を選ぶモニターが上級グループでは6割いたけれど、中級と初級グループでは約6割が(A)を選んでいる。Joshはバーベキューに来るトレーナーの例として紹介されているんだから、当然、彼もト

レーナーだよ。

😊 Joshの名前の後に、～ made him a minor celebrityとあったので頭が混乱しました。

😎 たいしたことないセレブってどんなセレブですか。

😎 ん？　あぁ、minor celebrityのこと？　このminorはポジティブな意味で使われているから「ちょっとした有名人」だよ。ジムのトレーナーなのに、プチ有名人になったということ。

😊 そうだったのか！

Questions 156-158 refer to the following e-mail.

E-Mail Message

To:	Loretta Wang <lwang@simpsonbeverages.com>
From:	Timothy Lennox <tlennox@simpsonbeverages.com>
Subject:	Marketing
Date:	September 17

Dear Loretta,

I have just received some information about the Western Professional Marketing (WPM) Convention in Sacramento. The theme this year is the use of social media for marketing, which is something that will be more and more important in the future. I would like to take a trip to Sacramento from October 12 to October 15 to attend the conference.

I am currently scheduled to train some new salespeople on those dates. However, I have spoken with Ms. Fayed and she has agreed to take care of that while I am away. When I get back from the conference, I will cover any topics that they miss.

The Web site of the event organizers is already offering tickets for the conference at $250 per head. I realize that this is not cheap, but I hope you will approve my application to buy one. Considering the potential for extra sales, I think this is a small expense.

Sincerely,

Timothy Lennox
Marketing Manager

(177w)

問題156-158は次のメールに関するものです。

宛先：Loretta Wang <lwang@simpsonbeverages.com>
送信者：Timothy Lennox <tlennox@simpsonbeverages.com>
件名：マーケティング
日付：9月17日

Lorettaさん

たった今、Sacramento で行われる Western Professional Marketing (WPM) Convention に関する情報を受け取ったところです。今年のテーマはソーシャルメディアのマーケティングへの活用で、これはこの先ますます重要になる事柄です。10月12日から10月15日まで Sacramento へ出張して、この会議に出席したいと思います。

私の今のところの予定では、この期間に数名の新しい販売員を教育することになっています。しかし、Fayed さんに相談して、私の留守中にこの件を引き受けてくれると言ってくれました。会議から戻ってから、彼らが聞きそこねた話があれば私がフォローするつもりです。

このイベントの主催者のウェブサイトではこの会議のチケットがすでに1人当たり250ドルで提供されています。これが安い額ではないことは承知していますが、私が1人分を申し込むことを承認していただければ幸いです。売り上げ増加の可能性を考えれば、これは小さな出費だと思います。

よろしくお願いします。

マーケティング部長
Timothy Lennox

☐ convention: 图 会議　☐ trip: 图 旅行　＊ここでは「出張」を示す　☐ conference: 图 会議　☐ currently: 副 現在、今
☐ be scheduled to ～: ～する予定になっている　☐ train: 動 ～を教育する　☐ salespeople: 图 販売員、営業担当者
☐ take care of ～: ～を引き受ける　☐ cover: 動 ～を扱う、～を取り上げる　☐ organizer: 图 主催者　☐ per head: 1人当たり
☐ approve: 動 ～を承認する　☐ application: 图 申請　☐ considering: 前 ～を考えれば、考慮すれば　☐ potential: 图 可能性
☐ extra: 形 追加の　☐ expense: 图 費用、出費

156. 正解：**B**　易 ■■■□□□□□ 難　選択率：(A) 8.2%　**(B) 85.5%**　(C) 4.3%　(D) 2.0%

Why did Mr. Lennox send the e-mail?
(A) To learn more about an upcoming event
(B) To request permission to attend a conference
(C) To explain the reason for a delay
(D) To ask for a transfer to a different department

□ upcoming: 形 来る、次の　□ permission: 名 許可
□ transfer: 名 異動

なぜLennoxさんは、このメールを出しましたか。
(A) 近く行われる催しについて詳しく知るために
(B) 会議への参加許可を求めるために
(C) 遅延の理由を説明するために
(D) 他の部署への異動を願い出るために

▶解説　第1段落でSacramentoで行われる会議の詳細について述べた後、❶でこの会議に出席するために出張したいとLennoxさんは申し出ています。また、第3段落❸で、このメールの宛先であるWangさんが、Lennoxさんの希望を承認する立場であることが分かります。oneは、会議に出席するためのチケットを指しています。よって、(B)が正解です。

---

157. 正解：**A**　易 ■■■■■□□□ 難　選択率：**(A) 42.0%**　(B) 14.9%　(C) 34.9%　(D) 7.5%

What has Ms. Fayed agreed to do?
(A) Train some new employees
(B) Accompany Mr. Lennox on a trip
(C) Take care of Mr. Lennox's clients
(D) Try some new marketing techniques

□ accompany: 動 ～に同行する
□ technique: 名 技術、手法

Fayedさんは何をすることに同意していますか。
(A) 数名の新入社員を教育する
(B) Lennoxさんの出張に同行する
(C) Lennoxさんの顧客の世話をする
(D) いくつかの新しいマーケティング手法を試す

▶解説　Lennoxさんは❷の前半で、会議の期間中、何人かの新しい販売員の研修を担うことになっていると述べています。その後、FayedさんがLennoxさんの留守中、その任務、つまり新入社員研修を引き受けることを了承したとありますので、(A)が正解です。

---

158. 正解：**C**　易 ■■■□□□□□ 難　選択率：(A) 5.5%　(B) 9.8%　**(C) 74.1%**　(D) 10.2%

What is indicated about Mr. Lennox?
(A) He is being transferred to the sales division.
(B) He has worked for Ms. Wang for many years.
(C) He considers the conference worth the admission fee.
(D) He has attended a WPM Convention in the past.

□ consider: 動 ～と見なす　□ worth: 形 ～の価値がある
□ admission fee: 入場料

Lennoxさんについて何が示されていますか。
(A) 彼は販売課へ異動する予定だ。
(B) 彼は長年Wangさんの下で働いている。
(C) 彼は、この会議が参加費の額に見合うものだと考えている。
(D) 彼はかつてWPM Conventionに参加したことがある。

▶解説　❹で、Lennoxさんは売上増加の可能性について述べています。この文のthisは、会議のチケット代である250ドルを指しています。売上増加のための出費なら、250ドルは小さな出費だと述べていることから、会議にそれだけの価値があると考えていることが分かります。よって、(C)が正解です。

((•)) ゼミ 生中継　😮 Hiro 😳 Mai 😄 Yasu 🎲 Dai 😸 Saki

157.
😮 上級グループの正答率は約70％あるけれど、中級グループでは37％に下がって、代わりに約4割が(C)を選んだみたい。ということは、(C)を消去できたかどうかに上級と中級の差が出たと思われる。

😸 Fayedさんの名前の直後に～ she has agreed to take care of that ...とあったので、take care ofに釣られて(C)にしました。thatが何を指すか慎重にチェックするべきでした。

😮 今、サキちゃんが言ったthatの中身を確認したら、1つ前の文に～

train some new salespeople ... があったので、(A)にしました。(C)はclientsが間違っています。

😮 その通り。Part 7が苦手と言う人は、時間が足りないから解けないと言う前に、時間があっても間違える原因を探る必要がある。サキ、自分がミスした原因は何だった？

😸 確認作業をサボったことです。

😮 それが収穫だよ。今後は気を付けてね。

Part 7 読解問題

Wilson's Crest Hotel

45 Portman Street
Arlington

The premier place to stay in Arlington

❶Thank you for choosing to stay at Wilson's Crest Hotel. We hope you enjoyed your visit to Arlington and that we will have an opportunity to serve you again on your return. ❷There are many wonderful places to visit in the area and our staff would be more than happy to recommend things to do on your next visit.

Please take a moment to let us know how we did. While Wilson's Crest Hotel takes great pride in its luxury and customer service, we know there is always room for improvement.

	Unsatisfactory	Satisfactory	Excellent
The helpfulness of front desk		X	
The location		X	
The lobby			X
The room size		X	

Additional comments: I found the room satisfactory. ❸However, I must mention that the décor was hardly fashionable, neither was it quaint nor antique. ❹This was in stark contrast with the lobby, which had obviously been recently refurbished and looked amazing.

Was this your first time staying at Wilson's Crest Hotel?   Yes _X_   No ___

What was the purpose of your visit to Arlington? ❺I was born and raised here, but I have been living in Ottawa for the past 20 years. My mother was the architect who designed this building and I wanted to come and admire her work.

❻**Name:** Sven Harbor

(225w)

問題159-162は次のアンケートに関するものです。

Wilson's Crest Hotel
45 Portman Street
Arlington

Arlingtonで一番の宿泊施設

Wilson's Crest Hotelでのご宿泊をお選びいただきまして、ありがとうございます。Arlingtonへのご旅行をお楽しみいただけたこと、また、お客さまが当地を再訪なさる機会に、私共があらためてお役に立てることを願っています。当地にはたくさんの素晴らしい名所がございますので、次回のご来訪の際には、私共の従業員が喜んでご案内させていただきたく存じます。

お手数ですが、私共のサービスに対するご感想をお知らせください。Wilson's Crest Hotelは、その豪華さとお客さまへのサービス内容を誇りにしておりますが、一方で常に改善の余地があることも承知しています。

	不満足	満足	大変満足
フロントの対応		×	
立地		×	
ロビー			×
客室の規模		×	

追加のご意見：部屋には満足しました。しかし、装飾はおしゃれとは言い難く、趣があるというわけでも古風というわけでもありませんでした。この点は、ロビーとは全く対照的でした。ロビーは見るからに最近改装されており、素晴らしい雰囲気でした。

今回、初めてWilson's Crest Hotelにご宿泊なさいましたか。
はい ×　いいえ ＿

Arlingtonへのご旅行の目的は何ですか。　私は当地に生まれ育ったのですが、過去20年間Ottawaに暮らしています。母が建築家としてこの建物を設計したので、ここへ来て母の仕事をじっくり見てみたいと思ったのです。

お名前：Sven Harbor

☐ survey: 图 調査、アンケート　☐ premier: 形 最高の、首位の　☐ opportunity: 图 機会　☐ serve: 動 ～の役に立つ
☐ recommend: 動 ～を勧める　☐ take a moment: 少し時間を取る　☐ take pride in: ～に誇りを持つ、～を自負する
☐ luxury: 图 豪華さ、ぜいたくさ　☐ room for ～: ～の余地　☐ improvement: 图 改善　☐ unsatisfactory: 形 不満足な
☐ satisfactory: 形 満足な　☐ excellent: 形 優れた、素晴らしい　☐ helpfulness: 图 助けになること　☐ front desk: フロント
☐ location: 图 立地　☐ additional: 形 追加の　☐ décor: 图 装飾、内装　☐ hardly: 副 とても～とは言えない　☐ fashionable: 形 おしゃれな
☐ neither A nor B: AもBもない　☐ quaint: 形 古風な趣のある　☐ antique: 形 古風な　☐ stark: 形 全くの　☐ contrast: 图 対比
☐ obviously: 副 明らかに　☐ recently: 副 最近の、最新の　☐ refurbish: 動 ～を改装する　☐ amazing: 形 素晴らしい　☐ purpose: 图 目的
☐ raise: 動 ～を育てる　☐ architect: 图 建築家　☐ design: 動 ～を設計する　☐ admire: 動 ～をほれぼれと眺める

Part 7 読解問題

---

159. 正解：**A**　易 ■■□□□□□ 難　選択率：**(A) 91.4%** (B) 0.4% (C) 2.4% (D) 5.1%

For whom is the survey intended?
(A) Hotel guests
(B) Conference attendees
(C) Travel agents
(D) Front desk staff

□ survey: 名 調査　□ attendee: 名 参加者、出席者

このアンケートは誰に向けられたものですか。
(A) ホテルの客
(B) 会議の出席者
(C) 旅行代理業者
(D) フロントの従業員

▶解説 冒頭の❶から、この文書がWilson's Crest Hotel の宿泊客に宛てたものであることが分かります。また、アンケート調査の項目からも、ホテルでの宿泊について尋ねられていることが分かります。よって、(A)が正解です。

---

160. 正解：**B**　易 ■■■■□□□ 難　選択率：(A) 5.1% **(B) 66.7%** (C) 19.2% (D) 8.2%

According to the survey, what can the business provide?
(A) Transportation to the airport
(B) Information about local attractions
(C) Chargers for several devices
(D) Cleaning for guests' clothing

□ transportation: 名 輸送　□ attraction: 名 観光名所、見もの
□ charger: 名 充電器　□ device: 名 機器

アンケートによると、この事業所は何を提供できますか。
(A) 空港への輸送
(B) 地元の観光名所に関する情報
(C) いくつかの機器に使える充電器
(D) 客の衣類の洗濯

▶解説 ❷で、この地域の特徴を挙げ、宿泊客の次の滞在時にはそこでできることをホテルの従業員が喜んで案内すると述べています。よって、(B)の「地元の観光名所に関する情報」が正解です。wonderful places to visit in the area が local attractions と言い換えられています。

---

161. 正解：**C**　易 ■■■□□□□ 難　選択率：(A) 23.5% (B) 2.4% **(C) 66.3%** (D) 7.5%

What does Mr. Harbor indicate about the room?
(A) Its equipment was out of order.
(B) It was too small.
(C) It was outdated.
(D) Its location was inconvenient.

□ equipment: 名 設備、機器　□ out of order: 故障して
□ outdated: 形 時代遅れの　□ inconvenient: 形 不便な

Harbor さんは部屋について何を述べていますか。
(A) 設備が故障していた。
(B) 狭すぎた。
(C) 流行遅れだった。
(D) 場所が不便だった。

▶解説 Harbor さんは部屋について、❸で不満を述べています。quaint と antique はどちらも、「古いが、趣がある」というプラスの意味を含むので、客室について「ただ古臭いだけだ」と考えたと判断できます。❹では、改装されたロビーとは対照的だと記述しています。よって、正解は (C) です。

---

162. 正解：**B**　易 ■■□□□□□ 難　選択率：(A) 0.8% **(B) 85.9%** (C) 7.8% (D) 4.7%

What is true about Mr. Harbor?
(A) He used a discount coupon.
(B) He grew up in Arlington.
(C) He accompanied a group of tourists.
(D) He worked on the building of Wilson's Crest Hotel.

□ discount coupon: 割引クーポン
□ accompany: 動 〜に付き添う

Harbor さんについて何が当てはまりますか。
(A) 彼は割引クーポンを使った。
(B) 彼は Arlington で育った。
(C) 彼は旅行者の一行を伴っていた。
(D) 彼は Wilson's Crest Hotel の建設に携わった。

▶解説 ❻の署名欄から、Harbor さんはこのアンケートの回答者であることが分かります。そのアンケートで彼が Arlington を訪問した目的を問われ、❺で「そこで生まれ育った」と回答していることから、(B)が正解です。(A)と(C)は述べられていません。ホテルの建設に携わったのは彼の母親なので、(D)も不適切です。

((●)) ゼミ 生 中継　　　（◎）Hiro （◎）Mai （◎）Yasu （◎）Dai （◎）Saki

160.

（◎）(C) の Chargers for several devices は文書にない情報だけど、選んだ人はいる？

（◎）選びました。

（◎）どうして？　充電器はどこにも登場しないよ。

（◎）ホテルなら充電器は貸してくれると思いました。

（◎）同感です。しかも、アーリントンはアメリカの街っぽいので、充電器は

絶対にあります。

（◎）それを言うんだったら、(A)も(D)も消去できないでしょ。設問に According to the survey とある場合、問題作成者は意図的にそれを使っている。受験者が不正解の選択肢を見て「これもあり得る。こっちもあり得る」と疑うのを防ぐためにね。

（◎）やられた〜。

TOEICよろず相談所　ヒロの部屋

⑪200問、2時間じゃ足りません！

TOEICを受けると、いつも全問を解く前に終わってしまうんですが、それが普通ですか？

リーディングセクションで時間切れになるのですよね。

そうです。最後はマークを適当に塗りつぶすだけです。

それをこの業界では「塗り絵」と呼びます。何問くらい塗り絵しますか。あと、現在のスコアはどれくらいですか。

スコアは600点で、塗り絵は20問くらいです。

正常です。600点レベルで、塗り絵しない人に会ったことがありません。**900点を取る人でも、塗り絵する人は結構います。**

何だか安心しました。ついでに変なことを聞いていいでしょうか。

どうぞ。

塗り絵をするならBがいいと聞いたのですが、本当ですか。

その質問はよく来ます（笑）　でも、ウソですよ。仮にPart 7の最後の20問を塗り絵するとします。選択肢は4つですから、Bが正解なのは4分の1なので5問だけです。多少のブレはあるでしょうが、Bだけがよく当たるなんてことはありません。

やはりそうですか。怪しいと思っていました。

個人的な体験から言えば、TOEICでは各記号がほぼ均等に正解になります。ですから、「どれを塗れば当たるか」を考える価値はありませんよ。

疑問が晴れました。ありがとうございました。

Part 7 読解問題

Questions 163-164 refer to the following notice.

Notice:

❶ This area is for Cosmos Financial Services' Staff to have meetings with clients and visitors.

- The area must be kept clean at all times. Please inspect the area after each meeting to ensure that it is ready for unexpected visits.
- ❷ The area can be reserved for up to one hour. If you would like to do so, please speak with Curtis Hyde. Check that no other staff member has reserved the room by checking the schedule posted on the door.
- ❸ This area is not to be used for discussion of sensitive personal information as it is a shared space. Private talks should be held in either Meeting Room 1 or Meeting Room 2.

(117w)

問題163-164は次の告知に関するものです。
告知
このエリアは、Cosmos Financial Services の従業員が顧客や来訪者とミーティングを行うためのものです。

・このエリアは、常にきれいに片付けておいてください。ミーティングが終わるたびにエリアを点検し、必ず不意の来訪者に対応できるようにしてください。

・このエリアは、最長1時間まで予約できます。予約したい場合には、Curtis Hyde に声を掛けてください。他の従業員がすでに部屋を予約していないことを、ドアに張り出された予定表を見て確認してください。
・このエリアは共有のスペースなので、機密性の高い個人情報に関わる話し合いには使えません。内密の話をする場合には、会議室1または会議室2を使用してください。

☐ inspect: 動 ～を点検する　☐ ensure: 動 ～を確実にする　☐ unexpected: 形 不意の　☐ visit: 名 訪問　☐ up to ～ : 最大で～まで
☐ schedule: 名 予定表　☐ post: 形 ～を掲示する　☐ sensitive: 形 機密の　☐ personal information: 個人情報　☐ shared: 形 共用の
☐ private: 形 内密の

163. 正解：**C**　易 ■■■□□□ 難　選択率：(A) 7.1%　(B) 4.7%　**(C) 82.0%**　(D) 6.3%

Why might an employee contact Mr. Hyde?
(A) To request that he restock cleaning supplies
(B) To sign in a visitor to the office
(C) To reserve a meeting area
(D) To schedule an employee evaluation

☐ restock: 動 ～を補充する　☐ cleaning supplies: 清掃用品、掃除道具　☐ schedule: 動 ～を予定する
☐ evaluation: 名 評価、査定

従業員がHydeさんに連絡を取るとしたら、その理由は何ですか。
(A) 彼に清掃用具の補充を依頼するために
(B) 来訪者を署名して登録の上、オフィスへ招き入れるために
(C) ミーティングの場所を予約するために
(D) 従業員の査定のスケジュールを組むために

▶解説 ❶でこのエリアが会議に使えることが述べられ、❷の前半に「このエリアは1時間まで予約できる」とあります。続けて、「そうしたい場合はCurtis Hydeに声を掛けるように」と述べられています。よって、(C)が正解です。

---

164. 正解：**D**　易 ■■□□□□ 難　選択率：(A) 3.1%　(B) 2.7%　(C) 13.3%　**(D) 80.8%**

What rule is applied to the use of the room?
(A) The carpets must be cleaned every month.
(B) The furniture must not be moved to another location.
(C) It should only be used if no other option is available.
(D) Sensitive information should not be discussed there.

☐ be applied to ～: ～に適用される
☐ furniture: 名 備品、家具　☐ option: 名 選択肢

この部屋を使う上でどんな規則が適用されますか。
(A) 必ず毎月じゅうたんを清掃しなければならない。
(B) 備品類を別の場所へ移動してはいけない。
(C) 他の選択肢がまったくない場合に限り使用してもよい。
(D) 機密性の高い情報についてそこで話してはいけない。

▶解説 この部屋の使用についてのルールに関する設問です。❸に、「このエリアは共有のスペースなので、機密性の高い個人情報に関わる話し合いには使えない」と明記されています。よって、(D)が正解です。

((•)) ゼミ 生中継　 Hiro　Mai　Yasu　Dai　Saki

163. ....
😀 設問がWhy mightで始まっている。Test 1で教えた格言を覚えている?
😮 あ、えっと……

😀 Why might のヒントは……
😎 ifにあり!
😀 その通り。例外はあるけれど、知っておけばきっと試験本番でも役に立つよ。

Questions 165-167 refer to the following letter.

Mr. Ramon Klukinski
LaTrobe Vocational College
Baltimore, MD 21208

Dear Mr. Klukinski,

I am interested in the position at LaTrobe Vocational College advertised in today's Herald Newspaper. I am currently the head of cleaning and facility maintenance at Goldman Convention Center, where I have been for the last five years. — [1] —. The center is open between the hours of 9:00 A.M. and 11:00 P.M. Therefore, in addition to my maintenance duties, I am required to manage the complicated schedules of people working different shifts.

I would like to work at LaTrobe Vocational College because the position suits my experience and skill set and also because the college is so close to my home. — [2] —. In fact, I am a graduate of the college and even worked there as an assistant to the groundskeeper during my final year of studies. — [3] —.

I have recently obtained an advanced certificate in building maintenance. — [4] —. This qualification will be particularly useful in maintaining the equipment and furnishings of your newly completed auditorium.

Please find enclosed my résumé and contact details.

Sincerely,

Paula Riser

Paula Riser

(190w)

問題**165-167**は次の手紙に関するものです。

Ramon Klukinski さま
LaTrobe Vocational College
Baltimore, MD 21208

Klukinski さま

私は、本日付のHerald Newspaper紙上で広告されているLaTrobe Vocational College での職に興味を持っています。私は現在、Goldman Convention Center で清掃と施設保守の責任者の立場にあり、この職に就いて5年になります。同センターの営業時間は午前9時から午後11時です。そのため、私は自分の保守作業に加えて、交代で勤務する従業員の複雑なスケジュールの管理も任されています。

私がLaTrobe Vocational College で働きたいと考えるのは、当該の職が自分の経験や技能に合っているからであり、また、同校が自宅に大変近いからでもあります。実は、私は同校の卒業生で、在学中の最終学年時にグラウンド管理人の補佐として働いたこともあります。

私は最近になって、ビル管理の上級資格を取得しました。これは、National Institute of Adult Learning を通じて6週間、オンラインで提供されたものでした。この資格は特に、貴校の新築の講堂にある機器や設備の保守管理に役立つでしょう。

同封の履歴書と連絡先詳細をご確認ください。

草々
Paula Riser

□ position: 图 職　□ currently: 圖 現在、今　□ head: 图 責任者　□ facility: 图 施設　□ maintenance: 图 保守、メンテナンス
□ therefore: 圖 従って　□ in addition to ～: ～に加えて　□ be required to ～: ～しなければならない　□ manage: 動 ～を管理する
□ complicated: 形 複雑な　□ shift: 图 シフト、交代勤務時間　□ suit: 動 ～に合う　□ experience: 图 経験　□ skill: 图 技能、技術
□ in fact: 実は　□ graduate: 图 卒業生　□ groundskeeper: 图 グラウンドの管理人　□ recently: 圖 最近　□ obtain: 動 ～を取得する
□ advanced: 形 上級の　□ certificate: 图 証明書、免許証　□ qualification: 图 資格　□ particularly: 圖 特に　□ equipment: 图 機器
□ furnishing: 图 （備え付けの）家具　□ newly: 圖 新たに、最近　□ auditorium: 图 講堂　□ enclosed: 形 同封されている
□ résumé: 图 履歴書　□ contact detail: 詳細な連絡先

165. 正解：**A**　易 ■■■■□□ 難　選択率：**(A) 61.6%** (B) 12.5% (C) 12.9% (D) 12.9%

For what position is Ms. Riser most likely applying?
(A) Janitor
(B) Lecturer
(C) Receptionist
(D) Research assistant

Riser さんは、どんな職に応募している可能性が最も高いですか。
(A) 管理人
(B) 講師
(C) 受付係
(D) 研究助手

▶解説　❶から Riser さんの現在の職務内容が清掃と施設保守であることが分かります。❷で、Riser さんは応募している職務にそれらの経験や技能が合っていると述べているため、Riser さんが応募しているのは「管理人」を意味する (A) だと判断できます。

---

166. 正解：**C**　易 ■■■■□□ 難　選択率：(A) 30.6% (B) 7.8% **(C) 40.4%** (D) 20.8%

What does Ms. Riser NOT mention about the college?
(A) It has recently added a performance space.
(B) She lives nearby.
(C) It offers attractive employee benefits.
(D) She has worked there before.

□ performance: 名 公演　□ nearby: 副 すぐ近くに
□ offer: 動 ～を提供する　□ attractive: 形 魅力的な
□ employee benefit: 福利厚生

Riser さんがこの大学について述べて<u>いない</u>ことは何ですか。
(A) 最近、公演のできる場所を新たに設けた。
(B) 彼女はその近隣に住んでいる。
(C) 職員に魅力的な福利厚生を提供している。
(D) 彼女はかつてそこで働いたことがある。

▶解説　第2段落にある❸が (B) に合致し、❹が (D) に合致します。❻の your newly completed auditorium から、この学校には新しい講堂があることが分かります。講堂は公演 (performance) などを行う場所なので、(A) の内容は正しいと言えます。(C) の employee benefits は「福利厚生」を指しますが、文書で触れられていません。

---

167. 正解：**D**　易 ■■■■□□ 難　選択率：(A) 4.7% (B) 12.5% (C) 33.3% **(D) 49.4%**

In which of the positions marked [1], [2], [3], and [4] does the following sentence best belong?

"It was a six-week course offered online through the National Institute of Adult Learning."
(A) [1]
(B) [2]
(C) [3]
(D) [4]

□ online: 副 オンラインで

次の文を当てはめるには、[1]、[2]、[3]、[4] と印が付けられた箇所のうちのどこが最もふさわしいですか。

「これは、National Institute of Adult Learning を通じて6週間、オンラインで提供されたものでした」
(A) [1]
(B) [2]
(C) [3]
(D) [4]

▶解説　ターゲット文にある six-week course offered online（オンラインで提供される6週間の講座）に関連する文書内の情報は❺です。ターゲット文を [4] の位置に入れると、Riser さんが保有するビル管理の資格は、6週間のオンライン講座に参加して取得したものだということになり、話の展開が自然に成立します。

ゼミ 生 中継　　Hiro　Mai　Yasu　Dai　Saki

165.
（Saki）サキ、Test 1 の4番で janitor を画像検索したよね。
（Saki）はい。あの時スマホで見た人の姿を思い浮かべながら、(A) を塗りました。

166.
（Dai）(A) と (C) の選択率が高い。この2つで迷った人は?
（Mai）はい。auditorium がヒントだったとは……。
（Yasu）同じく。(B) と (D) は見つけましたが。
（Saki）(A) の performance space と (C) の employee benefits を探しました。第2段落になくて不安になったのですが、第3段落の最後にある auditorium の言い換えが (A) だと気づいたんです。
（Dai）それで?

（Saki）うれしくなって、そのまま (A) を塗ってしまいました。
（Dai）本当に?　Test 1 で自分で言ったことを実行したんだね。「TOEIC あるあるランキング第6位」だけど、マイにとっては1位じゃない?
（Mai）はい、たぶんそうです。

167.
（Hiro）位置選択問題を解くための5つの視点のうち1つが役立つ。「代名詞」「副詞」「接続副詞」「the ＋名詞」「言い換え」のうち、どれか分かる?
（Mai）代名詞です。ターゲット文に It があります。
（Hiro）そう。他に this や their、these などがヒントになることもある。

Part 7 読解問題

Questions 168-171 refer to the following online chat discussion.

Col Simms [3:30 P.M.]: We need an article for the May issue. Another magazine has just published an article that's too similar to the one I was going to use. Do any of you have anything suitable?

Janice Rietz [3:31 P.M.]: I have an article on Dan Cross. He's an up-and-coming tennis player from Detroit. I spent a week there researching it. When is the deadline?

Col Simms [3:32 P.M.]: Sounds interesting. The deadline is Friday so you have two days.

Theo Ledbetter [3:35 P.M.]: I have an article, but I can't proofread it that soon. That's not long enough.

Col Simms [3:36 P.M.]: What's it about, Theo? I might be able to help.

Theo Ledbetter [3:37 P.M.]: It's on some rule changes the state basketball league is going to introduce. Would that be any good?

Col Simms [3:40 P.M.]: It's a good idea for an article, but the changes won't take effect until January. Let's consider that again in October.

Donna Papazian [3:42 P.M.]: I am about to write one about the popularity of watching games online. I don't think I could have it done by Friday, though.

Col Simms [3:45 P.M.]: Thanks, there's no flexibility on the deadline, I'm afraid. Janice, could you let me see the article you mentioned? I'll read it and let you know.

Janice Rietz [3:49 P.M.]: Sure thing. I won't be coming into the office today, though. Do you mind if I e-mail it to you?

Col Simms [3:50 P.M.]: Not at all.

(250w)

問題168-171は次のオンラインチャットに関するものです。

Col Simms [午後3時30分]：5月号向けに記事が1本必要だ。刊行されたばかりの他誌の記事が、使おうと思っていたものと酷似してるんだ。誰か、良さそうな記事を持ってないかな？

Janice Rietz [午後3時31分]：Dan Crossに関する記事があります。彼は新進気鋭のテニス選手で、Detroit出身です。同地で1週間、取材しました。締め切りはいつですか。

Col Simms [午後3時32分]：面白そうだね。締め切りは金曜日だから、あと2日ある。

Theo Ledbetter [午後3時35分]：私も1本書いていますが、そんなにすぐには校正できません。時間が足りません。

Col Simms [午後3時36分]：何についての記事なんだ、Theo？　私が手伝えるかもしれない。

Theo Ledbetter [午後3時37分]：州のバスケットボールリーグが導入を予定しているルール変更についてです。使えそうですか。

Col Simms [午後3時40分]：記事のネタとしてはいいが、その変更は1月まで適用されない。10月にあらためて考えよう。

Donna Papazian [午後3時42分]：1本書き始めるところです。オンラインでの試合観戦が増えていることについてです。ただし、金曜日までには書き終わらないと思います。

Col Simms [午後3時45分]：ありがとう、締め切りは絶対に動かせないと思うよ。Janis、言っていた記事を見せてもらえるかな？　目を通して、連絡する。

Janice Rietz [午後3時49分]：分かりました。でも、今日はオフィスへ行きません。メールで送っても構いませんか。

Col Simms [午後3時50分]：もちろん。

☐ article: 名 記事　☐ issue: 名 号　☐ publish: ～を出版する　☐ similar to ～: ～と似ている　☐ suitable: 形 適切な
☐ up-and-coming: 形 新進気鋭の　☐ deadline: 名 締め切り　☐ proofread: 動 ～を校正する　☐ league: 名 リーグ
☐ introduce: 動 ～を導入する　☐ take effect: 効力を発する、実施される　☐ consider: 動 ～を検討する　☐ popularity: 名 人気
☐ online: 副 オンラインで　☐ flexibility: 名 柔軟性、融通性　☐ let ～ know: ～に知らせる　☐ Sure thing.: もちろん。、いいとも。
☐ ～, though: ～ではあるが　☐ e-mail: 動 ～をメールで送る　☐ Not at all.: いいえ。、全然。

168. 正解：**C**　易 ■■■□□□□□ 難　選択率：(A) 1.2%　(B) 9.8%　**(C) 86.7%**　(D) 2.4%

At what type of business do the writers most likely work?
(A) A ticket agency
(B) A sports arena
(C) A publishing company
(D) A broadcasting studio

書き手たちはどんな業種に携わっている可能性が最も高いですか。
(A) チケット販売代理店
(B) スポーツ競技場
(C) 出版社
(D) 放送スタジオ

▶解説　チャットの参加者の勤務先が問われています。❶のan article（記事）やMay issue（5月号）といった語句、また、❷の「別の雑誌が、自分が使うつもりだった内容に似た記事を出した」といった記述から、彼らの勤務先は(C)の出版社だと考えられます。

---

169. 正解：**B**　易 ■■■■□□□□ 難　選択率：(A) 26.7%　**(B) 67.8%**　(C) 4.7%　(D) 0.8%

At 3:35 P.M., what does Mr. Ledbetter mean when he writes, "That's not long enough"?
(A) An article is too short.
(B) He needs more time.
(C) Few people have come to an event.
(D) The wrong items have been delivered.

午後3時35分に、Ledbetterさんはどのような意味で「時間が足りません」と書いていますか。
(A) 記事が短すぎる。
(B) 彼にはもっと時間が必要だ。
(C) 催しにほとんど人が来ていない。
(D) 誤った商品が配送された。

▶解説　Simmsさんが❹で「締め切りまで2日ある」と発言したのに対する応答の意味が問われています。Ledbetterさんは❺で「記事を持っているがそんなにすぐには校正できない」と述べて、That's not long enough.と発言しています。これは、「校正のための時間がもっと必要だ」と伝えていると考えるのが適切なので、(B)が正解です。

---

170. 正解：**D**　易 ■■■■■□□□ 難　選択率：(A) 11.4%　(B) 10.2%　(C) 9.4%　**(D) 68.6%**

According to the online chat discussion, what will happen next year?
(A) A tournament will be held in Detroit.
(B) An online service will be launched.
(C) Some athletes will retire.
(D) Some rules will be changed.

□ launch: 動 ～を開始する　□ athlete: 名 スポーツ選手

このオンラインチャットでの話し合いによると、来年何が起きますか。
(A) Detroitでトーナメントが行われるだろう。
(B) あるオンラインサービスが始まるだろう。
(C) 何人かのスポーツ選手が引退するだろう。
(D) いくつかのルールが変更されるだろう。

▶解説　❻で、Ledbetterさんが扱っている記事は、州のバスケットボールリーグが導入するルール変更についてだと述べられています。ただし、❼からその変更が実施されるのは1月であることが分かり、続けてその記事については10月に検討することを提案しているので、翌年の1月にルールが変更されると判断できます。よって、(D)が正解です。

---

171. 正解：**B**　易 ■■■□□□□□ 難　選択率：(A) 9.8%　**(B) 71.8%**　(C) 11.8%　(D) 5.5%

What is Ms. Rietz asked to do?
(A) Evaluate some potential suppliers
(B) Send a story about Dan Cross
(C) Investigate online gaming
(D) Take a business trip

□ evaluate: 動 ～を審査する　□ potential: 形 見込まれる
□ investigate: 動 ～を調べる
□ online gaming: オンラインゲーム

Rietzさんは何をするよう頼まれていますか。
(A) いくつかの見込みのある納入業者を審査する
(B) Dan Crossに関する記事を送る
(C) オンラインゲームについて調べる
(D) 出張に行く

▶解説　5月号に掲載する記事を検討した結果、Simmsさんは❽でRietzさんに、彼女が言及した記事を見せるよう要請しています。Rietzさんは❸でDan Crossについての記事を書いたと述べているので、(B)が正解です。

(((📡))) ゼミ🎤中継　😊 Hiro　😊 Mai　😊 Yasu　😊 Dai　😊 Saki

169.
😊 ターゲット文の直前にarticleが登場しているので、釣られて（A)にした人がいるんじゃない？　釣られ名人のサキはどうだった？

😊 また釣られました！　著者に笑われそうです。

😊 Ledbetterさんは、記事をそんなに早く校正できないと言ってから、That's not long enough.と発言している。だったら、記事が「長すぎる」と言うならともかく、「短すぎる」と言うのは変だよ。

😊 確かに……。時間的に短いと言っていたのですね。

171.
😊 2問付きチャットでも4問付きチャットでも、登場人物の名前を覚える必要はない。とにかくストーリーを理解することを優先すればいい。で、171番みたいに、特定の人物について問われたら、その時に改めて人名と発言をチェックすれば十分だよ。

😊 ヒントが遠い場所にあったので驚きました。

😊 ピンポイント型に見える設問なのに、このようにヒントが離れていることがある。だから、チャットは上から順にベタっと読む方がいい。ま、これはどの文書にも言えることだけど。

TOEICよろず相談所 ヒロの部屋

⑫英文を一発で理解したい

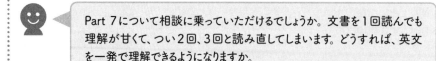

Part 7について相談に乗っていただけるでしょうか。文書を1回読んでも理解が甘くて、つい2回、3回と読み直してしまいます。どうすれば、英文を一発で理解できるようになりますか。

1回読んで英文を理解できない場合、いくつかの原因が考えられます。「知らない単語がある」とか「文構造を誤解している」などです。でも、多くの人に当てはまる原因は「読んでいない」ことです。

え、どういうことですか。

目に飛び込んでくる目立つ単語を拾いながら、ストーリーをでっち上げている人が非常に多いのです。「**文を読んでいる**」のではなく、「**たくさんの単語を見て想像をふくらませている**」イメージです。

あぁ、そうかもしれません…。

そういうことをすると、文書を読んでいるときは「分かったつもり」になっているのですが、設問を解こうとして選択肢を見ると自信がなくて読み直すことになります。

そうです。まさにそれです。どうすればいいですか。

すごくシンプルですが、英語を読んで理解する体験を増やしてください。「**解くために読む**」のではなく、「**理解するために読む**」体験です。

そもそも英語を読むのは試験日だけかも……

それだと少なすぎます。試験日に突然英語をたくさん読むのですよね。一発で理解できないのは当然です。TOEIC受験日が英語を読むのが最も少ない日と言えるくらい、読むのを習慣にしてください。

頑張ります！

Questions 172-175 refer to the following article.

A New Awareness of Healthy Eating

By Seth Olyphant, lifestyle reporter

❶ In recent years, there have been more and more television shows and books focusing on food, nutrition, and cooking. — [1] —. People are choosing ingredients at the supermarket differently. They are reading up on the health benefits of certain foods and they are becoming more critical of the options available on restaurant menus.

According to Kenny Bates of the Australian Consumer Association, it is having a real effect on which restaurants they choose to eat at and which they avoid. — [2] —. Once popular food chains are experiencing slumps while others are booking out months in advance. Restaurant owners are taking notice, and ❷ they are looking at replacing many dishes with more nutritional alternatives.

Nutritionists are finding it hard to keep up with the demand as they are asked to consult with restaurants, hotels, and caterers around the country. None more so than Isabella Scott, who is largely responsible for the change of attitude. — [3] —. ❸ Ms. Scott consulted and even shared screen time with celebrity chefs in many of the most popular broadcasts. In an interview for this article, she mentioned a new problem that restaurants are facing.

The trend that started here is now starting to take effect in many other countries and there is a demand for Australian chefs around the world. — [4] —. Becky Harmer from the Australian Restaurant Owners' Association says, ❹ "Many chefs at top restaurants are being offered excellent money to work in foreign countries. It is important that our culinary schools and vocational colleges prepare students for the changing expectations of their employers and the dining public."

(281w)

問題**172-175**は次の記事に関するものです。

健康的な食生活についての新たな認識
文　Seth Olyphant・生活様式リポーター

近年、食べ物や栄養、料理に的を絞ったテレビ番組や本がますます増えている。このことが、人々が口にするものについてより強い関心を持たせた。人々のスーパーマーケットでの食材の選び方が、今、変化している。彼らは、ある種の食べ物の健康上の効能について知識を深めており、レストランのメニューに並ぶ選択肢について、より批判的になっているのだ。

Australian Consumer Association の Kenny Bates によると、このことは彼らがどのレストランを選んで食事を取り、どの店を避けるかということに大きな影響を与えているという。かつて人気のあった外食チェーンが落ち込んでいる一方で、別の店には何カ月も前から予約が殺到している。レストランのオーナーらも状況に気づいており、多くの料理をより栄養価の高いものへと変更することを検討している。

栄養士たちは国中のレストランやホテル、仕出し業者から相談を受け、需要に応えるのが難しくなっている。その筆頭が Isabella Scott さんだ。彼女は、このような考え方の変化に対して大きな役割を果たしている。Scott さんは著名なシェフたちと意見を交換するばかりか、最も人気の高いテレビ番組の多くに、シェフらと一緒に出演した。今回の取材の中で、彼女はレストランが直面している新たな問題に触れた。

この国で生まれた潮流が、今、他の多くの国々に影響を及ぼし始めており、オーストラリア人シェフを求める声が世界中で上がっている。Australian Restaurant Owners' Association の Becky Harmer は、こう言う。「一流レストランの多くのシェフが多額の報酬を提示され、海外で働くようになっています。重要なのは、わが国の料理学校や専門学校が、学生たちを、彼らの雇用主や食事客の変わりゆく期待に応じて、訓練することなのです」

□ awareness: 图 意識、認識　□ recent: 形 最近の　□ focus on ～: ～に的を絞る　□ nutrition: 图 栄養　□ ingredient: 图 材料
□ differently: 副 異なって　□ read up on ～: よく読んで～に関する知識を得る　□ health benefit: 健康効果　□ certain: 形 特定の
□ critical of ～: ～についてうるさくて　□ option: 图 選択肢　□ have an effect on ～: ～に影響を及ぼす　□ avoid: 動 ～を避ける
□ food chain: 食品チェーン店、飲食チェーン店　□ experience: 動 ～を経験する　□ slump: 图 不振、不調　□ book out: 予約でいっぱいにする
□ in advance: 前もって　□ take notice: 自覚する　□ look at ～: ～を検討する　□ replace ～ with ...: ～を…に換える
□ nutritional: 形 栄養を供給する　□ alternative: 图 取って代わるもの、選択肢　□ nutritionist: 图 栄養士、栄養学者
□ keep up with ～: ～についていく、～に後れをとらない　□ demand: 图 要望、需要　□ consult with ～: ～と協議する、～に相談する
□ caterer: 图 仕出し業者　□ none more so than ～: ～の場合は特にそうである　□ largely: 副 大いに　□ responsible for ～: ～の責任を負って
□ attitude: 图 考え方　□ screen time: 出番　□ celebrity: 图 有名人　□ chef: 图 料理人　□ broadcast: 图 番組　□ interview: 图 取材
□ face: 動 ～に直面する　□ trend: 图 傾向、潮流　□ take effect: 効果を生じる　□ excellent: 形 素晴らしい　□ culinary school: 料理学校
□ vocational college: 専門学校　□ expectation: 图 期待　□ employer: 图 雇用主　□ dining public: 食事客

Part 7 読解問題

---

172. 正解：**A** 易 ■■■■■□□□ 難 選択率：**(A) 62.7%** (B) 9.8% (C) 15.7% (D) 9.8%

According to the article, what is probably happening in many Australian restaurants?
(A) They are updating their menus.
(B) They are changing their cleaning procedures.
(C) They are advertising for employees internationally.
(D) They are spending more on advertising.

□ update: 動 ～を更新する、最新のものにする
□ procedure: 名 手順　□ advertise for ～: ～を募集する
□ internationally: 副 国際的に

この記事によると、多くのオーストラリアのレストランで何が起きていそうですか。
(A) 店はメニューを刷新している。
(B) 店は清掃の手順を変えている。
(C) 店は国外に求人広告を出している。
(D) 店は広告に、より多くの費用をかけている。

▶解説 第1段落、第2段落全体で、消費者の健康に対する意識の変化から、食材選びやレストラン選びにも変化が見られると述べられています。それを受けて、❷で「レストランもより栄養価の高いものへと変更する動きがある」と述べられています。よって(A)の「メニューを刷新している」が正解です。

---

173. 正解：**C** 易 ■■■■□□□□ 難 選択率：(A) 7.1% (B) 21.6% **(C) 64.3%** (D) 5.1%

Who has appeared on several television shows?
(A) Seth Olyphant
(B) Kenny Bates
(C) Isabella Scott
(D) Becky Harmer

□ appear: 動 現れる、登場する

誰がいくつものテレビ番組に出演していますか。
(A) Seth Olyphant
(B) Kenny Bates
(C) Isabella Scott
(D) Becky Harmer

▶解説 ❸で、Scottさんが多くの人気番組で有名シェフたちと「screen timeを共有した」とあります。これはテレビ出演を意味するので、(C)が正解です。(A)のOlyphantさんはこの記事の執筆者です。(B)のBatesさんと(D)のHarmerさんは、それぞれ協会の専門家で、いずれもテレビ出演とは無関係です。

---

174. 正解：**D** 易 ■■■■□□□□ 難 選択率：(A) 10.2% (B) 11.8% (C) 18.0% **(D) 58.0%**

What is indicated about the chefs at many top restaurants?
(A) They are returning to culinary schools.
(B) They are making money from online videos.
(C) They are publishing their own recipe books.
(D) They are being offered employment overseas.

□ make money: 金をもうける　□ publish: 動 ～を出版する
□ recipe: 名 レシピ　□ overseas: 副 海外で

多くの一流レストランのシェフについて何が示されていますか。
(A) 彼らは料理学校へ戻っている。
(B) 彼らはオンライン動画で稼いでいる。
(C) 彼らは自分自身の料理本を出版している。
(D) 彼らは海外での雇用の機会を提示されている。

▶解説 オーストラリアのシェフに関する言及は第4段落にあります。Harmerさんの発言を引用する形で❹で「一流レストランの多くのシェフが多額の報酬を提示され、海外で働くようになっている」と述べられていることから、(D)が正解です。

---

175. 正解：**A** 易 ■■■■■□□□ 難 選択率：**(A) 38.8%** (B) 35.3% (C) 15.7% (D) 7.8%

In which of the positions marked [1], [2], [3], and [4] does the following sentence best belong?

"This has made people take a greater interest in what they are putting in their mouths."
(A) [1]
(B) [2]
(C) [3]
(D) [4]

□ take an interest in ～: ～に興味を持つ

次の文を当てはめるには、[1]、[2]、[3]、[4]と印が付けられた箇所のうちのどこが最もふさわしいですか。

「このことが、人々が口にするものについてより強い関心を持たせた」
(A) [1]
(B) [2]
(C) [3]
(D) [4]

▶解説 ターゲット文のThisが何を指すかを考えます。❶で「食べ物や栄養などに関するテレビ番組や本がますます増えている」と述べられています。この内容をThisで受けて、「このことが、人々が口にするものについてより強い関心を持たせた」と続けると自然な文脈が成立します。よって(A)が正解です。

((·)) ゼミ **生** 中継　　😊 Hiro　😊 Mai　😊 Yasu　🎲 Dai　😊 Saki

175. ⋯⋯⋯⋯⋯⋯⋯⋯⋯⋯⋯⋯⋯⋯⋯⋯⋯⋯⋯⋯⋯⋯

😊 このセットの中で、175番の正答率が極端に低い。

😊 [1]と[2]で迷いました。

😊 やはり、「5つの視点」が役立つ。167番と同様に、ここでも代名詞がヒント。人々が食べ物に関心を持つようなった原因が、ターゲット文にあるThisだから、空所の直前にそのような情報があるはず。

😊 それはそうですが、[2]でOKかと思いました。

😊 いや。1つ覚えて。基本的に、情報は1つの段落の中で「抽象から

具体へ流れる」という原則がある。ターゲット文と[2]の直前の文を比べて。どっちが抽象的?

😊 ターゲット文です。

😊 そう。[2]の直前の文はレストランの話をしている。ターゲット文はもっと抽象的で、人々が食べ物に興味を持ったと言っている。もし、ターゲット文を[2]に入れると、具体的な情報から抽象的な情報を導くことになる。

😊 確かに⋯⋯。原因と結果が逆になっちゃいますね。

235

Part 7 読解問題

Questions 176-180 refer to the following e-mail and itinerary.

	E-Mail Message
To:	Karina Chow <kchow@choweducation.com>
From:	Daniel Odanaka <dodanaka@dukecorporation.com>
Subject:	Learning Seminar
Date:	1 May
Attachment:	📎 Itinerary

Dear Ms. Chow,

My name is Daniel Odanaka and I have been put in charge of making the arrangements for your visit on 19 and 20 June. Unfortunately, Tim Whatley has had to take some time off work for personal reasons and I am filling in for him. I should let you know that both of the seminars on personal finance have sold out. It seems that the excellent reviews of your latest book on financial planning have also affected ticket sales.

I was able to arrange the station wagon you requested. I wonder if Mr. Whatley mentioned that Duke Corporation can provide a driver and car at no cost to you. Otherwise, considering the lack of parking in the city, you may prefer to rely on our excellent subway service as he proposed in a previous e-mail.

Judging from ticket sales, it appears that we could probably arrange a third appearance and draw a big enough audience to make a healthy profit. I have found an alternative venue, which is available in the afternoon of 21 June. Please let us know if you would like to take advantage of this situation.

You can contact me by e-mail or phone if there is anything else I can do to make your visit to Manchester go more smoothly.

Sincerely,

Daniel Odanaka

(238w)

問題176-180は次のメールと旅程表に関するものです。
宛先：Karina Chow <kchow@choweducation.com>
送信者：Daniel Odanaka <dodanaka@dukecorporation.com>
件名：学習セミナー
日付：5月1日
添付ファイル：Itinerary

Chow さま

Daniel Odanaka と申します。6月19日と20日のご訪問の手配を担当させていただいております。あいにく、Tim Whatley が個人的な理由でしばらく仕事を休んでおり、私が彼を代行しています。お知らせいたしますが、個人資産管理に関するセミナーは両方とも満席になっております。どうやら、ファイナンシャル・プランニングに関するあなたの最新刊書が大評判になっていることも、チケットの売れ行きに影響したようです。

ご依頼いただいたステーションワゴンを手配できました。Whatley が申し上げたかと存じますが、Duke Corporation では運転手付きでお車を無料で提供させていただくことも可能です。あるいは、市内に駐車場が少ないことを考えると、彼が前回のメールでご提案した、当市の便利な地下鉄サービスをご利用いただくほうがいいかもしれません。

チケットの売れ行きから判断しますと、おそらく3回目のセミナーを設けても、十分な数の聴衆を集め、大きな利益を上げることができるでしょう。候補となる新たな会場は見つけてあります。ここは6月21日の午後に利用可能です。この機会を生かしたければ、お知らせください。

Manchester へのご訪問をより円滑に進める上で、もし他に何か私ができることがあれば、メールか電話でご連絡ください。

よろしくお願いいたします。

Daniel Odanaka

□ itinerary: 图 旅程表　□ in charge of ~: ~を任されて　□ arrangement: 图 手配　□ unfortunately: 副 あいにく　□ take time off: 休みを取る
□ personal: 形 個人的な　□ fill in for ~: ~の代わりをする　□ personal finance: 個人資産管理　□ sell out: 完売する
□ financial planning: ファイナンシャル・プランニング　□ affect: 動 ~に影響を及ぼす　□ arrange: 動 ~を手配する
□ station wagon: ステーションワゴン　＊後部に広い荷物スペースのある乗用車　□ wonder if ~: ~ではないかと思う　□ at no cost: 無料で
□ otherwise: 副 そうでなければ　□ considering: 前 ~を考えれば　□ lack of ~: ~の不足、欠如　□ prefer to ~: ~することを好む、選ぶ
□ rely on ~: ~を当てにする　□ subway: 图 地下鉄　□ propose: 動 ~を提案する　□ previous: 形 前の　□ judge from ~: ~から判断する
□ appearance: 图 登場　□ draw an audience: 観客を集める　□ make a profit: 利益を上げる　□ healthy: 形 多くの、大量の
□ alternative: 形 新しい、代わりとなる　□ venue: 图 会場　□ take advantage of ~: ~を生かす　□ situation: 图 状況
□ contact: 動 ~に連絡する　□ smoothly: 副 円滑に

Itinerary — Karina Chow

(Revised 1 May)

Friday, 19 June
7:00 A.M. – Depart from Heathrow Airport
8:10 A.M. – Arrive at Manchester Airport (Pick up rental car)
10:00 A.M. - Planning meeting with representatives from Duke Corporation
❻ 2:30 P.M. – Check into the Grand Hotel
7:00 P.M. – Speaking engagement at Compton Event Centre
9:30 P.M. – Watch video recording of seminar

Saturday, 20 June
11:00 A.M. – Lunch with Carol Duncan from ARK Publishing
❼ 2:00 P.M. – Speaking engagement at Fort Congress Centre
6:00 P.M. – Dinner with Teri Wesley from Portsmouth University
8:45 P.M. – Depart from Manchester Airport (Return rental car)
9:50 P.M. – Arrive at Heathrow Airport

(100w)

旅程表——Karina Chow
（5月1日に修正）

6月19日 金曜日
午前7時—Heathrow 空港出発
午前8時10分—Manchester 空港到着（レンタカー借り出し）
午前10時—Duke Corporation の担当者らとの企画会議
午後2時30分—Grand Hotel へチェックイン
午後7時—Compton Event Centre で講演
午後9時30分—講演会のビデオ録画を視聴

6月20日 土曜日
午前11時—ARK Publishing の Carol Duncan と昼食
午後2時—Fort Congress Centre で講演
午後6時—Portsmouth 大学の Teri Wesley と夕食
午後8時45分—Manchester 空港出発（レンタカー返却）
午後9時50分—Heathrow 空港到着

☐ revise: 動 ～を修正する　☐ pick up ～: ～を受け取る　☐ planning meeting: 企画会議　☐ representative: 名 担当者、代理人
☐ speaking engagement: 講演の仕事　☐ video recording: ビデオ録画

Part 7 読解問題

176. 正解：D 易 ■■■□□□□ 難　選択率：(A) 9.4% (B) 12.9% (C) 20.8% **(D) 56.5%**

Where most likely does Mr. Odanaka work?
(A) At a limousine service
(B) At a convention center
(C) At an accommodation provider
(D) At an event promotions company

Odanakaさんはどこで働いている可能性が最も高いですか。
(A) リムジンサービス会社
(B) 会議場
(C) 宿泊施設提供会社
(D) イベント広報宣伝会社

▶解説 ❶でChowさんに対するOdanakaさんの役割が述べられています。その他、メールの第1段落でセミナーの売れ行きが良好だと述べ、第2段落でChowさん滞在中の移動手段を提示し、第3段落でセミナーの追加を提案していることから、Chowさんのセミナー全般を担当していると判断できます。正解は(D)です。

---

177. 正解：A 易 ■■□□□□□ 難　選択率：**(A) 73.3%** (B) 5.5% (C) 14.1% (D) 6.3%

What did Mr. Whatley recommend that Ms. Chow do?
(A) Use public transportation
(B) Look for a cheaper hotel
(C) Publish another book
(D) Call a travel agent

Whatleyさんは Chow さんに何をするよう勧めましたか。
(A) 公共交通機関を使う
(B) より安いホテルを探す
(C) 新たな本を出版する
(D) 旅行代理店へ電話する

☐ public transportation: 公共交通機関
☐ publish: 動 ～を出版する
☐ travel agent: 旅行代理店

▶解説 Whatleyさんは Odanaka さんの前に Chow さんを担当していた人です。❸から、「彼」が地下鉄での移動を Chow さんに提案していたことが分かります。その人物は同段落の前半に登場する Whatley さんを指すため、(A)の「公共交通機関を使う」が正解です。

---

178. 正解：B 易 ■■■□□□□ 難　選択率：(A) 10.6% **(B) 63.9%** (C) 16.1% (D) 7.8%

According to the e-mail, why might Ms. Chow want to extend her stay?
(A) To meet with a university professor
(B) To give another seminar
(C) To attend a book signing
(D) To do some sightseeing

メールによると、Chow さんが滞在期間を延長したがるとしたら、その理由は何ですか。
(A) 大学教授と会うために
(B) もう1回セミナーを開くために
(C) 本のサイン会に出席するために
(D) 観光するために

☐ extend: 動 ～を延長する　☐ book signing: 本のサイン会
☐ do sightseeing: 観光する

▶解説 チケットの売れ行きが好調なことから、❹で3回目のセミナー開催の可能性が述べられています。そして、❺には6月21日の会場に関する言及があります。確定済みのセミナーは6月19日と20日なので、6月21日にセミナーに登壇すれば、設問にある extend her stay に合致します。従って、彼女が滞在を延長するとすれば、追加のセミナーを開くためなので、(B)が正解です。

---

179. 正解：C 易 ■■■□□□□ 難　選択率：(A) 14.1% (B) 15.3% **(C) 63.1%** (D) 5.9%

What time is Ms. Chow scheduled to arrive at her accommodation on June 19?
(A) At 8:10 A.M.
(B) At 10:00 A.M.
(C) At 2:30 P.M.
(D) At 7:00 P.M.

Chow さんは6月19日の何時に宿泊場所に到着しますか。
(A) 午前8時10分に
(B) 午前10時に
(C) 午後2時30分に
(D) 午後7時に

▶解説 旅程表の6月19日の部分を参照します。❻で Grand Hotel へのチェックインが2:30 P.M. に予定されていることから、(C)が正解です。設問の accommodation は「宿泊施設」という意味で、ここでは Grand Hotel の言い換えです。(A)は空港への到着時間、(B)は Duke Corporation の担当者との会議の時間、(D)は Compton Event Centre における講演の時間です。

238

180. 正解：**C** 易 ■■■■■ 難 **選択率：**(A) 12.9% (B) 24.7% **(C) 52.9%** (D) 7.5%

What is indicated about the event at Fort Congress Centre?
(A) Its location has been changed.
(B) Ms. Chow will watch a performance there.
(C) Tickets are no longer available.
(D) It was advertised on the radio.

☐ performance: 名 公演 ☐ advertise: 動 ～を宣伝する

Fort Congress Centre での催しについて何が示されていますか。
(A) その場所が変更されている。
(B) Chow さんはそこで公演を見る。
(C) チケットはもう手に入らない。
(D) ラジオで宣伝された。

▶解説 2つの文書の情報を合わせて答える問題です。メールの❶と❷で、6月19日と20日のセミナーのチケットは両日とも売り切れていることが分かります。また、旅程表の❼で設問にあるFort Congress Centre は2日目のセミナー開催場所であることが分かります。従って、sold out を no longer available と言い換えた (C) が正解です。

((🗼)) ゼミ 生 中継   😀 Hiro 😊 Mai 😄 Yasu 😎 Dai 😺 Saki

178. ··········

😄 サキ、Why might のヒントは？

😺 if にあり!

😄 Chow さんが滞在を延長する可能性は、上の文書の第3段落に書かれていて、if もある。～ if you would like to take advantage of this situation. は、6月21日に3回目のセミナーをするなら、ということ。

😄 本当に Why might のヒントは if ですね。感動的です。

😺 例外はあるから気を抜いちゃダメだよ。

180. ··········

😄 一応、解けましたが、ヒントが最初の方にあるのが不思議な感じがしました。

😎 同じく。

😺 チケットの話は上の文書の前半にあるけれど、設問に具体的な会場名があるよね。Fort Congress Centre は2つ目の文書にしか登場しない。ということは、その会場がセミナーの会場であることを確認してから解くべきだよ。確認しなかった？

😀 しませんでした。

😎 (C) を塗った後で、一応、確認しました。

😺 ま、今回はラッキーだったね。

Part 7 読解問題

Questions 181-185 refer to the following e-mail and invoice.

E-Mail Message

To:	Gerald Comiskey <gcomiskey@barrontiling.com>
From:	Jane Whitman <jwhitman@clementprojects.com>
Date:	September 28
Subject:	234 Towers Road

Dear Mr. Comiskey,

❶ I am writing with regard to the apartment block at 234 Towers Road in Flinders. ❷ Clement Projects hired your company to tile all of the bathrooms. The understanding was that you would start work on September 19 and finish tiling all eight bathrooms by September 23. ❸ It was important that you do so because we had other workers coming in after you to fit cabinets, mirrors, and so on.

❹ Your delay in getting started on the work meant that we had other tradespeople waiting for you to finish. ❺ We were charged a high hourly rate to have these people wait for you until they could start work themselves. In the end, ❻ your employees were not done with the final bathroom until the afternoon of September 26. I have just received your invoice for the full amount of $59,623. As we suffered significant additional expenses as a result of the delays, ❼ I am hoping that you will offer us a discount on the work. If we cannot come to an ❽ acceptable arrangement, I will not be able to accept bids from Barron Tiling for any future projects. ❾ This includes the Montgomery Hotel project, which has more than 120 rooms.

Sincerely,

Jane Whitman

(222w)

問題181-185は次のメールと請求明細書に関するものです。

宛先：Gerald Comiskey <gcomiskey@barrontiling.com>
送信者：Jane Whitman <jwhitman@clementprojects.com>
日付：9月28日
件名：234 Towers Road

Comiskeyさま

このメールは、Flindersの234 Towers Roadにあるアパートの建物に関するものです。Clement Projectsは貴社に全浴室のタイル貼りを発注しました。合意事項は、貴社が9月19日に作業を開始し、9月23日までに全8室分の浴室にタイルを貼り終えるというものでした。貴社にそのとおりに作業していただくことは重要でした。というのも、貴社の作業後に他の業者を手配しており、棚や鏡の据え付けなどが行われることになっていたからです。

貴社の着工の遅れは、つまり他の作業員を貴社の作業完了まで待たせることになります。当社は高額の時給を支払った上で、そうした作業員らに仕事を開始できるまで待ってもらったのです。結局、貴社の従業員が最後の浴室の作業を終えたのは9月26日の午後でした。貴社から満額分5万9623ドルの請求書を受け取ったところです。当社は、この遅延の結果として多額の追加支出を余儀なくされましたので、貴社には作業費の値引きをお願いしたく存じます。もし納得のいく合意ができなければ、当方はこの先のいかなる工事案件についてもBarron Tilingからの入札をお受けできなくなります。これには、120室以上を擁するMontgomery Hotelの工事も含まれます。

よろしくお願いいたします。

Jane Whitman

☐ invoice: 名 請求明細書 ☐ with regard to ～: ～に関して ☐ hire: 動 ～を雇う ☐ tile: 動 ～にタイルを貼る ☐ understanding: 名 合意内容
☐ worker: 名 作業員 ☐ fit: 動 ～を取り付ける ☐ cabinet: 名 棚 ☐ ～, and so on: ～など ☐ delay: 名 遅れ ☐ tradespeople: 名 作業員
☐ charge: 動 ～を請求する ☐ hourly rate: 時給、1時間当たりの料金 ☐ in the end: 結局 ☐ suffer: 動 （損害）をこうむる
☐ significant: 形 かなりの、著しい ☐ additional: 形 追加の ☐ expense: 名 費用、出費 ☐ acceptable: 形 許容できる、納得のいく
☐ arrangement: 名 協定、取り決め ☐ bid: 名 入札 ☐ include: 動 ～を含む

Barron Tiling

27 Longmans Close, Seacrest

Invoice

For work carried out at: 234 Towers Road

❿ **Client:** Clement Projects   **Date of issue:** September 30

Address: 17 Bloomingdale Street, Brighton   **Payment due:** October 31

Item Description	Unit Price	Quantity	Subtotal
Tiling Bathroom (labor)	$3,699	8	$29,592.00
Tiling Bathroom (materials)	$3,399	8	$27,192.00
		Discount (10%)	-$5,678.40
		Tax	$2,555.28
		Total	$53,660.88

⓫

⓬ All work by Barron Tiling is covered by a ten-year guarantee on materials and workmanship.

Thank you for continuing to rely on Barron Tiling for your tiling needs.

(85w)

Barron Tiling
27 Longmans Close, Seacrest

請求明細書
作業場所：234 Towers Road
発注者：Clement Projects
所在地：17 Bloomingdale Street, Brighton
発行日：9月30日
支払期限：10月31日

品目説明	単価	数量	小計
浴室のタイル貼り（人件費）	3,699ドル	8	29,592.00ドル
浴室のタイル貼り（材料費）	3,399ドル	8	27,192.00ドル
値引き（10%）			－5,678.40ドル
税			2,555.28ドル
合計			53,660.88ドル
Barron Tiling が行う全作業について、材料および施工に10年保証が適用されます。			

引き続き、タイル貼りに関するご用命は Barron Tiling にお任せくださいますよう、よろしくお願いいたします。

☐ carry out ～ : ～を実行する   ☐ date of issue: 発行日   ☐ payment due: 支払期限   ☐ item description: 品目説明   ☐ unit price: 単価
☐ quantity: 图 数量   ☐ subtotal: 图 小計   ☐ labor: 图 労働   ☐ material: 图 資材、材料   ☐ guarantee: 图 保証   ☐ workmanship: 图 施工
☐ rely on ～ : ～に任せる

181. 正解：**B** 易 ■■■■□□ 難　選択率：(A) 27.5% **(B) 55.3%** (C) 8.6% (D) 7.1%

What kind of company does Ms. Whitman most likely work for?
(A) A real estate agency
(B) A construction company
(C) A hardware store
(D) An office furniture manufacturer

Whitman さんはどのような企業で働いている可能性が最も高いですか。
(A) 不動産会社
(B) 建設会社
(C) ホームセンター
(D) オフィス用家具メーカー

▶解説 メールの❷や❸でWhitmanさんの勤務先であるClement Projectsは、アパートのタイルの貼り替えや備品の備え付けなどの業務を外部の業者に委託している会社であることが分かります。このことから、(B)の建設会社だと判断できます。(A)は不動産の仲介をする代理店を指すため不適切です。

182. 正解：**D** 易 ■■■□□□ 難　選択率：(A) 11.0% (B) 19.2% (C) 15.7% **(D) 50.6%**

What is one purpose of the e-mail?
(A) To announce the outcome of a bidding
(B) To request an update on a project
(C) To recommend a superior service
(D) To explain the effects of a delay

□ outcome: 名 結果　□ bidding: 名 入札
□ superior: 形 優れた　□ effect: 名 影響

このメールの1つの目的は何ですか。
(A) 入札の結果を知らせること
(B) プロジェクトの最新情報を求めること
(C) 優れたサービスを勧めること
(D) 遅れの影響を説明すること

▶解説 メールの❹で「作業の遅れにより、他の業者を待たせることとなった」と述べ、続けて❺で「待っている間のコストがかかった」と不満が述べられています。よって、この手紙の目的の1つは、(D)の「遅れの影響を説明すること」です。

183. 正解：**C** 易 ■■■■□□ 難　選択率：(A) 3.9% (B) 30.2% **(C) 47.8%** (D) 15.7%

When was the tiling work at 234 Towers Road completed?
(A) On September 19
(B) On September 23
(C) On September 26
(D) On September 28

Towers Road 234番地のタイル貼り工事は、いつ完了しましたか。
(A) 9月19日に
(B) 9月23日に
(C) 9月26日に
(D) 9月28日に

▶解説 メールの件名や❶から、このメールが234 Towers Roadのアパートに関するものだと分かります。❷でBarron Tilingがタイル貼りの業務を受注したことが分かり、続く文に9月23日に完了予定だったとあります。しかし❻で、Barron Tilingの作業が26日の午後に終わったことが明記されているので、(C)が正解です。

184. 正解：**A** 易 ■■■■□□ 難　選択率：**(A) 46.3%** (B) 20.0% (C) 16.9% (D) 12.9%

What is probably true about Barron Tiling?
(A) It intends to bid on the Montgomery Hotel project.
(B) It is partially owned by Clement Projects.
(C) It uses locally sourced materials.
(D) It specializes in office buildings.

□ intend to ～: ～するつもりだ　□ bid: 動 入札する
□ partially: 副 部分的に　□ own: 動 ～を所有する
□ locally sourced: 地元で調達した、地元産の
□ specialize in ～: ～を専門にする

Barron Tiling について当てはまると思われることはどれですか。
(A) Montgomery Hotel の工事に入札するつもりだ。
(B) 部分的に Clement Projects 社に所有されている。
(C) 地元で調達した材料を使っている。
(D) オフィスビル専業である。

▶解説 2つの文書を参照します。❼でClement ProjectsはBarron Tilingに、値引きを要求しています。続けて❽で、同意が得られない場合、今後のプロジェクトで入札は受け付けないことと、❾でこれにはMontgomery Hotelのプロジェクトが含まれることが述べられています。請求明細書を見ると⓫で割引が適用されているので、Barron Tilingは今後も入札する意図があるとする(A)が正解です。

185. 正解：A 易 ■■■■ 難　選択率：**(A) 57.3%** (B) 13.3% (C) 18.0% (D) 8.2%

What is implied about the bathrooms in 234 Towers Road?
(A) They are covered by a ten-year guarantee.
(B) They failed to pass a safety inspection.
(C) They are designed for large families.
(D) They do not have any storage space.

□ fail to 〜: 〜しそこなう　□ pass: 動 〜に合格する
□ safety inspection: 安全審査
□ design: 動 〜を設計する　□ large family: 大家族
□ storage space: 収納スペース

Towers Road 234番地の浴室についてどのようなことが示唆されていますか。
(A) 10年保証が付いている。
(B) 安全検査に合格しなかった。
(C) 大家族向けに設計されている。
(D) 収納スペースがない。

▶解説 請求明細書の❿から、この請求明細書が234 Towers Roadの仕事に対するものだとが分かります。また⓬に、10年保証についての記述があります。よって、(A)が正解です。

((())) ゼミ 生中継　😀Hiro 😊Mai 😸Yasu 😑Dai 😺Saki

183.

😀 (B)を選んだ人は、第1段落にある9月23日に釣られたということ。それは「予定」で、実際に起きたことは第2段落にある。〜 your employees were not done ... until the afternoon of September 26. がヒント。あ、untilについて聞きたい。喫茶店が改装中だとしよう。The café will be closed until May 8. と店主が言ったら、5月8日は営業している?

😺 いいえ。5月8日は閉まっていると思います。

😀 実は、5月8日には営業している。日本語にすると「5月8日に再開す

るまでは休業している」が正しい。

😺 知りませんでした。

😸 「利用できない」とか「人がいない」といった内容を伝える場合は、untilの後ろに書かれた時点で状況が変わる、と覚えて。

😑 うちの会社のネイティブスピーカーが書く不在通知メールもそうです。I am out of the office until May 8. と書いたら、5月8日に出社します。「5月8日に戻るまでは不在」と伝えているらしいです。

😀 その通り。いかにもTOEICに登場しそうなセリフだね。

Part 7 読解問題

Questions 186-190 refer to the following online review, article, and letter to the editor.

www.ivebeenthere.com

Welcome to I've been there dot com.
Read reviews of local businesses written by their clients and customers.

Business: Neptune Sports and Leisure at Bay Town Shopping Center
Reviewed by: Rod Barkworth **Date:** June 18

I was at Neptune Sports and Leisure at Bay Town Shopping Center today. It was the day after opening and there were still a lot of people. It was especially surprising as it was a weekday. We had a great time. I especially enjoyed the climbing wall, the golf simulator, and the batting cage. The range of goods was excellent. Some of the brands I had never heard of, though. So, it is hard for me to comment on their quality. The prices seemed a little higher than I'm used to. Nevertheless, I bought a pair of running shoes and a new sweater.

(139w)

問題**186-190**は次のオンラインレビュー、記事と編集者への手紙に関するものです。

www.ivebeenthere.com
ようこそ、I've been there dot comへ。
地元の店舗・施設に関する顧客の批評をお読みください。

店舗：Bay Town Shopping CenterのNeptune Sports and Leisure
批評者：Rod Barkworth　日付：6月18日

今日、Bay Town Shopping CenterのNeptune Sports and Leisureへ行ってきました。開店日の翌日で、まだ人が大勢いました。平日だったので、非常に驚きました。私たちは楽しい一時を過ごしました。特に楽しんだのは、クライミングウォールとゴルフシミュレーター、バッティングケージです。品ぞろえは素晴らしいものでした。ただ、一度も聞いたことのないブランドのものもありました。なので、それらの品質についてはコメントしづらいところです。価格は自分のなじんだものよりも少し高いようでした。とはいえ、ランニングシューズ1足と新しいセーターを買いました。

☐ local business: 地元企業　☐ weekday: 图 平日　☐ have a great time: 楽しむ　☐ especially: 副 特に
☐ climbing wall: フリークライミング用の壁　☐ golf simulator: ゴルフのシミュレーター　☐ batting cage: バッティングケージ
☐ range of goods: 品ぞろえ、商品群　☐ excellent: 形 優れた　☐ quality: 图 品質　☐ nevertheless: 副 とはいえ、それにもかかわらず
☐ running shoes: ランニングシューズ　☐ sweater: 图 セーター

Bay Town (June 19)—Neptune Sports and Leisure has opened a store in the Bay Town Shopping Center. Neptune Sports and Leisure's success has been attributed to its competitive prices and the many enjoyable experiences on offer to customers. Every Neptune store has a climbing wall, running track and a batting cage, which are freely available to customers. Neptune has been generating a lot of interest through its innovative Internet marketing campaign, and the Bay Town Shopping Center location attracted record crowds to its opening.

In a move that hardly seemed necessary, free lunch vouchers for meals at nearby Gee's Healthy Eating were given to the first 50 people to show up. By 11 A.M., when they stopped counting, some 500 people had passed through the doors. They were there to enjoy the free facilities and check out the amazing variety of products and brands on offer.

(147w)

Bay Town（6月19日）── Neptune Sports and Leisure が Bay Town Shopping Center 内に店をオープンした。Neptune Sports and Leisure の成功の要因は、他店に負けない価格とたくさんの楽しい体験を客に提供することに起因すると考えられる。Neptune の各店には、クライミングウォールやランニングトラック、バッティングケージがあり、来店客が自由に利用できる。Neptune は、革新的なインターネットでのマーケティング・キャンペーンを通じて大いに人々の興味をか

き立ててきた。そして、Bay Town Shopping Center 店は、開店日に記録的な客足を呼び込んだ。

　戦略としてはほとんど不要に思えたが、近隣の Gee's Healthy Eating でのランチの無料クーポン券が開店から50人目までの来店客に配られた。午前11時に集計を終えるまでに、およそ500人が店舗の入り口をくぐり抜けていた。来店客は、店内で無料施設の利用を楽しみ、驚くほど多彩な取扱商品やブランド品をチェックした。

- □ attribute to ~: ~に起因すると考える　□ competitive: 形 競争力の高い　□ enjoyable: 形 楽しめる　□ on offer to ~: ~に提供されて
- □ running track: ランニングトラック　□ freely: 副 自由に　□ generate interest: 興味をかきたてる　□ innovative: 形 革新的な
- □ marketing campaign: マーケティング・キャンペーン　□ location: 名 店　□ attract crowds: 人々を集める　□ record: 形 記録的な
- □ in a move: 策として　□ hardly: 副 ほとんど~ない　□ necessary: 形 必要な　□ voucher: 名 クーポン　□ nearby: 形 近隣の
- □ show up: 現れる　□ pass through ~: ~を通る、~を通過する　□ facility: 名 施設　□ check out: ~を見る、チェックする
- □ amazing: 形 素晴らしい

Letters to the Editor

June 21 — I read the article about the opening of Neptune Sports and Leisure at Bay Town Shopping Center. The article almost appeared to be an advertisement for the store. I think that as it was intended as a news article, it should have taken a more critical stance. Bay Town already has Foreman Sports, which is an excellent sporting goods store that hires many young locals and has sponsored several of our sporting teams over the years. Neither of these deeds has been covered by the newspaper. Furthermore, the claim that prices are low is hard to accept as I found the prices to be 10 percent higher on average than Foreman Sports'.

— Samantha Riley

(120w)

編集者への手紙
6月21日 ──Bay Town Shopping Center の Neptune Sports and Leisure の開店に関する記事を読みました。記事は、ほとんどこの店の広告のようでした。報道記事を意図していた以上、もっと批判的な視点で書かれるべきだったと思います。Bay Town には、すでに Foreman Sports があります。ここは優れたスポーツ用品店で、多くの地元の若者

を雇用し、当地のスポーツチームのいくつかを何年にもわたって後援しています。これらの功績のいずれも、新聞で取り上げられたことはありません。その上、価格が安いとの記述は受け入れがたいものです。なぜなら、私が見た限り、同店の価格は Foreman Sports の価格よりも平均して10パーセント高いからです。

─── Samantha Riley

- □ advertisement: 名 広告、宣伝　□ intend: 動 ~を意図する　□ take a ~ stance: ~な立場を取る　□ critical: 形 批判的な
- □ sporting goods: スポーツ用品　□ locals: 名 地元の人々　□ sponsor: 動 ~を資金援助する、後援する　□ sporting team: スポーツチーム
- □ neither of ~: どちらの~もない　□ deed: 名 行い、功績　□ be covered by ~: (メディアなど)で取り上げられる
- □ furthermore: 副 さらに、その上　□ claim: 名 主張　□ accept: 動 ~を受け入れる　□ on average: 平均で

Part 7

▼ Reading Section

Part 7 読解問題

186. 正解：**A** 易 ■■■■■□ 難　選択率：**(A) 34.5%** (B) 31.0% (C) 27.1% (D) 2.7%

When was the grand opening of the new Neptune Sports and Leisure store?
(A) On June 17
(B) On June 18
(C) On June 19
(D) On June 20

Neptune Sports and Leisure の新店舗はいつ開店しましたか。
(A) 6月17日に
(B) 6月18日に
(C) 6月19日に
(D) 6月20日に

▶解説 ❶と❷の情報から、Barkworth さんが Neptune Sports and Leisure に行った日付が6月18日であることが分かります。また、❸で、Barkworth さんが店に行ったのはオープンした日の翌日であることが分かります。よって、店がオープンしたのは (A) の6月17日です。

---

187. 正解：**B** 易 ■■■■■□ 難　選択率：(A) 32.9% **(B) 32.2%** (C) 13.7% (D) 16.1%

What attraction is most likely unique to the Bay Town Shopping Center location?
(A) The climbing wall
(B) The golf simulator
(C) The batting cage
(D) The running track

□ unique to ～：～に特有の

Bay Town Shopping Center 店に特有のアトラクションは何である可能性が最も高いですか。
(A) クライミングウォール
(B) ゴルフシミュレーター
(C) バッティングケージ
(D) ランニングトラック

▶解説 2つの文書を参照して答えます。オンラインレビューの❹で Barkworth さんが挙げているものと、新聞記事の❻ですべての店に設置されているものとを比較すると、ゴルフシミュレーターはオンラインレビューにしか記載がありません。よって、(B) が正解です。

---

188. 正解：**D** 易 ■■■■■□ 難　選択率：(A) 20.0% (B) 18.4% (C) 20.0% **(D) 36.1%**

What is mentioned about the grand opening of the new Neptune Sports and Leisure store?
(A) It was timed to coincide with a popular local sporting event.
(B) The turnout was a disappointment to the organizers of the event.
(C) It had received extensive publicity on various local radio programs.
(D) Coupons for people to use at a local restaurant were provided.

□ time：[動] ～を良い時機に合わせる
□ coincide with ～：～と同時に起こる
□ sporting event：スポーツイベント
□ turnout：[名] 人出、参加者　□ disappointment：[名] 失望
□ receive extensive publicity：いたる所で評判になる

Neptune Sports and Leisure の開店について何が述べられていますか。
(A) 人気の高い地元のスポーツイベントと時期を合わせられた。
(B) 人出はイベントの主催者をがっかりさせた。
(C) 様々な地元のラジオ番組で大評判となった。
(D) 人々が地元のレストランで使えるクーポンが配られた。

▶解説 文書は3つとも Neptune Sports and Leisure store に触れているので、選択肢にある情報が記載されているか、しっかり確認する必要があります。記事の❼に、近くの Gee's Healthy Eating でのランチの無料クーポン券が提供されたと述べられています。vouchers を coupons と言い換えた (D) が正解です。(A) の「地元のスポーツイベント」や (B) の「イベントの主催者」、(C) の「ラジオ番組での評判に関する言及はありません。

---

189. 正解：**D** 易 ■■■■■□ 難　選択率：(A) 11.4% (B) 29.4% (C) 22.7% **(D) 31.0%**

What does Ms. Riley indicate about the article?
(A) It should have been published earlier.
(B) It was quite critical of a local business.
(C) It has appeared in another publication.
(D) It seemed to be promoting a business.

□ publish：[動] ～を発表する　□ appear：[動] 登場する
□ publication：[名] 出版物　□ promote：[動] ～を宣伝する

Riley さんは記事について何を指摘していますか。
(A) もっと早く発表されるべきだった。
(B) ある地元の事業者に対して非常に批判的だった。
(C) 別の出版物に載ったことがある。
(D) ある事業者を宣伝しているように見えた。

▶解説 Ms. Riley は編集者への手紙を書いた人物です。❽で「記事が店の宣伝のようだ」と述べられていることから、(D) が正解です。本文の appear と選択肢の seem は「～のようだ」という意味です。❽にある the store は Neptune Sports and Leisure を指し、選択肢では a business と言い換えられています。Riley さんは記事を批判していますが、記事は何も批判していないため、(B) は不適切です。

190. 正解：**C**　易 ■■■■■■■■ 難　選択率：(A) 9.8%　(B) 22.4%　**(C) 52.9%**　(D) 8.6%

About what do Mr. Barkworth and Ms. Riley agree?
(A) The job opportunities provided by Foreman Sports
(B) The little-known brands on offer at Neptune Sports and Leisure
(C) The higher prices at Neptune Sports and Leisure
(D) The lack of newspaper coverage of team sponsorship

☐ job opportunity: 雇用の機会
☐ little-known: 形 ほとんど知られていない
☐ lack: 名 不足、欠け
☐ coverage: 名 (メディアなどに) 取り上げられること、報道
☐ sponsorship: 名 スポンサーであること、後援

Barkworth さんと Riley さんは、何に関して意見が一致していますか。
(A) Foreman Sports が提供する雇用機会
(B) Neptune Sports and Leisure で売られているほとんど無名のブランド
(C) Neptune Sports and Leisure で提示される高めの価格
(D) チームの後援について取り上げる新聞記事がないこと

▶解説　オンラインレビューの❺と手紙の❾で、それぞれ Barkworth さんと Riley さんが価格について述べています。それによると、Neptune Sports and Leisure の商品価格は、他よりも高めだということで双方の意見が一致しています。よって、(C)が正解です。

🗼📻 ゼミ 生 中継　　　😀 Hiro 😳 Mai 😸 Yasu 😑 Dai 😺 Saki

187.
😀 あれ？　unique は「珍しい」みたいな意味だと思っていました。
😑 同じく。
😸 それもあるけど、be unique to 〜 は「〜に特有の」だよ。

189.
😸 ヒント情報で使われている appeared が、(C)にも仕込まれている。これがエサだね。釣られた人は？
😳 はい。エサに飛びついてしまいました。

😺 私は別のエサに飛びつきました。
😸 次の文にある critical が (B)にも入っている。
😳 はい。彼女の論調が批判的だったので、つい……。
😸 ところで、この critical は Test 1 の118番にあった critically とは違うよね。あそこでは critically acclaimed という形だった。意味を覚えている？
😺 「高く評価されている」でした。
😸 あと1回、Test 3 にも critical が出るよ。また違う意味で。

Questions 191-195 refer to the following letter, feedback form, and e-mail.

Kramer Construction

Office 7, 78 McDougal Street, Cincinnati 45268

August 5

Ms. Barbara Drazen:

The MacArthur Hotel in downtown Cincinnati has been demolished to make way for an even larger hotel and convention center. Because you previously used the conference rooms there, we thought you might be interested in helping us design an even better event space for the site. We intend to make the New MacArthur Hotel Cincinnati's premier location for large events.

With that end in mind, we have arranged an information session at our head office where we will explain the plans and receive feedback. We will pay for transportation and accommodation for a representative of your organization to take part. Please take a look at the invitation enclosed for details. We are looking forward to seeing you.

Sincerely,

Abramo Jenkins

Abramo Jenkins
Chief Designer — Kramer Construction

(140w)

問題191-195は次の手紙、評価記入用紙とメールに関するものです。

Kramer Construction
Office 7, 78 McDougal Street, Cincinnati 45268

8月5日

前略　Barbara Drazen さま

Cincinnati 中心部の MacArthur Hotel は取り壊され、さらに大規模なホテル兼会議場に生まれ変わろうとしています。貴社は以前、同ホテルの会議室をご利用されたことから、当社がさらに秀逸な催事場を同地向けに設計する上で、貴社にお力添えをいただけるのではないかと考えた

次第です。当社は New MacArthur Hotel を、Cincinnati 随一の大規模催事用施設にしたいと考えております。

そうした目標を織り込み、当社本社にて説明会を開く運びとなりました。会では今回の計画についてご説明し、ご意見を拝聴する予定です。貴社のご担当者にご出席いただくに当たっては、当社で交通費と宿泊費を負担させていただきます。同封の招待状で、詳細をご確認ください。お目に掛かれるのを楽しみにしております。

草々
Abramo Jenkins
設計主任——Kramer Construction

□ feedback form: 評価記入用紙　□ downtown: 名 中心街　□ demolish: 動 ～を取り壊す　□ make way for ～: ～に道を譲る
□ previously: 副 以前に　□ design: 動 ～を設計する　□ site: 名 用地、場所　□ intend to ～: ～するつもりである　□ premier: 形 最高の
□ end: 名 目的、目標　□ in one's mind: 心の中に、頭の中に　□ information session: 説明会　□ head office: 本社　□ take part: 参加する
□ enclose: 動 ～を同封する　□ detail: 名 詳細

Feedback Form
Kramer Construction — New MacArthur Hotel

Name: Wendy Tang　　　　　　**Company:** Gruber Publishing

Comments: I love the color scheme and layout of the conference center. I think that naming the conference rooms after local celebrities is a nice idea. However, I suggest that you use a numbering system instead. I also love the idea of having screens at the entrance of each room where event organizers can post messages for people arriving. Perhaps it would be nice to have a live video feed of the event broadcast on them so that latecomers can time their entrance.

ご意見記入用紙
Kramer Construction ― New MacArthur Hotel
お名前：Wendy Tang　社名：Gruber Publishing
ご意見：会議場の配色や配置は、とても気に入っています。会議室の名称に地元の著名人の名前を使うというのは、面白い着想だと思います。しかし、やはり規則的に番号を振ることをご提案します。また、各部屋

の入り口にスクリーンを設置し、イベントの主催者が到着する人たちへ向けた連絡事項を表示できるようにする、というアイデアもとてもいいと思います。もしかすると、イベントの様子を映した生映像をスクリーンに流せば、遅れてきた人が入室のタイミングを見計らえるかもしれません。

□ name: 動 〜に名を付ける　□ celebrity: 名 著名人　□ numbering system: 番号方式　□ color scheme: 配色、色彩設計
□ layout: 名 配置、レイアウト　□ entrance: 名 入り口　□ event organizer: イベント主催者　□ post: 動 〜を掲示する　□ perhaps: 副 おそらく
□ live: 形 生の　□ video feed: ビデオ画像　□ broadcast: 動 〜を放送する　□ latecomer: 名 遅れて来た人、遅刻者
□ time: 動 頃合いを見計らって〜を行う

E-Mail Message

To:	Antonio Damiano <adamiano@riseacademy.net>
From:	Juno Venn <jvenn@newmacarthurhotel.com>
Date:	July 2
Subject:	Availability

Dear Mr. Damiano,

Thank you for coming to see our facilities yesterday. I am glad you have chosen us as the venue for the Rise Academy Cooking Contest. I checked the availability of the two rooms you mentioned in your previous e-mail and found that both are available. I believe that Convention Room 3 would be the perfect choice considering the size of the audience. The adjacent room can seat no more than ninety people. Furthermore, it is equipped with the huge movable platform you need, which you can use at no extra charge. Please let me know if you would like us to reserve the room for you.

Sincerely,

Juno Venn ― New MacArthur Hotel

(130w)

宛先：Antonio Damiano <adamiano@riseacademy.net>
送信者：Juno Venn <jvenn@newmacarthurhotel.com>
日付：7月2日
件名：空き状況

Damiano さま

昨日は当施設の下見にご足労いただき、ありがとうございました。当施設を Rise Academy Cooking Contest の会場にお選びくださり、喜ばしく思っております。前回のメールでおっしゃっていた2部屋の予約状況を確認しましたところ、どちらもご利用いただけることが分かりました。聴衆の規模を考えると、会議室3をお選びいただくのが間違いないだろうと存じます。隣室の方だと、90名までしか着席できません。しかも、会議室3には、ご要望いただいている大きな可動式演壇が備え付けられており、追加料金無しでご利用いただけます。同会議室をご予約なさりたいかどうか、お知らせください。

よろしくお願いいたします。

Juno Venn ―― New MacArthur Hotel

□ facility: 名 施設、設備　□ venue: 名 会場　□ considering: 前 〜を考慮すれば　□ adjacent: 形 隣接した　□ seat: 動 〜を収容できる
□ furthermore: 副 さらに、その上　□ be equipped with 〜: 〜を備えている　□ huge: 形 巨大な、大規模な　□ movable: 形 動かせる、可動式の
□ platform: 名 演壇、舞台　□ at no extra fee: 追加料金なしで

Part 7 読解問題

---

191. 正解：A 易 ■■■■■□ 難　選択率：**(A) 32.5%** (B) 17.6% (C) 28.6% (D) 14.9%

What is one purpose of the letter?
(A) To explain a development project
(B) To announce the results of a survey
(C) To recommend an alternative service
(D) To invite prospective clients to a celebration

☐ alternative: 形 代わりの
☐ prospective: 形 見込みのある
☐ celebration: 名 祝賀会

手紙の1つの目的は何ですか。
(A) ある開発計画について説明すること
(B) ある調査結果を発表すること
(C) ある代替サービスを勧めること
(D) 見込み客を祝賀会に招待すること

▶解説 この手紙には、MacArthur Hotel の取り壊し・改築、会議場建設のお知らせと、その建設プロジェクトについての情報説明会への招待が含まれています。このうちの前者に相当する (A) が手紙の目的の1つと言えます。

---

192. 正解：B 易 ■■■■■□ 難　選択率：(A) 21.6% **(B) 42.7%** (C) 16.9% (D) 11.8%

In the letter, the word "end" in paragraph 2, line 1, is closest in meaning to
(A) completion
(B) goal
(C) limitation
(D) side

手紙の第2段落1行目にある「end」に最も意味が近いのは
(A) 完成
(B) 目標
(C) 制限
(D) 側面

▶解説 名詞 end には「目標」「終わり」「限度」「端」などの様々な意味があります。直前の❷で、New MacArthur Hotel を最高の場所にしたいという目標について述べています。設問にある end が含まれる文の With that ～ in mind は「その～を頭に入れて」という意味で、「～」の部分に「目標」を入れると文脈に合うことから、意味が最も近いのは、(B) の goal です。

---

193. 正解：D 易 ■■■■■□ 難　選択率：(A) 9.0% (B) 17.6% (C) 38.0% **(D) 27.1%**

According to the feedback form, where will screens probably be placed?
(A) On the counter at reception
(B) In front of every elevator
(C) At the entrance of the hotel
(D) By the door of each event space

☐ reception: 名 受付

評価記入用紙によると、スクリーンはどこに設置されると考えられますか。
(A) 受付のカウンターの上に
(B) 各エレベーターの前に
(C) ホテルの玄関に
(D) 各催事場の扉のそばに

▶解説 Tang さんは❹で、各会議室の入り口にスクリーンを置く案に賛成しています。この案はホテルの設計者によるもので、別案はどこにも書かれていません。会議室の入り口には通常ドアがあるので、(D) が正解です。

---

194. 正解：A 易 ■■■■■□ 難　選択率：**(A) 38.0%** (B) 21.2% (C) 20.0% (D) 12.2%

What is most likely true about the New MacArthur Hotel?
(A) It adopted Ms. Tang's suggestion.
(B) It was closed at the beginning of July.
(C) It hired a professional videographer.
(D) It has appointed a new general manager.

☐ adopt: 動 ～を採用する
☐ professional: 形 プロの　☐ videographer: 名 映像作家
☐ appoint: 動 ～を任命する　☐ general manager: 支配人

New MacArthur Hotel について何が最も当てはまりそうですか。
(A) Tang さんの提案を採用した。
(B) 7月初旬に閉館した。
(C) プロの映像作家を雇った。
(D) 新しい支配人を任命した。

▶解説 Tang さんは❸で、会場の名前に番号を使うことを勧めています。ホテル完成後に書かれたメールの❻には Convention Room 3 とあり、会場名に番号が使われていることが分かります。これらから、ホテル側は Tang さんの提案を受け入れたと推測できます。正解は (A) です。

250

195. 正解：C　易 ■■■■■■ 難　選択率：(A) 25.9%　(B) 23.5%　**(C) 25.9%**　(D) 16.1%

What is NOT indicated about the cooking contest?
(A) It will be held in the city center.
(B) It will require a large platform.
(C) It will be using two rooms.
(D) It will be attended by more than ninety people.

料理コンテストについて示されていないのは何ですか。
(A) 市の中心部で開かれるだろう。
(B) 大きな演壇を必要とするだろう。
(C) 2部屋使うことになるだろう。
(D) 90名以上が出席するだろう。

▶解説 メールの❺と❿から、料理コンテストは New MacArthur Hotel で開催されることが分かります。手紙の内容から New MacArthur Hotel は MacArthur Hotel を建て替えたもので、❶からホテルは市の中心部（downtown）にあると分かります。(A) はこれに合致します。(B) は❽から明らかです。Venn さんは会議室 3 を薦め、❼で「隣の部屋は 90 名までしか着席できない」と書いているので、(D) も正しい情報です。❻が料理コンテストは 1 部屋で足りることを示しますし、❾の room が単数形なので、(C) が正解です。

(((📡 ゼミ 生 中継　　　　　　　　　　　😺Hiro 😺Mai 😺Yasu 🎲Dai 😺Saki

191.
😺 (C) が魅力的かな。この手紙は設計の協力を過去のユーザーに依頼しているだけで、ホテルや会議室を推奨しているわけじゃない。完成前の建物は利用できないから、何かの代替サービスになるわけでもない。だから、(C) の recommend も alternative service も間違っている。

193.
😺 これも「釣り」だね。フォームにも (C) にも使われている at the entrance of がエサ。(C) はホテル自体の入り口だからダメ。

195.
😺 (A) をすぐに発見できた？
😺 はい。2文書参照型の設問がまだ1つしかなかったので、この問題のヒントは第1文書にあると予想したんです。
😺 その発想はナイス。実践的だよ。
😺 なるほど〜、頭いいなぁ。
😺 それで、いきなり (A) を塗ってしまいました。私の悪いクセです。
😺 また NOT 型でミスしたの？　Test 3 では繰り返さないように注意してね。

Part 7　▼ Reading Section

251

Questions 196-200 refer to the following letter, survey, and e-mail.

July 12

Dear Sir or Madam,

The Mansfield City Council is about to approve the construction of a train line that will pass through the center of Mansfield City. Mayor Noah Chavira, and others arguing in favor of the proposal point out that it will make it easier for tourists to get here. However, there is a compelling argument against the project. In addition to me, there are three other council members who hold that a train line would ruin the atmosphere of our town and make the area less attractive to tourists, who are contributing more and more to our economy. The proposed line is not only for passenger trains. Many freight trains would also be traveling through the town's center at all hours of the night.

We would like people living in the area to write in and put pressure on council members to vote against the plan at their next meeting; July 27. You can do so by filling out the enclosed survey and mailing it to the secretary of Mansfield City Council, Vince Marcel.

Sincerely,

Kendall Tesch
Council Member — Mansfield City Council

(186w)

問題196-200は次の手紙、アンケートとメールに関するものです。

7月12日

拝啓

Mansfield 市議会は、間もなく、Mansfield City の中心部を通る鉄道線の敷設を可決します。Noah Chavira 市長およびその他の提案賛成派は、鉄道敷設によって観光客が当地にアクセスしやすくなると述べています。しかし、この計画に反対する説得力のある主張があります。私に加えて3名の市議会議員は、こう考えています。鉄道線が敷かれるとこの町の雰囲気が壊され、当地の経済にますます寄与してくれている観光客にとって、町の魅力が薄れてしまうことになるだろう、と。提案され

ている鉄道線は旅客用に限定されていません。多くの貨物列車までもが、町の中心部を一晩中走り抜けることになるのです。

私たちは、当地の住民の方々に投書していただき、市議会議員らに圧力を掛けて、7月27日に開かれる次の議会で計画に反対票を投じるよう仕向けていただきたいと考えています。同封の調査票にご記入の上、Mansfield 市議会書記官の Vince Marcel 宛てに郵送していただければ結構です。

敬具

Kendall Tesch
議員——Mansfield 市議会

☐ survey: 图 調査、アンケート　☐ city council: 市議会　☐ approve: 動 ～を承認する　☐ train line: （鉄道の）路線
☐ pass through ～: ～を通る　☐ argue in favor of ～: ～に賛成の議論をする　☐ however: 副 しかしながら　☐ compelling: 形 説得力のある
☐ hold: 動 ～であると考える　☐ ruin: 動 ～を損なう　☐ atmosphere: 图 雰囲気　☐ attractive: 形 魅力的な　☐ contribute to ～: ～に貢献する
☐ freight train: 貨物列車　☐ at all hours of the night: 一晩中　☐ vote against ～: ～に反対票を投じる　☐ enclosed: 形 同封されている
☐ mail: 動 ～を郵送する　☐ secretary: 图 書記（官）、秘書（官）

Mansfield City Central Train Line Survey

Name: Colleen Donaldson   **Address:** Creek Street, Mansfield City

❻

Are you in favor of creating a railway through the city center?   ____ Yes _X_ No

Will the decision by council members affect the way you vote at the next election?

                                 _X_ Yes ____ No

A train line would:	____ Increase the number of visitors	_X_ Decrease the number of visitors	____ Have no effect on visitor numbers
❼ A better alternative to a train line is:	____ Shuttle buses from Glendale	❽ _X_ A subway line from Glendale	____ More parking in the city center

Comments: ❾ I think the best solution to the ongoing dispute is to build a subway line to connect Mansfield city center with the suburb of Glendale. Visitors coming from the airport could transfer at Glendale Station. A subway line would be a quieter option, and it would not harm the appearance of our wonderful town.

Thank you for participating in this survey. We also recommend sending an e-mail to the council member for your division.

(167w)

Mansfield City Central Train Line に関する調査票

お名前：Colleen Donaldson　ご住所：Creek Street, Mansfield City

市の中心部に鉄道線を通すことに賛成ですか。　__ はい　✕ いいえ

市議会議員の判断は、次の選挙でのあなたの投票行動に影響しますか。

                           ✕ はい　__ いいえ

鉄道線を敷設すると：	__ 来訪者の数が増える	✕ 来訪者の数が減る	__ 来訪者の数に影響は無い
鉄道線よりも望ましい選択肢は：	__ Glendale 発のシャトルバス	✕ Glendale 発の地下鉄	__ 市の中心部に駐車場を増設

ご意見：この論争を解決する最善策は、地下鉄を通すことだと思います。Mansfield の市の中心部と郊外の Glendale を結ぶ路線です。空港から来る旅行者は Glendale Station で乗り換えることができます。地下鉄線なら騒音がより低減される上、この町の素晴らしい景観を傷つけることもないでしょう。

この調査にご協力くださいまして、ありがとうございます。さらに、お住まいの地区の市議会議員宛てにメールを送られるようお勧めします。

☐ in favor of ～：～を支持して、～に賛成して　☐ create: 動 ～を作る、開発する　☐ decision: 名 決定　☐ affect: 動 ～に影響を与える
☐ election: 名 選挙　☐ increase: 動 ～を増やす　☐ decrease: 動 ～を減らす　☐ alternative: 名 取って代わるもの、代替案
☐ shuttle bus: シャトルバス　☐ subway line: 地下鉄路線　☐ solution: 名 解決策　☐ ongoing: 形 進行中の　☐ dispute: 名 論争
☐ suburb: 名 郊外　☐ transfer: 動 乗り換える　☐ option: 名 選択肢　☐ harm: 動 ～を害する　☐ appearance: 名 景観　☐ division: 名 地区

	E-Mail Message
To:	Henrietta Sales <division1@mansfieldcitycouncil.gov>
From:	Desmond Piatt <dpiatt@blueduck.com>
Subject:	Train line
Date:	July 13

Dear Ms. Sales,

As the Mansfield City Council representative for Division 1, it is up to you to stop this irreparable damage to our beautiful town. We must not allow the railway to go ahead. I urge you to join Kendall Tesch and other like-minded council members in their vote against the plan.

Sincerely,

Desmond Piatt
Resident

(74w)

宛先：Henrietta Sales <division1@mansfieldcitycouncil.gov>
送信者：Desmond Piatt <spiatt@blueduck.com>
件名：鉄道線
日付：7月13日

Sales さま

Division 1選出の Mansfield City 市議会議員として、私たちの美しい町に対するこのような不可逆的な損害を食い止められるかどうかが、あなたに委ねられています。私たちは、鉄道敷設計画を進めるわけにはいきません。私はあなたに、Kendall Tesch や彼女に同意する市議会議員たちに加わり、この計画に反対票を投じるよう、強く要請します。

よろしくお願いいたします。

Desmond Piatt
住民

□ representative: 图 代議員　□ up to ～: ～次第で　□ irreparable: 形 取り返しのつかない　□ go ahead: 先へ進む
□ urge ～ to ...: ～に…するよう要請する　□ like-minded: 形 同じ考えを持った

---

196. 正解：**C**　易 ▣▣▣▣▣▣ 難　選択率：(A) 11.0%　(B) 19.2%　**(C) 58.0%**　(D) 2.0%

What is mentioned about Mansfield City?
(A) Its population has decreased.
(B) Its airport was recently expanded.
(C) It is a growing tourist destination.
(D) It will host an upcoming sporting event.

□ population: 图 人口　□ recently: 副 最近
□ expand: 動 ～を拡張する　□ destination: 图 目的地
□ host: 動 ～を主催する　□ upcoming: 形 来る

Mansfield City について何が述べられていますか。
(A) 人口が減少している。
(B) 空港が最近、拡張された。
(C) 観光地として成長している。
(D) 近く開催されるスポーツの大会を主催する。

▶解説 手紙の❸で、鉄道の建設による悪影響について述べられています。町の経済にますます恩恵をもたらしている観光客の減少が考えられるとあり、Mansfield City が人気の観光地であることが分かります。よって (C) が正解です。

---

197. 正解：**D**　易 ▣▣▣▣▣▣ 難　選択率：(A) 14.5%　(B) 30.6%　(C) 15.3%　**(D) 29.4%**

Who is the intended recipient of the letter?
(A) A railway company representative
(B) A city council employee
(C) A member of a construction crew
(D) A resident of Mansfield City

□ recipient: 图 受取人　□ representative: 图 担当者
□ construction crew: 建設作業員

手紙は誰に宛てられたものですか。
(A) 鉄道会社の担当者
(B) 市議会の職員
(C) 建設作業員
(D) Mansfield City の住民

▶解説 ❶は不特定の人に宛てた手紙などの冒頭で使われる表現です。第2段落の❹には Mansfield City における鉄道建設に関して、この地域の住民にしてほしいことが述べられています。これらのことから、この手紙は特定の人物ではなく、Mansfield City の住民に宛てたものだと判断できます。よって、正解は (D) です。

198. 正解：A 易 ■■■■■□ 難   選択率：**(A) 15.3%** (B) 30.6% (C) 34.1% (D) 6.7%

What is suggested about Ms. Donaldson?
(A) She addressed an envelope to Vince Marcel.
(B) She wants to attract fewer visitors to Mansfield City.
(C) She attended a public discussion of construction plans.
(D) She is a local business owner.

□ address: 動 (郵便物などを～) に宛てる
□ envelope: 名 封書   □ public discussion: 公開討論会

Donaldson さんについて、何が示唆されていますか。
(A) 彼女は封書を Vince Marcel 宛てに送付した。
(B) 彼女は Mansfield City への来訪者数を減らしたがっている。
(C) 彼女は建設計画に関する公開討論会に参加した。
(D) 彼女は地元企業のオーナーだ。

▶解説 手紙と調査票を参照する問題です。Donaldson さんの名前はアンケートの❻にあります。このアンケートは、その内容から❺で言及されている、手紙に同封されたアンケートだと考えられます。手紙はアンケートを Marcel さんに郵送するよう求めているため、Donaldson さんはその通りにしたと考えられます。よって (A) が正解です。

---

199. 正解：D 易 ■■■■□□ 難   選択率：(A) 7.5% (B) 31.0% (C) 18.0% **(D) 31.4%**

What does Ms. Donaldson propose that Mansfield City do?
(A) Provide additional parking near the airport
(B) Conduct a survey of visitors
(C) Promote some of the city's attractions
(D) Construct a subway line

□ promote: 動 ～を宣伝する   □ subway line: 地下鉄路線

Donaldson さんは、Mansfield City に何をするよう提案していますか。
(A) 空港の近くに駐車場を増やす
(B) 来訪者を対象に調査を行う
(C) 市内の名所のいくつかを宣伝する
(D) 地下鉄を通す

▶解説 Donaldson さんは、❼の鉄道建設の代替案の欄で、地下鉄の案にチェックを入れています (❽)。また、❾のコメント欄でも、地下鉄の建設が最善だと述べているので、(D) が正解です。

---

200. 正解：B 易 ■■■■□□ 難   選択率：(A) 23.1% **(B) 39.2%** (C) 15.7% (D) 9.0%

What is probably true about Mr. Piatt?
(A) He is a member of the Mansfield City Council.
(B) He opposes the mayor's argument.
(C) He commutes to work by car.
(D) He had a meeting with Kendall Tesch.

□ oppose: 動 ～に反対する
□ commute to work: 通勤する

Piatt さんについて何が当てはまりそうですか。
(A) 彼は Mansfield 市議会の一員だ。
(B) 彼は市長の主張に反対している。
(C) 彼は車で通勤している。
(D) 彼は Kendall Tesch の打ち合わせをした。

▶解説 Piatt さんはメールの差出人です。メールの❿で鉄道の建設に反対であることを述べ、続く⓫で「同じように計画反対の考えを持つ議員に合流するよう求める」と述べています。一方、手紙の❷によれば、市長は鉄道建設を推進しています。これらの情報から、Piatt さんは市長の主張に反対していると判断できます。よって、(B) が正解です。

((◉)) ゼミ 生中継   😵 Hiro 😊 Mai 😎 Yasu 😐 Dai 😄 Saki

198.
😎 2文書参照型には常連パターンがある。「今週はカメラが半額」みたいな広告が出たとしよう。ダイ、次に何が起きる？

😐 え……。誰かが今週カメラを買う？

😎 そう。そして、その人について正しい情報が問われる。「割引を受けた」が正解。法則化すると、「X ならば Y だ」という条件が設定され、後で登場する人や会社が X を満たす。すると、Y が起きる。このパターンを「条件型」と呼ぼう。

😵 198番も似ていますね。

😎 手紙から、「アンケートに応じる人は、調査票を Marcel さんに送る」と言える。これが条件。第2文書によれば、Donaldson さんはアンケートに答えている。だから、(A) が正しいと分かる。

😐 なるほど。

😎 ただ、そもそも手紙に「条件」が載っていることに気づかなければ、解きようがない。だから、文書を「虫食い読み」しちゃいけないんだよ。忘れないでね。さて、Test 2 が終わった。リーディングセクションの正答数は？

😵 77問で、予想スコアは Test 1 とほぼ同じです。

😊 う～ん、55問。Part 5 が伸びなかったなぁ。

😐 49問です。あと5点で470点達成でした。

😎 ほら。Test 1 が終わったときに言ったよね。目標は射程圏内だって。サキは？

😄 53問です。合計は 400 から 550 までジャンプしました。

😎 みんな、ちゃんと復習してね。次は Test 3 に進もう。

Test 3
模擬試験 ③
解答と解説

お役立ちサイトやアプリのご案内

● ダウンロードセンター、ALCO：
模擬試験で使用した音声や復習用の音声をダウンロードできます。 （利用法は p.10、24）

● テスト採点センター：
簡単に答え合わせができます。（利用法は p.11）

● 動画センター：
全問題の解説が確認できます。（利用法は p.11）

※ QR コードを読み込む際は、他の QR コードを隠して
カメラを向けてください。

記号について

【品詞を表す】

名 名詞　動 動詞　形 形容詞　副 副詞
接 接続詞　前 前置詞　代 代名詞

※品詞が複数ある場合は、問題文での用法に合うものを1つ表示しています。

【ナレーターの性別や国籍を表す】
M: 男性ナレーター　W: 女性ナレーター

 アメリカ人　 カナダ人
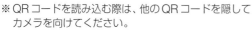 イギリス人　オーストラリア人

Test 3 成長記録シート

「3回チャレンジ法プラス」での正答数などの記録をつけて、成長を振り返りましょう。

1回目（勘を含む）

● 正答数

Part	正答数	
Part 1	／6	Listening 合計正答数
Part 2	／25	
Part 3	／39	
Part 4	／30	／100
Part 5	／30	Reading 合計正答数
Part 6	／16	
Part 7	／54	／100

● 換算スコアA

Listening ＿＿＿＿＿

Reading ＿＿＿＿＿

● 問題タイプ別正答数と正答率

Listening Section

正答数	正答数	正答率
L1：＿＿＿／16	（＿＿＿÷16）×100＝＿＿＿%
L2：＿＿＿／20	（＿＿＿÷20）×100＝＿＿＿%
L3：＿＿＿／15	（＿＿＿÷15）×100＝＿＿＿%
L4：＿＿＿／49	（＿＿＿÷49）×100＝＿＿＿%
L5：＿＿＿／15	（＿＿＿÷15）×100＝＿＿＿%

Reading Section

正答数	正答数	正答率
R1：＿＿＿／19	（＿＿＿÷19）×100＝＿＿＿%
R2：＿＿＿／19	（＿＿＿÷19）×100＝＿＿＿%
R3：＿＿＿／35	（＿＿＿÷35）×100＝＿＿＿%
R4：＿＿＿／25	（＿＿＿÷25）×100＝＿＿＿%
R5：＿＿＿／19	（＿＿＿÷19）×100＝＿＿＿%

年　月　日

1回目（勘を除く）

● 正答数

Part	正答数	
Part 1	／6	Listening 合計正答数
Part 2	／25	
Part 3	／39	
Part 4	／30	／100
Part 5	／30	Reading 合計正答数
Part 6	／16	
Part 7	／54	／100

● 換算スコアB

Listening ＿＿＿＿＿

Reading ＿＿＿＿＿

合　計 ＿＿＿＿＿

● 問題タイプ別正答数と正答率

Listening Section

正答数	正答数	正答率
L1：＿＿＿／16	（＿＿＿÷16）×100＝＿＿＿%
L2：＿＿＿／20	（＿＿＿÷20）×100＝＿＿＿%
L3：＿＿＿／15	（＿＿＿÷15）×100＝＿＿＿%
L4：＿＿＿／49	（＿＿＿÷49）×100＝＿＿＿%
L5：＿＿＿／15	（＿＿＿÷15）×100＝＿＿＿%

Reading Section

正答数	正答数	正答率
R1：＿＿＿／19	（＿＿＿÷19）×100＝＿＿＿%
R2：＿＿＿／19	（＿＿＿÷19）×100＝＿＿＿%
R3：＿＿＿／35	（＿＿＿÷35）×100＝＿＿＿%
R4：＿＿＿／25	（＿＿＿÷25）×100＝＿＿＿%
R5：＿＿＿／19	（＿＿＿÷19）×100＝＿＿＿%

年　月　日

2回目（勘を含む）

● 正答数

Part	正答数	
Part 1	／6	Listening 合計正答数
Part 2	／25	
Part 3	／39	
Part 4	／30	／100
Part 5	／30	Reading 合計正答数
Part 6	／16	
Part 7	／54	／100

● 換算スコアA

Listening ＿＿＿＿＿

Reading ＿＿＿＿＿

合　計 ＿＿＿＿＿

● 問題タイプ別正答数と正答率

Listening Section

正答数	正答数	正答率
L1：＿＿＿／16	（＿＿＿÷16）×100＝＿＿＿%
L2：＿＿＿／20	（＿＿＿÷20）×100＝＿＿＿%
L3：＿＿＿／15	（＿＿＿÷15）×100＝＿＿＿%
L4：＿＿＿／49	（＿＿＿÷49）×100＝＿＿＿%
L5：＿＿＿／15	（＿＿＿÷15）×100＝＿＿＿%

Reading Section

正答数	正答数	正答率
R1：＿＿＿／19	（＿＿＿÷19）×100＝＿＿＿%
R2：＿＿＿／19	（＿＿＿÷19）×100＝＿＿＿%
R3：＿＿＿／35	（＿＿＿÷35）×100＝＿＿＿%
R4：＿＿＿／25	（＿＿＿÷25）×100＝＿＿＿%
R5：＿＿＿／19	（＿＿＿÷19）×100＝＿＿＿%

年　月　日

2回目（勘を除く）

● 正答数

Part	正答数	
Part 1	／6	Listening 合計正答数
Part 2	／25	
Part 3	／39	
Part 4	／30	／100
Part 5	／30	Reading 合計正答数
Part 6	／16	
Part 7	／54	／100

● 換算スコアB

Listening ＿＿＿＿＿

Reading ＿＿＿＿＿

合　計 ＿＿＿＿＿

● 問題タイプ別正答数と正答率

Listening Section

正答数	正答数	正答率
L1：＿＿＿／16	（＿＿＿÷16）×100＝＿＿＿%
L2：＿＿＿／20	（＿＿＿÷20）×100＝＿＿＿%
L3：＿＿＿／15	（＿＿＿÷15）×100＝＿＿＿%
L4：＿＿＿／49	（＿＿＿÷49）×100＝＿＿＿%
L5：＿＿＿／15	（＿＿＿÷15）×100＝＿＿＿%

Reading Section

正答数	正答数	正答率
R1：＿＿＿／19	（＿＿＿÷19）×100＝＿＿＿%
R2：＿＿＿／19	（＿＿＿÷19）×100＝＿＿＿%
R3：＿＿＿／35	（＿＿＿÷35）×100＝＿＿＿%
R4：＿＿＿／25	（＿＿＿÷25）×100＝＿＿＿%
R5：＿＿＿／19	（＿＿＿÷19）×100＝＿＿＿%

年　月　日

3回目（勘を含む）　年　月　日

● 正答数

Part	正答数	
Part 1	／6	Listening 合計正答数
Part 2	／25	
Part 3	／39	
Part 4	／30	／100
Part 5	／30	Reading 合計正答数
Part 6	／16	
Part 7	／54	／100

● 換算スコアA

Listening ______

Reading ______

合　計 ______

● 問題タイプ別正答数と正答率

Listening Section

	正答数	正答数	正答率
L1：	____／16	(____÷16)×100＝____	%
L2：	____／20	(____÷20)×100＝____	%
L3：	____／15	(____÷15)×100＝____	%
L4：	____／49	(____÷49)×100＝____	%
L5：	____／15	(____÷15)×100＝____	%

Reading Section

	正答数	正答数	正答率
R1：	____／19	(____÷19)×100＝____	%
R2：	____／19	(____÷19)×100＝____	%
R3：	____／35	(____÷35)×100＝____	%
R4：	____／25	(____÷25)×100＝____	%
R5：	____／19	(____÷19)×100＝____	%

3回目（勘を除く）　年　月　日

● 正答数

Part	正答数	
Part 1	／6	Listening 合計正答数
Part 2	／25	
Part 3	／39	
Part 4	／30	／100
Part 5	／30	Reading 合計正答数
Part 6	／16	
Part 7	／54	／100

● 換算スコアB

Listening ______

Reading ______

合　計 ______

● 問題タイプ別正答数と正答率

Listening Section

	正答数	正答数	正答率
L1：	____／16	(____÷16)×100＝____	%
L2：	____／20	(____÷20)×100＝____	%
L3：	____／15	(____÷15)×100＝____	%
L4：	____／49	(____÷49)×100＝____	%
L5：	____／15	(____÷15)×100＝____	%

Reading Section

	正答数	正答数	正答率
R1：	____／19	(____÷19)×100＝____	%
R2：	____／19	(____÷19)×100＝____	%
R3：	____／35	(____÷35)×100＝____	%
R4：	____／25	(____÷25)×100＝____	%
R5：	____／19	(____÷19)×100＝____	%

弱点問題タイプ診断

Listening Section

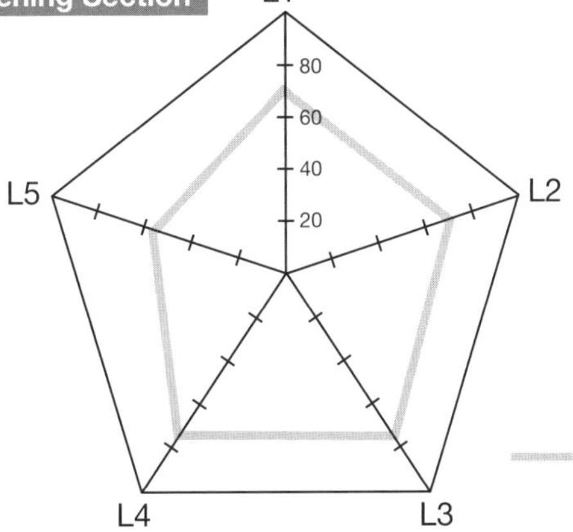
L1
80
60
40
20
L2
L3
L4
L5

Reading Section

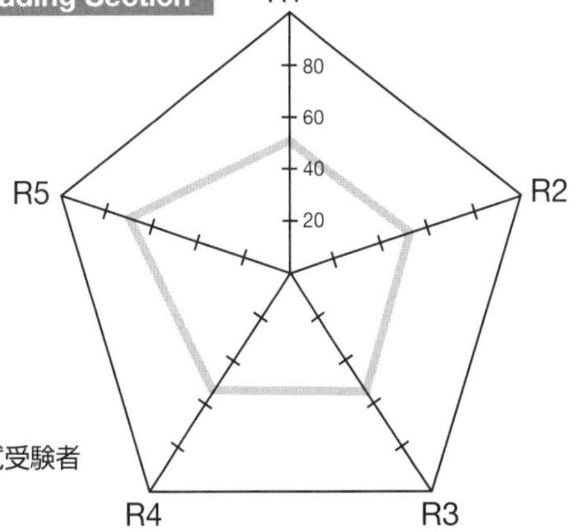
R1
80
60
40
20
R2
R3
R4
R5

モニタリング模試受験者平均正答率

参考資料：モニタリング模試実施データ

p.263に掲載された「スコア換算表」を作成するために、TOEIC L&Rテストの公式スコア保持者396名を対象に、Test 3と同じ問題を使用した模擬試験を実施しました。以下はその結果をまとめたものです。

	公式スコア平均	正答数平均	最低正答数	最高正答数	初級者レベル正答数	上級者レベル正答数
Listening	364.4	72.8	39	98	63問以下	83問以上
Reading	296.9	56.2	22	91	47問以下	67問以上

※表中の数字はモニタリング模試受験者396名のうち正常に受験したと認められたモニターの数値を基に算出しています。

※モニタリング模試受験者のうち、Listening Section、Reading Sectionそれぞれにおいて、正答数が少なかった25%を「初級者レベル」、多かった25%を「上級者レベル」と呼んでいます。

Test 3 解答＆問題タイプ一覧

答え合わせの手順

1. 正解を確認し、一覧表に正誤を記入する
自分の解答済のマークシートと解答一覧を突き合わせ、解答一覧内に正誤（○×）を記入しましょう。①～③は3回チャレンジ法プラス（p.12～参照）の1回目～3回目を表します。勘ボックスを利用した場合、勘ボックスの✔も転記します。

2. 間違えた問題の問題タイプ欄にチェックを入れる
間違えた問題もしくは正答したが勘ボックスに✔がある問題の「問題タイプ」欄に✔を記入します。

3. パートごとの正答数・問題タイプごとの正答数を数え、「成長記録シート」に記入する
パートごとの正答数（正誤欄の○の数）と勘を除く正答数（○の数—✔の付いた数）を数え、その数をp.258～の「成長記録シート」に記入しましょう。

4. 予想スコアと弱点問題タイプを算出する
p.263のスコア換算表を参照して実際のTOEIC L&Rテストでの予想スコアを算出し、「成長記録シート」に記入しましょう。また、問題タイプごとに誤答数（「問題タイプ」欄の✔の数）を転記し、正答率を算出して弱点問題タイプ／パートを把握しましょう。

Listening Section

問題番号	正解	問題タイプ	問題番号	正解	問題タイプ
Part 1			51	B	L4
1	D	L1	52	C	L4
2	B	L1	53	D	L4
3	C	L3	54	A	L2、L5
4	C	L1	55	D	L4
5	D	L3	56	A	L2
6	A	L3	57	A	L4
Part 2			58	D	L4
7	B	L1、L5	59	C	L2
8	B	L3	60	B	L4
9	C	L3	61	C	L4
10	A	L3	62	C	L2
11	A	L3	63	A	L4
12	B	L3	64	D	L4
13	C	L3	65	B	L4
14	B	L1	66	B	L4
15	B	L1、L5	67	A	L4
16	C	L1	68	A	L2
17	A	L3	69	C	L4
18	B	L1、L5	70	C	L4
19	A	L1、L5	**Part 4**		
20	B	L1	71	C	L4
21	B	L1、L5	72	B	L4
22	C	L3	73	D	L4
23	A	L3	74	D	L2
24	A	L1、L5	75	B	L4
25	B	L3	76	D	L4
26	C	L1、L5	77	D	L4
27	C	L3	78	B	L4
28	A	L3	79	A	L2、L5
29	C	L1、L5	80	A	L2
30	C	L1、L5	81	D	L4
31	A	L1、L5	82	C	L4
Part 3			83	C	L2
32	A	L2	84	A	L2、L5
33	B	L4	85	D	L4
34	C	L4	86	B	L2
35	A	L2	87	A	L4
36	C	L2、L5	88	D	L4
37	D	L4	89	A	L4
38	B	L2	90	C	L2、L5
39	D	L4	91	C	L4
40	B	L4	92	B	L2
41	A	L2	93	A	L4
42	B	L4	94	D	L4
43	C	L4	95	C	L4
44	B	L4	96	A	L4
45	D	L4	97	A	L4
46	D	L4	98	A	L4
47	D	L2	99	D	L4
48	C	L4	100	B	L4
49	A	L4			
50	A	L2			

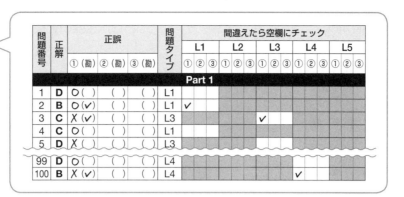

記入例

問題番号	正解	正誤 ①(勘)	正誤 ②(勘)	正誤 ③(勘)	問題タイプ	間違えたら空欄にチェック L1	L2	L3	L4	L5
Part 1										
1	D	○( )	( )	( )	L1					
2	B	○(✓)	( )	( )	L1	✓				
3	C	✗(✓)	( )	( )	L3			✓		
4	C	○( )	( )	( )	L1					
5	D	✗( )	( )	( )	L3					
99	D	○( )	( )	( )	L4					
100	B	✗(✓)	( )	( )	L4				✓	

Reading Section

問題番号	正解	正誤 ①(勘)	②(勘)	③(勘)	問題タイプ	問題番号	正解	正誤 ①(勘)	②(勘)	③(勘)	問題タイプ
Part 5						151	A	( )	( )	( )	R2
101	D	( )	( )	( )	R5	152	B	( )	( )	( )	R3
102	D	( )	( )	( )	R5	153	C	( )	( )	( )	R2
103	D	( )	( )	( )	R4	154	B	( )	( )	( )	R4
104	B	( )	( )	( )	R4	155	A	( )	( )	( )	R2
105	C	( )	( )	( )	R5	156	B	( )	( )	( )	R2
106	B	( )	( )	( )	R4	157	D	( )	( )	( )	R2
107	D	( )	( )	( )	R4	158	B	( )	( )	( )	R1
108	A	( )	( )	( )	R4	159	C	( )	( )	( )	R2
109	C	( )	( )	( )	R5	160	D	( )	( )	( )	R1
110	A	( )	( )	( )	R4	161	A	( )	( )	( )	R1
111	A	( )	( )	( )	R5	162	D	( )	( )	( )	R2
112	A	( )	( )	( )	R5	163	A	( )	( )	( )	R1
113	B	( )	( )	( )	R5	164	A	( )	( )	( )	R2
114	B	( )	( )	( )	R4	165	D	( )	( )	( )	R1、R3
115	C	( )	( )	( )	R5	166	C	( )	( )	( )	R1
116	D	( )	( )	( )	R4	167	B	( )	( )	( )	R3
117	A	( )	( )	( )	R5	168	A	( )	( )	( )	R1
118	C	( )	( )	( )	R4	169	D	( )	( )	( )	R2
119	D	( )	( )	( )	R4	170	B	( )	( )	( )	R1
120	B	( )	( )	( )	R4	171	C	( )	( )	( )	R1、R3
121	C	( )	( )	( )	R5	172	D	( )	( )	( )	R1
122	B	( )	( )	( )	R4	173	B	( )	( )	( )	R3
123	A	( )	( )	( )	R5	174	C	( )	( )	( )	R1、R3
124	B	( )	( )	( )	R4	175	C	( )	( )	( )	R3
125	C	( )	( )	( )	R5	176	A	( )	( )	( )	R1
126	C	( )	( )	( )	R5	177	D	( )	( )	( )	R3
127	A	( )	( )	( )	R4	178	D	( )	( )	( )	R2
128	B	( )	( )	( )	R4	179	C	( )	( )	( )	R3
129	A	( )	( )	( )	R5	180	C	( )	( )	( )	R2
130	D	( )	( )	( )	R4	181	B	( )	( )	( )	R1
Part 6						182	D	( )	( )	( )	R2
131	D	( )	( )	( )	R3、R4	183	A	( )	( )	( )	R3
132	A	( )	( )	( )	R3	184	A	( )	( )	( )	R1、R3
133	B	( )	( )	( )	R5	185	B	( )	( )	( )	R2
134	C	( )	( )	( )	R3、R4	186	D	( )	( )	( )	R2
135	B	( )	( )	( )	R3	187	D	( )	( )	( )	R3
136	A	( )	( )	( )	R3、R4	188	C	( )	( )	( )	R3
137	C	( )	( )	( )	R3、R4	189	C	( )	( )	( )	R3
138	D	( )	( )	( )	R3、R5	190	D	( )	( )	( )	R3
139	A	( )	( )	( )	R3、R4	191	C	( )	( )	( )	R1
140	D	( )	( )	( )	R4	192	B	( )	( )	( )	R2
141	C	( )	( )	( )	R3、R5	193	C	( )	( )	( )	R4
142	B	( )	( )	( )	R3	194	D	( )	( )	( )	R3
143	C	( )	( )	( )	R3、R4	195	A	( )	( )	( )	R1、R3
144	A	( )	( )	( )	R3、R5	196	B	( )	( )	( )	R2
145	D	( )	( )	( )	R3	197	C	( )	( )	( )	R2
146	B	( )	( )	( )	R5	198	B	( )	( )	( )	R1、R3
Part 7						199	A	( )	( )	( )	R2
147	A	( )	( )	( )	R2	200	A	( )	( )	( )	R1、R3
148	D	( )	( )	( )	R3						
149	B	( )	( )	( )	R3						
150	C	( )	( )	( )	R1、R3						

Test 3 マークシート状解答一覧

LISTENING SECTION

Part 1 / Part 2 / Part 3 / Part 4

READING SECTION

Part 5 / Part 6 / Part 7

Answer sheet (No. 1–200), columns A B C D

Test 3 スコア換算表

協力：アルク教育総合研究所

Listening Section

正答数	換算スコア	正答数	換算スコア
0	5	51	250
1	5	52	255
2	5	53	255
3	10	54	260
4	15	55	265
5	25	56	270
6	30	57	275
7	35	58	280
8	40	59	285
9	50	60	295
10	55	61	300
11	60	62	305
12	60	63	305
13	65	64	310
14	70	65	315
15	80	66	320
16	85	67	330
17	90	68	335
18	90	69	340
19	95	70	350
20	100	71	355
21	110	72	360
22	115	73	365
23	120	74	375
24	125	75	380
25	125	76	390
26	130	77	395
27	135	78	400
28	140	79	405
29	140	80	415
30	145	81	420
31	150	82	425
32	150	83	435
33	155	84	440
34	165	85	445
35	170	86	450
36	175	87	455
37	180	88	460
38	185	89	465
39	190	90	470
40	195	91	470
41	200	92	475
42	200	93	475
43	205	94	480
44	210	95	485
45	215	96	490
46	220	97	495
47	230	98	495
48	235	99	495
49	240	100	495
50	245		

Reading Section

正答数	換算スコア	正答数	換算スコア
0	5	51	280
1	5	52	280
2	5	53	285
3	5	54	290
4	5	55	295
5	5	56	300
6	5	57	310
7	5	58	315
8	10	59	325
9	20	60	330
10	25	61	340
11	30	62	345
12	40	63	350
13	45	64	355
14	55	65	360
15	60	66	365
16	70	67	370
17	75	68	370
18	80	69	375
19	90	70	380
20	95	71	380
21	105	72	385
22	110	73	395
23	120	74	405
24	125	75	410
25	130	76	415
26	140	77	420
27	145	78	430
28	155	79	435
29	160	80	440
30	170	81	440
31	175	82	445
32	180	83	450
33	190	84	455
34	195	85	460
35	205	86	465
36	210	87	470
37	215	88	470
38	225	89	475
39	230	90	480
40	240	91	485
41	245	92	485
42	245	93	490
43	250	94	495
44	255	95	495
45	260	96	495
46	265	97	495
47	265	98	495
48	270	99	495
49	275	100	495
50	275		

結果活用アドバイス

本書に登場するマイ、ヤス、ダイ、サキの4人の「換算スコア」を例に「弱点問題タイプ診断」の活用法をご紹介します。自分に最も近い人物の診断を参考に、今後の学習に役立ててください。

Listening Section

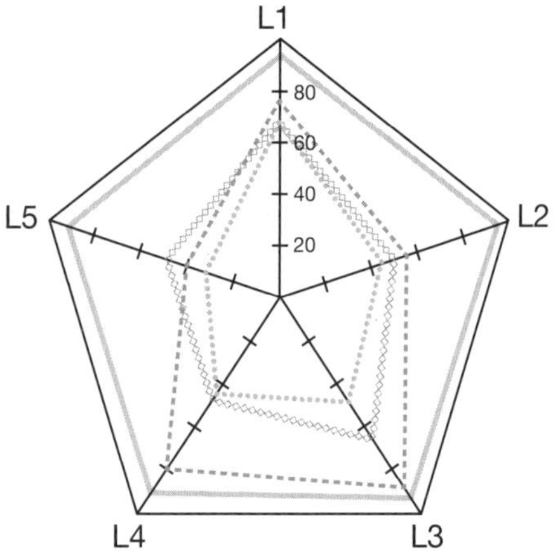

Reading Section

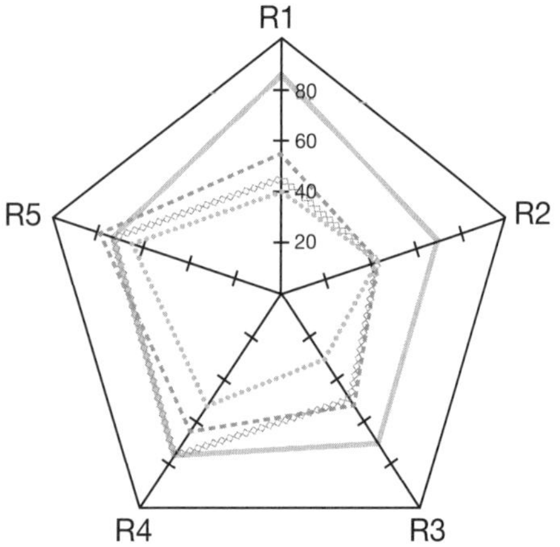

換算スコア

	Listening	Reading	合計
マイ	475	415	890
ヤス	380	315	695
ダイ	255	325	580
サキ	245	270	515

マイ、リスニングが475点だね。すごいじゃないか。

Part 3と4が簡単に感じました。本当にミスを5問まで減らすことができてうれしいです。音読練習を続けて良かったです。

練習しなかったPart 2も解きやすくなったよね。

はい。全問正解は難しいですが、楽になりました。

リーディングでは何が起きたの?

Part 7を先に解くのをやめて、通常通り最後にしました。

どうして? Test 2ではうまくいったのに。

結局、どんな順番で解いても時間が余るくらいの英語力を身につけることが一番大事だと思うんです。ですから、解く順番は気にしないことに決めました。これが私の「マイベスト」です。

マイのマイベストか。ジョークみたいだけど、本当にそれは大事な考え方だよ。いろんな学習法や攻略法に流されずに、自分に合うものを見つけて実践すること。そして、続けること。みんな忘れないでね。じゃ、次はヤス。

Part 5で25問も正解しました。

自分で自分に解説した?

はい。やって初めてその価値が分かりました。ぼんやり知っているだけだと、うまく解説できないです。自分が納得できるよう解説するには、しっかりした理解が必要だと分かりました。

換算点は695点だったよね。730点の達成は近いよ。では、次。ダイ、どうだった?

リーディングが大きく伸びました。Part 5の読み込みのおかげでしょうか。

そう。R4とR5が伸びているから、語彙と文法の力が上がったんだよ。Part 7はまだ厳しかっただろうけど。

はい、後半は相変わらず塗り絵でした。

それは仕方ない。ダイは近いうちに470点どころか600点もクリアできるよ。最後はサキ。どうだった?

下がりました。大学の試験があったので、あまり勉強できなかったんです。

そっか。ま、それは仕方ない。R3の低さを見ると、サキはPart 6でスコアを稼ぐのは難しいと思う。当面はPart 5と7を優先すればいい。仮にPart 6がボロボロでも、Part 5と7に時間を投入すれば、合計で600点のレベルには到達できるから。

分かりました。

一応、確認しておく。Test 4は、Test 1からTest 3までのコンテンツを「モノにした度」を測定するテストだから、徹底的に3つのテストを復習しておいてね。なるべく、解説ではなく英語の部分を繰り返し読んだり聞いたりしてほしい。脳ミソを英語漬けにする時間を毎日確保してね。

解説を確認し、間違えた問題は二度と間違えないようにきっちり復習しましょう。

Part 1 写真描写問題

1. DL↓130 🇬🇧 正解：**D** 易■■□□□□□難　選択率：(A) 6.3%　(B) 0.0%　(C) 0.0%　**(D) 93.7%**

(A) A woman is putting on a jacket.
(B) A woman is kneeling on a footpath.
(C) A woman is opening a window.
(D) A woman is vacuuming the floor.

☐ kneel: 動 膝をつく
☐ footpath: 名 小道、歩道
☐ vacuum: 動 ～に掃除機をかける

(A) 女性が上着を着ています。
(B) 女性が小道に膝をついています。
(C) 女性が窓を開けています。
(D) 女性が床に掃除機をかけています。

▶解説 女性が掃除機で床を掃除している様子を vacuuming the floor と表した (D) が正解です。女性はすでにジャケットを身に着けた状態なので、(A) は A woman is wearing a jacket. であれば適切ですが、身に着ける動作を表す putting on は不適切です。(B) と (C) も、動作の描写が適切ではありません。

2. DL↓131 🇦🇺 正解：**B** 易■■□□□□□難　選択率：(A) 0.4%　**(B) 91.1%**　(C) 3.0%　(D) 4.5%

(A) He's jogging through a park.
(B) He's taking tools out of a cart.
(C) He's riding a motor vehicle.
(D) He's raking up leaves into a pile.

☐ jog: 動 ジョギングする
☐ take ～ out of ...: …から～を取り出す
☐ tool: 名 道具
☐ cart: 名 カート、荷車
☐ motor vehicle: 自動車
☐ rake up ～: ～を書き集める
☐ pile: 名 積み重ねた山

(A) 彼は公園を通ってジョギングしています。
(B) 彼はカートから道具を取り出しています。
(C) 彼は自動車に乗っています。
(D) 彼は葉をかき集めて山にしています。

▶解説 男性が道具をカートから取り出している様子を taking tools out of a cart と表現した (B) が正解です。カートを抽象的に vehicle（乗り物）と表現することも可能ですが、男性は乗っていないため (C) の描写は不適切です。また、写真は公園のように見えますが、男性はジョギングをしているところでも、落ち葉をかき集めているところでもありません。

📻 ゼミ 生 中継

😎Hiro 🙂Mai 😮Yasu 😆Dai 😊Saki

1. ....

😎 さぁ、いよいよ最後の Test 3 だね。サキ、(D) を選べた？

😊 はい。ただ、彼女が立っている場所を floor と呼べるかどうか自信ありませんでした。この人、ベランダにいますよね。

😮 ベランダの床は floor だよ。ところで、(B) の kneeling は「膝をついている」だけど、正解として出ることがあるから忘れないで。

2. ....

😮 カートから道具を取り出しているのではなく、道具を乗せようとしてい

るのかもしれないと思いました。

😎 Part 1 は動画じゃないから真実は不明だよ。間違っていると言えなければ正解になる。言い換えると、不正解の選択肢には、確実にダメな理由がある。

😊 確かにそうですね。

😎 それより、動詞の rake を知ってた？ (D) では「かき集める」という動詞だけど、名詞で登場することもある Part 1 らしい単語だよ。

😆 画像検索しました。これは熊手ですね。

Part 1 写真描写問題

3. DL 133 🇬🇧 正解：**C** 易 ■■□□□□□ 難 選択率：(A) 0.4% (B) 1.1% **(C) 97.4%** (D) 1.1%

(A) A woman is pointing at a showcase.
(B) A woman is taking a bottle from a shelf.
(C) Some vegetables are on display in a store.
(D) Some baskets are being arranged in rows.

- [ ] point at ～: ～を指さす
- [ ] showcase: 名（ガラス張りの）陳列箱
- [ ] take ～ from ...: …から～を取る
- [ ] bottle: 名 瓶
- [ ] shelf: 名 棚
- [ ] on display: 陳列されて
- [ ] arrange: 動 ～を配置する
- [ ] in rows: 列を成して

(A) 女性が陳列箱を指さしています。
(B) 女性が棚から瓶を取っています。
(C) いくつかの野菜が店に陳列されています。
(D) いくつかのかごが列に並べられています。

▶解説 人物が大きく写っていない写真では、人物の動作とともに周りの様子に注目しましょう。正解は、野菜が並べられた状態を描写した(C)です。女性は、指を差す動作や、ボトルを棚から取り出す動作を行っていません。また、basket（かご）は列に並んでいますが、並べられている最中ではないため(D)は being が余計です。

---

4. DL 134 🇨🇦 正解：**C** 易 ■■■□□□□ 難 選択率：(A) 3.3% (B) 2.2% **(C) 86.6%** (D) 7.8%

(A) One of the men is inspecting a car.
(B) One of the men is greeting the audience.
(C) A band has gathered in the plaza.
(D) Some instruments are being carried away.

- [ ] inspect: 動 ～を点検する
- [ ] greet: 動 ～にあいさつする、～を出迎える
- [ ] gather: 動 集まる
- [ ] plaza: 名 広場
- [ ] instrument: 名 楽器
- [ ] carry away ～: ～を持ち去る

(A) 男性の1人が車を点検しています。
(B) 男性の1人が聴衆にあいさつしています。
(C) バンドが広場に集まっています。
(D) いくつかの楽器が持ち去られています。

▶解説 屋外で楽器を演奏している3人を「バンドが広場に集まっている」と描写した(C)が正解です。正解の選択肢の主語であるbandやmusicianといった楽器を演奏している人たちはPart 1に頻出します。車を点検している人や聴衆はいないため、(A)と(B)は不正解です。また、楽器は運ばれているところではないため、(D)の描写も不適切です。

((•)) 📻 ゼミ 生 中継   😊Hiro 😊Mai 😊Yasu 😎Dai 😊Saki

3. ....

😊 何かが1列になっていれば in a row と言えるけど、複数だと in rows と言える。

4. ....

😊 Test 2で、Part 1頻出の「日よけ3兄弟」を紹介したけれど、ここで別の3兄弟を紹介する。

😊 この3人が兄弟ですね。分かります。

😊 顔が似ているので、あり寄りのありですね。

😊 違う！ 彼らがいる場所に注目して。マイは分かる?

😊 あ、plaza ですね。

😊 そう。「広場3兄弟」だよ。スマホで画像検索して。まず、この plaza と patio を調べて。何が違う?

😊 plaza に比べると patio は「中庭」っぽいです。

😊 そう。その patio とほぼ同じなのが courtyard だよ。調べてみて。

😊 ほぼ同じですね。

😊 後で Part 7にも登場するよ。

5. ^{DL} 135 🇦🇺 正解：**D**　易 ■■□□□ 難　選択率：(A) 15.6%　(B) 4.8%　(C) 1.9%　**(D) 77.7%**

(A) Plants are being put into pots.
(B) Desk drawers have been pulled open.
(C) A chair is being pushed against a wall.
(D) Monitors have been set up side by side.

☐ plant: 图 植物
☐ put ～ into ...: ～を…に入れ込む
☐ pot: 图 鉢
☐ drawer: 图 引き出し
☐ pull ～ open: ～を手前に引いて開ける
☐ push ～ against ...: ～を…に押し付ける
☐ wall: 图 壁
☐ set up ～: ～を配置する
☐ side by side: 並んで

(A) 植物が鉢に植えられています。
(B) 机の引き出しが開けられています。
(C) 椅子が壁に押し付けられています。
(D) モニターが並んで配置されています。

▶解説 女性と女性がいる環境に注目しましょう。デスクの上にモニターが2台並べて設置されています。その様子を描写した(D)の「モニターが並んで配置されている」が正解です。plant（植物）やdesk drawer（デスクの引き出し）、chair（椅子）も写っていますが、選択肢にある動詞が表現している様子が写真と異なります。

6. ^{DL} 136 🇺🇸 正解：**A**　易 ■■□□□ 難　選択率：**(A) 78.8%**　(B) 1.5%　(C) 10.8%　(D) 8.9%

(A) Some bushes have been planted along a walkway.
(B) Pedestrians are crossing a road.
(C) A car has stopped at an intersection.
(D) Houses are crowded on a hillside.

☐ bush: 图 低木の茂み
☐ plant: 動 ～を植える
☐ walkway: 图 通路
☐ pedestrian: 图 歩行者
☐ cross: 動 ～を渡る、横断する
☐ intersection: 图 交差点
☐ crowd: 動 ～をぎっしり詰め込む
☐ hillside: 图 丘の斜面

(A) 低木の茂みがいくつか通路に沿って植えられています。
(B) 歩行者が道路を渡っています。
(C) 車が交差点に止まったところです。
(D) 家々がぎっしりと丘の斜面に建っています。

▶解説 歩道に沿って植えられたbushes（低木の茂み）を描写した(A)が正解です。(B)のpedestrians（歩行者）や、(C)のintersection（交差点）は写真に存在しません。また、写真にある家々はhillside（丘の斜面）に建てられていないため(D)の表現も不適切です。

((📡)) ゼミ生中継　😀Hiro 😊Mai 😄Yasu 😳Dai 😊Saki

5.
😀 人が目立っていても、周辺の物を描写する選択肢が正解になることもあるよ。

6.
😄 5番と違い、写真にないものが選択肢に登場しているから消去法を使いやすい。ダイは(A)を選べた？

😳 はい。ただ、bushesを知りません。
😄 複数形のまま画像検索して。単数形だと……
😊 あっ!
😄 そう、あの大統領が出てくる。

TOEICよろず相談所　ヒロの部屋

⑬イギリス英語に慣れるには？

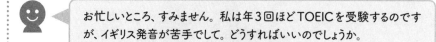

お忙しいところ、すみません。私は年3回ほどTOEICを受験するのですが、イギリス発音が苦手でして。どうすればいいのでしょうか。

目的次第です。どうして英語を学んでいるのですか。

うちの会社ではTOEIC受験が必須なので、私も受けています。ただ、提携会社がイギリスにあるので、出張や駐在も多いです。できれば、私もイギリスに駐在してみたいなと思っています。

コミュニケーションの手段として英語を学んでいるのですね。

そうです。

であれば、TOEICの音声は忘れてOKです。あれはプロのナレーターがスタジオで録音した音声なので、現実世界で聞こえる音声とは違います。

言われてみれば、そうですね。

イギリス英語であれ、アメリカ英語であれ、発音のバリエーションは数え切れません。現実世界のコミュニケーションを前提とするなら、**現実に生きている人たちが使う発音をすべて受け入れる姿勢が大切**です。それに、本当にイギリスで働く場合、話す相手はイギリス人とは限らないですよね。

はい。スペイン、ドイツ、ベルギーなどにも取引先があります。

であれば、なおさらです。**ネイティブスピーカーより、英語を使うノンネイティブスピーカーの方が何倍も多いのが現実**なので、発音にもそれだけバラエティーがあります。

いろんな発音に接する方法は、やはりインターネットですか。

YouTubeでもOKですし、映画やドラマの見放題サービスもいいと思います。えり好みせず、幅広くいろんな英語を吸収していってください。

Part 2 応答問題

---

7. DL 139 🇦🇺 🇬🇧　正解：**B**　易 ■■■■□□□ 難　選択率：(A) 26.0% **(B) 58.4%** (C) 15.6%

When will the coffee shop reopen?
(A) I don't have time today.
(B) The renovations have just begun.
(C) How about meeting at a coffee shop?

□ reopen: 動（店が）再び開く　□ renovation: 名 改築

コーヒーショップはいつ再開しますか。
(A) 今日は時間がありません。
(B) 改築は始まったばかりです。
(C) コーヒーショップで会うのはどうですか。

▶解説 When ～?でコーヒーショップの再開「時期」が問われています。それに対し、「改築は始まったばかり」と答えることで、営業はすぐには再開されないことを間接的に伝えている (B) が自然な応答です。

---

8. DL 140 🇨🇦 🇦🇺　正解：**B**　易 ■■□□□□□ 難　選択率：(A) 0.7% **(B) 98.9%** (C) 0.4%

How much did it cost to repair this window?
(A) As much as I can.
(B) Two hundred dollars.
(C) I guess so.

□ cost: 動 ～（の金額）がかかる
□ repair: 動 ～を修理する　□ guess: 動 ～だと思う

この窓を修理するのにいくらかかりましたか。
(A) できるだけたくさん。
(B) 200ドルです。
(C) そうだと思います。

▶解説 How much ～?で「金額」が問われているので、「200ドル」と答えた (B) が正解です。(A) には質問文にも登場する much がありますが、Part 2ではこのように同じ音、もしくは似た音を用いたワナが多用されるので注意しましょう。

---

9. DL 141 🇬🇧 🇺🇸　正解：**C**　易 ■■■■□□□ 難　選択率：(A) 17.8% (B) 22.3% **(C) 59.9%**

The posters will be delivered next week, right?
(A) They're weaker now.
(B) It's already closed.
(C) No, they're still being designed.

□ deliver: 動 ～を配達する　□ weak: 形 弱い
□ already: 副 すでに　□ closed: 形 閉まった
□ still: 副 まだ、今なお　□ design: 動 ～をデザインする

ポスターは来週配達されるんですよね?
(A) それらは今ではもっと弱いです。
(B) すでに閉まっています。
(C) いいえ、まだデザインされているところです。

▶解説 男性は「ポスターは来週配達されるよね」と述べ、同意を求めています。Noと否定し、「まだデザインの段階」と伝えることで、配達されない理由を説明している (C) が正解です。(A) は質問文のweekと似た音のweakerを用いた引っ掛けです。

---

10. DL 142 🇦🇺 🇬🇧　正解：**A**　易 ■■□□□□□ 難　選択率：**(A) 92.6%** (B) 2.6% (C) 4.8%

Which train should we catch when we go to Boston tomorrow?
(A) The 9:15 train would be the best.
(B) No, it didn't take three hours.
(C) With my supervisor.

□ catch: 動（列車などに）遅れないで乗る
□ supervisor: 名 監督者、上司

明日Bostonへ行くとき、どの電車に乗ればいいですか。
(A) 9時15分の電車が一番いいでしょう。
(B) いいえ、3時間はかかりませんでした。
(C) 私の上司とです。

▶解説 どの電車に乗るべきかが問われています。それに対し、「9時15分の電車」と答えている (A) が正解です。WH疑問文にYes/Noで答えることはできないので、(B) は不可です。(C) も「誰と」を答えているので、不正解です。

📡 ゼミ生中継　😀 Hiro 😊 Mai 😺 Yasu 🤖 Dai 😸 Saki

7.

😀 モニターの上級グループでは正答率91%だけど、中級グループでは50%近くに下がる。(A)のI don't have time today. が魅力的だった?

😊 最初の問題だから簡単だと思っていたら、Whenに答える応答がなくて焦りました。

😺 (A)のtimeが「いつ?」に関係しそうだから選んだのね。

😊 そう、それだけです。

😺 最初だからってなめちゃいけないよ。

9.

😀 Yes/No疑問文だから、Noで答えている (C) は選びやすいかな。サキはどれを選んだ?

😸 (B)です。「来週でしょ?」に対して、It's already ～は何となく流れが良くて選びました。「来週でしょ?」「もう到着したよ」みたいな。

😀 それは分かるけど、(B)は「もう閉まっている」だから会話が成立しないよ。「何となく流れがいい」をヒントにしちゃいけない。問題作成者はその心理を利用して不正解を作るから。

Part 2 応答問題

11. DL ▾ 143 🇦🇺 🇨🇦 正解：**A** 易 ▰▰▰▱▱▱ 難 選択率：(A) 62.8% (B) 1.9% (C) 35.3%

Do you have time to help me clean the
conference room this afternoon?
(A) I'll be free after two o'clock.
(B) A spacious room.
(C) I can't help it.

□ conference room: 会議室　□ free: 形 自由な
□ spacious: 形 広々とした　□ I can't help it.: 仕方がない。

今日の午後、会議室を掃除するの
を手伝ってもらう時間はあります
か。
(A) 2時以降は時間がありますよ。
(B) 広々とした部屋です。
(C) 仕方がないんです。

▶解説 「手伝う時間があるかどうか」と
Yes/No 疑問文で問うているのに対し、「2
時以降は時間がある」と応じている (A) が正
解です。Yes, I'll be free after two o'clock.
の Yes が省略された形です。

---

12. DL ▾ 144 🇦🇺 🇬🇧 正解：**B** 易 ▰▰▰▱▱▱ 難 選択率：(A) 18.2% **(B) 77.3%** (C) 4.5%

Where have all the plants gone?
(A) I've been transferred.
(B) We put them outside.
(C) In the afternoon.

□ transfer: 動 ～を異動させる　□ outside: 副 屋外へ

植物はみんなどこへ行ったんです
か。
(A) 私は異動になったんです。
(B) それらは屋外へ置きました。
(C) 午後にです。

▶解説 Where ～? で「場所」が問われてい
ます。plants（植物）の在りかを問われ、「屋
外に置いた」と答えた (B) が正解です。(A) の
「私が異動になった」や (C) の「午後に」で
は、植物の在りかを尋ねた質問への応答には
ならないため不正解です。

---

13. DL ▾ 145 🇨🇦 🇨🇦 正解：**C** 易 ▰▰▰▱▱▱ 難 選択率：(A) 13.4% (B) 2.6% **(C) 84.0%**

When was the company cafeteria repainted?
(A) Whenever you like.
(B) On the shelf.
(C) Just last week.

□ cafeteria: 名 カフェテリア、食堂
□ repaint: 動 ～を塗り直す
□ whenever: 接 ～する時にはいつでも

会社のカフェテリアはいつ塗り直
されたんですか。
(A) いつでもお好きなときに。
(B) 棚の上です。
(C) ちょうど先週です。

▶解説 When ～? で「時」を問うていま
す。カフェテリアがいつ塗り直されたかを
尋ねられて、「ちょうど先週」と答えている
(C) が正解です。

📡))) ゼミ 生 中継

😀 Hiro　😀 Mai　😀 Yasu　😎 Dai　😀 Saki

11.

😀 上級グループでは6%しか (C) を選んでいないのに、中級グループ
は約40%が選んでいる。Do you have time to help me ～に対し
て I can't help it. と応じると、me を it に置き換えることになる。

😣 かなり無礼ですね。

😀 通常、I can't help it. は「避けられない」とか「どうしようもない」とい
う意味だから、会話が成立しないよ。

12.

😀 (A) を「私が動かした」と勘違いした人いる?

😀 はい。そう思って選びました。

😀 (A) は異動のことだよ。人事異動。

😀 ジンジイドウ……?

😀 サキは知らないか。ダイ、教えてあげて。

😎 人事異動は、所属する部門が変わることです。国内営業部から海
外営業部に行くとか。

😀 分かりました。(A) は全然ダメですね。

13.

😀 例えば、「いつ塗り替える?」と希望を尋ねられたら、「いつでもいい」
の意味で (A) を言うことはできる。でも、この質問は過去の事実につ
いてだから「いつでもいい」は無理。

14. DL 146 正解：**B**　易 ▬▬▬ 難　選択率：(A) 5.2%　**(B) 91.8%**　(C) 3.0%

How far is it to the nearest supermarket?
(A) That's so convenient.
(B) Let me check the map.
(C) Yes, it opened last week.

□ far: 形 遠い　□ near: 形 近い
□ convenient: 形 便利な

一番近いスーパーマーケットまでどれくらい遠いですか。
(A) それはとても便利ですね。
(B) 地図を確認させてください。
(C) はい、先週開店しました。

▶解説 How far ～? で「距離」が問われているのに対し、(B)の「地図を確認する」が自然な応答です。質問の答えを知らない場合、「（何かの手段を使って）確認する」や「他の人に尋ねる」と述べるのは、Part 2にはよくある応答パターンです。

---

15. DL 147 正解：**B**　易 ▬▬▬ 難　選択率：(A) 10.8%　**(B) 81.0%**　(C) 8.2%

I don't like the color of the main lobby.
(A) I'll wear another shirt.
(B) We used a professional interior designer.
(C) Next to the entrance.

□ professional: 形 プロの、専門職の
□ interior designer: インテリア・デザイナー
□ next to ～: ～の隣に　□ entrance: 名 入り口

メインロビーの色が好きではありません。
(A) ほかのシャツを着ます。
(B) プロのインテリア・デザイナーを使いましたよ。
(C) 入り口の隣にです。

▶解説 「メインロビーの色が好きではない」という感想が述べられています。それに対し、「プロのインテリア・デザイナーを使った」と伝えることで、メインロビーがなぜその色になったのかを説明しようとしている(B)が自然な応答です。

---

16. DL 148 正解：**C**　易 ▬▬▬ 難　選択率：(A) 10.0%　(B) 36.8%　**(C) 53.2%**

Do you think the shipment will get here on time, or will it be late again?
(A) That's all we can do.
(B) I think you're probably right.
(C) Let's call the courier and find out.

□ shipment: 名 積み荷　□ on time: 時間通りに
□ late: 形 時間に遅れる　□ courier: 名 宅配便業者
□ find out: 確かめる

積み荷はここへ時間通りに着くと思いますか、それともまた遅れると思いますか。
(A) それが私たちにできるすべてです。
(B) あなたはおそらく正しいと思います。
(C) 宅配業者に電話をして確かめましょう。

▶解説 選択疑問文で「積み荷は時間通りに届くか、遅れるか」を尋ねています。「AかBか」と聞かれても、質問に答えられない場合に「他の人に確認する」と述べるのは、応答として自然です。ここでは「宅配業者に確認してみよう」と答えた(C)が正解です。

((∆)) ゼミ生中継　Hiro Mai Yasu Dai Saki

14.
😊 How far に限らず、ほぼ全てのWH疑問文には、このLet me ～で答えることができる。「XXで確認する」とか「XXさんに聞いてみる」とか、幅広く使える便利な表現だよ。

15.
😊 これは質問ではなく独り言だね。独り言への応答はいろいろあり得るから、消去法を使いにくい。でも、コツはある。(C)のような「前置詞＋名詞」が、独り言への正解になることはないと思っていい。言い換えると、主語と動詞を含む「文」が正解ってこと。

😮 あれ、どこかで聞いたことがあるなぁ。

😐 Test 1で聞きました。Whyに対しては、ほぼ確実に「文」が正解になるという話がありました。

😊 そう。「独り言とWhyには文が正解」と考えていいよ。

16.
😊 AかBかを問う選択疑問文だね。応答は、「どちらか1つを選ぶ」か「どちらも選ばない」になりがち。ここでは自分の意見を言わずに業者に聞こうと答えているから後者に該当する。サキは(C)を選べた？

😊 いいえ。courier が何のことか分からなくて、消去したはずの(B)を選びました。選びたくはなかったのですが……。

Part 2 応答問題

---

17. DL↓149 🇬🇧🇺🇸 　正解：**A**　易■■■■□□□□難　選択率：**(A) 67.7%**　(B) 6.7%　(C) 25.7%

Who's the man sitting in the waiting room?
(A) He's here to sell something.
(B) Not long.
(C) It's fine with me.

☐ waiting room: 待合室

待合室に座っている男性は誰ですか。
(A) 彼は何かを売りにここに来たんです。
(B) 長くはありません。
(C) 私は結構です。

▶解説 Who's (Who is) ～？で男性が「誰」なのかを問うています。「彼は何かを売りにここに来た」と男性の正体を説明した(A)が正解です。(B)の「長くはない」と、(C)の「私はそれでいい」は、どちらも「誰」への答えではありません。

---

18. DL↓150 🇨🇦🇺🇸 　正解：**B**　易■■■□□□□□難　選択率：(A) 26.8%　**(B) 62.1%**　(C) 10.8%

I'm afraid your watch is out of warranty.
(A) Yes, that's mine.
(B) I only bought it two months ago.
(C) Did you see the movie?

☐ I'm afraid ～: 残念ですが～　☐ out of ～: ～が切れて
☐ warranty: 名 保証

残念ですがお客さまの腕時計は保証が切れてしまっています。
(A) はい、それは私のものです。
(B) 2カ月前に買ったばかりですよ。
(C) 映画を見ましたか。

▶解説 I'm afraid ～（残念ながら）という表現を用いて、腕時計の保証が切れていることを伝えています。それに対し、「2カ月前に買ったばかりだ」と述べることで、「保証が切れているはずはない」ということを主張している(B)が自然な応答です。

---

19. DL↓151 🇨🇦🇦🇺 　正解：**A**　易■■■■■■□□難　選択率：**(A) 52.4%**　(B) 19.3%　(C) 28.3%

Why is the door to the gym locked?
(A) Mr. Moss has a key, doesn't he?
(B) Big enough for me.
(C) He's on his way, apparently.

☐ gym: 名 体育館　☐ lock: 動 ～に鍵を掛ける
☐ apparently: 副 どうやら

なぜ体育館へのドアに鍵が掛かっているんですか。
(A) Mossさんが鍵を持っていますよね？
(B) 私にとっては十分に大きいです。
(C) 彼はどうやら向かっているところです。

▶解説 ここでは「なぜドアに鍵が掛かっているのか」と述べることで、間接的に「ドアを開けたい」と伝えています。その意図をくみ取り、「Mossさんが鍵を持っているよね？」と返答し、ドアを開けるために必要な鍵の入手方法を伝えた(A)が自然な応答です。

(((📡))) ゼミ🅖中継　　😆Hiro 😊Mai 😎Yasu 🎲Dai 😀Saki

18.

😆 出た。Test 2の42番を覚えているかな。Part 3の意図問題として I only bought it a week ago. が出題されていたよね。

😊 確か、「1週間前に買ったばかりだから、返金してもらえるはず」という意図でした。

😆 会話の中で自然に使われるやりとりを引っこ抜いたのがPart 2だって実感できるよね。Part 2を得意にしたければ、Part 2形式にこだわった練習だけじゃなく、幅広く人間同士のコミュニケーションに接することが効果的だよ。

19.

😆 日本語でも同じだけど、Whyで質問する時、理由を知りたがっているとは限らない。この質問の意図は何だと思う？

😎 ドアを開けたいのかな。

😆 そうだろうね、たぶん。サキはどう思った？

😀 私はジムが人の名前だと思って……。適当にマークしました。

😆 仕方ない。Part 2では(C)を聞いた後に正解が分からなければ「勝負あり」だよ。適当でいいから、すぐにマークするのはかなり大切なことだよ。

20. DL 152 🇨🇦 🇺🇸　正解：**B**　易 ▮▮▮▮▯▯▯▯▯ 難　選択率：(A) 12.3% **(B) 73.6%** (C) 14.1%

Isn't Bridgit supposed to be on vacation?
(A) It was available yesterday.
(B) She's just got back from a trip.
(C) You opposed my plan.

☐ supposed to～：～することになっている
☐ on vacation: 休暇を取って
☐ get back from ～：～から戻る
☐ oppose: 動 ～に反対する

Bridgit は休暇を取っているはず
ではありませんでしたか。
(A) 昨日、入手可能でした。
(B) 彼女はちょうど旅行から戻っ
てきたところです。
(C) あなたは私の計画に反対しま
した。

▶解説 否定疑問文で「Bridgitは休暇を取っ
ているのではないか」と問うています。それ
に対し、「彼女は旅行から戻ってきたばか
り」とBridgitの状況を説明している (B) が
自然な応答です。(A) は It が何を指すかが不
明なので不正解です。

---

21. DL 153 🇦🇺 🇬🇧　正解：**B**　易 ▮▮▮▮▮▯▯▯▯ 難　選択率：(A) 12.3% **(B) 64.7%** (C) 23.0%

Do you know who designed this stadium?
(A) The game starts in an hour.
(B) It's amazing, isn't it?
(C) Yes, I'll stay there.

☐ design: 動 ～を設計する
☐ stadium: 名 スタジアム、競技場　☐ game: 名 試合
☐ amazing: 形 素晴らしい　☐ stay: 動 滞在する

このスタジアムを設計したのは誰
か知っていますか。
(A) 試合は1時間で始まります。
(B) 素晴らしいですよね。
(C) はい、そこに滞在します。

▶解説 質問者は設計した人物を尋ねること
で、「誰がこんなに素晴らしいスタジアムを
設計したのだろう」と感心する気持ちを表し
ています。その意図をくみ取り、「素晴らし
いよね」と答えることで女性の気持ちに同意
した (B) が正解です。

---

22. DL 154 🇬🇧 🇺🇸　正解：**C**　易 ▮▮▮▮▮▯▯▯▯ 難　選択率：(A) 17.5% (B) 25.7% **(C) 56.9%**

What's Larry been doing since he left us?
(A) You've done a great job.
(B) That's all right.
(C) He works at a library now.

☐ since: 接 ～して以来
☐ leave: 動 ～を去る　＊left は過去形
☐ great: 形 素晴らしい、すごい　☐ library: 名 図書館

Larry は私たちの元を去って以来
何をしているんですか。
(A) あなたは素晴らしい仕事をし
ました。
(B) それで大丈夫です。
(C) 彼は今、図書館で働いていま
す。

▶解説 「Larry は (会社等を) 去った後、何
をしているのか」という質問に対し、「今は
図書館で働いている」と答えた (C) が正解で
す。(A) は相手の成果をたたえる時の、(B) は
「大丈夫ですよ」と相手を許す時の表現で
す。

(((•))) ゼミ 生 中継　😀 Hiro 😀 Mai 😀 Yasu 😎 Dai 😀 Saki

21.

😀 質問が Do you ～? で、(C) だけが Yes で始まっている。それに、
stadium と stay の発音が似ている。分かりやすいエサが2つ。釣ら
れたのは誰?

😅 はい。釣られました。

😀 それにしても、(B) は質問に全く答えていないですね。

😀 そうだよ。Part 2 は「質問への答えはどれか」ではなく、「会話が成り
立つか」という観点で応答を聞く必要がある。

22.

😀 (B) が魅力的な不正解だったみたい。That's all right. を「彼は元
気だよ」と答えていると思ったのかな。

😎 その通りです。

Part 2 応答問題

23. DL 155 🇦🇺🇨🇦 正解：**A** 易▭▬▬▬▭▭ 難　選択率：(A) 56.9% (B) 17.1% (C) 26.0%

Isn't it time we conducted an employee evaluation?
(A) Oh, thanks for reminding me.
(B) It's just after one.
(C) Human resources department.

☐ conduct: 動 ～を実施する　☐ evaluation: 名 評価
☐ remind: 動 ～に思い出させる
☐ human resources department: 人事部

人事考課を実施する時期ではありませんか。
(A) ああ、思い出させてくれてありがとうございます。
(B) ちょうど1時すぎです。
(C) 人事部です。

▶解説 否定疑問文で「人事考課を実施する時期ではないか」と問うています。「思い出させてくれてありがとう」と答えることで、「確かにその通りだ」と伝えている (A) が正解です。

24. DL 156 🇬🇧🇦🇺 正解：**A** 易▭▬▬▭▭▭ 難　選択率：(A) 71.4% (B) 11.2% (C) 17.5%

We've only got five volunteers for the weekend.
(A) I'll see what I can do to help.
(B) I'm ready for my interview.
(C) That won't be enough time.

☐ weekend: 名 週末　☐ interview: 名 面接
☐ enough: 形 十分な

週末のボランティアが5人しかいません。
(A) 私に何ができるか検討してみます。
(B) 私は面接の準備ができています。
(C) それは十分な時間ではありません。

▶解説 「週末のボランティアは5人だけ」と述べることで、落胆の気持ちを伝えようとしています。その意図をくみ取り、「手伝うために何ができるか検討する」と返答し、男性をサポートする気持ちを伝えている (A) が正解です。

25. DL 157 🇨🇦🇬🇧 正解：**B** 易▭▭▭▭▬▭ 難　選択率：(A) 29.7% (B) 45.7% (C) 24.5%

Have you contacted the printer about the brochures?
(A) On page seven.
(B) Yes, they'll be ready by noon.
(C) When was it repaired?

☐ contact: 動 ～に連絡する　☐ printer: 名 印刷会社
☐ brochure: 名 パンフレット　☐ repair: 動 ～を修理する

パンフレットについて印刷会社に連絡しましたか。
(A) 7ページにです。
(B) はい、正午までに準備できます。
(C) いつ修理されたんですか。

▶解説 「パンフレットのことで印刷業者に連絡したのか」という問いに対し、Yesで「連絡した」と答えた上で、「それらを正午までには準備できる」と返答している (B) が正解です。(B) の they は、質問文にある名詞 brochures を指しています。

(((📡 ゼミ 生中継 　　　😀 Hiro 😺 Mai 🐵 Yasu 😎 Dai 😊 Saki

23.

😀 質問にある employee evaluation からの連想を利用したワナが、(C) だね。気づいた？

😊 はい。人事考課と言えば人事部をイメージします。

🐵 すみません。人事部は personnel department と習いましたが、違うのですか。

😀 いや、正しい。ただ会社によっては、human resources department と呼ばれるんだ。HRと略される場合もある。

24.

😀 (A) にある I'll see what I can do ～の I'll see は、目で何かを「見る」という意味ではない。ニュアンスが近いのは「検討する」とか「調べる」かな。

25.

😀 Part 2の中で正答率が最低なのがこれ。質問にある printer を日本語の「プリンター」だと勘違いすると、頭が混乱するよね。サキはどうだった？

😊 混乱して (C) にしました。プリンターと修理は相性がいい気がして……。

😎 同じく。

😀 確かに TOEIC ワールドではプリンターやコピー機はよく壊れるから修理との相性は悪くない。近年は冷蔵庫の方がよく壊れるけどね。

26. DL 158 正解：**C** 易■■■□□□□ 難　選択率：(A) 10.0%　(B) 31.6%　**(C) 58.4%**

I just called the tech department about the monitor.
(A) Thirty people took part.
(B) In just a few minutes.
(C) Don't tell me it's out of order again.

モニターについてちょうど技術部に電話しました。
(A) 30人が参加しました。
(B) ほんの2、3分で。
(C) まさかまた故障しているんじゃないでしょうね。

▶解説 「モニターのことで技術部に電話した」と報告しています。その報告を受け、「まさかまた故障しているのではないよね」と答え、「また何か問題が起きたのでは」と懸念を表している (C) が自然な応答です。

□ tech department: 技術部　＊tech は technology の略
□ take part: 参加する　＊took は take の過去形
□ Don't tell me ～ .: まさか～じゃないでしょうね。
□ out of order: 故障して

---

27. DL 159 正解：**C** 易■■■□□□□ 難　選択率：(A) 3.0%　(B) 10.8%　**(C) 86.2%**

What time does the concert begin?
(A) Yes, of course.
(B) In the auditorium.
(C) The ticket says 5:30.

コンサートは何時に始まりますか。
(A) はい、もちろん。
(B) ホールで。
(C) チケットに5時30分と書いてあります。

▶解説 What time ～? でコンサートの開始「時刻」を尋ねたのに対し、「チケットには5時30分と書かれている」と答えた (C) が正解です。WH で始まる疑問文には、(A) のように Yes/No で答えることはできません。「場所」を答えている (B) も不正解です。

□ auditorium: 图 ホール、観客席

---

28. DL 160 正解：**A** 易■■■□□□□ 難　選択率：**(A) 64.7%**　(B) 20.8%　(C) 14.5%

You know about the merger, don't you?
(A) Yes, it'll be announced soon.
(B) Sure, I'll be glad to.
(C) No, it's my turn.

合併について知っていますよね？
(A) はい、もうすぐ発表されます。
(B) もちろん、喜んで。
(C) いいえ、私の番です。

▶解説 「合併について知っているよね？」という問いに対し、Yes で「知っている」と伝え、「もうすぐ発表される」と述べた (A) が正解です。(B) の Sure と (C) の No は問題ありませんが、後の内容が質問とかみ合いません。

□ merger: 图 合併　□ glad to ～: 喜んで～する、～してうれしい
□ one's turn: ～の番

🎙))) ゼミ 生中継　　　Hiro　Mai　Yasu　Dai　Saki

26.
(Dai) (C) の Don't tell me ～は、文字通り「～を言うな」ではないよ。
(Saki) Don't tell me で「まさか～じゃないでしょうね」とオンライン辞書に載っています。
(Yasu) そうだったのか……。消去法で (C) を選ぼうと思っていたのに、(C) がダメだと思ったので、仕方なく (B) にしました。
(Dai) 決断の良さは認めよう。

27.
(Dai) これは簡単だったよね？　どう、サキ？
(Saki) What time だけ意識したら解けたので驚きでした。

28.
(Dai) この質問に Sure や No で答えることは可能だから、(B) と (C) が魅力的かな。実際、どちらかを選んだモニターが多い。サキ、M&A という言葉を知ってる？
(Saki) うっすら聞いたことがあります。
(Dai) その M が、質問にある merger の頭文字だよ。M&A は正式には、mergers and acquisitions で「合併と買収」のこと。
(Saki) Test 1 の Part 7 にもありましたね。Zeno Pharmaceuticals が Omicron Corporation を買収していました。
(Dai) よく覚えているね。
(Saki) たまたま昨日、復習したんです。

Part 2 応答問題

29. ^{DL} 161 🇨🇦 🇦🇺 正解：**C** 易■■■■□□□難 選択率：23.0% (B) 10.0% **(C) 66.9%**

Is there any flexibility on the price of these lights?
(A) I didn't expect to win a prize.
(B) One in each room.
(C) They're already heavily discounted.

☐ flexibility: 图 柔軟性、融通性　☐ light: 图 電灯
☐ expect to ～: ～することを期待する
☐ win: 動 (賞など) を勝ち取る　☐ prize: 图 賞
☐ heavily: 副 ひどく、激しく
☐ discount: 動 (価格) を割引する

これらの電灯の価格は融通がききますか。
(A) 私は賞を取るとは思っていませんでした。
(B) 各部屋に1つです。
(C) すでに大幅に値引きされているんです。

▶解説　「価格を融通してもらうことは可能か」という問いに対し、「すでに大幅に値引きされている」と答えることで、間接的に「これ以上の価格の変更 (値下げ) はできない」と伝えている (C) が正解です。

---

30. ^{DL} 162 🇬🇧 🇺🇸 正解：**C** 易■■■■□□□難 選択率：26.4% (B) 15.2% **(C) 58.4%**

Why don't we move to a brighter space?
(A) Very impressive.
(B) The shipping is free.
(C) The lobby is good for photos.

☐ Why don't we ～?: ～しませんか。
☐ move to ～: ～へ移動する　☐ bright: 形 明るい
☐ impressive: 形 印象的な　☐ shipping: 图 輸送料

もっと明るい場所に移動しませんか。
(A) とても印象的です。
(B) 送料は無料です。
(C) 写真を撮るにはロビーがいいです。

▶解説　Why don't we ～?は「～しませんか」と提案する表現です。「もう少し明るい場所へ移ろう」という提案を聞いて、今いる場所は写真を撮るのに向いていないことを察し、「写真を撮るにはロビーが適している」と返答した (C) が正解です。

---

31. ^{DL} 163 🇬🇧 🇨🇦 正解：**A** 易■■■■□□□難 選択率：**(A) 50.6%** (B) 20.4% (C) 29.0%

Where do you store the old documents?
(A) We have a new scanning system.
(B) Usually on Fridays.
(C) A confidential document.

☐ store: 動 ～を入れる、収容する
☐ scanning system: スキャンシステム
☐ confidential: 形 機密の

古い書類はどこに保管しているんですか。
(A) 新しいスキャンシステムがあるんです。
(B) たいてい毎週金曜日に。
(C) 機密書類です。

▶解説　Where ～?で古い書類を保管する「場所」を尋ねたのに対し、「新しいスキャンシステムがある」と述べ、古い書類はスキャンされることを伝えた (A) が正解です。(C) には質問文のdocumentsの単数形がありますが、質問の応答としては不適切です。

📡 ゼミ 生 中継　　　😀 Hiro　😀 Mai　😀 Yasu　😀 Oai　😀 Saki

30.

😀 この質問を聞いた時点では、どんな状況で会話が行われているか想像しにくいね。

😀 誰が話しているか見当が付きませんでした。

😀 でも、正解の応答を聞けば状況をイメージできる。たぶん、この人たちは写真撮影をしている。

31.

😀 質問はWhereだけど、Whenに聞こえると、(B)を選びたくなるよね。

😀 選んでしまいました。WH疑問文でミスしたのは痛いです。

😀 Part 2の後半は前半に比べると難しい問題が集まる傾向がある。仮に質問が簡単だと思っても、絶対に気を抜かないでね。集中力が切れそうになったら、大きく深呼吸して気持ちを立て直すといい。よし、これでPart 2は終わり。

TOEICよろず相談所　ヒロの部屋

⑭カンタンなはずの Part 2 が一番苦手です

 あのー、学校の先生から、リスニングのスコアは上がりやすいと聞きました。特に、Part 2 が簡単と聞きましたが、私は Part 2 が一番難しいと感じます。

Part 2 には簡単な問題がたくさん出ますよ。出題パターンが安定しているので、反復練習をすればすぐにスコアが伸びます。ただし、「満点を取りやすい」わけではありません。

 そうなんですね…私も模試なんかでも必ず5問くらい間違えます。そして「正解がない」と感じる問題が必ずあるんです。

ミスの数は5問程度ですか。であれば、Part 2 の練習をやめていいですよ。

 どういうことでしょうか。

「正解がない」と感じる問題があるということは、**会話の状況を瞬時に把握する力が足りない**ということです。Part 2 の形式に沿った練習を重ねても、その力はあまり伸びません。そもそも会話の状況が設定されていないので。

 なるほど。確かにそうですね。

Part 2 には「状況の理解」を試す問題がたくさん出るので、**様々な状況における人々のコミュニケーションを学ぶことが有効**です。Part 2 を楽勝で解ける人は、質問と正解の応答を聞いた瞬間に、その場面を脳裏に描くことができます。TOEIC用の教材だけでなく、海外ドラマや映画、または英会話を通じて純粋に「コミュニケーション」を学ぶことで、Part 2 が得意になった人が結構いますよ。「対策」を意識する必要はありません。

 分かりました。ありがとうございました。

Part 3 会話問題

DL 165 **Questions 32 through 34** refer to the following conversation.

W: Hi, Sunil. I've been looking for you. ❶ I have a friend who works at the museum and she gave me some tickets for ❷ the exhibition of ancient Egyptian artifacts that's coming up. Would you like to go with me?

M: I'd love to. I studied ancient history at university, you know?

W: That's why I thought of you. Look at this brochure. They are bringing over some really famous artifacts.

M: Wow. It looks amazing. It says here that ❸ the exhibition starts on March 23. That's still a month away.

W: Right. But actually, we can get into a preview on March 22 if you like.

M: Really? I can't wait! (106w/38 sec.)

□ exhibition: 图 展示、公開　□ ancient: 形 古代の　□ Egyptian: 形 エジプトの　□ artifact: 图 (考古学の) 遺物、埋蔵物
□ come up: やってくる　□ That's why ～: だから~なのだ　□ away: 副 (時間的に) 先で　□ preview: 图 内覧

問題32-34は次の会話に関するものです。
女：あら、Sunil。探してたのよ。博物館で働いている友達がいて、彼女が今度の古代エジプト埋蔵品展のチケットを何枚かくれたの。一緒に行かない?
男：ぜひ行きたいね。僕、大学で古代史を勉強してただろ?
女：だからあなたが思い浮かんだの。見て、このパンフレット。かなり有名な埋蔵品が展示されるわよ。
男：へえ。すごそうだね。ここに、展覧会の開始は3月23日って書いてあるよ。まだ1カ月先だ。
女：そう。でも実は、よければ3月22日の内覧会に入れるのよ。
男：本当? 待ち切れないよ!

---

32. 正解：A 易 ■■□□□□□□ 難　選択率：**(A) 97.0%** (B) 0.4% (C) 1.5% (D) 1.1%

What are the speakers discussing?
(A) An exhibit
(B) A film
(C) A contest
(D) A sporting event

話者たちは何について話していますか。
(A) 展覧会
(B) 映画
(C) コンテスト
(D) スポーツの試合

▶解説 女性が❷で「古代エジプト埋蔵品展」に言及し、男性に一緒に行かないかと誘っています。男性はそれに対し「ぜひ行きたい」と答え、続く内容も埋蔵品展の内容や日程なので、(A)が正解です。exhibitは名詞で「展覧会」という意味があり、exhibitionと同義です。

---

33. 正解：B 易 ■■■□□□□□ 難　選択率：(A) 10.8% **(B) 70.6%** (C) 13.4% (D) 5.2%

Where did the woman get the tickets?
(A) On the Internet
(B) From a friend
(C) At a ticket booth
(D) In a competition

女性はどこでチケットを入手しましたか。
(A) インターネットで
(B) 友達から
(C) チケット販売窓口で
(D) 競技会で

▶解説 設問文から女性はすでにチケットを持っていると分かり、女性が入手方法に言及すると考えられます。女性は❶で「博物館に勤務する友人からチケットをもらった」と述べており、(B)が正解です。

---

34. 正解：C 易 ■■■□□□□□ 難　選択率：(A) 1.9% (B) 10.8% **(C) 73.2%** (D) 14.1%

According to the man, when will the event begin?
(A) In a day
(B) In a week
(C) In a month
(D) In two months

男性によると、この催事はいつ始まりますか。
(A) 1日後に
(B) 1週間後に
(C) 1カ月後に
(D) 2カ月後に

▶解説 According to the manで設問が始まる場合、男性の発言にヒントがあります。男性はパンフレットを見ながら❸で「開始日はまだ1カ月も先だ」と待ち遠しい気持ちを表しており、正解は(C)です。選択肢のin ～は、「～後に」を意味する表現です。

(((ゼミ 生中継

(⚙) Hiro (⚙) Mai (⚙) Yasu (⚙) Dai (⚙) Saki

32.

(⚙) 話題が問われているということは、サキ、どういうこと?

(⚙) いったん無視して、2問目を意識しました。

(⚙) ナイス。2問目は明らかに細かい情報を求めているから、ヒントは1回しか聞こえない。しかも、かなり早いタイミングでI have a friend ～と言ったから2問目が少し解きにくい。

(⚙) 作戦大成功でした!

(⚙) やられた～。

34.

(⚙) ヒントの後、会話が終わるまでに8秒ほどあった。その時間に何をした?

(⚙) 34番の(C)の横に親指を置いて、32番から34番までの正解を(A)、(B)、(C)と記憶してから、マークを一気に3つ塗りました。

(⚙) 親指? え、どういうことですか?

(⚙) スリーフィンガー法だね。1問目の担当は左手の中指、2問目が人さし指、3問目が指親だよ。ヒントが聞こえる度にマークを塗らなくて済むから、設問と選択肢を見続けることができる。マイは前からこの方法を実践していたの?

(⚙) この本の解説動画を見て知りました。何度か試したら、自分に合うことが分かったので、最近はいつも実践しています。

278

166 Questions 35 through 37 refer to the following conversation.

M: Hello, Midwood Car Rentals. How may I help you?

W: Hi. ❶ I'd like to rent a car from next Friday through Sunday.

M: Certainly. What type of car would you prefer? We have–

W: Actually, I'm looking at your Web site now. Is a mid-size car available? I'm planning to take three people with me.

M: Well, those are very popular. Let me see. No... unfortunately, ❷ all of our mid-size cars are already booked for the weekend. How about one of our larger cars? They cost a little more, but you'll have a bit more room.

W: I see. I'll go with one of the larger models, then.

M: OK. ❸ Could I have your name and phone number, please?

(113w/41 sec.)

□ mid-size: 形 中型の □ unfortunately: 副 あいにく □ go with 〜: 〜を選ぶ

問題35-37は次の会話に関するものです。
男：はい、Midwood Car Rentalsです。ご用件を承りますが。
女：もしもし。車を1台、今度の金曜日から日曜日にかけて借りたいんです。
男：かしこまりました。どのような車種をご希望ですか。当店では――。
女：実は、今そちらのウェブサイトを見てます。中型車は借りられますか。私以外に3人乗る予定です。
男：そうですね、中型車は大変人気がありまして。お待ちください。駄目ですね……あいにく、中型車は全て週末は予約済みです。大きめの車はいかがですか。料金はやや上がりますが、車内にもう少し余裕がありますよ。
女：分かりました。では、大きめの車を1台お願いします。
男：かしこまりました。お名前とお電話番号をいただけますか。

---

35. 正解：**A** 易 ■■□□□□□□ 難 選択率：**(A) 99.2%** (B) 0.4% (C) 0.4% (D) 0.0%

Why is the woman calling?
(A) To reserve a vehicle
(B) To ask for directions
(C) To discuss a project
(D) To recommend a business

女性はなぜ電話をかけていますか。
(A) 乗り物を予約するために
(B) 道順を尋ねるために
(C) ある計画について話すために
(D) ある事業を勧めるために

▶解説 電話の目的が問われています。女性は❶で「次の金曜日から日曜日まで車を借りたい」と言っており、これをTo reserve a vehicle（乗り物を予約する）とした(A)が正解です。(C)のprojectは、通常「事業などの計画」という意味で用いる語なので、不適切です。

□ direction: 名 道順の案内 □ project: 名 計画、事業
□ recommend: 動 〜を勧める □ business: 名 店、会社

---

36. 正解：**C** 易 ■■■■■□□□ 難 選択率：(A) 11.2% (B) 46.1% **(C) 40.5%** (D) 2.2%

What does the man mean when he says, "those are very popular"?
(A) The price has gone up.
(B) A product is selling well.
(C) An option might be unavailable.
(D) Membership is required.

男性はどのような意味で「それらは大変人気がありまして」と言っていますか。
(A) 価格が上がっている。
(B) ある製品の売れ行きが良い。
(C) ある選択肢が利用できないかもしれない。
(D) 会員登録が必要だ。

▶解説 「中型車は借りられるか」という女性の発言を受けて、男性がthose are very popularと言っています。その後❷で「中型車は全て週末は予約済みだ」と述べているため、男性は中型車という選択肢が利用不可能かもしれないことを伝えようとしていると分かります。正解は(C)です。

□ option: 名 選択肢 □ membership: 名 会員であること

---

37. 正解：**D** 易 ■■□□□□□□ 難 選択率：(A) 10.4% (B) 4.5% (C) 7.1% **(D) 78.1%**

What is the woman asked to do?
(A) Make a payment
(B) Review some paperwork
(C) Choose an insurance package
(D) Provide her contact information

女性は何をするよう依頼されていますか。
(A) 支払いをする
(B) 書類を見直す
(C) 保険パックを選ぶ
(D) 自分の連絡先を提供する

▶解説 男性は❸でCould I 〜?に続けて「お名前と電話番号をいただけますか」と女性に依頼しています。「電話番号」をより抽象的なcontact information（連絡先）と言い換えた(D)が正解です。

□ review: 動 〜を見直す □ insurance package: 総合保険

ゼミ生中継

Hiro Mai Yasu Dai Saki

36. ....

😎 天国と地獄だよ。35番はモニターの正答率が最高だけど、36番はPart3で最低となっている。なぜ、(B)がダメか分かる？

😮 レンタカーはproductではないのですか。

😎 そう。それに、レンタカー屋は車を売っているわけではない。だから

sellingも間違っている。

😊 自信があったから、(C)まで読まなかった〜。

😆 35番の時点でレンタカーの話だと分かったので、こっちの(B)はおかしいと思いました。奇跡的に正解を選べました。

😎 お、やるじゃないか。

279

DL 167 **Questions 38 through 40** refer to the following conversation.

W: Hello. This is Rebecca Harris from Thornton Advertising. ❶ I'm calling regarding your application for the position on our production team. We'd like to meet with you.

M: Oh, great. I sent my portfolio on Wednesday. Has it arrived there yet?

W: Yes, it has. ❷ I've handed it over to the head of the production team and he will take a look at it over the weekend. ❸ The earliest we have available for an interview is Monday, I'm afraid. How does that sound?

M: ❹ Unfortunately, I have a full day planned on Monday. Do you have time on Tuesday?

W: ❺ Sure. How's 10 A.M.?

M: ❻ That sounds fine. (102w/42 sec.)

問題38-40は次の会話に関するものです。
女：もしもし。Thornton Advertising社のRebecca Harris です。当社の制作チームの職にご応募いただいている件で、電話を差し上げています。あなたにお目に掛かりたいと思いまして。
男：ああ、ありがとうございます。自分の作品集を水曜日にお送りしました。もう届いていますでしょうか。
女：はい、いただいています。制作チームの責任者に渡してあり、彼が週末をかけて拝見する予定です。面接が可能な日は、一番早くて月曜日になってしまうと思います。それでいかがでしょうか。
男：あいにく、月曜日には終日予定が入っています。火曜日にお時間をいただけますか。
女：結構です。午前10時でいかがですか。
男：それで結構です。

□ regarding: 前 ～に関して　□ application: 名 申し込み　□ position: 名 職、地位　□ production team: （番組などの）制作チーム
□ portfolio: 名 （代表作を収めた紙挟み式の）作品集、写真集　□ head: 名 （組織の）長

---

38. 正解：B 易 ■■■□□□□ 難　選択率：(A) 10.8%　**(B) 80.3%**　(C) 2.6%　(D) 5.6%

What is the purpose of the woman's call?
(A) To explain a procedure
(B) To set up an appointment
(C) To thank the man for some help
(D) To offer some advice

女性の電話の目的は何ですか。
(A) 手続きを説明すること
(B) 面談の約束を取ること
(C) 男性に、手助けしてくれたことへの感謝を伝えること
(D) アドバイスを与えること

▶解説 ❶から女性は、制作チームの求人応募者に電話していることが分かります。「お会いしたい」という発言から面接を希望していると考えられ、❸で月曜日の都合を尋ねているので、面接の日時を設定するために電話をかけていると分かります。正解は (B) です。

□ procedure: 名 手順　□ set up ～: ～を手配する

---

39. 正解：D 易 ■■■□□□□ 難　選択率：(A) 10.8%　(B) 12.3%　(C) 10.4%　**(D) 65.4%**

What does the woman say about the man's portfolio?
(A) It will be delivered tomorrow.
(B) It is heavier than expected.
(C) It does not contain the required materials.
(D) It will be viewed by a team leader.

女性は男性の作品集について何と言っていますか。
(A) 明日配送されるだろう。
(B) 思っていたよりも重い。
(C) 必要な資料が含まれていない。
(D) チームリーダーが目を通すだろう。

▶解説 自分の作品集を送ったと言う男性に女性は受け取ったと伝え、❷で「制作チームの責任者が週末に見る」と述べています。正解 (D) では、男性の作品集は「チームリーダーによって目を通される」と言い変えられています。

□ contain: 動 ～を含む　□ material: 名 資料　□ view: 動 ～を見る

---

40. 正解：B 易 ■■□□□□□ 難　選択率：(A) 3.7%　**(B) 92.9%**　(C) 1.5%　(D) 1.1%

When will the speakers most likely meet?
(A) On Monday
(B) On Tuesday
(C) On Wednesday
(D) On Friday

話者たちはいつ会う可能性が最も高いですか。
(A) 月曜日に
(B) 火曜日に
(C) 水曜日に
(D) 金曜日に

▶解説 月曜日の都合を尋ねられた男性は❹で予定があると答え、代わりに火曜日を提案しています。❺で女性が承諾して時間に言及しています。❻で男性も了承しているので、おそらく2人は火曜日に会うと考えられます。(B)が正解です。

((📡)) ゼミ 生 中継　😀 Hiro 😊 Mai 😆 Yasu 😎 Dai 😄 Saki

39.

😆 設問を見て。portfolioがある。Test 2の39番で、portfolioは重要語だって説明したよね。たまたま同じ問題番号だけど。

😊 portfolioには気づきました。でも、この問題は捨てました。

😀 え、どうして？

😄 選択肢が長くて読み切れないと思ったからです。それより、40番が

曜日だったので、しっかり聞かないとヤバイと思って、曜日に意識を向けました。

😆 曜日って言い換えられないから、聞き逃すと悔しいよね。

😎 なるほど。

😀 サキもマイも受験が上手になってきたね。

DL 168　Questions 41 through 43 refer to the following conversation.

W: My business has grown too large for our current premises so ❶I'm interested in renting somewhere a bit larger.

M: ❷There's a new building that's just been completed in Chevron. They have offices of all sizes. Would you like to take a look?

W: It sounds perfect. ❸What's the neighborhood like? Are there places to eat, and banks and things like that in the area?

M: ❹I have a detailed map on my computer. We could take a look and see if it has everything you need.　　　　(84w/31 sec.)

問題41-43は次の会話に関するものです。

女：私の会社は規模がだいぶ大きくなってしまい今の建物では手狭なので、どこかもう少し大きなところを借りたいのです。

男：完成したばかりの新しいビルがChevronにありますよ。あらゆる広さの事務所スペースが用意されています。ご覧になりますか。

女：とても良さそうですね。周辺はどんな感じかしら？　食事の場所とか銀行とか、そういったものがそのエリアにありますか。

男：詳しい地図が私のコンピューターに入っています。ちょっと見てみて、ご入り用のものが全てそろっているか調べられますよ。

□ business: 名 会社、店　□ current: 形 現在の　□ premise: 名（複数形で）建物
□ complete: 動 ～を完成させる　□ take a look: 見てみる　□ neighborhood: 名 近隣、界隈
□ detailed: 形 詳細な

41.　正解：A　易 ■■■□□□□ 難　選択率：**(A) 84.4%** (B) 2.6% (C) 10.8% (D) 1.9%

Who most likely is the man?
(A) A real estate agent
(B) A restaurant owner
(C) A construction worker
(D) A city official

□ real estate: 不動産　□ agent: 名 仲介者
□ construction: 名 建設　□ official: 名 公務員

男性は誰である可能性が最も高いですか。
(A) 不動産業者
(B) レストランの所有者
(C) 建設作業員
(D) 市の当局者

▶解説　❶でより広い賃貸物件を希望する女性に対し、男性は❷で「完成したばかりのビルの物件を見たいか」と尋ねています。物件に関する相談を受け、内覧を勧めるのは(A)の「不動産業者」だと考えられます。

42.　正解：B　易 ■■■□□□□ 難　選択率：(A) 10.0% **(B) 83.6%** (C) 3.0% (D) 3.3%

What does the woman ask about?
(A) Rental prices
(B) Nearby businesses
(C) Daily specials
(D) Local rules

□ nearby: 形 近くの　□ daily special: 日替わりの特別料理
□ local: 形 地元の

女性は何について尋ねていますか。
(A) 賃料
(B) 近隣の店
(C) 日替わり定食
(D) 地元の規則

▶解説　女性は❸で「周辺はどんな感じなのか」と尋ねた後、食事をする場所や銀行などの有無を確認しています。正解はそれをnearby businesses（近隣の店）と言い換えた(B)です。

43.　正解：C　易 ■■■□□□□ 難　選択率：(A) 1.9% (B) 5.9% **(C) 84.4%** (D) 7.4%

What will the man most likely do next?
(A) Check a menu
(B) Take a reservation
(C) Look at his computer
(D) Explain a system

男性はこの後何をする可能性が最も高いですか。
(A) メニューを調べる
(B) 予約を取る
(C) 自分のコンピューターを見る
(D) 仕組みを説明する

▶解説　近隣の状況について尋ねられた男性は❹で「自分のコンピューターに入っている詳しい地図で、必要なものがそろっているかどうか調べられる」と述べています。おそらくコンピューターを開いて女性に地図を見せると考えられるので、(C)が正解です。

(((ゼミ生中継)))　Hiro　Mai　Yasu　Dai　Saki

41.

😀 このような、登場人物を問う設問は頻出する。ここでは男性の職業が問われているけれど、ヒントはどこにあると思う？

😮 ケースバイケースだと思います。相手の発言にヒントがあってもおかしくないです。

😀 1つ言えるのは、自分で自分の職業を言う人はめったにいないということ。例えば、医者は患者に向かって「私は医者だ」とは言わない。

💀 そんな医者は病院に行った方がいいですね!

😀 だから、選択肢に並ぶ職業が、そのまま会話で聞こえる可能性は低い。関連語句がいくつかヒントとして登場するんだよ。

😊 私は会社から電話する時に「弥生証券の～です」と名乗ります。ですから、本人の発言がヒントになることもありそうです。

😀 それはそれでラッキーだよ。大事なのは、複数のヒントを元に、可能性が一番高そうな職業を推測することだよ。

Part 3 会話問題

DL 170 Questions 44 through 46 refer to the following conversation with three speakers.

W: Hi Robert. ❶I've decided to go to Madrid and speak with the management at Garcia Textile Company. ❷Recently, their quality has been dropping and I want to discuss it with them in person.

M1: Good idea. ❸I think it might be best if you take Philip with you, though. ❹He'll be replacing you next year and we should give him some more experience with this kind of thing.

W: Good point. Where is he?

M2: I'm right here. I heard what you were talking about.

W: Great. I'm leaving on Friday. Can you manage a trip with such short notice?

M2: It depends on whether or not I can find a flight.

W: You should be able to find something online. ❺I'll send you my schedule in a minute. (124w/40 sec.)

問題44-46は次の3人の話者による会話に関するものです。

女：ねえ、Robert。私、Madridへ行って、Garcia Textile Companyの経営陣と話してくることにしたわ。最近、あの会社の品質が落ちてるから、そのことについて直接会って話したいのよ。

男1：いい考えだね。ただし、Philipを一緒に連れて行くのが一番いいだろうと思う。彼は来年、君の後任になる予定だから、この種の経験をもっと積む方がいい。

女：いい指摘ね。彼はどこかしら？

男2：私ならここです。今のお話が耳に入りました。

女：良かったわ。私は金曜日に出発するの。こんな急な話だけど、出張の準備はできる？

男2：飛行機が取れるかどうかによりますね。

女：オンラインで何かしら取れるはずよ。私の予定をすぐに送るわ。

☐ decide to ～ : ～することを決める ☐ speak with ～ : ～と話をする ☐ management: 图 (集合的に) 経営陣、経営者側 ☐ quality: 图 品質
☐ drop: 動 下落する ☐ in person: 本人が直接に ☐ replace: 動 ～の後任となる ☐ experience: 图 経験 ☐ manage: 動 なんとかする
☐ trip: 图 旅行 ☐ notice: 图 通知、お知らせ ☐ depend on ～ : ～次第である ☐ whether or not ～ : ～か否か ☐ online: 副 オンラインで
☐ in a minute: すぐに

44. 正解：**B**　易 ■■■□□ 難　選択率：(A) 2.6%　**(B) 62.8%**　(C) 14.5%　(D) 20.1%

Why is the woman going to Madrid?
(A) To take a vacation
(B) To talk about a problem
(C) To inspect a construction
(D) To interview an applicant

□ inspect: 動 ～を視察する、立ち入り検査する
□ construction: 名 建設工事　□ interview: 動 ～と面接する
□ applicant: 名 応募者、候補者

なぜ女性はMadridへ行きますか。
(A) 休暇を取るために
(B) ある問題について話すために
(C) 工事を視察するために
(D) 応募者と面接するために

▶解説　女性は❶で「Madridへ行ってGarcia Textile Companyの経営陣と話をしてくることにした」と言い、❷では「最近品質が落ちてきているから直接話したい」と述べています。取引先の品質が下がることは問題だと言えるので、正解は(B)です。

---

45. 正解：**D**　易 ■■■□□ 難　選択率：(A) 28.3%　(B) 1.5%　(C) 8.2%　**(D) 61.7%**

What does Robert suggest doing?
(A) Contacting a travel agent
(B) Purchasing a guidebook
(C) Asking for a better price
(D) Taking a coworker

□ contact: 動 ～に連絡する　□ agent: 名 代理店
□ purchase: 動 ～を購入する　□ coworker: 名 同僚

Robertは何をするよう勧めていますか。
(A) 旅行代理店に連絡すること
(B) ガイドブックを買うこと
(C) より良い価格を要求すること
(D) 同僚を連れて行くこと

▶解説　冒頭で女性がRobertと呼び掛けており、答えた男性がRobertだと分かります。彼は❸でPhilipを一緒に連れて行くように勧めています。その理由は❹で「君の後任だから」だと分かります。これらのことからPhilipは2人の同僚だと判断できるので、(D)が正解です。

---

46. 正解：**D**　易 ■■□□□ 難　選択率：(A) 7.4%　(B) 11.2%　(C) 2.6%　**(D) 78.8%**

What does the woman say she will do?
(A) Update a Web site
(B) Speak with a supervisor
(C) Invite a client
(D) Provide her travel schedule

□ update: 動 ～を更新する、最新のものにする
□ supervisor: 名 監督者、上司
□ provide: 動 ～を提供する

女性は何をすると言っていますか。
(A) ウェブサイトを更新する
(B) 上司と話す
(C) 顧客を招く
(D) 自分の旅程を提示する

▶解説　❺で女性はPhilipに予定表を送ると言っていますが、これまでの会話からこれはPhilipが同行する出張のものだと分かります。正解はsend（送る）をprovide（提供する）と言い換えた(D)です。

(((📡))) ゼミ 生 中継　　　😀Hiro 🙂Mai 😮Yasu 😆Dai 😊Saki

44.
😀 抽象化に気づくことがポイントだね。quality has been droppingという表現が、(B)にあるproblemに合致すると見抜く必要がある。

45.
😀 設問に人名があると解きにくいかな。サキ、どう?
😊 あまり好きじゃないです。男性が2人いましたし。
😆 同じく。頭が混乱します。
😀 そっか。でも、安心していい。3人の会話では、誰かが名前を呼ばれたら、呼ばれた人は必ず直後に話す。だから、45番のように設問に人名がある場合、その名前が呼ばれた直後に話す人がヒントを言うと考えていい。ここでは、もっと後に聞こえるtripやflightを気にする必要はないよ。
😊 まさにそこに引っ掛かって、(A)を選びました。
😆 同じく。
😀 やはり。(A)の選択率が高いのはそのせいか。

283

Part 3 会話問題

DL 171 **Questions 47 through 49** refer to the following conversation.

M: ❶We've won the advertising contract for the Edinburgh Motor Show again this year.

W: That's great news, but to be honest, I'm a little surprised. ❷Attendance was down the last two years and I felt a little responsible.

M: I don't think that was our fault. The car companies didn't have any innovative products to show, so people lost interest. That's changed this time. ❸They all have electric cars coming out and some of the designs are really exciting.

W: So, ❹if the campaign doesn't attract a lot of visitors this time...

M: ❺We'll have to accept responsibility.　　　　　(94w/32 sec.)

□ attendance: 图 入場者数　□ fault: 图 責任　□ innovative: 形 革新的な

問題47-49は次の会話に関するものです。
男：今年もまた、うちがEdinburgh Motor Showの広告契約を取ったよ。
女：それは良い知らせね、でも正直なところ、ちょっと驚いたわ。過去2年間、来場者数が落ち込んでいたから、ちょっと責任を感じてたの。
男：それはうちのせいじゃなかったと思うよ。自動車メーカーが革新的な製品を全く発表しなかったから、皆、興味をなくしたんだ。今回は変わったよ。全社が電気自動車を出してくるし、そのデザインの中には本当にわくわくするものがあるんだ。
女：じゃあ、もしも今回、キャンペーンでたくさんの来場者を呼び込めなかったら……
男：うちが責任を負わなければならないだろうね。

---

47. 正解：**D**　易 ■■■■□□□□ 難　選択率：(A) 3.0% (B) 0.7% (C) 45.7% **(D) 50.6%**

Where do the speakers most likely work?
(A) At a sports arena
(B) At a radio station
(C) At a car manufacturer
(D) At an advertising firm

話者たちはどこで働いている可能性が最も高いですか。
(A) 競技場で
(B) ラジオ局で
(C) 自動車メーカーで
(D) 広告会社で

▶解説 男性は❶で「今年もMotor Showの広告契約を取った」と報告しています。参加者数やメーカーの製品について女性と話し、2人は❹❺で「集客に失敗すれば責任を負うべき」だと言っていることから、(D)の「広告会社」で働いていると判断できます。

---

48. 正解：**C**　易 ■■■□□□□□ 難　選択率：(A) 3.0% (B) 16.4% **(C) 73.2%** (D) 7.4%

What problem does the woman mention?
(A) The weather has been unfavorable.
(B) There is another event on the same day.
(C) Attendance has been low.
(D) Running costs have risen.

□ unfavorable: 形 好ましくない

女性はどんな問題を述べていますか。
(A) 天候が良くない。
(B) 別の催事が同じ日にある。
(C) 来場者数が落ち込んでいる。
(D) 維持費が上がっている。

▶解説 problem（問題）を問われた場合、ネガティブな情報が答えのヒントです。契約が取れたと聞いた女性は喜んだ後、正直少し驚いていると伝えています。❷で「過去2年間、来場者数が落ち込んでいたから」と続けており、(C)が正解です。

---

49. 正解：**A**　易 ■■□□□□□□ 難　選択率：**(A) 74.7%** (B) 7.8% (C) 14.5% (D) 3.0%

What does the man imply about this year's motor show?
(A) Some impressive products will be on show.
(B) Some manufacturers will not attend.
(C) It will be smaller than in previous years.
(D) It will be held indoors.

□ impressive: 形 印象的な　□ indoors: 副 屋内で

男性は今年のモーターショーについて何を示唆していますか。
(A) いくつかの印象的な製品が展示されるだろう。
(B) いくつかのメーカーが参加しないだろう。
(C) これまでの年よりも小規模なものになるだろう。
(D) 屋内で開催されるだろう。

▶解説 男性は、去年までのショーと今回は違うとして、❸で「全社が電気自動車を出す予定で、わくわくするデザインのものもある」と話しています。これをimpressive product（印象的な製品）と抽象的にまとめた(A)が正解です。

(((📡))) ゼミ生中継　　😎Hiro 😊Mai 😄Yasu 😎Dai 😊Saki

47.
😎(C)が魅力的な不正解。仮に彼らが車のメーカー勤務だったら、広告の契約を獲得した話はしないし、今年の入場者が少なければ自分たちの責任だとも言わないよね。単語ではなくストーリーを理解しているかどうかが問われている。

😊すみません、(D)はどんな会社ですか。ピンと来ません。

😎世の中には、イベントや商品の宣伝を専門的に引き受ける会社があるんだよ。テレビやインターネットを使ったり、ポスターなどの制作をしたりと、いろんな角度から宣伝を担当するのが主な仕事だよ。

48.
😎このAttendanceを覚えている？　Part 5に出ていたよね。

😐Test 1の119番です。

😎(C)と(D)で迷ったけど、45番から(D)が3連続していたので、ここは(C)にしました。

😎同じ記号が3つ続くと次は外したくなる。「TOEICあるあるランキング第3位」だよ。

DL 172 Questions 50 through 52 refer to the following conversation.

W: Excuse me. I bought this coffee maker set here a few days ago. I only opened the box up this morning, but when I did, I found that the color was wrong. The box says it's black, which is what I wanted, but the machine is actually dark brown. ❶ Can you exchange it for another?

M: Oh, I'm sorry about that. I don't know how that happened. I'd like to offer you a replacement, but ❷ we've had a clearance sale this week and we've sold out of that model. ❸ I can only offer you a refund, I'm afraid.

W: That'll do, then. ❹ I'll use the money to buy a different model.

M: Good idea. ❺ I think you'll be interested in some of the new ones we have in stock. (126w/44 sec.)

問題50-52は次の会話に関するものです。
女：すみません。このコーヒーメーカーのセットをここで数日前に買ったんです。今朝になってようやく箱を開けたんですが、見ると色が違っていました。箱には黒と書いてあって、それが欲しかった色なのに、実際には機械は焦げ茶色です。別のものと取り換えていただけますか。
男：ああ、それは申し訳ございません。どうしてそうなったのか分かりませんが。代わりの品物をお渡ししたいところですが、今週、在庫一掃セールを開催しておりまして、その型は売り切れてしまっています。返金で対応させていただくしかなさそうなのですが。
女：ならば、それで構いません。そのお金を使って別のモデルを買いますから。
男：名案ですね。当店で在庫している新製品の中に、興味を引かれるものがあると思いますよ。

□ exchange: 動 ～を交換する　□ replacement: 名 代替品
□ clearance sale: 在庫一掃セール　□ sell out ～: ～を売り切る　＊sold は sell の過去分詞
□ refund: 名 払い戻し　□ That'll do.: それで十分です。　□ stock: 名 在庫品

50. 正解：A 易 ■■■□□□□ 難　選択率：(A) 93.7% (B) 0.4% (C) 0.4% (D) 5.6%

What is the purpose of the woman's visit?
(A) To report a problem
(B) To request a manual
(C) To update her address
(D) To purchase a gift

女性の来店の目的は何ですか。
(A) ある問題を伝えること
(B) 説明書を要求すること
(C) 自分の住所を更新すること
(D) 贈答品を買うこと

▶解説 女性は、コーヒーメーカーのセットをこの店で数日前に買ったこと、箱に書いてあった色と実際の色が異なったことを述べた上で、❶で「取り換えてほしい」と述べています。よって、問題を報告することが来店の目的です。正解は (A) です。

51. 正解：B 易 ■■■□□□□ 難　選択率：(A) 5.9% (B) 88.1% (C) 3.0% (D) 2.6%

What has recently happened at the store?
(A) A change of management
(B) A clearance sale
(C) A policy revision
(D) An opening ceremony

最近この店で何がありましたか。
(A) 経営陣の交代
(B) 在庫一掃セール
(C) 方針の変更
(D) 開店セレモニー

▶解説 色が異なっていたことに対して謝罪していることから、男性は店員だと分かります。彼は❷で「在庫一掃セールを開催した」と述べており、これが最近店で起こったことです。(B) が正解です。

□ management: 名 （集合的に）経営陣、経営者側
□ policy: 名 方針　□ revision: 名 改訂

52. 正解：C 易 ■■■□□□□ 難　選択率：(A) 0.7% (B) 7.1% (C) 90.3% (D) 1.9%

What will the woman most likely do next?
(A) Check an online catalog
(B) Obtain proof of purchase
(C) Look at different models
(D) Go to another store

女性はこの後、何をする可能性が最も高いですか。
(A) オンラインカタログを調べる
(B) 購入証明書を取得する
(C) 別の型の品物を見る
(D) 別の店へ行く

▶解説 ❸で返金の申し出を受けた女性は、❹でそのお金を使って別の型のコーヒーメーカーを買う意思を表しています。さらに男性が❺で「在庫のある新製品に興味を持ってもらえると思う」と発言していることから、おそらく女性は違う型を見に行くと考えられますので、(C) が正解です。

□ obtain: 動 ～を手に入れる
□ proof of purchase: 購入証明書　＊レシートや領収書など

ゼミ生中継　Hiro　Mai　Yasu　Dai　Saki

50.
この3問は易しめだよね。TOEICワールドらしい現象が起きているけれど、サキ、何だと思う？

トラブル発生ですか。

そう。特にPart 3では問題が発生しがちだよ。ただし、その問題は40秒以内に解決する。他は？

客のクレーム。

いいね。不満を持つ客は多い。今回のクレームの原因は何だった？

色の間違いです。実際の試験でも、確かソファの色が間違っていた話を聞いた記憶があります。

おわびの印にクーポン券が登場すると、さらにTOEICワールドっぽいですね。

クーポン券はPart 4とPart 7の必須アイテムだよ。この本にも何回か登場しているよね。

DL 173 Questions 53 through 55 refer to the following conversation.

M: Hi, Nina. Have you found somewhere to live yet?

W: No, I'm still looking. I think it's time for me to buy a place. I've been renting for years.

M: ❶Well, my apartment is for sale. It's a bit small for me now that I have a family. Would you be interested?

W: Your apartment? You live on Davis Avenue! ❷I could walk to the office from there! But it might be too large and too expensive for me.

M: Well, there might be somewhere better in the area. ❸You should download a real estate app for your smartphone. They can usually give you an up-to-date list of properties available in any given area.

W: Sounds good. Do you have a specific app that you recommend?

(121w/43 sec.)

問題53-55は次の会話に関するものです。
男：やあ、Nina。住む所はもう見つかった？
女：いいえ、まだ探しているの。そろそろ家を買うべきなんだと思うわ。何年も賃借してるから。
男：実は、僕のマンションを売りに出してるんだ。今では僕にはちょっと手狭でね、もう家族がいるから。興味ある？
女：あなたのマンション？ Davis Avenue に住んでるんでしょ！ あそこからなら職場まで歩いて行けるわ！ でも、たぶん私には広過ぎるし、値が張り過ぎるかも。
男：まあ、あの地域には他にもっといい物件があるかもしれない。不動産アプリをスマートフォンにダウンロードするといいよ。たいてい、指定した地域で売りに出ている最新の物件リストを提供してくれるから。
女：良さそうね。お勧めの特定のアプリ、ある？

□ real estate: 不動産　□ up-to-date: 形 最新の　□ property: 名 不動産物件

---

53. 正解：D 易■■■□□□□□ 難　選択率：(A) 10.0% (B) 1.9% (C) 1.5% **(D) 86.2%**

Why does the man want to sell his apartment?
(A) He is moving to another town.
(B) It is far from some stores.
(C) There is not enough parking.
(D) It is too small for his family.

なぜ男性は自分のマンションを売りたがっていますか。
(A) 別の町へ引っ越す。
(B) いくつかの店から遠い。
(C) 十分な駐車スペースがない。
(D) 自分の家族にとって狭すぎる。

▶解説 男性がマンションを売りたい理由は、男性の発言にヒントがあります。❶で男性は「家族ができて手狭になったからマンションを売りに出している」と女性に伝えています。これを too small for his family と端的に表した (D) が正解です。

---

54. 正解：A 易■■■■□□□□ 難　選択率：**(A) 58.7%** (B) 18.6% (C) 11.2% (D) 11.2%

Why does the woman say, "You live on Davis Avenue"?
(A) To express excitement
(B) To suggest an alternative
(C) To turn down an offer
(D) To show her knowledge

なぜ女性は「Davis Avenue に住んでるんでしょ」と言っていますか。
(A) 興奮を言い表すために
(B) 代替案を提案するために
(C) 申し出を断るために
(D) 自分の知識を示すために

▶解説 ターゲット文は男性が売りに出しているマンションに興味はあるかと尋ねられた女性の発言です。続けて❷で「そこからなら職場まで歩いて行ける」と言っていることから、「住むことができたらうれしい」という気持ちを表していると言えます。これを excitement で表現した (A) が正解です。

□ excitement: 名 興奮　□ alternative: 名 代案　□ turn down ～: ～を断る

---

55. 正解：D 易■■■□□□□□ 難　選択率：(A) 8.2% (B) 14.9% (C) 11.5% **(D) 65.1%**

What does the man say the woman should do?
(A) Visit his office after work
(B) Make a phone call
(C) Rent a house
(D) Install an app

男性は、女性がどうするといいと言っていますか。
(A) 仕事の後、彼の事務所を訪ねる
(B) 電話をかける
(C) 家を借りる
(D) アプリをインストールする

▶解説 男性の提案の表現を待ち受けて聞きます。❸で You should ～（～するといい）に続けて、不動産アプリをダウンロードすることに言及しており、これが男性の提案です。「ダウンロードする」を「インストールする」と言い換えた (D) が正解です。

((( ))) ゼミ生中継　　Hiro　Mai　Yasu　Dai　Saki

54. ....

Saki サキ、ターゲット文のイントネーションを覚えている？

かなりうれしそうでした。

そうだね。あのイントネーションが耳に入れば、選択肢を絞り込めると思わない？

(A) は問題なさそうです。

本当だ。(C) は変ですね。あのイントネーションから、オファーを断っている姿は想像できないです。

このように、イントネーションが意図問題のヒントになることは決してレアじゃない。だから、声の調子にも注意を払ってリスニングの練習をするといい。

大学の先生は「気持ちを込めたモノマネ音読をしなさい」と言っています。

そう、まさにそれが効果的だよ。気持ちを込めると、ターゲット文を発言している話者の気持ちを理解することに通じるからね。意図問題が楽勝になるはずだよ。

174 **Questions 56 through 58** refer to the following conversation.

W: The new recruits will be starting next week, so ❶ we need to talk about the training workshop.

M: Right. I've reserved Meeting Room 1 for Monday and Tuesday and ❷ I sent an e-mail to the trainees telling them where it will be held. ❸ Would you like me to print out the manuals and handouts?

W: Yes, please. Don't do it yet, though. ❹ I want to make some changes to them first. We made a lot of changes to company policy last year and they haven't been reflected in the manuals or the presentations, yet. It'll take me a couple of days to check everything. Oh, and ❺ share the information about the location with the other instructors.　　　　　　　　　　(114w/38 sec.)

問題56-58は次の会話に関するものです。
女：新入社員たちが来週から働き始めるから、研修会について話さないと。
男：そうだね。第1会議室を月曜日と火曜日に押さえてあるし、研修生たちにメールを出して、どこで研修会が行われるか伝えたよ。マニュアルと配布資料をプリントアウトしようか。
女：ええ、お願い。でも、まだやらないで。最初に修正したいところがいくつかあるの。去年、会社の方針をたくさん変更したけど、それがマニュアルや説明資料にまだ反映されてないのよ。全てをチェックするのに2、3日かかりそうだわ。ああ、それと場所に関する情報を他の講師にも伝えておいて。

□ recruit: 图 新入社員　□ training workshop: 研修会　□ trainee: 图 訓練を受ける人　□ handout: 图 資料　□ reflect: 動 ～を反映する
□ presentation: 图 プレゼンテーション　＊ここではそれ用の資料のこと

Part 3　▼ Listening Section

---

56. 正解：**A**　易 ■■■□□□□ 難　選択率：**(A) 83.3%** (B) 12.3% (C) 3.3% (D) 0.7%

What is the conversation mainly about?
(A) A training workshop
(B) A recruitment plan
(C) A marketing strategy
(D) A company banquet

この会話は、主に何に関するものですか。
(A) 研修会
(B) 求人計画
(C) マーケティング戦略
(D) 会社の宴会

▶解説 女性は❶で「研修会について話す必要がある」と述べています。また男性が❷で「参加者に開催場所を知らせた」と報告し、女性は❺で「場所を他の講師にも伝えるように」と言っています。会話全体が研修会についての相談だと言えるので(A)が正解です。

□ recruitment: 图 (人員の) 補充、求人

---

57. 正解：**A**　易 ■■■■□□□ 難　選択率：**(A) 72.9%** (B) 10.8% (C) 13.8% (D) 2.6%

What does the man offer to do?
(A) Prepare some documents
(B) Check some inventory
(C) Review a proposal
(D) Calculate a budget

男性は何をすることを申し出ていますか。
(A) 書類を準備する
(B) 在庫を確認する
(C) 提案を再調査する
(D) 予算を計算する

▶解説 男性は❸でWould you like me to ～?(～しましょうか) という表現を用いて、マニュアルや配布資料をプリントアウトすることを申し出ています。それを「書類を準備する」と表現している(A)が正解です。

□ inventory: 图 (店内の) 全商品、在庫
□ calculate: 動 ～を計算する

---

58. 正解：**D**　易 ■■■■■□□ 難　選択率：(A) 3.0% (B) 21.6% (C) 10.0% **(D) 65.4%**

What does the woman say she will do?
(A) Create a shopping list
(B) Complete a report
(C) Evaluate a product
(D) Revise some materials

女性は何をするつもりだと言っていますか。
(A) 買い物のリストを作る
(B) 報告書を完成させる
(C) 製品を評価する
(D) いくつかの資料を修正する

▶解説 女性の❹の「それらに変更を加えたい」という発言は、プリントアウトを申し出た男性に対するもので、themはマニュアルなどを指しています。正解(D)ではmake changes toをrevise、マニュアルなどをmaterials (資料) と言い換えています。

□ evaluate: 動 ～を評価する　□ revise: 動 ～を修正する

(((📡))) ゼミ 生中継　　　　🎙Hiro 🎙Mai 🎙Yasu 🎙Dai 🎙Saki

56.

🎙 会話の冒頭でThe new recruits ～が聞こえるから、(B)に釣られそうになったかな。釣られ名人のサキはどうだった？

🎙 今回は大丈夫でした。話題が問われたので、後回しにしたのが良かったです。会話全体を聞くと、(B)のrecruitment planは全然ダメだと思いました。

🎙 いいね。受験の要領が良くなっている。

57.

🎙 設問は「申し出」の内容を尋ねているよね。このタイプの設問は頻出

する。そして、ヒントの出現方法にいくつかのパターンがある。相手のために何かすることを申し出る表現を知っているかな。

🎙 Let me ～ですか。

🎙 そう。I'll ～ for you. もそうだし、今回のようにWould you like me to ～? がヒントになることも多い。申し出の内容が問われていない場合でも、会話の中で誰かが何かを申し出ることはあるから、普段から申し出の表現に敏感になっておくと必ず役立つよ。

🎙 なるほど。

Part 3 会話問題

Questions 59 through 61 refer to the following conversation.

W: Waterfront Grill. How may I help you?

M: Hello. It's Martin Smith. ❶ I have an appointment to see Mr. Collins about some arrangements for a company banquet.

W: Right. ❷ I have you down for a meeting at 2 P.M. tomorrow.

M: Thanks. ❸ That's all I wanted to know.

W: Really?

M: Yeah– ❹ my computer has stopped working and I couldn't check my calendar.

W: Ah... OK, we'll see you tomorrow, Mr. Smith.

M: Oh, by the way, I was planning on driving in. Is there parking available in the building?

W: I'm afraid not, ❺ but there is usually plenty of parking available on the street outside. (98w/35 sec.)

□ arrangement: 名 手配　□ by the way: ところで　□ plenty of ～: 十分な～　□ outside: 副 外に

問題59-61は次の会話に関するものです。
女：Waterfront Grill です。ご用件を承ります。
男：もしもし。Martin Smith です。会社の宴会の手配の件でCollins さんとお会いする約束があるんですが。
女：はい。明日の午後2時のお打ち合わせということでお待ちしています。
男：ありがとう。それだけ知りたかったのです。
女：本当ですか。
男：ええ――私のコンピューターが作動しなくなって、カレンダーを確認できなかったものですから。
女：ああ……そうでしたか、では明日お待ちしております、Smith さま。
男：あ、ところで、車で伺うつもりなのです。建物の中に駐車できる場所はありますか。
女：あいにくございませんが、いつも外の通り沿いにたくさん駐車スペースが空いています。

---

59. 正解：C 易 ■■■□□□□□ 難　選択率：(A) 5.2% (B) 1.9% **(C) 91.4%** (D) 1.1%

Why is the man calling?
(A) To cancel a reservation
(B) To book a seat on a bus
(C) To confirm the time of an appointment
(D) To request an extension to a deadline

□ extension: 名 繰り延べ、延期　□ deadline: 名 締め切り

なぜ男性は電話をかけていますか。
(A) 予約をキャンセルするために
(B) バスの座席を予約するために
(C) 約束の時刻を確認するために
(D) 締め切りの延長を依頼するために

▶解説 男性が❶でMr. Collins との約束について言及し、女性は❷で「明日の午後2時に打ち合わせ予定だ」と答えています。それを聞いた男性が❸で「それだけ知りたかった」という発言から、彼は約束の確認をするために電話をかけたと考えられます。正解は(C)です。

---

60. 正解：B 易 ■■■□□□□□ 難　選択率：(A) 4.1% **(B) 84.4%** (C) 1.1% (D) 10.4%

What problem does the man mention?
(A) Traffic congestion
(B) A computer malfunction
(C) A flight delay
(D) A scheduling error

□ congestion: 名 渋滞　□ malfunction: 名 故障

男性はどんな問題を述べていますか。
(A) 交通渋滞
(B) コンピューターの不具合
(C) 航空便の遅延
(D) スケジュールの間違い

▶解説 男性は❹で「コンピューターが作動しなくなり、カレンダーを確認できなかった」と述べており、これが男性の言及している問題です。これをcomputer malfunction（コンピューターの不具合）と表現した(B)が正解です。

---

61. 正解：C 易 ■■■□□□□□ 難　選択率：(A) 4.5% (B) 2.2% **(C) 88.8%** (D) 4.5%

What does the woman say the man can do?
(A) Finalize a plan at a later date
(B) Send a text message to Mr. Collins
(C) Use some space near a building
(D) Borrow a company-owned car

□ finalize: 動 ～を確定する　□ text message: テキスト・メッセージ、携帯メッセージ　□ company-owned: 形 社有の

男性は何をできると女性は言っていますか。
(A) 後日、計画を仕上げる
(B) Collins さんへテキストメッセージを送る
(C) 建物付近のスペースを利用する
(D) 会社が所有する車を借りる

▶解説 男性から建物に駐車場があるか尋ねられた女性は❺で「外の通り沿いにたくさん駐車スペースが空いている」と述べています。これは、男性がその場所を使えることを伝える発言なので、(C)が正解です。

(((ゼミ生中継
Hiro　Mai　Yasu　Dai　Saki

60.

😎 Test 2の54番で、問題が問われたら、悪いことを連想させる単語がヒントになることが多いと言ったよね。ここではbroken やwrong といった直接的ヒントじゃなく、computer has stopped working だった。

😀 その直後にI couldn't check my calendar. って言ったので、そっちの方が悪い出来事に聞こえました。

😐 同じく。パソコンが止まること自体は必ずしも問題ではありません。カレンダーをチェックできないことの方が問題です。

😎 なるほど。カレンダーとスケジュールは関係が深いから、(D)のA scheduling error に釣られたモニターが約10%いたのか。

😀 自分も釣られました。

TOEICよろず相談所　ヒロの部屋

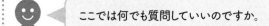

⑮スコアは910点ですが、全然話せません

ここでは何でも質問していいのですか。

英語学習に関することなら何でもOKですよ。

最近、TOEICで910点を取ったのですが、ちょっと驚いています。

910点とはすごいですね。おめでとうございます。

って言われるんですけど……実は、自分の英語力の低さに驚いているのです。900点を超えたのに、全然しゃべれません。

なるほど。よくある話です。でも、こう考えてはいかがですか。全然英語をしゃべれないのに、910点を取れたのは大成功だ、と。

でも、私は英語を話せるようになりたいので、素直に喜べません。900点を取るころには、英語をスラスラ話せているとイメージしていました。

ということは、英語を話せるようになりたくてTOEICを受験してきたのですね。そして、スコアが上がるのが面白くて「テスト対策」をしてきたのでしょうか。

はい、確かにそうです。

ここ1カ月の英語学習を振り返ってください。全体が100だとして、TOEIC対策を差し引くとどれだけ残りますか。

えっと、ゼロかもしれません。

「英語を話す練習」はしてこなかったのですね。であれば、話せないのは当然です。英語を話せるようになりたければ、その目的に沿ったトレーニングをしましょう。これから始めればいいではないですか。

あぁ…目からうろこが落ちました。これから頑張ります。

Part 3 会話問題

 Questions 62 through 64 refer to the following conversation and directory.

M: ❶I called earlier to ask about a book on modern European archi-tecture. ❷I was assured it was in stock but I can't find it.

W: Sure. ❸Can you give me the title of the book?

M: Yeah, it's called *Images of Europe*.

W: Hmm. So it's a book on architecture, right? Did you check the third floor?

M: Yes, I was just there, but I couldn't find it.

W: Oh, I know why. This is actually a collection of photographs of buildings in Europe. ❹I think it's in our travel section.

M: I see. I'll take a look there, then. (94w/35 sec.)

□ modern: 形 現代の　□ architecture: 名 建築　□ assure: 動 ～に断言する　□ in stock: 在庫の　□ title: 名 題名　□ actually: 副 実は
□ science: 名 科学

Directory	
Floor 4	Sciences
Floor 3	Architecture
Floor 2	Languages
❺**Floor 1**	Travel

案内板	
4階	科学
3階	建築
2階	言語
1階	旅行

問題62-64は次の会話と案内板に関するものです。

男：先ほど電話で、現代ヨーロッパ建築に関する本についてお伺いしたんです。間違いなく在庫があるということだったのですが、見つかりません。

女：かしこまりました。その本のタイトルを教えていただけますか。

男：ええ、『Images of Europe』というものです。

女：うーん。で、それは建築に関する本なのですね？　3階は探されましたか。

男：はい、今まで3階にいたのですが、見つかりませんでした。

女：ああ、理由が分かりました。これは実はヨーロッパの建物の写真集ですね。当店の旅行書の棚にあると思いますよ。

男：なるほど。じゃあ、そこを見てみます。

62. 正解：**C**   易▮▮▮▯▯▯▯難   選択率：(A) 6.3% (B) 10.4% **(C) 80.7%** (D) 2.6%

Who most likely is the woman?
(A) A school teacher
(B) An artist
(C) A shop clerk
(D) A translator

女性は誰である可能性が最も高いですか。
(A) 学校の先生
(B) 芸術家
(C) 店員
(D) 通訳者

▶解説 ❶から男性はある本について電話で問い合わせ、❷で在庫があると聞いたのに見つけられないことが分かります。そのため女性に助けを求めています。本の在庫がある職場で働く女性は書店の従業員であると考えられるので、(C)が正解です。

63. 正解：**A**   易▮▮▮▯▯▯▯難   選択率：(A) 84.8% (B) 2.2% (C) 3.3% (D) 9.7%

What information does the woman request?
(A) The title of a publication
(B) The number of visitors
(C) The date of an event
(D) The address of a building

☐ publication: 名 出版物

女性はどんな情報を求めていますか。
(A) 出版物のタイトル
(B) 来訪者数
(C) 催事の日付
(D) 建物の所在地

▶解説 女性は❸で書名を尋ねています。Can you give me ～？は依頼の表現で、これを使って情報を求めており、正解は(A)です。publication（出版物）は本、雑誌などの言い換えとして覚えておきたい単語です。

64. 正解：**D**   易▮▮▮▯▯▯▯難   選択率：(A) 0.7% (B) 13.4% (C) 1.1% **(D) 84.4%**

Look at the graphic. Which floor will the man go to next?
(A) Floor 4
(B) Floor 3
(C) Floor 2
(D) Floor 1

図表を見てください。男性はこの後、どの階へ行きますか。
(A) 4階
(B) 3階
(C) 2階
(D) 1階

▶解説 女性は❹で、男性が探している本は旅行書の棚にあると思うと述べています。それを受けて男性は、そこを見てみると答えています。案内板の❺から、旅行書は1階にあると分かるので、男性が次に行くのは(D)の「1階」です。

Part 3 ▼ Listening Section

((•)) ゼミ生中継   Hiro   Mai   Yasu   Dai   Saki

64.
不正解を選んだモニターのうちほとんどが、(B)の3階を選んでいる。予想通り。

そんな予想ができるのですか。

できる。問題作成者が使うテクニックを覚えている？ Test 2で話したやつ。

ダマシとボカシですか。

そう。ここでは、ダマシのテクニックに引っ掛かると、(B)を選ぶことになる。

私です。architecture が聞こえたのでダマされました。

サキ、その直後に何が聞こえた？

Did you check the third floor? です。ずばり「3階」が聞こえたので、なおさら(B)を選びたくなりました。

逆だよ。third floor が聞こえたということは、3階が正解になるはずがない。グラフィック問題は音情報だけでは解けないからね。

あ、そうでした。忘れていました……。

Part 3 会話問題

 178 **Questions 65 through 67** refer to the following conversation and seating chart.

W: OK, sir. ❶ We have a flight for Dallas leaving this evening at 7:25, and arriving at 9:30. Will you be carrying more than 20 kilograms of luggage?

M: No, that should be more than enough. ❷ Do you have any aisle seats still available?

W: Just one I'm afraid.

M: OK. ❸ I'll take it.

W: Great. You don't have much time to get to the airport so I suggest that you leave as soon as possible.

M: Thanks. ❹ I live near there so it shouldn't be a problem.

(82w/30 sec.)

問題65-67は次の会話と座席表に関するものです。
女：では、お客さま。今晩7時25分発、9時30分着のダラス行きの便がございます。20キロを超えるお荷物を持ち込まれるご予定ですか。
男：いいえ、そこまでにはならないはずです。通路側の席はまだ空いていますか。
女：1つだけしか無いようですが。
男：結構です。それを取ります。
女：かしこまりました。空港に到着していただくまでにあまり時間がありませんので、できるだけ早く出発なさることをお勧めします。
男：分かりました。私はその近くに住んでいるので、大丈夫なはずです。

□ flight: 名 飛行便、フライト　□ carry: 動 ～を持っていく　□ luggage: 名 手荷物　□ more than enough: 十二分で、十分過ぎる
□ aisle: 名 通路

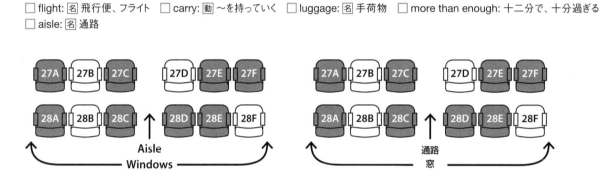

292

65. 正解：**B** 易 ■■■□□□□ 難 選択率：(A) 12.3% **(B) 79.6%** (C) 7.1% (D) 0.7%

When will the man's flight leave?
(A) This morning
(B) This evening
(C) Tomorrow morning
(D) Tomorrow afternoon

男性の乗る飛行機はいつ出発しますか。
(A) 今日の午前中
(B) 今日の夕刻
(C) 明日の午前中
(D) 明日の午後

▶解説 ❶で女性が、今夜7時25分発の便があることを男性に知らせています。荷物の重さや座席の選択について話が続いていることから、男性はこの便に搭乗すると推測でき、(B)が正解だと判断できます。

---

66. 正解：**B** 易 ■■□□□□□ 難 選択率：(A) 2.2% **(B) 90.3%** (C) 3.0% (D) 3.7%

Look at the graphic. Which seat will the man take?
(A) 27B
(B) 27D
(C) 28B
(D) 28F

図表を見てください。男性はどの席に座りますか。
(A) 27B
(B) 27D
(C) 28B
(D) 28F

▶解説 男性は❷で通路側の席を希望し、直後に女性から残り1席しかないことを伝えられています。そして、❸でその席を購入すると女性に告げていることから、男性が座るのは通路席だと分かります。選択肢の中で通路側の席は27Dだけなので、(B)が正解です。

---

67. 正解：**A** 易 ■■■■□□□ 難 選択率：**(A) 69.5%** (B) 5.9% (C) 21.6% (D) 2.6%

What does the man say about his home?
(A) It is near the airport.
(B) It is in Dallas.
(C) He will not have time to return there.
(D) He does not have an Internet connection.

□ return: 動 帰る

男性は自宅について何と言っていますか。
(A) 空港に近い。
(B) ダラスにある。
(C) そこへ戻る時間がない。
(D) インターネットにつながっていない。

▶解説 男性は❹で「その近くに住んでいるから大丈夫なはず」と言っています。これは女性が「なるべく早く空港に向かうべきだ」と助言したことへの返答です。よって、男性は空港の近くに住んでいることが分かります。正解は(A)です。

Part 3 ▶ Listening Section

(((📡))) ゼミ生中継 😎Hiro 😊Mai 😺Yasu 😎Dai 😸Saki

66.

😎 会話を聞く前に、黒と白のどちらが空席だと思った？

😸 白が空席です。航空会社のウェブサイトで座席指定すると、こんな画面が出てきます。

😎 選択肢にある座席番号をチェックしたら全部白い席だったので、男性は白い席を取ると予想しました。

😺 マイがやったように、選択肢にある4つの情報をグラフィックの中で探すようにチェックすると効率的だね。

😸 27Bと28Bは特徴を説明しにくいので、通路側か窓側が正解だと予想したら当たりました。

😺 ナイスな勘だね。ま、その調子で勘もリスニング力も磨いて。

67.

😎 上級グループでは正答率が95.5%だけど、初級グループでは49.3%しかない。多くが(C)を選んでいる。女性が後半でYou don't have much time to get to ～と言っていて、それが(C)に似ているからだね。聞こえた語句を含む選択肢に飛びつくと痛い目に遭う例だよ。

Part 3 会話問題

<DL>179</DL> **Questions 68 through 70** refer to the following conversation and list.

W: ❶ The last item on the agenda at today's meeting is the body soap housekeeping provides in each of the guest rooms.

M: Right. ❷ The supplier has started charging us too much and you wanted to use... Um... some other brand.

W: Yes. Aloe Soap. ❸ It is specially developed for accommodation providers. Furthermore, we can get it at half the price. It comes in four sizes–ranging from 100 milliliters up to a one-liter bottle. ❹ The one-liter bottle is too large for the shelf in the bathrooms, so I think we should go with the next size down.

M: Why not one of the smaller ones?

W: The larger bottles are better value for money.　　　(110w/40 sec.)

問題68-70は次の会話と表に関するものです。

女：今日の会議の最後の議題は、客室清掃部が各客室に備えるボディーソープについてです。

男：そうですね。納入業者の請求額が高くなり始めたので……えー……何か他のブランドのものを使いたいと。

女：はい。Aloe Soap です。これは宿泊業者向けに特別に開発されています。しかも、半値で入手できるのです。4つのサイズがあります──100ミリリットルから1リットルのボトルまでです。1リットルのボトルだと大き過ぎて浴室の棚に収まりませんので、1つ下のサイズのものにするのがいいと思います。

男：なぜさらに小さなものではないんですか。

女：大きめのボトルの方がコストパフォーマンスが良いのです。

□ item: 图 項目　□ agenda: 图 議題　□ housekeeping: 图 (ホテルなどの) 客室清掃部　□ provide: 動 ～を提供する
□ supplier: 图 供給業者　□ charge: 動 (人にある金額を)請求する　□ brand: 图 ブランド　□ specially: 副 特別に　□ develop: 動 ～を開発する
□ accommodation: 图 宿泊施設　□ furthermore: 副 なお、さらに　□ range from A to B: A から B まで及ぶ　□ go with ～: ～を選ぶ
□ better value for money: 割安な

ALOE SOAP	
Size	Volume
Mini	100ml
Small	300ml
❺ Regular	500ml
Large	1L

ALOE SOAP	
サイズ	量
極小	100ミリリットル
小	300ミリリットル
中	500ミリリットル
大	1リットル

68. 正解：A 易 ■■■□□□□□□ 難   選択率：**(A) 73.6%** (B) 7.1% (C) 13.0% (D) 6.3%

Where does the conversation most likely take place?
(A) At a hotel
(B) At a hair salon
(C) At a supermarket
(D) At a manufacturing plant

この会話はどこで交わされている可能性が最も高いですか。
(A) ホテルで
(B) 美容室で
(C) スーパーマーケットで
(D) 製造工場で

▶解説 女性が❶で「議題は各客室に備えるボディーソープに関して」だと述べています。さらに❸で宿泊業者向けに開発された製品の話をしており、これはホテルの社内会議であると判断できます。正解は(A)です。他の選択肢を避けるには、❶にあるguest rooms（客室）がヒントとなります。

---

69. 正解：C 易 ■■■□□□□□□ 難   選択率：(A) 7.8% (B) 7.1% **(C) 74.0%** (D) 11.2%

What does the man say about the supplier?
(A) It has won an award.
(B) It will redesign its logo.
(C) It has raised its prices.
(D) It will terminate a contract.

□ redesign: 動 ～を新しくデザインする □ logo: 名 ロゴ
□ raise: 動 （価格）を引き上げる □ terminate: 動 ～を終える

男性は納入業者について何と言っていますか。
(A) 賞を受賞した。
(B) 会社のロゴをデザインし直すだろう。
(C) 値上げした。
(D) 契約を解消するだろう。

▶解説 納入業者について男性は❷で触れています。請求が高額になってきているという内容から、納入業者は価格を上げたと言えるので、(C)が正解です。他ブランド製品について話し合ってはいますが、納入業者が契約を終えるとの発言はないため、(D)は不正解です。

---

70. 正解：C 易 ■■■■□□□□□ 難   選択率：(A) 3.7% (B) 20.1% **(C) 66.2%** (D) 9.7%

Look at the graphic. Which size will the speakers most likely choose?
(A) Mini
(B) Small
(C) Regular
(D) Large

図表を見てください。話者たちはどのサイズを選ぶ可能性が最も高いですか。
(A) 極小
(B) 小
(C) 中
(D) 大

▶解説 ❹で女性は、1リットルは浴室の棚に収まらないから、1サイズ小さいものにしようと提案しています。表を見ると、それは500ミリリットルの中サイズです（❺）。男性がより小さいサイズではない理由を尋ねると、女性は価格とのバランスの良さを挙げています。従って、中サイズが選ばれる可能性が最も高いため、正解は(C)です。

((📡)) **ゼミ生中継**   😺 Hiro 🐰 Mai 🐵 Yasu 🐶 Dai 🐱 Saki

70.

😺 ダマシとボカシに続く、問題作成者のテクニックを紹介するよ。その前に、解答の基本を確認しよう。選択肢とグラフィックに共通する情報を見つけることが大事だよね。そして、それ以外の情報がヒントになる。今回、会話で1リットルという情報が聞こえたけど、その後で何が起きた？

🐵 1リットルはダメだから、1つ小さいサイズにする話になりました。

😺 そう。1行ズレた場所に視線が誘導されたよね。これが「ズラシ」の

テクニックだよ。ズラシ以外に、ダマシとして smaller が登場していた。このエサにパクっと食いつくと、(B)を選んでしまう。初級グループの41.8%が釣られてしまった。問題作成者があの手この手で受験者を混乱させようとしているのが分かった？

🐶 意地悪ですね。

🐱 同感。

😺 では、Part 4 に行こう。

Part 4 説明文問題

DL 181 **Questions 71 through 73** refer to the following advertisement.

M: ❶Norton Community Center is pleased to announce that its relocation is now complete. To celebrate the reopening, we're holding a special event at our new building on April 15. We've invited Dave Broman, a retired mayor of Norton, who was one of the people responsible for the establishment of a community center in the first place. He recently published a book on his time as mayor and ❷he's agreed to talk to us about some of the contents. It should be an interesting talk. Tickets are free, but seating is limited. ❸Be sure to secure your seat through our Web site before they run out. Search online for the Norton Community Center.　　(112w/43 sec.)

問題71-73は次の宣伝に関するものです。
Norton Community Centerは、移転が完了したことをお知らせできることをうれしく思います。再開を祝して、新しい建物で4月15日に特別な催しを開催する予定です。当日はNortonの元市長、Dave Broman氏をお招きしています。氏は最初に地域センターの設立に尽力された方々の1人です。氏は先ごろ、市長時代のことをつづった著書を出版され、その内容の一部についてお話しいただけることになっています。興味深い講演となるでしょう。チケットは無料ですが、席に限りがあります。満席になる前に当センターのウェブサイトで席をご予約ください。オンラインでNorton Community Centerを検索してください。

☐ relocation: 图 移転　☐ celebrate: 動 ～を祝う　☐ retire: 動 退職する
☐ mayor: 图 市長　☐ establishment: 图 設立　☐ content: 图 中身、内容物
☐ seating: 图 座席　☐ secure: 動 ～を確保する　☐ run out: 売り切れる

---

71. 正解：C 易■■■□□□□□ 難　選択率：(A) 2.2% (B) 14.1% **(C) 80.7%** (D) 1.9%

What has the community center done recently?
(A) Hosted an auction
(B) Undergone renovations
(C) Moved to a new location
(D) Changed its opening hours

☐ undergo: 動 ～を受ける
☐ renovation: 图 修復、改築

この地域センターは最近、何をしましたか。
(A) オークションを主催した
(B) 改装工事を行った
(C) 新たな場所へ移転した
(D) 開館時間を変更した

▶解説 話者は❶で「Norton Community Centerの移転が完了した」ことを述べています。移転は「新たな場所へ移る」ことなので、(C)が正解です。

---

72. 正解：B 易■■■■□□□□ 難　選択率：(A) 16.7% **(B) 49.4%** (C) 10.4% (D) 22.7%

What has Mr. Broman agreed to do?
(A) Sign a contract
(B) Discuss a book
(C) Make a donation
(D) Answer questions

☐ donation: 图 寄付（金）

Bromanさんは何をすることに同意していますか。
(A) 契約書に署名する
(B) ある本について話す
(C) 寄付をする
(D) 質問に答える

▶解説 Bromanさんは最近本を出版した元市長です。❷でBromanさんが同意したことが述べられています。talk to usをdiscussで言い換えた(B)が正解です。discussは「～について話す」という意味でも使われます。

---

73. 正解：B 易■■□□□□□□ 難　選択率：(A) 1.9% **(B) 94.8%** (C) 1.1% (D) 1.1%

How can listeners obtain tickets?
(A) By buying a magazine
(B) By visiting a Web site
(C) By answering a survey
(D) By calling an organizer

聞き手はどのようにチケットを入手できますか。
(A) 雑誌を買うことで
(B) ウェブサイトにアクセスすることで
(C) アンケートに答えることで
(D) 主催者に電話することで

▶解説 話者は❸でBe sure to ～（～するように）と相手に念押しする表現を使って、ウェブサイトで席を確保するよう伝えているので、(B)が正解です。その後に、聞き手にインターネットで検索するよう促していることもヒントになります。

((•)) ゼミ 生 中継

(😊)Hiro (😊)Mai (😊)Yasu (😎)Dai (😊)Saki

71.
(😊) では、Part 4を始めよう。移転じゃなく改装だと思った人にとっては、(B)が魅力的かな。サキ、どれを選んだ？
(😊) (B)です。relocationを聞いてrenovationだと勘違いしました。

72.
(😊) ほら、discussが出た。あれは確か……
(😎) Test 1の148番です。

(😊) よく覚えているなぁ。モニターの正答率が5割を切ったのは、(B)を「本について議論する」と考えた人が多かったからだろうね。
(😎) Test 1の話を思い出して、(B)を選べました。
(😊) ナイス。他の選択肢は証拠がないね。
(😊) TOEICワールドでは、何かに出演するゲストが来場者やリスナーの質問に答えるのが普通なので、(D)を選んでしまいました。

DL 182 Questions 74 through 76 refer to the following talk.

W: ❶ I'm so glad that so many members of the press have come here today to hear this announcement from our company president. Mr. Drake will be on stage in a few minutes to talk about the development of our new smartphone and its revolutionary camera. I am permitted to tell you a few things, though. The new phone will be called the Ex-plus. And, ❷ it will be released to the public on September 20. Most excitingly, however, ❸ I can tell you that we've provided product samples for everyone attending the event today. ❹ Be sure to pick yours up as you leave the conference hall.　(104w/37 sec.)

問題74-76は次のトークに関するものです。
本日は弊社社長によるこの発表をお聞きいただくために、これほどたくさんの報道関係者にお集まりくださり、大変喜ばしく思います。Drakeが数分後に壇上で、弊社の新しいスマートフォンと、搭載される革新的なカメラの開発についてお話しいたします。ただし、私からも2、3お話しさせていただけることになっています。新しいスマートフォンはEx-plusと呼ばれます。そして、9月20日に発売される予定です。それはさておき、何よりも胸が躍ることに、本日この場にご参加いただいている全員に製品サンプルをご用意していることを、お知らせいたします。必ずご自分の分をお取りいただいてから、会議場を後にしてください。

□ press: 名 報道陣、記者　□ president: 名 社長　□ on stage: 壇上で
□ revolutionary: 形 革新的な、画期的な　□ release: 動 ～を発売する
□ to the public: 一般に、一般大衆に向けて　□ excitingly: 副 胸が躍ることに

74. 正解：D 易■■■□□□□難　選択率：(A) 1.1% (B) 14.1% (C) 7.1% **(D) 77.7%**

Where is the talk taking place?
(A) At a movie trade fair
(B) At a department meeting
(C) At an orientation session
(D) At a press conference

このトークはどこで行われていますか。
(A) 映画の見本市で
(B) 部内会議で
(C) 研修会で
(D) 記者会見で

▶解説 話者は❶で、「社長からの発表を聞くために多くの報道関係者が集まってくれてうれしい」と述べています。その後も、新製品の発表に関する内容が述べられているため、このトークは「記者会見」で行われていると判断できます。(D)が正解です。

□ take place: 起こる　□ trade fair: 見本市、展示会
□ session: 名 会合、集い　□ press conference: 記者会見

75. 正解：B 易■■□□□□□難　選択率：(A) 4.8% **(B) 78.4%** (C) 2.6% (D) 14.1%

What is planned for September 20?
(A) The company will change ownership.
(B) A new line of merchandise will go on sale.
(C) New employees will start work.
(D) A review will be published.

9月20日に何が予定されていますか。
(A) 会社の所有者が変わる。
(B) 新種の製品が発売される。
(C) 新入社員が働き始める。
(D) ある批評が出版される。

▶解説 この発表が新しいスマートフォンのものであること、そして商品名が発表された後、❷で「それは9月20日に発売される」と述べられています。よって、9月20日は新製品の発売日だということが分かるので、正解は(B)です。

□ ownership: 名 所有権　□ a new line of ～: ～の新製品、～の新種製品
□ merchandise: 名 商品　□ go on sale: 発売される、市場に出回る

76. 正解：D 易■■■□□□□難　選択率：(A) 5.9% (B) 8.6% (C) 17.5% **(D) 67.7%**

What are the listeners asked to do?
(A) Purchase protective clothing
(B) Bid for a contract
(C) Complete a customer survey
(D) Receive a sample as they leave

聞き手は何をするよう求められていますか。
(A) 保護服を買う
(B) ある契約に入札する
(C) 顧客アンケートに記入する
(D) 退出時にサンプルを受け取る

▶解説 ❸から、出席者全員に新製品のサンプルが配られることが分かります。その直後の❹でBe sure to ～（必ず～するように）と相手に念押しをする表現が続き、「会場を出る時にサンプルを受け取ることを忘れないように」と聞き手に伝えています。よって、(D)が正解です。

□ protective: 形 防護の　□ clothing: 名 衣服　□ bid: 動 入札する
□ complete: 動 ～に記入する　□ survey: 名 調査、アンケート

ゼミ生中継　Hiro Mai Yasu Dai Saki

75.
😀 設問に具体的な日付がある。日付は言い換えることができないから、トークの中で話者がそのまま言うと予測できるよね。日付以外に、どんな情報は言い換えられないと予測できる？
😀 曜日とか月でしょうか。
😀 そうだね。他にある？
😀 さっき出た、Bromanみたいな人名も言い換え不可能です。

😀 そう、固有名詞全般だね。固有名詞が聞き取れなくて苦手だと言う受験者は多いけど、やむを得ないと思う。大事なのは、それが名前であると認識できること。全ての固有名詞を聞き取れるようになる必要はないよ。
😀 ちょっと安心しました。
😀 72番や77番のように文字で確認できる場合は、聞く前に文字を見ておくと聞き取りやすくなる。

Part 4 説明文問題

DL 183 Questions 77 through 79 refer to the following telephone message.

W: Hi. This is Molly Taylor from Hampton Institute of Technology.
🇨🇦 ❶ I'm calling about the presentation you've agreed to give at our campus on Friday. We're really looking forward to hearing you speak. ❷ I just wanted to remind you to bring a receipt for any expenses you incur. ❸ This includes transportation and accommodation. ❹ I regret that we have not discussed any plans for after the presentation. Let me address that now. ❺ Today a few members of the staff mentioned that they'd like to take you out for dinner. I hope you'll consider the offer. Anyway, I'm looking forward to finally meeting with you face to face tomorrow.

(106w/46 sec.)

問題77-79は次の電話メッセージに関するものです。
もしもし。Hampton Institute of Technologyの Molly Taylor です。本学のキャンパスで金曜日に発表していただく件で、お電話を差し上げています。一同、あなたのお話を拝聴するのを大変楽しみにしております。お支払いいただく経費の領収書をお持ちくださるよう、お伝えするためにお電話しました。これには交通費と宿泊費が含まれます。発表を終えられてからの予定についてご相談しておらず申し訳ございません。この場でお知らせいたします。本日、スタッフ数名が、あなたを夕食にお連れしたいと申しておりました。この件をご検討いただければ幸いです。ともあれ、明日、いよいよ直接お会いできるのを楽しみにしております。

☐ incur: 動 (費用) を負担する ☐ regret: 動 ～を残念に思う ☐ face to face: 対面で

---

77. 正解：D 易 ■■■□□□ 難 選択率：(A) 4.8% (B) 4.8% (C) 5.9% **(D) 84.4%**

Why will the listener go to Hampton Institute of Technology?
(A) To meet with a candidate
(B) To take a class
(C) To collaborate on some research
(D) To give a presentation

なぜ聞き手は Hampton Institute of Technology へ行きますか。
(A) 候補者と会うために
(B) 授業を受けるために
(C) 研究に協力するために
(D) 発表を行うために

▶解説 Hampton Institute of Technology から電話していると話者が名乗った後の❶から、聞き手がそこで金曜日に講演を行う予定であることが分かります。よって、正解は (D) です。

☐ candidate: 名 候補者 ☐ collaborate: 動 協力する

---

78. 正解：B 易 ■■■□□□ 難 選択率：(A) 13.0% **(B) 54.3%** (C) 17.5% (D) 15.2%

What is the listener instructed to bring?
(A) A piece of identification
(B) A travel receipt
(C) An application form
(D) A research paper

聞き手は何を持ってくるよう指示されていますか。
(A) 身分証明書
(B) 旅費の領収書
(C) 申込用紙
(D) 研究論文

▶解説 話者は❷で聞き手に「支払った経費の領収書を持ってくる」よう念押しし、さらに❸で「それには交通費と宿泊費が含まれる」と述べています。よって、この内容を「旅費の領収書」と表した (B) が正解です。

☐ instruct ... to ～：…に～するよう指示する

---

79. 正解：A 易 ■■■■□□ 難 選択率：**(A) 45.7%** (B) 38.7% (C) 6.7% (D) 8.2%

What does the speaker mean when she says, "Let me address that now"?
(A) She wants to make some plans clear.
(B) She will give the listener her contact details.
(C) She believes there has been a misunderstanding.
(D) She thinks the listener has gone to the wrong location.

話者はどのような意図で「この場でお知らせいたします」と言っていますか。
(A) 予定をはっきりさせたい。
(B) 聞き手に自分の連絡先を伝えようとしている。
(C) 誤解が生じていると思っている。
(D) 聞き手が間違った場所へ行ってしまったと考えている。

▶解説 ❹から、話し手と聞き手は発表後の予定について話し合っていないことが分かります。この直後に Let me address that now. と言い、❺で話者は聞き手を食事に連れて行く案を伝えています。よって、ターゲット文は発表後の予定について話したいという意図を伝えるための発言です。これに合致するのは「予定をはっきりさせたい」を意味する (A) です。

☐ address: 動 ～に話し掛ける ☐ misunderstanding: 名 誤解

((•)) ゼミ生中継 😀 Hiro 😃 Mai 😸 Yasu 😎 Dai 😊 Saki

79.

😀 ターゲット文に代名詞の that があるから、それが何を指すか理解できていなければ解きにくい。モニターの上級グループでは正答率が9割近いけれど、中級では約4割、初級では約2割となっているから、やはり実力差がはっきり表れている。ダイは解けた？

😎 いいえ。address にいろんな意味がある気がして、考えているうちに次のトークが流れてきたので捨てました。

😀 確かに address には「～に対処する」以外に多くの意味がある。この本の中でも少なくとも3種類の意味が紹介されているから、復習時に見つけたらきちんと意味を確認してね。

DL ↓ 184 **Questions 80 through 82** refer to the following advertisement.

W: ❶ Tomorrow morning is the grand opening of Hobart's first ever Reed's Discount Store. To celebrate, we're giving lifetime membership cards to the first hundred people through the door. ❷ They entitle the holder to 10 percent off on all items in the store. They are really worth having. Over the years, this could amount to thousands of dollars in savings. Whether or not you get a card, there will be plenty to do. ❸ Come in and find out why Reed's is the nation's fastest growing discount store chain.　(87w/34 sec.)

問題80-82は次の宣伝に関するものです。
明朝、Hobart初のReed's Discount Storeがグランドオープンします。これを祝して、終身会員カードを先着100名さまに発行いたします。このカードがあれば店内の全商品が10パーセント引きになります。大変お得です。何年も続ければ、これが数千ドルの節約につながるかもしれません。カードの有無にかかわらず、お楽しみいただけることがたっぷりあります。ご来店いただき、なぜReed'sが国内一の急成長を遂げているディスカウントストアチェーンなのかを知ってください。

□ first ever: 史上初の　　□ lifetime: 形 生涯の、終身の　　□ membership card: 会員カード　　□ first ～ through the door: 来店者先着～人
□ entitle ... to ～: ... に～する権利を与える　　□ holder: 名 所有者　　□ over the years: 年月を重ねるごとに　　□ amount to ～: 結局～になる
□ saving: 名 節約　　□ whether or not ～: ～であろうとなかろうと

---

80. 正解：**A**　易 ■■□□□□ 難　　選択率：**(A) 95.2%** (B) 0.7% (C) 0.7% (D) 3.3%

What is being advertised?
(A) A grand opening
(B) An art competition
(C) An employment opportunity
(D) A catering service

何が宣伝されていますか。
(A) グランドオープン
(B) 美術コンテスト
(C) 雇用の機会
(D) 仕出しサービス

▶解説 ❶から、明日はReed's Discount Storeのグランドオープンの日だと分かります。その後もオープンを記念して行われる企画の内容が述べられていることからも、正解は(A)です。

□ opportunity: 名 機会　□ catering: 名 料理の仕出し

---

81. 正解：**D**　易 ■■□□□□ 難　　選択率：(A) 3.7% (B) 6.3% (C) 5.2% **(D) 84.4%**

What does the card enable people to do?
(A) Use a special room
(B) Obtain additional points
(C) Prove their identification
(D) Get price reductions

カードがあると人々は何ができますか。
(A) 特別室を利用する
(B) 追加ポイントを獲得する
(C) 身元を証明する
(D) 値引きを受ける

▶解説 会員カードが先着100名に発行されることが述べられた後、❷でそのカードについて「カードがあれば店内の全商品が10パーセント引きになる」と説明されています。よって、(D)が正解です。

□ enable ... to ～: …が～できるようにする
□ obtain: 動 ～を手に入れる　□ identification: 名 身元
□ reduction: 名 割引、値下げ

---

82. 正解：**C**　易 ■■■□□□ 難　　選択率：(A) 10.8% (B) 15.6% **(C) 55.4%** (D) 17.5%

What does the speaker say about the organization?
(A) It is based in Hobart.
(B) It manufactures its own products.
(C) It has been expanding.
(D) It advertises online.

話者はこの組織について何と言っていますか。
(A) Hobartを本拠地としている。
(B) 独自の製品を生産している。
(C) 拡大してきている。
(D) オンラインで宣伝している。

▶解説 設問内のorganizationはReed's Discount Storeを指します。❸で「国内一の急成長を遂げているディスカウントストアチェーン」と述べられています。よって、正解は(C)です。❶から、Hobartに初出店することが分かるので、(A)は不正解です。

□ organization: 名 組織、団体　□ be based in ～: ～を本拠地としている　□ manufacture: 動 ～を製造する
□ expand: 動 ～を拡大する

📡))) ゼミ 🔴生中継　　😀 Hiro　😶 Mai　😮 Yasu　🎲 Dai　😄 Saki

81.
😀 ヤス、割引と言えば英語で何？
😮 discountです！
😀 それが最初に思い浮かぶよね。たまたまこのトークではdiscountは使われていなかったけれど、discountとprice reductionは重要な言い換えだから絶対に忘れないでね。

82.
😀 このセットでは、この設問の正答率が低い。何が難しかった？
😄 どこでヒントが言われたか気づきませんでした。
😀 設問に具体的な言葉がないから、特定の情報に焦点を当てた聞き方ができないね。このタイプは「正しい情報はどれ?」と問うているから、即効性のある受験テクニックは存在しない。「しっかり聞いて理解するよう努める」ことが最重要だよ。

Part 4 説明文問題

Questions 83 through 85 refer to the following talk.

M: Could I have your attention, please? ❶ <u>The home we are standing in front of now is one of the most interesting on our walking tour of Calgary.</u> The house belonged to Wayne Baker, the world-renowned music composer. He created the soundtracks for some of the most popular movies ever made. We're leaving at two o'clock. So, ❷ <u>you'll only have a short time to choose souvenirs from the gift shop.</u> Oh, and remember, ❸ <u>many of the objects inside, including some priceless artworks, are very light sensitive.</u> ❹ <u>That's why photography is strictly prohibited.</u> Any questions? OK, let's go inside. (97w/37 sec.)

問題83-85は次のトークに関するものです。
ちょっとお聞きいただけますか。私たちが今前に立っている家は、このCalgaryの徒歩ツアーで最も興味深いものの1つです。この家はかつて、Wayne Baker という世界的に有名な作曲家のものでした。彼は、これまで製作された最も人気の高い映画のいくつかのサウンドトラックを手掛けました。ここを2時に出発します。ですから、ギフトショップでお土産をお選びいただくには短時間しかありませんよ。ああ、それからご留意いただきたいのですが、大変高価な芸術作品も含めて屋内の品物の多くは非常に光に敏感です。そういう理由で、写真撮影が固く禁じられています。何かご質問は？ では、中に入りましょう。

☐renowned: 形 有名な　☐composer: 名 作曲家　☐object: 名 物体　☐artwork: 名 手工芸品
☐sensitive: 形 敏感な、弱い　☐photography: 名 写真撮影　☐strictly: 副 厳しく　☐prohibit: 動 ～を禁止する

---

83. 正解: **C** 易■■■□□□□□□難 選択率: (A) 0.4% (B) 1.5% **(C) 85.9%** (D) 11.5%

Who most likely is the speaker?
(A) A bus driver
(B) A security guard
(C) A tour guide
(D) A museum director

話者は誰である可能性が最も高いですか。
(A) バスの運転手
(B) 警備員
(C) ツアーガイド
(D) 博物館長

▶解説 話者は❶で、「目の前の家はCalgary の徒歩ツアーで最も興味深いもの」と聞き手に紹介しています。その後も建物にまつわる人物や建物内での注意事項を説明していることから、話者は(C)の「ツアーガイド」だと考えられます。

---

84. 正解: **A** 易■■■■□□□□□難 選択率: **(A) 59.9%** (B) 11.2% (C) 11.9% (D) 15.6%

Why does the speaker say, "We're leaving at two o'clock"?
(A) To encourage listeners to hurry
(B) To explain a change to the schedule
(C) To advise listeners to stay longer
(D) To draw attention to a closing time

なぜ話者は「2時に出発します」と言っていますか。
(A) 聞き手たちを急がせるために
(B) 予定の変更を説明するために
(C) 聞き手たちにより長く滞在するよう助言するために
(D) 閉館時間に注意を向けさせるために

▶解説 話者は「2時に出発する」と設問の発言をした後、❷でお土産を買う時間が限られていることを説明しています。つまり、聞き手に急いでもらうことが話者の意図だと判断できるので、(A)が正解です。

☐draw attention to ～: ～に注意を引く

---

85. 正解: **D** 易■■■■□□□□□難 選択率: (A) 1.9% (B) 5.2% (C) 16.0% **(D) 75.1%**

What are listeners advised to do?
(A) Buy tickets online
(B) Enjoy a meal
(C) Read a product description
(D) Refrain from taking pictures

聞き手たちは何をするようアドバイスされていますか。
(A) チケットをオンラインで購入する
(B) 食事を楽しむ
(C) 商品説明を読む
(D) 写真撮影を控える

▶解説 話者は❸で、家の中にある物の多くは光に敏感であることを説明しています。続く❹で「それが理由で写真撮影が固く禁じられている」と述べています。よって、正解は(D)です。

☐description: 名 説明　☐refrain from ～: ～を控える

(((ゼミ 生 中継

😀Hiro 😊Mai 😄Yasu 😎Dai 😆Saki

84.
😀 意図問題の選択肢は長い。全て読むと時間がかかるから、縦に読む練習をすると役立つよ。例えば、ここではToを無視して、上からencourage listeners、explain a change、advise listeners、draw attentionのように。全体の半分しか読んでいないけど、トークを理解できていればexplain a changeとdraw attentionは不正解だと気づくよね。全部読むのに比べると時間を節約できる。

85.
😀 このように、TOEICワールドで働いているツアーガイドは、参加者に

禁止行為を伝えることがある。
😄 参加者に推奨することは言わないのですか。
😀 「楽しんで」みたいな当たり障りのないことは言うよ。
😎 土産店に立ち寄ることをゴリ押しすると読んだことがあります。
😀 読んだ？ そんな話をどこで読んだの？
😎 TOEICを舞台にしたミステリー小説があります。
😀 へぇ、そうなんだ。確かに、土産を買うよう勧めてくるツアーガイドはいる。きっと店からバックマージンをもらっているんだよ。

DL 187 **Questions 86 through 88** refer to the following announcement.

M: ❶ This is a message for passengers on Flight 283 for Hong Kong.
🇨🇦 ❷ We were scheduled to commence boarding 10 minutes from now. It doesn't look like that'll be possible. ❸ Due to the late arrival of a connecting flight, the departure of this aircraft has been delayed. At the moment, we expect to be able to commence boarding at 11:20. We apologize for the delay and we will do our best to minimize the effects. ❹ We ask that passengers remain near the departure gate as we will be announcing updates as information comes to hand.
(94w/37 sec.)

問題86-88は次のお知らせに関するものです。
香港行き283便の乗客の皆さまへお知らせいたします。今から10分後に搭乗を開始する予定でした。それが不可能な模様です。乗継便の到着の遅れが原因で、当機の出発が遅延しております。今のところ、11時20分に搭乗を開始できる見込みです。遅れをおわび申し上げますとともに、全力で影響を最小限に留める所存です。乗客の皆さまは、搭乗口付近から離れないようお願いいたします。新しい情報が入り次第、お知らせいたします。

□ schedule: 動 ～を予定に組み込む　□ commence: 動 ～を始める　□ boarding: 名 搭乗　□ connecting flight: 乗り継ぎ便
□ aircraft: 名 飛行機　□ expect to ～: ～を予期する　□ apologize: 動 謝る　□ do one's best: 全力を尽くす　□ minimize: 動 ～を最小限に抑える
□ remain: 動 （ある場所）にとどまる　□ departure gate: 出発ゲート、搭乗口　□ come to hand: 手に入る

---

86. 正解：**B**　易▪▪▪▪▫▫▫難　選択率：(A) 5.9%　**(B) 46.1%**　(C) 0.4%　(D) 45.7%

Where is the announcement being made?
(A) At a tourist information counter
(B) At a departure gate
(C) In a hotel lobby
(D) On an airplane

この告知はどこで行われていますか。
(A) 旅行者案内カウンターで
(B) 搭乗口で
(C) ホテルのロビーで
(D) 飛行機内で

▶解説 話者は❶で、「香港行き283便の乗客の皆さまへ」と呼び掛けています。また、❷で本来の搭乗開始までの時間を案内したり、最終文❹で乗客に departure gate（搭乗口）付近で待つように伝えたりしていることからも、正解は(B)です。

---

87. 正解：**B**　易▪▫▫▫▫▫▫難　選択率：(A) 1.5%　**(B) 94.1%**　(C) 1.5%　(D) 1.1%

What problem does the speaker mention?
(A) Some luggage has been lost.
(B) An aircraft has arrived late.
(C) A tour is overbooked.
(D) A suitcase is too large.

□ overbook: 動 定員以上の予約を受け付ける

話者はどのような問題に触れていますか。
(A) 手荷物が紛失した。
(B) 飛行機の到着が遅れた。
(C) ツアーの参加者数が定員を超えている。
(D) あるスーツケースが大き過ぎる。

▶解説 予定の搭乗開始時刻に飛行機に案内できないことが伝えられた後、❸で Due to ～（～が原因で）と理由を表す表現を使って、「乗継便の到着の遅れが原因」と説明されています。よって、正解は(B)です。

---

88. 正解：**D**　易▪▪▫▫▫▫▫難　選択率：(A) 0.7%　(B) 1.5%　(C) 2.2%　**(D) 93.7%**

Why are listeners asked to wait?
(A) To watch a video
(B) To receive some money
(C) To meet another employee
(D) To hear updated information

□ updated: 形 最新の

なぜ聞き手たちは待つように求められていますか。
(A) ビデオを見るために
(B) 金銭を受け取るために
(C) 別の従業員に会うために
(D) 新しい情報を聞くために

▶解説 話者は❹で、乗客に搭乗口付近にいるようお願いした後、その理由を「新しい情報が入り次第、お知らせする」と説明しています。よって、(D)が正解です。

(((•))) ゼミ生中継　🙂 Hiro　🙂 Mai　🙂 Yasu　🎲 Dai　🙂 Saki

86. ....
🙂 87番と88番は正答率が異様に高いのに、ここでミスしたモニターが多いみたいだよ。どうだった？
🙂 飛行機だと思って、(D)にしました。
🙂 空港を選ぶつもりで、(D)を塗りました。

🙂 まだ搭乗前だと分かったので、(B)にしました。
🎲 後半で departure gate が聞こえたので、(B)にしました。
🙂 理由はバラバラだな。前半にあった commence boarding を聞いた時点で、機内ではなく空港内で流れていると確定できるよ。

Part 4 説明文問題

DL 188 **Questions 89 through 91** refer to the following telephone message.

W: Hi. It's Tina Alvers from accounting. ❶ I'm calling about this order you've placed for some detergents, sponges, brooms, and mops. You've been instructed to clean up the office as part of our spring cleaning so I understand that it's all necessary, but I'm afraid I can't approve the purchase or reimburse you. Your department has already gone over its budget. ❷ In cases like this, you just need to get authorization from a supervisor before applying for reimbursement. Also, ❸ I noticed that you ordered the products from Hillside Mart. ❹ They're a little expensive. In the future, I suggest you use Brady's Grocery Store. We have membership there and they give us big discounts. (112w/48 sec.)

問題89-91は次の電話メッセージに関するものです。

もしもし。経理部のTina Alversです。あなたが今回注文した洗剤、スポンジ、ほうき、モップの件で電話しています。あなたは会社の春の大掃除の一環でオフィスの清掃を指示されているわけですから、これが全て必要であることは分かりますが、残念ながら私はこれらの購入を承認したり、精算したりはできません。あなたの部署はすでに予算を超過しています。このような場合、上長の許可を取ってから精算を申請する必要があります。それから、あなたは品物をHillside Martへ発注しましたね。あの店は少し高いんです。今後は、Brady's Grocery Storeを利用するようお勧めします。会社はあの店の会員になっているので、大幅な値引きを受けられるのです。

□ accounting: 名 経理部 　□ detergent: 名 洗剤 　□ sponge: 名 スポンジ
□ broom: 名 ほうき 　□ mop: 名 モップ 　□ reimburse: 動 ～に費用などを払い戻す
□ authorization: 名 許可、承認 　□ supervisor: 名 監督者、上司 　□ reimbursement: 名 精算、費用の払い戻し

---

89. 正解：A 易 ■■■□□□□ 難 　選択率：**(A) 84.4%** (B) 6.7% (C) 7.1% (D) 0.0%

What has the listener most likely ordered?
(A) Cleaning equipment
(B) Food supplies
(C) Stationery items
(D) Car parts

聞き手は何を発注した可能性が最も高いですか。
(A) 清掃用具
(B) 食料
(C) 事務用品
(D) 自動車部品

▶解説 ❶から、聞き手が「洗剤、スポンジ、ほうき、モップ」を注文したことが分かります。それらをまとめて「清掃用具」と表した(A)が正解です。

---

90. 正解：C 易 ■■■■■□ 難 　選択率：(A) 25.3% (B) 30.5% **(C) 28.3%** (D) 14.1%

Why does the speaker say, "Your department has already gone over its budget"?
(A) Better prices should be negotiated.
(B) A budget has been reduced recently.
(C) A different application process is necessary.
(D) Some goods must be returned to the store.

なぜ話者は「あなたの部署はすでに予算を超過しています」と言っていますか。
(A) もっと値切った方がよい。
(B) 最近、予算が減らされた。
(C) 他に必要な手続きがある。
(D) いくつかの商品を店に返品しなければならない。

▶解説 ターゲット文の後、❷で「このような場合、上長の許可を取ってから精算を申請する必要がある」と聞き手に手続きに関する説明がされています。よって、設問に引用された発言の理由は「他に必要な手続きがある」ことを伝えることだと判断できるので、(C)が正解です。

---

91. 正解：C 易 ■■□□□□ 難 　選択率：(A) 7.1% (B) 5.2% **(C) 79.9%** (D) 6.3%

What does the speaker say about Hillside Mart?
(A) It has a delivery service.
(B) It has a new catalog.
(C) Its prices are high.
(D) Its staff are very helpful.

話者はHillside Martについて何と言っていますか。
(A) 配送サービスがある。
(B) 新しいカタログがある。
(C) 価格が高い。
(D) 店員がとても親切だ。

▶解説 設問内のHillside Martという固有名詞を聞き逃さないようにしましょう。❸でHillside Martが言及され、その直後❹で「あの店は少し高い」と述べられています。よって、正解は(C)です。

((◤)) ゼミ 生 中継 　　　　Hiro Mai Yasu Dai Saki

89.

😀 サキ、このトークに出ているreimburseとかbudgetって何のことか分かる？　TOEICによく出る重要語だけど。

😶 あまりイメージできません。

😀 サキが会社で使う文房具を自分のお金で買ったとしよう。当然、会社に負担してもらいたいから、そういう申請をする。承認されたら、会社はサキが立て替えたお金を払い戻してくれる。この払い戻す行為

がreimburseだよ。

😶 そっか。アルバイト先のカフェから電車代を毎月もらっています。これもreimburseですね。

😀 その通り。で、このトークに出てくるbudgetは、聞き手が所属する部署が使っていい経費の上限のこと。例えば、年間100万円とかあらかじめ決まっているんだよ。日本語では「予算」と呼ばれている。

😶 分かりました。

↓189 **Questions 92 through 94** refer to the following excerpt from a meeting.

W: The next item on the agenda for today's meeting is to discuss a smartphone app. ❶Many of the readers of *Fishing Enthusiast Magazine* have been complaining that they don't want to carry around a magazine to read. These days, they would prefer to read on their devices. ❷I would like to offer them an app so that they can read our articles online. However, ❸there is a danger that they will not purchase a paper copy of our magazines if they can read them online. Furthermore, ❹our advertisers have informed me that they will not pay as much for online advertising. ❺I would like you all to take the next week to think about this issue and give a presentation on your ideas at the next weekly meeting.

(128w/46 sec.)

問題92-94は次の会議の一部に関するものです。
今日の会議の次の議題は、スマートフォンアプリを検討することです。『Fishing Enthusiast Magazine』の読者の多くが、雑誌を持ち歩いて読みたくないと苦情を寄せています。近年、読者は自分の電子機器で読む方がいいのです。私は、彼らに本誌の記事をオンラインで読めるよう、アプリを提供したいと思っています。ただし、リスクがあります。オンラインで記事を読むことができれば、読者は紙の本誌を買わなくなるでしょう。加えて、本誌の広告主たちは私に、オンライン広告に同額を払うつもりはないと伝えてきています。皆さんには、来週1週間かけてこの問題について考え、次の週例会議で考えを発表していただきたいと思います。

□ agenda: 图 議題　□ enthusiast: 图 ファン　□ a paper copy of ～: ～の印刷版　□ furthermore: 副 なお、さらに　□ as much: 同等に

---

92. 正解：**B**　易■■■□□□難　選択率：(A) 2.6%　**(B) 67.7%**　(C) 24.9%　(D) 2.6%

Who most likely is the speaker?
(A) A sporting goods store owner
(B) A magazine editor
(C) A software engineer
(D) A factory manager

話者は誰である可能性が最も高いですか。
(A) スポーツ用品店の店主
(B) 雑誌の編集者
(C) ソフトウェアの技術者
(D) 工場の管理者

▶解説 話者は❶で、読者からの苦情の話をしています。❷でour articles（私たちの記事）を読んでもらうための対策を提案したり、❸でour magazines（私たちの雑誌）と発言したりしていることから、話者は (B) の「雑誌の編集者」だと考えられます。

---

93. 正解：**A**　易■■■■□□難　選択率：**(A) 45.0%**　(B) 33.8%　(C) 8.6%　(D) 10.0%

What is the speaker's concern?
(A) Some advertising revenue will be lost.
(B) An app is not well designed.
(C) Some items are out of stock.
(D) A client will request a refund.

□ revenue: 图 収益　□ out of stock: 品切れ、在庫切れ
□ refund: 图 返金

話者の懸念は何ですか。
(A) いくつかの広告収入を失うだろう。
(B) あるアプリがうまく設計されていない。
(C) いくつかの商品の在庫が切れている。
(D) ある顧客が返金を要求するだろう。

▶解説 話者は❹で「本誌の広告主たちは私に、オンライン広告に（紙媒体と）同額を払うつもりはないと伝えてきてた」と述べています。この内容を、「広告収入を失う」と表した (A) が正解です。

---

94. 正解：**D**　易■■■□□□難　選択率：(A) 16.4%　(B) 5.6%　(C) 8.2%　**(D) 67.3%**

How are the listeners encouraged to show their ideas?
(A) By sending an e-mail
(B) By posting on a bulletin board
(C) By phoning the speaker
(D) By making a presentation

□ post: 動 ～を掲示する　□ bulletin board: 掲示板

聞き手たちは、どうやって自分の考えを示すよう促されていますか。
(A) メールを送ることで
(B) 掲示板に投稿することで
(C) 話者に電話することで
(D) 発表を行うことで

▶解説 話者は聞き手に❺で、来週1週間かけてこの問題について考えて、アイデアを次の週例会議で発表するように頼んでいます。従って、(D) が正解です。

Part 4 ▼ Listening Section

((♦)) 📡 ゼミ生中継　😀Hiro 😀Mai 😀Yasu 😎Dai 😀Saki

92. ....
😎 (C)を選んだ人は？
😀 エンジニアだと思いました。アプリが不評だからどうにかしようという話だと思ったので。
😀 エンジニアだとは思いませんでしたが、雑誌の編集者が売上とか広告収入を気にするのかどうか分かりませんでした。
😀 雑誌の編集者だからこそ、読者の声や売上を気にしているんだよ。

特に、広告は雑誌にとって超重要な収入源だから、その減少を編集者が心配するのは自然だし、当然、広告主の動向も気になる。

93. ....
😀 あれ？　アプリは未完成なのか……。
😎 未完成どころか作ることになっていないよ。だから、(B) は絶対に間違っている。

Part 4 説明文問題

Questions 95 through 97 refer to the following telephone message and menu.

W: Good morning, Tomoko. ❶This is Brenda from Robinson Brothers. ❷Thanks again for agreeing to cater our annual stockholders' meeting on such short notice. I have another request. Since some of the attendees are vegetarian, ❸we'd like to cancel the beef dish and replace it with something meatless, so there's at least one main dish for them. The vegetable casserole would be perfect. Everything else looks good. ❹Please e-mail me an updated estimate by five o'clock today. If you have any questions about the order or the event, call me at 211-555-4647. That's my mobile phone. Thank you. (97w/42 sec.)

問題95-97は次の電話メッセージとメニューに関するものです。

おはようございます、Tomoko。Robinson Brothers の Brenda です。弊社の年次株主総会へのお料理の提供を、大変急なお願いであるにもかかわらず承諾してくださったことに、あらためてお礼を言います。もう1つお願いがあります。出席者の中にベジタリアンがいるので、牛肉料理をキャンセルして、何か肉類を使わない料理に代えていただき、少なくとも1種類のメインディッシュを彼ら向けに用意したいのです。野菜キャセロールなら申し分ないでしょう。それ以外は全て大丈夫そうです。更新した見積書を、私宛てにメールで今日の5時までに送ってください。注文内容や総会について何かご質問があれば、211-555-4647にお電話ください。それが私の携帯電話の番号です。よろしくお願いします。

☐ cater: 動 〜に料理を提供する　☐ stockholder: 名 株主　☐ on short notice: 急な知らせで
☐ attendee: 名 出席者　☐ vegetarian: 形 菜食主義の　☐ dish: 名 料理
☐ replace A with B: A を B に代える　☐ meatless: 形 肉を含まない
☐ casserole: 名 鍋料理　☐ updated: 形 最新の　☐ estimate: 名 見積もり
☐ specialty: 名 名物、特製品

CATERING MENU	
Item	**Price per platter**
Specialty Garden Salad	$49
Vegetarian Casserole	$59
❺Beef Stroganoff	$79
Herb Roasted Pork	$89

仕出しメニュー	
品目	1皿当たりの価格
特製ガーデンサラダ	49ドル
ベジタリアン向けキャセロール	59ドル
ビーフ・ストロガノフ	79ドル
豚のハーブ焼き	89ドル

95. 正解：C 易 ■■■■■ 難　選択率：(A) 6.7%　(B) 23.0%　**(C) 59.1%**　(D) 7.1%

What event is Robinson Brothers going to hold?
(A) A company picnic
(B) An awards ceremony
(C) A shareholders' meeting
(D) A retirement party

Robinson Brothers は何の行事を実施しますか。
(A) 社内ピクニック
(B) 授賞式
(C) 株主総会
(D) 退職パーティー

▶解説 話者は❶で Robinson Brothers の Brenda だと名乗り、❷で「年次株主総会への料理の提供を承諾してくれてありがとう」とお礼を述べています。これらの発言から Robinson Brothers は株主総会を行うことが分かるので、(C) が正解です。

---

96. 正解：C 易 ■■■■■ 難　選択率：(A) 3.0%　(B) 42.0%　**(C) 48.3%**　(D) 2.2%

Look at the graphic. Which amount will no longer be charged?
(A) $49
(B) $59
(C) $79
(D) $89

☐ amount: 名 金額

図表を見てください。どの金額が請求されなくなりますか。
(A) 49 ドル
(B) 59 ドル
(C) 79 ドル
(D) 89 ドル

▶解説 話者は❸で「牛肉料理をキャンセルしたい」と述べています。メニューの❺から、牛肉を使用するメニューの価格は79ドルであることが分かります。つまり、請求されなくなる金額は (C) の「79ドル」です。(B) はベジタリアン向けキャセロールの価格です。これは牛肉料理に代わって注文されるため、請求される金額です。

---

97. 正解：A 易 ■■■■■ 難　選択率：**(A) 42.4%**　(B) 12.3%　(C) 15.6%　(D) 24.9%

What is the listener asked to do?
(A) Send a document
(B) Update a flyer
(C) Waive a fee
(D) Propose a solution

☐ update: 動 ～を更新する、最新のものにする
☐ flyer: 名 チラシ　☐ waive: 動 ～を免除する
☐ fee: 名 料金　☐ solution: 名 解決策、ツール

聞き手は何をするよう求められていますか。
(A) 書類を送る
(B) チラシを更新する
(C) 料金を免除する
(D) 解決策を提案する

▶解説 ❹に Please で始まる依頼表現があり、「更新した見積書をメールで送る」よう言われています。estimate（見積書）をより一般的な語、document（書類）に言い換えた (A) が正解です。

((( ))) ゼミ 生 中継　　😀 Hiro 👧 Mai 😀 Yasu 😎 Dai 😀 Saki

96.

😀 ダマシのテクニックが使われている。モニターの42%が (B) を選んでいるから、すごい破壊力だね。さて、(B) を選んだのは誰？

💀 こっちを見ないでください。(C) を選びましたよ。

😑 同じく。

😊 私も (C) です。beef をキャンセルすると言ってました。

😀 全員 (C) ですね。

😀 本当に？

💀 あれだけダマシのテクニックを教え込まれたら、さすがにミスしませんよ。

😀 マジで？　ま、全員正解で良かったよ。

97.

😀 聞き手が依頼されている内容が問われたら、当然、話者はトークの中で依頼表現を使っているはず。ここでは Please だけど、他にもある。例えば、Could you～？とか Would you mind ～？で始まる文がヒントになりがちだよ。

Part 4 説明文問題

Questions 98 through 100 refer to the following talk and graph.

M: I think it's time we talked about sales. ❶ I'm pleased to report that they're improving. However, the improvement is not across the board. Men's and women's clothing is selling well, but sales in some other departments have been way down. I think we're suffering because people are shopping online. There isn't much we can do about that. So, ❷ I suggest that we get rid of this department entirely. ❸ It takes 25 percent of our floor space and brings in only about six percent of our revenue. We need to sell as much of the current stock as possible to make way for the expansion of men's and women's clothing. It's May now, so I'll give you a couple of weeks for that. ❹ We'll make the change in June.

(128w/45 sec.)

問題98-100は次のトークとグラフに関するものです。
そろそろ売り上げについて話す時期だと思います。売り上げが伸びていると報告できることをうれしく思います。ただし、この伸びは全店にわたるものではありません。紳士服と婦人服はよく売れていますが、他の売り場のいくつかはかなり下がってきています。不振の原因は、人々がオンラインで買い物をしていることにあると思います。それについて、われわれができることは大してありません。そこで、この売り場を完全に廃止することを提案します。ここは当店の床面積の25パーセントを占めながら、利益のたった6パーセントほどしか稼ぎ出していないのです。われわれは、現状の在庫品をできるだけたくさん売り、紳士服・婦人服の売り場拡張に振り向ける必要があります。今は5月なので、その仕事に2週間差し上げます。変更は6月に行いましょう。

☐ across the board: 全体的に、おしなべて ☐ way: 副 はるかに
☐ down: 形 (売上が) 下がって、落ち込んで ☐ get rid of ～: ～を廃止する
☐ entirely: 副 完全に ☐ take: 動 ～を占める
☐ floor space: 床面積、売り場面積 ☐ bring in ～: (利益) をもたらす、稼ぐ
☐ revenue: 名 収益 ☐ stock: 名 在庫 ☐ make way for ～: ～のためにスペースを空ける
☐ expansion: 名 拡張 ☐ appliance: 名 電気製品 ☐ furniture: 名 家具

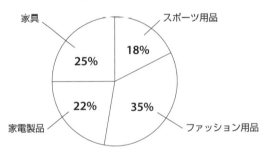

Floor Space Allocation

Furniture — ❺

Sporting Goods 18%

25%

Appliances 22%

Fashion 35%

割り当て床面積

家具 25%

スポーツ用品 18%

家電製品 22%

ファッション用品 35%

98. 正解：**A**　易 ■■■■□□□ 難　選択率：**(A) 66.5%**　(B) 3.0%　(C) 11.2%　(D) 11.5%

What does the speaker say about the company's sales?
(A) They have been improving.
(B) They have not been reported.
(C) They are difficult to anticipate.
(D) They are affected by the seasons.

話者はこの会社の売り上げについて何と言っていますか。
(A) 伸びてきている。
(B) 報告されていない。
(C) 予測が難しい。
(D) 季節の影響を受ける。

▶解説 話者は冒頭で今から売り上げについて話す時期だと述べ、❶で「それらは伸びている」と述べています。正解は (A) です。

□ anticipate: 動 ～を見込む
□ affect: 動 ～に悪影響を及ぼす

---

99. 正解：**D**　易 ■■■■■□□ 難　選択率：(A) 4.5%　(B) 34.2%　(C) 6.7%　**(D) 45.7%**

Look at the graphic. What category does the speaker suggest eliminating?
(A) Sporting Goods
(B) Fashion
(C) Appliances
(D) Furniture

図表を見てください。話者はどの部門の廃止を提案していますか。
(A) スポーツ用品
(B) ファッション
(C) 家電製品
(D) 家具

▶解説 選択肢は「部門」なので、トークでは円グラフの数字が述べられると予想できます。話者は❷で、get rid of this department entirely（この売り場を完全に廃止する）と述べています。これが設問では eliminate で言い換えられています。this department は、❸で「その部門は床面積の25パーセントを占める」と説明されています。円グラフの❺から25パーセントに該当するのは (D) の「家具」だと分かります。

□ category: 名 部門　□ eliminate: 動 ～を廃止する

---

100. 正解：**B**　易 ■■□□□□□ 難　選択率：(A) 5.6%　**(B) 77.7%**　(C) 5.2%　(D) 3.0%

When does the speaker say they should carry out the change?
(A) In May
(B) In June
(C) In July
(D) In August

話者はいつ変更を行うべきだと言っていますか。
(A) 5月に
(B) 6月に
(C) 7月に
(D) 8月に

▶解説 話者は最後に❹で「変更は6月に行おう」と述べているので、正解は (B) です。この「変更」は、家具売り場を廃止して、紳士服と婦人服の売り場を拡張することです。

□ carry out ～: ～を実施する

（（　）） ゼミ 生中継　　　　　　　　　　　Hiro　Mai　Yasu　Dai　Saki

99.

😀 ヤス、まさか、(B)のFashionを選んでないよね?

😵 え……。選びました。

😀 Men's and women'sclothingが聞こえたよね。そのイメージからFashionを連想したでしょ。で、(B)に飛びついた。違う?

😣 すみません! でも、Fashionという単語は聞こえませんでしたよ。ダマシじゃないです。

😀 まぁね。ダマシとボカシがミックスしたワナだね。でも、大事なのは円グラフの中のカテゴリー名ではなく数字の方を見ることだよ。

😄 分かりました!

😀 さて、リスニングセクションの正答数はどうだった?

😲 93問です。びっくりです。

😀 すごいね。後で詳しく聞かせてもらうよ。

😀 75問だ。Test 2より1問減ってしまった。

😑 自分は2問減って53問です。

😀 50問でした。換算点がTest 1の245点に逆戻りです。

😀 うーん…それも後で聞かせてもらおう。では、次はPart 5。

Part 5 短文穴埋め問題

---

101. 正解：**D** 易 ■■■■■□□□□ 難 選択率：(A) 3.2% (B) 0.8% (C) 0.8% **(D) 95.2%**

Mr. Onoda has recently sold the rights to his ------- to a major manufacturer.
(A) invent
(B) inventive
(C) inventively
(D) invention

Onodaさんは最近、自分の発明に関する権利を、ある大手メーカーに売却した。
(A) 動 ～を発明する
(B) 形 発明の才のある
(C) 副 独創的に
(D) 名 発明

▶解説 品詞の問題です。空所の前に代名詞の所有格his、後ろに前置詞toがあるので、hisの前にあるtoの目的語となる名詞を選びます。-tionは名詞を作る接尾辞なので、(D)のinventionが正解です。

□ right: 名 権利 □ major: 形 主要な
□ manufacturer: 名 製造業者、メーカー

---

102. 正解：**D** 易 ■■■□□□□□□ 難 選択率：(A) 2.0% (B) 8.4% (C) 2.4% **(D) 87.1%**

The equipment used by BFP Pool Care workers is not ------- own.
(A) they
(B) theirs
(C) them
(D) their

BFP Pool Careの従業員が使っている設備は、自社のものではない。
(A) 代 彼らが
(B) 代 彼らのもの
(C) 代 彼らを
(D) 代 彼らの

▶解説 代名詞の格が問われています。＜所有格＋own＞で「～自身のもの」の意味を表すので、正解は所有格である(D)のtheirです。この代名詞はworkersを指しています。

□ equipment: 名 設備 □ one's own: 自前のもの

---

103. 正解：**D** 易 ■■■■■□□□□ 難 選択率：(A) 8.4% (B) 10.0% (C) 22.9% **(D) 58.2%**

Once we obtain ------- of the number of guests, we will place an order with a catering company.
(A) supervision
(B) acquisition
(C) permission
(D) confirmation

招待客の人数の確認が取れ次第、私たちは仕出し業者に発注することになる。
(A) 名 監督
(B) 名 獲得
(C) 名 許可
(D) 名 確認

▶解説 空所直前にある動詞obtainの目的語を選択します。「人数の～が取れ次第、仕出し業者に発注する」の文意に合うのは、(D)のconfirmation（確認）です。

□ obtain: 動 ～を手に入れる
□ catering: 名 仕出し、ケータリング

---

104. 正解：**B** 易 ■■■■□□□□□ 難 選択率：(A) 32.1% **(B) 57.8%** (C) 5.6% (D) 4.4%

Bradman Software has been conducting research ------- new markets for robotics.
(A) by
(B) into
(C) besides
(D) out of

Bradman Softwareは、ロボット工学に関わる新たな市場についての研究を行っている。
(A) 前 ～によって
(B) 前 ～の中へ
(C) 前 ～の他に
(D) ～から

▶解説 空所後ろの名詞句new markets for roboticsは、直前の名詞researchの対象分野です。それを表すのは(B)のintoです。他に、＜research on ～＞でも同様の意味になります。

□ conduct: 動 ～を実施する □ robotics: 名 ロボット工学

ゼミ生中継

Hiro Mai Yasu Dai Saki

🧑 重要語句を中心に振り返っていこう。

103.

🧑 モニターの初級グループでは37.1％が(C)を選んでいる。ダイ、どれを選んだ？

😆 まさに(C)です。obtain permissionという組み合わせが良いと感じまして。

🧑 それは間違いないけど、後ろにつながらない。permission of the number of guestsだと意味不明になってしまう。

😆 101番と102番では空所の近くを見てサクっと解けたので、そのノリで解こうとしてしまいました。

🧑 TOEICはそれほど甘くないよ。

105. 正解：**C**　易 ■■■□□□□ 難　選択率：(A) 9.6%　(B) 0.4%　**(C) 88.8%**　(D) 1.2%

It has been ------- announced that Margaret Smith is the new head of public relations.
(A) official
(B) office
(C) officially
(D) officer

Margaret Smith が広報部の新たな責任者であると公式に発表された。
(A) 形 公式な
(B) 名 事務所
(C) 副 公式に
(D) 名 役人

▶解説 空所が現在完了形の受け身を表す been と announced に挟まれているので、空所には動詞を修飾する副詞が入ります。-ly は副詞を作る接尾辞です。従って、正解は (C) の officially です。

□ head: 名（組織の）長　□ public relations: 広報部

---

106. 正解：**B**　易 ■■■□□□□ 難　選択率：(A) 12.4%　**(B) 75.9%**　(C) 5.2%　(D) 6.4%

Before purchasing an item, please check the product ------- listed on the Web site.
(A) complications
(B) specifications
(C) renovations
(D) destinations

品物を購入なさる前に、ウェブサイトに記された製品仕様をご確認ください。
(A) 名 複雑さ
(B) 名 仕様
(C) 名 改修
(D) 名 目的地

▶解説 コロケーションの問題です。(B) の specifications は、product specifications で「製品仕様（書）」を意味します。これを入れると「商品を購入する前に〜を確認する」の文意に合います。

□ list: 動 〜を一覧表にする、リストアップする

---

107. 正解：**D**　易 ■□□□□□□ 難　選択率：(A) 0.8%　(B) 3.2%　(C) 3.6%　**(D) 92.4%**

Mr. Ford decided to use a conference room at the Central Hotel ------- the Douglas Center.
(A) but also
(B) although
(C) otherwise
(D) instead of

Ford さんは、Douglas Center の代わりに Central Hotel の会議室を使うことにした。
(A) 〜もまた
(B) 接 〜だが
(C) 副 さもないと
(D) 〜ではなく

▶解説 空所の後ろは名詞句 the Douglas Center のみなので、前置詞（句）を選択します。(D) を入れると「Douglas Center の代わりに Central Hotel の会議室を利用する」の意味が成り立ち、文意が通ります。

□ decide to 〜：〜することを決める

---

108. 正解：**A**　易 ■■■■■□□ 難　選択率：**(A) 30.5%**　(B) 28.5%　(C) 17.3%　(D) 23.3%

The remote-control camera was packaged -------, but the instruction book contained many errors.
(A) attractively
(B) formerly
(C) significantly
(D) conclusively

その遠隔操作カメラは美しく梱包されていたが、取扱説明書には多くの間違いが含まれていた。
(A) 副 魅力的に
(B) 副 かつては
(C) 副 大いに
(D) 副 結論的に

▶解説 直前の was packaged を修飾する語を選びます。2つの節を逆接の接続詞 but がつないでいます。後半「多くの間違いが含まれていた」から、前半は良い特徴を述べていると分かるので、(A) が正解です。

□ remote-control: 形 遠隔操作の　□ package: 動 〜を（容器に）入れる
□ instruction book: 取扱説明書

(((📻 ゼミ 生中継　　😀 Hiro　😊 Mai　😎 Yasu　🎲 Dai　🐵 Saki

106.

😎 もし、product が空所で、〜 check the ------- specifications という形で出題されても解けるかな。品詞問題だとしよう。

😀 選択肢は何ですか。

😎 produce や productive などが混ざっている。

🐵 形容詞を入れたくなります。

😎 そうだよね。いくら品詞問題が簡単でも、意味を無視して解こうとすると間違える。この product specifications は、見た目は2語だけど1語として認識する方がいい。「複合名詞」と呼ばれるものだね。実は日本語も同じで、例えば「健康診断」は「健康のための診断」だけど1語として認識するのが自然だよね。

108.

😎 (A) を選べた？

😊 はい。ちょっと変だと思ったのですが、他の選択肢がもっとおかしいので、消去法で (A) を選びました。

😎 (A) が変だと思ったのはなぜ？

😊 説明しにくいのですが、カンマの前と後の対比がしっくり来なかったです。

😎 変かな？　素敵な箱に入っていたけれど、説明書は間違いだらけだったんでしょ。問題ないよ。ヤスはどれを選んだ？

😎 しっかり包装されていたのかと思って、(B) にしました。

😎 それは firmly でしょ。スペルが違う。

😎 本当だ……。

Part5　▼　Reading Section

Part 5 短文穴埋め問題

109. 正解：**C** 易 ■■■□□□□ 難 選択率：(A) 6.8% (B) 13.3% (C) 76.3% (D) 3.6%

The ------- experience of the design team at G-Clef Cabinetry makes it Brisbane's most popular kitchen maker.
(A) collection
(B) collecting
(C) collective
(D) collectively

設計チームの豊富な体験のおかげでG-Clef CabinetryはBrisbane随一の評判を取るキッチン設備メーカーとなっている。
(A) 名 収集物
(B) 動 集めている（現在分詞）
(C) 形 集団的な
(D) 副 集合的に

▶解説 空所にはexperienceを伴って複合名詞を作る名詞か、名詞を修飾する形容詞が入ります。(A)を入れても複合名詞が成立しないため、形容詞の(C)が正解です。collective experienceは「経験の総和」を示し、ここでは設計チームの人員の経験が豊かであることが暗示されています。

---

110. 正解：**A** 易 ■■■■□□□ 難 選択率：(A) 52.2% (B) 6.4% (C) 15.7% (D) 25.7%

At the end of the lease, tenants are required to give the apartment a ------- cleaning.
(A) thorough
(B) sizable
(C) diverse
(D) defective

賃貸契約期間の終了時に、借り主は部屋を完全に清掃することが求められている。
(A) 形 完全な
(B) 形 かなり大きな
(C) 形 多様な
(D) 形 欠陥のある

▶解説 空所後ろにある名詞cleaningを修飾する語を選びます。アパートの借り主が最後に行う必要があるのは「完全な清掃」と考えるのが自然なので、(A)のthoroughが正解です。

□ lease: 名 賃貸借契約
□ tenant: 名 借家人、居住者

---

111. 正解：**A** 易 ■■■■■□□ 難 選択率：(A) 33.7% (B) 33.3% (C) 1.6% (D) 31.3%

Please submit your ------- letter to human resources if you would like reimbursement for evening classes.
(A) acceptance
(B) acceptable
(C) acceptability
(D) accepted

夜間授業料の払い戻しをご希望なら、合格通知を人事部へ提出してください。
(A) 名 受け入れ
(B) 形 受け入れられる
(C) 名 受容性
(D) 動 受け入れられた（過去分詞）

▶解説 コロケーションの問題です。(A)を選ぶと、acceptance letterで「合格通知」を意味する複合名詞が成り立ち、「払い戻しを希望する場合は、～を提出してください」の文意に合います。

□ human resources: 人事部
□ reimbursement: 名 払い戻し

 ゼミ 生中継 😀 Hiro 😶 Mai 😎 Yasu 🤓 Dai 😊 Saki

110.

😀 モニターに人気のあった不正解は(D)だけど、defectiveは「欠陥のある」だからダメ。「退去時に、欠陥のある清掃をする必要がある」なんて、おかしな話だよ。

😊 ただ、defective自体はTOEICでよく見る気がします。

😀 確かにそうだね。TOEICワールドでは、物を注文すると欠陥商品が届くことがあるからね。defective productという表現が頻出する。

111.

😀 106番で紹介した複合名詞がここにも登場している。選択率によれば、(B)と(D)が魅力的な不正解だね。ポイントは、acceptance letterを「合格通知」と認識できるかどうか。サキとダイは知っていた？

😊 いいえ。形容詞が正解だと思って、(B)にしました。

🤓 以前、研修費用の払い戻しを受けるために総務部に合格通知を提出したことがあります。が、日本語だったので、acceptance letterは知りませんでした。

😀 惜しい……。

112. 正解：**A**　易 ■■■□□□□ 難　選択率：**(A) 84.7%** (B) 6.8% (C) 3.6% (D) 4.8%

Part-time staff should be called ahead of their shift and informed of ------- their goals for the day are.
(A) what
(B) such
(C) why
(D) also

□ ahead of ～：～より前に
□ inform ～ of ...：～に…のことを知らせる

パートタイムの従業員は、勤務開始前に呼ばれて、何がその日の目標かを知らされることになっている。
(A) 代 何
(B) 形 そのような
(C) 副 なぜ
(D) 副 また

▶解説 空所から文末のareまでが直前の前置詞ofの目的語です。areの補語がないので、それを補って名詞節を完成させるには、(A)のwhatが適切です。

---

113. 正解：**B**　易 ■■■■□□□ 難　選択率：(A) 7.6% **(B) 35.7%** (C) 33.3% (D) 22.9%

Many businesses in Townsville urgently require ------- people due to the labor shortage.
(A) qualifying
(B) qualified
(C) to qualify
(D) to be qualified

□ urgently：副 至急、緊急に　□ due to ～：～が原因で
□ labor：名 労働者　□ shortage：名 不足

Townsvilleの多くの事業所が、人手不足のために、緊急に資質のある人を必要としている。
(A) 動 資格を与えている（現在分詞）
(B) 形 資格のある
(C) 資格を与えること（不定詞）
(D) 適任であること（受け身の不定詞）

▶解説 空所の前に述語requireが、後ろにその目的語peopleがあるので、空所にはpeopleを修飾する語が入ります。(B)を入れるとqualified people（資質のある人々）となり、文意が通ります。

---

114. 正解：**B**　易 ■■■■■□□ 難　選択率：(A) 15.3% **(B) 55.8%** (C) 10.0% (D) 18.9%

Remuneration for overtime work is made as a ------- payment from monthly wages.
(A) distinct
(B) separate
(C) nominal
(D) provisional

□ remuneration：名 報酬　□ overtime work：残業
□ payment：名 支払い　□ wage：名 賃金

残業代の支払いは、毎月の給料とは別の支払いとなる。
(A) 形 目立つ
(B) 形 別の
(C) 形 名目上の
(D) 形 暫定的な

▶解説 (B)のseparateは、＜separate ～ from ...＞で「…とは別の～」の意味を表します。「残業代の支払いは、毎月の給料とは～の支払いとなる」の文意に合うので、正解は(B)です。

Part5 ▶ Reading Section

((((((●))))) ゼミ 生中継　😎 Hiro 😊 Mai 😄 Yasu 🎲 Dai 😁 Saki

113.
😎 (C)が魅力的かな。もし、(C)が成り立つとすれば、Many businesses require to qualify people ～が成立する必要がある。でも、「～する必要がある」と言いたいのであれば、require toじゃない。マイ、どう使う？

😊 受動態のare required toです。または、need toでしょうか。

😎 その通り。それに、qualify peopleは、人々に資格を与えることを意味するから、「人手不足のせいで、多くの会社が人々に資格を与える必要がある」という変な内容になる。

114.
😄 この問題はどこで悩んだ？　separateとfromがセットで使われていることに気づくことが解答のポイント。ヤス？

😄 語彙レベルが高くて適当に(D)にしました。

😄 provisionalは「仮の」だから文意に合わない。確かに(C)と(D)は少しハイレベルだから必須単語とは言わない。でも、こうやって不正解として出題されると心が乱されるよね。だから目標スコアに関係なく、語彙力は高ければ高いほど有利だよ。当たり前だけど。

115. 正解：C 易 ■■■□□□□ 難　選択率：(A) 1.6% (B) 2.8% **(C) 79.5%** (D) 16.1%

The success of the project is -------
attributable to the hard work of all the people
involved.
(A) direction
(B) direct
(C) directly
(D) directed

☐ attributable to ～：〜に起因する
☐ involved: 形 関係して

この計画の成功は、関係者全員の大きな努力に直接起因するものだ。
(A) 名 方向
(B) 形 直接的な
(C) 副 直接的に
(D) 動 指示された（過去分詞）

▶解説 空所の前後に動詞isとその補語attributable があるので、空所には副詞が入ります。-ly は副詞を作る接尾辞なので、これで終わる (C) の directly が正解です。

116. 正解：D 易 ■■■■□□□ 難　選択率：(A) 26.5% (B) 5.6% (C) 9.2% **(D) 58.6%**

Employment conditions at Fairfield Industries
changed ------- the merger took place in
March.
(A) so that
(B) wherever
(C) even if
(D) when

☐ take place: 行われる

Fairfield Industries の雇用条件は、3月に合併が行われた時点で変更された。
(A) 〜するように
(B) 接 〜する所はどこでも
(C) 〜だとしても
(D) 接 〜する時に

▶解説 前後の節をつなぐ語を選択します。それぞれの節の時制が同じことから、(D) の when を入れると後半が時を表す従属節になり、「雇用条件は合併時に変更された」と文意が通ります。(A) が導く節では通常、助動詞か動詞の現在形が使われます。

117. 正解：A 易 ■■■■□□□ 難　選択率：**(A) 49.8%** (B) 46.2% (C) 2.8% (D) 1.2%

It is important the customer ------- with the
changes before we process the catering
order.
(A) agree
(B) agreement
(C) agreeable
(D) agreeably

☐ process: 動 〜を処理する　☐ catering: 名 仕出し、ケータリング

顧客が変更に同意した上で、仕出しの注文を処理することが重要だ。
(A) 動 同意する
(B) 名 同意
(C) 形 感じの良い
(D) 副 快く

▶解説 important の後ろの that が省略されている文です。仮主語として It があり、空所は the customer で始まる that 節に含まれています。that 節に動詞がないので、動詞の (A) が正解です。このように、重要性や必要性を表す形容詞を使う＜it is ～ that ... ＞の構文では、that 節内の動詞は原形を使います。

📡 ゼミ生中継　　　　　　😊 Hiro 😊 Mai 😊 Yasu 😊 Dai 😊 Saki

116.
😊 なぜか、中級グループでは40％が (A) を選んでいる。

😊 私も選びそうになりましたが、会社の雇用条件が変わることによって企業が合併するとは思えなかったので消しました。

😊 仮に、空所の後が so that the merger would take place だったら文法的には成立する。空所の前後の時制が同じであることが解答のポイントだよ。

117.
😊 品詞問題だから易しいはずだけど、サキはどれを選んだ？

😊 (B) です。文の構造が理解できませんでした。

😊 単純化すると、構造は It is important that A do B. だよ。

😊 あ、そういうことですか。that が省略されていたのですね。

118. 正解：**C**　易 ▮▮▮▯▯▯ 難　選択率：　(A) 12.0%　(B) 6.4%　(C) 55.4%　(D) 26.1%

-------, applicants will have more than three years'experience in the hotel industry.
(A) Mutually
(B) Fiercely
(C) Ideally
(D) Majorly

理想的には、応募者には3年以上ホテル業界で働いた経験が求められる。
(A) 副 互いに
(B) 副 激しく
(C) 副 理想的には
(D) 副 極めて

▶解説 空所に入る副詞は、文全体を修飾しています。「応募者は3年以上の経験が求められる」という内容に合うのは、(C) の Ideally（理想的には）です。

☐ applicant: 名 応募者、候補者　☐ industry: 名 産業界

---

119. 正解：**D**　易 ▮▮▮▯▯▯ 難　選択率：(A) 6.8%　(B) 14.5%　(C) 20.5%　(D) 58.2%

There are massive discounts on goods all ------- the store.
(A) against
(B) from
(C) under
(D) throughout

店の至る所にある商品が大幅に値引きされている。
(A) 前 ~に対して
(B) 前 ~から
(C) 前 ~の下に
(D) 前 ~の至る所に

▶解説 空所後の the store を伴って場所を表す語を選択します。(D) の throughout を入れると「店舗の至る所に」の意味が成り立ち、文意が通ります。

☐ massive: 形 大幅の

---

120. 正解：**B**　易 ▮▮▮▯▯▯ 難　選択率：(A) 11.6%　(B) 73.1%　(C) 6.8%　(D) 8.4%

Brad Myers is one of the most ------- people in the programming industry and his talks attract large audiences.
(A) celebratory
(B) influential
(C) tentative
(D) confidential

Brad Myers はプログラミングの世界で最も影響力のある人物の1人で、彼の話は大勢の聴衆を引き付ける。
(A) 形 祝賀の
(B) 形 影響力のある
(C) 形 暫定的な
(D) 形 機密の

▶解説 空所を含む前半は、後半の「Brad Myers の話は大勢の聴衆を引き付ける」と順接の接続詞 and でつながっています。直後の名詞 people を修飾して文意に合うのは (B) の influential（影響力のある）です。

☐ attract: 動 ~を引き付ける

---

121. 正解：**C**　易 ▮▮▯▯▯▯ 難　選択率：(A) 11.6%　(B) 2.8%　(C) 74.7%　(D) 10.8%

KJT Software has received a lot of complaints about the ------- of its new accounting package.
(A) stabilize
(B) stably
(C) stability
(D) stable

KJT Software 社は、同社の新しい会計ソフトの安定性に関する多くの苦情を受けている。
(A) 動 ~を安定させる
(B) 副 安定して
(C) 名 安定性
(D) 形 安定した

▶解説 空所は冠詞 the と前置詞 of に挟まれているので、about の目的語となる名詞を選択します。名詞を作る接尾辞 -ty で終わる (C) の stability が正解です。

☐ complaint: 名 苦情　☐ accounting: 名 経理
☐ package: 名 パッケージソフト

((≡)) ゼミ 生 中継　　　　　　　　　(😊)Hiro (😊)Mai (😊)Yasu (🎲)Dai (😊)Saki

119. ⋯⋯⋯⋯⋯⋯⋯⋯⋯⋯⋯⋯⋯⋯⋯⋯⋯⋯⋯⋯⋯⋯⋯⋯

(😊) サキ、前置詞の throughout を知っていた？

(😊) 見たことはあります。

(😊) 空間的にも時間的にも「あちこち」をイメージすればいい。
　　throughout the country は「国中の至る所で」だし、throughout the year は「1年を通じて」だね。じゃ、throughout the store はどうなる？

(😊) 「店中で」ですね。

(😊) そう。「あれもこれも割引してるよ〜」という状況だよ。

(😊) 空所の前に all があるせいで、頭が真っ白になりました。

(😊) これは副詞だから「あちこち」を強調しているだけだよ。

121. ⋯⋯⋯⋯⋯⋯⋯⋯⋯⋯⋯⋯⋯⋯⋯⋯⋯⋯⋯⋯⋯⋯⋯⋯

(😊) 問題文にある complaints を日本語で言えば何？

(😊) 文句です。

(😊) クレームとも言うよね。日本語のクレームは英語の claim から来たんだと思う。でも、英語の claim は何かを主張することを意味するだけで、必ずしも文句を意味するわけではない。だから、日本語のクレームに合致するのは complaint だと思えば無難だよ。

Part 5 短文穴埋め問題

122. 正解：**B**　易 ■■■■□■ 難　選択率：(A) 42.6% **(B) 40.6%** (C) 6.8% (D) 9.2%

Companywide cost-cutting at Cougar Auto has ------- to a drop in product quality and dependability.
(A) caused
(B) led
(C) invited
(D) proceeded

□ companywide: 形 全社的な
□ cost-cutting: 名 費用削減
□ dependability: 名 信頼性

Cougar Auto の全社的な経費節減の影響で、製品の品質と信頼性が下がっている。
(A) 動 ～を引き起こした
(B) 動 導いた
(C) 動 ～を招いた
(D) 動 進んだ

▶解説 空所直後に前置詞 to があります。＜ lead to ～＞で「（結果）につながる」の意味を表すことから、正解は (B) の led です。(A) は他動詞なので to が不要です。cause は他にも＜ cause A to B ＞や＜ cause ～ to 動詞＞の形で使われます。

123. 正解：**A**　易 ■■□□□□ 難　選択率：**(A) 75.5%** (B) 6.8% (C) 9.6% (D) 8.0%

Sherman Gallery provides certificates to prove that each piece is an ------- artwork.
(A) authentic
(B) authentically
(C) authenticate
(D) authenticity

□ certificate: 名 証明書　□ piece: 名 作品
□ artwork: 名 工芸品

Sherman Gallery が証明書を発行しているのは、個々の品が本物の芸術作品であることを証明するためだ。
(A) 形 本物の
(B) 副 確かに
(C) 動 ～が本物だと立証する
(D) 名 信ぴょう性

▶解説 空所の直前に冠詞 an、後ろに名詞 artwork があるので、artwork を修飾する形容詞を選択します。-ic は形容詞を作る接尾辞なので、これで終わる (A) の authentic が正解です。

124. 正解：**B**　易 ■■□□□□ 難　選択率：(A) 10.4% **(B) 81.1%** (C) 6.4% (D) 2.0%

There have been discussions ------- the organizing committee and representatives of several potential venues.
(A) during
(B) between
(C) through
(D) underneath

□ organizing committee: 組織委員会
□ representative: 名 代表者
□ potential: 形 可能性のある　□ venue: 名 会場

組織委員会といくつかの候補会場の代表者らとの間で、話し合いが行われている。
(A) 前 ～の期間中に
(B) 前 ～の間で
(C) 前 ～を通して
(D) 前 ～の下に

▶解説 空所の後ろでは、the organizing committee と representatives が並列の形でつながれています。「2者の間で話し合いがあった」と捉えるのが妥当なので、(B) の between が正解です。

(((( ))) ゼミ生中継　　　Hiro　Mai　Yasu　Dai　Saki

122.
- この問題は語法を問うている。中級グループでは54.4%が (A) を選び、正解の (B) を選んだのは35.2%だけ。
- caused が (A) にあるので、(B) を見ずに飛びついた人が多かったのではないでしょうか。
- その通り!
- (A) だけ見たとしても、caused to a drop という形が不適切だと気づ

かなきゃ。to が不要でしょ。
- はい……。速く解こうとして焦りました。
- ところで、r で始まる動詞を代わりに使うこともできる。ただし、空所の後の to が in だと想像して。ダイ、分かる?
- result ですか。
- そう、A が原因で B が結果なら、A resulted in B. と言える。

314

125. 正解：**C**　易 ■■■□□□□ 難　選択率：(A) 2.0%　(B) 6.4%　**(C) 90.8%**　(D) 0.8%

Ms. Dunn has ------- offered to share her sound-engineering experience with the theater's technical staff.
(A) grace
(B) gracious
(C) graciously
(D) graciousness

Dunn さんは、自分の音響技術に関する経験を劇場の技術陣に提供することを、快く申し出た。
(A) 名 品位
(B) 形 寛大な
(C) 副 寛大にも
(D) 名 寛大さ

▶解説 空所は has と offered に挟まれているので、空所には副詞が入ります。従って、副詞を作る接尾辞 -ly が付いている (C) の graciously が正解です。

☐ sound-engineering: 形 音響工学の
☐ technical: 形 技術の

---

126. 正解：**C**　易 ■■■■■■□ 難　選択率：(A) 35.3%　(B) 20.1%　**(C) 12.0%**　(D) 32.5%

Some participants made ------- critical observations about the validity of the health and safety workshop.
(A) its
(B) something
(C) rather
(D) themselves

参加者の中には、安全衛生研修会の有効性についてかなり批判的な見解を述べる者もいた。
(A) 代 それの
(B) 代 何か
(C) 副 かなり
(D) 代 彼ら自身

▶解説 空所から observations までが made の目的語なので、(A) か (C) が候補となります。its が指す名詞は文中になく、rather は「かなり」を意味する副詞として使えるため、(C) が正解です。

☐ critical: 形 批判的な　☐ observation: 名 意見
☐ validity: 名 有効性　☐ health and safety: 安全衛生

---

127. 正解：**A**　易 ■■■□□□□ 難　選択率：**(A) 65.5%**　(B) 16.5%　(C) 9.2%　(D) 8.8%

Trinidad brand sweaters are available ------- at Frampton Department Stores.
(A) exclusively
(B) eventually
(C) innovatively
(D) enthusiastically

Trindad ブランドのセーターは、Frampton Department Stores 限定で入手できる。
(A) 副 独占的に
(B) 副 最終的に
(C) 副 革新的に
(D) 副 熱狂的に

▶解説 空所後の at Frampton Department Stores を修飾する語を選択します。(A) の exclusively を選ぶと「Frampton Department Stores 限定で入手可能だ」の意味が成り立ち、文意が通ります。

Part 5 ▼ Reading Section

(((▲)))) ゼミ生中継　😊Hiro 😊Mai 😊Yasu 😎Dai 😊Saki

126.
😊 サキ、rather という言葉を知っているよね？
😊 知ってはいますが、rather than しか知りません。
😎 同じく。
😊 ヤス、どれを選んだ？
😊 (C) です。全部不正解に見えたので勘で塗っただけです。
😊 スマホで rather を調べてみて。例文をいくつか読むと、ニュアンスが伝わってくるよ。
😊 形容詞か副詞の前に rather が置かれている例が多いですね。

😊 この問題をミスしたこと自体は小さいことだよ。大事なのは、これをきっかけに知識を積み上げていくことだからね。

127.
😊 (A) が正解なのは分かりますが、(B) の eventually が正解にならないのはなぜですか。「あのセーターがついに手に入る」みたいな意味で成り立つ気がしました。
😊 その場合、eventually は available に対する副詞だから、置く場所が違う。あと、現在形の are と eventually を同時に使うのはおかしい。例えば、〜 sweaters will eventually be available at ... であれば問題ないよ。

128. 正解：**B** 易 ■■■■■■□ 難　選択率：(A) 10.0% **(B) 38.2%** (C) 42.2% (D) 9.6%

Employees may leave early on Fridays ------- their weekly production quota has been met.
(A) in spite of
(B) provided that
(C) in order that
(D) as much as

従業員は、週の生産ノルマを満たせば、金曜日には早く退社しても構わない。
(A) 〜にもかかわらず
(B) もし〜ならば
(C) 〜するために
(D) 〜と同程度に

▶解説　前後の節をつなぐ句を選びます。後半の「週の生産ノルマを満たす」は、前半の「従業員は金曜日には早く退社して構わない」の条件と判断できるので、(B)のprovided that（もし〜ならば）が正解です。

□ early: 副 予定よりも早く　□ production: 名 生産
□ quota: 名 割り当て分
□ meet: 動 〜を満たす ＊metは過去分詞

---

129. 正解：**A** 易 ■■■■■□□ 難　選択率：**(A) 68.7%** (B) 12.9% (C) 11.6% (D) 6.4%

The gym offers discounts at certain times of day ------- the number of visitors at any one time.
(A) to regulate
(B) has regulated
(C) is regulating
(D) was regulated

そのスポーツクラブでは、一度の来館者数を調整するために1日のある時間帯に割引料金を適用している。
(A) 調整するために
(B) 調整してきた
(C) 調整している
(D) 調整された

▶解説　空所の前に完成した主節があり、関係詞も接続詞も存在しません。そのため、(B)、(C)、(D)は不正解です。(A)を選べば、目的を表す副詞的用法の不定詞となり、「一度の来館者数を調整するために」の意味が成り立ちます。

□ certain: 形 一定の

---

130. 正解：**D** 易 ■■■■■□□ 難　選択率：(A) 26.1% (B) 23.3% (C) 14.9% **(D) 35.3%**

Before anyone is allowed to operate heavy machinery, they must pass a ------- test.
(A) feasibility
(B) preference
(C) determination
(D) competency

重機の操作を許可される前に、誰もが能力検定試験に合格しなければならない。
(A) 名 実現の可能性
(B) 名 好み
(C) 名 決断
(D) 名 能力

▶解説　「重機の操作を許可される前」に合格する必要がある試験は「能力検定試験」が自然なので、正解は(D)のcompetency（能力）です。

□ allow 〜 to ...: 〜に…することを許す
□ operate: 動 〜を操作する
□ heavy machinery: 重機
□ pass: 動 （試験など）に合格する

((((⚡)))) ゼミ 生 中継　😊 Hiro 😊 Mai 😊 Yasu 😎 Osi 😊 Saki

128.
😊 (B)と(C)で迷ったかな。ヤスはどれを選んだ？

😊 (C)です。(B)のprovided thatは意味を思い出せなくて、選べませんでした。

😊 (C)のin order thatは、みんなが知っているin order toと基本的には同じで、「〜のために」だよ。thatを使う場合は後ろに主語と動詞が続く。その点だけが違う。

😊 「金曜日に早く帰れるように、一生懸命に頑張る」みたいな内容をイメージして(C)にしました。

😊 おいおい、それは妄想だよ。問題文をちゃんと読んで。

130.
😊 (A)のfeasibilityは実現可能性と訳されることが多いけれど、空所に入れても意味が通じない。サキはどれを選んだ？

😊 (B)がperformanceに見えて、自信を持って選びました。実技試験のことだと思って……。

😊 設問と選択肢は慎重に読んで。では、Part 6に進もう。

TOEIC よろず相談所　ヒロの部屋

⑯ Part 7 を先に解く?

すみません、リーディングセクションについて聞きたいことがあるのですが、質問してよろしいでしょうか。

どうぞ。

Twitter を見ていたら、TOEIC は Part 7 から解くといいって誰かが書いていました。それって本当に効果的でしょうか。

人によります。文法と語彙に強い人、つまり、**Part 5 と Part 6 でスコアを稼げる人は Part 7 を最後に解けばいい**と思います。でも、「文法と語彙こそ苦手」という人も多いです。そして、解けない問題を解こうとして時間を浪費している人がかなりいます。そういう人は、Part 7 から取り組むと効果的だと思います。

なるほど。もし Part 7 から解く場合、どれくらいの時間を投入していいのでしょうか。

最大60分が目安です。それ以上使うと、Part 5 と Part 6 で悲惨なことが起きそうです。

確かにそうですね。

1つ大事なことがあります。それは「練習」です。**解く順番を変える場合は、模試を使って練習した方がいいです**。試験本番でいきなり試すと、マークミスをしたり、時間配分ができなくなったりして何かと危ないですからね。

了解しました。ありがとうございました。

Part 6 長文穴埋め問題

Questions 131-134 refer to the following information.

There are still tickets available for the ------- performance of *Jardin Verde* at the Lyric Theater in
131.

Hamilton.❶ The popular musical has been playing there for nearly six months and Friday, January

26 will be the last time it will be performed. -------.❷ It is highly recommended that anyone with an
132.

------- in live entertainment take this opportunity. The cast has won multiple awards for their work
133.

and newspaper reviews have been overwhelmingly positive. ------- January 26,❸ the theater will be
134.

closed for two weeks while they get ready for the next production — *Los Perros de Homero*.

(110w)

問題131-134は次の情報に関するものです。

Hamilton にある Lyric Theater での『Jardin Verde』の最終公演のチケットが、まだ入手できます。この人気のミュージカルは同劇場で6カ月近く上演されており、1月26日金曜日が最終公演日となる予定です。チケットは劇場の切符売り場またはウェブサイトで購入できます。生の舞台公演に興味のある人なら誰でも、この好機を逃さないよう、強くお勧めします。出演者たちはこの上演作で複数の賞を受賞しており、各紙の批評は圧倒的に好意的なものばかりです。1月26日以降、同劇場は2週間閉鎖され、その間、劇団は次の上演作――『Los Perros de Homero』の準備を行う予定です。

☐ performance: 图 公演　☐ play: 動 ～を上演する　☐ nearly: 副 ほぼ　☐ perform: 動 （劇）を上演する　☐ highly: 副 大いに、高く
☐ entertainment: 图 舞台公演　☐ opportunity: 图 機会　☐ multiple: 形 多数の　☐ overwhelmingly: 副 圧倒的に　☐ positive: 形 肯定的な
☐ get ready: 準備ができる　☐ production: 图 上演作品

131. 正解：D 易 ■■■□□□□ 難　選択率：(A) 6.4%　(B) 3.2%　(C) 3.6%　**(D) 86.7%**

(A) initial
(B) preview
(C) partial
(D) final

(A) 形 最初の
(B) 名 予告編
(C) 形 部分的な
(D) 形 最後の

▶解説　❶の情報から、*Jardin Verde* の公演は既に上演が開始されており、1月26日に最終公演を迎える予定であることが分かります。空所を含む文は、その最終公演日のチケットがまだ余っているという内容だと解釈できるので、(D) final を入れると文意が通ります。

---

132. 正解：A 易 ■■□□□□□ 難　選択率：**(A) 72.7%**　(B) 8.4%　(C) 5.6%　(D) 13.3%

(A) Tickets can be purchased from the box office or through the Web site.
(B) The show has been canceled due to an unfavorable response.
(C) The film will be available for home rental in six months.
(D) The theater will be torn down the following week.

(A) チケットは劇場の切符売り場またはウェブサイトで購入できます。
(B) 公演は、評判がかんばしくないために中止されました。
(C) この映画は、6カ月後には家庭用にレンタルできるようになります。
(D) この劇場は、翌週には取り壊される予定です。

□ unfavorable: 形 不都合な、不利な　□ response: 名 反響　□ rental: 名 賃貸
□ tear down 〜: 〜を取り壊す　＊torn は tear の過去分詞

▶解説　空所前❶で、*Jardin Verde* の公演日程について述べられており、空所後❷では、生の公演に足を運ぶことが勧められています。これら❶と❷の間に、チケットの購入方法を提示している (A) が入ると、自然な流れになります。❸によると2月に別の公演が始まるので、(D) は不適切です。

---

133. 正解：B 易 ■■■■□□□ 難　選択率：(A) 24.1%　**(B) 41.8%**　(C) 32.5%　(D) 1.6%

(A) interesting
(B) interest
(C) interested
(D) interestingly

(A) 形 興味深い
(B) 名 興味
(C) 形 興味のある
(D) 副 興味深く

▶解説　空所前に冠詞 an があり、直後に前置詞 in が続くので、空所には名詞が入ると判断できます。選択肢のうち、名詞は (B) interest（興味）のみなので、これが正解です。anyone with an interest in 〜 で「〜に興味がある人は誰でも」という意味です。

---

134. 正解：C 易 ■■■□□□□ 難　選択率：(A) 12.9%　(B) 21.7%　**(C) 59.4%**　(D) 6.0%

(A) Until
(B) On
(C) After
(D) At

(A) 前 〜まで
(B) 前 〜に
(C) 前 〜の後に
(D) 前 〜で

▶解説　❶から、1月26日が最終公演日だと分かります。さらに❸から、次の公演準備のために劇場が2週間閉まるという流れが把握できます。つまり、1月26日の最終公演が終わってからしばらくの間、劇場が閉まると解釈できるので、空所に入るのは (C) の After（〜の後に）です。

(((📡))) ゼミ 生 中継　　😊Hiro 😊Mai 😊Yasu 😊Dai 😊Saki

131.
😊 Part 6 に出る語彙問題の多くは、1文だけ読んでも解けないように作られている。広い視野を持って解くよう心掛けて。

132.
😊 この問題のように、文選択問題の (A) が正解だとしよう。(A) を読んだ時点で、すぐに (A) をマークする?

😊 私は (D) まで読んでから、(A) をマークします。

😊 読みますよね。そのせいで迷うこともありますが。

😊 それでいい。文選択問題は消去法で解くのが現実的だよ。不正解

の選択肢は「間違った情報」か「場違いな情報」だけど、正解の選択肢は「あってもなくてもいい情報」だから、明確な評価を下しにくい。面倒だけど、選択肢は全部読むのが無難だよ。

134.
😊 前置詞の問題だけど、空所を含む1文だけを読んでも解けない。ダイはどれを選んだ?

😊 (B) です。後ろに January 26 があるので On だと思いました。

😊 でも、その日は最終公演日だよね。前半の内容を忘れた?

😊 おそらく。

Part 6 長文穴埋め問題

Questions 135-138 refer to the following advertisement.

Qualified Accountant Needed
❶

------- . We are one of Canada's most successful accounting firms. The ------- retirement of one
135.   **136.**

of the branch's most senior employees puts us in need of a suitable replacement. You will be
❷

working with the accountant you will be replacing until she leaves the company. During that
❸

brief period, you will be expected to learn every aspect of the clients' accounts and come up

with strategies to manage their finances. ------- , we are looking for someone capable of making
137.

an immediate start. We ------- interviews between April 7 and April 11. If you would like to be
138.

considered, you should send in an application and résumé by April 1.
❹

(126w)

問題135-138は次の広告に関するものです。

求む、公認会計士

KLH Accounting では、Miami 支社に勤務する熟練の会計士を求めています。当法人はカナダで最も業績を上げている会計事務所の1つです。同支店の古参の会計士の1人が近く退職するため、ふさわしい後任者が必要です。あなたが引き継ぐことになる担当者が退職するまでの間、一緒に働いていただきます。その短期間に、顧客の経理に関するあらゆる側面を把握し、顧客の財務管理策を発案することが期待されています。そのため、すぐに勤務を開始できる方を求めています。4月7日から4月11日の間に面接を行います。選考へのご応募を希望される場合には、4月1日までに応募書類と履歴書をお送りください。

☐ qualified: 形 免許を受けた　☐ accountant: 名 会計士　☐ successful: 形 成功した　☐ accounting firm: 会計事務所　☐ retirement: 名 退職
☐ senior: 形 古参の、上位の　☐ suitable: 形 適切な　☐ replacement: 名 後任者　☐ replace: 動 ～を置き換える　☐ brief: 形 短い
☐ period: 名 期間　☐ aspect: 名 側面、状況　☐ account: 名 案件、取引　☐ come up with ～: ～を思いつく　☐ strategy: 戦略
☐ finance: 名 財政、財務　☐ capable: 形 能力がある　☐ immediate: 形 即時の　☐ send in ～: ～を送る　☐ résumé: 名 履歴書

135. 正解：B 易▰▰▰▱▱▱▱難 選択率：(A) 15.7% **(B) 64.7%** (C) 12.4% (D) 6.4%

(A) There is currently an entry-level position available in our organization.
(B) KLH Accounting is looking to hire an expert accountant for its Miami Branch.
(C) We are the state's top provider of certification for accountants.
(D) KLH is the perfect place to advertise your vacant positions.

(A) 当法人では現在、未経験で働ける職への求人を行っています。
(B) KLH Accounting は Miami 支社に勤務する熟練の会計士を求めています。
(C) 当法人は国内最大手の会計士認定機関です。
(D) KLH は、御社の求人広告を承る理想的な場です。

▶解説 ❶のタイトルから、公認会計士を募集していることが分かります。よって、本文全体の概要を端的に示した (B) が冒頭に来るのが適切です。初心者レベルの採用ではないので (A) は不正解です。KLH は会計士を探しているため (C) も間違いです。(D) は KLH が広告を出す場という内容が本文と合いません。

□ entry-level: 形 未経験の □ look to ~: ~しようとする □ expert: 形 専門の、熟練した
□ state: 名 州 □ certification: 名 資格 □ vacant: 形 空いている

136. 正解：A 易▰▱▱▱▱▱▱難 選択率：(A) - (B) - (C) - (D) -

(A) forthcoming
(B) occasional
(C) recent
(D) questionable

(A) 形 近々来る
(B) 形 時折の
(C) 形 最近の
(D) 形 疑わしい

▶解説 ❷で、新規採用者は退職する従業員と一緒に働くと述べられているので、退職予定の従業員はまだ辞めていないと判断できます。従って、「いずれ起きる」という意味を持つ (A) forthcoming が空所に入ります。(C) recent は過去の事柄を表すので不適切です。

137. 正解：C 易▰▰▱▱▱▱▱難 選択率：(A) 2.4% (B) 9.2% **(C) 85.5%** (D) 2.0%

(A) Insomuch as
(B) Alternatively
(C) Therefore
(D) In contrast

(A) ~なので
(B) 副 その代わりに
(C) 副 従って
(D) 対照的に

▶解説 ❸から、新規採用者には短期間で多くの引き継ぎ事項があることが分かります。また、空所後では、すぐに勤務を開始できる人材を探していると述べられています。空所前後は「理由と結論」の関係なので、空所には (C) の Therefore（従って）が入ります。

138. 正解：D 易▰▱▱▱▱▱▱難 選択率：(A) 5.2% (B) 3.2% (C) 0.8% **(D) 90.4%**

(A) have been holding
(B) held
(C) were held
(D) will be holding

(A) 行ってきた（現在完了進行形）
(B) 行った（過去形）
(C) 行われた（受け身の過去形）
(D) 行う予定だ（未来進行形）

▶解説 空所直後に目的語 interviews（面接）があるので、能動態である (A)、(B)、(D) が候補に挙がります。❹で4月1日までの応募を呼び掛けており、4月7日から11日に面接が行われるため、面接はまだ実施されていない未来の事柄だと判断できます。よって、(D) が正解です。

Part 6 ▼ Reading Section

(((📡))) ゼミ生中継 😀Hiro 😀Mai 😀Yasu 😀Dai 😀Saki

135.

😀 文書の先頭に文選択問題がある。どう思う?

😀 嫌な感じです。絶対に無理って思います。

😀 そうだよね。だから、いったん無視しよう。他の設問を解いてから、最後に戻って解けばいい。

136.

😀 いずれ辞める人の後任者を募集する広告だけど、多くのモニターが

(C) の recent を選んでいる。なぜだろう?

😀 誰かが辞めたから募集しているのだと何となく思いました。

😀 recent が近い将来を含むと思っていました。あと、(A) の意味を知らなかったので……。

😀 1つ重要なことを思い出そう。Part 6 に出る語彙問題は、1文だけ読んでも解けないことが多い。だから、解けたと思っても安心せず、別の文にヒントがあるかもしれないと警戒しよう。

Questions 139-142 refer to the following memo.

MEMO

To: Sales Managers
From: Pauline Jolly
Date: February 3
Subject: Evaluations

Dear sales managers,

❶ It is time for supervisors to conduct the annual employee evaluation. Between February 6 and February 12, sales managers should provide ------- to the people on their team using the **139.** downloadable form on the server. Please treat this as an opportunity to encourage salespeople. If someone on your team is underperforming, you should work with them to find the ------- of the **140.** problem. ❷ The company has produced a number of videos on sales techniques which may be of use in such cases. You can watch ------- online using the links on the company's Web site. -------. **141.** **142.**

Pauline Jolly

(126w)

問題**139-142**は次の回覧に関するものです。
回覧
宛先：営業部長
発信者：Pauline Jolly
日付：2月3日
件名：評価

営業部長各位

管理職による年1回の従業員評価を実施する時期になりました。2月6日から2月12日の間に、営業部長は各自の部下に評価を通達してくださ

い。評価には、サーバー上から評価票をダウンロードして、それを用いてください。この機会に、営業担当者たちに自信を与えてください。もし、部下の中に成績が低迷している者がいれば、本人と一緒に問題の原因究明に取り組んでください。会社はこれまで、こうしたケースに役立つかもしれない営業テクニックに関する動画を数多く制作してきました。それらの動画は、社のウェブサイト上のリンクを使って視聴できます。従業員には、動画を見るたびにアンケートに答えることが求められています。

Pauline Jolly

☐ sales manager: 名 営業部長　☐ evaluation: 名 評価　☐ conduct: 動 ～を実施する　☐ downloadable: 形 ダウンロードが可能な
☐ server: 名 サーバー　☐ treat A as B: AをBとして扱う　☐ encourage: 動 ～を元気づける　☐ salespeople: 名 営業スタッフ
☐ underperform: 動 十分に実力を発揮しない　☐ produce: 動 ～を制作する　☐ video: 名 動画　☐ technique: 名 技術

139. 正解：**A**　易■■■■■■難　選択率：**(A) 71.1%** (B) 13.7% (C) 8.4% (D) 6.4%

(A) feedback
(B) directions
(C) registration
(D) services

(A) 名 評価
(B) 名 指示
(C) 名 登録
(D) 名 サービス

▶解説 空所を含む1文だけでは正解が導けないので、文書全体から解答の手掛かりを探します。❶で、Jollyさんは営業部長に向けて、従業員のevaluation（評価）を行うよう依頼しています。これをfeedback（評価、意見）と言い換えた(A)が正解です。

---

140. 正解：**D**　易■■■■■■難　選択率：(A) 12.0% (B) 43.8% (C) 4.4% **(D) 39.8%**

(A) purpose
(B) reasoning
(C) blame
(D) source

(A) 名 目的
(B) 名 推論
(C) 名 非難
(D) 名 原因

▶解説 空所後にある of the problem（問題の）と相性が良いのは(D)のsource（源、原因）です。the cause of the problem、the reason for the problemも類似の表現です。(A)、(B)、(C)では文意が成立しません。

---

141. 正解：**C**　易■■■■■■難　選択率：(A) 22.9% (B) 1.2% **(C) 71.1%** (D) 4.4%

(A) it
(B) me
(C) them
(D) us

(A) 代 それを
(B) 代 私を
(C) 代 それらを
(D) 代 私たちを

▶解説 ❷から、会社が営業テクニックに関する数多くの動画を制作したことが分かります。空所には❷のa number of videosを受ける代名詞が入るので(C)のthemが正解です。(A) itは特定の1つのものを指す代名詞なので、ここでは適しません。

---

142. 正解：**B**　易■■■■■■難　選択率：(A) 13.7% **(B) 47.8%** (C) 13.7% (D) 24.5%

(A) Therefore, it is only relevant to people working in customer service.
(B) It is a requirement that employees fill out the survey after each viewing.
(C) By doing so, you could lower employee morale and make the situation worse.
(D) You must complete the entire process during January this year.

(A) 従って、それは顧客サービス部門で働いている人だけに関係があります。
(B) 従業員には、動画を見るたびにアンケートに答えることが求められています。
(C) そうすることで、従業員の士気を下げ、状況を悪化させてしまう可能性があります。
(D) 今年の1月中に全工程を完了させる必要があります。

▶解説 動画の視聴について述べられた後に続く内容としては、(B)の「動画を見るたびにアンケートに答えることが求められている」が話の流れとして自然です。

□ therefore: 副 従って　□ relevant to ～: ～に関係がある
□ customer service: 顧客サービス　□ requirement: 名 要求されるもの
□ fill out ～: ～に記入する　□ lower: 動 ～を下げる　□ morale: 名 士気
□ bad: 形 悪い　＊worseは比較級　□ complete: 動 ～を仕上げる　□ entire: 形 全部の
□ process: 名 手順、方法

((๑)) ゼミ 生 中継　😆Hiro 🐵Mai 🐵Yasu 🎲Dai 😆Saki

140. ⋯⋯⋯⋯⋯⋯⋯⋯⋯⋯⋯⋯⋯⋯⋯⋯
😆 魅力的な不正解は(B)のreasoningだけど、reasonと見間違えたのかな。誰か選んだ？

🐵 はい。見間違えたわけではありません。reasonもreasoningも同じだろうと思いました。

😆 同じじゃない。reasoningは「理由」ではなく、理由を付けて説明することや、論法のことだよ。仮に(B)がreasonだとしても、空所には入らないよ。

🐵 え。「問題の理由を見つける」となりませんか。

😆 reason for the problemだよ。前置詞が違う。

142. ⋯⋯⋯⋯⋯⋯⋯⋯⋯⋯⋯⋯⋯⋯⋯⋯
😆 多くのモニターが選んだ(D)がダメな理由ははっきりしている。この書類が書かれたのも、人事考課が実施されるのも2月だよね。なのに、(D)は人事考課を1月に完了するよう言っている。「間違った情報」だよ。

Part 6 長文穴埋め問題

Questions 143-146 refer to the following article.

(25 July) — As of 17 August this year, a new set of rules will be applied to all ------- work in the **143.** ① suburb of Port Melbourne. Existing structures can remain as they are. However, all new and ② ③ renovated structures must comply with a set of design standards determined by the city council. This legislation ------- the cultural identity and atmosphere of the area. The new set of standards **144.** ④ lists acceptable construction materials, design elements, and color schemes. -------. To discuss **145.** the rules or request an -------, you may call the city planner's office at 555-4834. **146.**

(104w)

問題143-146は次の記事に関するものです。
(7月25日) ―― 今年の8月17日付で、新たな一連の法規がPort Melbourne郊外における全ての建築工事に適用される。既存の建築物については、現状を維持できる。一方、あらゆる新築および改装建築物は、市の評議会によって決定された一連の設計基準に適合する必要がある。この法令によって、当該地域の文化的なアイデンティティーと雰囲気が保持されることになる。新たな基準の中には、認められる建築資材や設計要素、配色パターンが挙げられている。これは評議会のウェブサイトからダウンロードできる。規定に関する相談や例外措置の依頼については、555-4834番の都市計画管理者事務所宛てに電話で問い合わせることが可能だ。

☐ apply A to B : AをBに適用する ☐ suburb: 图 郊外 ☐ existing: 形 存在する ☐ structure: 图 建築物 ☐ remain: 動 〜のままでいる
☐ renovate: 動 〜を改装する ☐ comply with 〜 : (法律、基準) に従う ☐ standard: 图 基準 ☐ determine: 動 〜を決定する
☐ council: 图 評議会 ☐ legislation: 图 法律 ☐ cultural: 形 文化の ☐ atmosphere: 图 雰囲気 ☐ list: 動 〜を一覧表にする、リストアップする
☐ acceptable: 形 受諾しうる ☐ element: 图 要素 ☐ scheme: 图 案、構成 ☐ planner: 图 企画係

143. 正解：**C**　易 ■■■□□□□ 難　選択率：(A) 4.8%　(B) 6.4%　**(C) 70.7%**　(D) 17.3%

(A) cleaning
(B) advertising
(C) building
(D) consulting

(A) 名 清掃
(B) 名 広告
(C 名 建築
(D) 名 コンサルティング

▶解説　空所を含む1文のみでは、何の職種に向けた規則が適用されるのか判断できませんが、続く❷や❸のstructure（建築物）、❹のconstruction materials（建設資材）などのキーワードから、建築に関する話だと分かります。よって、(C) building（建築）が正解です。

144. 正解：**A**　易 ■■■■□□□ 難　選択率：**(A) 56.6%**　(B) 17.3%　(C) 21.7%　(D) 4.4%

(A) will preserve
(B) has preserved
(C) has been preserved
(D) preserved

(A) 動 保存するだろう（未来形）
(B) 動 保存してきた（現在完了形）
(C) 動 保存されてきた（受け身の現在完了形）
(D) 動 保存した（過去形）

▶解説　❶で、一連の規則が新たに適用される予定だと述べられています。このことから、まだルールの適用は始まっておらず、その法律によって地域の文化や雰囲気が保存されるのも先のことだと判断できます。従って、空所には未来を表す(A)のwill preserveが入ります。

145. 正解：**D**　易 ■■■■■□□ 難　選択率：(A) 14.1%　(B) 12.4%　(C) 21.3%　**(D) 52.2%**

(A) Fortunately, this does not affect homes which will be constructed this year.
(B) All communication regarding the regulations must be made in writing.
(C) People are free to choose any kind of architecture they like.
(D) It is available for download from the council website.

(A) 運よく、これは今年中に建築される予定の家屋には影響を与えない。
(B) この法令に関する全ての連絡は、書面で行われる必要がある。
(C) 人々は、自由に好みの種類の建築様式を選べる。
(D) これは評議会のウェブサイトからダウンロードできる。

▶解説　空所直前の❹の文では、新基準の内容が一覧化されていると記載されています。この情報を受けて、「それ（新しく決められた一連の基準）はウェブサイトからダウンロードできる」と情報を補足した(D)が正解です。

□ fortunately: 副 幸いにも　□ affect: 動 ～に悪影響を及ぼす　□ regarding: 前 ～に関して
□ regulation: 名 （通常複数形で）規則、法規　□ architecture: 名 建築様式

146. 正解：**B**　易 ■■□□□□□ 難　選択率：(A) 2.8%　**(B) 91.2%**　(C) 2.0%　(D) 4.0%

(A) except
(B) exception
(C) exceptional
(D) exceptionally

(A) 動 ～を除く
(B) 名 例外
(C) 形 例外的な
(D) 副 例外的に

▶解説　空所は冠詞anとカンマに挟まれているので、空所には名詞が入ると判断できます。選択肢の中で名詞は(B)のexception（例外、特例）です。

((🗼)) ゼミ 生中継　　　　Hiro　Mai　Yasu　Dai　Saki

145.

😀 あれ、(A)はダメですか。

😎 (A)は間違った情報だよ。文書の前半にall new and renovated structures must comply with a set of ～とあるから、住宅もstructureの一種である以上、新基準は住宅にも影響する。

😀 住宅だけ例外かと思いました。

😎 だったら、それを明示しなきゃ。「ただし、例外がある」とか「しかしながら」といった表現が必要。(A)はFortunatelyと言っているけど、新基準が住宅に影響しないのはfortunateなことじゃない。あくまでも市が

良いと思って作った基準だから、住宅に影響しないことは「幸運」ではない。もしそう言えるなら、逆に住宅以外の建物に新基準が適用されるのは「不運」ってことになるけど、そもそも運は関係ないよね。

😀 なるほど。分かりました。

😎 あと、(C)も完全に間違っている。新基準により家の設計などに制約が出るんだから、(C)の内容は真逆だよ。文書に矛盾する。

😀 やっぱり文選択問題は論理力を試しますね。苦手です。

😎 とにかく丁寧に英語を読む量を増やせば得意になるよ。では、Part 7に進もう。

Questions 147-148 refer to the following receipt.

McQueen Online Bookstore

Receipt # 99393-834893

Date of Purchase: May 28, 1:28 P.M.
For the amount of: $23.50
Payment for: Download of the eBook, *Getting around Estonia*
❶**Received from:** Chadwick Heller
❷**McQueen Points Remaining:** 64 *Valid until May 31 (3 days left)

Note: The above title may be downloaded for three years from the date of purchase. You may download it up to three times to any device registered in your name. ❸Purchase of this eBook also entitles the owner to receive 20 percent off on a physical copy of the book from McQueen Online Bookstore. ❹To take advantage of this offer, simply input the above receipt number into the voucher field at the checkout. Offer expires on November 28.

(120w)

問題**147-148**は次の領収書に関するものです。

McQueen Online Bookstore

領収書番号　99393-834893

ご購入日：5月28日　午後1時28分
お支払金額：23ドル50セント
ご購入品：電子書籍『Getting around Estonia』のダウンロード版
お支払者：Chadwick Heller

McQueen Points 残高：64　*5月31日まで有効（残り3日）

備考：上記タイトルは、ご購入日から3年間ダウンロードが可能です。お客さまのお名前が登録された機器に3回までダウンロードできます。また、本電子書籍をご購入いただいたお客さまは、同書の紙版をMcQueen Online Bookstoreでお求めいただく際に20パーセントの割引を受けられます。この特典をご利用いただくには、上記の領収書番号を精算画面のクーポン券欄に入力するだけです。特典の有効期限は11月28日です。

☐ date of purchase: 購入日　☐ eBook: 名 電子書籍　☐ remain: 動 残る　☐ valid: 形 有効な　☐ above: 形 上記の　☐ device: 名 機器
☐ register: 動 ～を登録する　☐ entitle ~ to ...: ～に…する権利を与える　☐ physical: 形 物質の　☐ copy: 名 (本の) 冊
☐ take advantage of ~: ～の特典を生かす　☐ simply: 副 単に　☐ input: 動 ～を入力する　☐ voucher: 名 クーポン券　☐ field: 名 欄
☐ checkout: 名 精算、会計　☐ expire: 動 失効する

147. 正解：**A**　易■■■■■■□難　選択率：**(A) 43.0%** (B) 10.4% (C) 36.5% (D) 9.2%

What is indicated about Mr. Heller?
(A) He may lose some points soon.
(B) He paid with a gift certificate.
(C) He used the store three years ago.
(D) He is waiting for an item to be shipped.

☐ gift certificate: 名 商品券
☐ ship: 動 ～を発送する

Hellerさんについて、何が示されていますか。
(A) 彼はもうすぐ何ポイントかを失うかもしれない。
(B) 彼は商品券で支払った。
(C) 彼は3年前にこの店を利用した。
(D) 彼は商品が配送されるのを待っている。

▶解説 Hellerさんの名前は❶に登場します。❶より上に載っている情報から、彼はMcQueen Online Bookstoreというオンライン書店で電子書籍を購入し、この領収書を受け取った人だと分かります。また、❷にはHellerさんが保有している店のポイントが6月になると失効する旨が記されています。それを「もうすぐポイントを失うかもしれない」と表現した (A) が正解です。

148. 正解：**D**　易■■■□□□□難　選択率：(A) 12.9% (B) 5.6% (C) 9.6% **(D) 71.5%**

How can Mr. Heller obtain a discount?
(A) By sending a copy of the receipt
(B) By registering his name with the seller
(C) By visiting a physical store
(D) By providing the receipt number

☐ obtain: 動 ～を得る
☐ seller: 名 売り主

Hellerさんは、どうすれば割引を受けられますか。
(A) 領収書の写しを送ることで
(B) 販売店に自分の名前を登録することで
(C) 実店舗へ行くことで
(D) 領収書番号を知らせることで

▶解説 ❸で電子書籍を購入した人を対象とする割引制度に言及しています。❹では「その利用するには receipt number（領収書番号）を精算画面に入力する必要がある」ことが分かります。従って (D) が正解です。

📻 ゼミ生中継　😎Hiro 🐵Mai 😺Yasu 🎲Dai 😊Saki

😎 このPart 7はどうだった？　試験本番もそうだけど、制限時間内に解き切るのは厳しいよね。
🐵 モニターも制限時間を守って解いたのですか。
😎 そう。易しい問題でも正答率が低いことがあるのは、時間がなくて適当に答えた人がいたからだよ。
🐵 だから後半は特に正答率が低いのですね。
😎 そういうこと。

147.
😎 では、147番から見ていこう。なぜか、(C) が人気のある不正解だね。たぶん、three yearsという情報が中盤に登場していて、(C) にも入っているから釣られたんだろうね。
😊 (A)にあるsoonが気になりました。4日後にポイントが消える場合、soonと言えますか。
😎 それは明確ではない。ただ、このような選択肢は試験によく出る。迷ったら、「不正解として通用するか？」と考えてみて。不正解とまでは言えないならば、問題作成者はそれを正解として作ったということだよ。
🎲 なるほど。

Part 7 読解問題

Questions 149-150 refer to the following text-message chain.

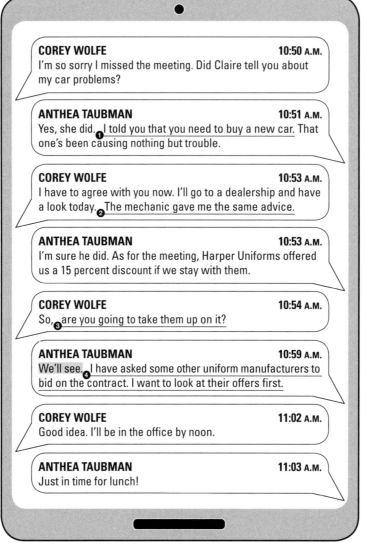

COREY WOLFE   10:50 A.M.
I'm so sorry I missed the meeting. Did Claire tell you about my car problems?

ANTHEA TAUBMAN   10:51 A.M.
Yes, she did. ❶I told you that you need to buy a new car. That one's been causing nothing but trouble.

COREY WOLFE   10:53 A.M.
I have to agree with you now. I'll go to a dealership and have a look today. ❷The mechanic gave me the same advice.

ANTHEA TAUBMAN   10:53 A.M.
I'm sure he did. As for the meeting, Harper Uniforms offered us a 15 percent discount if we stay with them.

COREY WOLFE   10:54 A.M.
So, ❸are you going to take them up on it?

ANTHEA TAUBMAN   10:59 A.M.
We'll see. ❹I have asked some other uniform manufacturers to bid on the contract. I want to look at their offers first.

COREY WOLFE   11:02 A.M.
Good idea. I'll be in the office by noon.

ANTHEA TAUBMAN   11:03 A.M.
Just in time for lunch!

(159w)

問題149-150は次のテキストメッセージのやりとりに関するものです。

COREY WOLFE 午前10時50分
ミーティングに出られなくて本当に申し訳ない。Claireは僕の車が故障したことを話してくれたのかな？

ANTHEA TAUBMAN 午前10時51分
うん、話してた。新しい車を買わないとって言ったじゃない。あの車は問題ばかり起こしてきたんだから。

COREY WOLFE 午前10時53分
認めざるを得ないな、こうなると。今日、ディーラーへ行って見てくるよ。修理工にも同じアドバイスをされたから。

ANTHEA TAUBMAN 午前10時53分
きっとそうでしょうね。ミーティングの件だけど、Harper Uniformsが、取引を継続する条件で15パーセント引きを提案してきたの。

COREY WOLFE 午前10時54分
で、その話に乗るつもり？

ANTHEA TAUBMAN 午前10時59分
まだ分からない。いくつか他の制服メーカーに頼んで、契約に入札してもらうことにしたの。まずは彼らの見積もりを見たいのよ。

COREY WOLFE 午前11時02分
いい考えだね。正午までには出社するよ。

ANTHEA TAUBMAN 午前11時03分
ランチに間に合うようにね！

☐ miss: 動 ～を欠席する   ☐ dealership: 名 販売特約店   ☐ mechanic: 名 修理工   ☐ as for ～: ～に関しては   ☐ stay with ～: ～を続ける
☐ uniform: 名 制服   ☐ take ～ up on ...: ～の（申し出など）に応じる   ☐ bid: 動 入札する   ☐ in time for ～: ～に間に合うように

149. 正解：**B**　易 ■■□□□□□ 難　選択率：(A) 0.8% **(B) 94.4%** (C) 1.2% (D) 3.2%

What did the mechanic advise Mr. Wolfe do?
(A) Update his contact details
(B) Purchase a new vehicle
(C) Create a customer account
(D) Go to a larger repair shop

□ account: 图 口座

修理工は Wolfe さんに何をする
よう助言しましたか。
(A) 連絡先情報を更新する
(B) 新しい車を買う
(C) 顧客口座を作る
(D) より大きな修理工場へ行く

▶解説 車のトラブルを伝えてきた Wolfe さ
んに対し Taubman さんは❶で、以前から
Wolfe さんに新しい車を買うよう勧めてい
た旨を述べています。それに対し Wolfe さ
んが❷で「修理工にも同じ助言をされた」と
応じていることから、修理工も新しい車を買
うように助言したのだと分かります。従っ
て、(B) が正解です。

---

150. 正解：**C**　易 ■■■■■□□ 難　選択率：(A) 14.9% (B) 21.3% **(C) 43.8%** (D) 19.3%

At 10:59 A.M., what does Ms. Taubman mean
when she writes, "We'll see"?
(A) She will take a good look at the product
quality.
(B) She wants to get Mr. Wolfe's opinion.
(C) She has not yet made up her mind.
(D) She thinks she has made the right decision.

□ make up one's mind: 決心する

午前10時59分に Taubman さ
んはどのような意味で「まだ分
からない」と書いていますか。
(A) 彼女は品質をよく見るつも
りだ。
(B) 彼女は Wolfe さんの意見を
聞きたい。
(C) 彼女はまだ決心していない。
(D) 彼女は、自分が正しい判断を
下したと思っていいる。

▶解説 We'll see. は、❸の「(取引を継続
すれば値引きするという申し出を)受け入れ
たのか」という質問に対する答えです。発言
の後の❹で、「他の制服メーカーにも入札を
頼んでいて、その見積もりを見たい」と伝え
ています。従って、まだ結論が出ていないと
分かるので、(C) が適切です。なお、ここで
の We'll see. は「様子を見て決める」という
意味の慣用表現です。

 ゼミ中継　　　 Hiro 👾 Mai 👾 Yasu 🎲 Dai 👾 Saki

150.

👾 この We'll see. は、一般的な会話にしょっちゅう登場する言い回しだ
よ。TOEIC の教材で見ることはあまりないけど。

👾 一般的な会話って、どこで見つけられますか。

👾 簡単だよ。映画とかドラマとか、そういう素材のこと。Netflix とか

Hulu って聞いたことある?

👾 あります。スマホに Hulu のアプリを入れてます。

👾 それだよ。好きな映画やドラマに没頭すれば、意図問題が簡単だと
思うようになるよ。もちろん、英会話に特化した教材でもいいけど。

👾 やってみます。

Part 7　Reading Section

Part 7 読解問題

Questions 151-154 refer to the following letter.

Randall Skin Care
45 Carlota Way
Mildura VIC 3502

27 June

Dear Shareholders,

Randall Skin Care has always been a market leader, and this has been linked to our increased investment in research and development and the close relationship that exists between that department and marketing, which is also getting extra funds. So, while it pains me to admit that profits are down this quarter, I can assure you that it is not because sales have declined.

In fact, quite the opposite is true. Sales have improved by some 8 percent since April. ❶The profit margin has been affected by an increase in production costs and a massive investment in product development. We believe that this is necessary from time to time in order to ensure the long-term success of our brand.

❷In the coming quarter, we intend to diversify the business by offering some new products such as deodorants and body soaps. ❸The product development and marketing departments will take a central role and some extra spending there now will surely pay off down the line. ❹We will also be spending a little more on customer service. As ❺online product reviews become more and more important, ensuring customer satisfaction is critical.

I would like to thank you for your patience during this time and assure you that the company's prospects are better than ever.

Sincerely,

Clara Braden

Clara Braden, CEO, Randall Skin Care

(234w)

問題151-154は次の手紙に関するものです。

Randall Skin Care
45 Carlota Way
Mildura VIC 3502

6月27日

前略　株主の皆さま

Randall Skin Careは常に市場をリードしてまいりました。そしてこのことは、当社の研究開発、および当該部門とマーケティング部門との間の緊密な関係の維持に対する投資拡大と結び付いており、それが、さらなる財源の確保にもつながっているのです。従って、残念ながら今四半期の利益が下がっていることは認めざるを得ませんが、それが売り上げの落ち込みに起因するものでないことは断言できます。

実のところ、正反対のことが起きています。売り上げは4月以降、8パーセントほど伸びているのです。利幅は、生産コストの増加と商品開発へ

の多額の投資の影響を受けてきました。当社の考えでは、自社ブランドの長期的な成功を確たるものにするには、こうしたことが時には必要です。

次の四半期に、当社は消臭剤やボディーソープといったいくつかの新製品を投入することで、ビジネスの多様化を図る考えでおります。商品開発部門とマーケティング部門が中核的な役割を担うようになり、そこでの現在の特別な支出は、将来間違いなく回収されることになるでしょう。当社はさらに、顧客サービスへの支出も増やすつもりです。オンラインの商品レビューの重要性がますます増す中で、顧客の満足を確保することは必要不可欠です。

現状へのご辛抱に感謝申し上げますとともに、当社の未来がこれまでになく明るいものになることをお約束いたします。

草々
Clara Braden、Randall Skin Care 最高経営責任者

□ shareholder: 图 株主　□ link: 動 ～を結び付ける　□ investment: 图 投資　□ close: 形 近い　□ exist: 動 存在する
□ fund: 图 資金　□ pain: 動 ～を苦しめる　□ admit: 動 ～を認める　□ quarter: 图 四半期　□ assure: 動 ～に断言する
□ decline: 動 減少する　□ quite the opposite: 全く逆　□ improve: 動 改善する　□ margin: 图 利幅　□ affect: 動 ～に影響を与える
□ massive: 形 きわめて多い　□ ensure: 動 ～を確実にする、～を確保する　□ long-term: 形 長期の　□ coming: 形 次の
□ diversify: 動 ～を多様化させる　□ deodorant: 图 体臭防止剤　□ role: 图 役割　□ spending: 图 支出　□ pay off: お金を回収する
□ down the line: 将来、そのうちに　□ critical: 形 重大な　□ patience: 图 辛抱強さ　□ prospect: 图 見通し

151. 正解：**A**　易 ■■■■■□□ 難　選択率：**(A) 53.8%** (B) 26.1% (C) 15.3% (D) 4.0%

According to the letter, why have profits dropped?
(A) Manufacturing costs have risen.
(B) Sales are declining.
(C) Advertising costs have risen.
(D) A new office was opened.

□ drop: 動 下がる
□ rise: 動 上がる　＊risen は過去分詞

この手紙によると、なぜ利益が落ち込んでいるのですか。
(A) 生産コストが上がった。
(B) 売り上げが落ちている。
(C) 広告費が上がった。
(D) 新しい事務所が開設された。

▶解説 ❶で、Randall Skin Care の利益が減少した理由は、生産コストの上昇と商品開発費への投資を強化したためだと分かります。production costs を manufacturing costs と言い換えた (A) が合致しています。第1段落の最後と第2段落の最初で売り上げが落ちたわけではないと強調しており、(B) は誤りです。

---

152. 正解：**B**　易 ■■■■□□□ 難　選択率：(A) 11.2% **(B) 63.1%** (C) 8.4% (D) 16.5%

Which department is NOT mentioned as receiving additional spending?
(A) Research and development
(B) Distribution
(C) Marketing
(D) Customer service

追加支出の対象として挙がっていないのはどの部門ですか。
(A) 研究開発
(B) 物流
(C) マーケティング
(D) 顧客サービス

▶解説 ❸で、同社の戦略上中心的役割を担う研究開発部門とマーケティング部門は、extra spending（特別な支出）を受ける旨が述べられています。さらに、❹では顧客サービス部門の支出も増やすと述べられています。よって、言及されていないのは (B) の「物流」です。

---

153. 正解：**C**　易 ■■□□□□□ 難　選択率：(A) 9.6% (B) 2.8% **(C) 85.1%** (D) 2.0%

What does the company intend to do next quarter?
(A) Reduce unnecessary spending
(B) Hire experts from abroad
(C) Expand into new product ranges
(D) Hold a meeting for shareholders

□ abroad: 名 外国

この会社は次の四半期に何をするつもりですか。
(A) 不必要な支出を削減する
(B) 国外の専門家を雇う
(C) 新たな商品分野に進出する
(D) 株主総会を開く

▶解説 ❷で次の四半期で取る対応策を説明しており、新製品を投入することによりビジネスを多様化する計画だと分かります。従って、diversify the business（ビジネスを多様化する）を Expand into new product ranges（新たな商品分野に拡大する）と表現した (C) が正解です。

---

154. 正解：**B**　易 ■■■■□□□ 難　選択率：(A) 15.3% **(B) 57.8%** (C) 10.4% (D) 16.1%

The word "critical" in paragraph 3, line 6, is closest in meaning to
(A) demanding
(B) essential
(C) negative
(D) sensitive

第3段落6行目にある「critical」に最も意味が近いのは
(A) 要求の多い
(B) 不可欠な
(C) 否定的な
(D) 敏感な

▶解説 critical は、❺の「オンラインの商品レビューの重要性が増しているため、顧客の満足を確保することが〜である」の「〜」に相当する部分です。critical が「不可欠な」や「重要な」という意味で用いられていると考えれば文意が通ります。それに最も近い意味を持つのは (B) の essential です。

((♦)) ゼミ 生 中継　　😀 Hiro 😊 Mai 😆 Yasu 🤓 Dai 😊 Saki

151.
😀 サキ、これはメールじゃなく手紙だよね。なぜだと思う？
😊 さぁ。大事な内容だからですか。
😀 株主向けだから。企業が株主にメッセージを出す場合、手紙を使うのが一般的なんだよ。
😊 そもそも、企業は株主のメールアドレスを知らないです。

152.
😆 文書の上から下までザッと読んだら、Distribution がどこにもなかったので、(B) を選びました。
😀 確かに。Distribution は登場していないから正解になる。ただ、そ

れに気づくには全部読む必要があるから、楽に解けるとは言えない。
😊 全部読むのはコスパが悪いですね。
😀 気持ちは分かるけど、他の設問もあるから、どっちみち全部読まされることになるよ。

154.
😀 出た。critical は Test 1 にも Test 2 にも違う意味で出ていたよね。覚えていなければ必ず復習してね。
🤓 前から3つ目のセットに同義語問題が出るのは普通ですか。
😀 よく気づいたね。同義語問題は、昔は後半に登場することが多かったけれど、近年はこのように前半に登場することもよくある。

Part 7 読解問題

Questions 155-157 refer to the following advertisement.

Volunteer at the Ralstow Community Fun Run!

If you are planning on taking part in the Ralstow Community Fun Run, you may be interested to learn that you can register for half price and avoid the selection process. As the event has grown in popularity, organizers now only accept about half of the applications they receive. ❶One way to ensure you are selected is to volunteer. Participants in the three and five-kilometer events will finish before the full and half marathon participants start, so if you take part in one of these runs, ❷you will have plenty of time to get to one of the drink stations and help other volunteers dispense water and other drinks for the half and full marathon. We are looking for 100 people to assist us with this work. If you are interested, fill out an online application at www.ralstowcfr.org. ❸It is necessary that you carry a mobile phone as you will be contacted on it by our chief organizer to finalize your application. It will also be used to coordinate your activities on the day of the fun run. Participants in the full and half marathon can also contact organizers to discuss other volunteer opportunities.

(201w)

問題155-157は次の広告に関するものです。

Ralstow Community Fun Run でボランティア活動を！

Ralstow Community Fun Run への参加をお考えなら、半額で登録でき、選抜の過程を飛び越えられると聞けば興味が湧くのではないでしょうか。当大会は人気が高まっているため、運営当局は現在、受けた応募の半数ほどしか受け入れていません。選ばれることを確実にする1つの方法は、ボランティアで働くことです。3キロ走および5キロ走の参加者は、フルマラソンやハーフマラソンの参加者がスタートする前にゴールすることになるので、上記のいずれかの種目に参加するのであれば、十分余裕を持って給水所の1つへ行き、他のボランティアスタッフを手伝って、水などの飲料をハーフマラソンやフルマラソンの走者に配ることができます。この仕事を手伝ってくださる方を100名募集しています。ご興味があれば、www.ralstowcfr.org でオンラインの申込用書式にご記入ください。これは、運営責任者がご応募を最終確認する際に、携帯電話へ連絡を差し上げるため、携帯電話の所持が必須です。また、マラソン大会当日に行動を指示させていだく際にも利用します。フルマラソンとハーフマラソンの参加者も、運営当局にご連絡の上、他のボランティア活動についてご相談いただけます。

☐ selection: 图 選考　☐ grow: 動 大きくなる　＊grown は過去分詞　☐ popularity: 图 人気　☐ application: 图 申し込み
☐ ensure: 動 ～を確実にする　☐ participant: 图 参加者　☐ take part in ～: ～に参加する　☐ dispense: 動 ～を分配する
☐ assist: 動 ～を手伝う　☐ fill out ～: ～に記入する　☐ mobile phone: 携帯電話　☐ finalize: 動 ～を終える
☐ coordinate: 動 ～をまとめる、～を調整する　☐ opportunity: 图 機会

155. 正解：**A**　易 ▬▬▬▬▬▬ 難　選択率：(A) **69.1%** (B) 26.5% (C) 4.0% (D) 0.4%

What is one benefit of volunteering?
(A) Guaranteed entry into the event
(B) Free runner registration
(C) An invitation to an after party
(D) A free T-shirt

□ benefit: 图 特典　□ guarantee: 動 〜を保証する

ボランティア活動の1つの特典は何ですか。
(A) 大会へのエントリーの保証
(B) 走者としての無料登録
(C) 大会後のパーティーへの招待
(D) 無料のTシャツ

▶解説 1文目と2文目では、このイベントは大変人気があるため、応募者の半分程度しか参加できない旨が書かれています。その後の❶で、確実に参加できるようにする手段としてボランティアで働くことを勧めているので、(A)が正解です。ensure you are selected（選ばれることを確実にする）を guaranteed entry（保証されたエントリー）という表現で言い換えています。

---

156. 正解：**B**　易 ▬▬▬▬▬▬ 難　選択率：(A) 2.4% (B) **90.0%** (C) 6.8% (D) 0.8%

What is one task volunteers will carry out at the Fun Run?
(A) Helping clean up garbage after the event
(B) Preparing beverages for participants
(C) Recording the runners' finishing times
(D) Directing traffic around the route

□ beverage: 图 飲み物

ボランティアスタッフがマラソン大会でこなす1つの仕事は何ですか。
(A) 大会後にごみ拾いを手伝うこと
(B) 参加者たちに飲み物を用意すること
(C) 走者たちの走行時間を記録すること
(D) コース周辺の交通整理をすること

▶解説 ❷で、他のボランティアスタッフを手伝って給水所で水などの飲料を走者に配ると説明されています。よって、water and other drinks（水などの飲料）を、より抽象的な beverages（飲み物）で言い換えた (B) が正解です。

---

157. 正解：**D**　易 ▬▬▬▬▬▬ 難　選択率：(A) 2.8% (B) 2.8% (C) 2.8% (D) **91.6%**

What condition must applicants satisfy to join the volunteers?
(A) They must supply an e-mail address.
(B) They must live in the Ralstow area.
(C) They must wear an official shirt.
(D) They must have a mobile phone.

参加者がボランティア活動に参加するために満たさなければならない条件は何ですか。
(A) メールアドレスを知らせなければならない。
(B) Ralstow 地区に住んでいなければならない。
(C) 公式シャツを身に着けなければならない。
(D) 携帯電話を持っていなければならない。

▶解説 ❸で、It is necessary that 〜（〜することが必要だ）という表現に続けて、「運営責任者が応募を最終確認する際に使うので、携帯電話の所持が必須」と記されています。他の条件には触れていません。

Part 7

((・∞・)) ゼミ生中継　😀Hiro 😊Mai 😎Yasu 🎲Dai 😄Saki

155.
😀 誰か、(B)を選んだ？
😎 選びました。registration に釣られた気がします。
😊 (B)は Free が間違っている。ボランティアになっても、エントリー費用は無料にならない。半額になるんだよ。

😄 正直、このフォントが読みにくくて途中で嫌になりました。
😎 そうだよね。内容が頭に入らなくなるよね。
🎲 同じく。
😀 まぁ、確かに読みにくいね。でも、それは全員同じだから我慢しなきゃ。慣れれば平気になるよ。

Questions 158-159 refer to the following e-mail.

To:	Chloe Tate <ctate@kingstondevelopments.com>
From:	Dougray Kumar <dkumar@kumarsculptures.com>
Subject:	45 Dolby Avenue
Date:	February 17

Dear Chloe,

❶ I am writing to let you know that I have just finished construction of the sculpture Kingston Developments commissioned for the courtyard of the office building you are constructing at 45 Dolby Avenue. When I spoke with you last week, you indicated that the site may not be ready for the piece to be installed. Regrettably, I need to have it shipped from my studio in Harrisford by February 27 so that I can commence work on my next project. ❷ If you are unable to accept delivery by then, I will be forced to keep it in a warehouse at your expense. Due to the size of the sculpture, this will cost as much as $450 per week. ❸ This condition was mentioned in our contract and I would like to avoid the situation if at all possible.

Please let me know if and when you can accept shipment of the sculpture. I will make all necessary shipping and installation arrangements to suit your schedule.

Kind regards,

Dougray Kumar
Kumar Sculptures

(189w)

問題158-159は次のメールに関するものです。

宛先：Chloe Tate <ctate@kingstondevelopments.com>
送信者：Dougray Kumar <dkumar@kumarsculptures.com>
件名：Dolby Avenue 45番地
日付：2月17日

Chloeさま

本メールにて、Kingston Developmentsよりご発注いただいた彫刻の製作が完了したことをお知らせします。彫刻は貴社がDolby Avenue 45番地に建設中のオフィスビルの中庭に設置するためのものです。先週、貴社とお話しした際、建設現場ではまだ彫刻を設置する準備が整っていない可能性があるとのことでした。あいにく、次の仕事に取り掛かるために当方は彫刻を2月27日までにHarrisfordにある自分の工房から運び出す必要があります。もし貴社がその日までに搬入を受け入れられない場合、当方は貴社のご負担で彫刻を倉庫に保管せざるを得なくなります。彫刻の大きさから、この保管費は週あたり450ドルにも上ります。この条件は貴社と交わした契約書に記載されており、当方としては、できることならそのような事態を避けたいと考えています。

貴社に彫刻の搬入を受け入れていただけるのか、いつなら受け入れ可能なのかをお知らせください。貴社のスケジュールに合わせて、当方で必要な配送および設置の手配を全て行います。

よろしくお願い申し上げます。

Dougray Kumar
Kumar Sculptures

☐ sculpture: 名 彫像　☐ commission: 動 ～を発注する　☐ courtyard: 名 中庭　☐ piece: 名 作品　☐ install: 動 ～を設置する
☐ regrettably: 副 残念ながら　☐ studio: 名 工房　☐ commence: 動 ～を開始する　☐ force: 動 ～を余儀なくさせる　☐ warehouse: 名 倉庫
☐ due to ～: ～のために　☐ cost: 動 ～（の金額）がかかる　☐ condition: 名 条件　☐ if at all possible: できることなら、万が一可能なら
☐ installation: 名 設置　☐ arrangement: 名 手配　☐ suit: 動 ～に合う

158. 正解：**B** 易 ■■■■■□□□ 難　選択率：(A) 3.6% **(B) 56.6%** (C) 18.5% (D) 20.5%

What is the purpose of the e-mail?
(A) To thank a client for paying a bill
(B) To provide an update on a project
(C) To invoice a customer for a service
(D) To ask for an extension to a deadline

☐ invoice: 動 ～に請求書を送る
☐ extension: 名 延期

このメールの目的は何ですか。
(A) 顧客に、請求額を支払ってくれたことへの礼を述べること
(B) プロジェクトの最新情報を伝えること
(C) 顧客にサービスの請求書を送ること
(D) 締め切りの延期を求めること

▶解説 ❶から、Kumarさんは彫刻が完成したことを伝えるためにメールを送っているのだと分かります。それを「プロジェクトの最新情報を提供すること」と表現した(B)が正解です。選択肢では、construction of the sculpture（彫刻の製作）がproject（プロジェクト）というより一般的な語で言い換えられています。

---

159. 正解：**C** 易 ■■■■■□□ 難　選択率：(A) 38.6% (B) 6.8% **(C) 49.8%** (D) 4.8%

What is mentioned in the contract?
(A) The sculpture must be ready by February 27.
(B) The artist must attend an unveiling event.
(C) The purchaser must pay a storage fee if it is incurred.
(D) The payment must be made in full within two months.

☐ unveiling: 名 除幕（式）　☐ purchaser: 名 購入者
☐ storage: 名 保管　☐ incur: 動 ～を課す

契約書には何が書かれていますか。
(A) 彫刻を2月27までに完成させなければならない。
(B) 製作者は除幕式に参加しなければならない。
(C) 購入者は、保管料が発生した場合には支払わなければならない。
(D) 2カ月以内に全額が支払われなければならない。

▶解説 ❷で、完成後すぐに彫刻を設置場所に運べず倉庫に保管する場合は、その費用は購入者が払うことが分かります。❸では「その条件は契約書で記載されている」と述べているので、(C)が契約で触れられている内容です。

((•)) ゼミ⏚中継　😊Hiro 😊Mai 😊Yasu 😎Dai 😊Saki

😊 ほら、Part 1で説明した「広場3兄弟」のうち、courtyardが1文目に出ている。重要単語を覚えるとどのパートでも役立つよ。

😎 確かに。

159.

😊 上級グループの正答率は75.8%だけど、中級グループでは48.8%に下がる。さらに初級グループでは25.8%しかない。中級と初級では、その分、(A)の人気が高い。2月27日は彫刻の完成期限ではなく、何の日？　ヤス？

😊 えっと、彫刻の発送日ですか。

😊 ま、そうだね。Kumarさんは、その日までに彫刻を発送したいと言っている。だから、(A)は内容自体が正しくない。

😊 それに、2月27日という日付が契約書に書かれているかどうか不明ですね。

😊 その通り。ところで、このストーリーの中で、彫刻はきちんと完成して納品できる準備が整っている。むしろ、受け取り側に問題があってすぐに納品できないらしいね。これはTOEICワールドでは珍しい現象かもしれない。あの世界では納品が遅れることの方が自然だからね。

Questions 160-162 refer to the following article.

Godfrey's on Maple Street

❶ This week, we are reviewing one of Napier's newest places to eat. Godfrey's on Maple Street is owned and run by two of the town's local sporting heroes — brothers, Mike and Ian Godfrey. The brothers are best known for their performances on the football field so it was with some skepticism in our hearts that we went to try the food.

We were pleasantly surprised when we entered. **❷** We expected that the walls would be decorated with photographs and news clippings from the owners' time as professional sports people. That was not the case at all. The interior decorator has done a wonderful job creating a bright cheerful atmosphere. The staff too were extremely friendly and welcoming.

As for the menu, this was another pleasant surprise. It seems that the brothers have taken ideas from the wonderful dining establishments they visited when representing their country at international sporting events. Unfortunately, this includes the prices. Nevertheless, everything is exotic and interesting and it is all extremely healthy. We believe that this is one of Napier's most exciting places to eat. **❸** It should also be mentioned that Godfrey's gives five percent of its profits to various local causes.

(200w)

問題160-162は次の記事に関するものです。

Maple Street の Godfrey's
今週は、Napier で最も新しい飲食店の1つをレビューしよう。Maple Street の Godfrey's を所有し経営しているのは、この町出身の2人のスポーツの英雄——Mike と Ian の Godfrey 兄弟だ。兄弟は何よりもフットボールの世界での活躍で知られているので、私たちは心中に一抹の不安を抱えつつ、試食に向かった。

店に入ると、うれしい驚きが待っていた。私たちが予想していたのは、壁が店主らのプロスポーツ選手時代の写真や新聞記事の切り抜きで飾られていることだった。しかし、全く違っていた。店内装飾を受け持った業者は素晴らしい仕事をこなし、明るく楽しそうな雰囲気を作り出していた。店員たちも大変親しみやすく、歓待してくれた。

メニューはと言えば、これがまたしてもうれしい驚きだった。どうやら兄弟は、国際試合で国の代表として訪れた先の優れた飲食店から着想を得ているようだ。残念なことに、それには価格水準も含まれてしまっているが。とはいえ、全てに異国情緒や興味をそそるものがあり、そしてどれもが極めてヘルシーだ。この店は、Napier で最も刺激的な飲食店の1つだと思う。さらに付け加えるべきことがある。Godfrey's は、収益の5パーセントを地元のさまざまな目的のために寄付しているのだ。

□ run: 動 ～を運営する　□ hero: 名 英雄　□ performance: 名 実績　□ skepticism: 名 懐疑的な見方　□ pleasantly: 副 心地よく
□ decorate: 動 ～を装飾する　□ clipping: 名 切り抜き　□ time: 名 時代　□ professional: 形 プロの　□ not the case: 事実と違う
□ interior: 名 内装　□ decorator: 名 装飾業者　□ atmosphere: 名 雰囲気　□ extremely: 副 極めて　□ welcoming: 形 歓迎する
□ dining establishment: 食事施設　□ unfortunately: 副 残念ながら　□ nevertheless: 副 それにもかかわらず　□ exotic: 形 異国情緒の
□ profit: 名 利益　□ cause: 名 目的

160. 正解：**D**　易 ■■■■□□ 難　選択率：(A) 2.8%　(B) 22.9%　(C) 6.0%　**(D) 67.9%**

Where would the article most likely be found?
(A) In a financial journal
(B) In a sports magazine
(C) In a company newsletter
(D) In a restaurant review

☐ financial: 形 金融の　☐ journal: 名 定期刊行物
☐ newsletter: 名 社内報

この記事はどこで目にする可能性が最も高いですか。
(A) 金融誌の中で
(B) スポーツ雑誌の中で
(C) 社内報の中で
(D) レストランのレビューの中で

▶解説　冒頭❶で、飲食店のレビューをすると述べられています。さらに第2段落では飲食店の雰囲気、第3段落ではメニューに言及して評価しています。最初から最後まで飲食店の話なので、飲食店のレビュー欄の記事だと考えられます。経営者は元スポーツ選手ですが、(B)のスポーツ雑誌の内容としては主題が不自然です。

---

161. 正解：**A**　易 ■■■■■■ 難　選択率：**(A) 28.5%**　(B) 14.9%　(C) 32.5%　(D) 24.1%

What is implied about the Godfrey brothers?
(A) They are not drawing attention to their sporting achievements.
(B) They are at the business every day.
(C) They were interviewed by the writers of the article.
(D) They are currently managing a professional sports team.

☐ achievement: 名 功績

Godfrey 兄弟について何が示唆されていますか。
(A) 彼らは、自分たちのスポーツでの功績に人目を引こうとはしていない。
(B) 彼らは毎日店にいる。
(C) 彼らは、この記事の筆者の取材を受けた。
(D) 彼らは今、あるプロスポーツチームを運営している。

▶解説　❷から、記事の筆者の予想に反して、プロスポーツ選手だった頃のオーナーの写真や記事は飲食店に飾られていなかったと分かります。従って、飲食店のオーナー達は過去の業績に注意を引こうとしていないと推測できるので、(A)が適切です。

---

162. 正解：**D**　易 ■■■■■□ 難　選択率：(A) 15.7%　(B) 6.0%　(C) 30.9%　**(D) 47.4%**

What is suggested about Godfrey's on Maple Street?
(A) It has many seasonal items.
(B) It is open seven days a week.
(C) It has reasonable prices.
(D) It has made charitable donations.

☐ seasonal: 形 季節の
☐ reasonable: 形 高くない、手頃な
☐ charitable: 形 慈善に関する
☐ donation: 名 寄付

Maple Street の Godfrey's について何が示されていますか。
(A) たくさんの季節の品を出している。
(B) 1週間、休みなく営業している。
(C) 手頃な価格を設定している。
(D) 慈善寄付を行った。

▶解説　❸から、この飲食店は収益の5パーセントを地元のために寄付していることが分かります。それを donations（寄付）と端的に言い表した(D)が正解です。第3段落で兄弟が世界中の優れた飲食店から着想を得たメニューに対する驚きを述べた後、Unfortunately, this includes the prices. と述べており、値段も一流並だった、つまり高いことが示唆されているので、(C)は誤りです。

((◎)) ゼミ 生 中継　　😎Hiro 😊Mai 😲Yasu 😑Dai 😄Saki

😎 記事が嫌いな受験者が多いのは知っているけれど、どうしてだろう？誰か教えて。

😊 理由は分かりませんが、理解するのが難しいです。

😑 語彙レベルが高いのではないかと。

😎 その傾向はある。あと、メールやチャットでは I が You に語るように書かれることが多い。そのスタイルだと理解しやすいけれど、記事はそうならない。ただ、記事は試験に絶対に出るから、慣れていくしかないよ。そもそも試験日を除いて、記事を英語で読む時間がどれくらいある？

😊😑 ……。

😎 ほら。試験日にしか記事を読まないのなら、試験中に厳しいと感じるのは当然だよ。

161.

😎 誰か、(C)を選んだ？　理由を教えてくれないかな。

😲 選びました。第2段落の最後で、店員さんがフレンドリーだって言っているので、記事を書いた人は店員に会っていますよね。

😎 それは正しい。でも、設問はこの店を経営している兄弟についてだよ。フレンドリーなのは The staff だよね。これは店の経営者やオーナーに対して使う言葉じゃない。

😲 あ、そういうことですか。分かりました。

Part 7 読解問題

Questions 163-165 refer to the following memo.

MEMO

To: All B&T Employees
From: Portia Tuttle
Date: November 17
Subject: December banquet

I just checked the schedule and noticed that the annual employee appreciation banquet is next month. This year, I have been put in charge of entertainment. — [1] —. I have been given a budget to hire an entertainer, but I would much rather put the money toward a lucky door prize and enjoy some entertainment from our colleagues.

— [2] —. If there is anyone who can perform a few songs on stage, I would love to hear from them. You can usually get me on extension 259. If there is more than one person or band interested in providing entertainment, I will either hold auditions or split the assigned time between two acts. — [3] —.

If no one expresses interest in this idea by Friday this week, I will contact Aprikana Talent Agents and ask them to provide a lounge singer for the evening. — [4] —. I think that would be a real disappointment because I had intended to arrange tickets for two for a stay at Astin Resort in Key West.

Sincerely,

Portia Tuttle

(191w)

問題163-165は次の連絡票に関するものです。

連絡票

宛先：全 B&T 従業員
発信者：Portia Tuttle
日付：11月17日
件名：12月の宴席

スケジュールを確かめたところ、毎年恒例の従業員謝恩夕食会が来月に迫っていることに気づきました。今年は、私がお楽しみ企画の担当になりました。エンターテイナーを手配する予算をもらってはいますが、むしろそのお金を抽選会の景品に振り向けて、余興の方は私たちの同僚に何か披露していただきたいと思うのです。

もし、どなたか壇上で2、3曲演奏してくださる方がいらっしゃるなら、ぜひお知らせください。私には、たいてい内線259番で連絡がつきます。お2人以上、あるいは2バンド以上が演奏をご希望であれば、私の方で審査させていただくか、または割当時間を2者の間で分けていただくようにします。

もし、今週の金曜日までにこの案に誰もご興味を示さない場合には、Aprikana Talent Agents に連絡を取って、その夜ラウンジ歌手を派遣してくれるよう手配します。その結果、今年は賞品の抽選がなくなってしまいます。それは大変残念なことだと思います。というのも、Key West の Astin Resort での1泊券を2枚、手配するつもりだったからです。

よろしくお願いいたします。

Portia Tuttle

□ appreciation: 名 感謝の気持ち　□ in charge of ～: ～の担当者で　□ rather: 副 むしろ　＊＜would rather ＋ 動詞＞の形で使われる
□ lucky door prize: 抽選でもらえる賞品　□ extension: 名 内線　□ band: 名 楽団、バンド　□ split: 動 ～を分ける
□ assign: 動 ～を割り当てる　□ act: 名 演目　□ intend to ～: ～するつもりである

163. 正解：**A**　易 ■■■■■■ 難　選択率：(A) 65.9% (B) 8.0% (C) 3.6% (D) 22.1%

What is the memo mainly about?
(A) Entertainment options for a company dinner
(B) Company policy with regard to hiring temporary staff members
(C) The following year's tentative work schedule
(D) Suggested themes for a corporate event

□ option: 名 選択肢　□ policy: 名 方針
□ with regard to ～: ～に関して
□ temporary: 形 一時的な
□ tentative: 形 暫定的な　□ theme: 名 主題
□ corporate: 形 法人の

この連絡票は、主に何に関するものですか。
(A) 会社の夕食会における、お楽しみ企画の選択肢
(B) 臨時雇用者に関する会社の方針
(C) 翌年の暫定的な業務予定
(D) 会社の催しに関するテーマの案

▶解説　Tuttleさんは❶で、「従業員謝恩夕食会の entertainment（余興）のための予算は、エンターテイナーに使うよりも抽選会の景品に使い、代わりに同僚のパフォーマンスの方が望ましい」と述べています。第2段落と第3段落にはそれぞれの案の具体的な情報が記載されています。よって、この連絡票は余興のためにできること（options）に関するものだと判断できます。(A)が正解です。

164. 正解：**A**　易 ■■■■■■ 難　選択率：(A) 61.0% (B) 6.8% (C) 23.7% (D) 7.2%

How should interested people contact Ms. Tuttle?
(A) By calling her on the telephone
(B) By sending her an e-mail
(C) By approaching her at her desk
(D) By sending her a text message

□ approach: 動 ～に近づく
□ text message: テキストメッセージ、携帯メッセージ

興味を持った人は、どうやってTuttleさんに連絡を取ればいいですか。
(A) 彼女に電話をかけることで
(B) 彼女にメールを送ることで
(C) 彼女の席へ行くことで
(D) 彼女にテキストメッセージを送ることで

▶解説　❷でTuttleさんは余興に参加したい人に対して、「内線259番で連絡がつきます」と述べていることから、(A)が適切です。ここでの extension は「内線」を意味しています。他の連絡方法には触れていません。

165. 正解：**D**　易 ■■■■■■ 難　選択率：(A) 16.9% (B) 19.3% (C) 15.7% (D) 47.4%

In which of the positions marked [1], [2], [3], and [4] does the following sentence best belong?

"As a result, there would be no lucky door prize this year."
(A) [1]
(B) [2]
(C) [3]
(D) [4]

次の文を当てはめるには、[1]、[2]、[3]、[4]と印が付けられた箇所のうちのどこが最もふさわしいですか。

「その結果、今年は賞品の抽選がなくなってしまいます」
(A) [1]
(B) [2]
(C) [3]
(D) [4]

▶解説　ターゲット文は、「その結果、今年は賞品の抽選はなくなるでしょう」という内容です。❶の情報から、予算はエンターテイナーか抽選会、どちらかの分しかないと推測できます。❸で、誰も余興に立候補しなかったらプロの歌手を派遣してもらう旨を述べています。その結果がターゲット文とすると文脈が通ります。正解は(D)です。[4] の後で、仮に抽選会を実施できた場合の景品の良さに触れているのもヒントです。

(( ))) ゼミ 生 中継　Hiro　Mai　Yasu　Dai　Saki

165.

😀 このターゲット文に大きいヒントがある。1つはAs a resultで、直前に何かの原因となる情報が記載されていると予想できる。あと1つ、助動詞のwouldもヒントだよ。ヤス、説明して。

👦 えっ……。仮定法か何かですか。

😀 そう。このターゲット文はwillではなくwouldを使っているから、ある状況を仮定して書かれている。どんな場合に抽選会がなくなるかを示す条件が直前に書かれているはずだよ。

😊 第3段落の先頭ですね。

😀 そう。「歌ってくれる社員がいなければ、タレント事務所に依頼する」という状況を想定しているよね。

😄 直後の文も I think that would be a real ～とwouldを使っていますね。

😀 そう。このwouldの存在意義に気づけば、(D)を選びやすい。こう考えると、文法力が高い方が、より正確な読解につながると言えるね。

😳 納得です。

Part 7 読解問題

Questions 166-167 refer to the following notice.

ATTENTION

❶The museum will open its doors later than usual on Wednesday, October 28. Officials from the city's Department of Health and Safety will be inspecting the museum's exits, alarms, and sprinkler system to ensure our compliance with city codes. This is scheduled to take place between 9:00 A.M. and 11:00 A.M. ❷We anticipate being able to welcome guests from 11:30 A.M. instead of the ❸usual 9:30 A.M. ❹If you need to make a special allowance for any tour companies who require access for a group earlier than that, please speak with the museum manager. Keep in mind that requests will be considered on a first come, first served basis. ❺Opening hours will be back to normal on Thursday.

Naveen Prasad — Assistant Manager

(123w)

問題166-167は次のお知らせに関するものです。

注意

当博物館は、10月28日水曜日、開館時刻を通常よりも遅らせる予定です。市のDepartment of Health and Safetyの職員が、博物館の非常口、警報装置および散水装置を検査し、当館が間違いなく市の基準を順守しているかを確認することになっています。これは午前9時から午前11時の間に実施される予定です。来館者を受け入れられるようになるのは通常の午前9時30分ではなく、午前11時30分からと見込んでいます。もし、団体向けにそれよりも早い入館を求めるツアー会社があって特別に許可する必要があれば、館長に相談してください。この許可要請は先着順に検討されることを念頭に置いてください。開館時間は木曜日には通常通りに戻ります。

Naveen Prasad──副館長

☐ attention: 名 注意　☐ official: 名 公務員、役人　☐ inspect: 動 ～を検査する　☐ alarm: 名 警報器　☐ ensure: 動 ～を確かめる
☐ compliance: 名 法令順守　☐ city code: 市の規則　☐ take place: 行われる　☐ anticipate: 動 ～を見込む　☐ allowance: 名 許容
☐ access: 名 入る権利　☐ consider: 動 ～を検討する　☐ on the first come, first served basis: 先着順に

166. 正解：**C**　易 ■■■■ ■ ■ 難　選択率：(A) 18.1%　(B) 6.0%　**(C) 56.6%**　(D) 18.9%

For whom is the notice intended?
(A) Tourists
(B) City officials
(C) Museum staff
(D) Tour company employees

このお知らせは誰に向けられたものですか。
(A) 観光客
(B) 市の職員
(C) 博物館の従業員
(D) ツアー会社の従業員

▶解説　前半で博物館の開館時間の変更や市の検査の詳細を説明していること、❷で「来館者を受け入れられるようになるのは午前11時30分からの見込み」と述べていることなどから、この告知は来館者を迎える立場の(C)、「博物館の従業員」を対象にしていると考えるのが自然です。なお、❹から、読み手がツアー会社から問い合わせを受ける可能性があると分かるので、(A)と(D)は不適切だと分かります。

---

167. 正解：**B**　易 ■ ■■■■ ■ 難　選択率：(A) 6.4%　**(B) 58.6%**　(C) 1.6%　(D) 32.9%

What time will the facility open on October 29?
(A) At 9:00 A.M.
(B) At 9:30 A.M.
(C) At 11:00 A.M.
(D) At 11:30 A.M.

□ facility: 名 施設

この施設は、10月29日には何時に開く予定ですか。
(A) 午前9時
(B) 午前9時30分
(C) 午前11時
(D) 午前11時30分

▶解説　❶で「10月28日水曜日は、通常よりも開館時間が遅い」と分かります。この開館時間が❷にある11時30分です。❸で通常の開館時間は9時30分だと分かります。さらに❺で、「木曜日には通常の開館時間に戻る」と述べられています。これらの情報から、設問にある10月29日は木曜日で、開館時間は通常の9時30分だと判断できます。(B)が正解です。

(((∆))) ゼミ 生 中継　　😀 Hiro　😊 Mai　😸 Yasu　🎲 Dai　😄 Saki

167.

😀 (D)を選んだ人は、中盤の〜 welcome guests from 11:30 A.M.という情報を見て11時半が正解だと思ったのかな。

😊 そうです。でも、これは10月28日の話ですね。設問を読み間違えました。

😀 設問は10月29日の開館時刻を問うているからね。ダイはどうして(D)を選んだの?

🎲 October 29という日付が設問にあるのに文書になかったので、印刷ミスだと判断し、October 28と読み替えました。

😊 ユニークすぎる判断だね、それは。確かにOctober 29は文書にないけど、October 28が水曜だから翌日の木曜のことを言っていると推測しなきゃ。

😄 文書にない日付が設問にいきなり使われることってありますよね。公式教材か何かで見たことがあります。

⑰ライティング力を上げたい

TOEICの勉強をしながらメールライティングの力を伸ばしたいのですが、可能でしょうか。うちの会社では英語のメールが飛び交うので、書く力が重要なのです。

それなら大丈夫です。TOEICの問題集や模試にはメールが多く含まれています。Part 6とPart 7です。

はい。それは知っていますが、問題を解くだけで本当に書く力が伸びるのでしょうか。

解くだけでは無理です。**一番のお勧めは「筆写」です。**実際に手を動かして書き写すシンプルな訓練ですが、ものすごく良い練習になります。「知っている」と「使える」は違いますよね。いくら単語やフレーズを知っていても、使えるとは限りません。筆写は、まさに「使う練習」です。

なるほど。やってみます。

できれば、「単語を1つずつ書き写す」のではなく「**文を書き写す**」という意識でやってください。長い文は途中で切ってもOKです。

分かりました。

そして、**コンテンツを少しずつ入れ替える**ともっと実践的な練習になります。例えば、営業部員が書いたメールを筆写する場合、商品名や店舗名などをご自身の職場に合わせて書き換えてみてはどうでしょう。そうすればリアリティーのあるメールになります。

おお！　それは良さそうです。ありがとうございました。

Questions 168-171 refer to the following information.

> # Sunny Castle Amusement Park
> ## Mobile Phones
>
> ❶ Employees of Sunny Castle Amusement Park are not allowed to carry their personal mobile phones with them while working in the amusement park grounds. — [1] —. All mobile phones can be kept in the lockers at the administration building. Otherwise, they may be left with the staff at the security desk near the main entrance. — [2] —. ❷ The rule only applies to employees who come in direct contact with park visitors. ❸ Therefore, the office staff is not obliged to conform.
>
> ❹ The park provides all staff members with company-owned mobile phones, which employees are expected to carry with them while on duty. — [3] —. You may not use this phone for personal calls nor may you install any unapproved applications. A list of approved applications is provided on the last page of this document. — [4] —. ❺ A more up-to-date version of the employee manual may be posted on the Web site. Check www.sunnycastleap.com/staff for updates.

(159w)

問題168-171 は次の案内に関するものです。

Sunny Castle Amusement Park
携帯電話について

Sunny Castle Amusement Park の従業員は、遊園地敷地内での勤務中に個人用の携帯電話を携行することを禁じられています。全ての携帯電話は、管理棟のロッカー内に保管できます。あるいは、正面入口近くの警備デスクで係員に預けても構いません。この規定が適用されるのは、来園者に直接応対する従業員だけです。従って、事務所内の勤務者が従う必要はありません。

当園は、全従業員に社有の携帯電話を支給しており、従業員はこれを勤務中に携行することになっています。それらは素晴らしい仕様の最新型のものです。この電話機を私用の通話に使ったり、未承認のアプリをインストールしたりすることはできません。承認済みのアプリの一覧は、本書類の最終ページに記載されています。従業員マニュアルの更新版が、ウェブサイトにアップされているかもしれません。www.sunnycastleap.com/staffで、情報の更新を確認してください。

□ allow: 動 ～を許可する　□ personal: 形 個人の　□ ground: 名 土地　□ administration: 名 管理　□ otherwise: 副 さもなければ
□ security desk: 警備デスク　□ apply: 動 適用する　□ visitor: 名 訪問者　□ oblige: 動 ～に義務付ける　□ conform: 動 従う
□ company-owned: 会社所有の　□ on duty: 勤務中　□ unapproved: 形 承認されていない　□ approved: 形 承認された
□ up-to-date: 形 最新の　□ post: 動 ～を載せる

Part 7 読解問題

---

168. 正解：**A** 易■■■■■■■■難　選択率：**(A) 85.5%** (B) 6.0% (C) 7.2% (D) 0.8%

Where would the information most likely be found?
(A) In an employee handbook
(B) In a newspaper article
(C) In a visitor information leaflet
(D) In a travel brochure

この情報は、どこに示されている可能性が最も高いですか。
(A) 従業員便覧の中に
(B) 新聞記事の中に
(C) 来園者向け案内書の中に
(D) 旅行パンフレットの中に

▶解説　冒頭の❶で、従業員が守るべき携帯電話使用のルールに言及しており、第2段落でもルールの詳細が説明されていることから、職員向け文書の一部だと推測できます。よって、この情報が掲載される場所としては(A)が妥当です。❺で、従業員マニュアルの新版があることに言及しているのもヒントになります。

---

169. 正解：**D** 易■■■■■■■■難　選択率：(A) 12.0% (B) 13.7% (C) 19.7% **(D) 54.2%**

What is implied about office staff at Sunny Castle Amusement Park?
(A) They can be contacted 24 hours a day.
(B) They cannot arrange group tours without advance notice.
(C) They recharge mobile phone batteries at the end of each shift.
(D) They do not communicate with patrons directly.

□ advance: 形 前もっての　□ recharge: 動 ～を再充電する
□ communicate: 動 連絡する　□ patron: 名 常連客

Sunny Castle Amusement Parkの事務所内勤務者について、どんなことが示唆されていますか。
(A) 彼らには24時間連絡が取れる。
(B) 彼らは事前通告なしに団体ツアーを手配できない。
(C) 彼らは毎勤務時間の終わりに携帯電話のバッテリーを充電する。
(D) 彼らは客と直接やり取りしない。

▶解説　第1段落前半で従業員の個人用携帯電話の使用に関する制限が説明されていますが、❷で「この規定が適用されるのは、来園者に直接応対する従業員だけ」だと分かります。続けて❸で「事務所内の勤務者が従う必要はない」と明記されています。つまり、内勤者は客と接することがないことを示唆しているので、(D)が正解です。

---

170. 正解：**B** 易■■■■■■■■難　選択率：(A) 4.8% **(B) 70.7%** (C) 8.0% (D) 15.7%

Why might someone visit the Web site?
(A) To obtain a list of show times
(B) To check changes to company policy
(C) To sign up for an information session
(D) To download the most recent newsletter

□ obtain: 動 ～を入手する　□ policy: 名 方針
□ information session: 説明会　□ newsletter: 社報

ウェブサイトにアクセスする人がいるとすれば、その理由は何ですか。
(A) ショーの時間の一覧を入手するために
(B) 会社の規定の変更を確認するために
(C) 説明会に申し込むために
(D) 最新の社報をダウンロードするために

▶解説　文書の終盤の❺で、ウェブサイトに最新の従業員マニュアルが掲載される可能性があると記されています。よって、会社の方針に変更があるかを確かめるためにウェブサイトを見る人がいると考えられます。正解は(B)です。

---

171. 正解：**C** 易■■■■■■■■難　選択率：(A) 4.0% (B) 8.8% **(C) 71.5%** (D) 15.3%

In which of the positions marked [1], [2], [3], and [4] does the following sentence best belong?

"They are recent models with excellent specifications."
(A) [1]
(B) [2]
(C) [3]
(D) [4]

□ excellent: 形 卓越した
□ specification: 名 仕様

次の文を当てはめるには、[1]、[2]、[3]、[4]と印が付けられた箇所のうちのどこが最もふさわしいですか。

「それらは素晴らしい仕様の最新型のものです」
(A) [1]
(B) [2]
(C) [3]
(D) [4]

▶解説　ターゲット文の主語である代名詞Theyは「素晴らしい仕様の最新型」のものであるはずです。これは通常、電子機器を描写する際に用いられる表現なので、この文書の主題である携帯電話を指していると推測できます。会社から貸与される携帯電話について述べられている❹の後に入れると、Theyがcompany-owned mobile phonesを指すことになり文脈が通ります。

((·)) ゼミ 生中継 　　　　　　　　　　Hiro　Mai　Yasu　Dai　Saki

169.

誰か、(D) を選べなかった理由を教えて。

park visitors と patrons が同じ人を指していることに気づきませんでした。patrons ってパトロンですよね。

日本語のパトロンは「後援者」だけど、英語の patrons は「常連客」も含むんだよ。

170.

Test 1 と Test 2 にもあった Why might だね。サキ、覚えているよね。

Why might のヒントは?

if にあり……、と言いたいですが、if がなかったです。

なかったね。Test 2 に出たとき、例外があるって言ったよね。

はい。これが例外だと気づきました。

(D) がダメな理由は、newsletter は関係ないことですか?

その通り。最新の従業員マニュアルはウェブサイトで入手可能だけど、newsletter はどこにも登場していない。

345

Part 7 読解問題

Questions 172-175 refer to the following online chat discussion.

Clyde Kang [3:30 P.M.]: As we discussed at last night's meeting, we have to let a few of our clients go. We're getting too busy to handle them all properly. I'm planning on calling Larusso University this afternoon to let them know. I would like to put them in touch with another reputable firm when I call. Any ideas?

Harry Larkin [3:31 P.M.]: I used to work at Ramsey Images. They were always very professional.

Jang-Mi Sin [3:31 P.M.]: That's true, but I don't think they're in business anymore.

Clyde Kang [3:33 P.M.]: Harry, I'm surprised you didn't know that. It's one of the reasons we've been so busy.

Derek Wilks [3:35 P.M.]: I hear that Galione Studios recently won an award for their work for Macchio Fashion.

Jang-Mi Sin [3:35 P.M.]: I have a friend who works there. He says they're in the same situation as we are. I doubt they're looking for extra work, either.

Harry Larkin [3:37 P.M.]: We haven't gotten any work from Larusso University recently. I don't think they'll be very concerned about the news.

Clyde Kang [3:45 P.M.]: They might. I heard that they have a big job coming up. I really don't want to put them in a difficult position.

Derek Wilks [3:46 P.M.]: Perhaps we should try to keep them as a client. How about hiring a dependable freelance photographer?

Clyde Kang [3:49 P.M.]: You might be right. Harry, can you recommend one of your old colleagues?

(245w)

問題172-175は次のオンラインチャットに関するものです。

Clyde Kang［午後3時30分］：昨夜の会議で話した通り、2、3の顧客を手放さなければならない。忙しくなってきていて、とても全ての顧客にきちんと対応できないからね。今日の午後にLarusso大学に電話して伝えるつもりだよ。彼らには、電話をかけたときに、別の評判のいい会社を紹介したいと思ってるんだ。どこがいいかな？

Harry Larkin［午後3時31分］：私はかつてRamsey Imagesに勤めていました。あそこはいつも、大変素晴らしい仕事をしていましたよ。

Jang-Mi Sin［午後3時31分］：その通りですが、今はもう営業していないと思います。

Clyde Kang［午後3時33分］：Harry、驚いたよ、君がそれを知らなかったとは。それが、うちがこれほど忙しくなっている理由の1つなんだ。

Derek Wilks［午後3時35分］：Galione Studiosが最近、Macchio Fashionの仕事で賞を取ったそうですよ。

Jang-Mi Sin［午後3時35分］：あの会社で働いている友人がいます。彼の話だと、あそこもうちと同じような状況だそうです。やはり、新たな仕事を求めているとは思えません。

Harry Larkin［午後3時37分］：Larusso大学からは、最近あまり仕事が来ていません。彼らは、今回の話を聞いてもさほど心配しないのではないでしょうか。

Clyde Kang［午後3時45分］：するかもしれない。あそこで近々、大きな仕事があると聞いたんだ。あまり彼らに困った状況に陥ってもらいたくはないね。

Derek Wilks［午後3時46分］：おそらく彼らは、顧客として手放さないようにした方がいいでしょう。信頼のおけるフリーのカメラマンを手配してはどうでしょうか。

Clyde Kang［午後3時49分］：それがいいかもしれないな。Harry、君の昔の同僚の誰かを推薦してもらえるかな？

☐ handle: 動 〜に対処する　☐ properly: 副 適切に　☐ let 〜 know: 〜に知らせる　☐ in touch with 〜: 〜と接触して
☐ reputable: 形 評判のいい　☐ firm: 名 会社　☐ in business: 事業を行って、営業して　☐ same 〜 as ...: …と同じ〜　☐ situation: 名 状況
☐ doubt: 動 〜とは思えない　☐ extra: 形 追加の　☐ perhaps: 副 おそらく　☐ How about 〜?: 〜はどうですか。　☐ dependable: 形 信頼できる
☐ freelance: 形 フリーの　☐ photographer: 名 写真家

Part 7 読解問題

172. 正解：**D** 易 ■■■■□□□ 難　選択率：(A) 14.5%　(B) 6.8%　(C) 9.2%　**(D) 68.7%**

Why did Mr. Kang start the online chat discussion?
(A) To ask for introductions to job seekers
(B) To announce the signing of a contract
(C) To thank employees for their hard work
(D) To get suggestions for a client referral

□ seeker: 图 探す人　□ referral: 图 紹介

なぜKangさんは、このオンラインチャットを始めましたか。
(A) 求職者への紹介を依頼するために
(B) 契約の締結を知らせるために
(C) 従業員の激務に謝意を表すために
(D) 顧客の紹介先を提案してもらうために

▶解説 ❶で顧客を手放す旨を確認し、❸では、その顧客に評判のいい会社を紹介したいと伝え、Any ideas?（どこがいいかな？）と尋ねています。この流れから、顧客の紹介先（a client referral）の提案を求めていると判断できるので、(D) が正解です。

---

173. 正解：**B** 易 ■■■■□□□ 難　選択率：(A) 7.6%　**(B) 65.1%**　(C) 8.8%　(D) 17.7%

What is implied about Galione Studios?
(A) It is hiring new staff.
(B) It is very busy.
(C) It took on a new client.
(D) It specializes in fashion photography.

□ take on ～: ～を引き受ける
□ specialize in ～: ～を専門とする

Galione Studiosについて何が示唆されていますか。
(A) 新しい人材を雇用している。
(B) 非常に多忙だ。
(C) 新しい顧客を得た。
(D) ファッション写真を専門としている。

▶解説 Galione Studiosの名前は❼に登場します。❽でSinさんがGalione Studiosも自分達の会社と同じような状況にあるらしいと伝えています。❷や❻の内容から、オンラインチャットの参加者たちの会社は非常に忙しいと分かるので、Galione Studiosについて示唆されている内容は (B) です。

---

174. 正解：**C** 易 ■■■■□□□ 難　選択率：(A) 23.3%　(B) 6.8%　**(C) 62.2%**　(D) 6.8%

At 3:45 P.M., why does Mr. Kang write, "They might"?
(A) He believes Ramsey Images will be interested in an offer.
(B) He sent some equipment away for repairs.
(C) He thinks Larusso University will be affected by a decision.
(D) He heard some news about a photography course.

□ equipment: 图 機器　□ affect: 動 ～に影響を与える

午後3時45分に、なぜKangさんは「するかもしれない」と書いていますか。
(A) 彼は、Ramsey Imagesが提案に興味を示すだろうと思っている。
(B) 彼は、ある装置を修理に出した。
(C) 彼は、Larusso大学が、ある決定の影響を受けるだろうと考えている。
(D) 彼は、ある写真講座に関する知らせを聞いた。

▶解説 They might. は、❾のLarusso大学からはあまり仕事がないので彼らは心配しないだろう、という趣旨のコメントに対する応答で、They might be concerned about the news. の be 以下が省略された形です。ターゲット文に続く❿では、大学で近々、大きな仕事があるため、そのときに困らせたくないと言っていることから、Kangさんは契約解除の決定によって大学は影響を受けるだろうと考えています。正解は (C) です。

---

175. 正解：**C** 易 ■■■□□□□ 難　選択率：(A) 16.9%　(B) 13.7%　**(C) 59.8%**　(D) 8.4%

What will Mr. Larkin most likely do next?
(A) Meet the hiring manager at Galione Studios
(B) Inquire about evening courses at Larusso University
(C) Contact a previous employee of Ramsey Images
(D) Renew a contract with Macchio Fashion

□ inquire: 動 尋ねる　□ renew: 動 ～を更新する

Larkinさんは次に何をする可能性が最も高いですか。
(A) Galione Studiosの採用責任者と会う
(B) Larusso大学の夜間講座について問い合わせる
(C) Ramsey Imagesの元従業員に連絡を取る
(D) Macchino Fashionとの契約を更新する

▶解説 Wilksさんが⓫でフリーのカメラマンを手配してはどうかと提案し、Kangさんが同意しています。そして⓬でLarkinさんに元同僚を紹介してほしいと述べています。❹から、Larkinさんの以前の勤務先はRamsey Imagesであること、❺から同社は営業していないことが分かります。これらからLarkinさんはRamsey Imagesの元社員に連絡を取ると判断できるので、(C) が正解です。

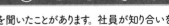

ゼミ 生中継

Hiro Mai Yasu Dai Saki

172. ....
😎 ヤス、(D)にあるreferralを覚えているかな。

🐼 はい、かすかに覚えています。

😎 referralは重要語だって言ったよね。

😀 Test 1の123番です。

😎 実は、近年は「リファラル」が日本語として定着しつつある。スマホで検索してみて。「リファラル採用」とか「リファラルリクルーティング」という言葉でヒットするはずだよ。

🐼 大学の先輩からその言葉を聞いたことがあります。社員が知り合いを会社に紹介して、採用されたら報奨金がもらえるそうですね。

😎 そういうこともある。TOEICワールドにも存在するシステムだよ。

174. ....
😎 モニターの20％以上が(A)を選んでいるけれど、これは惜しくない。大ハズレだよ。今、Ramsey Imagesは営業していないからね。

🐼 やっぱりそうか〜。

😎 では、ダブルパッセージに進もう。

349

Part 7 読解問題

Questions 176-180 refer to the following table of contents and interview from a magazine.

Software Developer's Monthly
February
Table of Contents

(54w)

問題176-180は次の目次と雑誌のインタビュー記事に関するものです。

Software Developer's Monthly
2月号
目次

☐ table of contents: 目次   ☐ editorial: 名 論説   ☐ editor: 名 編集者

An Interview with Verne Ramirez — founder of Ramirez Solutions
By Carmen Matei

Verne Ramirez recently sat down for an interview with Carmen Matei, one of the staff writers at *Software Developer's Monthly*. Matei arrived at the Skytop Hotel in central Taipei, where Ramirez was staying, and they met in the wonderful Clamshell Restaurant to talk about his exciting career.

Matei: Thank you for agreeing to this interview. Can you tell us why you're so far from home?

Ramirez: Not at all. I'm here to meet with a couple of young developers who are developing a smartphone application that can help you recognize locations from photographs and find them on a map. I'd like to use the technology in one of my company's upcoming software packages.

Matei: It sounds interesting. Can I ask how you got into software development?

Ramirez: Of course. I'm afraid it isn't a very interesting story. In high school, I asked a career counselor what the best paying jobs were. She mentioned medicine, law, and computers. I thought computers sounded the most fun of the three.

Matei: Did you have any experience programming before that?

Ramirez: None at all. Luckily, I was taught by Dr. Joseph Morgan at Kelston University. He really inspired me to try new things.

Matei: What do you wish you had known more about when you were starting out?

Ramirez: Many things, obviously. In particular, I wish I'd known more about choosing a good company to work for. I wasted a lot of time working in jobs where I learned nothing.

Matei: What a coincidence! One of our staff writers is working on an article about that for our February issue.

Ramirez: Well, I think everyone getting started in the industry should probably read it. It's important to plan your career well.

Matei: Speaking of plans, what do you have in mind for the next few years?

Ramirez: I'm getting ready to launch an online college where people from all over the world can learn computer programming. Instruction will be given by my employees, who are some of the most talented programmers in the industry.

(352w)

Verne Ramirez とのインタビュー —— Ramirez Solutions 創業者
聞き手：Carmen Matei
Verne Ramirez 氏が先頃、『Software Developer's Monthly』誌のスタッフライターの1人 Carmen Matei とのインタビューに応じてくれた。Matei は台北の中心部にある Skytop Hotel へ行き、そこに滞在中の Ramirez 氏と素晴らしい Clamshell Restaurant で対面し、氏の刺激的な経歴について話した。

Matei：このインタビューに応じてくださり、どうもありがとうございます。なぜ、このような遠い場所に来ていらっしゃるのですか。
Ramirez：どういたしまして。私がここに来ているのは、数名の若い開発者と会うためです。彼らが開発しているのはスマートフォン向けのアプリで、写真から場所を割り出して地図上に示してくれるものです。私はその技術を、自社の次のソフトウエア製品に使いたいと思っているのです。
Matei：面白そうですね。どのような経緯でソフトウエア開発の世界に身を投じられたのか、伺っても構いませんか。
Ramirez：もちろんです。大して面白い話ではないと思いますが。高校時代に、私は就職カウンセラーに尋ねたのです、どんな職業が最もお金を稼げるのかと。彼女が挙げたのは、医療、法律、そしてコンピューターの職でした。コンピューターが、その3つのうちで一番面白そうに思

えたのです。
Matei：それ以前にプログラミングの経験をお持ちだったのですか。
Ramirez：いいえ、全くなかったんです。運よく、私は Kelston 大学で Joseph Morgan 博士の指導を受けました。彼は私に、とにかく新しいことを試すよう仕向けてくれました。
Matei：駆け出しのころに、もっと知っていたらよかったのにと思われるのは、どんなことですか。
Ramirez：たくさんありますよ、もちろん。特に、もっと知っておけばよかったのにと思うのは、働きやすい会社の選び方についてです。私は、何も得るものがない職場で働くことで、多くの時間を無駄にしました。
Matei：何と、それは偶然ですね！ うちのライターの1人が、そのことに関する記事を担当しているのです。本誌の2月号に載ります。
Ramirez：ならば、この業界で働き始めようとしている人は皆、その記事を読んだほうがよさそうですね。自分の職業についてじっくり計画を練ることは大切です。
Matei：計画と言えば、この先の数年間、どのようなことをしようとお考えですか。
Ramirez：世界中の人がコンピューターのプログラミングを学ぶことができるオンライン大学の立ち上げを準備しています。講師を務めるのは私の会社の従業員たちで、業界で最も能力の高いプログラマーのうちの何名かです。

☐ founder: 名 創業者 ☐ developer: 名 開発者 ☐ recognize: 動 ～を認識する ☐ upcoming: 形 今度の ☐ medicine: 名 医学
☐ luckily: 副 幸運にも ☐ inspire: 動 ～に着想を与える ☐ obviously: 副 明らかに ☐ coincidence: 名 偶然

Part 7 読解問題

176. 正解：**A** 易 ■■■■■□□ 難 選択率：**(A) 71.9%** (B) 7.2% (C) 11.6% (D) 7.6%

For whom is the magazine most likely intended?
(A) Computer programmers
(B) Video game enthusiasts
(C) Hardware designers
(D) Appliance salespeople

□ enthusiast: 名 熱中している人
□ appliance: 名 電化製品　□ salespeople: 名 販売員

この雑誌は、どのような人を対象としている可能性が最も高いですか。
(A) コンピューターのプログラマー
(B) テレビゲームの愛好者
(C) ハードウエアの設計者
(D) 家電製品の販売員

▶解説 ❶で月刊誌のタイトルがSoftware Developer's Monthlyだと分かります。また❷に「プログラミング業界のニュース」という記事があることから、ソフトウエア開発者、つまり (A) のコンピューターのプログラマーを対象とした雑誌だと推測できます。

---

177. 正解：**D** 易 ■■■■■□□ 難 選択率：(A) 14.5% (B) 28.9% (C) 17.3% **(D) 36.1%**

What is indicated about Mr. Ramirez?
(A) He often stays at the Skytop Hotel.
(B) He will give interviews to multiple magazines.
(C) He is negotiating a merger with another company.
(D) He is in Taipei to negotiate a business deal.

□ multiple: 形 複数の　□ negotiate: 動 ～を交渉する
□ merger: 名 合併　□ deal: 名 取引

Ramirezさんについて、何が示されていますか。
(A) 彼はよく Skytop Hotel に宿泊する。
(B) 彼は複数の雑誌のインタビューに応じるつもりだ。
(C) 彼は別の企業と合併の交渉をしている。
(D) 彼はビジネス取引の交渉をするために台北にいる。

▶解説 Ramirez さんは、2文書目でインタビューを受けている人物です。❹からRamirezさんは現在台北に滞在中であることが分かり、❺と❻から自社で採用したいと考えている新技術を開発しているプログラマーに会うために来たことが分かります。それらを「ビジネス取引の交渉をするために台北にいる」と言い表した (D) が正解です。

---

178. 正解：**D** 易 ■■■■■□□ 難 選択率：(A) 19.3% (B) 14.5% (C) 42.2% **(D) 22.5%**

What attracted Mr. Ramirez to his current field?
(A) Positive experiences from his childhood
(B) The opportunities for extended holidays
(C) The prospect of working with Dr. Morgan
(D) The promise of high financial reward

□ current: 形 現在の　□ field: 名 分野
□ positive: 形 積極的な　□ childhood: 名 子供時代
□ opportunity: 名 機会　□ prospect: 名 見通し
□ financial: 形 金銭上の　□ reward: 名 褒美

どのようなことが、Ramirezさんを現在の業種に導いたのですか。
(A) 幼少期の前向きな経験
(B) 長期休暇の機会
(C) Morgan博士と働く見通し
(D) 高収入を得られるという確約

▶解説 ソフトウエア開発に興味を抱いたきっかけを聞かれ、Ramirezさんは❼で高校時代のカウンセラーが、最も収入が高い職種の1つとしてコンピューターを挙げたことだと答えています。よって、彼が現在の職業を選んだ理由は (D) です。Ramirezさんは Morgan 博士と一緒に働きたかったとは答えていないので、(C) は不正解です。

---

179. 正解：**C** 易 ■■■■■□□ 難 選択率：(A) 12.9% (B) 24.1% **(C) 50.6%** (D) 10.0%

On what page of the magazine is the article Ms. Matei mentions?
(A) Page 7
(B) Page 8
(C) Page 19
(D) Page 22

Mateiさんが触れた記事は、雑誌の何ページに載っていますか。
(A) 7ページ
(B) 8ページ
(C) 19ページ
(D) 22ページ

▶解説 ❽でRamirezさんは「良い会社の選び方を知っていればよかった」と後悔している旨を述べ、Mateiさんは❾で、同僚のライターがそれに関係する記事を書いていると応じています。「会社の選び方」は、目次の❸にある Finding the Right Employer（良い雇用主を見つけるには）に一致するため、(C) が正解です。

180. 正解：**C**　易 ■■■■ ■ 難　選択率：(A) 10.0%　(B) 23.3%　**(C) 58.6%**　(D) 5.2%

What will Mr. Ramirez do soon?
(A) Publish a book on his life as a company president
(B) Teach a course to university students
(C) Establish an educational institution
(D) Purchase land for a new company headquarters

Ramirez さんは、もうすぐ何をするつもりですか。
(A) 会社社長としての自分の人生に関する本を出版する
(B) 大学生に講義する
(C) 教育機関を設立する
(D) 新しい会社の本社のために土地を買う

▶解説　⑩で Ramirez さんは「世界中の人がプログラミングを学ぶことができるオンライン大学の立ち上げを準備中だ」と述べています。online college（オンラインの大学）を educational institution（教育機関）と抽象的に表現している (C) が正解です。

□ publish: 動 ～を出版する　□ establish: 動 ～を設立する
□ institution: 名 機関　□ headquarters: 名 本社

((≋)) ゼミ 生 中継　　　　　　(≋) Hiro (≋) Mai (≋) Yasu (≋) Dai (≋) Saki

177.

(≋) このインタビューは、文字は多いけれど、会話調だから理解するのは易しかったでしょ？

(≋) そうですね。記事や手紙に比べれば読みやすいです。

(≋) ヤス、177番の (D) を選べた？

(≋) いいえ。時間切れになると思って焦っていたので、適当に (B) を塗りました。

(≋) このような、選択肢照合型を解くには時間がかかるから、残り時間が少なくなったら優先的に捨てていいよ。What is indicated about XXX? という形をしているから、すぐに判別できる。

178.

(≋) サキ、(C) にした？　大人気の不正解なんだけど。

(≋) 選びました。Dr. Morgan について、He really inspired me to try new things. と言っているので、これがヒントだと思いました。

(≋) おいおい、ちょっと待ってよ。(C) は The prospect of working with Dr. Morgan だよ。Dr. Morgan は大学の先生だから、もし、(C) が正解ならば、Ramirez さんは大学の先生になりたかったことになる。

(≋) 選択肢をよく読んでいませんでした。

(≋) もっと手前で、インタビュアーが Can I ask how you got into software development? と質問しているよね。これへの答えが、Ramirez さんがソフト開発の仕事を目指した動機だよ。

Part 7 読解問題

Questions 181-185 refer to the following article and ticket.

GILMORE (February 10) — Gilmore City has recently cleared and developed a large area of parkland in Mulberry Hills. This land has been used to create a new fashion district known as the Gilmore Fashion District or GFD. Gilmore has been associated with a growing number of fashion labels over the years. City leaders are hoping that fashion design and production will become one of the town's major industries. To encourage businesses to move into the new district and provide them a financial boost, the council has agreed to subsidize the rent for the first five years of every lease. As a result, businesses will be able to save up to 50 percent on rent and benefit from being in one of the most attractive locations businesses in this industry could hope for.

Besides the obvious financial advantages, companies will benefit from a connection with the newly founded Balmoral College of Art. The publicly owned college is located within the GFD and has agreed to provide a space for all of the city's fashion shows. The college's 640 square-meter function hall is available for free for approved events. According to Cheryl Dominic from Zebra Garments, one of the first companies to move to the GFD, the event hall has been an excellent venue for her company's promotional events.

So far, the only way to rent an office in the GFD has been to receive an invitation from the GFD administrators. Soon, however, administrators will be accepting applications from other businesses. There are conditions on the type and size of company that is allowed to move into the GFD and interested people can learn more about them by following the links on the Web site.

(283w)

問題181-185は次の記事とチケットに関するものです。

GILMORE（2月10日）―― Gilmore市は先ごろ、Mulberry Hillsの広大な公園用地を整地、開発した。この一帯を利用して、Gilmore Fashion DistrictまたはGFDの名で知られる新興ファッション地区が生まれようとしている。Gilmoreは何年にもわたり、増加するファッションブランドと提携してきた。市の有力者たちは、ファッションデザインとファッション品の生産が、この市の主要産業の1つになることを期待している。この新興地区に事業者を誘致し、財政支援を行うために、市議会はあらゆる賃貸契約に対して最初の5年間、賃料を助成することを承認している。その結果、事業者は賃料を最大で5割まで節減することが可能となり、この業種の事業者が望み得る最も魅力的な場所の1つに進出するという恩恵を手にできるのだ。

目に見える財務上の利得に加えて、事業者は新たに開校したBalmoral College of Artからも恩恵を受けられることになる。この公立大学はGFD地区内にあり、市で催されるあらゆるファッションショーのために会場を提供することに同意している。同校の640平方メートルの講堂で、承認を受けた催事を無料で開催できるのだ。GFDに進出した第1陣事業者の1つZebra GarmentsのCheryl Dominicさんによると、この催事場は同社の販促イベントにうってつけの会場だという。

これまでのところ、GFDで事業場所の貸与を受ける唯一の方法は、GFD管理当局から招致してもらうことだ。しかし、程なく管理当局は、それ以外の事業者からの申請を受け付ける予定だ。事業者の種別や規模に関する条件があり、それに基づいてGFDへの進出が許可される。興味のある人は、ウェブサイト上のリンクをたどれば詳細情報を入手できる。

Admit One

The Annual Gilmore Fashion Show
See exciting designs created exclusively in the GFD!
7:00 P.M. to 10:00 P.M., June 16

This ticket has been provided for **Noelle Peabody** of **Crisp Fashion**.

This is a free ticket provided for employees of businesses displaying items in the show. Please note that this ticket is non-transferable. As a result, you may be asked to show identification at the entrance. A detailed map of the event's location, as well as contact details of the organizers, are printed on the back.

(88w)

1名さま有効

年次 Gilmore Fashion Show
GFD だけで生み出された素晴らしいデザインをご覧ください！
6月16日　午後7時から午後10時まで

本券は Crisp Fashion の Noelle Peabody さまに発行されています。

これは無料入場券で、ショーで商品を披露する事業者の従業員に発行されるものです。本券は譲渡できませんのでご注意ください。そのため、入り口で身分証明書の提示を求められることがあります。イベント会場の詳細地図、および主催者の連絡先詳細は、裏面に印刷されています。

□ admit: 動 ～に入ることを許す　＊入場券などに書かれた admit one は「1名有効」の意味　□ exclusively: 副 独占的に
□ display: 動 ～を展示する　□ note: 動 ～に注意する　□ non-transferable: 形 譲渡できない　□ identification: 名 身分証明書
□ detailed: 形 詳細な

181. 正解：**B** 易 ■■■■■■□ 難　選択率：(A) 16.1%　**(B) 41.0%**　(C) 16.9%　(D) 22.9%

What is most likely true about the GFD?
(A) It was inspired by a project in another town.
(B) The land was previously used for recreation.
(C) The cost of rent there is rising.
(D) It offers excellent views of the city.

□ inspire: 動 ～に着想を与える　□ previously: 副 以前
□ view: 名 眺望

GFD について最も当てはまりそうなことはどれですか。
(A) 別の町の計画に触発された。
(B) 敷地がかつてレクリエーションに使われていた。
(C) 同地の賃貸料は上がっている。
(D) 町の素晴らしい景観を味わえる。

▶解説 ❶で、Gilmore は parkland（公園用地）を開発して GFD を建設したと述べられています。このことから、GFD の土地は以前レクリエーションに使われていた場所だと判断できるので、(B) が正解です。(A) の他の町のプロジェクト、(C) の賃貸料の上昇、(D) の景観には言及されていません。

---

182. 正解：**D** 易 ■■■■■■□ 難　選択率：(A) 12.4%　(B) 18.5%　(C) 20.5%　**(D) 45.4%**

Why was the GFD created?
(A) To raise funds through charity events
(B) To reduce traffic in the city center
(C) To provide jobs for college graduates
(D) To foster a growing industry

□ raise: 動 （資金など）を募る　□ fund: 名 資金
□ charity: 名 慈善　□ reduce: 動 ～を減らす
□ traffic: 名 交通量　□ graduate: 名 卒業生
□ foster: 動 ～を育成する

なぜ GFD は造られましたか。
(A) 慈善イベントを通じて資金を集めるために
(B) 市の中心部の交通量を減らすために
(C) 大学の卒業生に就職先を提供するために
(D) 成長産業を育成するために

▶解説 記事の❷から、Gilmore が何年にもわたり、増加するファッションブランドと提携してきたことが分かります。さらに❸に「市の有力者たちはファッション業界が市の主要産業になることを期待している」とあり、そのために市が助成金を出すことが❹で述べられています。これらの点を「成長産業を育成する」と表現した (D) が正解です。

---

183. 正解：**A** 易 ■■■■■■□ 難　選択率：**(A) 28.5%**　(B) 19.7%　(C) 35.3%　(D) 14.1%

What is suggested about Zebra Garments?
(A) It was invited to the district by GFD Administration.
(B) It hires students from Balmoral College of Art.
(C) It provided initial funding for the GFD.
(D) It has submitted an entry to the Gilmore Fashion Show.

□ initial: 形 最初の

Zebra Garments について、何が示されていますか。
(A) GFD 管理当局によってこの地区に招致された。
(B) Balmoral College of Art の学生を雇っている。
(C) GFD に初期投資した。
(D) Gimore Fashion Show への参加を申請している。

▶解説 ❻から Zebra Garments はすでに GFD に移転していること、❼から記事が書かれた時点では GFD administrators（GFD 管理当局）から誘致を受けた会社しか移転できないことが分かるので、正解は (A) です。

---

184. 正解：**A** 易 ■■■■■■□ 難　選択率：**(A) 16.9%**　(B) 30.9%　(C) 21.7%　(D) 26.5%

What is implied about Ms. Peabody?
(A) She will visit Balmoral College of Art.
(B) She works for a business outside the GFD.
(C) She will judge garments in the Gilmore Fashion Show.
(D) She is one of the administrators of the GFD.

□ judge: 動 ～を評価する　□ garment: 名 衣服

Peabody さんについて、何が示唆されていますか。
(A) 彼女は Balmoral College of Art を訪問するだろう。
(B) 彼女は GFD 地区外の事業所で働いている。
(C) 彼女は Gilmore Fashion Show で衣服を審査するだろう。
(D) 彼女は GFD の管理当局者の1人だ。

▶解説 チケットの❽と❾から、Peabody さんは The Annual Gilmore Fashion Show のチケットを受け取った人物だと分かります。一方、記事の❺から、Gilmore でのファッションショーはすべて、ある大学で行われることが分かります。その大学とは、❺の直前で述べられている Balmoral College of Art です。つまり Peabody さんはそこを訪れる予定だと示唆されているので、(A) が正解です。

185. 正解：**B**　易 ■■■■□□ 難　選択率：(A) 13.7%　**(B) 51.8%**　(C) 24.9%　(D) 6.4%

According to the ticket, what should ticket holders refrain from doing?
(A) Driving to the venue
(B) Selling their tickets
(C) Calling the event organizer
(D) Video recording the show

□ refrain from 〜：動 〜を控える
□ venue: 名 会場

チケットの記載によると、チケットの所有者は何をしてはいけませんか。
(A) 車を運転して会場へ行くこと
(B) チケットを販売すること
(C) イベントの主催者に電話をかけること
(D) ショーをビデオ撮影すること

▶解説 ❿に、チケットは譲渡不可と記載されています。よって、チケットの持ち主が避けるべきことは、(B)の「チケットを販売すること」です。(A)の交通手段、(C)の電話での連絡、(D)のビデオ撮影への言及はありません。

(((ฺ)))) ゼミ 生中継　　　😊 Hiro 😊 Mai 😊 Yasu 😊 Dai 😊 Saki

181.

😊 parklandになじみがなかったので、(B)を選びにくかったですが、他の選択肢は全く根拠がないので(B)にしました。

😊 parklandは人々が利用できる緑地のこと。recreationは「気晴らし」とか「娯楽」だから、(B)は明示された根拠から合理的に推測できる。それに、設問はWhat is most likely true 〜?だから、正しい情報が問われているのではなく、最もマシな情報を選ぶことが求められている。(B)は完璧に正確な情報ではないけれど、正解としては疑いようがない。

😊 なるほど。

183.

😊 Zebra Garments が登場した直後に one of the first companies とある。その first と、(C)にある initial がほぼ同じ意味だから、(C)は魅力的な不正解だと思う。

😊 そう考えました。よく分かりますね。

184.

😊 遠く離れた3つの情報を関連付ける必要があったね。Balmoral College of Art が全部のファッションショーの会場であることが重要なヒントだよ。Peabodyさんが行くショーは、その一部だね。こうやって、「全部」と「一部」を利用した2文書参照型の設問は、必ず出題されるから慣れておくといいよ。

Part 7 読解問題

Questions 186-190 refer to the following schedule, online application, and e-mail.

---

www.hansencc.org

Upcoming Events at the Hansen Community Center (March)

Ikebana — From 3:00 P.M. March 5, 12, 19, and 26 (Wednesdays)
The art of traditional Japanese flower arrangement is not only a lot of fun, it is a great way to add a sense of sophistication to any interior. Come and learn from Ichiho Fukuzaki, an expert certified by the National Ikebana Association of Japan.

Secretarial Skills Classes — From 2:00 P.M. March 6, 8, 13, 15, 20, 22, 27, and 29 (Thursdays and Saturdays)
Participants who complete this month-long course will receive a certificate in Basic Secretarial Skills from Bobson Community College.
Note: The teacher hired to provide this class is no longer available. Unless we can find a very experienced teacher with qualifications in word processing, spreadsheets, office administration, and corporate communications, this course may be canceled. Please contact Hansen Community Center Administration to apply.

Hansen Jazz Club — From 8:00 P.M. March 3 and 17
This popular association meets twice a month to discuss jazz, share information, and enjoy performances by members.

Thorne Gardening Society — From 9:00 A.M. March 2, 9, 16, and 23 (Sundays)
Members of the Thorne Gardening Society gather on Sundays to discuss gardening and organize the Annual Thorne Gardening Competition, a hugely popular event in Hansen. They are always looking for new members. Contact the society at tgs@hopeone.org for details on becoming a member.

If you would like to use the Hansen Community Center for your event, please contact the chief scheduler at 555-2394. Please note it is necessary to submit a photographic identification when reserving a space. Until March 31, programs will be provided on the seventh and eighth floors except the one in the evening, which will be held on the sixth floor. However, due to the renovation work, they will all be conducted on the ninth floor next month.

(306w)

問題186-190は次の予定表、オンライン応募フォームとメールに関するものです。

Hansen Community Center での近日開催イベント (3月)

生け花——3月5日、12日、19日、26日 (水曜日)、午後3時から
伝統的な日本の生け花の技法は、大いに楽しめるばかりか、どんな部屋にも洗練された感覚を付け加えられる優れた方法です。National Ikebana Association of Japan 公認の専門家、Ichiho Fukuzaki の手ほどきを受けに来てください。

秘書技能クラス——3月6日、8日、13日、15日、20日、22日、27日、29日 (木曜日と土曜日)、午後2時から
この1カ月コースを修了した参加者は、Bobson Community College から基礎秘書技能の修了証が授与されます。
備考: このクラスの担当者として採用された講師は都合がつかなくなっています。ワープロ、表計算ソフト、業務管理、企業広報に関する資格を持つ経験豊富な講師が見つからなければ、このコースは休止される可能性があります。Hansen Community Center 管理課へご連絡の上、ご応募ください。

Hansen ジャズクラブ——3月3日と17日、午後8時から
この人気の会合は月に2回開かれ、ジャズについて語り合ったり、情報交換したり、参加者の演奏を楽しんだりします。

Thorne ガーデニング協会——3月2日、9日、16日、23日 (日曜日)、午前9時から
Thorne ガーデニング協会の会員は日曜日に集まり、ガーデニングについて語り合うとともに、Hansen で大変人気の高い催しである年次 Thorne Gardening 品評会を主催します。同会は常に新しいメンバーを募集しています。tgs@hopeone.org の同会宛てにご連絡の上、入会の詳細をご確認ください。

ご自身の催事に Hasen Community Center をご利用になりたい場合、555-2394のスケジュール管理者長にご連絡ください。会場を予約する場合、写真付きの身分証明書の提示が必要なことにご留意ください。3月31日までは、プログラムは7階と8階で開催されます。ただし夜間のものは6階で開催されます。しかし、改修作業のため、翌月からはすべて9階で実施されます。

☐ traditional: 形 伝統的な ☐ sense: 名 感覚 ☐ sophistication: 名 洗練 ☐ expert: 名 専門家 ☐ certified: 形 公認の
☐ secretarial: 形 秘書の ☐ skill: 名 技能 ☐ complete: 動 〜を修了する ☐ certificate: 名 修了証、証明書 ☐ qualification: 名 資格
☐ word processing: ワープロ ☐ spread sheet: 表計算ソフト ☐ office administration: 業務管理 ☐ corporate communication: 企業広報
☐ association: 名 会合 ☐ photographic: 形 写真の ☐ renovation: 名 修復、改築

ONLINE APPLICATION

Position:	Teacher of Secretarial Course
Applicant name:	Travis Waldron
Address:	12 Schreiber Drive, West Vandros
Contact number:	555-4932
Self-introduction:	❿I graduated from the Mnuchin School of Business last month, so I believe I am well qualified for the position. I have excellent word processing and spreadsheets skills as evidenced by my Level 5 certificates in both. Furthermore, the course I took at Mnuchin School of Business covers the topics of corporate communications and office administration in great depth.

(80w)

オンライン応募フォーム

職種：	秘書コースの教員
応募者氏名：	Travis Waldron
住所：	12 Schreiber Drive, West Vandros
連絡先電話番号：	555-4932
自己紹介：	私は Mnuchin School of Business を先月卒業しましたので、自分がこの職に適任だと考えています。いずれの能力検定でも Level 5 の証明書が裏付けている通り、ワープロと表計算関連の技能に秀でています。加えて、私が Mnuchin School of Business で履修した課程は、企業広報や業務管理といったテーマについて深く掘り下げるものでした。

□ qualified: 形 資格のある　□ evidence: 動 ～を証明する　□ cover: 動 ～を取り扱う

E-Mail Message

To:	director@hansencc.org
From:	scha@smilenet.com
Date:	March 21
Subject:	Contact details

Hello,

⓫I'm considering joining the jazz club from April, but I could not see the organizer's contact details on the Web site. Could you please either give them to me or forward this e-mail to them so that they can reply to me directly?

Sincerely,

Sarah Cha

(59w)

宛先：director@hansencc.org
送信者：scha@smilnet.com
日付：3月21日
件名：連絡先詳細

こんにちは、

4月からジャズクラブに参加したいと考えているのですが、主催者の詳しい連絡先がウェブサイト上に見つかりませんでした。ご教示いただくか、もしくは私に直接返事できるよう、このメールを同会宛てに転送していただけますか。

よろしくお願いいたします。

Sarah Cha

186. 正解：**D** 易 ■■■■■■■ 難　選択率：(A) 10.4% (B) 40.2% (C) 19.7% **(D) 25.3%**

According to the schedule, which event is looking to increase its size?
(A) Ikebana
(B) Secretarial Skills Classes
(C) Hansen Jazz Club
(D) Thorne Gardening Society

予定表によると、どのイベントが規模を拡大しようとしていますか。
(A) 生け花
(B) 秘書技能クラス
(C) Hansen ジャズクラブ
(D) Thorne ガーデニング協会

▶解説 予定表には、3月に開催される4つのイベントの情報が掲載されています。❻で「Thorne Gardening Societyは常に新メンバーを募集している」ことが分かるので、(D) が正解です。設問のincrease its sizeは「参加者を増やす」ことを意味しています。

---

187. 正解：**D** 易 ■■■■■■■ 難　選択率：(A) 30.1% (B) 20.5% (C) 24.9% **(D) 19.3%**

What is implied about Ms. Fukuzaki?
(A) She is training an apprentice.
(B) She advertised her course in a newspaper.
(C) She is the founder of a national association.
(D) She has submitted identification to the community center.

☐ train: 動 ～を訓練する　☐ apprentice: 名 見習い
☐ founder: 名 創業者　☐ national: 形 全国的な
☐ association: 名 協会

Fukuzaki さんについて、どんなことが示唆されていますか。
(A) 彼女は弟子を1人、訓練している。
(B) 彼女は自分の講座を新聞で宣伝した。
(C) 彼女は、ある全国的な団体の創設者だ。
(D) 彼女は身分証明書を地域センターに提示している。

▶解説 Fukuzaki さんは❶に登場し、その前後の情報から生け花の講師だと分かりますが、それに合う選択肢はありません。そこで、全てのイベント主催者に共通の情報が書かれている最後の段落に注目します。❼に、Hansen Community Center の部屋を予約するには写真付き身分証明書の提出が必要だと記載されているので、Fukuzaki さんも提出したことが推測でき、(D) が正解です。

---

188. 正解：**C** 易 ■■■■■■ 難　選択率：(A) 19.7% (B) 24.9% **(C) 40.6%** (D) 8.4%

What is NOT mentioned about the Hansen Jazz Club?
(A) It has regular meetings.
(B) It is a well-liked club.
(C) It provides free membership.
(D) It hosts performances by members.

☐ regular: 形 定期的な　☐ well-liked: 形 人気のある

Hansen ジャズクラブについて述べられていないのはどれですか。
(A) 定期的に会合を開いている。
(B) 人気のあるクラブだ。
(C) 無料で会員になれる。
(D) 会員に演奏の機会を提供している。

▶解説 Hansen Jazz Club の情報が記載されているのは予定表の第3段落です。選択肢の(A)は❹、(B)は❸、(D)は❺の情報とそれぞれ一致しています。(C)の「無料で入会できる」は本文で言及されていません。

---

189. 正解：**C** 易 ■■■■■■ 難　選択率：(A) 17.7% (B) 32.1% **(C) 29.7%** (D) 14.5%

What is suggested about Mr. Waldron?
(A) He takes part in one of the events at the community center.
(B) He taught a class at the Mnuchin School of Business.
(C) He has insufficient experience for the position.
(D) He was notified of the vacant position by Ms. Cha.

☐ take part in ～: ～に参加する
☐ insufficient: 形 不十分な　☐ notify: 動 ～に知らせる

Waldron さんについて、どんなことが示唆されていますか。
(A) 彼は地域センターでのイベントの1つに参加している。
(B) 彼は Mnuchin School of Business で、ある授業を受け持った。
(C) 彼は、この職に就くには経験不足だ。
(D) 彼は欠員について Cha さんから知らされた。

▶解説 Waldron さんは、オンラインの応募フォームに記入した人です。❿から、Waldron さんは前月にビジネススクールを卒業したと分かります。予定表の❷を見ると、秘書技能クラスの講師は「経験豊富な講師 (a very experienced teacher)」である必要があります。卒業間もない Waldron さんに教授経験はないと推測できるので、(C) が正解です。

190. 正解：**D** 易 ■■■■■ 難　選択率：(A) 30.1%　(B) 21.7%　(C) 17.7%　(D) 22.9%

Where would Ms. Cha attend her first session?
(A) On the sixth floor
(B) On the seventh floor
(C) On the eighth floor
(D) On the ninth floor

Chaさんは、どこで最初の集会に参加しますか。
(A) 6階で
(B) 7階で
(C) 8階で
(D) 9階で

▶解説 まず、⓫でChaさんは4月からジャズクラブに参加したいと述べています。Hansen Jazz Club を含む全プログラムの会場は予定表の最終段落に記載されていて、❽で3月31日までの会場が述べられています。さらに❾でHowever, と続き、変更があることが示唆されます。「翌月、つまり4月からは全プログラムが9階で行われる」とありますので、Chaさんが参加する見込みのジャズクラブの初回は(D)の9階で行われることが分かります。

((( ))) ゼミ 生 中継　　Hiro　Mai　Yasu　Dai　Saki

187.
(A)を選んだ人いるよね？　Fukuzakiさんが見習いを訓練しているとは、どこにも書かれていないし、合理的にそんな推測ができる根拠もない。彼女は生け花の専門家であることは確実だけど、それだけで、見習いを訓練していると判断するのは妄想だよ。

190.
ほら、これも184番のような「全部」と「一部」を利用している。4月は全てのプログラムが9階で実施される前提がある中で、プログラムの一部であるジャズクラブに関する情報を探して解くタイプだよね。

焦っていたので、1つ目の文書の最後は読み飛ばしていました。

Test 2でも言ったように、Part 7で「虫食い読み」はダメだよ。読まないエリアを作ると解けない問題が結構あるから。

Part 7　▼ Reading Section

Part 7 読解問題

Questions 191-195 refer to the following e-mail, text message, and invoice.

To: Franz Zabka <fzabka@parkersoftware.com>
From: Steve Criss <scriss@vestatech.com>
CC: Dorothy Warner <dwarner@vestatech.com>
Subject: New project
Date: October 8

Dear Mr. Zabka,

At Vesta Tech, we are planning on creating a new tablet computer, which will allow users to attach a variety of camera lenses. It will be referred to as the FlexLens Project. We intend to hire Parker Software to create the software for the tablet computer. As we are still in the planning stages, **I would like to ask you to come to our office in Atlanta to act as a consultant for our designers and engineers.** They need to understand the requirements of the software creators before they decide on the device's hardware specifications. Because I am insisting that everyone assigned to the project attend, **the only two dates we have available this month are Thursday, October 26 and Tuesday, October 31.**

My personal assistant, Dorothy Warner will be available to meet you at the airport. You can text message her at (232) 555-8389.

According to our agreement, Parker Software does not bill us for this kind of preliminary meeting unless the project is later abandoned and we do not offer you a programming contract. Regardless of whether or not this project goes ahead, I would like to pay for your travel costs. Please pass your receipts to Ms. Warner when you arrive. She will take care of the reimbursement before you leave.

Sincerely,

Steve Criss
President — Vesta Tech

(241w)

問題191-195は次のメール、テキストメッセージと請求明細書に関するものです。

宛先：Franz Zabka <fzabka@parkersoftware.com>
送信者：Steve Criss <scriss@vestatech.com>
CC：Dorothy Warner <dwarner@vestatech.com>
件名：新規プロジェクト
日付：10月8日

Zabka さま

私ども Vesta Tech では、新しいタブレット型コンピューターの開発を計画しています。これは、ユーザーがさまざまなカメラレンズを取り付けられるものです。FlexLens Project と命名される予定です。当社は Parker Software に、このタブレット型コンピューター向けのソフトウエアの開発をお願いしたいと考えています。まだ計画段階ですので、当社の Atlanta のオフィスへお越しいただき、こちらの設計者や技術者のためにコンサルタント業務をしていただきたく存じます。彼らはソフトウエア開発側の要件を理解した上で、このデバイスのハード面の仕様を決定する必要があります。当該プロジェクトに関わる全員に同席を求めておりますため、今月、当方に好都合な日は、次の2日しかありません。10月26日木曜日と10月31日火曜日です。

私の個人秘書 Dorothy Warner に、空港へお迎えに伺わせるつもりです。彼女宛てに (232) 555-8389 へテキストメッセージをお送りいただけます。

契約により、Parker Software からは、のちにプロジェクトが中止になり当社がプログラミングの契約をご提示しない場合を除き、この種の事前協議についてのご請求をいただいておりません。今回のプロジェクトでは、話が進展するか否かにかかわらず、ご出張費をお支払いしたく存じます。到着時に Warner に領収書をお渡しください。彼女が、お帰りまでに精算の手続きをいたします。

よろしくお願いいたします。

Steve Criss
社長——Vesta Tech

□ attach: 動 〜を取り付ける　□ refer to 〜 as ...: 〜を…と呼ぶ　□ act as 〜: 〜の役を務める　□ consultant: 名 相談役
□ requirement: 名 要件　□ device: 名 機器　□ specification: 名 仕様　□ assign: 動 〜を割り当てる　□ bill: 動 〜に請求する
□ preliminary: 形 予備の　□ abandon: 動 〜を中止する　□ regardless of 〜: 〜にもかかわらず　□ go ahead: 前進する
□ take care of 〜: 〜を処理する　□ reimbursement: 名 払い戻し

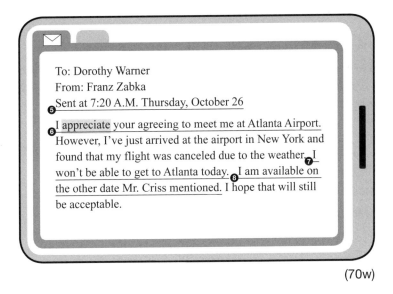

To: Dorothy Warner
From: Franz Zabka
❺Sent at 7:20 A.M. Thursday, October 26

❻I appreciate your agreeing to meet me at Atlanta Airport. However, I've just arrived at the airport in New York and found that my flight was canceled due to the weather. ❼I won't be able to get to Atlanta today. ❽I am available on the other date Mr. Criss mentioned. I hope that will still be acceptable.

(70w)

宛先：Dorothy Warner
送信者：Franz Zabka
10月26日、木曜日、午前7時20分に送信済み

Atlanta空港でお出迎えくださるとのこと、感謝申し上げます。ただ、ちょうどNew Yorkの空港に着いたところなのですが、私の乗る便が、天候が理由で欠航になったことが分かりました。今日中にはAtlantaに到着できません。Crissさんがおっしゃっていた別の日であれば、私も都合をつけられます。そのような変更を、まだご了承いただければ幸いです。

□ acceptable: 形 受け入れることができる

Parker Software
24 Muriel Lane, Queens, NY
Invoice

Client: Vesta Tech　　**Date:** November 30　　**Project:** FlexLens

Service	Hourly Rate	Semi Total
❾Meeting with Vesta Tech Employees (5 hour preliminary meeting in October)	$270	$1,350.00
Transportation and Accommodation	N/A	$0.00
	Tax	$162.00
	Total	$1,512.00

(43w)

Parker Software
24 Muriel Lane, Queens, NY
請求明細書

請求先：Vesta Tech　　**日付**：11月30日　　**案件**：FlexLens

サービス内容	時間単価	小計
Vesta Techの従業員との会議 （10月の5時間にわたる予備会議）	270ドル	1350ドル
交通費および宿泊費	適用外	0ドル
	税	162ドル
	合計	1512ドル

□ hourly rate: 1時間あたりの料金　□ semi total: 小計　□ transportation: 名 交通費　□ accommodation: 名 宿泊費

---

191. 正解：**C** 易 ■■■■■■ 難 選択率：(A) 15.3% (B) 26.9% **(C) 35.7%** (D) 15.3%

What is the purpose of the e-mail?
(A) To provide a sample of a software program
(B) To request an interview with an applicant
(C) To arrange a consultation
(D) To promote a business

☐ consultation：名 相談 ☐ promote：動 ～を宣伝する

メールの目的は何ですか。
(A) ソフトウエアプログラムの見本を提供すること
(B) 応募者との面接を依頼すること
(C) 相談の場を設けること
(D) 事業を宣伝すること

▶解説 メールの❶で、Criss さんは Parker Software の Zabka さんに、Vesta Tech でのコンサルタント業務をしてほしいと要請しています。よって、(C) が正解です。

---

192. 正解：**B** 易 ■■■■■■ 難 選択率：(A) 16.5% **(B) 38.2%** (C) 28.5% (D) 8.8%

Whose contact details did Mr. Criss provide to Mr. Zabka?
(A) A company president's
(B) A secretary's
(C) A software developer's
(D) An engineer's

Criss さんは、誰の連絡先の詳細を Zabka さんに伝えましたか。
(A) ある会社社長の
(B) ある秘書の
(C) あるソフトウエア開発者の
(D) ある技術者の

▶解説 メールの❸で Criss さんが Warner さんを自分の assistant だと紹介し、連絡先を伝えています。assistant を secretary と言い換えた (B) が正解です。

---

193. 正解：**C** 易 ■■■■■■ 難 選択率：(A) 7.6% (B) 24.1% **(C) 48.2%** (D) 12.0%

In the text message, the word "appreciate" in paragraph 1, line 1, is closest in meaning to
(A) enhance
(B) take account of
(C) feel grateful for
(D) admire

テキストメッセージの第1段落1行目にある「appreciate」に最も意味が近いのは
(A) ～を高める
(B) ～を考慮に入れる
(C) ～に感謝する
(D) ～を称賛する

▶解説 ❻で Zabka さんは、Warner さんが空港に迎えに来てくれることに対して感謝しています。よって最も意味が近いのは、(C) の feel grateful for です。

---

194. 正解：**D** 易 ■■■■■■ 難 選択率：(A) 8.0% (B) 17.3% (C) 30.5% **(D) 36.5%**

When did Mr. Zabka most likely arrive in Atlanta?
(A) On October 8
(B) On October 9
(C) On October 26
(D) On October 31

Zabka さんはいつ Atlanta に到着した可能性が最も高いですか。
(A) 10月8日に
(B) 10月9日に
(C) 10月26日に
(D) 10月31日に

▶解説 メールの❷で、Criss さんが都合の良い日時を知らせています。Zabka さんからのテキストメッセージは、❺の情報から候補日の1つ、26日に送られたものだと分かります。❼に「今日（＝26日）はアトランタに行けなくなった」とあり、❽で「もう1つの候補日でもいい」と知らせています。これらの情報から、Zabka さんがアトランタに行くのは (D) の10月31日であると判断できます。

---

195. 正解：**A** 易 ■■■■■■ 難 選択率：**(A) 16.9%** (B) 24.5% (C) 31.7% (D) 18.5%

What is implied about Vesta Tech?
(A) It did not go ahead with the FlexLens Project.
(B) It is not recognized as a major brand.
(C) It has an office in New York.
(D) It charged Parker Software for transportation costs.

☐ recognize：動 ～を認識する ☐ major：形 主要な
☐ charge：動 ～に請求する

Vesta Tech についてどんなことが示唆されていますか。
(A) FlexLens Project を推進しなかった。
(B) 大手のブランドとは認識されていない。
(C) New York に事務所を構えている。
(D) Parker Software に交通費を請求した。

▶解説 メールの❹に「契約により、のちにプロジェクトが中止にならない限り、Cater Software からの事前協議に対する請求はされない」と明記されています。しかし、請求明細書の❾によれば、事前協議に対する請求がなされています。このことから、Vesta Tech 社は、FlexLens プロジェクトを中止したことが推測できます。よって、(A) が正解です。

ゼミ生中継

194.

🙂 10月26日にZabkaさんがアトランタに行けなかったのは分かりますが、10月31日に本当に行ったのでしょうか。

😊 いい点に気づいたね。厳密には、第3文書もヒントになっているよ。請求項目に「10月の事前協議」って書かれている。

🙂 あ、本当ですね。

195.

😊 この設問はVesta Techについて問うていることをしっかり認識することが大切。(C)はParker Softwareに関する情報だよね。

🙂 え、Vesta Techはどこにあるんですか。

😊 アトランタだよ。第1文書にも第2文書にも書かれている。第3文書によれば、おそらくParker SoftwareはNew Yorkにある。

😊 交通費は10月31日の当日に支払われたのですよね。メールの最後に交通費は当日払うとありました。

😊 そうだよ。だから、Parker Softwareが発行した請求書では交通費がゼロになっている。(D)は、Vesta Techが主語だから全くダメ。Parker Softwareに交通費を請求する理由がない。

😌 なるほど。ゆっくり読めば理解できます。

Part 7 読解問題

Questions 196-200 refer to the following Web page and e-mails.

https://www.colbertcatering.com/faq

Welcome to Colbert Catering

Home	Events	Menus	**FAQ**

What is the largest event you can cater?
We can cater to groups of up to 500. However, it should be noted that not all menus will be available to such large groups. For example, the "deluxe menu" and the "food of the world menu" are only available to groups of under 300 and 200 people respectively.

Do you offer discounts to frequent customers?
We offer discounts for select customers based on the amount they spend at Colbert Catering rather than their frequency. ❶People who spend more than $2,000 in any quarter will receive 10 percent off in the following quarter.

What are Colbert Catering's business hours?
Our office hours are from 9:00 A.M. to 5:00 P.M., Monday to Friday. However, Colbert Catering is able to serve its clients 24 hours a day, seven days a week. ❷Some penalty rates apply on weekends, public holidays, and between the hours of 9:00 P.M. to 9:00 A.M.

How far can Colbert Catering deliver food?
Colbert Catering is based in Vernon. Generally speaking, ❸we only provide catering to addresses within 30 kilometers of our facility.

Are alternatives available for people with allergies?
❹We can substitute ingredients where necessary. Please fill out a special request form on the Web site.

(215w)

問題196-200は次のウェブページと2通のメールに関するものです。

https://www.colbertcatering.com/faq

Colbert Cateringのウェブサイトへようこそ
ホーム　イベント　メニュー　よくある質問

ケータリングが可能なイベントの最大規模はどのくらいですか。
500名さまの集まりまでサービス可能です。ただし、そこまで大規模な場合、全てのメニューをご用意できるわけではないことをご了承ください。例えば、「デラックスメニュー」と「世界の料理メニュー」は、それぞれ300名未満、200名未満の集まりでしかご利用いただけません。

利用頻度の高い顧客に割引は提供されますか。
限られたお客さまに割引を提供しておりますが、ご利用頻度ではなくColbert Cateringへお支払いいただく金額に基づいて決めさせていただいています。四半期あたり2000ドルを超える額をお支払いくださるお客さまは、翌四半期に10パーセント引きでご利用いただけます。

Colbert Cateringの営業時間はどうなっていますか。
当店の営業時間は、月曜日から金曜日の午前9時から午後5時までです。ただしColbert Cateringでは、24時間、週に7日サービスのご提供が可能です。週末、祝祭日、および午後9時から午前9時の間のサービスには、追加料金がかかります。

Colbert Cateringはどの程度遠くまで料理を配送できますか。
Colbert CateringはVernonを本拠としています。おおむね、当店がケータリングを提供するのは、当店から30キロメートル以内の場所に限られます。

アレルギーを持つ人向けの代替メニューはありますか。
必要に応じて、材料の代替が可能です。ウェブサイト上の特別依頼欄にご記入ください。

□ catering: 名 出前、ケータリング　□ cater: 動 料理を提供する　□ respectively: 副 それぞれ　□ frequent: 形 頻繁な　□ select: 形 限定された
□ frequency: 名 頻度　□ quarter: 名 四半期　□ following: 形 次の　□ business hour: 営業時間　□ serve: 動 (店の人が客の)注文を聞く
□ penalty rate: 時間外割増金　□ apply: 動 適用される　□ public holiday: 祝祭日　□ be based in ~: ~を本拠地としている
□ generally speaking: 一般的に言えば　□ facility: 名 施設　□ alternative: 名 代替案　□ allergy: 名 アレルギー
□ substitute: 動 ~を取り替える　□ ingredient: 名 材料　□ where necessary: 必要に応じて　□ fill out ~: ~に記入する

To: Trish Bryson <tbryson@colbertcatering.com>
From: Abu Markov <amarkov@firecoot.com>
Date: October 11
Subject: Party catering

Dear Ms. Bryson,

Thank you for providing catering for my party so expertly last night. The Colbert Catering staff were all extremely professional and the food and drinks were very high quality. I was also impressed with your value for money. I feel that I received higher quality food for about 10 percent less than the previous caterer charged. Well done! I have recommended your services to my neighbor, who I expect will contact you later today for an appointment.

The real purpose of my e-mail, however, is to let you know that your team has left some equipment behind. This morning I found a silver tray with the Colbert Catering logo on it in my kitchen.

Sincerely,

Abu Markov

(134w)

宛先：Trish Bryson <tbryson@colbertcatering.com>
送信者：Abu Markov <amarkov@firecoot.com>
日付：10月11日
件名：パーティーのケータリング

Brysonさま

昨夜は私のパーティーに素晴らしいケータリングをご提供くださり、ありがとうございました。Colbert Cateringのスタッフは皆、大変プロ意識を持っており、食べ物も飲み物の非常に質の高いものでした。また、コストパフォーマンスの高さにも感銘を受けました。以前頼んだ仕出し業者よりも質の高い料理を、10パーセントほど安く食べられたように感じています。素晴らしい！　そちらのサービスを隣人にも勧めておきましたので、今日、後ほど、面会予約の連絡が行くだろうと思います。

ところで、このメールの本当の目的は、そちらのスタッフが備品をお忘れになったことをお伝えすることです。今朝、Colbert Cateringのロゴが入った銀のトレーをわが家の台所で見つけました。

よろしくお願いいたします。

Abu Markov

☐ expertly: 副 上手に　☐ extremely: 副 極めて　☐ professional: 形 プロの　☐ quality: 名 品質　☐ impressed: 形 感銘を受けて
☐ value for money: 支払った金額よりも値打ちがあると思えるもの　☐ caterer: 名 仕出し業者　☐ later today: 今日中に
☐ leave ~ behind: ~を置き去りにする　☐ equipment: 名 備品

```
┌─────────────────────────────────────────────────────────────┐
│ ▤▤▤               E-Mail Message                        ▤▤▤ │
├──────────┬──────────────────────────────────────────────────┤
│   To:    │ Trish Bryson <tbryson@colbertcatering.com>       │
├──────────┼──────────────────────────────────────────────────┤
│  From:   │ Valerie Yasser <vyasser@swandive.com>            │
├──────────┼──────────────────────────────────────────────────┤
│  Date:   │ October 11                                       │
├──────────┼──────────────────────────────────────────────────┤
│ Subject: │ Appointment request                              │
└──────────┴──────────────────────────────────────────────────┘
```

Dear Ms. Bryson,

I was handed your business card by Abu Markov, who praised your services highly. I would like to set up an appointment to discuss arrangements for a business luncheon I am planning. ❼ It will be held in the conference room in my office at 34 Prince Street, Vernon. It will be a group of around 30 business executives and I would like to serve one of your high-end menu plans. ❽ I am aware that one of the guests is allergic to shrimp and another to coconut. Can you accommodate special menu requests?

Please contact me on 832-555-3472 to discuss an appointment time.

Sincerely,

Valerie Yasser
President — Swandive Trading

(127w)

宛先：Trish Bryson <tbryson@colbertcatering.com>
送信者：Valerie Yasser <vyasser@swandive.com>
日付：10月11日
件名：予約のお願い

Brysonさま

そちらの名刺をAbu Markovから預かった者です。彼は、貴店のサービスを絶賛していました。一度お目に掛かって、計画しているビジネス昼食会の手配についてご相談したいと思っています。会は、VernonのPrince Street 34番地にある私の職場の会議室で開かれる予定です。約30名の企業幹部が集まることになっており、貴店の最高級メニューのコースの1つを振る舞いたいと考えています。招待客の1人に小エビの、別の1人にココナッツのアレルギーがあることが分かっています。特別メニューの要望にお応えいただけますでしょうか。

832-555-3472までご連絡ください。お目にかかる日時についてお話ししたく存じます。

よろしくお願いいたします。

Valerie Yasser
社長──Swandive Trading

☐ hand: 動 ～を手渡す　☐ praise: 動 ～を称賛する　☐ set up ～: ～を手配する　☐ luncheon: 名 昼食会　☐ around: 前 おおよそ
☐ executive: 名 役員　☐ serve: 動 （食事）を出す　☐ high-end: 形 最高級の　☐ aware: 形 ～を知っている
☐ allergic: 形 アレルギー体質の　☐ accommodate: 動 ～を受け入れる

Test 1   Test 2   **Test 3**

196. 正解：**B**   易■■■■■□難   選択率：(A) 18.5% **(B) 45.8%** (C) 17.3% (D) 7.6%

Who is eligible for a discount?
(A) People who frequently use Colbert Catering
(B) People who spend over a certain amount
(C) People who sign up for a membership plan
(D) People who recommend Colbert Catering to others

誰が割引を受けられますか。
(A) 頻繁に Colbert Catering を利用する人々
(B) 一定の金額以上を支払う人々
(C) 会員制度に申し込む人々
(D) Colbert Catering を他の人に勧める人々

☐ eligible for ～：～にふさわしい
☐ sign up for ～：～に申し込む

▶解説 割引に言及されているのは、ウェブページの第2段落です。❶に「四半期内に2000ドルを超える金額を支払うと、次の四半期で10パーセントの割引を受けられる」と記されているので、これを over a certain amount（一定以上の金額）と言い換えた (B) が正解です。

---

197. 正解：**C**   易■■■■■□難   選択率：(A) 16.5% (B) 23.3% **(C) 38.2%** (D) 9.6%

According to the Web page, why might Colbert Catering charge an additional fee?
(A) The client lives outside the Vernon central business district.
(B) A combination of two menus is required.
(C) A job is scheduled for a national holiday.
(D) The number of guests is too small.

ウェブページによると、Colbert Catering が追加料金を求めるとすれば、その理由は何ですか。
(A) 客が Vernon 中心部の商業地区から外れた所に住んでいる。
(B) 2つのメニューの組み合わせが求められる。
(C) サービスが祝祭日に予定されている。
(D) 招待客の数が少なすぎる。

☐ district: 名 地域 ☐ combination: 名 組み合わせ

▶解説 ウェブページの❷で、週末や休日 (weekends, public holidays) には割増料金が適用されると述べられています。(C) の a national holiday はこれに該当するので、これが正解です。ケータリングが可能な範囲については❸で述べられていますが、(A) の範囲外に対する料金については記載がありません。

---

198. 正解：**B**   易■■■■■■難   選択率：(A) 13.3% **(B) 24.1%** (C) 26.9% (D) 23.7%

What is implied about Mr. Markov?
(A) He tried to contact a sales representative after 5:00 P.M.
(B) His home is within 30 kilometers of Colbert Catering.
(C) His event attracted over 300 guests.
(D) He ordered more than $2,000 worth of catering in the previous quarter.

Markov さんについて、何が示唆されていますか。
(A) 彼は午後5時以降に営業担当者と連絡を取ろうとした。
(B) 彼の家は Colbert Catering から30キロメートル以内にある。
(C) 彼の会には300人以上が集まった。
(D) 彼は前四半期に、2000ドル以上相当のケータリングサービスを発注した。

☐ sales representative: 営業担当者
☐ worth: 名 相当する量

▶解説 Markov さんは1つ目のメールを書いた人物で、❺から Colbert Catering の利用者だと分かります。❻では、同社のトレーが自宅の台所に置き忘れられていたと伝えており、パーティーは Markov さんの自宅で行われたと推測できます。ウェブページの❸で、会社の30キロ圏内でしかケータリングをしないと述べられているため、(B) が正解です。

---

199. 正解：**A**   易■■■■■□難   選択率：**(A) 24.1%** (B) 27.3% (C) 22.5% (D) 13.7%

What is indicated about Ms. Yasser's event?
(A) It will be held in a commercial building.
(B) It has a very restrictive budget.
(C) It was catered by Colbert Catering last year.
(D) It will have the maximum number of guests.

Yasser さんの会について、何が示されていますか。
(A) 商業ビル内で催されるだろう。
(B) 予算が非常に制限されている。
(C) 昨年、Colbert Catering にケータリングしてもらった。
(D) 最大限の数の招待客が集まるだろう。

☐ commercial: 形 商業の ☐ restrictive: 形 制限の
☐ budget: 名 予算 ☐ maximum: 形 最大の

▶解説 Yasser さんは2つ目のメールの差出人で、❼から、会社の会議室を使った昼食会を計画していることが分かります。会社が入居するのは商業ビルだと考えられるため、(A) が正解です。

Part 7 ▼ Reading Section

369

Part 7 読解問題

What will Ms. Yasser most likely be required to do?
(A) Fill out an online form
(B) Give directions to her company
(C) Amend the number of attendees
(D) Call another branch of Colbert Catering

□ direction: 图 道順の指示　□ amend: 動 ～を修正する
□ attendee: 图 参加者　□ branch: 图 支店

Yasserさんは何をするように求められる可能性が最も高いですか。
(A) オンラインフォームに記入する
(B) 自分の会社への道案内をする
(C) 参加者の人数を変更する
(D) Colbert Catering の別の支店に電話をかける

▶解説 Yasser さんは、❽で「食物アレルギーのある招待客のために特別なメニューを提供してくれるか」を尋ねています。ウェブページの❹で、「必要があれば材料を変更できる」と述べられ、希望する場合は特別依頼欄に記入するよう求められています。これらから、(A) が正解です。

(((▲))) ゼミ 生 中継　😀 Hiro 😀 Mai 😀 Yasu 😀 Dai 😀 Saki

198. ....

😀 文書を正確に理解しないと、(D) を選びたくなる。

😀 選びました。Markovさんは10%の割引を受けましたよね。

😀 いや、彼はそんなことは書いていない。以前のケータリング会社と比べて10%安く済んだのに、食事はベターだったと書いているだけだよ。よく読んで。

😀 ～ less than the previous caterer charged. となっています。割引じゃなかったのですね。

😀 (B) まで読んで選んだから、(D) は読まなかった。ラッキー。

😀 お疲れさま。Test 3 も終わったね。結果はどうだった？

😀 76問で、換算スコアは890点でした。

😀 58問です。

😀 逆転させていただきました。59問です。合計は580点。

😀 目標の470点を大きく超えたね。サキは？

😀 48問です。合計は550から515に下がりました。

😀 じゃあ、結果を元に個別にアドバイスをするよ。

TOEICよろず相談所　ヒロの部屋

⑱試験当日は何をするのがいいですか

 明日、TOEICの公開テストを受けるのですが、何をしたらいいでしょうか。ギリギリですみません。

 いえいえ。今日は遅いですから、もう寝てください。一夜漬けは意味ないですよ。そして朝から、公式教材の音声を聞いてください。ETSのロゴマークが入っているTOEIC本を持っていますか。

 はい。公式の問題集を持っています。

 では、その音声をスマホなどに入れて、朝起きたらリスニングセクションをやってください。

 え、全部ですか。

 いえ、好きなパートだけでいいです。特になければ、Part 2だけでいいですよ。Part 2は音声だけで取り組めますから。公式教材に登場するナレーターは、公開テストにも出てくるのでお勧めです。

 分かりました。

 音を聞く目的は、**脳ミソを英語漬け**にすることなので、聞きながら日本語に訳さないでくださいね。それより、聞こえた英語を口頭でリピートする方がいいです。

 単語帳を試験会場に持っていくのはアリですか。

 アリですが、知らない単語を覚えようとはしないでください。**試験直前に知らない単語をいくつか覚えたところで役立つことはまずないです。**知っている情報にだけ目を通して気分を落ち着かせる方が有意義だと思いますよ。

 遅い時間にありがとうございました。明日、頑張ってきます。

 Good luck!

Test 4
模擬試験 ④
解答

お役立ちサイトやアプリのご案内

●ダウンロードセンター、ALCO：
模擬試験で使用した音声や復習用の音声をダウンロードできます。　　　　　　　（利用法は p.10、24）

●テスト採点センター：
簡単に答え合わせができます。（利用法は p.11）

記号について

【品詞を表す】
名 名詞　　動 動詞　　形 形容詞　　副 副詞
接 接続詞　前 前置詞　代 代名詞
※品詞が複数ある場合は、問題文での用法に合うものを1つ表示しています。

【ナレーターの国籍を表す】
🇺🇸 アメリカ人　　🇨🇦 カナダ人
🇬🇧 イギリス人　　🇦🇺 オーストラリア人

Test 4 結果記録シート

TEST 4の結果を記録しましょう。繰り返し取り組んだ場合は、2回目、3回目の記録もつけてください。

1回目（勘を含む）

● 正答数

Part	正答数		
Part 1	／6	Listening 合計正答数	
Part 2	／25		
Part 3	／39		
Part 4	／30		／100
Part 5	／30	Reading 合計正答数	
Part 6	／16		
Part 7	／54		／100

● 換算スコアA

Listening ＿＿＿＿＿

Reading ＿＿＿＿＿

合　計 ＿＿＿＿＿

● 問題タイプ別正答数と正答率

Listening Section

正答数	正答数	正答率
L1：＿＿＿＿／16	（＿＿＿＿÷16）×100＝＿＿＿＿％	
L2：＿＿＿＿／20	（＿＿＿＿÷20）×100＝＿＿＿＿％	
L3：＿＿＿＿／15	（＿＿＿＿÷15）×100＝＿＿＿＿％	
L4：＿＿＿＿／49	（＿＿＿＿÷49）×100＝＿＿＿＿％	
L5：＿＿＿＿／15	（＿＿＿＿÷15）×100＝＿＿＿＿％	

Reading Section

正答数	正答数	正答率
R1：＿＿＿＿／20	（＿＿＿＿÷20）×100＝＿＿＿＿％	
R2：＿＿＿＿／20	（＿＿＿＿÷20）×100＝＿＿＿＿％	
R3：＿＿＿＿／35	（＿＿＿＿÷35）×100＝＿＿＿＿％	
R4：＿＿＿＿／25	（＿＿＿＿÷25）×100＝＿＿＿＿％	
R5：＿＿＿＿／19	（＿＿＿＿÷19）×100＝＿＿＿＿％	

年　月　日

1回目（勘を除く）

● 正答数

Part	正答数		
Part 1	／6	Listening 合計正答数	
Part 2	／25		
Part 3	／39		
Part 4	／30		／100
Part 5	／30	Reading 合計正答数	
Part 6	／16		
Part 7	／54		／100

● 換算スコアB

Listening ＿＿＿＿＿

Reading ＿＿＿＿＿

合　計 ＿＿＿＿＿

● 問題タイプ別正答数と正答率

Listening Section

正答数	正答数	正答率
L1：＿＿＿＿／16	（＿＿＿＿÷16）×100＝＿＿＿＿％	
L2：＿＿＿＿／20	（＿＿＿＿÷20）×100＝＿＿＿＿％	
L3：＿＿＿＿／15	（＿＿＿＿÷15）×100＝＿＿＿＿％	
L4：＿＿＿＿／49	（＿＿＿＿÷49）×100＝＿＿＿＿％	
L5：＿＿＿＿／15	（＿＿＿＿÷15）×100＝＿＿＿＿％	

Reading Section

正答数	正答数	正答率
R1：＿＿＿＿／20	（＿＿＿＿÷20）×100＝＿＿＿＿％	
R2：＿＿＿＿／20	（＿＿＿＿÷20）×100＝＿＿＿＿％	
R3：＿＿＿＿／35	（＿＿＿＿÷35）×100＝＿＿＿＿％	
R4：＿＿＿＿／25	（＿＿＿＿÷25）×100＝＿＿＿＿％	
R5：＿＿＿＿／19	（＿＿＿＿÷19）×100＝＿＿＿＿％	

年　月　日

2回目（勘を含む）

● 正答数

Part	正答数		
Part 1	／6	Listening 合計正答数	
Part 2	／25		
Part 3	／39		
Part 4	／30		／100
Part 5	／30	Reading 合計正答数	
Part 6	／16		
Part 7	／54		／100

● 換算スコアA

Listening ＿＿＿＿＿

Reading ＿＿＿＿＿

合　計 ＿＿＿＿＿

● 問題タイプ別正答数と正答率

Listening Section

正答数	正答数	正答率
L1：＿＿＿＿／16	（＿＿＿＿÷16）×100＝＿＿＿＿％	
L2：＿＿＿＿／20	（＿＿＿＿÷20）×100＝＿＿＿＿％	
L3：＿＿＿＿／15	（＿＿＿＿÷15）×100＝＿＿＿＿％	
L4：＿＿＿＿／49	（＿＿＿＿÷49）×100＝＿＿＿＿％	
L5：＿＿＿＿／15	（＿＿＿＿÷15）×100＝＿＿＿＿％	

Reading Section

正答数	正答数	正答率
R1：＿＿＿＿／20	（＿＿＿＿÷20）×100＝＿＿＿＿％	
R2：＿＿＿＿／20	（＿＿＿＿÷20）×100＝＿＿＿＿％	
R3：＿＿＿＿／35	（＿＿＿＿÷35）×100＝＿＿＿＿％	
R4：＿＿＿＿／25	（＿＿＿＿÷25）×100＝＿＿＿＿％	
R5：＿＿＿＿／19	（＿＿＿＿÷19）×100＝＿＿＿＿％	

年　月　日

2回目（勘を除く）

● 正答数

Part	正答数		
Part 1	／6	Listening 合計正答数	
Part 2	／25		
Part 3	／39		
Part 4	／30		／100
Part 5	／30	Reading 合計正答数	
Part 6	／16		
Part 7	／54		／100

● 換算スコアB

Listening ＿＿＿＿＿

Reading ＿＿＿＿＿

合　計 ＿＿＿＿＿

● 問題タイプ別正答数と正答率

Listening Section

正答数	正答数	正答率
L1：＿＿＿＿／16	（＿＿＿＿÷16）×100＝＿＿＿＿％	
L2：＿＿＿＿／20	（＿＿＿＿÷20）×100＝＿＿＿＿％	
L3：＿＿＿＿／15	（＿＿＿＿÷15）×100＝＿＿＿＿％	
L4：＿＿＿＿／49	（＿＿＿＿÷49）×100＝＿＿＿＿％	
L5：＿＿＿＿／15	（＿＿＿＿÷15）×100＝＿＿＿＿％	

Reading Section

正答数	正答数	正答率
R1：＿＿＿＿／20	（＿＿＿＿÷20）×100＝＿＿＿＿％	
R2：＿＿＿＿／20	（＿＿＿＿÷20）×100＝＿＿＿＿％	
R3：＿＿＿＿／35	（＿＿＿＿÷35）×100＝＿＿＿＿％	
R4：＿＿＿＿／25	（＿＿＿＿÷25）×100＝＿＿＿＿％	
R5：＿＿＿＿／19	（＿＿＿＿÷19）×100＝＿＿＿＿％	

年　月　日

● 正答数

Part	正答数	
Part 1	／6	Listening 合計正答数
Part 2	／25	
Part 3	／39	
Part 4	／30	／100
Part 5	／30	Reading 合計正答数
Part 6	／16	
Part 7	／54	／100

● 換算スコアA

Listening ＿＿＿＿＿
Reading ＿＿＿＿＿
合　計 ＿＿＿＿＿

● 問題タイプ別正答数と正答率

Listening Section

正答数	正答数	正答率
L1：＿＿＿／16	（＿＿＿÷16）×100＝＿＿＿ ％
L2：＿＿＿／20	（＿＿＿÷20）×100＝＿＿＿ ％
L3：＿＿＿／15	（＿＿＿÷15）×100＝＿＿＿ ％
L4：＿＿＿／49	（＿＿＿÷49）×100＝＿＿＿ ％
L5：＿＿＿／15	（＿＿＿÷15）×100＝＿＿＿ ％

Reading Section

正答数	正答数	正答率
R1：＿＿＿／20	（＿＿＿÷20）×100＝＿＿＿ ％
R2：＿＿＿／20	（＿＿＿÷20）×100＝＿＿＿ ％
R3：＿＿＿／35	（＿＿＿÷35）×100＝＿＿＿ ％
R4：＿＿＿／25	（＿＿＿÷25）×100＝＿＿＿ ％
R5：＿＿＿／19	（＿＿＿÷19）×100＝＿＿＿ ％

● 正答数

Part	正答数	
Part 1	／6	Listening 合計正答数
Part 2	／25	
Part 3	／39	
Part 4	／30	／100
Part 5	／30	Reading 合計正答数
Part 6	／16	
Part 7	／54	／100

● 換算スコアアB

Listening ＿＿＿＿＿
Reading ＿＿＿＿＿
合　計 ＿＿＿＿＿

● 問題タイプ別正答数と正答率

Listening Section

正答数	正答数	正答率
L1：＿＿＿／16	（＿＿＿÷16）×100＝＿＿＿ ％
L2：＿＿＿／20	（＿＿＿÷20）×100＝＿＿＿ ％
L3：＿＿＿／15	（＿＿＿÷15）×100＝＿＿＿ ％
L4：＿＿＿／49	（＿＿＿÷49）×100＝＿＿＿ ％
L5：＿＿＿／15	（＿＿＿÷15）×100＝＿＿＿ ％

Reading Section

正答数	正答数	正答率
R1：＿＿＿／20	（＿＿＿÷20）×100＝＿＿＿ ％
R2：＿＿＿／20	（＿＿＿÷20）×100＝＿＿＿ ％
R3：＿＿＿／35	（＿＿＿÷35）×100＝＿＿＿ ％
R4：＿＿＿／25	（＿＿＿÷25）×100＝＿＿＿ ％
R5：＿＿＿／19	（＿＿＿÷19）×100＝＿＿＿ ％

弱点問題タイプ診断

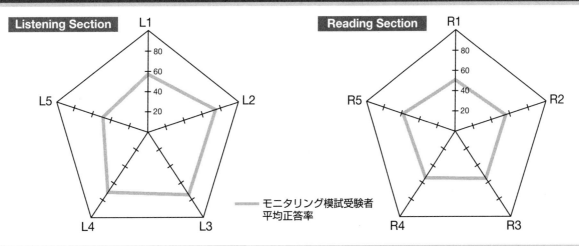

Listening Section

Reading Section

モニタリング模試受験者平均正答率

参考資料：モニタリング模試実施データ

p.379に掲載された「スコア換算表」を作成するために、TOEIC L&Rテストの公式スコア保持者335名を対象に、Test 1と同じ問題を使用した模擬試験を実施しました。以下はその結果をまとめたものです。

	公式スコア平均	正答数平均	最低正答数	最高正答数	初級者レベル正答数	上級者レベル正答数
Listening	370.3	69.7	26	97	61問以下	80問以上
Reading	318.3	55.2	23	98	42問以下	66問以上

※表中の数字はモニタリング模試受験者335名のうち正常に受験したと認められたモニターの数値を基に算出しています。
※モニタリング模試受験者のうち、Listening Section、Reading Sectionそれぞれにおいて、正答数が少なかった25％を「初級者レベル」、多かった25％を「上級者レベル」と呼んでいます。

Test 4 解答＆問題タイプ＆出題元一覧

答え合わせの手順

1. 正解を確認し、一覧表に正誤を記入する
自分の解答済のマークシートと解答一覧を突き合わせ、解答一覧内に正誤（○×）を記入しましょう。勘で答えた場合、勘ボックスに✔を入れます。

2. 間違えた問題の問題タイプ欄にチェックを入れる
間違えた問題もしくは正答したが勘ボックスに✔がある問題の「問題タイプ」欄に✔を記入します。

3. パートごとの正答数・問題タイプごとの正答数を数え、「結果記録シート」に記入する
パートごとの正答数（正誤欄の○の数）と勘を除く正答数（○の数ー✔の付いた数）を数え、その数をp.374〜の「結果記録シート」に記入しましょう。

4. 予想スコアと弱点問題タイプを算出する
p.379のスコア換算表を参照して実際のTOEIC L&Rテストでの予想スコアを算出し、p.374〜の「結果記録シート」に記入しましょう。間違えた問題や✔の付いた問題は、出題元を参照して復習しましょう。

Listening Section

番号	正解	正誤(勘)	タイプ	L1	L2	L3	L4	L5	出題元 Test	Q	解説	国籍	音声
Part 1													
1	D	( )	L1						3	1	265		194
2	B	( )	L1						2	2	149		195
3	B	( )	L3						1	3	34		197
4	A	( )	L3						3	6	267		198
5	D	( )	L1						2	5	151		199
6	C	( )	L3						1	6	35		200
Part 2													
7	C	( )	L3						2	8	152		203
8	B	( )	L3						1	9	37		204
9	A	( )	L3						3	17	272		205
10	B	( )	L3						1	15	39		206
11	B	( )	L3						2	25	157		207
12	C	( )	L3						3	13	270		208
13	A	( )	L3						1	21	41		209
14	C	( )	L1、L5						2	23	157		210
15	A	( )	L3						1	30	44		211
16	C	( )	L3						3	22	273		212
17	B	( )	L3						2	12	153		213
18	B	( )	L1、L5						1	23	42		214
19	C	( )	L1						2	13	153		215
20	C	( )	L1、L5						1	10	37		216
21	A	( )	L3						2	14	154		217
22	B	( )	L1、L5						3	21	273		218
23	B	( )	L1、L5						2	24	157		219
24	A	( )	L3						3	28	275		220
25	B	( )	L1、L5						2	21	156		221
26	A	( )	L1、L5						3	24	274		222
27	C	( )	L1						1	29	44		223
28	C	( )	L1						3	20	273		224
29	A	( )	L1、L5						2	31	159		225
30	C	( )	L1、L5						3	30	276		226
31	C	( )	L1、L5						1	26	43		227
Part 3													
32	B	( )	L2						2	35	162		229
33	A	( )	L4						2	36			
34	D	( )	L4						2	37			
35	B	( )	L2						1	59	56		230
36	D	( )	L4						1	60			
37	B	( )	L2						1	61			
38	A	( )	L4						3	35	279		231
39	C	( )	L2、L5						3	36			
40	D	( )	L4						3	37			
41	C	( )	L4						1	35	47		232
42	A	( )	L4						1	36			
43	D	( )	L4						1	37			
44	A	( )	L2						3	41	281		234
45	B	( )	L4						3	42			
46	C	( )	L4						3	43			
47	D	( )	L4						1	47	52		235
48	C	( )	L4						1	48			
49	A	( )	L4						1	49			
50	B	( )	L2						2	53	170		236
51	B	( )	L4						2	54			
52	C	( )	L2、L5						2	55			
53	A	( )	L2						3	56	287		237
54	A	( )	L4						3	57			
55	D	( )	L4						3	58			
56	D	( )	L4						2	38	164		238
57	A	( )	L4						2	39			
58	D	( )	L4						2	40			
59	C	( )	L2						1	38	48		239
60	A	( )	L4						1	39			
61	C	( )	L4						1	40			
62	A	( )	L4						2	62	174		240
63	B	( )	L4						2	63			
64	D	( )	L4						2	64			
65	C	( )	L4						1	62	58		242
66	D	( )	L4						1	63			
67	A	( )	L4						1	64			
68	A	( )	L2						3	68	294		243
69	C	( )	L4						3	69			
70	C	( )	L4						3	70			
Part 4													
71	D	( )	L2						2	71	181		245
72	B	( )	L4						2	72			
73	D	( )	L4						2	73			
74	A	( )	L4						3	89	302		246
75	C	( )	L2、L5						3	90			
76	C	( )	L4						3	91			
77	B	( )	L2						1	77	66		247
78	A	( )	L4						1	78			
79	D	( )	L4						1	79			
80	B	( )	L2						3	92	303		248
81	A	( )	L4						3	93			
82	D	( )	L4						3	94			
83	B	( )	L2						2	83	186		250
84	C	( )	L4						2	84			
85	A	( )	L4						2	85			
86	A	( )	L2						1	86	69		251
87	B	( )	L4						1	87			
88	A	( )	L2、L5						1	88			
89	B	( )	L2						3	80	299		252
90	D	( )	L4						3	81			
91	D	( )	L4						3	82			
92	A	( )	L2						2	86	187		253
93	B	( )	L4						2	87			
94	A	( )	L2、L5						2	88			
95	D	( )	L4						1	98	74		254
96	C	( )	L4						1	99			
97	B	( )	L4						1	100			
98	D	( )	L4						3	98	306		255
99	D	( )	L4						3	99			
100	B	( )	L4						3	100			

※「出題元」欄はその問題が出題されたTestと問題番号を、「解説」欄は解説が掲載されているページ数を、「音声」欄はトラック番号を表します。

記入例

番号	正解	正誤(勘)	タイプ	L1	L2	L3	L4	L5	TEST	Q	解説	国籍	音声
				間違えたら空欄にチェック					出題元				
Part 1													
1	D	O( )	L1						3	1	265	[flag]	193
2	B	O(v)	L1	v					2	2	149	[flag]	194
3	B	X(v)	L3			v			1	3	34	[flag]	197
4	A	O( )	L3						3	6	267	[flag]	198
5	D	X	L1						2	5	151	[flag]	199
99	D	O( )	L4						3	99			
100	B	X(v)	L4				v		3	100			

Reading Section

番号	正解	正誤(勘)	タイプ	R1	R2	R3	R4	R5	Test	Q	解説
				間違えたら空欄にチェック					出題元		
Part 5											
101	D	( )	R5						3	102	308
102	A	( )	R4						2	112	197
103	B	( )	R5						1	113	80
104	B	( )	R4						1	102	77
105	C	( )	R5						2	130	202
106	A	( )	R4						3	127	315
107	D	( )	R5						2	107	195
108	D	( )	R4						3	107	309
109	C	( )	R5						1	121	82
110	A	( )	R4						3	108	309
111	C	( )	R5						2	109	196
112	A	( )	R4						1	110	79
113	A	( )	R5						3	112	311
114	B	( )	R4						2	106	195
115	A	( )	R5						3	111	310
116	B	( )	R4						1	104	78
117	C	( )	R5						2	103	194
118	B	( )	R4						1	122	82
119	C	( )	R5						3	126	315
120	B	( )	R4						1	114	80
121	D	( )	R5						2	121	199
122	D	( )	R4						3	130	316
123	A	( )	R5						1	129	84
124	B	( )	R4						2	119	199
125	D	( )	R5						1	119	82
126	D	( )	R4						3	128	316
127	D	( )	R5						2	125	201
128	C	( )	R4						1	118	81
129	A	( )	R5						3	117	312
130	B	( )	R4						2	120	199
Part 6											
131	A	( )	R3、R5						2	139	208
132	B	( )	R3、R4						2	140	
133	D	( )	R3						2	141	
134	C	( )	R3、R4						2	142	
135	A	( )	R3、R4						3	139	322
136	D	( )	R4						3	140	
137	C	( )	R3、R5						3	141	
138	B	( )	R3						3	142	
139	A	( )	R3						1	139	90
140	B	( )	R5						1	140	
141	D	( )	R3、R4						1	141	
142	A	( )	R3、R4						1	142	
143	C	( )	R5						2	131	204
144	D	( )	R3、R4						2	132	
145	A	( )	R3、R4						2	133	
146	B	( )	R3						2	134	
Part 7											
147	A	( )	R2						3	147	326
148	D	( )	R3						3	148	
149	D	( )	R2						2	149	214
150	D	( )	R4						2	150	

番号	正解	正誤(勘)	タイプ	R1	R2	R3	R4	R5	Test	Q	解説
				間違えたら空欄にチェック					出題元		
151	A	( )	R2						2	151	
152	C	( )	R1						1	149	96
153	D	( )	R2						1	150	
154	A	( )	R1						3	163	338
155	A	( )	R2						3	164	
156	D	( )	R1、R3						3	165	
157	B	( )	R1						2	154	218
158	C	( )	R2						2	155	
159	B	( )	R3						3	149	328
160	C	( )	R1、R3						3	150	
161	D	( )	R1						1	162	108
162	A	( )	R3						1	163	
163	D	( )	R2						1	164	
164	B	( )	R2						2	172	232
165	C	( )	R2						2	173	
166	D	( )	R2						2	174	
167	A	( )	R1、R3						2	175	
168	A	( )	R2						3	151	330
169	B	( )	R3						3	152	
170	C	( )	R2						3	153	
171	B	( )	R4						3	154	
172	B	( )	R1						1	158	104
173	D	( )	R2						1	159	
174	B	( )	R3						1	160	
175	B	( )	R1、R3						1	161	
176	B	( )	R1						2	181	240
177	D	( )	R1						2	182	
178	C	( )	R3						2	183	
179	A	( )	R1、R3						2	184	
180	A	( )	R3						2	185	
181	B	( )	R1						3	181	354
182	D	( )	R2						3	182	
183	A	( )	R3						3	183	
184	A	( )	R1、R3						3	184	
185	B	( )	R2						3	185	
186	A	( )	R3						2	186	244
187	B	( )	R1、R3						2	187	
188	D	( )	R3						2	188	
189	D	( )	R2						2	189	
190	C	( )	R3						2	190	
191	B	( )	R1						1	191	132
192	C	( )	R1						1	192	
193	A	( )	R3						1	193	
194	C	( )	R2						1	194	
195	D	( )	R1、R3						1	195	
196	B	( )	R2						3	196	366
197	C	( )	R2						3	197	
198	B	( )	R1、R3						3	198	
199	A	( )	R2						3	199	
200	A	( )	R1、R3						3	200	

Test 4 マークシート状解答一覧

LISTENING SECTION

No.	ANSWER (A B C D)	No.	ANSWER (A B C)	No.	ANSWER (A B C)
Part 1		Part 2			
1		11		21	
2		12		22	
3		13		23	
4		14		24	
5		15		25	
6		16		26	
7		17		27	
8		18		28	
9		19		29	
10		20		30	

No.	ANSWER (A B C)	No.	ANSWER (A B C D)	No.	ANSWER (A B C D)
31		Part 3			
32		41		51	
33		42		52	
34		43		53	
35		44		54	
36		45		55	
37		46		56	
38		47		57	
39		48		58	
40		49		59	
		50		60	

No.	ANSWER (A B C D)	No.	ANSWER (A B C D)	No.	ANSWER (A B C D)
61		Part 4			
62		71		81	
63		72		82	
64		73		83	
65		74		84	
66		75		85	
67		76		86	
68		77		87	
69		78		88	
70		79		89	
		80		90	

No.	ANSWER (A B C D)
91	
92	
93	
94	
95	
96	
97	
98	
99	
100	

READING SECTION

No.	ANSWER (A B C D)	No.	ANSWER (A B C D)	No.	ANSWER (A B C D)
Part 5					
101		111		121	
102		112		122	
103		113		123	
104		114		124	
105		115		125	
106		116		126	
107		117		127	
108		118		128	
109		119		129	
110		120		130	

No.	ANSWER (A B C D)	No.	ANSWER (A B C D)	No.	ANSWER (A B C D)
Part 6				Part 7	
131		141		151	
132		142		152	
133		143		153	
134		144		154	
135		145		155	
136		146		156	
137		147		157	
138		148		158	
139		149		159	
140		150		160	

No.	ANSWER (A B C D)	No.	ANSWER (A B C D)	No.	ANSWER (A B C D)
161		171		181	
162		172		182	
163		173		183	
164		174		184	
165		175		185	
166		176		186	
167		177		187	
168		178		188	
169		179		189	
170		180		190	

No.	ANSWER (A B C D)
191	
192	
193	
194	
195	
196	
197	
198	
199	
200	

Test 4 スコア換算表

協力：アルク教育総合研究所

Listening Section

正答数	換算スコア	正答数	換算スコア
0	5	51	280
1	5	52	285
2	5	53	290
3	5	54	295
4	10	55	300
5	20	56	305
6	25	57	310
7	30	58	315
8	35	59	320
9	40	60	325
10	45	61	330
11	50	62	335
12	60	63	335
13	65	64	340
14	70	65	345
15	80	66	350
16	85	67	355
17	95	68	360
18	105	69	365
19	115	70	370
20	120	71	375
21	125	72	380
22	130	73	385
23	135	74	390
24	140	75	390
25	145	76	395
26	150	77	400
27	155	78	410
28	160	79	415
29	165	80	420
30	170	81	425
31	175	82	430
32	180	83	435
33	185	84	440
34	195	85	445
35	200	86	445
36	205	87	450
37	210	88	455
38	220	89	460
39	225	90	465
40	230	91	470
41	235	92	475
42	240	93	480
43	245	94	490
44	250	95	495
45	250	96	495
46	255	97	495
47	260	98	495
48	265	99	495
49	270	100	495
50	275		

Reading Section

正答数	換算スコア	正答数	換算スコア
0	5	51	290
1	5	52	295
2	5	53	305
3	10	54	310
4	20	55	320
5	25	56	325
6	25	57	330
7	30	58	335
8	30	59	335
9	35	60	340
10	40	61	340
11	40	62	345
12	45	63	350
13	50	64	355
14	60	65	355
15	65	66	360
16	70	67	360
17	80	68	365
18	85	69	370
19	90	70	370
20	95	71	375
21	100	72	375
22	105	73	380
23	110	74	380
24	115	75	385
25	120	76	390
26	125	77	395
27	130	78	400
28	135	79	405
29	140	80	410
30	145	81	415
31	155	82	420
32	160	83	425
33	170	84	430
34	175	85	435
35	180	86	440
36	190	87	445
37	195	88	450
38	200	89	455
39	210	90	460
40	215	91	465
41	220	92	470
42	230	93	475
43	235	94	480
44	240	95	480
45	250	96	490
46	255	97	495
47	265	98	495
48	270	99	495
49	275	100	495
50	285		

結果活用アドバイス

本書に登場するマイ、ヤス、ダイ、サキの4人の換算スコアを例に「弱点問題タイプ診断」の活用法をご紹介します。自分に最も近い人物の診断を参考に、今後の学習に役立ててください。

Listening Section

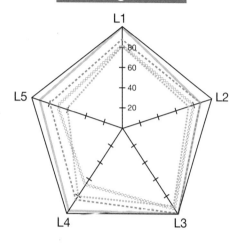

Reading Section

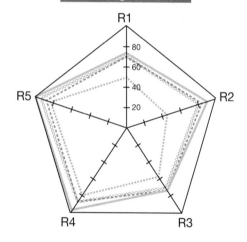

換算スコア

		Listening	Reading	合計
——	マイ	495	450	945
-----	ヤス	455	425	880
××××××	ダイ	395	415	810
....	サキ	420	365	785

さて、Test 4の結果はどうだったかな。これまでに解いたことがある問題でも、意外とたくさん間違えたでしょ。

リスニングで発音が変わっていましたよね。ナレーターが違うだけで、新しい問題のように感じました。

マイはリスニングで97問も正答したのか。かなり徹底的に復習したんだね。

はい、1つもミスしない自信がありましたが、ダメでした。リーディングで12問も間違えたのが信じられません。

Part 7で11問ミスか。じゃ、その11問を振り返って、正解の根拠がどれなのか、そして、不正解の選択肢がなぜ不正解なのか1つ1つ確認して。日本語訳に頼らず、英語だけを見てね。

分かりました。解説も読まずにやってみます。

ヤスはTest 4をやって何か気づいたことはある?

あります。何度も同じ模試を繰り返すと、答えを覚えてしまうと思っていたのですが、大きな間違いでした。

その通り。本当に答えを覚えてしまうなら、Test 4で全問正解するはずだからね。

悔しいので、全問正解できるまで何度でも再挑戦します。

その姿勢が大事だよ。次はダイ。たくさん間違えたね。

はい。ただ、810点という数字を見ると何だかうれしいです。もしかすると、実力でこれだけ取れる日が来るのかも、と。

きっと来るよ。400点前後だった人が800点を超えた例はいくらでもある。将来、ダイの会社がもっと高いスコアを求めてくるかもしれないし、業務で英語を使う日が来る可能性だってあるよね。

その通りです。

この本の中身を吸収すればビジネス現場で必ず役立つから、Test 4で満点が取れるくらいに今後も学習を続けていって。

了解しました。

サキはどうだった?

Test 3の復習が甘かったので、だいたい予想通りの結果です。1つ聞きたいのですが、L5は、どんな問題ですか。

Part 2に10問ほど出る遠まわしに答える応答と、Part 3と4の意図問題5問だよ。どうして?

私の4回の成績を見るとL5がいつも最低なんです。

L5は難易度が高いから、今は気にしなくていい。それより、サキは英語の基礎となる語彙と文法に注力する必要がある。Test 1の後で言ったように、英文を丁寧に読んで品詞や語順に注意を払って。分からないことは高校時代に使った文法の参考書で調べるといいよ。R5が文法だから、これが80%を切らないレベルを目指そう。

分かりました。ありがとうございました。

さて、これでTest 4も終わり。お疲れさま。

さいごに

ついにゼミの最終日。
講義を終えたヒロから4人にメッセージが伝えられる。

みんな来週の公開テストを受けるよね。今回のゼミで学んだことをきちんと実践すれば目標は達成できるよ。とりあえず、ゼミは今日で終わり。最後に感想を聞かせて。たまにはダイから。

最初は、できないことが多くて辛かったです。ただ、**勉強すればするほど結果が良くなっていった**ので、TOEIC は面白いと思うようになりました。

いいね。マイは？

リスニング力が上がったことを実感しています。YouTube で聞く**ナマ英語がだんだん聞き取れる**ようになってきました。

音読の効果だよ。マイはスコアアップを目的に英語を学んでいるわけじゃないから、教材とは別に**リアルな英語に触れる時間も増やしていって**。そのうちスピーキングのゼミにも来てね。

はい、楽しみにしています。

ヤスはどうだった？

集中力と忍耐力がついた気がします。

英語に没頭する時間が増えたからだね。海外での買い付けに行かせてもらえるようになったら教えてね。最後にサキ。初めて受講してどうだった？

楽しかったです。**独学だと気づかないことがたくさんあった**ので、ゼミに来て良かったです。あと、講義動画のおかげで、スキマ時間の勉強がめちゃ増えました。

教えるのも楽しかったよ。ところで、みんな、次に集まる日はいつか覚えている？

スコア発表の日です。

そう。みんなでスマホを見ながら「せーの」でスコアを確認しよう。目標達成者には、なんと、高級寿司がおごられる。

マジですか！

達成しなかった人がおごるんだよ。

えーーーーーっ!?

冗談だよ（笑）

まったく、もう。

最後に、映画 Back to the Future からこの言葉を引用してみんなに贈るよ。*If you put your mind to it, you can accomplish anything.* **気持ちを込めて全力で取り組めば、何だって達成できる**。みんな、受講してくれてありがとう。では、解散。

ありがとうございました！

『　　あとがき　　』

　この「究極の模試プロジェクト」に着手したのは1年2カ月前です。そのとき、心に誓いました。「いい模試」であるだけでなく「楽しい学習体験の場」を作ろうと。良質な教材があふれかえる今、読者が求めるものは「質の高さ」は当然として、「学習を続けたくなる環境」や「楽しさ」のはず。それらを実現するための「楽しい学習体験の場」を提供することにコミットしようと決めたのです。

　「楽しい学習体験の場」を作るために取り組んだのが、本全体を1つの物語に仕立て上げることと、思わず読みたくなる「ゼミ生中継」を作ることです。5人のキャラクターの会話を通して、模試に取り組むあなたもきっと感じた戸惑いや体験を先回りして文字にしました。それを可能にしたのは、50名を超えるモニターの「リアルな声」です。東京、名古屋、大阪、神戸で開催されたイベントの参加者に、模試を受けた直後にディスカッションをしてもらい、それを録音した音源をボクが何十時間も聞いて、マイたちのセリフに盛り込んでいきました。普通のTOEIC教材の学習では得られない、仲間がいるような楽しい感覚をあなたに味わっていただけたことを願っています。

　本書の制作に当たり、多くの方にご協力いただきました。全員のお名前を掲載することができないのが残念ですが、以下の方々に厚く御礼を申し上げます。オンラインで4つの模試を受験してくださった約1500名の皆さん、フォーカスグループに参加してくださった約50名の皆さん、多くのアイデアを提案してくださった「究極の模試制作集団」の皆さん、ツイッターでアンケートに答えてくださった皆さん。

　さらに、モニター用イベントの主催、問題作成、解説執筆、写真提供、動画の検証など、多くのご協力をいただいた以下の方々に、特別な感謝の気持ちを伝えたいと思います。（敬称略・五十音順）
浅場眞紀子、石川綾美、石橋敦子、泉裕美、和泉有香、上原ちとせ、梅島義博、江藤友佳、大西由紀子、勝山庸子、加藤草平、工藤郁子、倉本淑子、後藤理恵子、澤野祥子、下窄称美、下山智裕、田岡千明、堤康博、天満嗣雄、豊馬桃子、番場直之、船橋由紀子、真弓真理、丸岡幸子、本山浩子、矢津裕子、山下莉加、山本直実
そして、600問以上の問題作成に加え、英語に関する多くのアドバイスをくれた盟友ロス・タロック。皆さんの力なしに、本書を完成させることはできませんでした。深く感謝します。

　最後まで読んでくださったあなたに贈ろうと思っていたメッセージを「さいごに」でヒロに取られてしまったので、別の言葉を贈ります。

Your goal is within your reach.

第247回TOEIC L&R公開テスト実施日に

ヒロ前田

著者プロフィール

ヒロ前田 Hiro Maeda

TOEIC受験力UPトレーナー。神戸大学経営学部卒。大人のための勉強スペース「T'z英語ラウンジ」経営。2003年5月に講師として全国の企業・大学で指導を開始。'05年にはTOEIC対策指導者を養成する講座をスタートし、トレーナーを務めている。'08年グランドストリーム株式会社を設立。TOEIC® L&Rテストの受験回数は120回を超え、47都道府県で公開テストを受験する「全国制覇」を'17年5月に達成。取得スコアは15点から990点まで幅広い。著書に『TOEIC® L&Rテスト 究極のゼミ』シリーズ（アルク）、『TOEIC® テスト900点。それでも英語が話せない人、話せる人』（KADOKAWA）等、共著に『TOEIC® L&Rテスト 直前の技術』、『TOEIC®テスト 新形式問題やり込みドリル』（アルク）等がある。

●ヒロ前田が質問に答えます　本書の読者専用LINEアカウント

TOEIC® L&Rテスト　究極の模試600問+

発行日：2020年 3 月10日（初版）
　　　　2024年10月25日（第7刷）

著者：ヒロ前田

編集：株式会社アルク 出版編集部
編集協力：中村理恵、藤田くる美、溝口優美子
翻訳：株式会社オフィスLEPS岡本茂紀
校正：Peter Branscombe、Margaret Stalker、渡邉真理子
表紙・本文デザイン：伊東岳美
ナレーション：【アメリカ】Howard Colefield、Karen Haedrich、Josh Keller
　　　　　　　【カナダ】Andree Dufleit、Nadia Jaskiw、Jon Mudryj
　　　　　　　【イギリス】Nadia McKechnie、Guy Perryman
　　　　　　　【オーストラリア】Sarah Greaves、Brad Holmes、Jason Takada
録音・編集：一般財団法人英語教育協議会（ELEC）
動画撮影・編集：合同会社ADD9
DTP：朝日メディアインターナショナル株式会社、伊東岳美
印刷・製本：大日本印刷株式会社

発行者：天野智之
発行所：株式会社アルク
　　　　〒141-0001　東京都品川区北品川6-7-29 ガーデンシティ品川御殿山
　　　　Website：https://www.alc.co.jp/

地球人ネットワークを創る

アルクのシンボル
「地球人マーク」です。

TOEIC® L&Rテスト 究極の模試600問⁺ Test 1 マークシートA-1 （勘ボックスあり）

実施日： 　年　　月　　日

	Part 1	Part 2	Part 3	Part 4	Listening 計	Part 5	Part 6	Part 7	Reading 計
	/6	/25	/39	/30	/100	/30	/16	/54	/100
					/495				/495
					換算スコア				換算スコア

LISTENING SECTION

Part 1
No.	ANSWER A B C D 勘
1	Ⓐ Ⓑ Ⓒ Ⓓ ☐
2	Ⓐ Ⓑ Ⓒ Ⓓ ☐
3	Ⓐ Ⓑ Ⓒ Ⓓ ☐
4	Ⓐ Ⓑ Ⓒ Ⓓ ☐
5	Ⓐ Ⓑ Ⓒ Ⓓ ☐
6	Ⓐ Ⓑ Ⓒ Ⓓ ☐

Part 2
No.	ANSWER A B C 勘
7	Ⓐ Ⓑ Ⓒ ☐
8	Ⓐ Ⓑ Ⓒ ☐
9	Ⓐ Ⓑ Ⓒ ☐
10	Ⓐ Ⓑ Ⓒ ☐
11	Ⓐ Ⓑ Ⓒ ☐
12	Ⓐ Ⓑ Ⓒ ☐
13	Ⓐ Ⓑ Ⓒ ☐
14	Ⓐ Ⓑ Ⓒ ☐
15	Ⓐ Ⓑ Ⓒ ☐
16	Ⓐ Ⓑ Ⓒ ☐
17	Ⓐ Ⓑ Ⓒ ☐
18	Ⓐ Ⓑ Ⓒ ☐
19	Ⓐ Ⓑ Ⓒ ☐
20	Ⓐ Ⓑ Ⓒ ☐
21	Ⓐ Ⓑ Ⓒ ☐
22	Ⓐ Ⓑ Ⓒ ☐
23	Ⓐ Ⓑ Ⓒ ☐
24	Ⓐ Ⓑ Ⓒ ☐
25	Ⓐ Ⓑ Ⓒ ☐
26	Ⓐ Ⓑ Ⓒ ☐
27	Ⓐ Ⓑ Ⓒ ☐
28	Ⓐ Ⓑ Ⓒ ☐
29	Ⓐ Ⓑ Ⓒ ☐
30	Ⓐ Ⓑ Ⓒ ☐
31	Ⓐ Ⓑ Ⓒ ☐

Part 3
No.	ANSWER A B C D 勘
32	Ⓐ Ⓑ Ⓒ Ⓓ ☐
33	Ⓐ Ⓑ Ⓒ Ⓓ ☐
34	Ⓐ Ⓑ Ⓒ Ⓓ ☐
35	Ⓐ Ⓑ Ⓒ Ⓓ ☐
36	Ⓐ Ⓑ Ⓒ Ⓓ ☐
37	Ⓐ Ⓑ Ⓒ Ⓓ ☐
38	Ⓐ Ⓑ Ⓒ Ⓓ ☐
39	Ⓐ Ⓑ Ⓒ Ⓓ ☐
40	Ⓐ Ⓑ Ⓒ Ⓓ ☐
41	Ⓐ Ⓑ Ⓒ Ⓓ ☐
42	Ⓐ Ⓑ Ⓒ Ⓓ ☐
43	Ⓐ Ⓑ Ⓒ Ⓓ ☐
44	Ⓐ Ⓑ Ⓒ Ⓓ ☐
45	Ⓐ Ⓑ Ⓒ Ⓓ ☐
46	Ⓐ Ⓑ Ⓒ Ⓓ ☐
47	Ⓐ Ⓑ Ⓒ Ⓓ ☐
48	Ⓐ Ⓑ Ⓒ Ⓓ ☐
49	Ⓐ Ⓑ Ⓒ Ⓓ ☐
50	Ⓐ Ⓑ Ⓒ Ⓓ ☐
51	Ⓐ Ⓑ Ⓒ Ⓓ ☐
52	Ⓐ Ⓑ Ⓒ Ⓓ ☐
53	Ⓐ Ⓑ Ⓒ Ⓓ ☐
54	Ⓐ Ⓑ Ⓒ Ⓓ ☐
55	Ⓐ Ⓑ Ⓒ Ⓓ ☐
56	Ⓐ Ⓑ Ⓒ Ⓓ ☐
57	Ⓐ Ⓑ Ⓒ Ⓓ ☐
58	Ⓐ Ⓑ Ⓒ Ⓓ ☐
59	Ⓐ Ⓑ Ⓒ Ⓓ ☐
60	Ⓐ Ⓑ Ⓒ Ⓓ ☐
61	Ⓐ Ⓑ Ⓒ Ⓓ ☐
62	Ⓐ Ⓑ Ⓒ Ⓓ ☐
63	Ⓐ Ⓑ Ⓒ Ⓓ ☐
64	Ⓐ Ⓑ Ⓒ Ⓓ ☐
65	Ⓐ Ⓑ Ⓒ Ⓓ ☐
66	Ⓐ Ⓑ Ⓒ Ⓓ ☐
67	Ⓐ Ⓑ Ⓒ Ⓓ ☐
68	Ⓐ Ⓑ Ⓒ Ⓓ ☐
69	Ⓐ Ⓑ Ⓒ Ⓓ ☐
70	Ⓐ Ⓑ Ⓒ Ⓓ ☐

Part 4
No.	ANSWER A B C D 勘
71	Ⓐ Ⓑ Ⓒ Ⓓ ☐
72	Ⓐ Ⓑ Ⓒ Ⓓ ☐
73	Ⓐ Ⓑ Ⓒ Ⓓ ☐
74	Ⓐ Ⓑ Ⓒ Ⓓ ☐
75	Ⓐ Ⓑ Ⓒ Ⓓ ☐
76	Ⓐ Ⓑ Ⓒ Ⓓ ☐
77	Ⓐ Ⓑ Ⓒ Ⓓ ☐
78	Ⓐ Ⓑ Ⓒ Ⓓ ☐
79	Ⓐ Ⓑ Ⓒ Ⓓ ☐
80	Ⓐ Ⓑ Ⓒ Ⓓ ☐
81	Ⓐ Ⓑ Ⓒ Ⓓ ☐
82	Ⓐ Ⓑ Ⓒ Ⓓ ☐
83	Ⓐ Ⓑ Ⓒ Ⓓ ☐
84	Ⓐ Ⓑ Ⓒ Ⓓ ☐
85	Ⓐ Ⓑ Ⓒ Ⓓ ☐
86	Ⓐ Ⓑ Ⓒ Ⓓ ☐
87	Ⓐ Ⓑ Ⓒ Ⓓ ☐
88	Ⓐ Ⓑ Ⓒ Ⓓ ☐
89	Ⓐ Ⓑ Ⓒ Ⓓ ☐
90	Ⓐ Ⓑ Ⓒ Ⓓ ☐
91	Ⓐ Ⓑ Ⓒ Ⓓ ☐
92	Ⓐ Ⓑ Ⓒ Ⓓ ☐
93	Ⓐ Ⓑ Ⓒ Ⓓ ☐
94	Ⓐ Ⓑ Ⓒ Ⓓ ☐
95	Ⓐ Ⓑ Ⓒ Ⓓ ☐
96	Ⓐ Ⓑ Ⓒ Ⓓ ☐
97	Ⓐ Ⓑ Ⓒ Ⓓ ☐
98	Ⓐ Ⓑ Ⓒ Ⓓ ☐
99	Ⓐ Ⓑ Ⓒ Ⓓ ☐
100	Ⓐ Ⓑ Ⓒ Ⓓ ☐

READING SECTION

Part 5
No.	ANSWER A B C D 勘
101	Ⓐ Ⓑ Ⓒ Ⓓ ☐
102	Ⓐ Ⓑ Ⓒ Ⓓ ☐
103	Ⓐ Ⓑ Ⓒ Ⓓ ☐
104	Ⓐ Ⓑ Ⓒ Ⓓ ☐
105	Ⓐ Ⓑ Ⓒ Ⓓ ☐
106	Ⓐ Ⓑ Ⓒ Ⓓ ☐
107	Ⓐ Ⓑ Ⓒ Ⓓ ☐
108	Ⓐ Ⓑ Ⓒ Ⓓ ☐
109	Ⓐ Ⓑ Ⓒ Ⓓ ☐
110	Ⓐ Ⓑ Ⓒ Ⓓ ☐
111	Ⓐ Ⓑ Ⓒ Ⓓ ☐
112	Ⓐ Ⓑ Ⓒ Ⓓ ☐
113	Ⓐ Ⓑ Ⓒ Ⓓ ☐
114	Ⓐ Ⓑ Ⓒ Ⓓ ☐
115	Ⓐ Ⓑ Ⓒ Ⓓ ☐
116	Ⓐ Ⓑ Ⓒ Ⓓ ☐
117	Ⓐ Ⓑ Ⓒ Ⓓ ☐
118	Ⓐ Ⓑ Ⓒ Ⓓ ☐
119	Ⓐ Ⓑ Ⓒ Ⓓ ☐
120	Ⓐ Ⓑ Ⓒ Ⓓ ☐
121	Ⓐ Ⓑ Ⓒ Ⓓ ☐
122	Ⓐ Ⓑ Ⓒ Ⓓ ☐
123	Ⓐ Ⓑ Ⓒ Ⓓ ☐
124	Ⓐ Ⓑ Ⓒ Ⓓ ☐
125	Ⓐ Ⓑ Ⓒ Ⓓ ☐
126	Ⓐ Ⓑ Ⓒ Ⓓ ☐
127	Ⓐ Ⓑ Ⓒ Ⓓ ☐
128	Ⓐ Ⓑ Ⓒ Ⓓ ☐
129	Ⓐ Ⓑ Ⓒ Ⓓ ☐
130	Ⓐ Ⓑ Ⓒ Ⓓ ☐

Part 6
No.	ANSWER A B C D 勘
131	Ⓐ Ⓑ Ⓒ Ⓓ ☐
132	Ⓐ Ⓑ Ⓒ Ⓓ ☐
133	Ⓐ Ⓑ Ⓒ Ⓓ ☐
134	Ⓐ Ⓑ Ⓒ Ⓓ ☐
135	Ⓐ Ⓑ Ⓒ Ⓓ ☐
136	Ⓐ Ⓑ Ⓒ Ⓓ ☐
137	Ⓐ Ⓑ Ⓒ Ⓓ ☐
138	Ⓐ Ⓑ Ⓒ Ⓓ ☐
139	Ⓐ Ⓑ Ⓒ Ⓓ ☐
140	Ⓐ Ⓑ Ⓒ Ⓓ ☐

Part 7
No.	ANSWER A B C D 勘
141	Ⓐ Ⓑ Ⓒ Ⓓ ☐
142	Ⓐ Ⓑ Ⓒ Ⓓ ☐
143	Ⓐ Ⓑ Ⓒ Ⓓ ☐
144	Ⓐ Ⓑ Ⓒ Ⓓ ☐
145	Ⓐ Ⓑ Ⓒ Ⓓ ☐
146	Ⓐ Ⓑ Ⓒ Ⓓ ☐
147	Ⓐ Ⓑ Ⓒ Ⓓ ☐
148	Ⓐ Ⓑ Ⓒ Ⓓ ☐
149	Ⓐ Ⓑ Ⓒ Ⓓ ☐
150	Ⓐ Ⓑ Ⓒ Ⓓ ☐
151	Ⓐ Ⓑ Ⓒ Ⓓ ☐
152	Ⓐ Ⓑ Ⓒ Ⓓ ☐
153	Ⓐ Ⓑ Ⓒ Ⓓ ☐
154	Ⓐ Ⓑ Ⓒ Ⓓ ☐
155	Ⓐ Ⓑ Ⓒ Ⓓ ☐
156	Ⓐ Ⓑ Ⓒ Ⓓ ☐
157	Ⓐ Ⓑ Ⓒ Ⓓ ☐
158	Ⓐ Ⓑ Ⓒ Ⓓ ☐
159	Ⓐ Ⓑ Ⓒ Ⓓ ☐
160	Ⓐ Ⓑ Ⓒ Ⓓ ☐
161	Ⓐ Ⓑ Ⓒ Ⓓ ☐
162	Ⓐ Ⓑ Ⓒ Ⓓ ☐
163	Ⓐ Ⓑ Ⓒ Ⓓ ☐
164	Ⓐ Ⓑ Ⓒ Ⓓ ☐
165	Ⓐ Ⓑ Ⓒ Ⓓ ☐
166	Ⓐ Ⓑ Ⓒ Ⓓ ☐
167	Ⓐ Ⓑ Ⓒ Ⓓ ☐
168	Ⓐ Ⓑ Ⓒ Ⓓ ☐
169	Ⓐ Ⓑ Ⓒ Ⓓ ☐
170	Ⓐ Ⓑ Ⓒ Ⓓ ☐
171	Ⓐ Ⓑ Ⓒ Ⓓ ☐
172	Ⓐ Ⓑ Ⓒ Ⓓ ☐
173	Ⓐ Ⓑ Ⓒ Ⓓ ☐
174	Ⓐ Ⓑ Ⓒ Ⓓ ☐
175	Ⓐ Ⓑ Ⓒ Ⓓ ☐
176	Ⓐ Ⓑ Ⓒ Ⓓ ☐
177	Ⓐ Ⓑ Ⓒ Ⓓ ☐
178	Ⓐ Ⓑ Ⓒ Ⓓ ☐
179	Ⓐ Ⓑ Ⓒ Ⓓ ☐
180	Ⓐ Ⓑ Ⓒ Ⓓ ☐
181	Ⓐ Ⓑ Ⓒ Ⓓ ☐
182	Ⓐ Ⓑ Ⓒ Ⓓ ☐
183	Ⓐ Ⓑ Ⓒ Ⓓ ☐
184	Ⓐ Ⓑ Ⓒ Ⓓ ☐
185	Ⓐ Ⓑ Ⓒ Ⓓ ☐
186	Ⓐ Ⓑ Ⓒ Ⓓ ☐
187	Ⓐ Ⓑ Ⓒ Ⓓ ☐
188	Ⓐ Ⓑ Ⓒ Ⓓ ☐
189	Ⓐ Ⓑ Ⓒ Ⓓ ☐
190	Ⓐ Ⓑ Ⓒ Ⓓ ☐
191	Ⓐ Ⓑ Ⓒ Ⓓ ☐
192	Ⓐ Ⓑ Ⓒ Ⓓ ☐
193	Ⓐ Ⓑ Ⓒ Ⓓ ☐
194	Ⓐ Ⓑ Ⓒ Ⓓ ☐
195	Ⓐ Ⓑ Ⓒ Ⓓ ☐
196	Ⓐ Ⓑ Ⓒ Ⓓ ☐
197	Ⓐ Ⓑ Ⓒ Ⓓ ☐
198	Ⓐ Ⓑ Ⓒ Ⓓ ☐
199	Ⓐ Ⓑ Ⓒ Ⓓ ☐
200	Ⓐ Ⓑ Ⓒ Ⓓ ☐

※解答一覧→本冊p.28〜参照

TOEIC® L&Rテスト 究極の模試600問+ Test 1 マークシート A-2 (勘ボックスあり)

実施日： 　年　　月　　日

	Part 1	Part 2	Part 3	Part 4	Listening 計	Part 5	Part 6	Part 7	Reading 計
換算スコア	/6	/25	/39	/30	/100	/30	/16	/54	/100
					/495		換算スコア		/495

LISTENING SECTION

Part 1

No.	ANSWER (A B C D 勘)
1	Ⓐ Ⓑ Ⓒ □
2	Ⓐ Ⓑ Ⓒ □
3	Ⓐ Ⓑ Ⓒ □
4	Ⓐ Ⓑ Ⓒ □
5	Ⓐ Ⓑ Ⓒ □
6	Ⓐ Ⓑ Ⓒ □
7	Ⓐ Ⓑ Ⓒ □
8	Ⓐ Ⓑ Ⓒ □
9	Ⓐ Ⓑ Ⓒ □
10	Ⓐ Ⓑ Ⓒ □

Part 2 (No. 11–30) — ANSWER A B C 勘

Part 3 (No. 31–40) — ANSWER A B C 勘; (No. 41–70) — ANSWER A B C D 勘

Part 4 (No. 71–100) — ANSWER A B C D 勘

READING SECTION

Part 5 (No. 101–130) — ANSWER A B C D 勘

Part 6 (No. 131–146) — ANSWER A B C D 勘

Part 7 (No. 147–200) — ANSWER A B C D 勘

TOEIC® L&Rテスト 究極の模試600問+ Test 1 マークシートA-3 （勘ボックスあり）

実施日 :　　　年　　　月　　　日

Part 1	Part 2	Part 3	Part 4	Listening 計
/ 6	/ 25	/ 39	/ 30	/ 100

換算スコア 　/ 495

Part 5	Part 6	Part 7	Reading 計
/ 30	/ 16	/ 54	/ 100

換算スコア 　/ 495

※解答一覧→本冊p.28〜参照

LISTENING SECTION

Part 1

No.	ANSWER A B C D 勘
1	Ⓐ Ⓑ Ⓒ Ⓓ □
2	Ⓐ Ⓑ Ⓒ Ⓓ □
3	Ⓐ Ⓑ Ⓒ Ⓓ □
4	Ⓐ Ⓑ Ⓒ Ⓓ □
5	Ⓐ Ⓑ Ⓒ Ⓓ □
6	Ⓐ Ⓑ Ⓒ Ⓓ □

Part 2

No.	ANSWER A B C 勘
7	Ⓐ Ⓑ Ⓒ □
8	Ⓐ Ⓑ Ⓒ □
9	Ⓐ Ⓑ Ⓒ □
10	Ⓐ Ⓑ Ⓒ □
11	Ⓐ Ⓑ Ⓒ □
12	Ⓐ Ⓑ Ⓒ □
13	Ⓐ Ⓑ Ⓒ □
14	Ⓐ Ⓑ Ⓒ □
15	Ⓐ Ⓑ Ⓒ □
16	Ⓐ Ⓑ Ⓒ □
17	Ⓐ Ⓑ Ⓒ □
18	Ⓐ Ⓑ Ⓒ □
19	Ⓐ Ⓑ Ⓒ □
20	Ⓐ Ⓑ Ⓒ □
21	Ⓐ Ⓑ Ⓒ □
22	Ⓐ Ⓑ Ⓒ □
23	Ⓐ Ⓑ Ⓒ □
24	Ⓐ Ⓑ Ⓒ □
25	Ⓐ Ⓑ Ⓒ □
26	Ⓐ Ⓑ Ⓒ □
27	Ⓐ Ⓑ Ⓒ □
28	Ⓐ Ⓑ Ⓒ □
29	Ⓐ Ⓑ Ⓒ □
30	Ⓐ Ⓑ Ⓒ □
31	Ⓐ Ⓑ Ⓒ □

Part 3

No.	ANSWER A B C D 勘
32	Ⓐ Ⓑ Ⓒ Ⓓ □
33	Ⓐ Ⓑ Ⓒ Ⓓ □
34	Ⓐ Ⓑ Ⓒ Ⓓ □
35	Ⓐ Ⓑ Ⓒ Ⓓ □
36	Ⓐ Ⓑ Ⓒ Ⓓ □
37	Ⓐ Ⓑ Ⓒ Ⓓ □
38	Ⓐ Ⓑ Ⓒ Ⓓ □
39	Ⓐ Ⓑ Ⓒ Ⓓ □
40	Ⓐ Ⓑ Ⓒ Ⓓ □
41	Ⓐ Ⓑ Ⓒ Ⓓ □
42	Ⓐ Ⓑ Ⓒ Ⓓ □
43	Ⓐ Ⓑ Ⓒ Ⓓ □
44	Ⓐ Ⓑ Ⓒ Ⓓ □
45	Ⓐ Ⓑ Ⓒ Ⓓ □
46	Ⓐ Ⓑ Ⓒ Ⓓ □
47	Ⓐ Ⓑ Ⓒ Ⓓ □
48	Ⓐ Ⓑ Ⓒ Ⓓ □
49	Ⓐ Ⓑ Ⓒ Ⓓ □
50	Ⓐ Ⓑ Ⓒ Ⓓ □
51	Ⓐ Ⓑ Ⓒ Ⓓ □
52	Ⓐ Ⓑ Ⓒ Ⓓ □
53	Ⓐ Ⓑ Ⓒ Ⓓ □
54	Ⓐ Ⓑ Ⓒ Ⓓ □
55	Ⓐ Ⓑ Ⓒ Ⓓ □
56	Ⓐ Ⓑ Ⓒ Ⓓ □
57	Ⓐ Ⓑ Ⓒ Ⓓ □
58	Ⓐ Ⓑ Ⓒ Ⓓ □
59	Ⓐ Ⓑ Ⓒ Ⓓ □
60	Ⓐ Ⓑ Ⓒ Ⓓ □
61	Ⓐ Ⓑ Ⓒ Ⓓ □
62	Ⓐ Ⓑ Ⓒ Ⓓ □
63	Ⓐ Ⓑ Ⓒ Ⓓ □
64	Ⓐ Ⓑ Ⓒ Ⓓ □
65	Ⓐ Ⓑ Ⓒ Ⓓ □
66	Ⓐ Ⓑ Ⓒ Ⓓ □
67	Ⓐ Ⓑ Ⓒ Ⓓ □
68	Ⓐ Ⓑ Ⓒ Ⓓ □
69	Ⓐ Ⓑ Ⓒ Ⓓ □
70	Ⓐ Ⓑ Ⓒ Ⓓ □

Part 4

No.	ANSWER A B C D 勘
71	Ⓐ Ⓑ Ⓒ Ⓓ □
72	Ⓐ Ⓑ Ⓒ Ⓓ □
73	Ⓐ Ⓑ Ⓒ Ⓓ □
74	Ⓐ Ⓑ Ⓒ Ⓓ □
75	Ⓐ Ⓑ Ⓒ Ⓓ □
76	Ⓐ Ⓑ Ⓒ Ⓓ □
77	Ⓐ Ⓑ Ⓒ Ⓓ □
78	Ⓐ Ⓑ Ⓒ Ⓓ □
79	Ⓐ Ⓑ Ⓒ Ⓓ □
80	Ⓐ Ⓑ Ⓒ Ⓓ □
81	Ⓐ Ⓑ Ⓒ Ⓓ □
82	Ⓐ Ⓑ Ⓒ Ⓓ □
83	Ⓐ Ⓑ Ⓒ Ⓓ □
84	Ⓐ Ⓑ Ⓒ Ⓓ □
85	Ⓐ Ⓑ Ⓒ Ⓓ □
86	Ⓐ Ⓑ Ⓒ Ⓓ □
87	Ⓐ Ⓑ Ⓒ Ⓓ □
88	Ⓐ Ⓑ Ⓒ Ⓓ □
89	Ⓐ Ⓑ Ⓒ Ⓓ □
90	Ⓐ Ⓑ Ⓒ Ⓓ □
91	Ⓐ Ⓑ Ⓒ Ⓓ □
92	Ⓐ Ⓑ Ⓒ Ⓓ □
93	Ⓐ Ⓑ Ⓒ Ⓓ □
94	Ⓐ Ⓑ Ⓒ Ⓓ □
95	Ⓐ Ⓑ Ⓒ Ⓓ □
96	Ⓐ Ⓑ Ⓒ Ⓓ □
97	Ⓐ Ⓑ Ⓒ Ⓓ □
98	Ⓐ Ⓑ Ⓒ Ⓓ □
99	Ⓐ Ⓑ Ⓒ Ⓓ □
100	Ⓐ Ⓑ Ⓒ Ⓓ □

READING SECTION

Part 5

No.	ANSWER A B C D 勘
101	Ⓐ Ⓑ Ⓒ Ⓓ □
102	Ⓐ Ⓑ Ⓒ Ⓓ □
103	Ⓐ Ⓑ Ⓒ Ⓓ □
104	Ⓐ Ⓑ Ⓒ Ⓓ □
105	Ⓐ Ⓑ Ⓒ Ⓓ □
106	Ⓐ Ⓑ Ⓒ Ⓓ □
107	Ⓐ Ⓑ Ⓒ Ⓓ □
108	Ⓐ Ⓑ Ⓒ Ⓓ □
109	Ⓐ Ⓑ Ⓒ Ⓓ □
110	Ⓐ Ⓑ Ⓒ Ⓓ □
111	Ⓐ Ⓑ Ⓒ Ⓓ □
112	Ⓐ Ⓑ Ⓒ Ⓓ □
113	Ⓐ Ⓑ Ⓒ Ⓓ □
114	Ⓐ Ⓑ Ⓒ Ⓓ □
115	Ⓐ Ⓑ Ⓒ Ⓓ □
116	Ⓐ Ⓑ Ⓒ Ⓓ □
117	Ⓐ Ⓑ Ⓒ Ⓓ □
118	Ⓐ Ⓑ Ⓒ Ⓓ □
119	Ⓐ Ⓑ Ⓒ Ⓓ □
120	Ⓐ Ⓑ Ⓒ Ⓓ □
121	Ⓐ Ⓑ Ⓒ Ⓓ □
122	Ⓐ Ⓑ Ⓒ Ⓓ □
123	Ⓐ Ⓑ Ⓒ Ⓓ □
124	Ⓐ Ⓑ Ⓒ Ⓓ □
125	Ⓐ Ⓑ Ⓒ Ⓓ □
126	Ⓐ Ⓑ Ⓒ Ⓓ □
127	Ⓐ Ⓑ Ⓒ Ⓓ □
128	Ⓐ Ⓑ Ⓒ Ⓓ □
129	Ⓐ Ⓑ Ⓒ Ⓓ □
130	Ⓐ Ⓑ Ⓒ Ⓓ □

Part 6

No.	ANSWER A B C D 勘
131	Ⓐ Ⓑ Ⓒ Ⓓ □
132	Ⓐ Ⓑ Ⓒ Ⓓ □
133	Ⓐ Ⓑ Ⓒ Ⓓ □
134	Ⓐ Ⓑ Ⓒ Ⓓ □
135	Ⓐ Ⓑ Ⓒ Ⓓ □
136	Ⓐ Ⓑ Ⓒ Ⓓ □
137	Ⓐ Ⓑ Ⓒ Ⓓ □
138	Ⓐ Ⓑ Ⓒ Ⓓ □
139	Ⓐ Ⓑ Ⓒ Ⓓ □
140	Ⓐ Ⓑ Ⓒ Ⓓ □
141	Ⓐ Ⓑ Ⓒ Ⓓ □
142	Ⓐ Ⓑ Ⓒ Ⓓ □
143	Ⓐ Ⓑ Ⓒ Ⓓ □
144	Ⓐ Ⓑ Ⓒ Ⓓ □
145	Ⓐ Ⓑ Ⓒ Ⓓ □
146	Ⓐ Ⓑ Ⓒ Ⓓ □

Part 7

No.	ANSWER A B C D 勘
147	Ⓐ Ⓑ Ⓒ Ⓓ □
148	Ⓐ Ⓑ Ⓒ Ⓓ □
149	Ⓐ Ⓑ Ⓒ Ⓓ □
150	Ⓐ Ⓑ Ⓒ Ⓓ □
151	Ⓐ Ⓑ Ⓒ Ⓓ □
152	Ⓐ Ⓑ Ⓒ Ⓓ □
153	Ⓐ Ⓑ Ⓒ Ⓓ □
154	Ⓐ Ⓑ Ⓒ Ⓓ □
155	Ⓐ Ⓑ Ⓒ Ⓓ □
156	Ⓐ Ⓑ Ⓒ Ⓓ □
157	Ⓐ Ⓑ Ⓒ Ⓓ □
158	Ⓐ Ⓑ Ⓒ Ⓓ □
159	Ⓐ Ⓑ Ⓒ Ⓓ □
160	Ⓐ Ⓑ Ⓒ Ⓓ □
161	Ⓐ Ⓑ Ⓒ Ⓓ □
162	Ⓐ Ⓑ Ⓒ Ⓓ □
163	Ⓐ Ⓑ Ⓒ Ⓓ □
164	Ⓐ Ⓑ Ⓒ Ⓓ □
165	Ⓐ Ⓑ Ⓒ Ⓓ □
166	Ⓐ Ⓑ Ⓒ Ⓓ □
167	Ⓐ Ⓑ Ⓒ Ⓓ □
168	Ⓐ Ⓑ Ⓒ Ⓓ □
169	Ⓐ Ⓑ Ⓒ Ⓓ □
170	Ⓐ Ⓑ Ⓒ Ⓓ □
171	Ⓐ Ⓑ Ⓒ Ⓓ □
172	Ⓐ Ⓑ Ⓒ Ⓓ □
173	Ⓐ Ⓑ Ⓒ Ⓓ □
174	Ⓐ Ⓑ Ⓒ Ⓓ □
175	Ⓐ Ⓑ Ⓒ Ⓓ □
176	Ⓐ Ⓑ Ⓒ Ⓓ □
177	Ⓐ Ⓑ Ⓒ Ⓓ □
178	Ⓐ Ⓑ Ⓒ Ⓓ □
179	Ⓐ Ⓑ Ⓒ Ⓓ □
180	Ⓐ Ⓑ Ⓒ Ⓓ □
181	Ⓐ Ⓑ Ⓒ Ⓓ □
182	Ⓐ Ⓑ Ⓒ Ⓓ □
183	Ⓐ Ⓑ Ⓒ Ⓓ □
184	Ⓐ Ⓑ Ⓒ Ⓓ □
185	Ⓐ Ⓑ Ⓒ Ⓓ □
186	Ⓐ Ⓑ Ⓒ Ⓓ □
187	Ⓐ Ⓑ Ⓒ Ⓓ □
188	Ⓐ Ⓑ Ⓒ Ⓓ □
189	Ⓐ Ⓑ Ⓒ Ⓓ □
190	Ⓐ Ⓑ Ⓒ Ⓓ □
191	Ⓐ Ⓑ Ⓒ Ⓓ □
192	Ⓐ Ⓑ Ⓒ Ⓓ □
193	Ⓐ Ⓑ Ⓒ Ⓓ □
194	Ⓐ Ⓑ Ⓒ Ⓓ □
195	Ⓐ Ⓑ Ⓒ Ⓓ □
196	Ⓐ Ⓑ Ⓒ Ⓓ □
197	Ⓐ Ⓑ Ⓒ Ⓓ □
198	Ⓐ Ⓑ Ⓒ Ⓓ □
199	Ⓐ Ⓑ Ⓒ Ⓓ □
200	Ⓐ Ⓑ Ⓒ Ⓓ □

TOEIC® L&Rテスト 究極の模試600問+ Test 2 マークシートA-1 (勘ボックスあり)

実施日： 　　年　　月　　日

	Part 1	Part 2	Part 3	Part 4	Listening 計	Part 5	Part 6	Part 7	Reading 計
	/6	/25	/39	/30	/100	/30	/16	/54	/100
換算スコア					/495		換算スコア		/495

LISTENING SECTION

Part 1

No.	ANSWER
1	A B C D 勘
2	A B C D 勘
3	A B C D 勘
4	A B C D 勘
5	A B C D 勘
6	A B C D 勘
7	A B C 勘
8	A B C 勘
9	A B C 勘
10	A B C 勘

Part 2

No.	ANSWER
11	A B C 勘
12	A B C 勘
13	A B C 勘
14	A B C 勘
15	A B C 勘
16	A B C 勘
17	A B C 勘
18	A B C 勘
19	A B C 勘
20	A B C 勘

No.	ANSWER
21	A B C 勘
22	A B C 勘
23	A B C 勘
24	A B C 勘
25	A B C 勘
26	A B C 勘
27	A B C 勘
28	A B C 勘
29	A B C 勘
30	A B C 勘

No.	ANSWER
31	A B C 勘
32	A B C 勘
33	A B C D 勘
34	A B C D 勘
35	A B C D 勘
36	A B C D 勘
37	A B C D 勘
38	A B C D 勘
39	A B C D 勘
40	A B C D 勘

Part 3

No.	ANSWER
41	A B C D 勘
42	A B C D 勘
43	A B C D 勘
44	A B C D 勘
45	A B C D 勘
46	A B C D 勘
47	A B C D 勘
48	A B C D 勘
49	A B C D 勘
50	A B C D 勘

No.	ANSWER
51	A B C D 勘
52	A B C D 勘
53	A B C D 勘
54	A B C D 勘
55	A B C D 勘
56	A B C D 勘
57	A B C D 勘
58	A B C D 勘
59	A B C D 勘
60	A B C D 勘

No.	ANSWER
61	A B C D 勘
62	A B C D 勘
63	A B C D 勘
64	A B C D 勘
65	A B C D 勘
66	A B C D 勘
67	A B C D 勘
68	A B C D 勘
69	A B C D 勘
70	A B C D 勘

Part 4

No.	ANSWER
71	A B C D 勘
72	A B C D 勘
73	A B C D 勘
74	A B C D 勘
75	A B C D 勘
76	A B C D 勘
77	A B C D 勘
78	A B C D 勘
79	A B C D 勘
80	A B C D 勘

No.	ANSWER
81	A B C D 勘
82	A B C D 勘
83	A B C D 勘
84	A B C D 勘
85	A B C D 勘
86	A B C D 勘
87	A B C D 勘
88	A B C D 勘
89	A B C D 勘
90	A B C D 勘

No.	ANSWER
91	A B C D 勘
92	A B C D 勘
93	A B C D 勘
94	A B C D 勘
95	A B C D 勘
96	A B C D 勘
97	A B C D 勘
98	A B C D 勘
99	A B C D 勘
100	A B C D 勘

READING SECTION

Part 5

No.	ANSWER
101	A B C D 勘
102	A B C D 勘
103	A B C D 勘
104	A B C D 勘
105	A B C D 勘
106	A B C D 勘
107	A B C D 勘
108	A B C D 勘
109	A B C D 勘
110	A B C D 勘

No.	ANSWER
111	A B C D 勘
112	A B C D 勘
113	A B C D 勘
114	A B C D 勘
115	A B C D 勘
116	A B C D 勘
117	A B C D 勘
118	A B C D 勘
119	A B C D 勘
120	A B C D 勘

No.	ANSWER
121	A B C D 勘
122	A B C D 勘
123	A B C D 勘
124	A B C D 勘
125	A B C D 勘
126	A B C D 勘
127	A B C D 勘
128	A B C D 勘
129	A B C D 勘
130	A B C D 勘

Part 6

No.	ANSWER
131	A B C D 勘
132	A B C D 勘
133	A B C D 勘
134	A B C D 勘
135	A B C D 勘
136	A B C D 勘
137	A B C D 勘
138	A B C D 勘
139	A B C D 勘
140	A B C D 勘

No.	ANSWER
141	A B C D 勘
142	A B C D 勘
143	A B C D 勘
144	A B C D 勘
145	A B C D 勘
146	A B C D 勘
147	A B C D 勘
148	A B C D 勘
149	A B C D 勘
150	A B C D 勘

Part 7

No.	ANSWER
151	A B C D 勘
152	A B C D 勘
153	A B C D 勘
154	A B C D 勘
155	A B C D 勘
156	A B C D 勘
157	A B C D 勘
158	A B C D 勘
159	A B C D 勘
160	A B C D 勘

No.	ANSWER
161	A B C D 勘
162	A B C D 勘
163	A B C D 勘
164	A B C D 勘
165	A B C D 勘
166	A B C D 勘
167	A B C D 勘
168	A B C D 勘
169	A B C D 勘
170	A B C D 勘

No.	ANSWER
171	A B C D 勘
172	A B C D 勘
173	A B C D 勘
174	A B C D 勘
175	A B C D 勘
176	A B C D 勘
177	A B C D 勘
178	A B C D 勘
179	A B C D 勘
180	A B C D 勘

No.	ANSWER
181	A B C D 勘
182	A B C D 勘
183	A B C D 勘
184	A B C D 勘
185	A B C D 勘
186	A B C D 勘
187	A B C D 勘
188	A B C D 勘
189	A B C D 勘
190	A B C D 勘

No.	ANSWER
191	A B C D 勘
192	A B C D 勘
193	A B C D 勘
194	A B C D 勘
195	A B C D 勘
196	A B C D 勘
197	A B C D 勘
198	A B C D 勘
199	A B C D 勘
200	A B C D 勘

※解答一覧→本冊p.144〜参照

TOEIC® L&Rテスト 究極の模試600問⁺ Test 2 マークシートA-2 （勘ボックスあり）

実施日： 　年　　月　　日

	Part 1	Part 2	Part 3	Part 4	Listening 計
	/ 6	/ 25	/ 39	/ 30	/ 100
				換算スコア	/ 495

	Part 5	Part 6	Part 7	Reading 計
	/ 30	/ 16	/ 54	/ 100
			換算スコア	/ 495

※解答一覧→本冊p.144〜参照

LISTENING SECTION

Part 1

No.	ANSWER A B C D 勘
1	Ⓐ Ⓑ Ⓒ Ⓓ □
2	Ⓐ Ⓑ Ⓒ Ⓓ □
3	Ⓐ Ⓑ Ⓒ Ⓓ □
4	Ⓐ Ⓑ Ⓒ Ⓓ □
5	Ⓐ Ⓑ Ⓒ Ⓓ □
6	Ⓐ Ⓑ Ⓒ Ⓓ □

Part 2

No.	ANSWER A B C 勘
7	Ⓐ Ⓑ Ⓒ □
8	Ⓐ Ⓑ Ⓒ □
9	Ⓐ Ⓑ Ⓒ □
10	Ⓐ Ⓑ Ⓒ □
11	Ⓐ Ⓑ Ⓒ □
12	Ⓐ Ⓑ Ⓒ □
13	Ⓐ Ⓑ Ⓒ □
14	Ⓐ Ⓑ Ⓒ □
15	Ⓐ Ⓑ Ⓒ □
16	Ⓐ Ⓑ Ⓒ □
17	Ⓐ Ⓑ Ⓒ □
18	Ⓐ Ⓑ Ⓒ □
19	Ⓐ Ⓑ Ⓒ □
20	Ⓐ Ⓑ Ⓒ □
21	Ⓐ Ⓑ Ⓒ □
22	Ⓐ Ⓑ Ⓒ □
23	Ⓐ Ⓑ Ⓒ □
24	Ⓐ Ⓑ Ⓒ □
25	Ⓐ Ⓑ Ⓒ □
26	Ⓐ Ⓑ Ⓒ □
27	Ⓐ Ⓑ Ⓒ □
28	Ⓐ Ⓑ Ⓒ □
29	Ⓐ Ⓑ Ⓒ □
30	Ⓐ Ⓑ Ⓒ □
31	Ⓐ Ⓑ Ⓒ □

Part 3

No.	ANSWER A B C D 勘
32	Ⓐ Ⓑ Ⓒ Ⓓ □
33	Ⓐ Ⓑ Ⓒ Ⓓ □
34	Ⓐ Ⓑ Ⓒ Ⓓ □
35	Ⓐ Ⓑ Ⓒ Ⓓ □
36	Ⓐ Ⓑ Ⓒ Ⓓ □
37	Ⓐ Ⓑ Ⓒ Ⓓ □
38	Ⓐ Ⓑ Ⓒ Ⓓ □
39	Ⓐ Ⓑ Ⓒ Ⓓ □
40	Ⓐ Ⓑ Ⓒ Ⓓ □
41	Ⓐ Ⓑ Ⓒ Ⓓ □
42	Ⓐ Ⓑ Ⓒ Ⓓ □
43	Ⓐ Ⓑ Ⓒ Ⓓ □
44	Ⓐ Ⓑ Ⓒ Ⓓ □
45	Ⓐ Ⓑ Ⓒ Ⓓ □
46	Ⓐ Ⓑ Ⓒ Ⓓ □
47	Ⓐ Ⓑ Ⓒ Ⓓ □
48	Ⓐ Ⓑ Ⓒ Ⓓ □
49	Ⓐ Ⓑ Ⓒ Ⓓ □
50	Ⓐ Ⓑ Ⓒ Ⓓ □
51	Ⓐ Ⓑ Ⓒ Ⓓ □
52	Ⓐ Ⓑ Ⓒ Ⓓ □
53	Ⓐ Ⓑ Ⓒ Ⓓ □
54	Ⓐ Ⓑ Ⓒ Ⓓ □
55	Ⓐ Ⓑ Ⓒ Ⓓ □
56	Ⓐ Ⓑ Ⓒ Ⓓ □
57	Ⓐ Ⓑ Ⓒ Ⓓ □
58	Ⓐ Ⓑ Ⓒ Ⓓ □
59	Ⓐ Ⓑ Ⓒ Ⓓ □
60	Ⓐ Ⓑ Ⓒ Ⓓ □
61	Ⓐ Ⓑ Ⓒ Ⓓ □
62	Ⓐ Ⓑ Ⓒ Ⓓ □
63	Ⓐ Ⓑ Ⓒ Ⓓ □
64	Ⓐ Ⓑ Ⓒ Ⓓ □
65	Ⓐ Ⓑ Ⓒ Ⓓ □
66	Ⓐ Ⓑ Ⓒ Ⓓ □
67	Ⓐ Ⓑ Ⓒ Ⓓ □
68	Ⓐ Ⓑ Ⓒ Ⓓ □
69	Ⓐ Ⓑ Ⓒ Ⓓ □
70	Ⓐ Ⓑ Ⓒ Ⓓ □

Part 4

No.	ANSWER A B C D 勘
71	Ⓐ Ⓑ Ⓒ Ⓓ □
72	Ⓐ Ⓑ Ⓒ Ⓓ □
73	Ⓐ Ⓑ Ⓒ Ⓓ □
74	Ⓐ Ⓑ Ⓒ Ⓓ □
75	Ⓐ Ⓑ Ⓒ Ⓓ □
76	Ⓐ Ⓑ Ⓒ Ⓓ □
77	Ⓐ Ⓑ Ⓒ Ⓓ □
78	Ⓐ Ⓑ Ⓒ Ⓓ □
79	Ⓐ Ⓑ Ⓒ Ⓓ □
80	Ⓐ Ⓑ Ⓒ Ⓓ □
81	Ⓐ Ⓑ Ⓒ Ⓓ □
82	Ⓐ Ⓑ Ⓒ Ⓓ □
83	Ⓐ Ⓑ Ⓒ Ⓓ □
84	Ⓐ Ⓑ Ⓒ Ⓓ □
85	Ⓐ Ⓑ Ⓒ Ⓓ □
86	Ⓐ Ⓑ Ⓒ Ⓓ □
87	Ⓐ Ⓑ Ⓒ Ⓓ □
88	Ⓐ Ⓑ Ⓒ Ⓓ □
89	Ⓐ Ⓑ Ⓒ Ⓓ □
90	Ⓐ Ⓑ Ⓒ Ⓓ □
91	Ⓐ Ⓑ Ⓒ Ⓓ □
92	Ⓐ Ⓑ Ⓒ Ⓓ □
93	Ⓐ Ⓑ Ⓒ Ⓓ □
94	Ⓐ Ⓑ Ⓒ Ⓓ □
95	Ⓐ Ⓑ Ⓒ Ⓓ □
96	Ⓐ Ⓑ Ⓒ Ⓓ □
97	Ⓐ Ⓑ Ⓒ Ⓓ □
98	Ⓐ Ⓑ Ⓒ Ⓓ □
99	Ⓐ Ⓑ Ⓒ Ⓓ □
100	Ⓐ Ⓑ Ⓒ Ⓓ □

READING SECTION

Part 5

No.	ANSWER A B C D 勘
101	Ⓐ Ⓑ Ⓒ Ⓓ □
102	Ⓐ Ⓑ Ⓒ Ⓓ □
103	Ⓐ Ⓑ Ⓒ Ⓓ □
104	Ⓐ Ⓑ Ⓒ Ⓓ □
105	Ⓐ Ⓑ Ⓒ Ⓓ □
106	Ⓐ Ⓑ Ⓒ Ⓓ □
107	Ⓐ Ⓑ Ⓒ Ⓓ □
108	Ⓐ Ⓑ Ⓒ Ⓓ □
109	Ⓐ Ⓑ Ⓒ Ⓓ □
110	Ⓐ Ⓑ Ⓒ Ⓓ □
111	Ⓐ Ⓑ Ⓒ Ⓓ □
112	Ⓐ Ⓑ Ⓒ Ⓓ □
113	Ⓐ Ⓑ Ⓒ Ⓓ □
114	Ⓐ Ⓑ Ⓒ Ⓓ □
115	Ⓐ Ⓑ Ⓒ Ⓓ □
116	Ⓐ Ⓑ Ⓒ Ⓓ □
117	Ⓐ Ⓑ Ⓒ Ⓓ □
118	Ⓐ Ⓑ Ⓒ Ⓓ □
119	Ⓐ Ⓑ Ⓒ Ⓓ □
120	Ⓐ Ⓑ Ⓒ Ⓓ □
121	Ⓐ Ⓑ Ⓒ Ⓓ □
122	Ⓐ Ⓑ Ⓒ Ⓓ □
123	Ⓐ Ⓑ Ⓒ Ⓓ □
124	Ⓐ Ⓑ Ⓒ Ⓓ □
125	Ⓐ Ⓑ Ⓒ Ⓓ □
126	Ⓐ Ⓑ Ⓒ Ⓓ □
127	Ⓐ Ⓑ Ⓒ Ⓓ □
128	Ⓐ Ⓑ Ⓒ Ⓓ □
129	Ⓐ Ⓑ Ⓒ Ⓓ □
130	Ⓐ Ⓑ Ⓒ Ⓓ □

Part 6

No.	ANSWER A B C D 勘
131	Ⓐ Ⓑ Ⓒ Ⓓ □
132	Ⓐ Ⓑ Ⓒ Ⓓ □
133	Ⓐ Ⓑ Ⓒ Ⓓ □
134	Ⓐ Ⓑ Ⓒ Ⓓ □
135	Ⓐ Ⓑ Ⓒ Ⓓ □
136	Ⓐ Ⓑ Ⓒ Ⓓ □
137	Ⓐ Ⓑ Ⓒ Ⓓ □
138	Ⓐ Ⓑ Ⓒ Ⓓ □
139	Ⓐ Ⓑ Ⓒ Ⓓ □
140	Ⓐ Ⓑ Ⓒ Ⓓ □

Part 7

No.	ANSWER A B C D 勘
141	Ⓐ Ⓑ Ⓒ Ⓓ □
142	Ⓐ Ⓑ Ⓒ Ⓓ □
143	Ⓐ Ⓑ Ⓒ Ⓓ □
144	Ⓐ Ⓑ Ⓒ Ⓓ □
145	Ⓐ Ⓑ Ⓒ Ⓓ □
146	Ⓐ Ⓑ Ⓒ Ⓓ □
147	Ⓐ Ⓑ Ⓒ Ⓓ □
148	Ⓐ Ⓑ Ⓒ Ⓓ □
149	Ⓐ Ⓑ Ⓒ Ⓓ □
150	Ⓐ Ⓑ Ⓒ Ⓓ □
151	Ⓐ Ⓑ Ⓒ Ⓓ □
152	Ⓐ Ⓑ Ⓒ Ⓓ □
153	Ⓐ Ⓑ Ⓒ Ⓓ □
154	Ⓐ Ⓑ Ⓒ Ⓓ □
155	Ⓐ Ⓑ Ⓒ Ⓓ □
156	Ⓐ Ⓑ Ⓒ Ⓓ □
157	Ⓐ Ⓑ Ⓒ Ⓓ □
158	Ⓐ Ⓑ Ⓒ Ⓓ □
159	Ⓐ Ⓑ Ⓒ Ⓓ □
160	Ⓐ Ⓑ Ⓒ Ⓓ □
161	Ⓐ Ⓑ Ⓒ Ⓓ □
162	Ⓐ Ⓑ Ⓒ Ⓓ □
163	Ⓐ Ⓑ Ⓒ Ⓓ □
164	Ⓐ Ⓑ Ⓒ Ⓓ □
165	Ⓐ Ⓑ Ⓒ Ⓓ □
166	Ⓐ Ⓑ Ⓒ Ⓓ □
167	Ⓐ Ⓑ Ⓒ Ⓓ □
168	Ⓐ Ⓑ Ⓒ Ⓓ □
169	Ⓐ Ⓑ Ⓒ Ⓓ □
170	Ⓐ Ⓑ Ⓒ Ⓓ □
171	Ⓐ Ⓑ Ⓒ Ⓓ □
172	Ⓐ Ⓑ Ⓒ Ⓓ □
173	Ⓐ Ⓑ Ⓒ Ⓓ □
174	Ⓐ Ⓑ Ⓒ Ⓓ □
175	Ⓐ Ⓑ Ⓒ Ⓓ □
176	Ⓐ Ⓑ Ⓒ Ⓓ □
177	Ⓐ Ⓑ Ⓒ Ⓓ □
178	Ⓐ Ⓑ Ⓒ Ⓓ □
179	Ⓐ Ⓑ Ⓒ Ⓓ □
180	Ⓐ Ⓑ Ⓒ Ⓓ □
181	Ⓐ Ⓑ Ⓒ Ⓓ □
182	Ⓐ Ⓑ Ⓒ Ⓓ □
183	Ⓐ Ⓑ Ⓒ Ⓓ □
184	Ⓐ Ⓑ Ⓒ Ⓓ □
185	Ⓐ Ⓑ Ⓒ Ⓓ □
186	Ⓐ Ⓑ Ⓒ Ⓓ □
187	Ⓐ Ⓑ Ⓒ Ⓓ □
188	Ⓐ Ⓑ Ⓒ Ⓓ □
189	Ⓐ Ⓑ Ⓒ Ⓓ □
190	Ⓐ Ⓑ Ⓒ Ⓓ □
191	Ⓐ Ⓑ Ⓒ Ⓓ □
192	Ⓐ Ⓑ Ⓒ Ⓓ □
193	Ⓐ Ⓑ Ⓒ Ⓓ □
194	Ⓐ Ⓑ Ⓒ Ⓓ □
195	Ⓐ Ⓑ Ⓒ Ⓓ □
196	Ⓐ Ⓑ Ⓒ Ⓓ □
197	Ⓐ Ⓑ Ⓒ Ⓓ □
198	Ⓐ Ⓑ Ⓒ Ⓓ □
199	Ⓐ Ⓑ Ⓒ Ⓓ □
200	Ⓐ Ⓑ Ⓒ Ⓓ □

TOEIC® L&Rテスト 究極の模試600問+ Test 2 マークシートA-3 (勘ボックスあり)

実施日： 　　年　　月　　日

	Part 1	Part 2	Part 3	Part 4	Listening 計	Part 5	Part 6	Part 7	Reading 計
	/6	/25	/39	/30		/30	/16	/54	
換算スコア					/495		換算スコア		/495
					/100				/100

LISTENING SECTION

Part 1 — No. 1〜6 (ANSWER: A B C 勘)

Part 2 — No. 7〜31 (ANSWER: A B C 勘)

Part 3 — No. 32〜70 (ANSWER: A B C D 勘)

Part 4 — No. 71〜100 (ANSWER: A B C D 勘)

READING SECTION

Part 5 — No. 101〜130 (ANSWER: A B C D 勘)

Part 6 — No. 131〜146 (ANSWER: A B C D 勘)

Part 7 — No. 147〜200 (ANSWER: A B C D 勘)

※解答一覧→本冊p.144〜参照

TOEIC® L&Rテスト 究極の模試600問⁺　Test 3 マークシートA-1 （勘ボックスあり）

実施日：　　年　　月　　日

	Part 1	Part 2	Part 3	Part 4	Listening 計
	/ 6	/ 25	/ 39	/ 30	/ 100
				換算スコア	/ 495

	Part 5	Part 6	Part 7	Reading 計
	/ 30	/ 16	/ 54	/ 100
			換算スコア	/ 495

LISTENING SECTION

Part 1

No.	ANSWER A B C D 勘
1	Ⓐ Ⓑ Ⓒ Ⓓ ☐
2	Ⓐ Ⓑ Ⓒ Ⓓ ☐
3	Ⓐ Ⓑ Ⓒ Ⓓ ☐
4	Ⓐ Ⓑ Ⓒ Ⓓ ☐
5	Ⓐ Ⓑ Ⓒ Ⓓ ☐
6	Ⓐ Ⓑ Ⓒ Ⓓ ☐

Part 2

No.	ANSWER A B C 勘
7	Ⓐ Ⓑ Ⓒ ☐
8	Ⓐ Ⓑ Ⓒ ☐
9	Ⓐ Ⓑ Ⓒ ☐
10	Ⓐ Ⓑ Ⓒ ☐
11	Ⓐ Ⓑ Ⓒ ☐
12	Ⓐ Ⓑ Ⓒ ☐
13	Ⓐ Ⓑ Ⓒ ☐
14	Ⓐ Ⓑ Ⓒ ☐
15	Ⓐ Ⓑ Ⓒ ☐
16	Ⓐ Ⓑ Ⓒ ☐
17	Ⓐ Ⓑ Ⓒ ☐
18	Ⓐ Ⓑ Ⓒ ☐
19	Ⓐ Ⓑ Ⓒ ☐
20	Ⓐ Ⓑ Ⓒ ☐
21	Ⓐ Ⓑ Ⓒ ☐
22	Ⓐ Ⓑ Ⓒ ☐
23	Ⓐ Ⓑ Ⓒ ☐
24	Ⓐ Ⓑ Ⓒ ☐
25	Ⓐ Ⓑ Ⓒ ☐
26	Ⓐ Ⓑ Ⓒ ☐
27	Ⓐ Ⓑ Ⓒ ☐
28	Ⓐ Ⓑ Ⓒ ☐
29	Ⓐ Ⓑ Ⓒ ☐
30	Ⓐ Ⓑ Ⓒ ☐
31	Ⓐ Ⓑ Ⓒ ☐

Part 3

No.	ANSWER A B C D 勘
32	Ⓐ Ⓑ Ⓒ Ⓓ ☐
33	Ⓐ Ⓑ Ⓒ Ⓓ ☐
34	Ⓐ Ⓑ Ⓒ Ⓓ ☐
35	Ⓐ Ⓑ Ⓒ Ⓓ ☐
36	Ⓐ Ⓑ Ⓒ Ⓓ ☐
37	Ⓐ Ⓑ Ⓒ Ⓓ ☐
38	Ⓐ Ⓑ Ⓒ Ⓓ ☐
39	Ⓐ Ⓑ Ⓒ Ⓓ ☐
40	Ⓐ Ⓑ Ⓒ Ⓓ ☐
41	Ⓐ Ⓑ Ⓒ Ⓓ ☐
42	Ⓐ Ⓑ Ⓒ Ⓓ ☐
43	Ⓐ Ⓑ Ⓒ Ⓓ ☐
44	Ⓐ Ⓑ Ⓒ Ⓓ ☐
45	Ⓐ Ⓑ Ⓒ Ⓓ ☐
46	Ⓐ Ⓑ Ⓒ Ⓓ ☐
47	Ⓐ Ⓑ Ⓒ Ⓓ ☐
48	Ⓐ Ⓑ Ⓒ Ⓓ ☐
49	Ⓐ Ⓑ Ⓒ Ⓓ ☐
50	Ⓐ Ⓑ Ⓒ Ⓓ ☐
51	Ⓐ Ⓑ Ⓒ Ⓓ ☐
52	Ⓐ Ⓑ Ⓒ Ⓓ ☐
53	Ⓐ Ⓑ Ⓒ Ⓓ ☐
54	Ⓐ Ⓑ Ⓒ Ⓓ ☐
55	Ⓐ Ⓑ Ⓒ Ⓓ ☐
56	Ⓐ Ⓑ Ⓒ Ⓓ ☐
57	Ⓐ Ⓑ Ⓒ Ⓓ ☐
58	Ⓐ Ⓑ Ⓒ Ⓓ ☐
59	Ⓐ Ⓑ Ⓒ Ⓓ ☐
60	Ⓐ Ⓑ Ⓒ Ⓓ ☐
61	Ⓐ Ⓑ Ⓒ Ⓓ ☐
62	Ⓐ Ⓑ Ⓒ Ⓓ ☐
63	Ⓐ Ⓑ Ⓒ Ⓓ ☐
64	Ⓐ Ⓑ Ⓒ Ⓓ ☐
65	Ⓐ Ⓑ Ⓒ Ⓓ ☐
66	Ⓐ Ⓑ Ⓒ Ⓓ ☐
67	Ⓐ Ⓑ Ⓒ Ⓓ ☐
68	Ⓐ Ⓑ Ⓒ Ⓓ ☐
69	Ⓐ Ⓑ Ⓒ Ⓓ ☐
70	Ⓐ Ⓑ Ⓒ Ⓓ ☐

Part 4

No.	ANSWER A B C D 勘
71	Ⓐ Ⓑ Ⓒ Ⓓ ☐
72	Ⓐ Ⓑ Ⓒ Ⓓ ☐
73	Ⓐ Ⓑ Ⓒ Ⓓ ☐
74	Ⓐ Ⓑ Ⓒ Ⓓ ☐
75	Ⓐ Ⓑ Ⓒ Ⓓ ☐
76	Ⓐ Ⓑ Ⓒ Ⓓ ☐
77	Ⓐ Ⓑ Ⓒ Ⓓ ☐
78	Ⓐ Ⓑ Ⓒ Ⓓ ☐
79	Ⓐ Ⓑ Ⓒ Ⓓ ☐
80	Ⓐ Ⓑ Ⓒ Ⓓ ☐
81	Ⓐ Ⓑ Ⓒ Ⓓ ☐
82	Ⓐ Ⓑ Ⓒ Ⓓ ☐
83	Ⓐ Ⓑ Ⓒ Ⓓ ☐
84	Ⓐ Ⓑ Ⓒ Ⓓ ☐
85	Ⓐ Ⓑ Ⓒ Ⓓ ☐
86	Ⓐ Ⓑ Ⓒ Ⓓ ☐
87	Ⓐ Ⓑ Ⓒ Ⓓ ☐
88	Ⓐ Ⓑ Ⓒ Ⓓ ☐
89	Ⓐ Ⓑ Ⓒ Ⓓ ☐
90	Ⓐ Ⓑ Ⓒ Ⓓ ☐
91	Ⓐ Ⓑ Ⓒ Ⓓ ☐
92	Ⓐ Ⓑ Ⓒ Ⓓ ☐
93	Ⓐ Ⓑ Ⓒ Ⓓ ☐
94	Ⓐ Ⓑ Ⓒ Ⓓ ☐
95	Ⓐ Ⓑ Ⓒ Ⓓ ☐
96	Ⓐ Ⓑ Ⓒ Ⓓ ☐
97	Ⓐ Ⓑ Ⓒ Ⓓ ☐
98	Ⓐ Ⓑ Ⓒ Ⓓ ☐
99	Ⓐ Ⓑ Ⓒ Ⓓ ☐
100	Ⓐ Ⓑ Ⓒ Ⓓ ☐

READING SECTION

Part 5

No.	ANSWER A B C D 勘
101	Ⓐ Ⓑ Ⓒ Ⓓ ☐
102	Ⓐ Ⓑ Ⓒ Ⓓ ☐
103	Ⓐ Ⓑ Ⓒ Ⓓ ☐
104	Ⓐ Ⓑ Ⓒ Ⓓ ☐
105	Ⓐ Ⓑ Ⓒ Ⓓ ☐
106	Ⓐ Ⓑ Ⓒ Ⓓ ☐
107	Ⓐ Ⓑ Ⓒ Ⓓ ☐
108	Ⓐ Ⓑ Ⓒ Ⓓ ☐
109	Ⓐ Ⓑ Ⓒ Ⓓ ☐
110	Ⓐ Ⓑ Ⓒ Ⓓ ☐

Part 6

No.	ANSWER A B C D 勘
111	Ⓐ Ⓑ Ⓒ Ⓓ ☐
112	Ⓐ Ⓑ Ⓒ Ⓓ ☐
113	Ⓐ Ⓑ Ⓒ Ⓓ ☐
114	Ⓐ Ⓑ Ⓒ Ⓓ ☐
115	Ⓐ Ⓑ Ⓒ Ⓓ ☐
116	Ⓐ Ⓑ Ⓒ Ⓓ ☐
117	Ⓐ Ⓑ Ⓒ Ⓓ ☐
118	Ⓐ Ⓑ Ⓒ Ⓓ ☐
119	Ⓐ Ⓑ Ⓒ Ⓓ ☐
120	Ⓐ Ⓑ Ⓒ Ⓓ ☐
121	Ⓐ Ⓑ Ⓒ Ⓓ ☐
122	Ⓐ Ⓑ Ⓒ Ⓓ ☐
123	Ⓐ Ⓑ Ⓒ Ⓓ ☐
124	Ⓐ Ⓑ Ⓒ Ⓓ ☐
125	Ⓐ Ⓑ Ⓒ Ⓓ ☐
126	Ⓐ Ⓑ Ⓒ Ⓓ ☐
127	Ⓐ Ⓑ Ⓒ Ⓓ ☐
128	Ⓐ Ⓑ Ⓒ Ⓓ ☐
129	Ⓐ Ⓑ Ⓒ Ⓓ ☐
130	Ⓐ Ⓑ Ⓒ Ⓓ ☐

Part 7

No.	ANSWER A B C D 勘
131	Ⓐ Ⓑ Ⓒ Ⓓ ☐
132	Ⓐ Ⓑ Ⓒ Ⓓ ☐
133	Ⓐ Ⓑ Ⓒ Ⓓ ☐
134	Ⓐ Ⓑ Ⓒ Ⓓ ☐
135	Ⓐ Ⓑ Ⓒ Ⓓ ☐
136	Ⓐ Ⓑ Ⓒ Ⓓ ☐
137	Ⓐ Ⓑ Ⓒ Ⓓ ☐
138	Ⓐ Ⓑ Ⓒ Ⓓ ☐
139	Ⓐ Ⓑ Ⓒ Ⓓ ☐
140	Ⓐ Ⓑ Ⓒ Ⓓ ☐
141	Ⓐ Ⓑ Ⓒ Ⓓ ☐
142	Ⓐ Ⓑ Ⓒ Ⓓ ☐
143	Ⓐ Ⓑ Ⓒ Ⓓ ☐
144	Ⓐ Ⓑ Ⓒ Ⓓ ☐
145	Ⓐ Ⓑ Ⓒ Ⓓ ☐
146	Ⓐ Ⓑ Ⓒ Ⓓ ☐
147	Ⓐ Ⓑ Ⓒ Ⓓ ☐
148	Ⓐ Ⓑ Ⓒ Ⓓ ☐
149	Ⓐ Ⓑ Ⓒ Ⓓ ☐
150	Ⓐ Ⓑ Ⓒ Ⓓ ☐
151	Ⓐ Ⓑ Ⓒ Ⓓ ☐
152	Ⓐ Ⓑ Ⓒ Ⓓ ☐
153	Ⓐ Ⓑ Ⓒ Ⓓ ☐
154	Ⓐ Ⓑ Ⓒ Ⓓ ☐
155	Ⓐ Ⓑ Ⓒ Ⓓ ☐
156	Ⓐ Ⓑ Ⓒ Ⓓ ☐
157	Ⓐ Ⓑ Ⓒ Ⓓ ☐
158	Ⓐ Ⓑ Ⓒ Ⓓ ☐
159	Ⓐ Ⓑ Ⓒ Ⓓ ☐
160	Ⓐ Ⓑ Ⓒ Ⓓ ☐
161	Ⓐ Ⓑ Ⓒ Ⓓ ☐
162	Ⓐ Ⓑ Ⓒ Ⓓ ☐
163	Ⓐ Ⓑ Ⓒ Ⓓ ☐
164	Ⓐ Ⓑ Ⓒ Ⓓ ☐
165	Ⓐ Ⓑ Ⓒ Ⓓ ☐
166	Ⓐ Ⓑ Ⓒ Ⓓ ☐
167	Ⓐ Ⓑ Ⓒ Ⓓ ☐
168	Ⓐ Ⓑ Ⓒ Ⓓ ☐
169	Ⓐ Ⓑ Ⓒ Ⓓ ☐
170	Ⓐ Ⓑ Ⓒ Ⓓ ☐
171	Ⓐ Ⓑ Ⓒ Ⓓ ☐
172	Ⓐ Ⓑ Ⓒ Ⓓ ☐
173	Ⓐ Ⓑ Ⓒ Ⓓ ☐
174	Ⓐ Ⓑ Ⓒ Ⓓ ☐
175	Ⓐ Ⓑ Ⓒ Ⓓ ☐
176	Ⓐ Ⓑ Ⓒ Ⓓ ☐
177	Ⓐ Ⓑ Ⓒ Ⓓ ☐
178	Ⓐ Ⓑ Ⓒ Ⓓ ☐
179	Ⓐ Ⓑ Ⓒ Ⓓ ☐
180	Ⓐ Ⓑ Ⓒ Ⓓ ☐
181	Ⓐ Ⓑ Ⓒ Ⓓ ☐
182	Ⓐ Ⓑ Ⓒ Ⓓ ☐
183	Ⓐ Ⓑ Ⓒ Ⓓ ☐
184	Ⓐ Ⓑ Ⓒ Ⓓ ☐
185	Ⓐ Ⓑ Ⓒ Ⓓ ☐
186	Ⓐ Ⓑ Ⓒ Ⓓ ☐
187	Ⓐ Ⓑ Ⓒ Ⓓ ☐
188	Ⓐ Ⓑ Ⓒ Ⓓ ☐
189	Ⓐ Ⓑ Ⓒ Ⓓ ☐
190	Ⓐ Ⓑ Ⓒ Ⓓ ☐
191	Ⓐ Ⓑ Ⓒ Ⓓ ☐
192	Ⓐ Ⓑ Ⓒ Ⓓ ☐
193	Ⓐ Ⓑ Ⓒ Ⓓ ☐
194	Ⓐ Ⓑ Ⓒ Ⓓ ☐
195	Ⓐ Ⓑ Ⓒ Ⓓ ☐
196	Ⓐ Ⓑ Ⓒ Ⓓ ☐
197	Ⓐ Ⓑ Ⓒ Ⓓ ☐
198	Ⓐ Ⓑ Ⓒ Ⓓ ☐
199	Ⓐ Ⓑ Ⓒ Ⓓ ☐
200	Ⓐ Ⓑ Ⓒ Ⓓ ☐

※解答一覧→本冊p.260～参照

TOEIC® L&Rテスト 究極の模試600問+ Test 3 マークシートA-2 （勘ボックスあり）

実施日 ：　　　　年　　　月　　　日

	Part 1	Part 2	Part 3	Part 4	Listening 計	Part 5	Part 6	Part 7	Reading 計
	/6	/25	/39	/30		/30	/16	/54	
換算スコア					/495			換算スコア	/495
					Listening 計				/100

LISTENING SECTION

Part 1 — No. 1〜6 ANSWER A B C D 勘

Part 1 / Part 2 — No. 7〜10, 11〜20, 21〜30, 31〜40 ANSWER A B C 勘

Part 3 — No. 41〜50, 51〜60, 61〜70 ANSWER A B C D 勘

Part 4 — No. 71〜80, 81〜90, 91〜100 ANSWER A B C D 勘

READING SECTION

Part 5 — No. 101〜110, 111〜120, 121〜130, 131〜140, 141〜150 ANSWER A B C D 勘

Part 6 — No. 131〜140, 141〜150 ANSWER A B C D 勘

Part 7 — No. 151〜160, 161〜170, 171〜180, 181〜190, 191〜200 ANSWER A B C D 勘

※解答一覧→本冊p.260〜参照

TOEIC® L&Rテスト 究極の模試600問⁺ Test 3 マークシートA-3 （勘ボックスあり）

実施日： 　　年　　月　　日

	Part 1	Part 2	Part 3	Part 4	Listening 計
	/ 6	/ 25	/ 39	/ 30	/ 100
換算スコア					/ 495

	Part 5	Part 6	Part 7	Reading 計
	/ 30	/ 16	/ 54	/ 100
換算スコア				/ 495

LISTENING SECTION

Part 1 / Part 2

No.	ANSWER A B C D 勘	No.	ANSWER A B C 勘	No.	ANSWER A B C 勘
1	Ⓐ Ⓑ Ⓒ Ⓓ ☐	11	Ⓐ Ⓑ Ⓒ ☐	21	Ⓐ Ⓑ Ⓒ ☐
2	Ⓐ Ⓑ Ⓒ Ⓓ ☐	12	Ⓐ Ⓑ Ⓒ ☐	22	Ⓐ Ⓑ Ⓒ ☐
3	Ⓐ Ⓑ Ⓒ Ⓓ ☐	13	Ⓐ Ⓑ Ⓒ ☐	23	Ⓐ Ⓑ Ⓒ ☐
4	Ⓐ Ⓑ Ⓒ Ⓓ ☐	14	Ⓐ Ⓑ Ⓒ ☐	24	Ⓐ Ⓑ Ⓒ ☐
5	Ⓐ Ⓑ Ⓒ Ⓓ ☐	15	Ⓐ Ⓑ Ⓒ ☐	25	Ⓐ Ⓑ Ⓒ ☐
6	Ⓐ Ⓑ Ⓒ Ⓓ ☐	16	Ⓐ Ⓑ Ⓒ ☐	26	Ⓐ Ⓑ Ⓒ ☐
7	Ⓐ Ⓑ Ⓒ ☐	17	Ⓐ Ⓑ Ⓒ ☐	27	Ⓐ Ⓑ Ⓒ ☐
8	Ⓐ Ⓑ Ⓒ ☐	18	Ⓐ Ⓑ Ⓒ ☐	28	Ⓐ Ⓑ Ⓒ ☐
9	Ⓐ Ⓑ Ⓒ ☐	19	Ⓐ Ⓑ Ⓒ ☐	29	Ⓐ Ⓑ Ⓒ ☐
10	Ⓐ Ⓑ Ⓒ ☐	20	Ⓐ Ⓑ Ⓒ ☐	30	Ⓐ Ⓑ Ⓒ ☐

Part 3

No.	ANSWER A B C 勘	No.	ANSWER A B C D 勘	No.	ANSWER A B C D 勘
31	Ⓐ Ⓑ Ⓒ ☐	41	Ⓐ Ⓑ Ⓒ Ⓓ ☐	51	Ⓐ Ⓑ Ⓒ Ⓓ ☐
32	Ⓐ Ⓑ Ⓒ Ⓓ ☐	42	Ⓐ Ⓑ Ⓒ Ⓓ ☐	52	Ⓐ Ⓑ Ⓒ Ⓓ ☐
33	Ⓐ Ⓑ Ⓒ Ⓓ ☐	43	Ⓐ Ⓑ Ⓒ Ⓓ ☐	53	Ⓐ Ⓑ Ⓒ Ⓓ ☐
34	Ⓐ Ⓑ Ⓒ Ⓓ ☐	44	Ⓐ Ⓑ Ⓒ Ⓓ ☐	54	Ⓐ Ⓑ Ⓒ Ⓓ ☐
35	Ⓐ Ⓑ Ⓒ Ⓓ ☐	45	Ⓐ Ⓑ Ⓒ Ⓓ ☐	55	Ⓐ Ⓑ Ⓒ Ⓓ ☐
36	Ⓐ Ⓑ Ⓒ Ⓓ ☐	46	Ⓐ Ⓑ Ⓒ Ⓓ ☐	56	Ⓐ Ⓑ Ⓒ Ⓓ ☐
37	Ⓐ Ⓑ Ⓒ Ⓓ ☐	47	Ⓐ Ⓑ Ⓒ Ⓓ ☐	57	Ⓐ Ⓑ Ⓒ Ⓓ ☐
38	Ⓐ Ⓑ Ⓒ Ⓓ ☐	48	Ⓐ Ⓑ Ⓒ Ⓓ ☐	58	Ⓐ Ⓑ Ⓒ Ⓓ ☐
39	Ⓐ Ⓑ Ⓒ Ⓓ ☐	49	Ⓐ Ⓑ Ⓒ Ⓓ ☐	59	Ⓐ Ⓑ Ⓒ Ⓓ ☐
40	Ⓐ Ⓑ Ⓒ Ⓓ ☐	50	Ⓐ Ⓑ Ⓒ Ⓓ ☐	60	Ⓐ Ⓑ Ⓒ Ⓓ ☐

Part 4

No.	ANSWER A B C D 勘	No.	ANSWER A B C D 勘	No.	ANSWER A B C D 勘
61	Ⓐ Ⓑ Ⓒ Ⓓ ☐	71	Ⓐ Ⓑ Ⓒ Ⓓ ☐	81	Ⓐ Ⓑ Ⓒ Ⓓ ☐
62	Ⓐ Ⓑ Ⓒ Ⓓ ☐	72	Ⓐ Ⓑ Ⓒ Ⓓ ☐	82	Ⓐ Ⓑ Ⓒ Ⓓ ☐
63	Ⓐ Ⓑ Ⓒ Ⓓ ☐	73	Ⓐ Ⓑ Ⓒ Ⓓ ☐	83	Ⓐ Ⓑ Ⓒ Ⓓ ☐
64	Ⓐ Ⓑ Ⓒ Ⓓ ☐	74	Ⓐ Ⓑ Ⓒ Ⓓ ☐	84	Ⓐ Ⓑ Ⓒ Ⓓ ☐
65	Ⓐ Ⓑ Ⓒ Ⓓ ☐	75	Ⓐ Ⓑ Ⓒ Ⓓ ☐	85	Ⓐ Ⓑ Ⓒ Ⓓ ☐
66	Ⓐ Ⓑ Ⓒ Ⓓ ☐	76	Ⓐ Ⓑ Ⓒ Ⓓ ☐	86	Ⓐ Ⓑ Ⓒ Ⓓ ☐
67	Ⓐ Ⓑ Ⓒ Ⓓ ☐	77	Ⓐ Ⓑ Ⓒ Ⓓ ☐	87	Ⓐ Ⓑ Ⓒ Ⓓ ☐
68	Ⓐ Ⓑ Ⓒ Ⓓ ☐	78	Ⓐ Ⓑ Ⓒ Ⓓ ☐	88	Ⓐ Ⓑ Ⓒ Ⓓ ☐
69	Ⓐ Ⓑ Ⓒ Ⓓ ☐	79	Ⓐ Ⓑ Ⓒ Ⓓ ☐	89	Ⓐ Ⓑ Ⓒ Ⓓ ☐
70	Ⓐ Ⓑ Ⓒ Ⓓ ☐	80	Ⓐ Ⓑ Ⓒ Ⓓ ☐	90	Ⓐ Ⓑ Ⓒ Ⓓ ☐

No.	ANSWER A B C D 勘
91	Ⓐ Ⓑ Ⓒ Ⓓ ☐
92	Ⓐ Ⓑ Ⓒ Ⓓ ☐
93	Ⓐ Ⓑ Ⓒ Ⓓ ☐
94	Ⓐ Ⓑ Ⓒ Ⓓ ☐
95	Ⓐ Ⓑ Ⓒ Ⓓ ☐
96	Ⓐ Ⓑ Ⓒ Ⓓ ☐
97	Ⓐ Ⓑ Ⓒ Ⓓ ☐
98	Ⓐ Ⓑ Ⓒ Ⓓ ☐
99	Ⓐ Ⓑ Ⓒ Ⓓ ☐
100	Ⓐ Ⓑ Ⓒ Ⓓ ☐

READING SECTION

Part 5

No.	ANSWER A B C D 勘	No.	ANSWER A B C D 勘	No.	ANSWER A B C D 勘
101	Ⓐ Ⓑ Ⓒ Ⓓ ☐	111	Ⓐ Ⓑ Ⓒ Ⓓ ☐	121	Ⓐ Ⓑ Ⓒ Ⓓ ☐
102	Ⓐ Ⓑ Ⓒ Ⓓ ☐	112	Ⓐ Ⓑ Ⓒ Ⓓ ☐	122	Ⓐ Ⓑ Ⓒ Ⓓ ☐
103	Ⓐ Ⓑ Ⓒ Ⓓ ☐	113	Ⓐ Ⓑ Ⓒ Ⓓ ☐	123	Ⓐ Ⓑ Ⓒ Ⓓ ☐
104	Ⓐ Ⓑ Ⓒ Ⓓ ☐	114	Ⓐ Ⓑ Ⓒ Ⓓ ☐	124	Ⓐ Ⓑ Ⓒ Ⓓ ☐
105	Ⓐ Ⓑ Ⓒ Ⓓ ☐	115	Ⓐ Ⓑ Ⓒ Ⓓ ☐	125	Ⓐ Ⓑ Ⓒ Ⓓ ☐
106	Ⓐ Ⓑ Ⓒ Ⓓ ☐	116	Ⓐ Ⓑ Ⓒ Ⓓ ☐	126	Ⓐ Ⓑ Ⓒ Ⓓ ☐
107	Ⓐ Ⓑ Ⓒ Ⓓ ☐	117	Ⓐ Ⓑ Ⓒ Ⓓ ☐	127	Ⓐ Ⓑ Ⓒ Ⓓ ☐
108	Ⓐ Ⓑ Ⓒ Ⓓ ☐	118	Ⓐ Ⓑ Ⓒ Ⓓ ☐	128	Ⓐ Ⓑ Ⓒ Ⓓ ☐
109	Ⓐ Ⓑ Ⓒ Ⓓ ☐	119	Ⓐ Ⓑ Ⓒ Ⓓ ☐	129	Ⓐ Ⓑ Ⓒ Ⓓ ☐
110	Ⓐ Ⓑ Ⓒ Ⓓ ☐	120	Ⓐ Ⓑ Ⓒ Ⓓ ☐	130	Ⓐ Ⓑ Ⓒ Ⓓ ☐

Part 6 / Part 7

No.	ANSWER A B C D 勘	No.	ANSWER A B C D 勘	No.	ANSWER A B C D 勘
131	Ⓐ Ⓑ Ⓒ Ⓓ ☐	141	Ⓐ Ⓑ Ⓒ Ⓓ ☐	151	Ⓐ Ⓑ Ⓒ Ⓓ ☐
132	Ⓐ Ⓑ Ⓒ Ⓓ ☐	142	Ⓐ Ⓑ Ⓒ Ⓓ ☐	152	Ⓐ Ⓑ Ⓒ Ⓓ ☐
133	Ⓐ Ⓑ Ⓒ Ⓓ ☐	143	Ⓐ Ⓑ Ⓒ Ⓓ ☐	153	Ⓐ Ⓑ Ⓒ Ⓓ ☐
134	Ⓐ Ⓑ Ⓒ Ⓓ ☐	144	Ⓐ Ⓑ Ⓒ Ⓓ ☐	154	Ⓐ Ⓑ Ⓒ Ⓓ ☐
135	Ⓐ Ⓑ Ⓒ Ⓓ ☐	145	Ⓐ Ⓑ Ⓒ Ⓓ ☐	155	Ⓐ Ⓑ Ⓒ Ⓓ ☐
136	Ⓐ Ⓑ Ⓒ Ⓓ ☐	146	Ⓐ Ⓑ Ⓒ Ⓓ ☐	156	Ⓐ Ⓑ Ⓒ Ⓓ ☐
137	Ⓐ Ⓑ Ⓒ Ⓓ ☐	147	Ⓐ Ⓑ Ⓒ Ⓓ ☐	157	Ⓐ Ⓑ Ⓒ Ⓓ ☐
138	Ⓐ Ⓑ Ⓒ Ⓓ ☐	148	Ⓐ Ⓑ Ⓒ Ⓓ ☐	158	Ⓐ Ⓑ Ⓒ Ⓓ ☐
139	Ⓐ Ⓑ Ⓒ Ⓓ ☐	149	Ⓐ Ⓑ Ⓒ Ⓓ ☐	159	Ⓐ Ⓑ Ⓒ Ⓓ ☐
140	Ⓐ Ⓑ Ⓒ Ⓓ ☐	150	Ⓐ Ⓑ Ⓒ Ⓓ ☐	160	Ⓐ Ⓑ Ⓒ Ⓓ ☐

No.	ANSWER A B C D 勘	No.	ANSWER A B C D 勘	No.	ANSWER A B C D 勘
161	Ⓐ Ⓑ Ⓒ Ⓓ ☐	171	Ⓐ Ⓑ Ⓒ Ⓓ ☐	181	Ⓐ Ⓑ Ⓒ Ⓓ ☐
162	Ⓐ Ⓑ Ⓒ Ⓓ ☐	172	Ⓐ Ⓑ Ⓒ Ⓓ ☐	182	Ⓐ Ⓑ Ⓒ Ⓓ ☐
163	Ⓐ Ⓑ Ⓒ Ⓓ ☐	173	Ⓐ Ⓑ Ⓒ Ⓓ ☐	183	Ⓐ Ⓑ Ⓒ Ⓓ ☐
164	Ⓐ Ⓑ Ⓒ Ⓓ ☐	174	Ⓐ Ⓑ Ⓒ Ⓓ ☐	184	Ⓐ Ⓑ Ⓒ Ⓓ ☐
165	Ⓐ Ⓑ Ⓒ Ⓓ ☐	175	Ⓐ Ⓑ Ⓒ Ⓓ ☐	185	Ⓐ Ⓑ Ⓒ Ⓓ ☐
166	Ⓐ Ⓑ Ⓒ Ⓓ ☐	176	Ⓐ Ⓑ Ⓒ Ⓓ ☐	186	Ⓐ Ⓑ Ⓒ Ⓓ ☐
167	Ⓐ Ⓑ Ⓒ Ⓓ ☐	177	Ⓐ Ⓑ Ⓒ Ⓓ ☐	187	Ⓐ Ⓑ Ⓒ Ⓓ ☐
168	Ⓐ Ⓑ Ⓒ Ⓓ ☐	178	Ⓐ Ⓑ Ⓒ Ⓓ ☐	188	Ⓐ Ⓑ Ⓒ Ⓓ ☐
169	Ⓐ Ⓑ Ⓒ Ⓓ ☐	179	Ⓐ Ⓑ Ⓒ Ⓓ ☐	189	Ⓐ Ⓑ Ⓒ Ⓓ ☐
170	Ⓐ Ⓑ Ⓒ Ⓓ ☐	180	Ⓐ Ⓑ Ⓒ Ⓓ ☐	190	Ⓐ Ⓑ Ⓒ Ⓓ ☐

No.	ANSWER A B C D 勘
191	Ⓐ Ⓑ Ⓒ Ⓓ ☐
192	Ⓐ Ⓑ Ⓒ Ⓓ ☐
193	Ⓐ Ⓑ Ⓒ Ⓓ ☐
194	Ⓐ Ⓑ Ⓒ Ⓓ ☐
195	Ⓐ Ⓑ Ⓒ Ⓓ ☐
196	Ⓐ Ⓑ Ⓒ Ⓓ ☐
197	Ⓐ Ⓑ Ⓒ Ⓓ ☐
198	Ⓐ Ⓑ Ⓒ Ⓓ ☐
199	Ⓐ Ⓑ Ⓒ Ⓓ ☐
200	Ⓐ Ⓑ Ⓒ Ⓓ ☐

※解答一覧→本冊p.260〜参照

TOEIC® L&Rテスト 究極の模試600問＋ Test 4 マークシート

実施日： 　年　　月　　日

	Part 1	Part 2	Part 3	Part 4	Listening計	Part 5	Part 6	Part 7	Reading計
換算スコア	/6	/25	/39	/30	/100	/30	/16	/54	/100
					/495			換算スコア	/495

LISTENING SECTION

Part 1 — No. 1–6 ANSWER (A B C D), No. 7–10 ANSWER (A B C)

Part 2 — No. 11–40 ANSWER (A B C)

Part 3 — No. 41–70 ANSWER (A B C D)

Part 4 — No. 71–100 ANSWER (A B C D)

READING SECTION

Part 5 — No. 101–130 ANSWER (A B C D)

Part 6 — No. 131–146 ANSWER (A B C D)

Part 7 — No. 147–200 ANSWER (A B C D)

※解答一覧→本冊p.376〜参照

TOEIC® L&Rテスト 究極の模試600問⁺ マークシートA （勘ボックスあり）

実施日： ____年 ____月 ____日

	Part 1	Part 2	Part 3	Part 4		Listening 計
	/ 6	/ 25	/ 39	/ 30		/ 100
					換算スコア	/ 495

	Part 5	Part 6	Part 7		Reading 計
	/ 30	/ 16	/ 54		/ 100
				換算スコア	/ 495

LISTENING SECTION

Part 1

No.	ANSWER A B C D 勘
1	Ⓐ Ⓑ Ⓒ Ⓓ □
2	Ⓐ Ⓑ Ⓒ Ⓓ □
3	Ⓐ Ⓑ Ⓒ Ⓓ □
4	Ⓐ Ⓑ Ⓒ Ⓓ □
5	Ⓐ Ⓑ Ⓒ Ⓓ □
6	Ⓐ Ⓑ Ⓒ Ⓓ □
7	Ⓐ Ⓑ Ⓒ □
8	Ⓐ Ⓑ Ⓒ □
9	Ⓐ Ⓑ Ⓒ □
10	Ⓐ Ⓑ Ⓒ □

Part 2

No.	ANSWER A B C 勘
11	Ⓐ Ⓑ Ⓒ □
12	Ⓐ Ⓑ Ⓒ □
13	Ⓐ Ⓑ Ⓒ □
14	Ⓐ Ⓑ Ⓒ □
15	Ⓐ Ⓑ Ⓒ □
16	Ⓐ Ⓑ Ⓒ □
17	Ⓐ Ⓑ Ⓒ □
18	Ⓐ Ⓑ Ⓒ □
19	Ⓐ Ⓑ Ⓒ □
20	Ⓐ Ⓑ Ⓒ □

No.	ANSWER A B C 勘
21	Ⓐ Ⓑ Ⓒ □
22	Ⓐ Ⓑ Ⓒ □
23	Ⓐ Ⓑ Ⓒ □
24	Ⓐ Ⓑ Ⓒ □
25	Ⓐ Ⓑ Ⓒ □
26	Ⓐ Ⓑ Ⓒ □
27	Ⓐ Ⓑ Ⓒ □
28	Ⓐ Ⓑ Ⓒ □
29	Ⓐ Ⓑ Ⓒ □
30	Ⓐ Ⓑ Ⓒ □

Part 3

No.	ANSWER A B C 勘
31	Ⓐ Ⓑ Ⓒ □
32	Ⓐ Ⓑ Ⓒ □
33	Ⓐ Ⓑ Ⓒ □
34	Ⓐ Ⓑ Ⓒ □
35	Ⓐ Ⓑ Ⓒ □
36	Ⓐ Ⓑ Ⓒ □
37	Ⓐ Ⓑ Ⓒ □
38	Ⓐ Ⓑ Ⓒ □
39	Ⓐ Ⓑ Ⓒ □
40	Ⓐ Ⓑ Ⓒ □

No.	ANSWER A B C D 勘
41	Ⓐ Ⓑ Ⓒ Ⓓ □
42	Ⓐ Ⓑ Ⓒ Ⓓ □
43	Ⓐ Ⓑ Ⓒ Ⓓ □
44	Ⓐ Ⓑ Ⓒ Ⓓ □
45	Ⓐ Ⓑ Ⓒ Ⓓ □
46	Ⓐ Ⓑ Ⓒ Ⓓ □
47	Ⓐ Ⓑ Ⓒ Ⓓ □
48	Ⓐ Ⓑ Ⓒ Ⓓ □
49	Ⓐ Ⓑ Ⓒ Ⓓ □
50	Ⓐ Ⓑ Ⓒ Ⓓ □

No.	ANSWER A B C D 勘
51	Ⓐ Ⓑ Ⓒ Ⓓ □
52	Ⓐ Ⓑ Ⓒ Ⓓ □
53	Ⓐ Ⓑ Ⓒ Ⓓ □
54	Ⓐ Ⓑ Ⓒ Ⓓ □
55	Ⓐ Ⓑ Ⓒ Ⓓ □
56	Ⓐ Ⓑ Ⓒ Ⓓ □
57	Ⓐ Ⓑ Ⓒ Ⓓ □
58	Ⓐ Ⓑ Ⓒ Ⓓ □
59	Ⓐ Ⓑ Ⓒ Ⓓ □
60	Ⓐ Ⓑ Ⓒ Ⓓ □

No.	ANSWER A B C D 勘
61	Ⓐ Ⓑ Ⓒ Ⓓ □
62	Ⓐ Ⓑ Ⓒ Ⓓ □
63	Ⓐ Ⓑ Ⓒ Ⓓ □
64	Ⓐ Ⓑ Ⓒ Ⓓ □
65	Ⓐ Ⓑ Ⓒ Ⓓ □
66	Ⓐ Ⓑ Ⓒ Ⓓ □
67	Ⓐ Ⓑ Ⓒ Ⓓ □
68	Ⓐ Ⓑ Ⓒ Ⓓ □
69	Ⓐ Ⓑ Ⓒ Ⓓ □
70	Ⓐ Ⓑ Ⓒ Ⓓ □

Part 4

No.	ANSWER A B C D 勘
71	Ⓐ Ⓑ Ⓒ Ⓓ □
72	Ⓐ Ⓑ Ⓒ Ⓓ □
73	Ⓐ Ⓑ Ⓒ Ⓓ □
74	Ⓐ Ⓑ Ⓒ Ⓓ □
75	Ⓐ Ⓑ Ⓒ Ⓓ □
76	Ⓐ Ⓑ Ⓒ Ⓓ □
77	Ⓐ Ⓑ Ⓒ Ⓓ □
78	Ⓐ Ⓑ Ⓒ Ⓓ □
79	Ⓐ Ⓑ Ⓒ Ⓓ □
80	Ⓐ Ⓑ Ⓒ Ⓓ □

No.	ANSWER A B C D 勘
81	Ⓐ Ⓑ Ⓒ Ⓓ □
82	Ⓐ Ⓑ Ⓒ Ⓓ □
83	Ⓐ Ⓑ Ⓒ Ⓓ □
84	Ⓐ Ⓑ Ⓒ Ⓓ □
85	Ⓐ Ⓑ Ⓒ Ⓓ □
86	Ⓐ Ⓑ Ⓒ Ⓓ □
87	Ⓐ Ⓑ Ⓒ Ⓓ □
88	Ⓐ Ⓑ Ⓒ Ⓓ □
89	Ⓐ Ⓑ Ⓒ Ⓓ □
90	Ⓐ Ⓑ Ⓒ Ⓓ □

No.	ANSWER A B C D 勘
91	Ⓐ Ⓑ Ⓒ Ⓓ □
92	Ⓐ Ⓑ Ⓒ Ⓓ □
93	Ⓐ Ⓑ Ⓒ Ⓓ □
94	Ⓐ Ⓑ Ⓒ Ⓓ □
95	Ⓐ Ⓑ Ⓒ Ⓓ □
96	Ⓐ Ⓑ Ⓒ Ⓓ □
97	Ⓐ Ⓑ Ⓒ Ⓓ □
98	Ⓐ Ⓑ Ⓒ Ⓓ □
99	Ⓐ Ⓑ Ⓒ Ⓓ □
100	Ⓐ Ⓑ Ⓒ Ⓓ □

READING SECTION

Part 5

No.	ANSWER A B C D 勘
101	Ⓐ Ⓑ Ⓒ Ⓓ □
102	Ⓐ Ⓑ Ⓒ Ⓓ □
103	Ⓐ Ⓑ Ⓒ Ⓓ □
104	Ⓐ Ⓑ Ⓒ Ⓓ □
105	Ⓐ Ⓑ Ⓒ Ⓓ □
106	Ⓐ Ⓑ Ⓒ Ⓓ □
107	Ⓐ Ⓑ Ⓒ Ⓓ □
108	Ⓐ Ⓑ Ⓒ Ⓓ □
109	Ⓐ Ⓑ Ⓒ Ⓓ □
110	Ⓐ Ⓑ Ⓒ Ⓓ □

No.	ANSWER A B C D 勘
111	Ⓐ Ⓑ Ⓒ Ⓓ □
112	Ⓐ Ⓑ Ⓒ Ⓓ □
113	Ⓐ Ⓑ Ⓒ Ⓓ □
114	Ⓐ Ⓑ Ⓒ Ⓓ □
115	Ⓐ Ⓑ Ⓒ Ⓓ □
116	Ⓐ Ⓑ Ⓒ Ⓓ □
117	Ⓐ Ⓑ Ⓒ Ⓓ □
118	Ⓐ Ⓑ Ⓒ Ⓓ □
119	Ⓐ Ⓑ Ⓒ Ⓓ □
120	Ⓐ Ⓑ Ⓒ Ⓓ □

Part 6

No.	ANSWER A B C D 勘
121	Ⓐ Ⓑ Ⓒ Ⓓ □
122	Ⓐ Ⓑ Ⓒ Ⓓ □
123	Ⓐ Ⓑ Ⓒ Ⓓ □
124	Ⓐ Ⓑ Ⓒ Ⓓ □
125	Ⓐ Ⓑ Ⓒ Ⓓ □
126	Ⓐ Ⓑ Ⓒ Ⓓ □
127	Ⓐ Ⓑ Ⓒ Ⓓ □
128	Ⓐ Ⓑ Ⓒ Ⓓ □
129	Ⓐ Ⓑ Ⓒ Ⓓ □
130	Ⓐ Ⓑ Ⓒ Ⓓ □

No.	ANSWER A B C D 勘
131	Ⓐ Ⓑ Ⓒ Ⓓ □
132	Ⓐ Ⓑ Ⓒ Ⓓ □
133	Ⓐ Ⓑ Ⓒ Ⓓ □
134	Ⓐ Ⓑ Ⓒ Ⓓ □
135	Ⓐ Ⓑ Ⓒ Ⓓ □
136	Ⓐ Ⓑ Ⓒ Ⓓ □
137	Ⓐ Ⓑ Ⓒ Ⓓ □
138	Ⓐ Ⓑ Ⓒ Ⓓ □
139	Ⓐ Ⓑ Ⓒ Ⓓ □
140	Ⓐ Ⓑ Ⓒ Ⓓ □

Part 7

No.	ANSWER A B C D 勘
141	Ⓐ Ⓑ Ⓒ Ⓓ □
142	Ⓐ Ⓑ Ⓒ Ⓓ □
143	Ⓐ Ⓑ Ⓒ Ⓓ □
144	Ⓐ Ⓑ Ⓒ Ⓓ □
145	Ⓐ Ⓑ Ⓒ Ⓓ □
146	Ⓐ Ⓑ Ⓒ Ⓓ □
147	Ⓐ Ⓑ Ⓒ Ⓓ □
148	Ⓐ Ⓑ Ⓒ Ⓓ □
149	Ⓐ Ⓑ Ⓒ Ⓓ □
150	Ⓐ Ⓑ Ⓒ Ⓓ □

No.	ANSWER A B C D 勘
151	Ⓐ Ⓑ Ⓒ Ⓓ □
152	Ⓐ Ⓑ Ⓒ Ⓓ □
153	Ⓐ Ⓑ Ⓒ Ⓓ □
154	Ⓐ Ⓑ Ⓒ Ⓓ □
155	Ⓐ Ⓑ Ⓒ Ⓓ □
156	Ⓐ Ⓑ Ⓒ Ⓓ □
157	Ⓐ Ⓑ Ⓒ Ⓓ □
158	Ⓐ Ⓑ Ⓒ Ⓓ □
159	Ⓐ Ⓑ Ⓒ Ⓓ □
160	Ⓐ Ⓑ Ⓒ Ⓓ □

No.	ANSWER A B C D 勘
161	Ⓐ Ⓑ Ⓒ Ⓓ □
162	Ⓐ Ⓑ Ⓒ Ⓓ □
163	Ⓐ Ⓑ Ⓒ Ⓓ □
164	Ⓐ Ⓑ Ⓒ Ⓓ □
165	Ⓐ Ⓑ Ⓒ Ⓓ □
166	Ⓐ Ⓑ Ⓒ Ⓓ □
167	Ⓐ Ⓑ Ⓒ Ⓓ □
168	Ⓐ Ⓑ Ⓒ Ⓓ □
169	Ⓐ Ⓑ Ⓒ Ⓓ □
170	Ⓐ Ⓑ Ⓒ Ⓓ □

No.	ANSWER A B C D 勘
171	Ⓐ Ⓑ Ⓒ Ⓓ □
172	Ⓐ Ⓑ Ⓒ Ⓓ □
173	Ⓐ Ⓑ Ⓒ Ⓓ □
174	Ⓐ Ⓑ Ⓒ Ⓓ □
175	Ⓐ Ⓑ Ⓒ Ⓓ □
176	Ⓐ Ⓑ Ⓒ Ⓓ □
177	Ⓐ Ⓑ Ⓒ Ⓓ □
178	Ⓐ Ⓑ Ⓒ Ⓓ □
179	Ⓐ Ⓑ Ⓒ Ⓓ □
180	Ⓐ Ⓑ Ⓒ Ⓓ □

No.	ANSWER A B C D 勘
181	Ⓐ Ⓑ Ⓒ Ⓓ □
182	Ⓐ Ⓑ Ⓒ Ⓓ □
183	Ⓐ Ⓑ Ⓒ Ⓓ □
184	Ⓐ Ⓑ Ⓒ Ⓓ □
185	Ⓐ Ⓑ Ⓒ Ⓓ □
186	Ⓐ Ⓑ Ⓒ Ⓓ □
187	Ⓐ Ⓑ Ⓒ Ⓓ □
188	Ⓐ Ⓑ Ⓒ Ⓓ □
189	Ⓐ Ⓑ Ⓒ Ⓓ □
190	Ⓐ Ⓑ Ⓒ Ⓓ □

No.	ANSWER A B C D 勘
191	Ⓐ Ⓑ Ⓒ Ⓓ □
192	Ⓐ Ⓑ Ⓒ Ⓓ □
193	Ⓐ Ⓑ Ⓒ Ⓓ □
194	Ⓐ Ⓑ Ⓒ Ⓓ □
195	Ⓐ Ⓑ Ⓒ Ⓓ □
196	Ⓐ Ⓑ Ⓒ Ⓓ □
197	Ⓐ Ⓑ Ⓒ Ⓓ □
198	Ⓐ Ⓑ Ⓒ Ⓓ □
199	Ⓐ Ⓑ Ⓒ Ⓓ □
200	Ⓐ Ⓑ Ⓒ Ⓓ □

TOEIC® L&Rテスト 究極の模試600問+ マークシートB

実施日： 　　　年　　　月　　　日

	Part 1	Part 2	Part 3	Part 4	Listening 計
	/6	/25	/39	/30	/100

換算スコア 　/495

	Part 5	Part 6	Part 7	Reading 計
	/30	/16	/54	/100

換算スコア 　/495

LISTENING SECTION

Part 1

No.	ANSWER A B C D
1	Ⓐ Ⓑ Ⓒ Ⓓ
2	Ⓐ Ⓑ Ⓒ Ⓓ
3	Ⓐ Ⓑ Ⓒ Ⓓ
4	Ⓐ Ⓑ Ⓒ Ⓓ
5	Ⓐ Ⓑ Ⓒ Ⓓ
6	Ⓐ Ⓑ Ⓒ Ⓓ
7	Ⓐ Ⓑ Ⓒ
8	Ⓐ Ⓑ Ⓒ
9	Ⓐ Ⓑ Ⓒ
10	Ⓐ Ⓑ Ⓒ

Part 2

No.	ANSWER A B C
11	Ⓐ Ⓑ Ⓒ
12	Ⓐ Ⓑ Ⓒ
13	Ⓐ Ⓑ Ⓒ
14	Ⓐ Ⓑ Ⓒ
15	Ⓐ Ⓑ Ⓒ
16	Ⓐ Ⓑ Ⓒ
17	Ⓐ Ⓑ Ⓒ
18	Ⓐ Ⓑ Ⓒ
19	Ⓐ Ⓑ Ⓒ
20	Ⓐ Ⓑ Ⓒ

No.	ANSWER A B C
21	Ⓐ Ⓑ Ⓒ
22	Ⓐ Ⓑ Ⓒ
23	Ⓐ Ⓑ Ⓒ
24	Ⓐ Ⓑ Ⓒ
25	Ⓐ Ⓑ Ⓒ
26	Ⓐ Ⓑ Ⓒ
27	Ⓐ Ⓑ Ⓒ
28	Ⓐ Ⓑ Ⓒ
29	Ⓐ Ⓑ Ⓒ
30	Ⓐ Ⓑ Ⓒ

No.	ANSWER A B C
31	Ⓐ Ⓑ Ⓒ
32	Ⓐ Ⓑ Ⓒ

Part 3

No.	ANSWER A B C D
33	Ⓐ Ⓑ Ⓒ Ⓓ
34	Ⓐ Ⓑ Ⓒ Ⓓ
35	Ⓐ Ⓑ Ⓒ Ⓓ
36	Ⓐ Ⓑ Ⓒ Ⓓ
37	Ⓐ Ⓑ Ⓒ Ⓓ
38	Ⓐ Ⓑ Ⓒ Ⓓ
39	Ⓐ Ⓑ Ⓒ Ⓓ
40	Ⓐ Ⓑ Ⓒ Ⓓ

No.	ANSWER A B C D
41	Ⓐ Ⓑ Ⓒ Ⓓ
42	Ⓐ Ⓑ Ⓒ Ⓓ
43	Ⓐ Ⓑ Ⓒ Ⓓ
44	Ⓐ Ⓑ Ⓒ Ⓓ
45	Ⓐ Ⓑ Ⓒ Ⓓ
46	Ⓐ Ⓑ Ⓒ Ⓓ
47	Ⓐ Ⓑ Ⓒ Ⓓ
48	Ⓐ Ⓑ Ⓒ Ⓓ
49	Ⓐ Ⓑ Ⓒ Ⓓ
50	Ⓐ Ⓑ Ⓒ Ⓓ

No.	ANSWER A B C D
51	Ⓐ Ⓑ Ⓒ Ⓓ
52	Ⓐ Ⓑ Ⓒ Ⓓ
53	Ⓐ Ⓑ Ⓒ Ⓓ
54	Ⓐ Ⓑ Ⓒ Ⓓ
55	Ⓐ Ⓑ Ⓒ Ⓓ
56	Ⓐ Ⓑ Ⓒ Ⓓ
57	Ⓐ Ⓑ Ⓒ Ⓓ
58	Ⓐ Ⓑ Ⓒ Ⓓ
59	Ⓐ Ⓑ Ⓒ Ⓓ
60	Ⓐ Ⓑ Ⓒ Ⓓ

No.	ANSWER A B C D
61	Ⓐ Ⓑ Ⓒ Ⓓ
62	Ⓐ Ⓑ Ⓒ Ⓓ
63	Ⓐ Ⓑ Ⓒ Ⓓ
64	Ⓐ Ⓑ Ⓒ Ⓓ
65	Ⓐ Ⓑ Ⓒ Ⓓ
66	Ⓐ Ⓑ Ⓒ Ⓓ
67	Ⓐ Ⓑ Ⓒ Ⓓ
68	Ⓐ Ⓑ Ⓒ Ⓓ
69	Ⓐ Ⓑ Ⓒ Ⓓ
70	Ⓐ Ⓑ Ⓒ Ⓓ

Part 4

No.	ANSWER A B C D
71	Ⓐ Ⓑ Ⓒ Ⓓ
72	Ⓐ Ⓑ Ⓒ Ⓓ
73	Ⓐ Ⓑ Ⓒ Ⓓ
74	Ⓐ Ⓑ Ⓒ Ⓓ
75	Ⓐ Ⓑ Ⓒ Ⓓ
76	Ⓐ Ⓑ Ⓒ Ⓓ
77	Ⓐ Ⓑ Ⓒ Ⓓ
78	Ⓐ Ⓑ Ⓒ Ⓓ
79	Ⓐ Ⓑ Ⓒ Ⓓ
80	Ⓐ Ⓑ Ⓒ Ⓓ

No.	ANSWER A B C D
81	Ⓐ Ⓑ Ⓒ Ⓓ
82	Ⓐ Ⓑ Ⓒ Ⓓ
83	Ⓐ Ⓑ Ⓒ Ⓓ
84	Ⓐ Ⓑ Ⓒ Ⓓ
85	Ⓐ Ⓑ Ⓒ Ⓓ
86	Ⓐ Ⓑ Ⓒ Ⓓ
87	Ⓐ Ⓑ Ⓒ Ⓓ
88	Ⓐ Ⓑ Ⓒ Ⓓ
89	Ⓐ Ⓑ Ⓒ Ⓓ
90	Ⓐ Ⓑ Ⓒ Ⓓ

No.	ANSWER A B C D
91	Ⓐ Ⓑ Ⓒ Ⓓ
92	Ⓐ Ⓑ Ⓒ Ⓓ
93	Ⓐ Ⓑ Ⓒ Ⓓ
94	Ⓐ Ⓑ Ⓒ Ⓓ
95	Ⓐ Ⓑ Ⓒ Ⓓ
96	Ⓐ Ⓑ Ⓒ Ⓓ
97	Ⓐ Ⓑ Ⓒ Ⓓ
98	Ⓐ Ⓑ Ⓒ Ⓓ
99	Ⓐ Ⓑ Ⓒ Ⓓ
100	Ⓐ Ⓑ Ⓒ Ⓓ

READING SECTION

Part 5

No.	ANSWER A B C D
101	Ⓐ Ⓑ Ⓒ Ⓓ
102	Ⓐ Ⓑ Ⓒ Ⓓ
103	Ⓐ Ⓑ Ⓒ Ⓓ
104	Ⓐ Ⓑ Ⓒ Ⓓ
105	Ⓐ Ⓑ Ⓒ Ⓓ
106	Ⓐ Ⓑ Ⓒ Ⓓ
107	Ⓐ Ⓑ Ⓒ Ⓓ
108	Ⓐ Ⓑ Ⓒ Ⓓ
109	Ⓐ Ⓑ Ⓒ Ⓓ
110	Ⓐ Ⓑ Ⓒ Ⓓ

No.	ANSWER A B C D
111	Ⓐ Ⓑ Ⓒ Ⓓ
112	Ⓐ Ⓑ Ⓒ Ⓓ
113	Ⓐ Ⓑ Ⓒ Ⓓ
114	Ⓐ Ⓑ Ⓒ Ⓓ
115	Ⓐ Ⓑ Ⓒ Ⓓ
116	Ⓐ Ⓑ Ⓒ Ⓓ
117	Ⓐ Ⓑ Ⓒ Ⓓ
118	Ⓐ Ⓑ Ⓒ Ⓓ
119	Ⓐ Ⓑ Ⓒ Ⓓ
120	Ⓐ Ⓑ Ⓒ Ⓓ

No.	ANSWER A B C D
121	Ⓐ Ⓑ Ⓒ Ⓓ
122	Ⓐ Ⓑ Ⓒ Ⓓ
123	Ⓐ Ⓑ Ⓒ Ⓓ
124	Ⓐ Ⓑ Ⓒ Ⓓ
125	Ⓐ Ⓑ Ⓒ Ⓓ
126	Ⓐ Ⓑ Ⓒ Ⓓ
127	Ⓐ Ⓑ Ⓒ Ⓓ
128	Ⓐ Ⓑ Ⓒ Ⓓ
129	Ⓐ Ⓑ Ⓒ Ⓓ
130	Ⓐ Ⓑ Ⓒ Ⓓ

Part 6

No.	ANSWER A B C D
131	Ⓐ Ⓑ Ⓒ Ⓓ
132	Ⓐ Ⓑ Ⓒ Ⓓ
133	Ⓐ Ⓑ Ⓒ Ⓓ
134	Ⓐ Ⓑ Ⓒ Ⓓ
135	Ⓐ Ⓑ Ⓒ Ⓓ
136	Ⓐ Ⓑ Ⓒ Ⓓ
137	Ⓐ Ⓑ Ⓒ Ⓓ
138	Ⓐ Ⓑ Ⓒ Ⓓ
139	Ⓐ Ⓑ Ⓒ Ⓓ
140	Ⓐ Ⓑ Ⓒ Ⓓ

No.	ANSWER A B C D
141	Ⓐ Ⓑ Ⓒ Ⓓ
142	Ⓐ Ⓑ Ⓒ Ⓓ
143	Ⓐ Ⓑ Ⓒ Ⓓ
144	Ⓐ Ⓑ Ⓒ Ⓓ
145	Ⓐ Ⓑ Ⓒ Ⓓ
146	Ⓐ Ⓑ Ⓒ Ⓓ
147	Ⓐ Ⓑ Ⓒ Ⓓ
148	Ⓐ Ⓑ Ⓒ Ⓓ
149	Ⓐ Ⓑ Ⓒ Ⓓ
150	Ⓐ Ⓑ Ⓒ Ⓓ

Part 7

No.	ANSWER A B C D
151	Ⓐ Ⓑ Ⓒ Ⓓ
152	Ⓐ Ⓑ Ⓒ Ⓓ
153	Ⓐ Ⓑ Ⓒ Ⓓ
154	Ⓐ Ⓑ Ⓒ Ⓓ
155	Ⓐ Ⓑ Ⓒ Ⓓ
156	Ⓐ Ⓑ Ⓒ Ⓓ
157	Ⓐ Ⓑ Ⓒ Ⓓ
158	Ⓐ Ⓑ Ⓒ Ⓓ
159	Ⓐ Ⓑ Ⓒ Ⓓ
160	Ⓐ Ⓑ Ⓒ Ⓓ

No.	ANSWER A B C D
161	Ⓐ Ⓑ Ⓒ Ⓓ
162	Ⓐ Ⓑ Ⓒ Ⓓ
163	Ⓐ Ⓑ Ⓒ Ⓓ
164	Ⓐ Ⓑ Ⓒ Ⓓ
165	Ⓐ Ⓑ Ⓒ Ⓓ
166	Ⓐ Ⓑ Ⓒ Ⓓ
167	Ⓐ Ⓑ Ⓒ Ⓓ
168	Ⓐ Ⓑ Ⓒ Ⓓ
169	Ⓐ Ⓑ Ⓒ Ⓓ
170	Ⓐ Ⓑ Ⓒ Ⓓ

No.	ANSWER A B C D
171	Ⓐ Ⓑ Ⓒ Ⓓ
172	Ⓐ Ⓑ Ⓒ Ⓓ
173	Ⓐ Ⓑ Ⓒ Ⓓ
174	Ⓐ Ⓑ Ⓒ Ⓓ
175	Ⓐ Ⓑ Ⓒ Ⓓ
176	Ⓐ Ⓑ Ⓒ Ⓓ
177	Ⓐ Ⓑ Ⓒ Ⓓ
178	Ⓐ Ⓑ Ⓒ Ⓓ
179	Ⓐ Ⓑ Ⓒ Ⓓ
180	Ⓐ Ⓑ Ⓒ Ⓓ

No.	ANSWER A B C D
181	Ⓐ Ⓑ Ⓒ Ⓓ
182	Ⓐ Ⓑ Ⓒ Ⓓ
183	Ⓐ Ⓑ Ⓒ Ⓓ
184	Ⓐ Ⓑ Ⓒ Ⓓ
185	Ⓐ Ⓑ Ⓒ Ⓓ
186	Ⓐ Ⓑ Ⓒ Ⓓ
187	Ⓐ Ⓑ Ⓒ Ⓓ
188	Ⓐ Ⓑ Ⓒ Ⓓ
189	Ⓐ Ⓑ Ⓒ Ⓓ
190	Ⓐ Ⓑ Ⓒ Ⓓ

No.	ANSWER A B C D
191	Ⓐ Ⓑ Ⓒ Ⓓ
192	Ⓐ Ⓑ Ⓒ Ⓓ
193	Ⓐ Ⓑ Ⓒ Ⓓ
194	Ⓐ Ⓑ Ⓒ Ⓓ
195	Ⓐ Ⓑ Ⓒ Ⓓ
196	Ⓐ Ⓑ Ⓒ Ⓓ
197	Ⓐ Ⓑ Ⓒ Ⓓ
198	Ⓐ Ⓑ Ⓒ Ⓓ
199	Ⓐ Ⓑ Ⓒ Ⓓ
200	Ⓐ Ⓑ Ⓒ Ⓓ

TOEIC® L&R テスト 究極の模試600問+
模擬試験 ④
Test 4

受験日	年　　月　　日
開始時間	時　　　分
Listening Section 終了時間	時　　　分
Reading Section 終了時間	時　　　分

◆Listening Section の音声は、ダウンロードしてご利用ください。詳しくは本冊のp.10に掲載されています。【Test 4】の音声を利用します。所要時間は**約46分**です。

◆解答には本冊巻末のマークシートを使用してください。テスト採点センター（本冊p.11）もご利用いただけます。

◆解答一覧は本冊p.376～にあります。

テスト採点
センター

使用する音声ファイル一覧

Listening Section、Part 1 Directions	193_T4_P1_Dir.mp3
Part 1 No.1～No.6	194_T4_P1_01.mp3～200_T4_P1_06.mp3
Part 2 Directions	201_T4_P2_Dir.mp3
Part 2 No.7～No.31	202_T4_P2_07.mp3～227_T4_P2_31.mp3
Part 3 Directions	228_T4_P3_Dir.mp3
Part 3 No.32～No.70	229_T4_P3_32-34.mp3～243_T4_P3_68-70.mp3
Part 4 Directions	244_T4_P4_Dir.mp3
Part 4 No.71～No.100	245_T4_P4_71-73.mp3～255_T4_P4_98-100.mp3

矢印の方向に引くと、この冊子を取り外すことができます。

LISTENING TEST

In this section, your ability to understand spoken English will be shown. The Listening test consists of four parts and will take approximately 45 minutes. Directions will be given for each part. By following the directions you hear, select the best possible answer and mark your answers on your answer sheet. Please refrain from writing anything in your test book.

PART 1

Directions: In this part, you will see a picture in your test book and hear four statements. After hearing each statement, select the one statement you think is the best description for the picture. Then, mark the answer on your answer sheet. You will only hear the statements one time, and they will not be printed in your test book.

Statement (B), "They're sitting side by side," best describes the picture. Therefore, you should choose answer (B) and mark it on your answer sheet.

1.

2.

GO ON TO THE NEXT PAGE ➤

3.

4.

GO ON TO THE NEXT PAGE

4

5.

6.

GO ON TO THE NEXT PAGE

PART 2

Directions: In this part, you will hear a question or statement. You will then hear three alternative responses to the question or statement. They will all be spoken in English. You will only hear them one time, and they will not be printed in your test book. Choose the best response to each question and mark the letter (A), (B), or (C) on your answer sheet.

7. Mark your answer on your answer sheet.

8. Mark your answer on your answer sheet.

9. Mark your answer on your answer sheet.

10. Mark your answer on your answer sheet.

11. Mark your answer on your answer sheet.

12. Mark your answer on your answer sheet.

13. Mark your answer on your answer sheet.

14. Mark your answer on your answer sheet.

15. Mark your answer on your answer sheet.

16. Mark your answer on your answer sheet.

17. Mark your answer on your answer sheet.

18. Mark your answer on your answer sheet.

19. Mark your answer on your answer sheet.

20. Mark your answer on your answer sheet.

21. Mark your answer on your answer sheet.

22. Mark your answer on your answer sheet.

23. Mark your answer on your answer sheet.

24. Mark your answer on your answer sheet.

25. Mark your answer on your answer sheet.

26. Mark your answer on your answer sheet.

27. Mark your answer on your answer sheet.

28. Mark your answer on your answer sheet.

29. Mark your answer on your answer sheet.

30. Mark your answer on your answer sheet.

31. Mark your answer on your answer sheet.

Directions: In this part, you will hear conversations between two or more people. You will be asked to answer three questions about what the speakers say in each conversation. You will only hear the conversations one time, and they will not be printed in your test book. Choose the best response to each question and mark the letter (A), (B), (C), or (D) on your answer sheet.

32. What kind of business do the men work for?

(A) A cleaning service
(B) A solar power company
(C) A construction firm
(D) An Internet service provider

33. What do the men imply about the job?

(A) It will take a long time.
(B) It will be carried out on another day.
(C) It has been assigned to a different team.
(D) It was requested by a company executive.

34. What does the woman ask the men to do?

(A) Lock the door
(B) Return her keys
(C) Take out some garbage
(D) Send a text message

35. Where most likely are the speakers?

(A) In a restaurant kitchen
(B) At a home improvement store
(C) At a food market
(D) At a souvenir shop

36. What does the man offer the woman?

(A) A discount
(B) A guided tour
(C) Gift wrapping
(D) Some samples

37. According to the man, what will happen next month?

(A) The business will be closed.
(B) An item will become available.
(C) A new location will open.
(D) Job applications will be accepted.

38. Why is the woman calling?

(A) To reserve a vehicle
(B) To ask for directions
(C) To discuss a project
(D) To recommend a business

39. What does the man mean when he says, "those are very popular"?

(A) The price has gone up.
(B) A product is selling well.
(C) An option might be unavailable.
(D) Membership is required.

40. What is the woman asked to do?

(A) Make a payment
(B) Review some paperwork
(C) Choose an insurance package
(D) Provide her contact information

41. What does the woman want the man to do?

(A) Choose a color scheme
(B) Interview a candidate
(C) Accept a delivery
(D) Write a report

42. What does the man ask the woman about?

(A) An arrival time
(B) The amount of a bill
(C) The cost of some materials
(D) A mailing address

43. What does the woman say she will do?

(A) Read some reviews
(B) See an accountant
(C) Hire a decorator
(D) Make a phone call

Test 4

GO ON TO THE NEXT PAGE

44. Who most likely is the man?

(A) A real estate agent
(B) A restaurant owner
(C) A construction worker
(D) A city official

45. What does the woman ask about?

(A) Rental prices
(B) Nearby businesses
(C) Daily specials
(D) Local rules

46. What will the man most likely do next?

(A) Check a menu
(B) Take a reservation
(C) Look at his computer
(D) Explain a system

47. Why did the woman contact the man's company?

(A) To request a replacement invoice
(B) To express thanks for a favor
(C) To announce the cancellation of a product
(D) To have some garbage removed

48. What does the man say he must do?

(A) Provide a refund
(B) Review some reports
(C) Charge an additional fee
(D) Take a vacation

49. What will the woman do this week?

(A) Replace some equipment
(B) Speak at a workshop
(C) Take employees on a trip
(D) Watch a movie

50. Where do the speakers most likely work?

(A) At an assembly plant
(B) At a shipping facility
(C) At a legal office
(D) At a hotel

51. What problem does the man mention?

(A) Some guests will arrive late.
(B) Some products have been broken.
(C) A machine is too expensive.
(D) A deadline has passed.

52. What does the woman mean when she says, "They won't like that"?

(A) Product quality has dropped.
(B) Extra work will be assigned.
(C) A request is unacceptable.
(D) A warranty will expire.

53. What is the conversation mainly about?

(A) A training workshop
(B) A recruitment plan
(C) A marketing strategy
(D) A company banquet

54. What does the man offer to do?

(A) Prepare some documents
(B) Check some inventory
(C) Review a proposal
(D) Calculate a budget

55. What does the woman say she will do?

(A) Create a shopping list
(B) Complete a report
(C) Evaluate a product
(D) Revise some materials

56. Who is Jules Martinez?

(A) A guest speaker
(B) A sales representative
(C) A council inspector
(D) A photographer

57. What problem does the woman mention?

(A) A portfolio has not been submitted.
(B) A kitchen has not been cleaned.
(C) Some information is inaccurate.
(D) Some equipment is out of order.

58. What is the man asked to do?

(A) Request some repairs
(B) Fill out a form
(C) Purchase a replacement
(D) Change an appointment

59. What is the topic of the conversation?

(A) Office equipment
(B) Employee training
(C) A meeting location
(D) Customer feedback

60. What does the woman ask about?

(A) The location of a hotel
(B) The name of a business
(C) The date of an event
(D) The availability of a client

61. What will the woman most likely do next?

(A) Pick up a client
(B) Announce some survey results
(C) Reserve a table
(D) Change her appointment

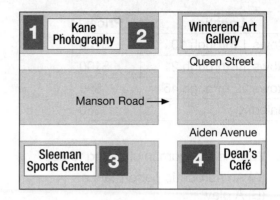

62. Why will the woman borrow the man's car?

(A) To go shopping
(B) To meet a client
(C) To make a delivery
(D) To return home

63. Look at the graphic. In which parking lot does the man say he left the car?

(A) Parking Lot 1
(B) Parking Lot 2
(C) Parking Lot 3
(D) Parking Lot 4

64. What does the man ask the woman to do?

(A) Have the car washed
(B) Pay the parking fee
(C) Bring back a receipt
(D) Refill the fuel tank

GO ON TO THE NEXT PAGE

Location	Price
Rows 1 through 10	$120
Rows 11 through 21	$100
Rows 22 through 45	$90
Balcony	$60

65. What is the woman planning to see?

(A) An acrobatic performance
(B) A play
(C) A concert
(D) A ballet

66. Look at the graphic. How much will the woman be required to pay for each ticket?

(A) $120
(B) $100
(C) $90
(D) $60

67. What does the man advise the woman to do?

(A) Arrive early
(B) Eat beforehand
(C) Purchase a T-shirt
(D) Bring an umbrella

ALOE SOAP	
Size	Volume
Mini	100ml
Small	300ml
Regular	500ml
Large	1L

68. Where does the conversation most likely take place?

(A) At a hotel
(B) At a hair salon
(C) At a supermarket
(D) At a manufacturing plant

69. What does the man say about the supplier?

(A) It has won an award.
(B) It will redesign its logo.
(C) It has raised its prices.
(D) It will terminate a contract.

70. Look at the graphic. Which size will the speakers most likely choose?

(A) Mini
(B) Small
(C) Regular
(D) Large

Directions: In this part, you will hear some talks given by a single person. You will be asked to answer three questions about what the speaker says in each talk. You will only hear the talks one time, and they will not be printed in your test book. Choose the best response to each question and mark the letter (A), (B), (C), or (D) on your answer sheet.

71. What is about to take place?

(A) A sales presentation
(B) A college introduction
(C) A book reading
(D) A seminar

72. Who is scheduled to speak?

(A) College professors
(B) Career counselors
(C) Artists
(D) Journalists

73. What are the audience members encouraged to do?

(A) Take notes
(B) Complete evaluation forms
(C) Open brochures
(D) Ask questions

74. What has the listener most likely ordered?

(A) Cleaning equipment
(B) Food supplies
(C) Stationery items
(D) Car parts

75. Why does the speaker say, "Your department has already gone over its budget"?

(A) Better prices should be negotiated.
(B) A budget has been reduced recently.
(C) A different application process is necessary.
(D) Some goods must be returned to the store.

76. What does the speaker say about Hillside Mart?

(A) It has a delivery service.
(B) It has a new catalog.
(C) Its prices are high.
(D) Its staff are very helpful.

77. What is the occasion for the speech?

(A) A book signing
(B) A management workshop
(C) A trade show
(D) A retirement celebration

78. What has Ms. Dawe received recognition for?

(A) Writing a helpful book
(B) Reducing departmental spending
(C) Completing a successful career
(D) Founding a profitable business

79. What is Ms. Dawe planning to do in the future?

(A) Produce a television program
(B) Take a job at a university
(C) Relocate to a new city
(D) Lead a department

80. Who most likely is the speaker?

(A) A sporting goods store owner
(B) A magazine editor
(C) A software engineer
(D) A factory manager

81. What is the speaker's concern?

(A) Some advertising revenue will be lost.
(B) An app is not well designed.
(C) Some items are out of stock.
(D) A client will request a refund.

82. How are the listeners encouraged to show their ideas?

(A) By sending an e-mail
(B) By posting on a bulletin board
(C) By phoning the speaker
(D) By making a presentation

GO ON TO THE NEXT PAGE ➡

Test 4

83. Who is George Wallace?

(A) A producer
(B) A writer
(C) A singer
(D) A videographer

84. What are listeners asked to do when they call?

(A) Suggest a title for a song
(B) Talk about an experience
(C) Name one of George Wallace's works
(D) Guess the location of a film set

85. What will the winner be given?

(A) A copy of a new book
(B) An invitation to a party
(C) An autographed album
(D) A ticket to a workshop

86. Where is the announcement being made?

(A) In a supermarket
(B) In a sporting goods store
(C) In a hardware store
(D) In an electronics shop

87. What does the speaker say about the business?

(A) It is open until late.
(B) It has won an award.
(C) It is holding a seasonal sale.
(D) It is employing new staff.

88. Why does the speaker say, "You really don't want to be last in line"?

(A) There is a limited number of the goods available.
(B) It will take a long time to serve customers.
(C) The store will close very soon.
(D) The line will extend outdoors.

89. What is being advertised?

(A) A grand opening
(B) An art competition
(C) An employment opportunity
(D) A catering service

90. What does the card enable people to do?

(A) Use a special room
(B) Obtain additional points
(C) Prove their identification
(D) Get price reductions

91. What does the speaker say about the organization?

(A) It is based in Hobart.
(B) It manufactures its own products.
(C) It has been expanding.
(D) It advertises online.

92. What is the purpose of the message?

(A) To make a complaint
(B) To announce a schedule
(C) To request a change
(D) To explain a delay

93. What does the speaker ask about?

(A) Ticket prices
(B) Workshop topics
(C) Parking allocation
(D) Accommodation options

94. What does the speaker imply when she says, "I hope this isn't a repeat of last year"?

(A) The same problem occurred in the past.
(B) The schedule looks similar to the previous year's.
(C) She did not receive an invitation to a prior event.
(D) Few people are showing interest in an event.

Departments	Section Leaders
Design	Nadia Becker
Marketing	Ahmed Lloyd
Administration	Daisy Chang
Customer Service	Simon Logan

Floor Space Allocation

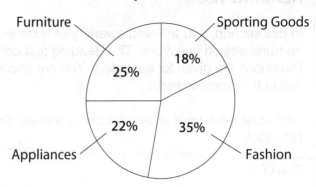

95. What is being distributed to staff members?

(A) Security passes
(B) Stationery items
(C) Work vests
(D) Annual bonuses

96. Look at the graphic. Where do the listeners most likely work?

(A) In design
(B) In marketing
(C) In administration
(D) In customer service

97. What does the speaker say about Ms. Chang?

(A) She will change departments.
(B) She is in a meeting.
(C) She has not arrived at work yet.
(D) She has a doctor's appointment.

98. What does the speaker say about the company's sales?

(A) They have been improving.
(B) They have not been reported.
(C) They are difficult to anticipate.
(D) They are affected by the seasons.

99. Look at the graphic. What category does the speaker suggest eliminating?

(A) Sporting Goods
(B) Fashion
(C) Appliances
(D) Furniture

100. When does the speaker say they should carry out the change?

(A) In May
(B) In June
(C) In July
(D) In August

This is the end of the Listening Test. Turn to Part 5 in your test book.

Test 4

GO ON TO THE NEXT PAGE

READING TEST

In this section, you will read a variety of texts and answer several different types of reading comprehension questions. The Reading test consists of three parts and will take 75 minutes. Directions are given for each part. You are encouraged to answer as many questions as possible within the time allowed.

You must mark your answers on your answer sheet. Please refrain from writing anything in your test book.

PART 5

Directions: The following sentences are incomplete. Select the most appropriate word or phrase from the choices (A), (B), (C), and (D), and mark your answer on your answer sheet.

101. The equipment used by BFP Pool Care workers is not ------- own.
(A) they
(B) theirs
(C) them
(D) their

102. The Bellmax store at Hastings Mall is expected to reopen ------- next month.
(A) early
(B) really
(C) mostly
(D) quickly

103. Attractions at Megaworld Theme Park have ------- inspections for safety issues.
(A) regularly
(B) regular
(C) regulate
(D) regulation

104. The section meeting was ------- to finish at 5:00 P.M. but carried on for two hours longer.
(A) forced
(B) supposed
(C) refused
(D) postponed

105. West Motors and Brix City will split the cost ------- for the Kelly Park renovation evenly.
(A) requiring
(B) is required
(C) required
(D) having required

106. Trinidad brand sweaters are available ------- at Frampton Department Stores.
(A) exclusively
(B) eventually
(C) innovatively
(D) enthusiastically

107. ------- of an interview Mr. Gaines gave before he became famous were discovered by a local journalist.
(A) Record
(B) Recorded
(C) Recording
(D) Recordings

108. Mr. Ford decided to use a conference room at the Central Hotel ------- the Douglas Center.
(A) but also
(B) although
(C) otherwise
(D) instead of

109. *Lime Sky* is far ------- to receive an award than any other music video in the competition.

(A) most likely
(B) likely
(C) more likely
(D) likelihood

110. The remote-control camera was packaged -------, but the instruction book contained many errors.

(A) attractively
(B) formerly
(C) significantly
(D) conclusively

111. Inspectors have identified ------- issues that must be rectified before the reopening.

(A) every
(B) neither
(C) several
(D) another

112. Glasgow Catering has always provided ------- levels of food quality for our in-flight meals.

(A) satisfactory
(B) protective
(C) periodical
(D) lengthy

113. Part-time staff should be called ahead of their shift and informed of ------- their goals for the day are.

(A) what
(B) such
(C) why
(D) also

114. ------- to the Woodhill Art Competition must be delivered in person by August 19.

(A) Compositions
(B) Submissions
(C) Establishments
(D) Refunds

115. Please submit your ------- letter to human resources if you would like reimbursement for evening classes.

(A) acceptance
(B) acceptable
(C) acceptability
(D) accepted

116. Hotel guests are given a coconut juice drink immediately ------- arrival.

(A) over
(B) upon
(C) beyond
(D) across

117. Managers at Glacier Tools are ------- required to travel internationally.

(A) frequented
(B) frequency
(C) frequently
(D) frequent

118. Details of the advertisement's production schedule will be ------- to the crew by the director.

(A) informed
(B) distributed
(C) suspended
(D) advised

119. Some participants made ------- critical observations about the validity of the health and safety workshop.

(A) its
(B) something
(C) rather
(D) themselves

120. ------- the updates are installed, users should be able to start using the software.

(A) Whether
(B) Now that
(C) So
(D) As far as

GO ON TO THE NEXT PAGE ➤

121. The ------- of Monday's meeting is to decide on a route for the walkathon.
(A) objectively
(B) objecting
(C) objection
(D) objective

122. Before anyone is allowed to operate heavy machinery, they must pass a ------- test.
(A) feasibility
(B) preference
(C) determination
(D) competency

123. The president of Dixon Foods praises divisions ------- successfully reduce their use of paper.
(A) that
(B) if
(C) whom
(D) how

124. ------- adequate promotion, Ms. Walker's book should be a national bestseller.
(A) Once
(B) Given
(C) Moreover
(D) According to

125. ------- at this year's summer concert was higher than organizers had expected.
(A) Attend
(B) Attending
(C) Attendees
(D) Attendance

126. Employees may leave early on Fridays ------- their weekly production quota has been met.
(A) in spite of
(B) provided that
(C) in order that
(D) as much as

127. The company president is extremely ------- to the needs of the various sections.
(A) attends
(B) attentively
(C) attention
(D) attentive

128. Greg Silva is the chief editor of the ------- acclaimed magazine *Indoor Outdoor*.
(A) mindfully
(B) personally
(C) critically
(D) virtually

129. It is important the customer ------- with the changes before we process the catering order.
(A) agree
(B) agreement
(C) agreeable
(D) agreeably

130. All requests for information will receive a ------- response from our customer service personnel.
(A) durable
(B) swift
(C) previous
(D) constant

16

PART 6

Directions: Some of the following sentences are incomplete. Select the most appropriate word, phrase, or sentence from the choices (A), (B), (C), and (D), and mark your answer on your answer sheet.

Questions 131-134 refer to the following article.

Newcomer in the fast food industry

In just under 12 months, Lin Mian Chinese Food ------- a major competitor in the fast food
                                              131.

industry. This has surprised many of the industry's experts.

Chinese food has always been popular with diners. They have ------- enjoyed dining at Chinese
                                                           132.

restaurants or ordering deliveries. On the other hand, fast food has been most commonly

associated with burgers, pizza, and chicken. -------. There are now more than 200 Lin Mian
                                             133.

restaurants nationwide, and that number is growing.

Lin Mian is seen as a tasty healthy option. -------, it has been recognized by the National Healthy
                                            134.

Eating Association. A meal at Lin Mian has around 20 percent less salt and fat than the equivalent

at a hamburger restaurant.

---

131. (A) has become
(B) will become
(C) to become
(D) had become

132. (A) subsequently
(B) traditionally
(C) rarely
(D) creatively

133. (A) Lin Mian will open soon in both
countries.
(B) This was generally expected.
(C) The plan has to be abandoned due to
certain problems.
(D) Lin Mian is changing that.

134. (A) Nevertheless
(B) Instead
(C) In fact
(D) Similarly

GO ON TO THE NEXT PAGE ▶

MEMO

To: Sales Managers

From: Pauline Jolly

Date: February 3

Subject: Evaluations

Dear sales managers,

It is time for supervisors to conduct the annual employee evaluation. Between February 6 and

February 12, sales managers should provide ------- to the people on their team using the
135.

downloadable form on the server. Please treat this as an opportunity to encourage salespeople.

If someone on your team is underperforming, you should work with them to find the ------- of the
136.

problem. The company has produced a number of videos on sales techniques which may be of

use in such cases. You can watch ------- online using the links on the company's Web site. -------.
137.   138.

Pauline Jolly

---

135. (A) feedback
(B) directions
(C) registration
(D) services

136. (A) purpose
(B) reasoning
(C) blame
(D) source

137. (A) it
(B) me
(C) them
(D) us

138. (A) Therefore, it is only relevant to people working in customer service.
(B) It is a requirement that employees fill out the survey after each viewing.
(C) By doing so, you could lower employee morale and make the situation worse.
(D) You must complete the entire process during January this year.

-------. In accordance with a company-wide push to reduce spending, every department was set
139.

a goal of 10 percent, which ------- except one were able to achieve. The accounting department
140.

did manage to cut spending a little. However, their expenses were ------- so low that the goal may
141.

have been unrealistic. Their modest achievement was made by switching their paper supplier.

The new supplier, Ascot Paper offered to undercut the price of the previous supplier by five

percent. According to our calculations, the ------- will result in a saving of around €1,600 per year.
142.

139. (A) Expenditure is down this quarter.
(B) Running costs should increase as the
     company grows.
(C) No objectives have been met since last
     year.
(D) We are no longer using paper.

140. (A) each
(B) all
(C) neither
(D) other

141. (A) likewise
(B) quite
(C) indeed
(D) already

142. (A) change
(B) campaign
(C) program
(D) closure

GO ON TO THE NEXT PAGE

Test 4

To: Steven Rand <srand@speedway.com>
From: FF Internet Customer Service <cs@ffinternet.com>
Date: March 6
Subject: Overdue account

Dear Mr. Rand,

It has come to our attention that payment for your Internet ------- for February is overdue. You
143.

agreed to have the fee automatically deducted from your bank account on the 1st of every month.

We attempted to make a ------- on March 1. However, the request was denied by your bank. We
144.

will try again on March 20 as stipulated in the agreement. Please make sure you have sufficient

funds in the account by then.

If you are ------- using this bank account, you can switch to payment by credit card by changing
145.

your payment information on your Account page by March 20. -------.
146.

Sincerely,

Mary Cole

Customer Service — FF Internet

---

143. (A) connective
(B) connect
(C) connection
(D) connectively

144. (A) difference
(B) concession
(C) decision
(D) withdrawal

145. (A) no longer
(B) still
(C) just
(D) at present

146. (A) Please note that the due date for payment will be announced soon.
(B) In this case, we will take payment for February and March on April 1.
(C) You are encouraged to reapply next time a vacant position becomes available.
(D) To make things easier, you could consider automatic payment in future.

Directions: In this part, you will read a selection of texts, such as advertisements, e-mails, and instant messages. Each text or set of texts is followed by several questions. Select the most appropriate answer for each question and mark the letter (A), (B), (C), or (D) on your answer sheet.

Questions 147-148 refer to the following receipt.

McQueen Online Bookstore

Receipt # 99393-834893

Date of Purchase: May 28, 1:28 P.M.
For the amount of: $23.50
Payment for: Download of the eBook, *Getting around Estonia*
Received from: Chadwick Heller
McQueen Points Remaining: 64 *Valid until May 31 (3 days left)

Note: The above title may be downloaded for three years from the date of purchase. You may download it up to three times to any device registered in your name. Purchase of this eBook also entitles the owner to receive 20 percent off on a physical copy of the book from McQueen Online Bookstore. To take advantage of this offer, simply input the above receipt number into the voucher field at the checkout. Offer expires on November 28.

---

147. What is indicated about Mr. Heller?

(A) He may lose some points soon.
(B) He paid with a gift certificate.
(C) He used the store three years ago.
(D) He is waiting for an item to be shipped.

148. How can Mr. Heller obtain a discount?

(A) By sending a copy of the receipt
(B) By registering his name with the seller
(C) By visiting a physical store
(D) By providing the receipt number

Join the Bronson Wilderness Society (BWS)

Our society of wilderness enthusiasts meets every weekend for a variety of activities around Orchid Bay. These include bushwalks, bird watching, volunteer cleanups, and educational seminars. Our members come from all walks of life and this variation is what helps make the group exciting and fulfilling for all participants. We are currently looking for new members to join and bring more fresh ideas and variety to the society.

Membership costs only $200 annually and it affords members discounts at many local businesses such as Drysdale's Leisure Center, where you can save as much as $10 a month. Other participating businesses include Randolph All Sports, Hooper Health Food, and Kreese Camping Goods.

Before they apply for full membership, interested people are offered a free three-month trial membership to help them make up their minds. The secretary of the society, Philomena Driscoll, provides information sessions about the society at our office in Strathpine. Please call her at 555-8423 to schedule an appointment.

149. What is indicated about BWS members?
(A) They have special skills.
(B) They all own local businesses.
(C) They were all introduced by other members.
(D) They have diverse backgrounds.

150. The word "affords" in paragraph 2, line 1, is closest in meaning to
(A) spares
(B) admits
(C) manages
(D) grants

151. Why are people instructed to call Ms. Driscoll?
(A) To learn more about an association
(B) To apply for membership
(C) To submit to an assessment
(D) To volunteer to help at an event

Drummond (September 6) — Blake Hawthorne, the president of Zeno Pharmaceuticals, announced today that he had finished negotiations for a takeover of Omicron Corporation. He stated that Zeno Pharmaceuticals would completely absorb the smaller company and that all their products would simply be rebranded.

Both companies have their headquarters and production facilities in Drummond so the change is not expected to have a very profound effect on staff members, who should be able to continue in their current positions albeit at a different address.

"I'll be retiring as soon as the deal is formalized" said Melissa Raver, the current CEO of Omicron Corporation. "I am very happy with the arrangement and expect the company to experience even greater prosperity as a result" she added.

152. What is the article mainly about?

(A) A new product
(B) A temporary closure
(C) A corporate merger
(D) An advertising strategy

153. What is indicated about Omicron Corporation?

(A) It has recently reported record profits.
(B) It has received an industry award.
(C) It is moving away from Drummond.
(D) It will have a change in leadership.

Test 4

GO ON TO THE NEXT PAGE

MEMO

To: All B&T Employees
From: Portia Tuttle
Date: November 17
Subject: December banquet

I just checked the schedule and noticed that the annual employee appreciation banquet is next month. This year, I have been put in charge of entertainment. — [1] —. I have been given a budget to hire an entertainer, but I would much rather put the money toward a lucky door prize and enjoy some entertainment from our colleagues.

— [2] —. If there is anyone who can perform a few songs on stage, I would love to hear from them. You can usually get me on extension 259. If there is more than one person or band interested in providing entertainment, I will either hold auditions or split the assigned time between two acts. — [3] —.

If no one expresses interest in this idea by Friday this week, I will contact Aprikana Talent Agents and ask them to provide a lounge singer for the evening. — [4] —. I think that would be a real disappointment because I had intended to arrange tickets for two for a stay at Astin Resort in Key West.

Sincerely,

Portia Tuttle

154. What is the memo mainly about?

(A) Entertainment options for a company dinner
(B) Company policy with regard to hiring temporary staff members
(C) The following year's tentative work schedule
(D) Suggested themes for a corporate event

155. How should interested people contact Ms. Tuttle?

(A) By calling her on the telephone
(B) By sending her an e-mail
(C) By approaching her at her desk
(D) By sending her a text message

156. In which of the positions marked [1], [2], [3], and [4] does the following sentence best belong?

"As a result, there would be no lucky door prize this year."

(A) [1]
(B) [2]
(C) [3]
(D) [4]

Venus Fitness Center
Twin Pines Mall
772 Coleman Rd., Seattle, WA 98563

May 2

Mr. Diego Sanchez
63 Gibson Street
Seattle, WA 98112

Dear Mr. Sanchez,

I am happy to announce that next Friday, May 11 is the tenth anniversary of Venus Fitness Center. To celebrate, we are holding a barbecue on the grassed area at the rear of the gym. All members are invited and food and drink will be supplied by the center. You can even bring along a friend to join in the celebrations for free.

All of the trainers will be there to lend a hand and socialize with members. Even Josh Kruger, whose work with several movie stars has made him a minor celebrity, has agreed to attend.

I have been put in charge of organizing the event. People who wish to attend should send me a text message with the words, "I'm in" to my mobile phone at 823 555 3495. Please also mention whether or not you will be bringing a friend.

Sincerely,

Beth Hays

Beth Hays
Member Services — Venus Fitness Center

157. What is the purpose of the letter?
  (A) To offer a discount membership
  (B) To announce a special event
  (C) To recommend a new program
  (D) To congratulate a successful candidate

158. Who is Josh Kruger?
  (A) A movie star
  (B) A founder of a gym
  (C) A physical trainer
  (D) A customer service agent

GO ON TO THE NEXT PAGE

COREY WOLFE   10:50 A.M.
I'm so sorry I missed the meeting. Did Claire tell you about my car problems?

ANTHEA TAUBMAN   10:51 A.M.
Yes, she did. I told you that you need to buy a new car. That one's been causing nothing but trouble.

COREY WOLFE   10:53 A.M.
I have to agree with you now. I'll go to a dealership and have a look today. The mechanic gave me the same advice.

ANTHEA TAUBMAN   10:53 A.M.
I'm sure he did. As for the meeting, Harper Uniforms offered us a 15 percent discount if we stay with them.

COREY WOLFE   10:54 A.M.
So, are you going to take them up on it?

ANTHEA TAUBMAN   10:59 A.M.
We'll see. I have asked some other uniform manufacturers to bid on the contract. I want to look at their offers first.

COREY WOLFE   11:02 A.M.
Good idea. I'll be in the office by noon.

ANTHEA TAUBMAN   11:03 A.M.
Just in time for lunch!

159. What did the mechanic advise Mr. Wolfe do?

(A) Update his contact details
(B) Purchase a new vehicle
(C) Create a customer account
(D) Go to a larger repair shop

160. At 10:59 A.M., what does Ms. Taubman mean when she writes, "We'll see"?

(A) She will take a good look at the product quality.
(B) She wants to get Mr. Wolfe's opinion.
(C) She has not yet made up her mind.
(D) She thinks she has made the right decision.

For more than 30 years, Cameron Associates has been helping our clients in the business world grow their companies and develop mutually beneficial relationships with people and organizations in both the public and private sectors.

Our vast network of connections enables us to put our clients together with both suppliers and clients whose needs and capabilities are a perfect match. Our clients also have complete access to the database of résumés on our job search Web site, ZipJobs.com, which is the most popular and highly rated in the country. Our team of consultants are also excellent motivational speakers and can be relied on to give your workforce the boost it needs when things are not going as well as they should. Please view the testimonials from our many satisfied customers on our Web site at www.cameronassociates.com.

We have just expanded our business, which means we now have the means to take on new clients. If you think your company could use the services of the United States' top consultancy firm, why not give us a call? One of our representatives will be happy to thoroughly explain our services and pricing structure so that you can make an informed decision. Call 405-555-8489 to arrange a free consultation.

Cameron Associates

161. What is the purpose of the information?

(A) To notify current clients of a change in pricing structure
(B) To describe a company's standards of customer service
(C) To advertise career opportunities
(D) To promote a company's services

162. What is NOT provided by Cameron Associates?

(A) Financial advice
(B) Professional introductions
(C) Recruitment services
(D) Employee motivational talks

163. What has Cameron Associates done recently?

(A) It has launched a new service.
(B) It has changed its address.
(C) It has won an award.
(D) It has grown.

Test 4

GO ON TO THE NEXT PAGE

A New Awareness of Healthy Eating

By Seth Olyphant, lifestyle reporter

In recent years, there have been more and more television shows and books focusing on food, nutrition, and cooking. — [1] —. People are choosing ingredients at the supermarket differently. They are reading up on the health benefits of certain foods and they are becoming more critical of the options available on restaurant menus.

According to Kenny Bates of the Australian Consumer Association, it is having a real effect on which restaurants they choose to eat at and which they avoid. — [2] —. Once popular food chains are experiencing slumps while others are booking out months in advance. Restaurant owners are taking notice, and they are looking at replacing many dishes with more nutritional alternatives.

Nutritionists are finding it hard to keep up with the demand as they are asked to consult with restaurants, hotels, and caterers around the country. None more so than Isabella Scott, who is largely responsible for the change of attitude. — [3] —. Ms. Scott consulted and even shared screen time with celebrity chefs in many of the most popular broadcasts. In an interview for this article, she mentioned a new problem that restaurants are facing.

The trend that started here is now starting to take effect in many other countries and there is a demand for Australian chefs around the world. — [4] —. Becky Harmer from the Australian Restaurant Owners' Association says, "Many chefs at top restaurants are being offered excellent money to work in foreign countries. It is important that our culinary schools and vocational colleges prepare students for the changing expectations of their employers and the dining public."

164. According to the article, what is probably happening in many Australian restaurants?

(A) They are updating their menus.
(B) They are changing their cleaning procedures.
(C) They are advertising for employees internationally.
(D) They are spending more on advertising.

165. Who has appeared on several television shows?

(A) Seth Olyphant
(B) Kenny Bates
(C) Isabella Scott
(D) Becky Harmer

166. What is indicated about the chefs at many top restaurants?

(A) They are returning to culinary schools.
(B) They are making money from online videos.
(C) They are publishing their own recipe books.
(D) They are being offered employment overseas.

167. In which of the positions marked [1], [2], [3], and [4] does the following sentence best belong?

"This has made people take a greater interest in what they are putting in their mouths."

(A) [1]
(B) [2]
(C) [3]
(D) [4]

Randall Skin Care
45 Carlota Way
Mildura VIC 3502

27 June

Dear Shareholders,

Randall Skin Care has always been a market leader, and this has been linked to our increased investment in research and development and the close relationship that exists between that department and marketing, which is also getting extra funds. So, while it pains me to admit that profits are down this quarter, I can assure you that it is not because sales have declined.

In fact, quite the opposite is true. Sales have improved by some 8 percent since April. The profit margin has been affected by an increase in production costs and a massive investment in product development. We believe that this is necessary from time to time in order to ensure the long-term success of our brand.

In the coming quarter, we intend to diversify the business by offering some new products such as deodorants and body soaps. The product development and marketing departments will take a central role and some extra spending there now will surely pay off down the line. We will also be spending a little more on customer service. As online product reviews become more and more important, ensuring customer satisfaction is critical.

I would like to thank you for your patience during this time and assure you that the company's prospects are better than ever.

Sincerely,

Clara Braden

Clara Braden, CEO, Randall Skin Care

Test 4

168. According to the letter, why have profits dropped?

(A) Manufacturing costs have risen.
(B) Sales are declining.
(C) Advertising costs have risen.
(D) A new office was opened.

169. Which department is NOT mentioned as receiving additional spending?

(A) Research and development
(B) Distribution
(C) Marketing
(D) Customer service

170. What does the company intend to do next quarter?

(A) Reduce unnecessary spending
(B) Hire experts from abroad
(C) Expand into new product ranges
(D) Hold a meeting for shareholders

171. The word "critical" in paragraph 3, line 6, is closest in meaning to

(A) demanding
(B) essential
(C) negative
(D) sensitive

GO ON TO THE NEXT PAGE

Kevin Woods [3:30 P.M.]:
Hi guys. We discussed hiring someone in the power line maintenance division. What's the status on that?

Sung-Yong Lee [3:31 P.M.]:
I'm already working on it. I've advertised the position and received a bunch of résumés. I need someone to interview the applicants with me. Who's available on both March 23 and 24?

Kevin Woods [3:34 P.M.]:
Great work Sung-Yong. I'll join you if no one else is available.

Mel Chapel [3:36 P.M.]:
I'm busy on March 23. I have to help with the installation of the new generators in Hill Valley.

Denise Porter [3:38 P.M.]:
How about Rob McMillan? He's back from Maine. If he's not available, I'll do it.

Mel Chapel [3:42 P.M.]:
He's on vacation until March 26.

Kevin Woods [3:45 P.M.]:
Well, it looks like that's a plan. Whoever you choose for the position, please make sure they have a Class 1 electrician's license. We don't have time to train someone.

Sung-Yong Lee [3:46 P.M.]:
That reminds me. No matter who we choose, we'll need to provide employee orientation.

Mel Chapel [3:49 P.M.]:
I took care of that last time. It won't require any preparation for me to do it again.

Kevin Woods [3:52 P.M.]:
Thanks, Mel. Let's schedule that when we decide on the start date.

172. Where do the writers most likely work?

(A) At a fitness center
(B) At an electric company
(C) At a department store
(D) At a financial institution

173. Why does Mr. Woods praise Mr. Lee?

(A) He helped train some new employees.
(B) He has received a new qualification.
(C) He made a useful suggestion.
(D) He has made progress on a task.

174. Who will most likely assist Mr. Lee with the interview?

(A) Rob McMillan
(B) Denise Porter
(C) Mel Chapel
(D) Kevin Woods

175. At 3:49 P.M., why does Ms. Chapel write, "I took care of that last time"?

(A) She thinks it is another staff member's turn.
(B) She is ready to conduct an orientation.
(C) She has a lot of projects to complete.
(D) She would like to try something new.

GO ON TO THE NEXT PAGE

Test 4

```
┌─────────────────────────────────────────────────────────────────────┐
│                         E-Mail Message                                │
├──────────┬──────────────────────────────────────────────────────────┤
│ To:      │ Gerald Comiskey <gcomiskey@barrontiling.com>              │
├──────────┼──────────────────────────────────────────────────────────┤
│ From:    │ Jane Whitman <jwhitman@clementprojects.com>               │
├──────────┼──────────────────────────────────────────────────────────┤
│ Date:    │ September 28                                               │
├──────────┼──────────────────────────────────────────────────────────┤
│ Subject: │ 234 Towers Road                                           │
└──────────┴──────────────────────────────────────────────────────────┘
```

Dear Mr. Comiskey,

I am writing with regard to the apartment block at 234 Towers Road in Flinders. Clement Projects hired your company to tile all of the bathrooms. The understanding was that you would start work on September 19 and finish tiling all eight bathrooms by September 23. It was important that you do so because we had other workers coming in after you to fit cabinets, mirrors, and so on.

Your delay in getting started on the work meant that we had other tradespeople waiting for you to finish. We were charged a high hourly rate to have these people wait for you until they could start work themselves. In the end, your employees were not done with the final bathroom until the afternoon of September 26. I have just received your invoice for the full amount of $59,623. As we suffered significant additional expenses as a result of the delays, I am hoping that you will offer us a discount on the work. If we cannot come to an acceptable arrangement, I will not be able to accept bids from Barron Tiling for any future projects. This includes the Montgomery Hotel project, which has more than 120 rooms.

Sincerely,

Jane Whitman

Barron Tiling
27 Longmans Close, Seacrest
Invoice

For work carried out at: 234 Towers Road
Client: Clement Projects
Address: 17 Bloomingdale Street, Brighton

Date of issue: September 30
Payment due: October 31

Item Description	Unit Price	Quantity	Subtotal
Tiling Bathroom (labor)	$3,699	8	$29,592.00
Tiling Bathroom (materials)	$3,399	8	$27,192.00
		Discount (10%)	-$5,678.40
		Tax	$2,555.28
		Total	$53,660.88

All work by Barron Tiling is covered by a ten-year guarantee on materials and workmanship.

Thank you for continuing to rely on Barron Tiling for your tiling needs.

176. What kind of company does Ms. Whitman most likely work for?

(A) A real estate agency
(B) A construction company
(C) A hardware store
(D) An office furniture manufacturer

177. What is one purpose of the e-mail?

(A) To announce the outcome of a bidding
(B) To request an update on a project
(C) To recommend a superior service
(D) To explain the effects of a delay

178. When was the tiling work at 234 Towers Road completed?

(A) On September 19
(B) On September 23
(C) On September 26
(D) On September 28

179. What is probably true about Barron Tiling?

(A) It intends to bid on the Montgomery Hotel project.
(B) It is partially owned by Clement Projects.
(C) It uses locally sourced materials.
(D) It specializes in office buildings.

180. What is implied about the bathrooms in 234 Towers Road?

(A) They are covered by a ten-year guarantee.
(B) They failed to pass a safety inspection.
(C) They are designed for large families.
(D) They do not have any storage space.

GO ON TO THE NEXT PAGE →

GILMORE (February 10) — Gilmore City has recently cleared and developed a large area of parkland in Mulberry Hills. This land has been used to create a new fashion district known as the Gilmore Fashion District or GFD. Gilmore has been associated with a growing number of fashion labels over the years. City leaders are hoping that fashion design and production will become one of the town's major industries. To encourage businesses to move into the new district and provide them a financial boost, the council has agreed to subsidize the rent for the first five years of every lease. As a result, businesses will be able to save up to 50 percent on rent and benefit from being in one of the most attractive locations businesses in this industry could hope for.

Besides the obvious financial advantages, companies will benefit from a connection with the newly founded Balmoral College of Art. The publicly owned college is located within the GFD and has agreed to provide a space for all of the city's fashion shows. The college's 640 square-meter function hall is available for free for approved events. According to Cheryl Dominic from Zebra Garments, one of the first companies to move to the GFD, the event hall has been an excellent venue for her company's promotional events.

So far, the only way to rent an office in the GFD has been to receive an invitation from the GFD administrators. Soon, however, administrators will be accepting applications from other businesses. There are conditions on the type and size of company that is allowed to move into the GFD and interested people can learn more about them by following the links on the Web site.

Admit One

The Annual Gilmore Fashion Show
See exciting designs created exclusively in the GFD!
7:00 P.M. to 10:00 P.M., June 16

This ticket has been provided for **Noelle Peabody** of **Crisp Fashion**.

This is a free ticket provided for employees of businesses displaying items in the show. Please note that this ticket is non-transferable. As a result, you may be asked to show identification at the entrance. A detailed map of the event's location, as well as contact details of the organizers, are printed on the back.

181. What is most likely true about the GFD?

(A) It was inspired by a project in another town.
(B) The land was previously used for recreation.
(C) The cost of rent there is rising.
(D) It offers excellent views of the city.

182. Why was the GFD created?

(A) To raise funds through charity events
(B) To reduce traffic in the city center
(C) To provide jobs for college graduates
(D) To foster a growing industry

183. What is suggested about Zebra Garments?

(A) It was invited to the district by GFD Administration.
(B) It hires students from Balmoral College of Art.
(C) It provided initial funding for the GFD.
(D) It has submitted an entry to the Gilmore Fashion Show.

184. What is implied about Ms. Peabody?

(A) She will visit Balmoral College of Art.
(B) She works for a business outside the GFD.
(C) She will judge garments in the Gilmore Fashion Show.
(D) She is one of the administrators of the GFD.

185. According to the ticket, what should ticket holders refrain from doing?

(A) Driving to the venue
(B) Selling their tickets
(C) Calling the event organizer
(D) Video recording the show

GO ON TO THE NEXT PAGE

Test 4

www.ivebeenthere.com

Welcome to I've been there dot com.
Read reviews of local businesses written by their clients and customers.

Business: Neptune Sports and Leisure at Bay Town Shopping Center
Reviewed by: Rod Barkworth   **Date:** June 18

I was at Neptune Sports and Leisure at Bay Town Shopping Center today. It was the day after opening and there were still a lot of people. It was especially surprising as it was a weekday. We had a great time. I especially enjoyed the climbing wall, the golf simulator, and the batting cage. The range of goods was excellent. Some of the brands I had never heard of, though. So, it is hard for me to comment on their quality. The prices seemed a little higher than I'm used to. Nevertheless, I bought a pair of running shoes and a new sweater.

Bay Town (June 19) — Neptune Sports and Leisure has opened a store in the Bay Town Shopping Center. Neptune Sports and Leisure's success has been attributed to its competitive prices and the many enjoyable experiences on offer to customers. Every Neptune store has a climbing wall, running track and a batting cage, which are freely available to customers. Neptune has been generating a lot of interest through its innovative Internet marketing campaign, and the Bay Town Shopping Center location attracted record crowds to its opening.

In a move that hardly seemed necessary, free lunch vouchers for meals at nearby Gee's Healthy Eating were given to the first 50 people to show up. By 11 A.M., when they stopped counting, some 500 people had passed through the doors. They were there to enjoy the free facilities and check out the amazing variety of products and brands on offer.

Letters to the Editor

June 21 — I read the article about the opening of Neptune Sports and Leisure at Bay Town Shopping Center. The article almost appeared to be an advertisement for the store. I think that as it was intended as a news article, it should have taken a more critical stance. Bay Town already has Foreman Sports, which is an excellent sporting goods store that hires many young locals and has sponsored several of our sporting teams over the years. Neither of these deeds has been covered by the newspaper. Furthermore, the claim that prices are low is hard to accept as I found the prices to be 10 percent higher on average than Foreman Sports'.

— Samantha Riley

186. When was the grand opening of the new Neptune Sports and Leisure store?

(A) On June 17
(B) On June 18
(C) On June 19
(D) On June 20

187. What attraction is most likely unique to the Bay Town Shopping Center location?

(A) The climbing wall
(B) The golf simulator
(C) The batting cage
(D) The running track

188. What is mentioned about the grand opening of the new Neptune Sports and Leisure store?

(A) It was timed to coincide with a popular local sporting event.
(B) The turnout was a disappointment to the organizers of the event.
(C) It had received extensive publicity on various local radio programs.
(D) Coupons for people to use at a local restaurant were provided.

189. What does Ms. Riley indicate about the article?

(A) It should have been published earlier.
(B) It was quite critical of a local business.
(C) It has appeared in another publication.
(D) It seemed to be promoting a business.

190. About what do Mr. Barkworth and Ms. Riley agree?

(A) The job opportunities provided by Foreman Sports
(B) The little-known brands on offer at Neptune Sports and Leisure
(C) The higher prices at Neptune Sports and Leisure
(D) The lack of newspaper coverage of team sponsorship

GO ON TO THE NEXT PAGE

SANDER'S PRODUCTIONS
772 Rockatanski Road • Boise • ID 83644

March 23

Ms. Lawrence,

Thank you so much for putting me in touch with Todd Jensen. We were having difficulty finding someone with his qualifications and it felt like a miracle when you suddenly contacted us and explained his situation. He has been doing an excellent job on the Francis Inn television commercials. The project reminds me of the time we worked together on the Heathcliff Hotel advertising campaign.

If there is anything we can do to repay the favor, do not hesitate to let me know. I look forward to seeing you at this year's Producers' Conference in Boulder. I hear that Freda Watts is presenting. We attended her lectures at Kamloops University. It is great to see that she is finally getting the industry recognition she deserves.

Sincerely,

Reg Garibaldi

Reg Garibaldi

To: Reg Garibaldi <rgaribaldi@sandersproductions.com>
From: Carrie Lawrence <clawrence@eaglevl.com>
Subject: Instructional videos
Date: June 17

Dear Reg,

I have been communicating with Mr. Jensen of late and he informs me that you have secured a contract to shoot a series of instructional videos and need a second crew to cover the workload. While we have not received a formal invitation, I would like to offer our services as a subcontractor. I remember that our previous collaboration was regarded as a great success, and I hope that we can repeat that this time.

Best regards,

Carrie
Eagle Video Labs

ACVPA

Annual Corporate Video Production Awards Ceremony
Event Schedule (Confidential Information for Committee Members ONLY)
Chandler Plaza Hotel, December 2

Time	Event	Presenter
7:00 P.M.~7:10 P.M.	**Opening Speech** **By:** ACVPA President Sam Whitehall	
7:10 P.M.~7:40 P.M.	**Dinner Service**	
7:40 P.M.~7:50 P.M.	Award for Best Regional Advertisement **Recipient:** Voorhees Video	Presented by: Creed Norris
7:50 P.M.~8:00 P.M.	Award for Best Public Service Announcement **Recipient:** Undecided	Presented by: Undecided
8:00 P.M.~8:10 P.M.	Award for Best Instructional Video **Recipient:** Sanders Productions/Eagle Video Labs	Presented by: Luke Moore
8:10 P.M.~8:20 P.M.	Award for Best Memorial Video **Recipient:** Undecided	Presented by: Undecided
8:20 P.M.~8:40 P.M.	**Closing Speech** **By:** ACVPA Founder Cindy DuPont	

191. Why did Mr. Garibaldi write to Ms. Lawrence?

(A) To offer a suggestion for a title
(B) To express appreciation for an introduction
(C) To remind her of a condition in her contract
(D) To suggest she submit her work for evaluation

192. Who most likely is Ms. Watts?

(A) A conference organizer
(B) A software engineer
(C) A university lecturer
(D) A factory manager

193. What is indicated about the Heathcliff Hotel advertising campaign?

(A) It was considered a success.
(B) It will be completed in March.
(C) It has had its budget reduced.
(D) It is being managed by Mr. Jensen.

194. What will happen on December 2?

(A) Transportation will be provided for guests.
(B) Mr. Norris will receive an award.
(C) Chandler Plaza Hotel will host a ceremony.
(D) A committee member will greet the audience.

195. What is suggested about Mr. Garibaldi?

(A) He is a member of the awards committee.
(B) He will provide training to Mr. Jensen.
(C) He will give a presentation at ACVPA.
(D) He accepted Ms. Lawrence's business proposal.

GO ON TO THE

https://www.colbertcatering.com/faq

Welcome to Colbert Catering

Home	Events	Menus	**FAQ**

What is the largest event you can cater?
We can cater to groups of up to 500. However, it should be noted that not all menus will be available to such large groups. For example, the "deluxe menu" and the "food of the world menu" are only available to groups of under 300 and 200 people respectively.

Do you offer discounts to frequent customers?
We offer discounts for select customers based on the amount they spend at Colbert Catering rather than their frequency. People who spend more than $2,000 in any quarter will receive 10 percent off in the following quarter.

What are Colbert Catering's business hours?
Our office hours are from 9:00 A.M. to 5:00 P.M., Monday to Friday. However, Colbert Catering is able to serve its clients 24 hours a day, seven days a week. Some penalty rates apply on weekends, public holidays, and between the hours of 9:00 P.M. to 9:00 A.M.

How far can Colbert Catering deliver food?
Colbert Catering is based in Vernon. Generally speaking, we only provide catering to addresses within 30 kilometers of our facility.

Are alternatives available for people with allergies?
We can substitute ingredients where necessary. Please fill out a special request form on the Web site.

To: Trish Bryson <tbryson@colbertcatering.com>
From: Abu Markov <amarkov@firecoot.com>
Date: October 11
Subject: Party catering

Dear Ms. Bryson,

Thank you for providing catering for my party so expertly last night. The Colbert Catering staff were all extremely professional and the food and drinks were very high quality. I was also impressed with your value for money. I feel that I received higher quality food for about 10 percent less than the previous caterer charged. Well done! I have recommended your services to my neighbor, who I expect will contact you later for an appointment.

of my e-mail, however, is to let you know that your team has left some equipment behind.
a silver tray with the Colbert Catering logo on it in my kitchen.

E-Mail Message

To:	Trish Bryson <tbryson@colbertcatering.com>
From:	Valerie Yasser <vyasser@swandive.com>
Date:	October 11
Subject:	Appointment request

Dear Ms. Bryson,

I was handed your business card by Abu Markov, who praised your services highly. I would like to set up an appointment to discuss arrangements for a business luncheon I am planning. It will be held in the conference room in my office at 34 Prince Street, Vernon. It will be a group of around 30 business executives and I would like to serve one of your high-end menu plans. I am aware that one of the guests is allergic to shrimp and another to coconut. Can you accommodate special menu requests?

Please contact me on 832-555-3472 to discuss an appointment time.

Sincerely,

Valerie Yasser
President — Swandive Trading

196. Who is eligible for a discount?

(A) People who frequently use Colbert Catering
(B) People who spend over a certain amount
(C) People who sign up for a membership plan
(D) People who recommend Colbert Catering to others

197. According to the Web page, why might Colbert Catering charge an additional fee?

(A) The client lives outside the Vernon central business district.
(B) A combination of two menus is required.
(C) A job is scheduled for a national holiday.
(D) The number of guests is too small.

198. What is implied about Mr. Markov?

(A) He tried to contact a sales representative after 5:00 P.M.
(B) His home is within 30 kilometers of Colbert Catering.
(C) His event attracted over 300 guests.
(D) He ordered more than $2,000 worth of catering in the previous quarter.

199. What is indicated about Ms. Yasser's event?

(A) It will be held in a commercial building.
(B) It has a very restrictive budget.
(C) It was catered by Colbert Catering last year.
(D) It will have the maximum number of guests.

200. What will Ms. Yasser most likely be required to do?

(A) Fill out an online form
(B) Give directions to her company
(C) Amend the number of attendees
(D) Call another branch of Colbert Cat

Stop! This is the end of the test. If you finish before time is called, you may go back to Parts 5, 6, 7 and check your work.

NO TEST MATERIAL ON THIS PAGE

NO TEST MATERIAL ON THIS PAGE

NO TEST MATERIAL ON THIS PAGE

『TOEIC® L&R テスト 究極の模試600問＋』別冊④

PC：7019067

発行：株式会社アルク

無断複製および配布禁止

43